MW00852394

# Messerschmitt Me 262
# Development & Politics

# MESSERSCHMITT
## DEVELOPMENT & POLITICS ME 262

### Dan Sharp

TEMPEST
BOOKS

DAN SHARP is the author of more than a dozen books about aircraft and aviation, specialising
in archival research on German Second World War aircraft development.
He graduated with a Bachelor of Arts degree in history from the University of Liverpool
before starting a career in publishing. He lives in Nottinghamshire.

Published in Great Britain by Tempest Books
an imprint of Mortons Books Ltd.
Media Centre
Morton Way
Horncastle LN9 6JR
www.mortonsbooks.co.uk

First printed in 2022
Second edition © 2024 by Tempest Books

All rights reserved. No part of this publication may be reproduced or transmitted in any form or by any means, electronic or mechanical
including photocopying, recording, or any information storage retrieval system without prior permission in writing from the publisher.
ISBN 978-1-911658-27-6

The right of Dan Sharp to be identified as the author of this work has been asserted in accordance with the Copyright, Designs and
Patents Act 1988.

Typeset by Jayne Clements (jayne@hinoki.co.uk), Hinoki Design and Typesetting

Original cover artwork by Piotr Forkasiewicz

Acknowledgements
Thanks to Stephen Walton, Steve Coates, David Schwartz, Elizabeth Borja, Oliver Thiele, J Richard Smith, Hermione Giffard, Mikael
Gersel, Michael Baumgartl, Dan O'Connell, Steve O'Hara, Ian Fisher and Calum Douglas.

*For Calum Douglas*

# Contents

# Introduction

THIS BOOK is about the design and wartime development of the Messerschmitt Me 262 jet fighter.

Its aim is to study this process in detail while setting it within the broader context of arms procurement for the Luftwaffe during the Second World War.

As such, it seeks to explain not only the technological development of the aircraft itself but also to examine the discussions and decision-making processes taking place within the German Air Ministry, within the Luftwaffe, within the Messerschmitt company and within other organisations which would determine the course of that development as well as preparations for the type's entry into full series production.

Three concurrent and overlapping threads are central to the book's chronological narrative—the project and development work undertaken by Messerschmitt, first in Augsburg and later in Oberammergau; the flight testing undertaken at Lechfeld and elsewhere, and the high level meetings and discussions concerning the aircraft. Reference is also made, where appropriate, to Me 262 production.

The chronology itself can be loosely divided into four stages. The German Air Ministry commissioned Messerschmitt to begin work on a jet fighter design during the summer of 1938 and the project itself, under the internal company designation P 65 or P 1065, commenced at the start of April 1939. An order for three prototypes was placed in March 1940, increasing to 20 prototypes by July. This two year period encapsulates the first stage of Me 262 development.

The heavy losses suffered by the Luftwaffe during the Battle of Britain in the summer of 1940 provoked urgent demands for better equipment and effectively forced Messerschmitt to suspend much of its experimental and project activity, concentrating instead on upgrades for existing types and expedited preparations for the replacement of the Bf 110 with the new Me 210.[1] The Me 262, with just one airworthy prototype built, was put on the back burner and remained there as the engine manufacturers struggled to come up with a jet unit reliable enough for flight testing.

Fallout from the Me 210's failure in early 1942 rocked the Messerschmitt company to its core. With attention focused elsewhere, the Me 262 programme was neglected to the extent that by the beginning of 1943 Junkers was complaining that it had airworthy engines ready to test but no airframes to put them in. This two-and-a-half year period of drift was the second stage of the Me 262's development.

The third stage, beginning in early 1943, would see increasing interest in the Me 262 from the German Air Ministry and the Luftwaffe. Messerschmitt began updating the design and commenced numerous developmental programmes with the goal of increasing and expanding its capabilities. Preparations for full series production of the type as a fighter-bomber, alongside the Bf 109 or its direct successor, commenced but a critical shortage of jig and tool makers, combined with the process of compulsory conscription to the army, severely hampered this process. Then a fumbled conference with Adolf Hitler resulted in an order that the Me 262 could only be built and operated as a pure bomber.

The final stage of development would see the bomber-only order loosened and then reversed towards the end of 1944, with attention switching to how best the Me 262 might be equipped to destroy Allied bomber formations—both during the day and at night. Threads of research begun during the third stage of development matured into a range of schemes for arming the aircraft with high-calibre cannon and/or rocket-propelled weapons, as well as plans to radically alter the airframe for improved aerodynamic performance and greater range.

## JETS VERSUS PISTON ENGINES

The story of the engine that would eventually power the series production model Me 262, the Jumo 004 B-1, runs in parallel to that of the airframe—though it is not the main focus of this book. The German Air Ministry was quick to support jet engine development as a means of propulsion specifically for fighter aircraft. It was the Ministry which commissioned Messerschmitt to begin working on the jet fighter concept and the Ministry which contracted Messerschmitt first to design a jet fighter, then to begin building prototypes. Far from being an innovation which originated with the company, and which the company subsequently championed in the face of official indifference, the intertwined jet engine and jet fighter programmes were driven by the German government via the usual processes of business in the aviation industry—requirements, specifications and paid contracts for work.

The jet engine's potential benefits were clear to the Ministry's engineers and decision makers: it was lighter than the equivalent piston engine, offering a potentially high power-to-weight ratio, and presented a significantly smaller profile which greatly reduced aerodynamic drag when compared to piston engines with their large propellers and bulky radiators.

While other manufacturers encountered great difficulties with their jet engine designs, the development team at Junkers Flugzeug und Motorenwerke, led by Dr Anselm Franz, enjoyed early success with their 004 A series engines and had more than enough examples to power the handful of early Me 262 prototypes made by Messerschmitt.

The 004 B-1 was not originally intended to become the Me 262's production model powerplant but it did work sufficiently well to make series production viable. It also utilised a minimal quantity of strategic materials compared to the 004 A. Mishandled in operation, its service life could be woefully short,[2] yet it does not seem to have been any more dangerous in service than the Luftwaffe's piston engines—which were badly affected by shortages of critical materials such as nickel.

Part of the Me 262's problem was that Germany did not seek to replace its expensive piston engines with a very large number of cheaper jet engines, choosing instead to keep piston engines and their associated fighters in large scale production until the very end. Some attempts were made to cancel the Bf 109, as mentioned before and described in much greater detail later, but none were successful. And the Fw 190 was never scheduled for cancellation.

Indeed, the economic arguments in favour of building jet engines and jet fighters appear to have had little influence on the decision-making process of those in power—particularly since the Me 262, the only available jet fighter airframe, was relatively large and needed two jet engines, making it slightly more expensive overall than the equivalent single seat fighter powered by one piston engine.[3]

Those who spoke in favour of adopting jet fighters typically did so on the basis of their outright performance superiority over piston engine fighters. As this book will show, this argument is made repeatedly in high level meetings where engine design and development is discussed. The Me 262, though slow to accelerate, was faster than any other fighter and it was even thought that, owing to compressibility, it might not be possible to make an aircraft go much faster than the 1,000km/h of which the Me 262 was capable, albeit in a steep dive. In the aerial combat environment of the Second World War, outright speed trumped any other quality a fighter might possess and as such the Me 262 represented a clear performance advantage—even though it was more expensive and time-consuming to build than a piston engine fighter. It could also carry a heavier armament than a piston engine fighter, with its weapons conveniently grouped together in an easily detachable nose, and could fly on cheaper, less refined, fuels than were needed for a piston engine.

Those who successfully argued in favour of retaining piston engine fighters drew attention to jet fighters' low endurance range, to their high fuel consumption and to the additional training required by those who would fly them—particularly pilots who lacked experience in operating a twin-engine machine. Crucially, and perhaps most persuasively, they also pointed out that the production lines, supply chains and manufacturing groups which built the piston engine fighters had become so firmly established that reequipping them with all-new jigs and tooling, setting up new supply chains and switching the hundreds of subcontractors over to new sets of components would cause huge disruption to the German war effort, not to mention requiring a Herculean feat of reorganisation. Fighter production would be offline for months at a time when the Luftwaffe urgently needed every aircraft it could lay its hands on.

## A SKEWED HISTORY

This book seeks to provide a new history of the Me 262 which draws extensively on archival material and as such owes little or nothing to earlier works on the same subject.

The cliched adage that history is written by the victors appears to have been true for the Me 262—though only with respect to who was wielding the pen, since what was actually recorded for posterity would be dictated by one particular group of 'losers'. More than a year after the war's end, in January 1947, the United States Strategic Bombing Survey (USSBS) Aircraft Division produced a hefty report entitled Messerschmitt AG Augsburg, Germany Over-All-Report, which included a 14-page appendix on the history and development of the Me 262.

USSBS reports were typically based on a mishmash of interviews with German personnel, captured documents and Allied wartime intelligence documents compiled and commented upon with the goal of emphasising the role played by American bomber groups in winning the war. In this way they differed from otherwise similar USSAF Technical Intelligence reports, which lacked that particular axe to grind and tended therefore to present purely factual information. In this case, the Over-All-Report appears to have been based largely on information supplied by Messerschmitt company personnel. Since the report was made available to the public, it would go on to form the foundation upon which many post-war histories of the Me 262 were constructed.

Some of the sentiments and opinions expressed within this influential document are worth noting before reading the remainder of the present book. The Over-All-Report states that Germany's "inability to bring the [Me 262] into operation in any appreciable numbers can be attributed in a considerable degree to the failure of the German Air Force and Air Ministry in their planning and judgement, and to political

intervention into the purely technical fields of aircraft production and tactical disposition of operational aircraft. To this can be added the effects of our strategic bombing on Me 262 production, our low-level attacks on completed aircraft and the German inability to solve completely the technical problems inherent in turbojet propulsion design."

It goes on: "The Me 262 project was initiated in 1938, when the Air Ministry requested Messerschmitt to design an aircraft capable of a speed of 500mph, to be powered by a turbojet. The development of the turbojet engine was also an Air Ministry project and was scheduled to be ready by December 1939. The Messerschmitt designs were finished and submitted to the Air Ministry in June 1939 and in July 1940 three experimental airframes were finished. At this time, Ernst Udet, in his belief that the war had been won already, favoured abandoning the Me 262 project altogether."

Meanwhile, "Junkers had been working on the development of a turbojet engine, to be known as the '004'. This entire jet engine had not impressed Field Marshal Milch, who openly questioned the value of even carrying on experiments in turbojet engines. Despite the indifference of the Air Ministry, Junkers continued its work and in June 1942 was able to send Messerschmitt several '004' engines to be used experimentally.

"The Me 262 was rebuilt for the Junkers engines and the aircraft was flown in July 1942 with results which greatly enthused the Messerschmitt officials, who felt then that everything possible should be done at once to get the aircraft into quantity mass production."

But the Air Ministry remained uninterested. "The Messerschmitt officials were shocked by this indifference and made numerous appeals to the Luftwaffe staff, picturing the possibilities of the plane. Most of these communications went unanswered. Finally the Luftwaffe staff replied that there was no real need for such an aircraft and the numbers scheduled for production were sufficient for the experiments they would make in combat.

"Without active support from the Air Ministry or the Luftwaffe, the Messerschmitt company found it impossible, at this time, to set up an adequate production line, or even to carry out the needed additional research and design."

Evidently, "the period from July 1942 until spring 1943 was frittered away in exchanges, memoranda and futile visits to Berlin by Messerschmitt officials. Mr Voigt, a Messerschmitt official, attributed this neglect of Germany's most promising aircraft to the prevailing feeling of fear in government circles and unwillingness to risk political security, a psychology engendered by the German system of rigid dictatorship."

The report credits Galland with demanding "the immediate mass production of the Me 262, side by side with conventional fighters" but even when production had been approved "the Air Ministry seemed unwilling to give the project realistic backing by assigning the necessary tools, materials and personnel. This was particularly true for jig and tool construction".

Indeed, "throughout 1943 the battle between Messerschmitt and the Air Ministry went on. Milch continued to question the value of the aircraft and refused to scrap production of any other type to provide the Me 262 programme with the needed resources".

The USSBS's informants were also scathing of Junkers and its engines: "Throughout 1944 bottlenecks existed in certain items as a result of transport difficulties, bombing of industry and the advances of Allied armies. Landing gear, fuel pumps, forged parts and thin sheet steel were problems. The delivery of power units, however, caused the greatest amount of anxiety at the Messerschmitt works. It was often the case that finished airframes had to wait for the power plants to arrive."

Junkers director Walter Cambeis was also evidently interviewed by the USSBS team and "stated that he had always been opposed to rushing the '004' engine into production as he realised that it was not fully developed and he had no sympathy with the politicians who were dictating to the aircraft industry. Finally, as the course of the war began to go so obviously against Germany, he lost all interest in prolonging the struggle and no longer exerted himself to further research or to meet production schedules. He stated that by this sort of passive sabotage he felt that he was best serving his country in shortening the war".

The accuracy or otherwise of these various statements may be judged when set against the information presented in this book.

**THE DECISIVE MOMENT**

The history of the Me 262 from early 1943 until the end of the war, defined as the third and fourth stages of the type's development in this book, may be regarded as a cautionary tale about the attempted introduction of radical technological change in a time of national crisis.

The expenditure of resources on designing and building the Me 262 represented a speculative investment in emerging technologies at the end of the 1930s—a time when the German Air Ministry under Ernst Udet sought to capitalise on any opportunity for potential performance advantage over the equipment operated by foreign powers.

The beginning of the Second World War saw a sharp refocusing of resources on existing equipment and the shock of engaging with an enemy whose technology was of equal or superior quality during the Battle of Britain only served to intensify that focus. The seeds planted under Udet's regime continued to grow, however, and when the Me 262 emerged as a viable product at the beginning of 1943, the decision makers of the Air Ministry and the Luftwaffe were faced with an acute dilemma: how far were they willing to go with this revolutionary new innovation?

More than three years of warfare on an increasingly global scale, with the associated demands placed on the German economy in general and the aircraft manufacturing industry in particular, had resulted in worrying shortages of war-critical materials such as aluminium alloy, nickel and chromium. A lack of skilled labour had been exacerbated by ongoing rounds of arbitrary conscription, with jig and toolmakers being in particularly short supply. In addition, existing aircraft production lines had become hidebound, with even small changes to existing systems resented by those charged with ensuring production quotas were filled.

Putting the Me 262 into mass production without changing the existing assembly lines was likely to result in intolerable economic strain. Changing the existing assembly lines was likely to result in a shortage of fighters for the Luftwaffe at a time when such a shortage could have dire consequences for the war effort. Neither option was particularly appealing to the Air Ministry but the third option, to do nothing and leave the status quo intact, does not seem to have been considered.

Adopting the aircraft would create significant challenges for the Luftwaffe too. From a maintenance standpoint, ground crews had a wealth of experience in handling piston engine types but the jet was something entirely new—and particularly unforgiving of any errors made due to inexpert attention. There was also the question of supplies; depots were full of spares, tools, manuals and handling gear associated with the existing piston engine types. Introducing the Me 262 would require a whole new inventory of parts and equipment.

Training aircrew represented, if anything, an even greater difficulty. Most of the Luftwaffe's pilots were experienced in managing a single-engine aircraft. Converting to the twin-engine Me 262 would require training on twin-engine piston types before pilots got anywhere near the jet itself. Once able to competently fly a machine with two engines, pilots would be faced with the daunting task of coaxing the Me 262 into the air—a feat which required great care and an abnormally long take-off run if damage to the aircraft's engines or a serious accident were to be avoided. Landings, particularly when flying on one engine or when short of fuel, were similarly fraught with peril for the inexperienced.

Pilots would also have to learn new combat tactics if the Me 262 were to be employed as a fighter, since it relied heavily on its insurmountable speed advantage for success. Attempting the turning combat they were used to was likely to result in swift defeat.

Unlike the Luftwaffe's other fighters, the Me 262 had not been built to a Luftwaffe requirement and its specification had been decided by the Air Ministry. It had been designed as a pure fighter, although some thought had previously been given to its employment as a reconnaissance machine—a role to which it was well suited since jet engines were less prone to excessive vibration than piston engines.

It was presented as a single seater with neither bomb attachment points nor a bombsight and as such the Luftwaffe evidently gave no thought to its employment for other combat roles.

Beyond the Air Ministry, responsible for procurement, and the Luftwaffe, the Ministry's 'customer', there were two further interested parties: Messerschmitt, the manufacturer, and Adolf Hitler—the Nazi dictator among whose many undesirable qualities was an unnerving tendency towards micromanagement in areas where he lacked even the most basic technical knowledge.

The sudden focus on the Me 262 at the beginning of 1943 raised unique concerns for Messerschmitt as a private and independent company.[4] Having long since established itself as Germany's main manufacturer of piston engine fighters, it abruptly came to realise that it had inadvertently developed a new product which rendered most of its own existing products obsolete. And not just those products already in production—but also its intended Bf 109 successors, the already-failing Me 309 and that type's hastily cobbled together replacement the Me 209. At the same time the company was in the process of losing a lucrative contract to build the Luftwaffe's new piston engine fast bomber type, its twin fuselage Bf 109 Zw having lost out to Dornier's Do 335.

The challenge now facing Messerschmitt was how to proceed with the Me 262 while preserving its existing line of business as far as possible.

When it came to arms procurement, Hitler had focused much of his attention up to this point on armoured vehicles for the German Army; aircraft development had been left to the discretion of Göring and his staff. During the course of 1943 however, the Führer would pay increasingly close attention to the development of aircraft too—principally jet aircraft and bombers. He had his own ideas about the Me 262 and approached its development from his own unique perspective.

While it could be said that all four parties had the same broad intent, in that they all wanted to do what was best to help Germany win the war, each had their own individual goals: the Air Ministry wanted to find a way of bringing the Me 262 to mass production with minimal disruption. The Luftwaffe wanted a new fighter with unsurpassed performance. Messerschmitt wanted to build the Me 262 without compromising its overall profitability and Hitler wanted a fast jet bomber that could be used to repel an Allied invasion force before it gained a foothold on the Continent.

It goes without saying that the Me 262 made little impact when it came to helping Germany win the war and this book will show that of the four parties concerned, only Messerschmitt could be said to have achieved its goal. The Air Ministry faced such an uphill struggle in trying to establish production lines for the Me 262 that it gave up its own independence in exchange for the expertise of Albert Speer's Ministry of Armaments and War Production. The Luftwaffe would be forced to operate the Me 262 as a bomber for months when it desperately needed it as a fighter and Hitler's vision of the Me 262 whizzing over the invasion beaches on D-Day, dropping bombs onto disembarking troop formations, was destined to remain unrealised. Messerschmitt, on the other hand, was able to continue building the Bf 109 en masse and in parallel to the Me 262 until the end of the war.

# Origins:
# 1938 to January 1941

INDUSTRIALIST ERNST Heinkel hired inventor Hans von Ohain to build him a working jet engine in April 1936—and for more than two years Ernst Heinkel Flugzeugwerke (EHF) was the sole company in Germany designing jet aircraft, including fighters.

This de facto monopoly only applied to airframes however, with the German Air Ministry, the Reichsluftfahrtministerium (RLM), encouraging four other firms, BMW, Bramo, Daimler-Benz and Junkers to create their own gas turbines for aircraft propulsion.

Junkers had begun designing its own jet aircraft[1] by July 1938 and that October the RLM decided to officially make Messerschmitt AG the second jet fighter manufacturer.

According to an RLM report entitled Current Status and Future Development Work in the Field of High-Speed Flight With Jet Engines,[2] dated October 14, 1938: "Until now, only EHF was entrusted with this [designing jet fighters], partly for reasons of confidentiality. However, it now seems appropriate to entrust another aircraft factory with the development of fast single-seaters.

"This comes into consideration on the basis of preparatory work [carried out by] the company Messerschmitt AG ... An extension of the development to a

second aircraft factory also seems appropriate in order to avoid a monopoly of EHF in this area."

The "preparatory work" had apparently begun some months earlier. Woldemar Voigt, later to become head of Messerschmitt's Projects Office, recalled hearing about the work ongoing at Heinkel[3] and that "... during the course of 1938, we, at Messerschmitt, were informed by the RLM that BMW, too, was working on this sensational new development. We were asked to submit studies on the potential performance to be achieved by a fighter powered by the gas turbine and the thrust requirement for such an aircraft."

Unfortunately, "the eventual size of the engine was still very much a matter for speculation" and the company was forced to make its calculations on the basis of rather sketchy data supplied by BMW. Eventually "we concluded that our total thrust requirement for a single-seater with the specified armament and a 30-minute endurance at combat altitude was 610kg.

"Since both the engine weight formula and manufacturing considerations seemed to favour smaller engines, we suggested to the RLM that the proposed fighter should have two gas turbine engines of about 700lb (315kg) each.

"We had not, at this stage, sketched out any firm design proposals and we had seriously underestimated the drag divergence Mach number and, in consequence, the speed for which the projected aeroplane was to be designed ... In the event, the Technical Office of the RLM elected to go for very much higher thrust levels, both BMW and Junkers—the latter having meanwhile entered the turbojet picture—aiming at a static thrust in the order of 1,500lb (680kg).

"Such a value was certainly much higher than that demanded by the twin-engined aeroplane that we envisaged at that time, but the decision at least enabled us to commence serious design studies and the higher thrust requested by the RLM was to prove a boon in the event ... The actual configuration of Projekt 1065, or the Me 262 as it was eventually to be designated, evolved from a series of quite different design studies, the drawings of which unfortunately no longer exist".

Messerschmitt commenced the design of what would become the Me 262 in late 1938 under the project designation P 1065,[4] working through a wide range of different layouts—all of them featuring a tailwheel arrangement rather than the tricycle configuration that would later become a hallmark of the Me 262.

"The nosewheel undercarriage had only just been demonstrated by the Douglas DC-4 and was still very much a radical innovation, and it was obvious that our aeroplane would have radical features enough without adding an innovatory undercarriage," remembered Voigt.

"In view of the high thrust level stipulated for the new turbojets by the RLM, our first design studies were based on the use of a single BMW TL-Strahltriebwerk—as the new power plant was then known[5]—as we felt that one engine would be the optimum for a single-seat fighter of the prescribed characteristics."

In fact, the earliest known jet fighter specification sent to Messerschmitt by the RLM actually required the use of just one engine. This document, Preliminary Technical Guidelines for Fast Fighter Planes with Jet Engines,[6] was sent to the company on January 3, 1939.

In addition to a single jet engine and a single seater layout, two different configurations were expected: fast fighter and interceptor. A full-vision cockpit canopy was "desirable" and a pressure cabin was needed for the interceptor version.

Armament was to be two MG 17s with 1,000 rounds each, plus one 20mm MG 151 with 500 rounds for the standard fast fighter version and the same guns but fewer rounds for the interceptor—500 per MG 17 and 250 for the MG 151. In both cases these had to be installed in the fuselage if possible or close to it if not.

The radio set would be a standard Fu G VII as fitted to the Bf 109 E and a flare gun with six rounds was also needed, along with a seat belt and parachute.

Top speed was to be 900km/h with a landing speed not above 120km/h if possible. Endurance at full power was one hour for the fast fighter and half an hour for the interceptor. Rate of climb performance was "still to be determined". Stress rating was H 5—the standard fighter category—and the airframe was to be of all-metal construction, although "simple and cheap construction is required. The construction effort for the series must not exceed 3,000 hours". No details of the engine, its manufacturer or its likely performance were included.

With a single engine, Voigt recalled, "arranging the power plant in the fuselage with its intake in the extreme nose and efflux duct in the tail was the logical first stage[7] but was soon discarded as we felt that, in view of the large wetted areas involved, the weight of sheet metal demanded by the lengthy ducting and the boundary layer that would be generated in the intake duct with reduction in total pressure in the engine inlet as a result, this could scarcely be the optimum layout.

"We then endeavoured to reduce the total wetted area and to materially shorten the ducting by investigating a twin-tailboom arrangement rather similar to that eventually adopted for de Havilland's Vampire. This was even less successful in our view as, although duct length had been somewhat reduced, the external wetted surface area was, in fact, greater and the airflow over the upper and lower wing surfaces was now disturbed at three places (i.e. by the central nacelle and the two booms).

"The next evolutionary stage was a pod-and-boom configuration not unlike that to be adopted several years later for the Projekt 1101, although without the swept surfaces [wings] and nosewheel undercarriage of the later design. From the performance viewpoint this arrangement appeared to be the optimum that we could achieve with a single-engined aeroplane. At the expense of a fairly long intake duct we reduced the fuselage cross section and total wetted area to a minimum."[8]

Again, there were concerns about the undercarriage, with Voigt remembering it as a "nightmare". The wheels retracted into the fuselage, interfering with the engine installation and wing structure, and the tailwheel was in the way of the engine exhaust. As a result, "somewhat reluctantly, we began to consider the possibilities of reverting to our earliest proposal of a twin-engined design".

The first twin-engine configuration examined was "basically a straightforward low-wing aeroplane with the engine nacelles mounted conventionally on the wings. The main undercarriage members retracted into the wing/fuselage intersection, one main member being arranged to retract into a well forward of the single mainspar and the other into a well aft of the spar.

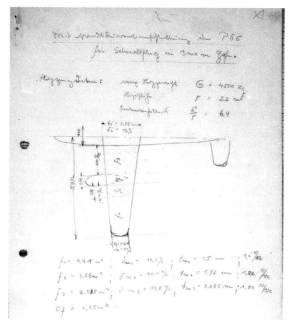

*Sketch made by Hans Hornung in April 1939 showing the earliest known version of the Messerschmitt P 65 with a tubular fuselage, straight wings and tailplanes, and a teardrop shape denoting the wing-mounted jet engine.*

"From the viewpoint of drag, this arrangement seemed optimum, but it was unacceptable to us structurally for the attachment points had of necessity to be situated unreasonably far aft for a tailwheel aircraft and we could find no satisfactory method of handling the wing and fuselage forces and moments in the areas cut up by the retracted wheels."

A chart prepared by Messerschmitt staff immediately after the war cites April 1, 1939, as the official first day of the project to create what would become the Me 262.[9] Messerschmitt engineer Hans Hornung wrote out a set of notes detailing the aircraft design on April 13, 1939.[10]

He began with a sketch showing the single-seater with a slender tapering fuselage, straight wings similar to those of the Bf 109 and straight tailplanes. The wing was shown with a teardrop-shaped protrusion at mid-span denoting the engines. Wingspan was 11.9m, wing area was 22m², weight was given as 4,500kg and top speed was projected at 840km/h.

These figures placed the aircraft between the contemporary single-engine Bf 109 E and twin-engine Bf 110 C in size, but closer to the 109. Clearly the size, shape and even appearance of the type's engines was still uncertain, while the undercarriage continued to pose difficulties.

"Another stepping stone before we reached the configuration submitted to the RLM," recalled Voigt, "was a design essentially similar to the contemporary Heinkel jet fighter project (which was to materialize as the He 280) except that we still adhered to the tailwheel

undercarriage whereas the Heinkel team was being somewhat more adventurous in this respect.

"The two members of our main undercarriage folded inward, the wheels turning about 50-degrees in relation to their oleo legs and fitting into the contours of the fuselage. While this design looked good from the aerodynamic point of view, we had two reasons for continuing our search. Firstly the undercarriage was overly complex, would be expensive to manufacture and would probably be trouble-prone in the field, and, secondly, the mid-wing arrangement resulted in three closely-spaced aerodynamic disturbances on the under surfaces [the lower part of the fuselage and the lower part of each engine nacelle] and we suspected that we might encounter considerable transonic drag."

The Messerschmitt team altered the design of the undercarriage mainwheels so that they would fold inwards from the wings towards the fuselage without turning—simply lying flat instead. But since the landing gear together with the wheels was wider than the relatively thin wings, this meant the wheels would protrude above the upper surface of the wing—necessitating a bulge at the wing roots.

Therefore, Voigt wrote, "in order to provide an aerodynamic fairing for the retracted wheels, the fuselage was given what was essentially a triangular cross section, the base of the triangle being wide enough to accommodate the wheel wells. An incidental advantage of such a cross section was that, with the apex of the triangle near the pilot's eye level, a good field of vision was provided from the cockpit".

Messerschmitt formally submitted its P 1065 design proposal to the RLM for consideration on June 7, 1939.[11] Nothing of this submission appears to have survived—no drawings and no data—yet it would appear that the P 1065 as submitted had changed little from the configuration sketched out by Horning two months earlier. Certainly, by the end of September 1939, wing area was still 22m² with wingspan presumably also the same[12]—though maximum take-off weight had decreased to 4,321kg.[13] Voigt remembered this initial submission featuring the low-wing layout and triangular fuselage cross section, though the latter seems to have remained a contentious issue for some months afterwards.

The Second World War began on September 1, 1939, and less than three weeks later, on September 20, Messerschmitt's Project Office produced a three-page document entitled Technical Conditions for P 65.[14] In line with the original requirement, this stated that the aircraft was to perform two roles: fighter for use against air targets and "as an interceptor with fuel for 15 minutes

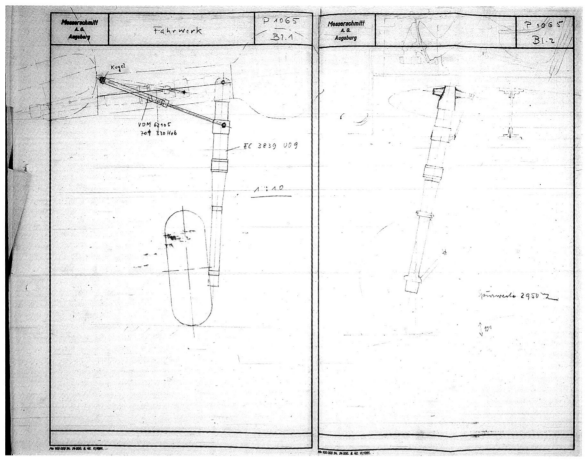

*Messerschmitt sketches showing the P 1065's undercarriage mainwheel arrangement. The positioning of the wheels meant that a fuselage with a triangular cross section was necessary.*

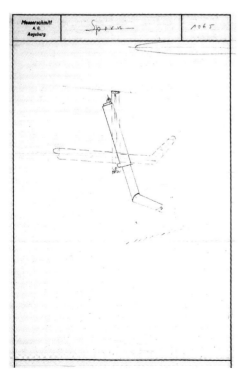

*The P 1065's uncomplicated tailwheel and its position relative to the tailplanes.*

of flight time at 6,000m altitude—use against air targets".

It was necessary that "the installation of different engine models must be possible without major structural changes". It was also to have a pressure cabin capable of maintaining a constant cabin temperature from 3.5km up to 10km altitude. Canopy defrosting and de-fogging was essential.

There were three options for armament: four MG 17s with 800 rounds each plus two MG 151s with 400 rounds each; two MG 17s with 800 rounds each plus three MG 151s with 400 rounds each, or one "large-calibre weapon (P 30/7 or 30/8)"[15] with 100 rounds plus two MG 151s or four MG 17s. All three options were for installation in the aircraft's nose. The gunsight would be a Revi C 12 C, the radio would be a Fu GVII and a flare gun would be included for the pilot with six rounds.

The aircraft would have two fuel tanks—an armoured one at the front and a "replaceable metal tank or sealing rivets" at the rear. Under "safety devices", the sheet lists a seat belt, back parachute with oxygen and dive brakes. Under "performance", it rather vaguely states "maximum speed as high as possible" but landing speed must be below 140km/h; take-off run below 600m; one hour

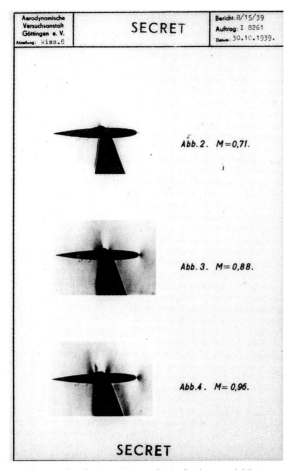

*Photographs showing Messerschmitt fuselage model being tested at different speeds in the AVA's wind tunnel.*

endurance at 6,500m altitude and 85% throttle as a standard fighter. Again in line with the January 3 requirement, the airframe was to be "all-metal construction. Simple and cheap construction is required".

Nine days later, on September 29, 1939, a new data sheet was issued[16] outlining three different variants, referred to as P 65 I, P 65 II and Interzeptor. These appear to have been the original June 1939 design (P 65 I), a version with new smaller wings (P 65 II) and the required interceptor variant, now essentially the P 65 II with a reduced fuel load.

Where the P 65 I had a wing area of 22m², the P 65 II's was reduced to 18.5m². The effect of this was to reduce maximum take-off weight from 4,321kg to 4,235kg at the cost of increasing landing speed from 130km/h to 150km/h, or from 154km/h to 177km/h if the aircraft was being forced to land with its full fuel and munitions load.

Both P 65 I and P 65 II would have sufficient fuel for one minute's start at 130% power, an unspecified time climbing at 100% power, five minutes of air combat at 130% power and 55 minutes' flying time at 85% power. When used as an interceptor, P 65 II would only have enough fuel for 25 minutes' total flying time.

Armament was now reduced to just two options: "Weapons I: 3 x MG 151 with 400 rounds (2 x MG 17 with 800 rounds)" or "Weapons II: 1 x 30/7. 2 MG 17 with 800 rounds". The design still included a pressure

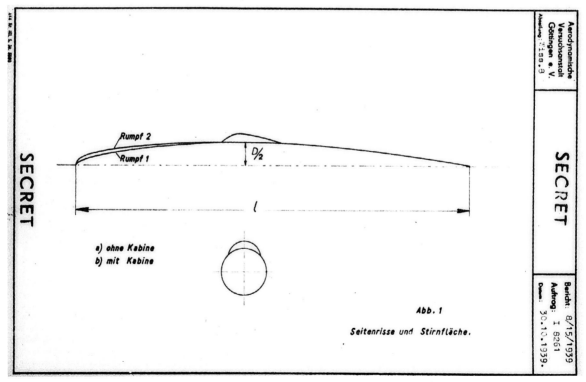

*AVA wind tunnel model sketch showing two different fuselage forms tested on Messerschmitt's behalf.*

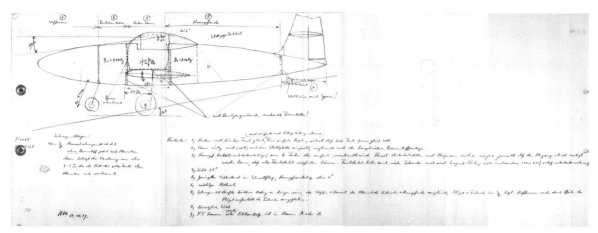

*Willy Messerschmitt's drawing of the P 1065, dated October 17, 1939. Although it features a mid-wing layout and an oval fuselage cross-section, the design also includes a nosewheel—in addition to the tailwheel—and the soon-to-be familiar fuel tank layout.*

cabin for all variants and now both night lighting and an Fu G 18 were listed as equipment. Both fuel tanks would now be given armour protection.

A slightly different version of the same data sheet[17] was issued the following day, September 30, which deleted the interceptor variant and stated that armour protection would be provided for "all three" fuel tanks. The "Weapons I" armament options was now given as "1 x MG 151 with large calibre and 200 rounds. 2 x MG 151 with 400 rounds", while "Weapons II" remained the same. Maximum speed was included this time and the figures make clear what Messerschmitt hoped to achieve by giving the aircraft smaller wings: "Max speed at 3,000m with 100% performance—P 65 I = 840km/h, P 65 II = 915km/h. With 130% performance—P 65 I = 950km/h, P 65 II = 975km/h."

Between October 8 and October 10, Willy Messerschmitt together with company engineers Rolf von Chlingensperg and Riclef Schomerus went on a brief P 1065-related business trip.[18] First they travelled to Berlin for meetings with the RLM and jet engine manufacturer Bramo,[19] then on to the Aerodynamische Versuchsanstalt (AVA) at Göttingen.

At the RLM, Messerschmitt asked for the aircraft's ammunition requirement to be reduced, since carrying so much ammo was hampering flight endurance,[20] and for the fuel reserve to be reduced from 10 minutes' worth down to five. Technical Office representative Hans-Martin Antz agreed to both requests. It was noted that Junkers was continuing with "the construction of equipment" and "Junkers, like Bramo, will deliver two units on July 1". Messerschmitt's meeting summary notes that "we must contact Junkers as soon as possible to adjust to P 65"—in other words it would be necessary to liaise with Junkers about how best to install its jet engines within the Messerschmitt airframe.

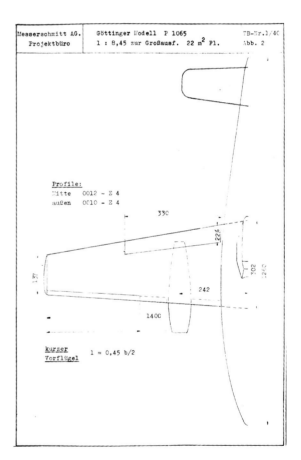

*Messerschmitt company drawing of an AVA model showing the 22m² wing designed for the P 1065.*

At Bramo's offices, the jet engines it was building and their controls were discussed. Intriguingly, the Messerschmitt meeting summary says: "We demanded that the pivotability should not result in any delay in deliveries from BMW. In contrast to earlier statements, BMW now believes that the pivotability would result in a delay in the deadline. Then I did without the swivelling option for the first engines."[21]

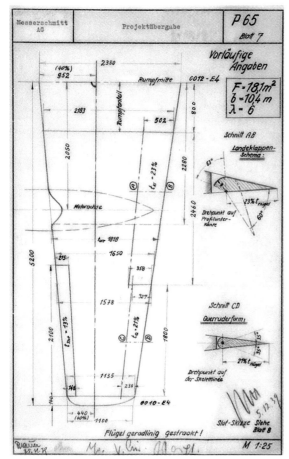

*Wing design for the P 1065 with 18.1m²
area, dated November 25, 1939 and signed by
Willy Messerschmitt ten days later.*

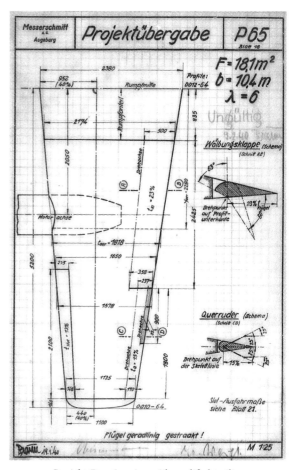

*Straight P 1065 wing with modified trailing
edge surfaces and a refined turbojet outline,
from a page dated January 19, 1940.*

Finally, at the AVA, "the timing of our wind tunnel measurements was discussed and the possibility of producing further models for P 65 in the workshop was clarified".

Schomerus drafted the official trip summary report on October 13 and on October 17 Professor Messerschmitt himself produced a sketch that he labelled 'P 1065'. This showed remarkable foresight in some respects—the canopy was similar to what would appear on the series production model Me 262 and a nosewheel was drawn in too, as well as the tailwheel—but the fuselage was mid-wing and oval in layout.

Whether Voigt was mistaken in recalling that the June 7 submission had the low-wing, triangular fuselage cross section layout, or whether that layout was indeed submitted and Professor Messerschmitt simply regarded the more conventional mid-wing/oval layout as superior is unclear. Either way, Messerschmitt's Project Office seems to have spent the last two weeks of October 1939 comparing and contrasting the merits and drawbacks of oval versus triangular cross section fuselages. And the mid-wing versus low-wing layout comparisons ran into December 1939.

A report issued on October 27 listed the advantages of an oval fuselage cross section[22] as 0.4m² smaller wing area required, smaller tailplanes possible and visibility over the fuselage centreline better by half a degree. The advantages of the triangular fuselage cross section[23] were much more extensive: a 2.3m² smaller total surface area, a 0.12m² smaller frontal area, slightly smaller fin possible, less wing panelling required, 6% lower wing root bending moment, lots of space for the control rods down the sides of the pressure cabin, a maximum of five weapons possible in the nose compared to four for the oval fuselage, normal landing gear retraction, normal landing gear covers, and better installation options for a nose wheel.

On October 30, the AVA released some results from wind tunnel tests carried out for Messerschmitt on a pair of fuselage shapes at high subsonic speeds—from Mach 0.65 up to Mach 0.95.[24] Both fuselages were cylindrical with a cockpit bulge about halfway along on the upper surface but they differed in the shape of their nose—one was sharper and the other blunter and more rounded.

The December 15 report on mid-wing versus low-wing layout[25] gave the advantages of the former as

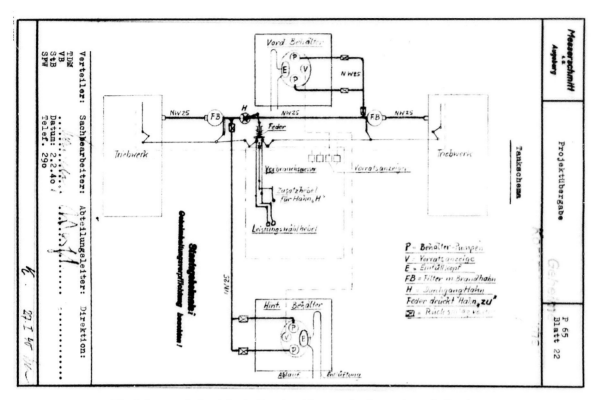

*The fuel system designed for the P 1065, with two tanks, front and rear, feeding the two engines. The addition of a third tank had already been discussed by this time.*

"low thrust" and "lower overall height (undercarriage)". This was based on the assumption that the engines would be mounted centrally within the wings, rather than slung below them.

The advantages of a low-wing configuration were "larger possible elevation of the tailplanes in relation to the wing (downdraft, temperature)"—in other words moving the tailplanes away from the hot engine exhausts—"smallest overall dimensions (length), tanks of the same size, better view (downwards and to the side over the engines), belly landings, lower overspeed (effectiveness of fillets on the leading edge of the wing), less interference between the fuselage and the engine nacelles, reduced exposure to temperature on the fuselage and almost horizontal fuselage axis (landing gear)".

## PROJEKTÜBERGABE P 65

Meanwhile, work had already started on a 20-page document entitled Projektübergabe P 65 or 'project delivery P 65'.[26] Many of the pages in the only known surviving copy of this report have different dates on them, with pages adding updated design data evidently inserted later. The earliest page is the first one, dated November 9, 1939. This suggests that an 18m² area wing is now the preferred design, though the original 22m² area wing is also mentioned. The mainwheel size is given as 770 x 270. The next oldest page, Page 2 from November 21,

gives details of the 380 x 150 tailwheel.

Pages 4 and 5, both dated November 25, give details of the new wing design—the area of which is now given as 18.1m². Also mentioned for the first time is a drawing number—1065.00-26.[27]

Page 3, evidently first drafted on November 27, lists special equipment for the P 1065 V1—the first prototype. The aircraft was to have a detachable silk brake parachute filling a 110 litre space in the fuselage behind the rear fuel tank and the nose would be filled with 150kg of ballast to represent a full weapons load.

A fully equipped but non-functional pressure cabin would be installed too, as would an ejection seat and dive brakes. Two Bramo/BMW P 3302 engines would be fitted, each weighing 533kg including auxiliary equipment, and it was reported that "the question of which prototype and with which load assumptions the nose wheel can be used for is still open".

None of the pages within Projektübergabe P 65 has a date which falls within December 1939 but according to Voigt, there was a meeting on December 1, 1939, between BMW, the RLM at the Luftwaffe test centres to discuss installation of the P 3302 and the P 3304 in the P 1065 This included questions about how the engines could be attached, the fuel system they would need and the instrumentation.

On December 19, a P 1065 mock-up was inspected

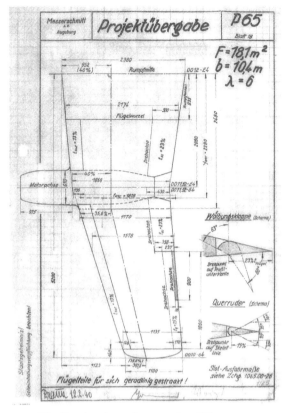

*The P 1065 wing as it appeared on February 12, 1940—the outer section now being swept back to resolve centre of gravity issues arising from BMW's longer-than-expected turbojet design.*

and approved[28] and on January 15, after a hiatus lasting more than six weeks, another round of Projektübergabe P 65 revisions and additions commenced with a detailed description of the ejection seat to be installed.[29] This essentially comprised a cylinder of compressed air and a piston which, when activated using a handle on the seat near the pilot's knees, propelled the seat upwards with a force of 5g, reaching a final speed of 8.5m per second.

The handle would only become 'live' once the aircraft's canopy had been ejected, but Professor Messerschmitt suggested that the seat release should also require a two-step movement to prevent accidental activation.

Even as work on the P 1065 progressed, the Project Office sketched out an alternative design in parallel—the P 1070.[30] This smaller twin-jet fighter's straight wings[31] were to have an overall span of just 8.3m, compared to 10.4m for the P 1065, with an area of 13m² compared to 18m². Overall length was 7.2m compared to 10.65m. Despite the Project Office's earlier aversion to the nose-wheel layout, the P 1070 was to have exactly that. The P 1070's existence would be brief, however, with no further work in evidence after January 22.

A P 1065 cockpit interior mock-up was meanwhile inspected on January 18[32] and on January 24 another

page was added to Projektübergabe P 65 giving provisional details of the cockpit canopy structure.[33] The 'first version' of this would be attached using four lever locks, only those on the left being unfastened for access to the cockpit—effectively allowing the canopy to hinge open to the right. It was noted that it might be necessary to provide the canopy with double glazing, the design of which would be available within 10-14 days.

On January 27, a further addition to Projektübergabe P 65, page 14, gave details of the fuselage nose.[34] Seventeen drawing numbers were cited, suggesting that the design was increasingly moving towards preparations for the first prototype. The same page pointed out that accessibility for adjusting the weapons, even when the lower part of the fuselage was closed, "must be guaranteed by means of hand holes". The weapons mounts needed to be vibration-proof and further changes to their arrangement were to be expected following test firings.

A report separate from the Projektübergabe, produced on January 30, 1940, examined options for building the aircraft's tailplanes.[35] Three different proposals were listed, one of them to use the same structure as had been used for the Me 210. More than a week later, on February 8, 1940, a meeting was held at Messerschmitt's Augsburg headquarters to discuss project definition and construction status of the P 65.[36] Only four men were present—Willy Messerschmitt himself, Joseph Helmschrott, von Chlingensperg and Rudolf Seitz. Seitz, a member of Voigt's team, would continue to work on the P 65/Me 262 on and off for much of the war.

The meeting summary includes the earliest known mention of swept outer wings for the aircraft and indicates that the V1's wings would be unique: "For V1 the Bramo 3302 engine is hung under the wing, for all subsequent models the engines are installed centrally in the wing."

Voigt later recalled that the reason for choosing swept outer wings had nothing to do with high-speed aerodynamics: "BMW soon ascertained that its turbojet would be still larger and appreciably heavier than the company's least sanguine revised calculations had suggested, thus presenting us with serious centre of gravity problems. Aircraft development had progressed too far for us to dramatically revise its layout and we were forced to introduce what we considered a somewhat inelegant 'fix' in the form of swept outer wing panels to resolve the CG difficulties presented by the heavier engines.

"Thus, it was to be purely fortuitous that the Me 262 was to become the world's first operational fighter featuring wing sweepback; a radical departure that, at this stage at least, reflected no attempt to reduce the effects of compressibility."[37]

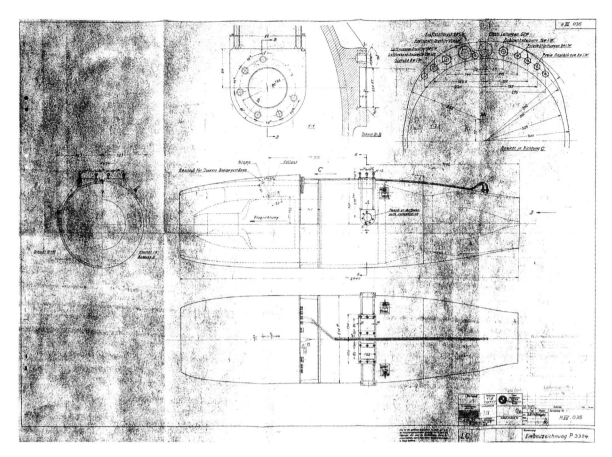

*BMW's ill-fated P 3304 turbojet design as it appeared in March 1940. The company
initially intended to focus its jet engine development on this type.*

However, it is worth noting that Voigt also remembered disliking the configuration where the engines were mounted centrally in the wing—yet the original period document shows this was still the preferred layout.

He said: "The other design change accompanying this 'fix' was in the actual positioning of the engine. We had never been really happy with the arrangement whereby the engine was mounted centrally on the wing. It had been obvious from the outset that the structure wrapped around the engine was going to be quite heavy and also expensive.

"Now, with further revised estimates of engine size and weight, the nacelle diameter was coming out so large that Projekt 1065 no longer looked as aerodynamically favourable as we had expected. We were forced to face the fact that the wing of our aeroplane was simply too small to make an in-wing installation of the engine rewarding.

"We had earlier considered the possibility of mounting the engine under the wing, but, perhaps as a result of a latent suspicion that this configuration offered too simple a solution to our problems, had devoted most attention to the in-wing arrangement. Now we finally reverted to underslung engine nacelles and had arrived

by a somewhat circuitous route at the definitive configuration—a low-mounted wing embodying sweepback and carrying the engine nacelles underslung."

Also discussed during the meeting of February 8 were the ramifications that positioning the engines under the wings would have for the tail unit. According to the summary, the existing triangular tail unit was designed to suit a layout where the engines were in the wings rather than under them and as a result "it is to be expected that the VI's stability at full throttle with underslung engines is low". If the tail unit needed altering then it would be necessary to build a new one, rather than changing the existing one. It was noted that while the fin and tailplanes would be covered with Dural sheets, the rudder would be covered with fabric.

On February 15, a fifteenth page was added to the Projektübergabe which detailed a 'final' wing design with an area of 18.1m² and a span of 10.4m.[38] Details of flaps, ailerons and slots were given but the dive brakes were to be detailed separately.

Page 3 of the Projektübergabe, the project guidelines, was then superseded on February 17 by Pages 3a and 3b.[39] The brake parachute previously mentioned would now only require 90 litres of space in the fuselage rather than

110 but the dive brakes, ejection seat and fully equipped but non-functional pressure cabin remained the same. It was noted that "additional monitoring devices are required to test the engines (still needs to be clarified by the engine manufacturer)" and no weights were given for the underwing mounted engines this time.

Where it was originally projected that 150kg of ballast would need to go into the fuselage nose to represent the weight of the production model's guns and ammunition, now "the fuselage nose remains without weapons ... no ballast is required in their place". The first P 1065 would not be fitted with radio equipment and it had evidently been decided that one P 1065 prototype would trial a nosewheel arrangement after all—but exactly which one remained undetermined. No order had yet been officially placed for any P 1065 prototypes, yet it appears that Messerschmitt had already been told such an order was imminent.

A new Page 8 inserted on the same day further elaborated on the engine situation for the V1: "Given the position of the engine relative to the spar, no ballast is likely to be required in place of the weapons."[40] For the P 65 series production model, the P 3304 engine would be installed but "the locating of the engine in the front wing position has not yet been clarified; negotiations with BMW Spandau are ongoing about this and about the line connections". For both the V1 and the series production model, "to better accommodate the landing gear connection, the engines are now arranged at a distance of ~2,080mm from the centre of the fuselage".

At this stage BMW was planning to focus its development effort entirely on the P 3304—building only two P 3302s in order to gain "general knowledge about the behaviour of turbojets". However, under pressure from the RLM's Technical Office this total was increased to four.[41]

Willy Messerschmitt wrote to General-Ingenieur Gottfried Reidenbach at the Technical Office on February 19, 1940,[42] to make it plain that delays were to be expected.

The heading of his letter was "P 65 Deadline" and he wrote: "We inform you that we are constantly coordinating our own dates with the delivery dates communicated to us by the engine supplier [BMW] via the RLM. Since we were last given the date of delivery for the engine of July 1, 1940, based on our telephone inquiry to RLM-LC 3 (H. Schelp) on February 16, 1940, we will ensure that the airframe is ready by the time the engine is received.

"We have so far postponed the earlier dates that we had intended, as it is not necessary to finish the airframe before the engines arrive. This measure has made it possible for us to continuously incorporate corrections after receiving the results from the wind tunnel testers.

"If you agree, we will continue to do this in the future. We would therefore ask you to inform us about the delivery dates of the engines, if there are still postponements to be expected.

"The assembly date of course depends on the condition in which the engine arrives, i.e. whether it corresponds to the construction documents known to us, or more or less deviates from them. If the process is reasonably correct, the aircraft may be ready to fly by the end of July 1940. However, we believe that with the novelty of the engine, difficulties will arise which will lead to a corresponding postponement of the flight clearance date. Since we have not yet had such an engine in hand, it is extremely difficult to say more precisely.

"We are not sure whether Siebel will guarantee the dates that we carefully estimate based on our experience. If this is not the case, I would ask you to arrange for Siebel to send some of the design engineers here in order to carry out the construction work here until it is completed."

Messerschmitt's policy of declining to complete an airframe before its intended engines had been delivered would have consequences for the P 1065/Me 262 programme later on. And it appears that he was relying on an infusion of engineers borrowed, via the RLM, from the Halle-based Siebel Flugzeugwerke company to get the work completed—rather than using his own staff.

The January 24 Projektübergabe note about the cockpit canopy was superseded exactly a month later on February 24.[43] Now the canopy structure was to be double glazed—though not immediately. The description states: "The current single pane design must, under all circumstances, be carried out in such a way that a double pane can be installed without any structural changes."

Additionally, it was foreseen that a purely electrical windscreen de-icing system would not be possible, so a combined electrical/hot air system was being designed whereby "hot air ... from the nozzle area of the engines is, with the help of a blower, piped through an approx. 100mm thick line to a gap approx. 10mm wide and 200mm long in front of the windscreen" for de-icing. Although, "the final definition of this system can ... only take place after the test results have been received".

Finally, in the centre section of the canopy structure, the first pane of Plexiglass on the left "is to be designed as a pressure-tight hinged or sliding window".

The RLM placed an order for three P 1065 prototypes powered by BMW turbojets on March 1, 1940.[44]

A new Page 1 was added to the Projektübergabe on

*Artistic rendering of the P 1065 in flight from the build description issued by Messerschmitt on March 21, 1940.*

*The P 1065 shown at rest. The tailwheel arrangement mattered less if the engines were mounted within the wings.*

*Access to the P 1065's weapon's bay was to be straightforward and convenient thanks to a novel tilting nose arrangement.*

*Forward view of the P 1065 with its tail mounted on a jack, showcasing its triangular*
*fuselage cross section as well as the ports for its trio of MG 151 cannon.*

March 6—superseding the original of November 9, 1939, to give more details of the main landing gear.[45] Take-off weight was now given as 4,440kg plus or minus two per cent and landing speed with 90% take-off weight was 188km/h. Tyre pressure for the 770 x 270 mainwheels was 3.75 atmospheres. A new Page 3 was also inserted on the same day,[46] stating that the V1's fuel tanks would now be medium-weight 16mm-thick sack tanks rather than rigid structures and the V1's wing area had been set at 20m². Lastly, also on March 6, a new Page 14 noted that "the weapons bay can be swivelled; the pivoting takes place by means of a hand crank located on the tiltable part of the structure". New drawings would be provided showing the tilting arrangement—which involved the whole nose pivoting upwards to reveal the weapons, their mountings and their ammunition boxes.[47]

The last addition to Projektübergabe P 65 was on March 15 with a further change to the ballast requirement. Now 50kg of dead weight would need to be put in the nose, since the engines were going to be shifted rearwards by 12.5cm and 4kg of ballast was needed for every centimetre moved. It was still expected that the series production model would have its P 3304 engines built into its wings rather than hung below them.

## PROJEKTBAUBESCHREIBUNG

A new P 1065 build description—effectively a brochure featuring numerous artistic renderings of how the aircraft could be expected to look when built—was issued by Messerschmitt on March 21, 1940.[48] This summed up all the development undertaken thus far as it applied purely to the series production model. It would be a tail-dragger of all-metal construction with its engines built into the leading edges of its wings.

Constructed to the highest stress group, H 5, the aircraft's engines, continuous wing unit and tail unit could be removed for transportation on standard 12m railway wagons.

*Another drawing from the March 1940 description, this time a cutaway showing the P 1065's cockpit tub, retracted undercarriage positions, twin fuel tanks and weapons bay.*

*P 1065 fuselage component breakdown. This basic arrangement would change little as the type's development progressed.*

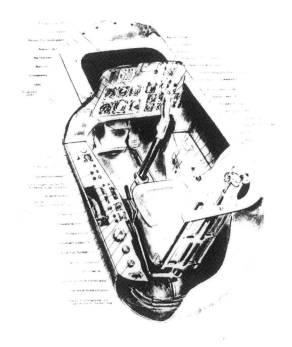

*Layout of the P 1065's pressurised*
*cockpit—including an ejection seat.*

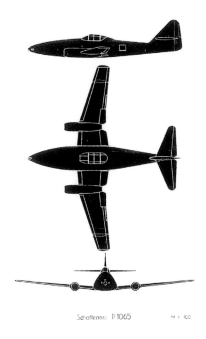

*Three-view drawing of the P 1065 from*
*the March 1940 description.*

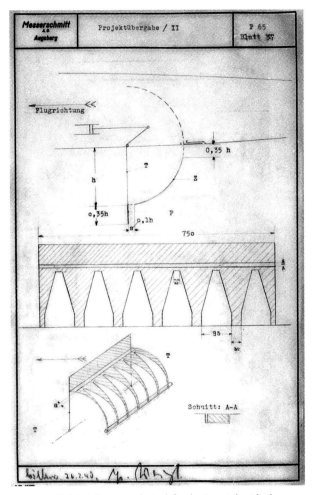

*A cylindrical form was devised for the P 1065's airbrakes,*
*shown in this drawing dated February 26, 1940.*

The undercarriage track width was roughly 2.95m and the mainwheels retracted inwards hydraulically and could be manually extended in an emergency. The lining of the wheel wells was attached to the wing struts and the covers were controlled via pressurised oil cylinders. In the cockpit, the landing gear position could be checked using a 12-bulb display with accompanying buzzer.

The wheel size remained 770 x 270 with individual brake cylinders controlled by the pilot using Bf 109 F foot pedals and the swivelling tailwheel had a 380 x 150 tyre with a spring strut.

At the tail end of the aircraft, the rudder and elevators would be fabric-covered, with the tailplanes mounted on the fin. Inside the cockpit, the elevators and ailerons would be operated by the control column mounted on a torsion tube, with the rudder controlled by a Bf 109 F foot lever. Trimming the rudder involved turning a handwheel.

The continuous wing unit was attached to the fuselage from below at four points and was a single-spar low-rib design but "otherwise the well-known Messerschmitt smooth sheet metal construction". There would be an air brake in the wing centre section on both sides of the fuselage, actuated using a thumb switch on the throttle. Unusually, "by exchanging different end caps, the wing surface area can be changed from 20m² to 18m² for flight tests".

The type would have two BMW P 3304 engines, each providing 600kg of thrust at sea level, which would be started "by means of an outboard starting system". Each would have its own throttle with three

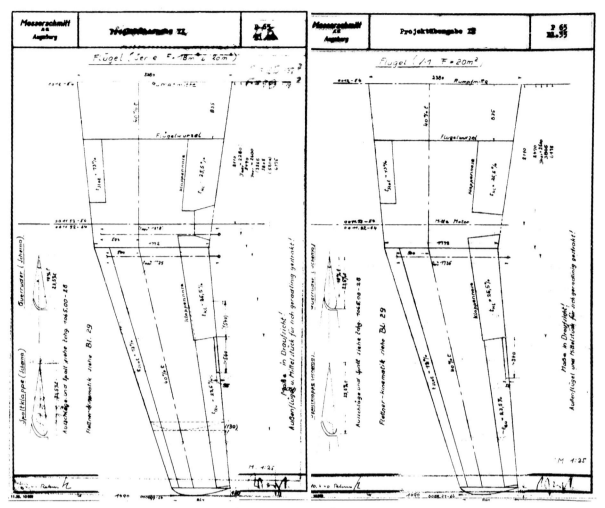

*Diagrams showing how the 18m² could become a 20m² wing with the addition of a new end cap.*

positions—overdrive, normal thrust to idle (throttleable), and quick stop. The latter was to be used in the event of engine failure.

Fuel would be carried in "two exchangeable, protected sack tanks of the same size, each with a capacity of approx. 860 litres. They can be removed by means of covers on the underside of the fuselage". Each tank would incorporate two electrically operated pumps.

In the cockpit, the pilot sat on a seat parachute with high-altitude breathing apparatus which itself sat on an ejection seat, as outlined in Projektübergabe P 65. The cockpit canopy was also as previously described—locked down at four points, opening to the right and capable of sustaining a pressure corresponding to 3,000m altitude all the way up to 10,000m. The whole cabin would be heated using compressed air from the engines.

The dashboard would have gauges to monitor the fuel level, fuel flow, lubricant pressure and engine speed. Other flight instruments were as standard. A built-in flare launcher could be fired using buttons on the left side of the dashboard and an on-board oxygen system

would be provided. The pilot also had the use of a compass, on-board clock and map pocket.

Electrical power would come from two 1,000W generators, with an outboard electrical connection on the right side of the fuselage. The radio systems, FuG XXV and optionally FuG XVII or FuG XVIII, would be mounted on a frame behind the rear fuel tank, with the antenna stretched from the fuselage to the fin.

Only one armament was specified—three MG 151s with 250 rounds each in the nose. Two were positioned next to one another, with the third above them on a tray covering the ammunition boxes, and hand holes were provided for manual adjustment by the ground crew without the need to fully open the compartment. Empty belts and cartridges would be collected in boxes which had flaps that opened downwards for emptying. An ESK 2000 gun camera would be installed at the top of the weapons bay.

Two sets of performance data were given—with and without the extended wing end caps. The extended caps, for the 20m² wing area, gave a wingspan of 12.35m,

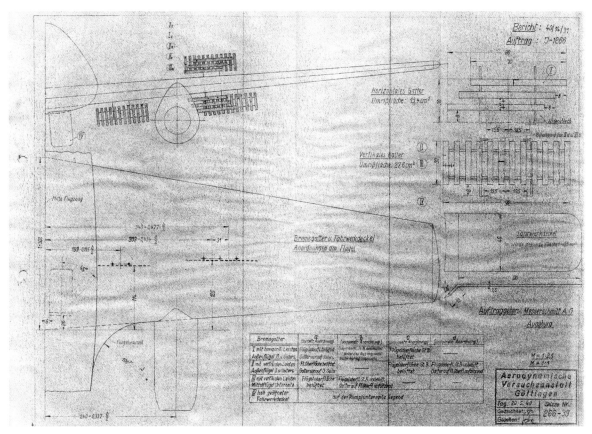

*AVA diagram showing different potential positions for the P 1065's redesigned gate-type airbrakes.*

while the standard 18m² area wings had a span of 10.4m. In both cases, fuselage length remained 10.6m and height was 2.8m. The longer caps increased take-off weight from 4,442kg to 4,498kg and cut top speed from 870km/h to 857km/h, both achieved at 6km altitude.

Maximum endurance, using minimum performance, was the same for both at one hour and 14 minutes. Time to climb to 6km was five minutes 36 seconds with the standard wings or five minutes 42 seconds with the wing extensions. The only real advantage of the longer wings, seemingly, was a reduced landing speed—from 148km/h to 141km/h, assuming a landing weight of 3,300kg in both cases.

## PROJEKTÜBERGABE II P 65

Even as the last few pages were being added to Projektübergabe P 65, work commenced on a second document labelled Projektübergabe II P 65. This was much longer at 76 pages and again its pages bore various different dates, ranging from February 26 to May 8, 1940, but the majority were from a single date—March 5.

While much of the information it contains mirrors that presented in the Projektbaubeschreibung of March 21, and some pages are seemingly copies of pages from Projektübergabe P 65 with newer dates added, it does offer a few additional details. For example Page 36, dated

February 29, 1940, explains the form and operation of the air brakes.[49] These would consist of two perforated cylindrical surfaces, one installed on the upper surface of each wing between the engine nacelle and the fuselage just behind the wing spar. When the pilot activated the system, both surfaces would rotate out of the wing, then rotate back into the wing when they were no longer needed. According to the report, "it is to be expected that the demand will be made to continuously extend and retract the brake".

Page 4, from March 5, noted that the tightly riveted pressure cabin, which included no thermal insulation, would have 80mm of armour protection built into its front wall.[50] And Page 44 revealed that each of the aircraft's two fuel tanks would supply a different engine unless one suffered battle damage and leaked—in which case the pilot could use a lever to activate a valve routing fuel from a single tank to both engines.[51]

Page 60, also from March 5, indicated that the FuG XXV's rod antenna on the underside of the fuselage would be coupled to the landing gear, so that when the gear was extended the antenna would retract. Furthermore, "the previously planned arrangement of the wire antenna (stretched from the fuselage to the fin) still requires approval from the E-Stelle [Luftwaffe test centres]". Another March 5 sheet, Page 63, mentioned in

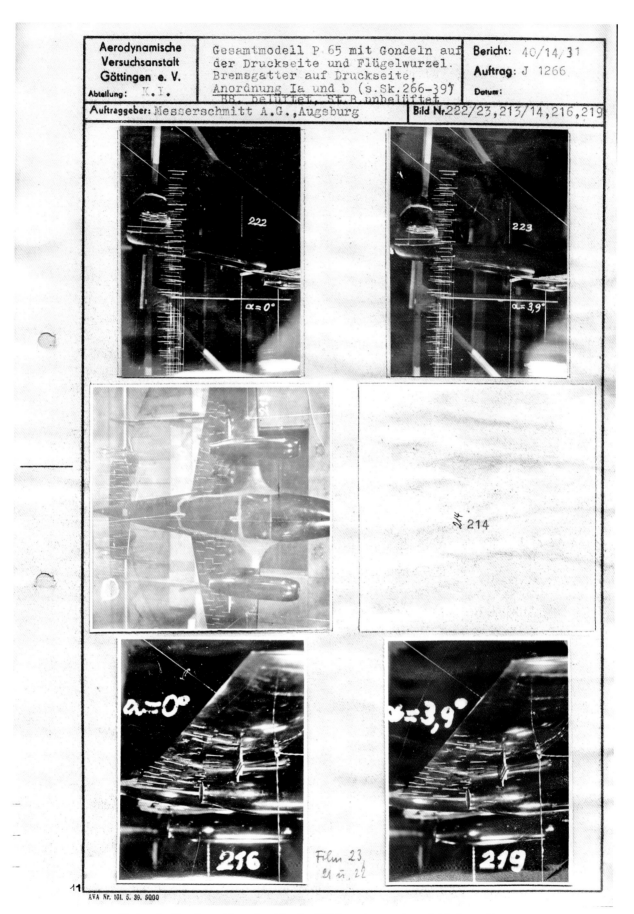

*Photos of a P 1065 model employed by the AVA in testing a variety of airbrake positions.*

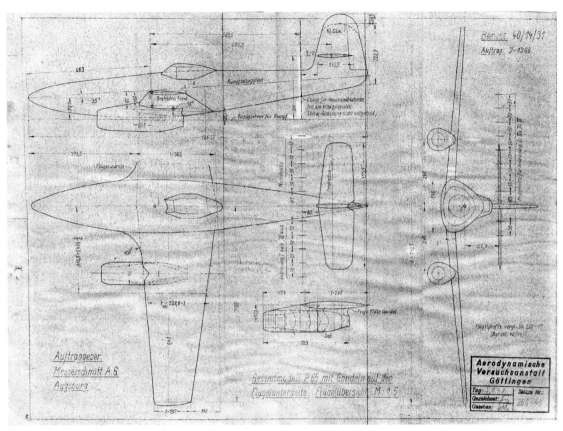

*P 1065 wind tunnel model with the engine nacelles now positioned below the wings. The outer wing sweepback already decided upon by Messerschmitt has not yet been incorporated into the model.*

passing that "the gun bay contains 3 MG 151s, the space provided for 2 additional MG 17s cannot be built in",[52] and Page 71 of April 22 contributed a note on cockpit ventilation for the V1: "For cabin ventilation, an adjustable flap must be provided on the fuselage in the area of positive pressure (immediately in front of the cabin structure ...) and an outlet opening in the area of the greatest negative pressure (on the canopy structure)."[53]

The Siebel personnel promised back in February had been allocated to the P 1065 project but suspicions soon arose that they were not, in fact, the professional engineers and draughtsmen expected. Willy Messerschmitt wrote to Antz at the RLM's Technical Office on May 3, 1940, to complain: "Dear Mr Antz! I have a little worry that you may be able to help me allay. I was supposed to get the Siebel design office. The people from Siebel made available to me generally do not make a very good impression.

"I have also heard from other sources that the best efforts of the Siebel office are being used for other purposes and that some are also working for the Heinkel company. Therefore, I am sending you a list of the draftsmen and designers who, according to the Siebel company, are meant to be available. These work partly

in Halle and partly here for the P 65 and other tasks.

"I would be indebted to you if you would make it possible to check whether the engineers and draughtsmen on the list are really all engineers and draughtsmen from Siebel. Unfortunately I have no way of doing this myself."

Evidently a second P 1065 project offer was made to the RLM by the Messerschmitt on May 15, 1940,[54] but exactly what this consisted of, and how it differed in detail from the original pitch which had won an order for three prototypes, is unclear.

Meanwhile, the P 1065's air brakes had been reconsidered by May 6, with the original cylindrical design being switched for flat rectangular perforated surfaces with an area of 0.3 to 0.5m$^2$ on the underside of the wing on both sides. For the P 65 prototypes there would even be adjustable intermediate positions between the fully deployed and fully retracted states. The number and shape of the perforations had yet to be determined.[55]

More detail concerning the fuel tanks was also added at this time—the flexible sack type tanks would only be used for gasoline. If the aircraft was to be powered by diesel oil, sheet metal tanks with leak protection would be used. And where the two pumps fitted to the V1 would operate at a rate of 1,000 litres per hour, the

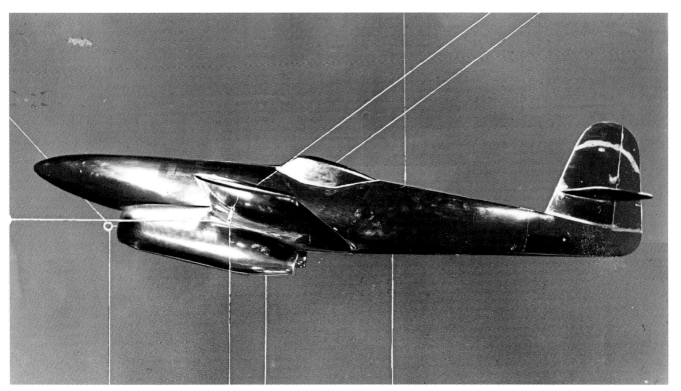

*Photograph of the actual model tested by the AVA up to July 1940.*

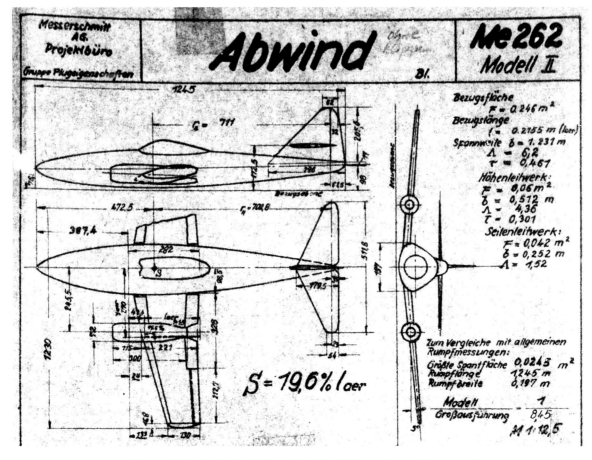

*Messerschmitt sketch of a wind tunnel model with the engine nacelles mounted*
*mid-wing—the arrangement still intended for the production model.*

*Messerschmitt P 1065 model. The fuselage has the familiar Me 262 shape but the wings remain significantly different from those that would eventually enter series production.*

series production model would have pumps capable of supplying 1,500 litres per hour.[56]

## PROJEKTÜBERGABE III P 65

The earliest known reference to Messerschmitt's decision to begin flight-testing the Me 262 V1 prototype without jet engines can be found on the first page of Projektübergabe III, dated May 30, 1940.[57]

This has the heading "V1 with Jumo 210 G installation" and under "task" it is stated that in order "to test the airframe, a normal engine is to be installed in the fuselage instead of the weapons". The Jumo 210 G was notable for introducing fuel injection to the series and had powered the short-lived Bf 109 C variant, a handful of which had served in Spain with the Condor Legion during early 1938. By May 1940 it was still a relatively modern engine but one that was no longer required for the front line.

The page noted that the water radiator installation for the powerplant should be like that of the Bf 109 D, with the oil cooler either beside or in front of it and the oil tank itself positioned within the aircraft's forward fuel tank. Fuel for the piston engine would be drawn from the rear tank. The propeller would also be the same as

that fitted to Bf 109 Ds and an experimental spinner ordered by the Project Office had already been delivered.

Evidently BMW supplied Messerschmitt with installation details for its P 3302 engines on June 20[58] and the following day the V1's planned fuel system arrangement was amended with the addition of Projektübergabe III page 4, which now gave details of the "V1 mit Jumo 210 G und 2 x TL 3302".[59] The jet engines would be suspended below the wings and fed fuel from the rear fuselage tank. The piston engine in the nose would be supplied from the forward fuselage tank, which would be reshaped for the prototype to accommodate only 500 litres of fuel, rather than the originally planned 860 litres.

On July 1, the date when BMW was supposed to deliver the first P 3302 jet engines to Messerschmitt, the RLM issued a new C-Amts-Programm Lieferplan or production schedule which had the P 1065 literally pencilled in at the bottom. Heinkel's twin-jet competitor for the Messerschmitt design, the He 280, appeared typed in mid-table.[60] It showed that 20 examples of each aircraft were planned, with the first P 1065 now expected in September 1940, followed by two more in October, three in November, five in December, five in January 1941 and four in February 1941. The He 280 timetable required two aircraft to be completed in August 1940, three in September, then five in each of October, November and December.

Six days later, the AVA issued a report on wind tunnel tests it had conducted on at least nine different air brake designs for the P 1065.[61] Some showed them installed on the wing underside, some on the upper surface of the wing, some inboard of the engine nacelles and some outboard. At around the same time, the AVA was also evidently testing different engine nacelle configurations for the aircraft. Models with underwing nacelles were tested as well as models with the nacelles attached to the upper surface of the wing—protruding from the wing on either side of the cockpit.[62]

Meanwhile, BMW had been struggling with the P 3304 turbojet. According to a company report of February 1941,[63] which retrospectively assessed the engine's progress: "… very considerable difficulties arose in the workshop during the production of the 3304 jet engine, which led to the realisation that series production was not possible without significant design changes.

"This fact, combined with the initially very good successes on the test bench of the much simpler to produce P 3302, led to the number of prototype P 3302s being increased to 10 in the middle of the year. Short-term demands of Technical Office for pre-production 0-series engines then led to the planned production of another 40 engines on the basis of P 3302."

The next update to Projektübergabe III was on July 22, when some centre of gravity calculations were added as page 8, but apart from that virtually nothing seems to have been done on the P 1065 at Messerschmitt itself between the end of June and the middle of October 1940—a hiatus of three and a half months on the project.

At BMW, a plan was drawn up in August to demonstrate the P 3302 to Reichsmarschall Hermann Göring in October—which had an unfortunate knock-on effect for the P 3304. According to a company report: "In order to achieve this goal, all work on P 3304 was largely stopped in favour of the P 3302 until around mid-October. All this resulted in the fact that the delivery date for P 3304, which was originally in June 1940, had to be postponed to mid-January 1941."[64]

On September 26, 1940, Professor Messerschmitt wrote again to Reidenbach at RLM's Technical Office, to explain why so little had been done: "Due to the stressful work given to our design office and our experimental team as a result of the war requirements, we have been forced to pull workers out of prototype programmes that are to be completed later and are not yet at the front.

"We do this in the following order: the Me 210 is disturbed as little as possible. The P 65 follows. First and foremost, workers will only be removed from the Me 209. The Me 261 does not currently require any designers and is completed in operation as a filling work.

"For the reasons mentioned above, we are not able to give exact dates for our future prototypes. We would be extremely grateful if you could get us design engineers on loan from other companies and ask you to check whether the Siebel engineers are partially or fully available again now or later."[65]

Despite Messerschmitt's pledge to only remove workers from the ongoing Me 209 development programme,[66] the evidence speaks for itself: the P 1065 had been put on hold. During this period—essentially the duration of the Battle of Britain—the company was putting much of its collective effort into developing and supporting the Bf 109 and Bf 110, while trying to concentrate whatever capacity might be left over on preparing the already-troubled Me 210 to succeed the latter.

It was not until October 15 that three further pages were added to P 65's Projektübergabe III. The new page 9 discussed flaps and ailerons, as well as stating that two independent valves would be provided for emergency actuation of the landing gear and landing flaps using compressed air.[67]

Page 10, stated to be a supplement to pages 70-71b of Projektübergabe II, added very little, reiterating that "the postponement of the delivery date for the TL 3302 engines led to the installation of the Jumo 210 G as an auxiliary engine for testing the flight characteristics; the 3302 engines are then hung under the wing".[68]

Page 11 gave some insight into the ongoing difficulties BMW was experiencing when it came to building engines reliable enough for flight testing. It said: "Dummy engine. After completion of the flight tests to determine the characteristics of the wing without the nacelles, dummy engines are to be provided optionally on the lower and upper side of the wing as well as in the centre; position the dummies in the direction of flight for all three cases, if possible according to the later position of the engines."[69] In other words, Messerschmitt was preparing to flight test the P 1065 V1 with mock-ups of BMW P 3302 engine nacelles slung below its wings, attached to their leading edges or even fixed above them. The same page pointed out that it needed to at least be possible to retrofit the V1 with an ejection seat when one became available.

Two weeks later, on November 1, 1940, a replacement page 4 was issued which did little other than further reduce the size of the forward fuel tank to just 200 litres.[70] Evidently the pressure on the Project Office had eased somewhat by this point since Willy Messer-schmitt now committed its resources to an entirely new project—the design of a long-range bomber intended as a natural extension of the Me 261 extreme-range transport project.[71]

Nevertheless, Messerschmitt wrote to the Luftwaffe's chief engineer Generalstabsing. Lucht on November 29, 1940, to say: "For me, the lack of designers is actually the only thing that prevents me from completing such tasks [the further development of a long-range recon-naissance/bomber design] quickly. The few designers that I have are almost all busy with carrying out the ongoing improvements, change instructions, etc., of the two models running in series [Bf 109 and Bf 110].

"But I am convinced that today there are still a lot of design engineers at other companies who are not involved in war-related work. Wouldn't it be possible for me to get a number of designers from such companies?

"Unfortunately, none of these tasks can be solved by French or other foreign designers, since in connection with the rapid new and further development of aircraft, the greatest possible secrecy is necessary to prevent the enemy from keeping up."[72]

More weeks then passed with few changes made to the P 1065 until, on December 17, there was further discussion of fitting a nosewheel. Helmschrott wrote a memo to Voigt and others stating that suspension travel for the nosewheel arrangement needed to be re-exam-ined and static tests were required to see whether and how often the wheel itself and the leg it was attached to could withstand shocks consistent with the aircraft's maximum allowable descent speed and a 50% fuel load.[73]

Up to this point, even though a nosewheel had been included in a drawing by Willy Messerschmitt in October 1939, and adding one to a prototype had been discussed in February 1940, it was still expected that the P 1065 would be a conventional tail-dragger—with two undercarriage mainwheels and a tailwheel. Now it seems to have been firmly decided that a nosewheel would eventually become part of the design.

A 14th page was added to Projektübergabe III on January 8, 1941, which said: "According to Prof. Messer-schmitt's decision, the weapons bay is to be designed in such a way that a nosewheel can be installed. Drawing 1065.00-163 serves as the construction documentation for this. Drawings 1065.00-131-147, 152, 153, 156 and page 63 of Projektübergabe II are therefore now invalid."

By this time, construction of the V1 prototype appears to have been well under way—through exactly when manufacturing of parts and their assembly commenced is unclear. It is conceivable that this had started way back in February 1940 or even earlier, since at that time

Messerschmitt had been planning to have the completed prototype ready in time for the anticipated delivery of BMW's engines on July 1.[74]

A day earlier, on January 7, 1941, Messerschmitt had written to the Generalluftzeugmeister, Ernst Udet, to further expand on the note he sent Lucht in Novem-ber.[75] He wrote: "I am currently working on a design, based on the experience with the 261 and using a large number of components of the 261, which covers around 20,000km. Two-thirds of the fuel would be carried internally, the rest would be discardable. Appropriate defensive armament and the possibility of accommo-dating bombs and camera equipment will be provided.

"I have the impression that such an aircraft will become an important weapon for the Air Force. Actu-ally we're already too late for it, because the USA now has long-range bombers, even if they don't have this range. It would be quite possible to push through such a development exceptionally quickly ... if special meas-ures are taken."

Messerschmitt sent Voigt a memo[76] on January 10 to relay some bad news: "Subject: Me 262. According to a message from BMW, Munich, dated 7.1.41, delivery of the engines is not expected anytime soon. Reasonably reliable dates cannot be set. For this reason, the 262 should only be accelerated in construction to the extent that is important for testing of flight characteristics and performance.

"The following programme is therefore established: 1. V1 will continue to be made ready to fly at an accel-erated rate. 2. With only a few engineers, the design office sets out the design of the weapons bay with nose-wheel and for conversion of the mainwheels to suit that arrangement, in order to test the nosewheel landing properties using one of V1-V3 (on this occasion the nose is to get a towing hook). 3. Mr Helmschrott will provide a rough draft overview drawing of the nose-wheel arrangement on January 13, 1941.

"Mr Seitz urgently procures two cold rocket motors (later an additional two each for V2 and V3). Preliminary February 1.

"4. The following wings are to be prepared: a) standard swept form, b) final swept wing."

In addition to indicating the aircraft's state of devel-opment at this time, Messerschmitt's memo also appears to be the earliest known use of the RLM number 8-262 for the P 1065. Whether the number had been formally allocated at this point is uncertain but from this point on, 'P 65' and 'P 1065' are used less and less frequently in company documents and elsewhere.

The following day, Messerschmitt reverted to using 'P 65' when writing to the company's chief design engineer Richard Bauer—presumably because Bauer would not yet have known what he was talking about if he had referred to the 'Me 262'.[77] This memo was headed "Construction documents P 65" and it said: "All documents for V1, V2 and V3 should have been delivered to you. However, a number of variants are still to be expected for these three aircraft, as they are to be used exclusively for flight characteristics and later engine tests. I ask for the completion dates for the individual aircraft to be determined."

The 20 prototypes optimistically scheduled by the RLM just six months earlier had been boiled down to just three—and none of them had been completed. Requirements placed on the company during the Battle of France and the ensuing Battle of Britain had dramatically delayed the programme of airframe development, while Messerschmitt's engine-building partner for the P 1065/Me 262, BMW, had similarly failed to supply the powerplants essential for a full flight test programme.

By mid-January 1941, the only way forward was to complete the Me 262 V1 and commence flight testing using its nose-mounted Jumo 210 G piston engine. Attempts would be made to secure a pair of Walter RII-209 'cold' rocket motors,[78] providing 750kg of thrust each, which would enable testing at higher speeds and airframe development was expected to progress towards a tricycle undercarriage and swept-back wings.

# Distractions:
# January 1941 to May 1942

**B**MW'S DECLARATION that its jet engines would not be ready for delivery in the foreseeable future had left the Me 262 programme in limbo by mid-January 1941.

The company had found, during P 3302 test runs at 9,000rpm, that all the blades of the seventh compressor stage broke due to resonance vibrations. Changing them evidently required new dies, which took several months to manufacture.

In addition, the engine's original uncooled nozzle failed to withstand the temperatures to which it was exposed and had to be replaced with a cooled version. The combustion chamber was also found to have a very uneven temperature distribution, which made a complete redesign necessary.

Just manufacturing the combustion chamber in the first place caused difficulties. It was originally made using welded sheet metal—but this was found to cause unacceptable warping so "in order to achieve a reasonably adequate dimensional accuracy, very expensive and cumbersome equipment had to be made, which of course also had a time-consuming effect on the development".[1]

Then there were problems with seized axial thrust bearings, which necessitated a huge increase in oil circulation, and issues with unreliable Leistritz fuel pumps

*BMW learned how to build turbojets the hard way with its troublesome P 3302 unit.*

which "constantly ate" their bearings.[2]

In other words, learning how to design and build a working turbojet from scratch without any previous experience to draw on was proving to be a Herculean task.

Construction of the first Me 262 prototype continued but Messerschmitt's Project Office remained heavily

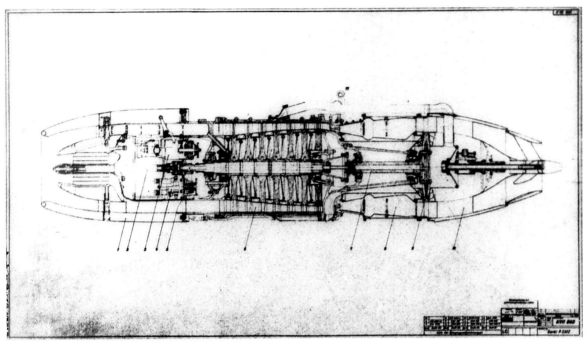

*The internal workings of the BMW P 3302.*

burdened by a backlog of war-essential tasks. Yet elsewhere within the company another advanced project was going from strength to strength.

Working in parallel to Voigt's team was Abteilung L—effectively a second project office within Messerschmitt AG that was tasked first and foremost with designing and building a rocket-propelled interceptor.

During the summer of 1940 Abteilung L, led by charismatic swept-wing and rocket propulsion pioneer Alexander Lippisch, had been testing the DFS 194 at the Luftwaffe's Peenemünde experimental station. This was a glider fitted with a Walter HWK RI-203 rocket motor and on June 3, 1940, it had made its first powered flight.

Although restricted to a maximum speed of 550km/h due to the glider's structural limits, the tests showed huge potential and resulted in plans for a new aircraft stressed for much greater speeds, the Me 163 V4,[3] being given a higher priority rating.[4]

There seems to have been a degree of not-entirely-friendly rivalry between the Project Office and Abteilung L, and it must have been galling for Woldemar Voigt to see Lippisch succeeding in spectacular fashion—the DFS 194 roaring off the runway at Peenemünde was evidently quite a sight—while the much-delayed Me 262 V1 languished engineless in the company's workshops.

On January 20, Willy Messerschmitt issued a list of nonessential new 'commissions' which were to be deleted from the schedule completely "in order to relieve the Project Office".[5] These included, among other things, the design of pressure cabins for the Bf 109 F, Me 210 and Me 262.

However, the same list also stated that a programme of Me 210 simplification and "new proposals for Series 2 must be carried out urgently. A deferment is not conceivable". It is likely, in fact, that most of the company's design and development resources—excluding Abteilung L—were being poured into the Me 210 programme at this point, since it was deemed critically important for the war and was in the process of going wrong.

The Me 163 V4 was completed in February and made its first towed flight at Augsburg on February 13, 1941. It was a small, lightweight, swept-wing machine which lacked even a traditional undercarriage—taking off on a jettisonable wheeled dolly and landing on an extendable skid. It also had a good lift-to-drag ratio and was highly manoeuvrable. Even as a glider, in the hands of its regular test pilot Heini Dittmar it could reportedly perform stunts and extreme manoeuvres that few other aircraft could match.

As an experimental airframe however, it was designed with only enough space on board for the bare essentials—the pilot, the engine when it became available and sufficient fuel for short test flights. There would be no internal armament fitted and additional fuel was not required.

The Me 262 V1, on the other hand, was a big sturdy machine designed to accommodate two engines and a substantial fuel load. There was room in the nose for the Jumo 210 G only because the aircraft had been intended as the prototype for a production model combat aircraft with cannon in that position.

*The Messerschmitt Me 163 V4. While Voigt's Project Office concentrated on preparing the Me 210 for service, Abteilung L enjoyed success with this innovative new aircraft.*

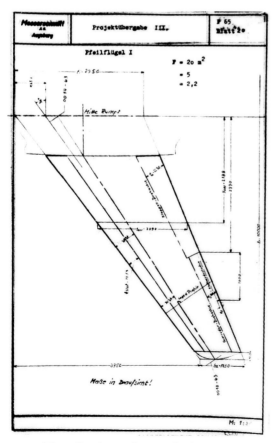

*The earliest known drawing of a fully swept wing for the Me 262, circa April 1941.*

As glide-tests of the Me 163 V4 commenced and construction of the Me 262 V1 neared completion, in February 1941, events were taking place elsewhere which would later come to draw attention still further away from the Me 262 development programme.

Engineer Günther Diedrich at aero engine manufacturer Argus Motoren had constructed a rudimentary four-wheeled testbed for a tube-shaped pulsejet and had begun driving it on a test track—reaching speeds of up to 100km/h. The only obstacle to achieving greater speeds, Diedrich would later recall,[6] was the length of the test track.

Another engineer, Paul Schmidt, had commenced pulsejet development in Germany at his own company in Munich in 1930—evolving the tube shape and its key features—but in 1940 the RLM "strove for cooperation between the firms of Schmidt and Argus and paved the way for mutual visits and exchange of experience"[7] in pulsejet development. However, once Argus had received Schmidt's data and the basic details of his design, it decided to carry forward the development without him. Diedrich solved several problems that Schmidt had struggled to overcome and created what would later be designated the Argus-Schmidt As 014 pulsejet.[8]

On February 25, 1941, the RLM issued a specification for a new single-seat fighter.[9] This appears to have called for an aircraft powered by the new DB 603 engine—a

*Argus pulsejet undergoing flight tests*
*attached to a Gotha Go 145 trainer.*

development of the DB 601. Competing designs were produced by Focke-Wulf and Messerschmitt, with the Messerschmitt design becoming the Me 309.[10] Work on the Me 209 as the successor to the Bf 109 had not yet ceased entirely but it was winding down. The 309 seems to have shown great promise and quickly supplanted the 209 as the 109's heir apparent, increasingly occupying Messerschmitt's designers and engineers as the year wore on.

Meanwhile, BMW had formulated a new delivery schedule for its P 3302 engines—with the first pair of VI-10 prototypes with 400kg thrust due for delivery to Messerschmitt in March 1941, followed by a pair providing 600kg thrust in June 1941 and then four more 600kg thrust units for a total of eight engines by August 1941.[11]

In March, with the still-engineless Me 163 V4 now regularly looping, diving and soaring above Messerschmitt's Augsburg factory, Voigt's team finally found themselves with sufficient time to begin work on developing the Me 262's aerodynamics. Another sheet, Page 15, was finally added to Projektübergabe III on April 4, 1941, this time giving details of a proposed 'Pfeilflügel' or swept wing for the type. It would have a wing area of 20m², a span of just 10m and a sweepback of 35°.

A conference was held on April 8 to further discuss the installation of Walter rocket motors in the Me 262.[12]

Work on the Me 262 VI had finally been completed by this time and build quality must have been high because an examination on April 17, prior to its first test flight,[13] identified only six minor issues—the wing end caps were not connected tightly enough to the wings' internal structure; aileron deflection was found to be relatively large; the inner aileron mass balance lever was very flexible laterally—more so than on a Bf 109; the tailplane end caps also needed to be more tightly attached; there was a suspicion that the screws used to fasten together the two halves of the tailfin might be too weak and the electrical switch used to actuate the tail control surfaces had a relatively high adjustment speed.

At 7.35pm on April 18, Flugkapitän Fritz Wendel took

the aircraft up for its first flight albeit powered only by its Jumo 210 G. This would be the first of more than 40 such tests without the use of jet engines, which continued into September 1941.

As flight testing of the Me 262 VI continued, examining issues including centre of gravity placement, slack in the cockpit controls, play in the control surfaces, elevator vibrations and performance with different wing slat positions, the Project Office seems to have turned its attention away from the Me 262 almost entirely. Evidently knowledge of Schmidt's pulsejet experiments had passed to Messerschmitt and both the propulsion system's potential and its seemingly imminent availability appear to have aroused a keen interest within Voigt's department.

After producing a handful of calculations on the potential performance of the piston engine Me 262 VI supplemented by a pair of 500kg thrust pulsejets,[14] it now focused on designing a small, lightweight, swept-wing fighter powered by Schmidt pulsejets under the designation P 1079—a direct competitor for Abteilung L's rocket-propelled interceptor project.

All of the Project Office's work at this stage seems to have focused on the apparent potential of Schmidt's tubes – whether Messerschmitt was even aware of the practical experiments being carried out by Diedrich at Argus is unclear.

Voigt's team spent much of May, June and July 1941 studying numerous different layouts for the P 1079 aircraft—the end result of which was a report entitled 'Flugzeuge mit Strahlrohren' in July.[15] At least 21 variants, many with highly unusual features but all with the same swept-back wings, were outlined—most of them small and powered by just a single pulsejet motor. They were also hard at work on designing the Me 309, which itself now boasted radical design features such as a laminar wing, tricycle undercarriage, ejection seat and retractable radiator.

A further distraction from the Me 262 appeared on April 26, 1941, in the form of an order for 30 of the long-range bombers Willy Messerschmitt had pitched to Udet three and a half months earlier, now under the designation Me 264.[16] It would be necessary to drive through the design and development of this large project on top of all the company's other commitments.

By mid-July, three months later, the attention of Messerschmitt's Project Office was almost entirely focused on other lines of research and development. Even so, work continued elsewhere. Flight test data was steadily accumulating from the Me 262 VI and on July 24 the AVA delivered a new report on wind tunnel tests of 35° swept wings for the type.[17]

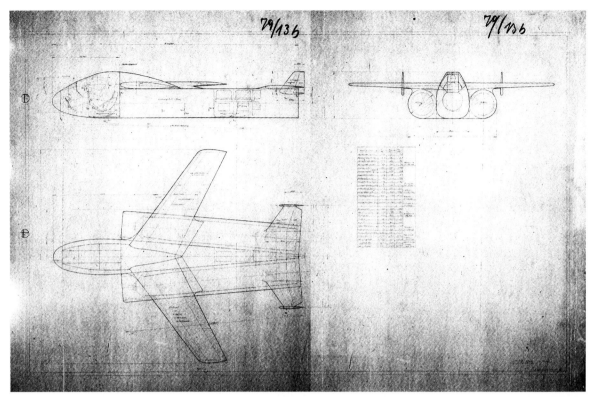

*P 1079/13b—one of at least 21 designs for a pulsejet-powered fighter drawn up by the Messerschmitt Project Office during the spring and summer of 1941.*

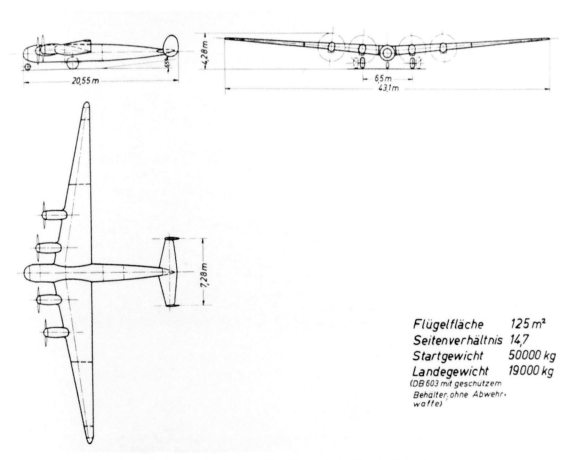

Flügelfläche        125 m²
Seitenverhältnis  14,7
Startgewicht        50000 kg
Landegewicht      19000 kg
(DB 603 mit geschutzem
Behälter, ohne Abwehr-
waffe)

*A very basic three-view drawing of the Messerschmitt Me 264 design from 1941.*

*The Me 309 was a promising design for a
Bf 109 replacement in August 1941—and received
much more attention than the Me 262.*

*The jet-engineless Messerschmitt Me 262 V1 as viewed
from the rear—its twin-bladed prop is clearly visible.*

The following day, despite the fact that there had been
almost no meaningful advancement of the Me 262's
design for more than seven months (in fact, beyond the
decision to fit a nosewheel, almost nothing had changed
for more than a year) the RLM reaffirmed its interest
in the type by changing its order from 20 prototypes to
five prototypes plus 20 series production model aircraft.[18]

Two pilots from the Luftwaffe's Rechlin test
centre—Heinrich Beauvais and Paul Bader—flew the
Me 262 V1 on August 4 and on August 8 Udet was
shown an Me 262 prototype—presumably also the
V1—fitted with a pair of wooden mock-up jet engines.[19]

Messerschmitt's attention remained elsewhere,
however; the Me 309 brochure was produced in
August and five prototype Me 309s had been ordered
by August 14.[20] The type was described as a "Jagd-Ein-
sitzer", single-seat fighter, but with the additional role
of "Stuka-Jäger"—dive-bomber/fighter. It was to have a
maximum take-off weight of 3,500kg or 4,100kg overload including a single 500kg bomb. Wing area was to
be 15.9m$^2$ with a wingspan of 11.05m. A top speed of
630km/h was predicted, with the aircraft's DB 603 H
burning 100 octane fuel.

That same day Willy Messerschmitt sent a memo
to the company's test section to complain about the
lacklustre results being achieved from the Me 262 V1
test flight programme.[21] Referring to test flight report
No. 262 02 L 41 of August 7, he wrote: "The results of
the experiment are incomprehensible, the values are
considerably worse than the wind tunnel measurements with small nominal values. Has it been established
whether the aircraft can even be pulled to the largest
angle of attack? What further tests can be carried out
to achieve the real maximum lift coefficients?

"The test flights were carried out between June 18
and July 7, yet the test report was not made out until

August 7 and it did not come to me until August 13. I ask
for suggestions as to which measures must be taken
to prepare the test reports in a considerably shorter
time. This processing period means an unnecessary loss
of time and prevents the tests from being repeated in
good time."

Messerschmitt's sudden interest in the Me 262 after
months of apparent neglect may have been prompted by
an event which took place the day before, on August 13.
The Me 163 V4, transferred to Peenemünde in July, had
now been fitted with its HWK RI-203 rocket motor
and had successfully made its first powered flight.

This ought to have been a cause for celebration within
the Messerschmitt company, but instead it seems to have
dramatically deepened a growing divide between Professor Messerschmitt and Voigt on one side and Lippisch on
the other. Emboldened by this breakthrough, Lippisch
evidently went to Ernst Udet with a set of demands.

He wanted Abteilung L to enjoy parity of status with
Voigt's office and to be provided with its own bespoke
premises at Obertraubling—around 140km to the north-
east of Augsburg, not far from the company's Regensburg plant; he wanted the aircraft he designed to bear his
name—redesignating the Me 163 as the Li 163; and since
production of further 163s was to be accelerated, he also
wanted to take an unspecified number of personnel from
Augsburg with him to make this possible.[22]

Udet agreed to all of these measures. Willy Messerschmitt, however, seems to have taken exactly the
opposite view. On August 28, Messerschmitt himself,
Lippisch, Messerschmitt advisory board chairman Theo
Croneiss, company production director Fritz Hentzen
and the head of the RLM's Technical Office Gottfried
Reidenbach attended a pre-arranged meeting to discuss
these points and Udet's acquiescence to them.

Reidenbach "accepted Professor Messerschmitt's
objections to moving Abteilung L to Obertraubling
and agreed that Abteilung L should remain in Augsburg.
He asked whether Lippisch and Voigt's project offices

*Photograph of the Me 262 V1 from Messerschmitt report No. 262 02 L 41 of August 7. Willy Messerschmitt personally reprimanded the company's test section over its lateness and its "incomprehensible" findings.*

*The Me 262 V1's cockpit canopy from another photo which appears in Messerschmitt report No. 262 02 L 41.*

would have equal status within the organisation under Professor Messerschmitt and whether the design office and prototype workshop would support both project offices to the same degree.

"Brigadeführer Croneiss and Direktor Hentzen answered both questions in the affirmative. Oberst-Ing. Reidenbach said he was satisfied with this solution."[23]

The following day Croneiss, Hentzen and Reidenbach met without Messerschmitt or Lippisch present, but with Hans-Martin Antz in attendance. They essentially agreed that Abteilung L would indeed remain at Augsburg and that Messerschmitt should speak to Udet personally about Lippisch having his name applied to Abteilung L-designed aircraft.[24]

Furthermore, Croneiss "handed over the description of the enlarged version of the Me 163 to Herr Antz for further attention". This appears to be a reference to a project description published two days earlier, on August 27, by Abteilung L entitled 'Projectbaubeschreibung Li P 05 Interceptor'.[25] The foreword states: "On the basis the flight experiences and characteristics test of the Me 163 V4 the present project was developed as a massive enlargement of the tried and tested pattern." The interceptor detailed did indeed look like a scaled-up Me 163 V4, powered by four rocket motors instead of just one and armed with four MG 151/20 cannon.

Receiving this, "Herr Antz informed the meeting that the project office chief Voigt had submitted a project closely resembling that of Abteilung L. He had received a drawing of P 1079/13c, dated August 11, 1941, and an accompanying description of an aircraft, which although not tailless, had a sharply swept-back wing and was powered by a jet engine. Herr Antz remarked that when Herr Voigt had handed over this information he had said that if this project were developed it would not be necessary to build the Me 163 and the interceptor".

Voigt and Lippisch appear to have been engaged in an increasingly bitter rivalry, with the former attempting to derail the latter's rocket interceptor with his department's pulsejet-powered swept-wing fighter project. Lippisch himself had demonstrated to Messerschmitt that he was not a team player—bypassing the company's leadership and going directly to Udet, while making unprecedented demands and setting conditions that the company would have found difficult to meet.

All this considered, it seems unlikely to have been a coincidence that Messerschmitt sent Voigt a memo

*Exhaust assembly of the Me 262 V1's Jumo 210 G.*

*The Me 262 V1's chin radiator.*

*Me 262 V1 cylindrical oil cooler. This was removed when the aircraft was used for timed trials.*

simply headed "Interceptor" on August 29, with a copy also sent to Seitz.[26] It said: "Based on the verbal consultation, please check whether it is possible to meet the following conditions with the Me 262: 1. For the start and ascent to 8,000m in 80 seconds there are [rocket] motors for 6gr/sec. available. For a further 10 minutes you can then use a considerably smaller [rocket] motor of about 400kg, maybe even less, extremely high speed flight being dispensed with. Please calculate the necessary climbing thrust, the resulting amount of fuel and the total weight if three weapons and a FuG 16 radio system are installed.

"2. An attempt should be made to assemble and accommodate Argus or Schmidt motors in batteries (later in the wing). The advantage of the smaller devices is better space utilisation. In addition, the large number

of devices has the further advantage that they are less susceptible to battle damage and safer in the event of failure of one or the other device. Please contact me on this matter Tuesday, September 2, 1941."

In other words, consideration was being given to whether the Me 262 could conceivably become an interceptor without jet engines by utilising a large rocket motor for a fast climb with a smaller motor for cruising at altitude—or an interceptor powered exclusively by batteries of wing-mounted pulsejets as originally envisioned back in April.

The Me 262 had two major advantages as an interceptor over Lippisch's P 05—it was already the subject of an RLM production order and it already existed as a flying prototype. Lippisch's Me 163 V4 was only an experimental aircraft, albeit one with a viable engine.

Yet the Me 262 V1's airframe, regardless of its engines, remained underdeveloped. The flight test programme had evidently revealed at least one basic weakness of its design—the cockpit canopy. Willy Messerschmitt wrote a memo on September 2, 1941,[27] claiming that "the 262 canopy is curved and is said to have very poor visibility. The canopy of the Heinkel machine should also be curved but affords a very good view. The poor visibility can only be due to poor manufacturing. Please clarify what can be done to get decent windows and let us know."

That same day, Voigt's team appears to have begun sketching out designs for an interceptor variant of the Me 262 as requested.[28] These initially took the form of the Me 262 W1 and Me 262 W2. The W1 was to be powered by a pair of 500kg thrust pulsejets[29] while the W2 would have a pair of Walter rocket motors. Very few further details about either design appear to have survived.

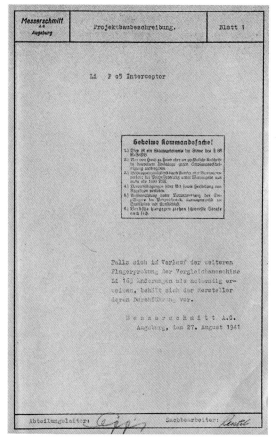

*Title page of Alexander Lippisch's P 05 interceptor description, which refers to the Me 163 as the 'Li 163'—a sign of growing division within the company.*

Manoeuvrability experiments were carried out with the Me 262 VI at the Rechlin test centre during September and it was discovered that, at speeds above 300km/h, the aircraft was less agile than expected. Consequently, the hinge axis of the ailerons was shifted and the rudder surface area was correspondingly enlarged.[30]

Attention continued to focus primarily on the promising Me 309. A two-day inspection of a cockpit mock-up took place on September 11-12, 1941, with only minor amendments required, such as repositioning the pedals and compass, the addition of a variometer, and the inclusion of a small personal luggage space for the pilot.[31] By September 22, the order for five Me 309 prototypes had been supplemented by an additional order for 15 0-series pre-production machines. This was more than either the Augsburg or Regensburg factories could handle, so negotiations began to transfer Bf 108 production from Regensburg to the Potez company in France.[32]

A production schedule was drawn up which would see the VI-V5 prototypes built in Augsburg, the first flying in March 1942, and the 15 pre-production

machines assembled at Regensburg—though all parts would be manufactured at or sourced via Augsburg.[33]

By now, with BMW having missed deadline after deadline for delivery of its turbojet engines, serious thought was being given to equipping the Me 262 with the rival Jumo-produced unit, known as the T1, instead. On September 26, 1941, the RLM asked Messerschmitt to investigate whether the fighter could be converted into a reconnaissance machine if the armament was deleted and a camera was installed—and if so, whether it could be powered by a pair of Jumo T1s.[34] Presumably this work was intended to provide a potential alternative to the development of a dedicated jet-propelled reconnaissance aircraft then under way at Arado.

Like the Me 262, Arado's design, designated E 370, was to be powered by a pair of BMW turbojets.[35] It had a long cigar-shaped fuselage, straight wings and a landing skid instead of a wheeled undercarriage in order to free up more space for internal fuel tanks.

Having both the Me 262 and E 370 dependent on BMW's much-delayed turbojets was asking for trouble, and with no airframes yet earmarked for Jumo's engine, it must have seemed like a sensible precaution to commission a variant of the Me 262 powered by the T1.

A production schedule drawn up on October 7 by Anselm Franz, who was leading the T1's development at Junkers' Otto Mader Werk facility, indicates that the RLM had now ordered enough T1s to power 20 Me 262 fighters by August 1942—a total of 60 engines, including 20 spare units.[36]

Messerschmitt submitted its design for the Me 262 reconnaissance machine to the RLM on October 21 and nearly a fortnight later, on November 4, the RLM requested the completion of 10 pre-production Me 262s between June and October 1942.[37]

In mid-November 1941, BMW was finally able to deliver a pair of P 3302 VI-10 prototypes to Messerschmitt for installation into the Me 262 VI[38] but they do not seem to have inspired a great deal of confidence since work on preparing a variety of alternative propulsion systems for the type continued and it was deemed appropriate to retain the aircraft's nose-mounted Jumo 210 G for safety's sake.

A new but short-lived Me 262 interceptor design, the Me 262 J, was the subject of some discussion and calculations from November 10 to November 12, 1941. Little is known about this design except that it had a new nose, could have been a two-seater, was armed with two MG 151/20 cannon, carried five or six separate fuel tanks and had a Walter rocket motor for propulsion.[39] It also appears to have been proposed with somewhat smaller wings than those of the series production model—16m²

*Perspective drawing of Abteilung L's P 05 interceptor, which Lippisch intended to develop from the purely experimental (at this time) Me 163.*

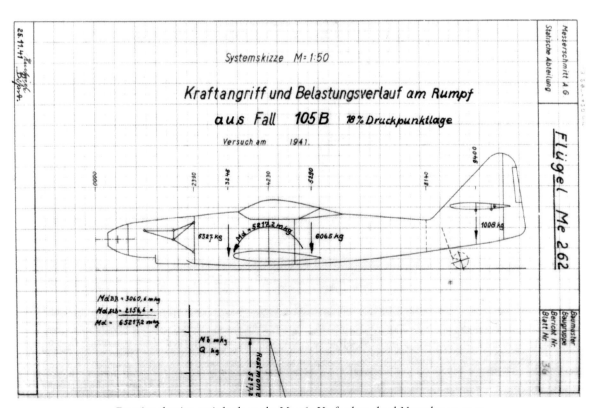

*Drawing showing static loads on the Me 262 V1 fuselage, dated November 25, 1941.*

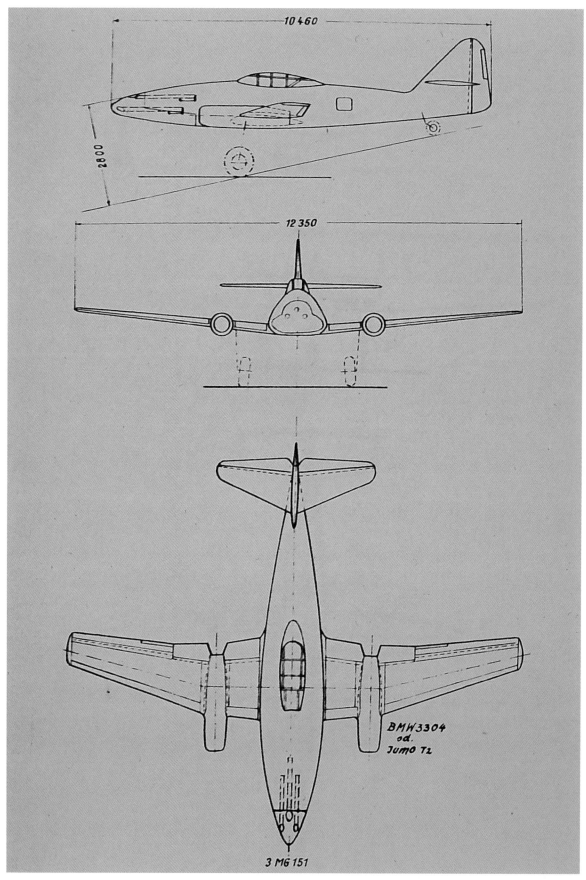

*Three-view drawing of the Me 262 from a January 1, 1942, document showing every aircraft then in development. The engines are shown as mid-wing and either two BMW 3304s or two Jumo T2s.*

in area compared to 20m².

By now Willy Messerschmitt had been able to set aside the rift with Lippisch, though the matter was by no means settled. But another festering sore within the Messerschmitt company was about to become a gaping wound—with dire consequences for the professor himself and for the Luftwaffe.

## THE BIGGEST DISTRACTION

The delivery schedule for the Me 210 heavy fighter had slipped and slipped again throughout 1941 as Messerschmitt's engineers struggled to overcome the type's problems. It suffered from a tendency to ground loop, its DB 601 engines kept inexplicably catching fire, it porpoised in level flight—making it difficult to aim its guns, and it suffered from unacceptable elevator buffeting with its dive brakes extended.

The Luftwaffe desperately needed a replacement for its outdated Bf 110 heavy fighters and put pressure on Udet to get the Me 210 fixed and put into service. Udet had done everything he could think of to make Messerschmitt aware of this urgency and to try and reach a solution, but to no avail.

As a last ditch effort he commissioned Henschel's technical director and well-known troubleshooter Karl Frydag to visit Messerschmitt's Augsburg headquarters on November 17, 1941, to investigate whether, from a technical standpoint, the Me 210 would ever become a viable combat aircraft. Then, on the day, perhaps even as Frydag was walking around the factory, Udet committed suicide by shooting himself in the head.

The position of Generalluftzeugmeister was assumed by the State Secretary for Aviation, Generalfeldmarschall Erhard Milch, and it took him a few weeks to get a grip on all the many threads of development that Udet had set in motion—offering a brief respite to the embattled Messerschmitt.

Willy Messerschmitt wrote a memo to Voigt and Seitz on December 12, 1941, expressing his unease at the sheer length of the Jumo T1 turbojet now planned for the Me 262. He wrote: "I fear that in the long run the Junkers engine will cause difficulties since it has to be installed too far forward because of its size. The nose wheel solution would therefore be very good. Perhaps when we have the nose wheel some of the weapons could be built into the wing."[40]

That same day, Milch convened one of his first department head meetings, with all of the RLM's most senior officials in attendance, and the top item on the agenda was the Me 210.[41] Frydag presented the results of his investigation—stating that the Me 210 would be "a useable aircraft". Majors Walter Storp, the Luftwaffe's

RLM liaison, and Edgar Petersen, commander of the Luftwaffe's test centres, agreed with this assessment.

Evidently the RLM's Technical Office had already decided what changes were needed to fix the Me 210 and 300 of the 400 examples due to be built by May 1942 would have these changes made to them. The remaining 100 would not be fit for frontline duties but would instead be used for training purposes.

In order to make the specified changes, Messerschmitt would be given production assistance and the use of "300 high-quality technical personnel, from January 15, 1942". Technical management staff would be provided by Messerschmitt.

Further desirable changes, which could not be implemented initially due to the tight timeframe, would be made to a projected second series, starting in August 1942.

It was reported that the Luftwaffe's high command had "announced that the Me 210 will be used primarily as a low-level attack aircraft[42] in 1942". This meant that it would operate as a light bomber, without the need to dive and thereby eliminating any issues arising from the use of the aircraft's dive brakes—though this also meant additional armour would need to be fitted to protect the aircraft from ground fire.

Petersen pointed out that the fuselage needed to be lengthened to prevent spins and that there needed to be an increase in operational safety of the fuselage-mounted remote-controlled gun turrets. Finally, it was bluntly stated that "the aircraft has a tendency to stall suddenly. The stall is without warning, so operational losses among the troops must be expected. The troops are to be instructed about this during the briefing".

Dramatically changing the Me 210 from a heavy fighter/dive-bomber to a low-level attack aircraft was a radical step. The Luftwaffe officer or officers[43] who had made this decision presumably thought they were helping the RLM by giving the aircraft what they saw as a less demanding role—but it simply led to more problems.

During a separate meeting at the RLM on December 17, 1941, Seitz explained that work on the P 1079 pulsejet fighter, perhaps now seen as a more viable prospect than the Me 262, was proceeding.

At the end of 1941, the RLM produced a production schedule of the turbojets intended for installation in the Me 262, from BMW, Jumo and Heinkel.[44] BMW was scheduled to deliver one P 3302 prototype in February 1942, another in March and two in April. Jumo was to deliver one prototype T1 in February, two in March, one in each of April, May, June and July, then two in August and two in September.

Then BMW was contracted to supply 40 pre-production P 3302s—beginning with three in October

1942, then another five in November, followed by eight in December, January, February and March 1943. Pre-production model Jumo T1s were due for delivery commencing with two in July 1942, then four in August, and then another six every month from September through to August 1943. The Heinkel HeS 8 was also earmarked for the Me 262—with pre-production model deliveries starting in June 1942.

A lengthy document was produced on January 1, 1942, which gave a comprehensive update on every aircraft development project then in progress—including the Me 262.[45] It noted that the series production model would be powered by two BMW P 3304s or two Jumo T2s,[46] that it would be armed with three MG 151s and that its design included a pressure cabin.

Its all-up weight would be 4,500kg with 1,320kg of fuel. Wing area was 20m² and wingspan was 12.35m. Top speed was expected to be 857km/h and landing speed was 141km/h at a landing weight of 3,300kg. Endurance without bombs at 6km altitude and 830km/h was 45 minutes or 54 minutes at 660km/h. No figure was given for endurance with bombs.

The competing He 280 was listed alongside, powered by two HeS 8 turbojets, but a short and rather prophetic note beneath the listing read "equipping with Junkers engines not possible".

The same document also listed the Bf 110 C, D, E, F-2, F-3, F-4, G-2, G-3 and G-4, Me 109 F-4, F-4tr and G-1, Me 210 A-1, B-1, C-1 and D-1, Me 310, Me 309, Me 163 A-1 and B-1, Me 321, Me 323 D-1, D-2 and D-5, Me 261 and Me 264. This gave some indication of just how much work Messerschmitt had in progress.

On January 8, 1942, Fritz Wendel flew the Jumo 210 G-powered Bf 110 V8, which had been modified as a jet test-bed with a single BMW P 3302 prototype slung beneath the fuselage.[47] The flight lasted only six minutes—from 3.01pm to 3.07pm.

At the RLM department heads meeting of January 13, 1942,[48] there was a reminder that the General Staff requirement was for two Me 210 squadrons with armour for low level attack by April 1, 1942. The meeting heard that the Messerschmitt company was due to begin refitting the aircraft in just two days and was demanding the armour plates.[49]

However, "the dates given for supplying the die-pressed and tempered armour plates given are not acceptable. Manufacturing the dies alone is expected to take six to eight weeks. The date requested by the General Staff must be kept under all circumstances.

"Some of the aircraft must therefore initially be equipped with armour which is welded together from straight plates or is simply bent sheet metal. The effectiveness of this welded construction must be roughly equivalent to the final version".

Whether anyone genuinely believed that this somewhat hairbrained scheme for bringing the Me 210 into service would work is unclear. Those with any knowledge of aircraft design and manufacturing would have known all too well that it was destined to fail.

The intensification of Me 210 manufacturing effort, particularly at Regensburg, now had a knock-on effect for the Me 309. The Regensburg plant manager, Karl Linder, wrote a memo to his staff on January 10, stating that it was now highly unlikely that the 309 pre-production series would be built there and that all 309-related work should cease.[50] A second blow was dealt on January 13 when the RLM's Technical Office announced that the Jumo 213 was "the only engine to be considered for fighters".[51] Work had already commenced on tentative plans to install the 213 in the 309 but now it would be necessary to speed up this process dramatically, with the partly finished Me 309 V3 forward fuselage being repurposed as a mock-up for the 213 installation.[52]

By now both BMW P 3302s had been installed in the Me 262 V1 and static vibration testing had commenced, with an interim report on progress being produced on January 16.[53]

Four days later there was another RLM department heads meeting. Frydag reported that in the best case scenario, 160 armoured Me 210s would be delivered to the Luftwaffe by the end of April—but "Messerschmitt gave less favourable dates".[54] Within seven days the production schedule had already slipped and it was clear that the Luftwaffe General Staff's requirement would not be met. The RLM meeting on January 27 heard that "by May 15, 240 aircraft are to be delivered to the set schedule. A prerequisite for adherence to the schedule is the allocation of Lechfeld airfield, including hangar space, to Messerschmitt" but "the efforts of the Technical Office [to secure this] have so far been unsuccessful".[55]

Even as the Me 210 programme began to topple over, tests commenced on a feature evidently unique to the first Me 262 prototype—its ejection seat. No subsequent 262 is known to have had one. Testing began in early February with a protective screen covering the rest of the aircraft to prevent damage. Film footage was shot which indicated the curved flight path of the seat and dummy pilot as they were ejected. It was soon revealed that aluminium alloy launch rails were satisfactory but an alternative made from steel "showed the marks of seizing, which affected the height of the ejection".[56]

A mock-up of the Me 262 reconnaissance variant was inspected by personnel from Rechlin and the RLM on February 5 and it was decided that one of

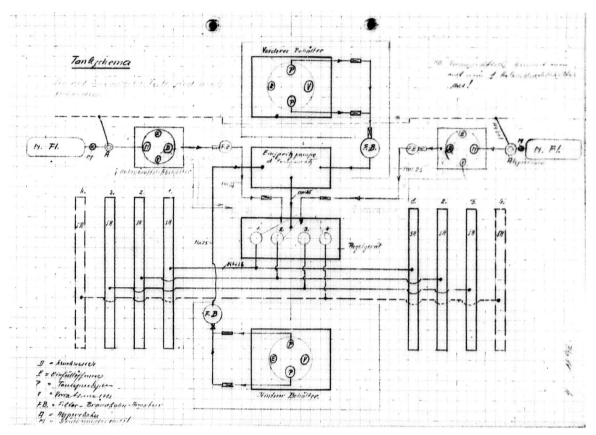

*Fuel system planned for an Me 262 powered by eight Argus pulsejets—four under each wing.*

the pre-production Me 262s should be built to that design.[57] Meanwhile, final testing of the Me 262 V1's P 3302 engines continued with a strength check of the connection between the engines and the airframe.[58]

At the RLM management meeting on February 10 it was ominously reported that the "Me 210 is judged very badly at the front. The Me 210 programme will probably have to be changed". The Technical Office was to submit proposals for how to proceed by February 14.[59]

Three prototypes of the P 1079 had by now been ordered but with Messerschmitt clearly overburdened it was decided on February 17, 1942, that a separate organisation, the Deutsche Forschungsanstalt für Segelflug (DFS) based at Ainring, should take over their construction.[60] On February 24, Messerschmitt agreed to hand over the work[61] and that same day it was confirmed that Henschel had taken over the supply of armour plates for the armoured Me 210, now being referred to as the Me 210 S.[62]

Milch and Luftwaffe Chief of Staff Generalleutnant Hans Jeschonnek both attended a meeting with Reichsmarschall Hermann Göring on March 6 and Jeschonnek outlined the seriousness of the situation.[63] The Me 210s delivered to his men so far were unfit for purpose. He said: "Crews cannot be expected to fly the Me 210. It enters a flat spin very easily, the cause

of which is unexplained. Then there are considerable difficulties with the engine installation. Two fires have already broken out in mid-air. The machine easily overturns, leading to the death of the crews. It is extremely questionable whether the use of the Me 210 can be expected at all this spring."

Milch reported that Willy Messerschmitt wanted to try fixing the aircraft by lengthening its fuselage and would personally give a presentation outlining this proposal on March 9. However, he went on, "if the Me 210 fails, it must be clarified whether production of the Me 109 and Me 110 can be increased. The six Me 210 groups planned for the spring must be equipped with the Me 109 and Me 110 instead. The necessary armour increases must be carried out on time".

In other words, the Luftwaffe desperately needed low-level high-speed bombers and if the Me 210 would be unavailable then Bf 109s and Bf 110s would have to be pressed into service in that role instead. There was also another factor to consider—a direct order from Adolf Hitler that a high-speed bomber be brought into service. Milch said: "In order to comply with the Führer's wish to be able to use a high-speed bomber in some form, the Me 109 was thought of, which can carry 250kg bombs, up to a maximum of 500kg. With additional fuel tanks it can be brought to a range of 1,300km."

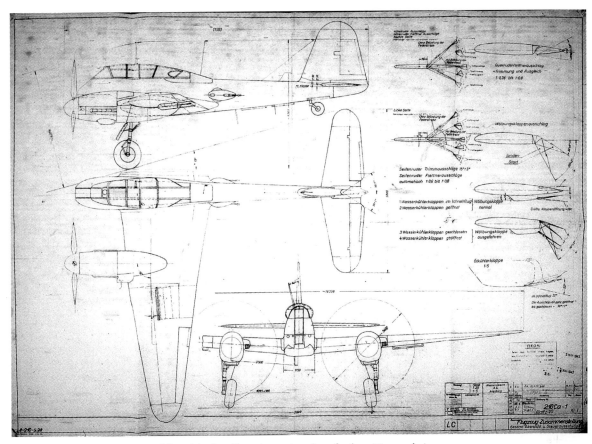

*The original problematic 11.183m long fuselage Me 210 design.*

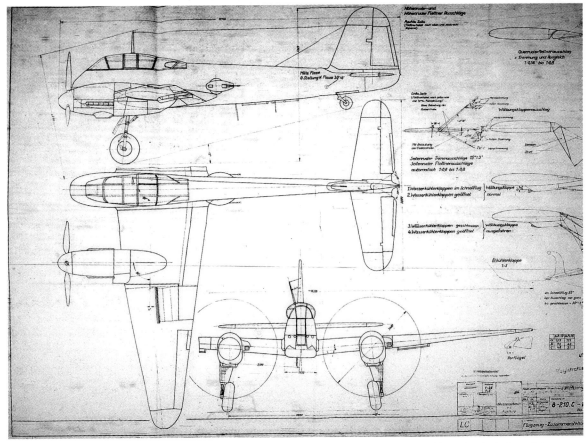

*The revised 12.133m long fuselage Me 210. Lengthening the fuselage cured the worst of the problems that had plagued the type.*

Göring tersely responded: "I agree."

Finally, Milch stated that if it were possible to wait until 1943, the Arado Ar 240 would be available. Göring ordered that "the Arado is to be examined immediately regarding its use as a replacement for the Me 210. At the same time, the possible increase in [Bf 109 and Bf 110] production must be checked".

The Me 210 programme, into which huge investments of time, money and precious resources had been ploughed, was now dangerously close to outright cancellation. The RLM department heads meeting of March 17, 1942, heard that "the aim is for a decision to be made about the further construction of the Me 210 by 1.5.42".[64]

## FIRST FLIGHT WITH JETS

It was against this backdrop that, on the evening of March 25, 1942, the Me 262 V1 finally made its first jet-powered flight at Augsburg. Pilot Fritz Wendel had spent just over half an hour that afternoon conducting turning tests in Me 210 NE+BH and then had to wait nearly five hours for the jet prototype to be ready.

During initial taxiing, both engines cut out when their throttles were moved back too far. Having restarted the engines, Wendel found that he needed 800-900m of runway to get airborne, taking off at 7.29pm. After climbing for 20 seconds, he levelled and the airspeed rose to 400-450km/h. However, Wendel then found that he could not reduce the engines' revs.

Attempting to throttle back resulted in the failure of the port side fuel injector and subsequent extremely rough running of that engine. After cutting it, Wendel then accidentally also cut the starboard engine too by backing it off too much. Despite a high rate of descent, he managed to land normally—albeit breaking the shock struts of the aircraft's main landing gear in the process.

In his report, he concluded that "in its present condition the aircraft cannot be handled by an average pilot". The whole flight lasted just five minutes.[65]

This disappointing experience, however, was just a sideshow to what was happening elsewhere within the Messerschmitt company. Neither Willy Messerschmitt himself nor the RLM were focused on the Me 262—with all eyes turned instead to the rapidly unravelling Me 210 disaster.

That same day, March 25, Messerschmitt felt compelled to broadcast a message to all company employees through the factory public address system at Augsburg, reassuring them that, whatever they had heard, everything would be all right.

He said: "Comrades! Since rumours about the Me 210 matter which contradict the facts are being spread

in the factory and in the city, I consider it necessary, as far as I can for reasons of confidentiality at all, to give some clarifications.

"On Monday, March 9, a meeting took place[66] with the Reichsmarschall of the Greater German Reich [Göring], in which the Luftwaffe presented a number of requests for changes to the aircraft type mentioned, which are still considerably greater than the current changes made in Landsberg. The Reichsmarschall has decided that these changes should be started, tested and implemented immediately. In order to avoid unnecessary advance notice and thus larger, later changes, some of our comrades were used for work on other types of our constructions for this reason.

"Of course, in the interests of secrecy, I cannot inform you about details of the nature of these changes and the purpose for which they are carried out.

"All I can tell you is that the rumours that are spread are not true. In particular, rumours that I personally would have fallen out of favour with the Reichsmarschall are completely out of thin air, which you can already see from the fact that the Reichsmarschall has ordered that I should get more workers in the Construction Office to carry out my plans.

"I ask you, my comrades, to work as far as you have the opportunity to correct the rumours that have spread."

It would soon transpire, however, that the worst was yet to come, particularly for Willy Messerschmitt personally. The following day, before the results of Wendel's abortive Me 262 V1 flight test had been disseminated, Rechlin and RLM personnel made another inspection of the Me 262 reconnaissance version mock-up and called for the pilot's seat to be repositioned for improved cockpit visibility—necessitating a new mock-up.[67] This was followed on March 31 by a conference with Rechlin and RLM staff concerning the Me 262's armour and fuel tank protection.[68] That same day a report was produced by Messerschmitt on the pulsejet-powered P 1079, now officially designated Me 328, which emphasised its suitability as a fighter.[69]

An appendix of sorts was added to Me 262 Projektübergabe III in April 1942 which proposed fitting the second prototype, Me 262 V2, with Argus pulsejets as an alternative means of propulsion.[70]

The aircraft was to have six 150kg thrust pulsejet tubes, with the possibility of installing two more at a later date. There would initially be three beneath each wing, spaced at least 150mm apart and suspended 100mm from the lower surface of the wing on elasticated mounts.

According to the report "the combination of two or more SR in a common nacelle is to be planned for later. If necessary, it should be possible to attach SR to the underside and top of the wing. It should also be possible to install four more powerful SRs with about 450mm diameter around 400kg thrust using the same fittings".

Evidently the Me 262 V2 would need only minor modifications to accommodate the new propulsion system—particularly landing flap cutouts. It would also require 50 litres of compressed air for pressurising the fuel system, taps for regulating the flow of fuel in flight and various additional cockpit gauges. No armament was to be fitted.

## MESSERSCHMITT'S CENSURE

The Me 210 was back on the agenda of the RLM management meeting on April 14, 1942, and Milch called on Technical Office chief Wolfgang Vorwald to give an update.[71] Vorwald opened with "I can only report that the aircraft that should have been made ready for testing have been delayed considerably, until April 20 ... the delay is mainly down to the fact that Messerschmitt has made various changes ... the landing gear is strengthened, and the landing gear mountings in the wings have been revised again. The decision [on whether to continue with Me 210 production] can therefore only be made on May 15 at the earliest".

Frydag, still heavily involved in attempts to resolve the Me 210's problems, reported that Messerschmitt's director of production Fritz Hentzen "gets new things every day ... Messerschmitt assails him with changes, and he is helplessly at the mercy of it".

Then the Luftwaffe's chief engineer, Generalstabsingenieur Roluf Lucht, interjected: "Why not take away the management from Messerschmitt? Until he is subordinated to someone else, nothing can be done. Right now he is the prime minister and he has the majority."

Milch replied: "You don't have to worry ... in the worst case, I will confiscate the plant and assign Messerschmitt to a general manager. Nowadays that is easily possible."

As he thought about it, this idea seemed to appeal to Milch. He then mused: "[Friedrich] Seiler as chairman of the [Messerschmitt company] supervisory board is tough. Lucht, order Seiler to come and see me on Friday morning. Maybe Mr Frydag can be there. The 210 may run as it likes, but there is no way that it can come into series production this year."

Just five days later on April 19, during a meeting at the Reichsjägerhof Rominten—Göring's hunting lodge on the Rominter Heath in East Prussia—the Reichsmarschall ordered the cancellation of the Me 210.[72] According to the meeting minutes: "Field Marshal Milch gives a lecture on the aircraft delivery situation. The Me 210 will no longer have any significant impact

in 1942, whether it will be delivered at all depends on the testing. Once this has been completed, the series can only start again in four months ... Mr Reichsmarschall deletes the Me 210 from the programme. The engines and equipment are to be used for other manufacturing, the rest to be sent to scrap. However, the intended testing should still be carried out in order to gain general technical experience."

On April 21, the RLM meeting took place as usual and there was some discussion about the Me 210's intended testing. In the meantime, however, Milch had apparently had his talk with Seiler and explained to him that Willy Messerschmitt was being removed from his position as company chairman and chief executive. The job of travelling over to Augsburg and telling Messerschmitt to his face had fallen to Lucht—who evidently relished the task.

He told the meeting: "I want to report on my visit to Augsburg. I carried out the action on command. The whole situation was catastrophic. I found Messerschmitt completely broken. He was physically very down and very agitated. The negotiations could hardly be carried out at a high level. He was crying his eyes out. Seiler was there. They all fell on Seiler like a pack, including Croniess.

"Croneiss has in no way balanced the matter as was necessary, or as he has usually done, because in my opinion he feels offended by Seiler. Hentzen and Rohrluh play no role at all; they live entirely in fear of their lord. Messerschmitt is running the whole show ... he alone says what goes; he undoubtedly has the majority together with the baroness. The gentlemen are not able to assert themselves against him because they feel like his employees and not as equal opponents."

Evidently as soon as Messerschmitt's loyal colleagues discovered that Seiler had been forewarned of the purpose for Lucht's visit, they had turned on him. Seiler found himself caught between Milch and the RLM on one side and Willy Messerschmitt on the other who, as Lucht pointed out, personally owned 35.2% of the company's stock and was in a relationship with Baroness Lilly von Michel-Raulino—who led the group of investors holding the remaining 64.8%.[73]

Lucht told the meeting that, despite Messerschmitt's removal from the key offices of his own company being framed as something the Government wanted, "it is viewed as a Seiler action, and people just cannot be dissuaded from that; they just don't believe what they are told anymore".

The cancellation of the Me 210 also had severe consequences for the Messerschmitt company financially, with the lost contract and the huge sums spent on parts evidently pushing it towards the brink of bankruptcy.

Fighter ace Adolf Galland, who had been promoted to General der Jagdflieger, Inspector of Fighters, on December 5, 1941, attended the RLM GL meeting on April 27 eager to know what was happening to the various next generation piston engine fighters then in development. He was particularly concerned about the Me 309 and whether it could make up for the shortfall created by the failure of the Me 210.[74]

Reidenbach said: "After the Messerschmitt bankruptcy, we have to be very careful. The machine isn't in production, the engine isn't there yet, and the prototype isn't flying either." A discussion about the Jumo 213 followed and he then said: "The [Fw] 190 with 213 is slightly better in terms of performance than the 109 G with [DB] 605, but worse than the 309."

Milch replied: "I have determined the following. We are having a 109 built with a Jumo 213, i.e. not a 309 but initially the old 109, as an alternative solution. The following could happen: the engine becomes available but the 309 is not ready for it. But you could then deliver the 109 with the engine."

Galland retorted: "Why can't you deliver this machine [Me 309] with this engine?"

Milch said: "The engine is not there yet. Let us assume that the engine comes a little later, not until 1944. Then it can happen that the engine comes on at that moment but the airframe is not there yet. So I said: we'll take the 109 as it is and try it out with this engine next. Then, in any case, when the engine comes, this machine would run with this engine."

The Jumo 213-engined Bf 109 was to be designated Bf 109 H[75] but, Reidenbach noted, it would be largely a new aircraft since the existing 109 airframe could not easily be adapted to the new powerplant. The 109 H with Jumo 213 was deemed a non-starter at this time.

At meeting of Messerschmitt's board of directors on April 30 it was unanimously decided that "Professor Willy Messerschmitt will carry out his duties as senior design engineer of the company for the duration of the war." Croneiss became chief executive and operations director for the Augsburg works, while Seiler became chairman of the board.[76]

Milch was entirely unaware that by playing this card at this time, by making Willy Messerschmitt a scapegoat for the Me 210's failure, he had significantly undermined his own authority. Given the circumstances, and at face value, it does not seem unreasonable that Messerschmitt should have been made to carry the can for what was objectively a total disaster. And removing the leader/owner of a large aviation company was not without

precedent—most notably it had happened to Hugo Junkers in 1934.

But Milch had failed to account for a general perception at the time that he held a personal grudge against the professor[77] and that, in light of this, his decision to arbitrarily demote and humiliate Messerschmitt could easily be viewed as unjust. And he had similarly underestimated Messerschmitt's perceived importance to the war effort as well as the esteem in which he was held by Adolf Hitler.[78]

Later, when Milch was attempting to get Me 262 production started early, he would be overruled by Hitler acting on Messerschmitt's behalf—letting him know in no uncertain terms that he was powerless to act against the Führer's favourites. Milch's first thought had been to remove Messerschmitt as an obstacle—but he had instead made Messerschmitt perhaps the biggest and most immovable obstacle he would face going forward.

At the company, Messerschmitt may have lost his titles but he seems to have lost none of his authority. There were tangible changes however. His senior managers, including Seiler and Croneiss, do appear to have shouldered more responsibility for production matters and administration—freeing up Messerschmitt to concentrate more on what he did best: designing aircraft.

And in spite of everything, at the GL meeting on May 5, 1942, Petersen reported that testing of Me 210s with extended fuselages had "found that the properties of the modified aircraft tend to be more those of a fast bomber than an attack aircraft or reconnaissance aircraft".[79] Milch responded: "I received a letter in which I was told that the flight characteristics of the aircraft were absolutely perfect, despite the high speed." The letter was then read out, though the stenographer recording the meeting did not note its contents.

There was another issue which came into play—the Hungarians, having signed a deal to build the Me 210 under licence, wanted to get started. Vorwald told the meeting he had "sent them an official notification that the 210 will probably not work" but despite this "they are now continuing to build the 210. The decision on this question can ultimately only be made by the Reichsmarschall [Göring]. The Hungarians supply us with two thirds of what they build".

Müller noted: "We're getting a total of 500 to 600 machines, distributed until mid-1945."

Milch seems reluctantly to have accepted that, given this enormous freebie and the positive test results reported by Petersen's test pilots, "maybe we will be very happy when we get these machines after all. It is necessary, however, that we have the development department here for the next meeting in 14 days so that they can explain to us what the situation is with the 110, 210 and 310 family and we can think about how things should go on; because the 210 is not just the loss of a machine, but the failure of an entire development".

Apparently swallowing his pride, Milch reported to Göring on May 9, four days later, that "the flight characteristics of the Me 210 were correct due to the lengthened fuselage and modification of the tail unit and the installation of slots".[80] Jeschonnek stated that the Me 210 needed to be tested immediately by his staff and Storp mentioned that the Me 210's speed had so far been 20-30km above that of the Bf 110. Göring then "postponed the order to dismantle the Me 210 until the test results were received". The Me 210 programme would now continue, with the type eventually being redesignated Me 410.

The tide had begun to turn in Messerschmitt's favour at last after months of acrimony and disruption.

# 3

# Turning point:
# May 1942 to May 1943

ITH MUCH of the Messerschmitt company preoccupied by the Me 210, the low-priority Me 262 programme had continued to drift through the first half of 1942.

Despite humbling Willy Messerschmitt with demotion, Milch pressed ahead with a course of action apparently calculated to undermine what remained of his authority. During a meeting with Göring on May 21,[1] he told the Reichsmarschall that "the idea was taken up to develop a successor for the Ju 188 on the basis of the designs by Lippisch and Horten. Lippisch is not in the right place at Messerschmitt.

"It is intended to set up his own design office together with the Horten brothers and to affiliate them with Messerschmitt AG until further notice. It remains to be seen whether this should still be the case when the planning is ready for series production."

Göring was "astonished" that the RLM wasn't already backing the development of tailless piston engine and jet bomber types based on the concepts of Lippisch and his fellow 'flying wing' pioneers Reimar and Walter Horten. It was concluded that "Lippisch and Horten come together, are spatially separated from Messerschmitt, and receive full support from GL.[2] The start of series production can be expected in two and a half years at the earliest. If this project succeeds, it could

mean the replacement of the Ju 188."

It is unclear just how far Milch himself was enthusiastic about the potential of tailless aircraft and how far he was pushing this plan purely because he knew it would sew dissent within Messerschmitt, further driving a wedge between Willy Messerschmitt and Lippisch, the head of his second project office. Certainly, nothing immediately came of the proposal although it would eventually bear fruit.

Meanwhile, within Voigt's office attention had returned briefly to plans for the Me 262's pressurised cockpit and a short report was produced in May which described the use of paste to cover rivets and create an airtight seal. The same paste would also be used between sheets of metal before riveting and this method had been found effective.[3]

There was bad though unsurprising news on May 29; following Wendel's disastrous flight with BMW P3302s just over two months earlier, when the RLM took the decision to limit Me 262 prototype production to just five examples. The total order remained tentatively at 20 aircraft, but the other 15 would only be approved for construction following successful flight testing of the first five.[4]

Ten days earlier the RLM had produced a fighter production chart which showed that the Me 309 was

*The Me 262 V3, which made the type's first flight using Jumo-made turbojets on July 18, 1942.*

due to commence series production in June 1944 with output reaching 60 aircraft per month by December 1944. A year later, by the end of December 1945, Me 309 production was expected to hit 800 a month, with the DB 605-engined Bf 109 shrinking from 600 per month in May 1945 down to just 200 by December. The BMW 801-engined Fw 190 was due to be phased out entirely by July 1944, with the Jumo 213-engined Fw 190 continuing at a rate of 240 per month thereafter.[5] There was no mention of jet aircraft.

Messerschmitt sent a single representative—Hilber—to a meeting to discuss jet engine installation in the Me 262, referred to throughout as either the P 65 or P 1065, on June 9, 1942, at the RLM's offices in Berlin.[6] It was noted that BMW's P 3302 pre-production 0-series and Junkers' T2 series were expected to commence deliveries in mid-1943 and that they would have "uniform fittings for mounting on the airframe to facilitate interchangeability. Since Messerschmitt has not yet had any experience with central [wing] installation and this is not to be expected in the near future, the fittings are intended for installation under the wing". The attachment points were being designed so that in each case the nacelle would sit only 20mm from the underside of the wing to provide as much ground clearance as possible. It was further noted that the BMW engine weighed around 550kg while the Jumo T2 was 650kg. Hilber reported: "BMW and Junkers will send the drafts to the airframe companies involved [an Arado representative was also present at the meeting] by June 29, 1942. The comments of the airframe companies should be available by July 7, 1942 at another meeting in the Technical Office. I mentioned that there are currently no people available for the development of the P 1065."

Precisely when Jumo delivered a pair of T1 prototype turbojets to Messerschmitt is unclear. Voigt would recall in the 1970s that the Me 262 V3 had been "completed with two Jumo 109-004 TLs" on June 1, 1942—which would presumably mean that the engines were delivered some time before then.[7] However, various historians have subsequently given delivery dates ranging from June 1[8] to early July 1942.[9]

Whatever the case, confidence in the T1 must have been high since there was no suggestion that a nose-mounted piston engine would be needed this time.

The date of the Me 262 V3's first flight, powered by those Jumo engines, is verified by numerous sources. Fritz Wendel climbed into the cockpit at Leipheim early on the morning of July 18, 1942. Initially, he encountered great difficulty in getting airborne because the aircraft's nose-high tailsitter attitude masked the control surfaces.[10] However, by jabbing the brakes at the right moment during the take-off run he was able to raise the tail—introducing airflow over the control surfaces and allowing him to take off. Even so, taking off needed 650m of runway.

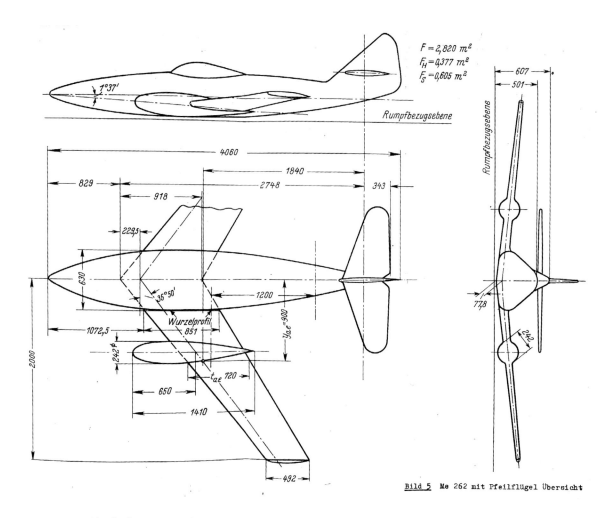

$F = 2{,}820\ m^2$
$F_H = 0{,}377\ m^2$
$F_S = 0{,}605\ m^2$

*Sketch of Me 262 wind tunnel model with 35° swept back wings from Puffert's July 20, 1942, report.*

Wendel made his first flight at 8.40am, lasting 12 minutes, and a second at 12.05pm, lasting 13 minutes. On both occasions the engines reportedly performed satisfactorily. Franz produced his own report on the flight for Jumo, stating: "Two test flights were conducted with the Me 262 fighter equipped with two T1 turbojet engines.

"Both flights up to 3.5km altitude and at flying speeds up to 720km/h were terminated without any engine difficulties. The pilot was satisfied with engine performance, but stopping the aircraft after landing was difficult because of the missing propeller brake effect."[11]

There was no joyous celebration however. As Messerschmitt vice-president and commercial director Rakan Kokothaki recalled shortly after the war: "The big event of the first flight of the Me 262 with two Junkers 004 jet units on the 17th [sic] of July, 1942, went by completely unobserved. Because of the general agitation incited anew against Messerschmitt [owing to the Me 210 debacle], no official recognition was given to this very important event."[12]

The Project Office's Hans Joachim 'Jochen' Puffert

had meanwhile been working on wind tunnel tests of an Me 262 model with 35° swept-back wings and his report was produced on July 20, 1942.[13] He found that the best aerodynamic performance was achieved with a continuous sweep of the wing's leading edge; the Me 262 up to this point had retained a straight leading edge between the fuselage and the engine with only the outer section being swept back.

By July 29 the Me 262 V1 was back in action and making test flights—presumably using just its piston engine. Wendel flew it for 15 minutes on the 29th and again for 19 minutes on August 4. He also continued flights with the V3, taking it up for 18 minutes on August 1, 20 minutes on August 7 and another 20 minutes on August 11. During this time he discovered an issue with elevator vibrations at high speeds.[14] The vibrations began at 550km/h and became increasingly bad before reaching a peak at 620km/h. Stability was neutral in horizontal flight at full throttle but the aircraft was unstable when climbing.

The RLM's response to these relatively trouble-free test flights was to send over Beauvais from the Rechlin

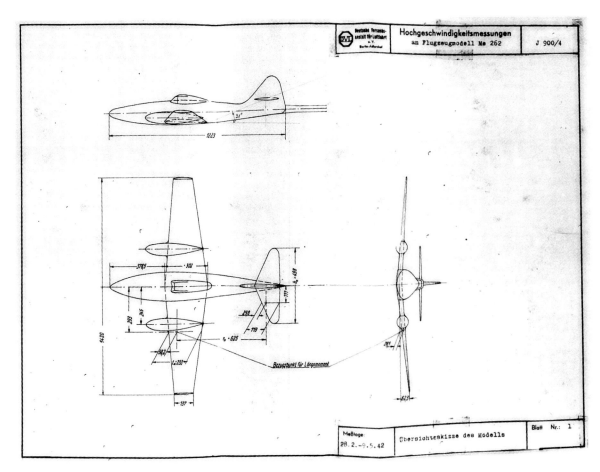

*All attention may have been focused on the Me 210 but work on the Me 262 never entirely ceased.*
*This image shows a wind tunnel model tested by the DVL from February 28 to May 9, 1942.*
*The resulting report would not be delivered to Messerschmitt until September 12.*

test centre to fly the V3. He arrived at Leipheim on August 11 and after instruction from Wendel on the tail-lifting procedure attempted a take-off.[15] Unfortunately, he had failed to gather sufficient speed and crashed off the end of the runway into a cornfield, wrecking the aircraft and putting a complete halt to the Me 262 jet-propelled flight test programme for six weeks—since the V2 had no engines and the V1 could only soldier on with its piston engine.

Nevertheless, on August 12, 1942, Messerschmitt was finally given leave to proceed with the 15 machines that had hung in the balance since May 29. There would now be ten prototypes and ten pre-production machines in total.[16] V1 would be reequipped with pulsejets, V2 would be fitted with Jumo T1s, V3 would be rebuilt, V4 and V5 would be completed in January and March 1943 and work on the all-new V6-V10 would begin in May 1943.

The V11-V20 pre-production machines would test the new tricycle undercarriage, pressure cabin, dive brakes, armour for both pilot and fuel tanks, radio and IFF equipment and armament options of three MG 151s or two MG 151s and one MK 103.

During the flight test programme's downtime, on September 12, the Messerschmitt engineers received a detailed report on experiments conducted in the DVL's high-speed wind tunnel.[17] A straight-winged Me 262 model had been used with nodules on the wing leading edges, rather than below them, to represent the engines.

If anything, this was another example of the low priority under which the Me 262 programme had been progressing. The model was an outdated design and the actual tests had been carried out between February 28 and May 9, 1942—which meant it had taken more than four months to write and deliver the report.

On October 1, fitted with a new pair of Jumo T1s, the Me 262 V2 finally made its first flight from Lechfeld—which had a much longer runway than Leipheim. Wendel flew it at 9.23am for 20 minutes and from 10.35am it was flown for a further 16 minutes by Beauvais.[18]

By this time the RLM appears to have become keenly aware of the Me 262's potential. The day after the V2's first flight, the number of pre-production aircraft on order was increased to 30—to be delivered by the end

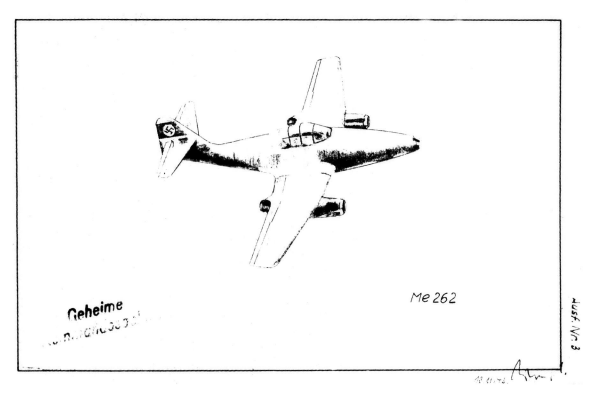

*Very basic drawing of the Me 262 with underwing engines which appeared within the project description of November 20, 1942.*

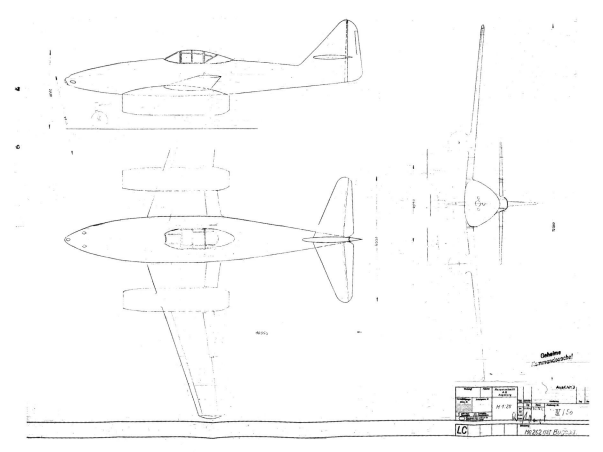

*The first version of the Me 262's nosewheel design as seen in the November 20, 1942, project description. Both the attachment point and the strut form would be revised over the coming months. The nose shows apertures for three MG 151s and at the very tip a housing for an ESK 2000 gun camera.*

*The Messerschmitt Me 309 was planned as the direct successor to the Bf 109.*

of 1943. Given the company's manifold other manufacturing commitments, many of which had considerably higher priority than the Me 262, the company's officials responded that only ten could feasibly be built over the next 15 months.[19]

Meanwhile, Wendel was now rapidly racking up flights on the Me 262 V2, with 19 minutes on October 2, 27 minutes on October 29, 33 minutes on November 2 and another 33 on November 4. At around this time it seems to have become clear that there could be a long wait for spare undercarriage parts to complete repairs on the V3. Therefore, the decision was made to cannibalise the V1 in order to get the V3 fixed and flying again.[20] Even then the V3 would not be ready until March 22, 1943.

The Project Office had evidently also found time to continue its work on the Me 262. The first new project description since March 1940's P 65 brochure was published on November 20, 1942—after a gap of more than two years and eight months, notwithstanding the sparse and perhaps never completed Projektübergabe III.[21]

This described the Me 262 as a twin-engine 'Verfolgungsjäger' or 'pursuit fighter' with all-metal construction, and armament of three MG 151 cannon with 250 rounds each in its nose and at the very tip of its nose an ESK 2000 gun camera.

From front to back, the airframe contained the gun bays, forward fuel tank, pressurised cockpit, rear fuel tank and tail unit. The undercarriage was hydraulically actuated, with main wheels measuring 770mm x 270mm and the nosewheel 560 x 200.

The flight controls were standard push-rods linked to the pilot's control column and the wings had a

*The Me 309 V1 undergoes maintenance on the hardstanding while the Me 262 V1, sitting on jacks because its undercarriage had been borrowed by Me 262 V3, lurks in the shadows of the hangar. The wings in the foreground were evidently destined for the Me 309 V4.*

continuous sweep back from root to tip. The engines were Jumo T1 units and would be suspended beneath the wings on either side of the fuselage.

The armoured fuel tanks were flexible bags, each containing 860 litres and served by two electrical pumps. The tank assemblies could be accessed and removed via covers on the underside of the fuselage.

Equipment consisted of an ejection seat with seat parachute and built-in breathing apparatus. The pressure cabin would be barrel-shaped within the fuselage and would be heated using compressed air taken from the engines. The radio system would be installed as a unit behind the rear fuel tank—the antenna stretching from the cockpit canopy to the fin.

Within the cockpit, the landing gear, electrical devices and signalling equipment controls would be positioned to the left and right sides of the pilot's seat, with engine monitoring, flight monitoring and navigation equipment on the instrument panel in front of the pilot.

Wingspan was 12.35m, the same as in 1940, overall length was 10.46m (a reduction of 120mm), height was 2.8m and wing area was 20m². Equipped weight was 3,405kg, compared to the 2,872kg projected back in March 1940—an increase of 533kg. Projected pilot weight had increased from 90kg to 100kg, fuel load was oddly given as 1,320kg, which was the same as it had been 32 months earlier even though the aircraft's fuel tank capacity had by now increased to 1,720kg. Total take-off weight was 5,090kg, compared to 4,442kg previously.

Top speed was 858km/h at an altitude of 6km with

120% thrust, time to climb to 6km at 100% thrust was six minutes and 30 seconds, and range at 6km was 620-960km. Maximum flight time was 48 minutes and landing speed was 148km/h.

All of this, it was noted, was based on an expectation that the engines would be lightened by 200kg compared to their prototype form and that the airframe would be lightened by 200kg.

## FROM ME 309 TO ME 209

By December 1942, the three Me 262 prototypes completed to date had flown fewer than 50 times between them since April 1941, only 15 of those flights being made under jet propulsion. In contrast, the Me 309 V1 prototype, which had first become airborne on the same day as the Me 262V3, July 18, 1942, had made more than 80 flights—mostly with Karl Baur or Fritz Wendel at the controls. The Me 309V2 had also been completed and flown by Baur on November 29—although its nosewheel collapsed on landing and it was written off.

As the chosen successor to the Bf 109, the Me 309 had enjoyed top priority both for prototype construction and flight testing between July and December 1942—leaving the Me 262 prototypes to be tinkered with as and when there was time to do so.

However, the RLM had become increasingly aware of the jet's potential, perhaps thanks to Beauvais' reports, and on December 2 the company was "urged ... to complete first nosewheel-equipped machines earlier than previously planned, increase size and accelerate delivery of pre-production batch" with a target

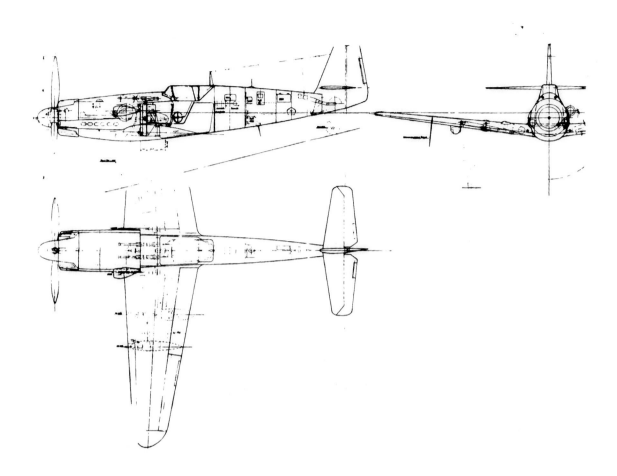

*With the Me 309 programme having turned into another failure, albeit a less costly one than that of the Me 210,*
*Messerschmitt concocted the Me 209—effectively a heavily modified and upgraded Bf 109—as its replacement.*

production of at least 20 aircraft per month from 1944.[22]

Wendel continued to fly the V2, reporting on December 9—reiterating that "take-off with the tail wheel is very difficult when the slipstream is missing. It is recommended to equip the aircraft with a nosewheel". Furthermore, "the aircraft has good longitudinal stability when the engines are idling; however, the stability decreases with increasing speed. The forces acting on the ailerons are too high".[23]

The following day, December 10, Milch launched what he called the Vulkan programme—which aimed to give development priority to key jet- and rocket-propelled fighters, missile and bombs, as well as the engines that would power them.[24] These included the Me 163, Me 262, He 280, Me 328 and Ar 234, as well as the BMW 003, formerly the P 3302, the Jumo 004, formerly the T1, DB 007, HeS 011, Argus 014, BMW 018 and Argus 024.

As usual though, the main focus of Messerschmitt's attention remained elsewhere. Back in June, Milch had started a competition for a new fast bomber design, with entries from "Lippisch, Junkers, Blohm & Voss, Focke-Wulf and others".[25] Lippisch was still a Messerschmitt employee, despite machinations to alter his relationship

with the company, and so a competing design was entered from the main Project Office.

By December, this design—the Me 109 Zwilling—seemed the most likely to succeed. It consisted of two Bf 109 airframes positioned side by side, connected by constant chord wing and tail pieces. The aerodynamic advantages offered by this layout were clear—it resulted in a twin-engine aircraft without the drag created by a central fuselage. Even better, it relied in large part on components that were already being mass produced.

Another alternative offered by the company was the Me 309 Zwilling, which was based on the same principle but used two Me 309 fuselages instead. If the Me 309 went into mass production as planned, this design would enjoy the same shared component advantage.

By this time Willy Messerschmitt, concentrating even more closely on leading his company's projects and engineering teams, had become increasingly interested in taking a modular approach to design—creating new aircraft for a diverse range of roles from existing components.

Both the Me 109 Zw and Me 309 Zw were discussed at a meeting of the RLM's aircraft development committee, led by Milch, on December 12.[26]

Ten days later, it was clear that another Messerschmitt development programme was in trouble. During an RLM management meeting on December 22, it was reported that switching from the Bf 109 to the Me 309 would leave a gaping hole in the monthly fighter output figure. Keeping the Bf 109 G would, together with the Fw 190, result in the Luftwaffe having 3,000 single seaters on its books by the end of 1944. Switching to the Me 309 would leave the Luftwaffe with just 1,700.[27] The Me 309 was a completely new design and would require a whole new set of components, new jigs and new production lines with the associated retraining of workers—which would all take time.

Further nails were driven into the Me 309's coffin at the management meeting on December 29.[28] RLM staff engineer Walter Friebel reported: "The General der Jagdflieger [Galland] saw the 309 while inspecting the Messerschmitt works and wrote a report on the performance, saying that the machine does not look particularly good and is not very promising for the future."

Milch responded: "Because the climbing performance is worse than with the G." Friebel replied that the Me 309's climbing performance was indeed worse than that of the Bf 109 G—because it had more armour, better armament, a heavier undercarriage and a heavier engine. But both the 309 airframe and its DB 603 engine were at the beginning of their development with much room for improvement and refinement whereas, he said, the 109 and its DB 605 had little left to give.

Milch was entirely unimpressed by this explanation and dismissed it as "not interesting". He was sceptical too that the DB 603 would ever realise its projected 2,000 PS output and noted that the Me 309 production series would not begin until October 1943 and then only in small numbers, with a significant output not being reached before the second half of 1944.

As of January 1, 1943, just one Me 262 prototype continued to fly—Me 262 V2, with Me 262 V1 having donated its undercarriage to Me 262 V3, which was still having it fitted. The Me 309 was in imminent danger of cancellation and the Me 109 Zwilling fast bomber was heading for a final decision crunch meeting on January 8. At around this time Dornier was allowed to submit a new design and the meeting was pushed back to January 19.[29] In the event, it did not go well for Messerschmitt. A head-to-head comparison of the Me 109 Zwilling and Dornier's new DoP 231 saw the Dornier design winning the contract. It would soon receive the formal designation Do 335.

The following day, January 20, 1943, Willy Messerschmitt met with Galland and Wolfgang Vorwald, head of the RLM's Technical Office and offered them a new option: a Bf 109 fitted with a DB 603 instead of the Me 309. It would have a wide-set undercarriage, heavy armament and similar performance to that of the 309—at only 25% of the production cost. Prototypes could be ready later in the year, with a pre-production series commencing no later than the beginning of 1944.[30]

Galland and Vorwald agreed that this would indeed be an improvement and as a result the Me 309 was cancelled and the resources that had been marshalled to bring it into production would now be switched to the new design, known initially as the Bf 109/603.[31]

Just five days earlier, on January 15, an internal Messerschmitt report had been produced which compared the projected performance of the Me 309 against that of a Bf 109 G equipped with a DB 603 engine and a radiator setup similar to that of the Me 309.[32] This showed that the 109/603 would weigh 132kg less than the Me 309 and would only be 4km/h slower at an altitude of 3km. And if the 109/603 was given the Me 309's wings, its speed would be increased by 9km/h—making it faster than the Me 309.

Messerschmitt had seized upon this opportunity to replace the failing 309 with something that could utilise numerous existing components, making it cheaper and quicker to build, while offering practically the same level of performance. In fact, Messerschmitt had been studying the possibility of equipping the Bf 109 with either the DB 603 or Jumo 213 since at least November 1941.[33]

Vorwald announced the decision to press ahead with the Bf 109/603 at the RLM development conference on January 21 and during the same meeting it was reported for the first time that the Me 262 was to be built in large quantities—with an eventual target of 100 aircraft per month. Evidently "special action for this is to be obtained from the Reichsmarschall".[34] The Me 262's erstwhile competitor, the He 280, was now to be restricted to just 100 aircraft in total.

By February 2, the Bf 109/603 had been redesignated Me 209. While it was mostly composed of standard 109 G parts, it did require some significant modifications to existing components and some entirely new parts—particularly for its wings and tail. And while designing these, the project office seems to have drawn on data generated by the extensive test programme carried out for the original Me 209 from 1938 to 1941, making the reallocation of the name particularly apt.

## COMPLETE REDESIGN

Nine months after initially trying and failing to extract Alexander Lippisch from the Messerschmitt company,

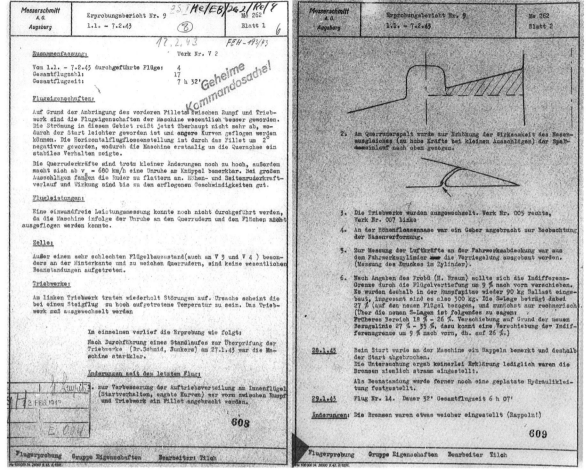

*Messerschmitt Me 262 test summary report covering the period January 1 to February 7, 1943. A diagram at the top of the second page shows the position of V2's new fillet, which gave its wing continuous sweepback from root to tip.*

Milch restated this objective during his management meeting on February 11, 1943, but this time Lippisch was to take the Me 262 with him when he left.[35] The official minutes of the meeting recorded: "The Generalfeldmarschall [Milch] orders that after the programme has been approved [Studie 1014—the next major phase of aircraft development for the Luftwaffe], the development forces are to be concentrated on the rapid implementation of the tasks set out in the programme and the other development projects are largely to be cancelled.

"Special emphasis is also placed on the further development of jet aircraft and jet engines. The construction capacity of Messerschmitt will be extremely strained for the next few years due to the current tasks (Me 209, 328, 163, 262, 410). The Generalfeldmarschall considers it necessary to divide up these tasks, in the sense that Messerschmitt concentrates primarily on Me 209 and 410 and jet aircraft may be relocated to a separate plant under the leadership of Lippisch and Horten.

"Director Frydag suggests the Siebel company for this, as there would be a good management system for carrying out the new constructive work ... Likewise, it is considered necessary to separate the design and manufacture of the jet engines from the factories making piston engines. The entire workforce that is now busy with this work [in separate locations and working for separate companies] would have to be brought together in these plants. Corresponding investigation in this direction is still to be carried out and dealt with in a further discussion."

Up to now, early February 1943, the Messerschmitt company had paid only scant regard to the Me 262 project. Extremely slow progress had been made, punctuated by lengthy bouts of indifference and delays caused by a string of new projects being jumped to the front of the development queue; by an ongoing lack of parts which should have been relatively easy to source—such as undercarriage components—and by distractions ranging from urgent war work to friction with the RLM.

Despite the outstanding order for 20 prototypes dating back to July 1940, only a handful of airframes had been built and fewer still were available for testing at any given time. If a prototype was lost, there was no direct replacement available, nor was there a supply of spares

*Just as Messerschmitt had struggled with the Me 210 and neglected the Me 262, so too had Heinkel struggled with the He 177 bomber and neglected its Me 262 jet fighter rival, the He 280. On March 19, 1943, company representative Siegfried Günter asked for its cancellation to free up resources for the He 177.*

on hand for repairs. Messerschmitt had ordered enough parts to keep the programme alive but not enough to drive it forward.

It might be assumed that this state of affairs could be blamed on a shortage of engines from Jumo, but Junkers does not appear to have had much difficulty in supplying 004 prototype engines when an airframe was available to accommodate them during the late 1942 to early 1943 period. Indeed, the contemporary documents contain no complaints about an engine shortage at this time—when it would have been extremely easy for Messerschmitt to highlight this as an issue had it been the case.

Yet now, finally, with the RLM practically shoving Messerschmitt along, development of the Me 262 was gathering pace.

On February 11, the same day that Milch outlined his plan to remove the Me 262 from Messerschmitt, an experimental Me 262 fuselage drop test was evidently carried out over Chiemsee in Bavaria—with the assistance of personnel from Munich-based 4. Flak-Brigade, rather than Messerschmitt staff.[36] The wingless test vehicle was carried up to 6,000m above the lake, beneath the wing of the Me 323 S-9, and released. A maximum speed of 870km/h was recorded as its descent reached

an altitude of 2,000m but its parachute then failed to deploy and it was destroyed when it hit the water at around 800km/h.

A meeting took place on February 13 at the RLM in Berlin to ensure that the series production model Me 262's airframe strength was adequate for various manoeuvres, such as taking off, landing and diving.[37] This was conducted by just two Messerschmitt personnel, and one RLM staff member.

Flight testing of the Me 262 V2—still the sole airworthy example—continued throughout February with changes and improvements being made incrementally to its tail surfaces, landing gear and fuselage. A large fillet was now added to the wing between the engine and the fuselage which resulted in a straight leading edge all the way from the wingroot to the wingtip. This provided improved take-off performance and greater manoeuvrability in turns once airborne.[38]

There were also numerous parts failures—including problems with the variometer, control stick, elevator balance weight, tail wheel, oil tank, left slat, wingtip ferrules, pitot tube and engine cowlings. Testing was dogged by strong vibrations in the ailerons and wings between 690km/h and 710km/h, the origin of which could not be determined.[39] Unsuccessful attempts were made to cure the problem by inserting felt strips into the aileron slots. In addition, the pitot tube was relocated and damping nozzles were added to the conduits leading to the fuel pressure gauges.[40] It was also discovered at this time that the Me 262 could be flown safely on only one engine when a fault was discovered that caused the 004 to cut out suddenly when rapidly throttled back.[41]

Discussions between Messerschmitt, the RLM and the Rechlin test centre led to a document known as Protokoll Nr. 9 being issued on March 4, 1943. This called for nothing short of a complete redesign of the Me 262,[42] the first step being to draw up different armament options for the aircraft. By March 6 it was reported that plans were in place to patch up the Me 262 V1 and convert it to Jumo 004s. Me 262 V3 was complete except for the installation of its landing gear, Me 262 V4 was awaiting landing gear components and work was now ongoing on the V6-V10 prototypes, though "the final delivery dates for the Junkers T1 and T2 engines are still pending".[43]

A day earlier, Vorwald had chaired the RLM's development meeting and Milch's plan to relocate the Me 262 was discussed.[44] Dr Georg Pasewaldt, Vorwald's immediate subordinate, said: "It would be a case of whether the Siebel capacity might be in question. At that time, the 262 or 410 were planned for Siebel. The gentlemen were with me and spoke out in favour of the 262. I think that in any case [however,] one will leave that in Augsburg in accordance with the suggestion that was recently made to Generalfeldmarschall [Milch] by Seiler. They didn't really dare to approach the 410, apparently because of the stalls, etc. Siebel was apparently unsure of that. Otherwise you could think of the 264 or something similar to Siebel."

Vorwald replied: "You mean to relocate the 410 from Messerschmitt to Siebel?" Pasewald said that this was what Messerschmitt wanted and Vorwald said, "with the 410 I still see anger".

## MORE ENGINES THAN AIRFRAMES

The various armament options proposed by Messerschmitt for the Me 262 were discussed during the development meeting on March 19, this time with Milch back at the helm.[45] Galland said: "The first solution, three MG 151/20 is extremely bad." Pasewaldt replied: "That will hardly come into play. It is only planned to represent something as a weapon. This is a temporary thing that is only produced in smaller numbers."

Milch asked Galland which option he liked best and Galland replied: "The solution with the MK 103."

Later on, the He 280 was an agenda item and Heinkel's leading project engineer Siegfried Günter was present to participate in the discussion. Milch asked him: "When will the first [production model] aircraft come? When is the operational aircraft coming? When can the aircraft be used?"

Günter replied, apparently despondently: "The series of 300 examples should have the same armament: two MK 108 and two MG 151/20. There is not yet any work capacity available for this series. In the spring and summer of 1944, 13 prototype machines are to be built."

Generalingenieur Walter Hertel from the Technical Office engines section said: "According to the planning, delivery is due from March 1944." Günter replied: "I am not aware of that."

Milch: "Is the machine with the engine so clear that you can plan for that?"

Günter: "Nothing is clear about the machine. The engine is too weak and is out of the question. The BMW engine has not yet flown and has not yet been delivered. We have two test models with a Jumo engine. We only made experiments of this."

Friebel: "I can report that ... the capacity for a jet aircraft has been secured. It does not necessarily have to be the 280. Capacity was only kept open to bring one jet aircraft to production as quickly as possible."

Milch: "So far, it has not been possible to say of any one aircraft that it will come in the foreseeable future."

Günter: "Since the 262 is planned with the Jumo engine, according to the information provided by the test centres, I would suggest that we not build the 280 series, but instead only build the 13 prototypes in order to gain broad experience and to get some test vehicles for the engines, i.e. BMW and Jumo. We want to free up constructive capacity for the 177. We would like to put the designers that we now have on the 280 on the 177."

Milch: "That's what the working group for jet engines does. We want to see what they're doing today. It's sad I don't have this yet."

Hertel's subordinate Schelp responded: "Jumo T1 was intended for the 262 and 280. We have engines but no airframes. The first prototype has long gone to Rechlin. It ran for 30 hours without problems, then flew with a Ju 88 for 30 hours, also without problems. We don't have any airframes."

Milch: "Why doesn't the engine fit into the Heinkel?"

Schelp: "The first airframe [He 280 with Jumo 004] from Heinkel flew for the first time three days ago."

Someone shouted in the background, recorded by the stenographer, "It was only a makeshift conversion!"

Schelp: "All of this is undoubtedly new territory, we cannot know what will happen when series production begins. We are constantly pushing this forward to get to the next problem."

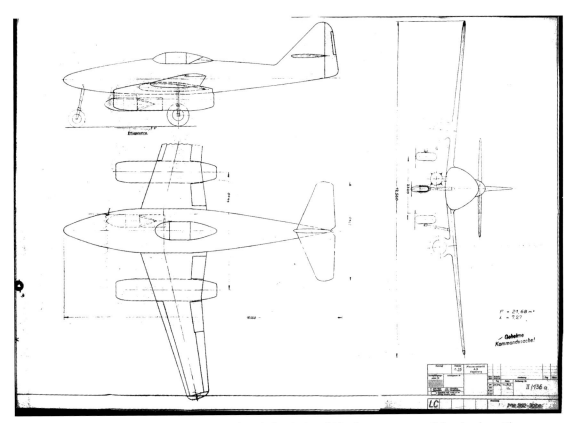

*The Me 262 as it appears in Messerschmitt's description of March 25, 1943: as a fighter-bomber with a revised nosewheel strut and revised canopy compared to the design as it appeared in November of the previous year. The aircraft's dimensions—wingspan and length—remain the same.*

Milch: "I only see the problem in the engines and not in the airframes. They have to be tried out."

Schelp: "We have engines there without being able to test them. The first pilot series of [Jumo 004] A units has almost been delivered; the pre-production series of the B-engine starts in July. In terms of status and development, these engines have achieved more than we expected."[46]

This conversation is remarkable for two reasons. Firstly, it shows that Heinkel, critically short of resources and under pressure to get the He 177 heavy bomber into service, wanted to see its own He 280 jet fighter cancelled. Secondly, it shows that there were more Jumo 004 turbojets available than there were airframes to test them in, with the prototype 004 A series having been nearly completed and with preparations for the 004 B pre-production series well under way. Turbojets were sitting around idle, waiting to be installed in aircraft that had not yet been constructed.

The following day, its undercarriage in place at last, the Me 262 V3 re-joined the test programme at Messerschmitt and on March 22, at the next RLM development meeting, Technical Office jet specialist Hans-Martin Antz gave a comprehensive update on the status of both the Me 262 and He 280.[47] He reiterated the suggestion that the He 280 be "deferred" and noted that according to a plan supplied by Messerschmitt, "it would be possible to deploy 40 Me 262 aircraft by the end of 1944". Furthermore, "the armament, which was originally planned with three MG 151/20, is currently being modernised and based on the latest demands of the General der Jagdflieger. It will certainly be possible to accommodate four MK 108 in the nose.

"We are currently investigating the possibility of installing it in the wings, as well as the use of the MK 103. The aircraft is equipped with a pressurized cabin, so it can also be used at high altitudes. No firm information can yet be given about the performance of the engine at peak altitude."

Schelp then discussed the engines again: "We have two solutions available: the Junkers solution and the BMW solution. In the beginning we didn't even know what kind of trouble we would get ... It is possible that the Junkers engine can be brought into three different construction stages.

"The A-engine was purely a test device, where no major emphasis was placed on weight. The pilot series of 40 pieces, which was ordered, is practically delivered ... Then the engine was redesigned according to series production requirements and in order to be able

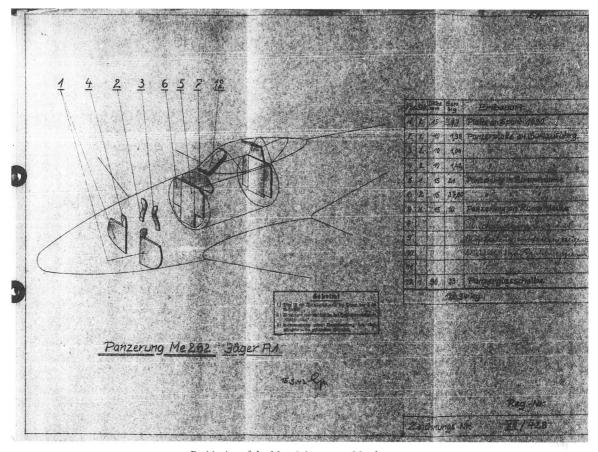

*Positioning of the Me 262's armour, March 1943.*

to address the question of fuel economy at the same time. This concerns the Junkers 004 B engine. Here the performance [thrust] has been increased to 840kg on the test stand and to 730kg at 150m/sec on the ground, i.e. 900km per hour. The first engines of the pre-production series have already been delivered in these designs. The first two pieces of the small series production run should start in July of this year.

"... At the moment there are no test stands for these engines that would enable us to check the performance in the different flight conditions. So we had to go to a Ju 88 and hang it underneath to be able to demonstrate the performance. The first engine was delivered to Rechlin a long time ago, has run for 30 hours on the test stand without any inconvenience, and has been attached to the Ju 88 in this form and ran another 30 hours in a test flight without further ado.

"Breakdowns and dips [in performance] did not occur in the development of the engine. But that doesn't mean that no glitches are to be expected during the introduction. But we hope to get to the difficulties as quickly as possible, which will certainly become noticeable in longer flight tests. The pilot series for this engine is in progress. The only negative I see is that we don't have any test vehicles where we can install the engine.

"Junkers has made various planning studies on how a series is to be delivered and has also taken the view that the working hours required for such an engine would decrease significantly per engine in a large series production run."

Turning to the BMW 003, Schelp said that "difficulties have arisen here ... because various problems were not yet known at all. Today, however, these difficulties can largely be considered to have been overcome. The first two engines ... are ready and can be delivered. Since they are designed for the same performance [as the 004], they have the same connection not only in the suspension, but also in the connection line on the throttle, with the exception of the cover, so they can absolutely be exchanged.

"Since the BMW engine has been approached a little sharper, this engine does not have the same further development options as the Junker engine. Junkers has offered that the switchover of the series, if it runs, to the 004 C would be possible as early as mid-1944. The BMW engine will have a starting thrust of 900kg, i.e. 100kg less than the Junkers engines."

He said it was "not yet clear whether the Me 262 with the BMW engine will have significantly worse flight performance than with the Junkers engine".

*Gesamtmodell mit PT1000, Gondelverkleidung 1, Gondeleinlauf N*

*Anordnung der Waffen unter dem Rumpf*

 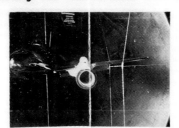 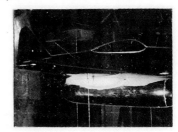

*Waffeneinbau über der Gondel (Flügeloberseite) | innen — Waffen zwischen Flügel und Gondel — außen*

*Undated photographs showing an Me 262 wind tunnel model with modifications to represent new weapons positions in the wings or under the fuselage.*

After a brief discussion about Heinkel's problems with the He 280, Milch mentioned that there were other jet aircraft types listed in his briefing notes besides the Me 262 and He 280. Pasewaldt said: "Yes, but only these two types in this order of magnitude. If I may touch on the engine question, I would like to say that the engines that have been designed are definitely not built for nothing. In my opinion, there are quite simple installation options, which can be the quick solution for single-engine jet aircraft; these can be created quite quickly under certain circumstances."

He noted that it would be wrong to think that the jet engines could be operated without malfunctions, but they were quick and cheap to make and could be replaced easily—which was not the case with piston engines.

During yet another RLM management meeting, on March 23,[48] Vorwald explained that at Messerschmitt it had become necessary to switch some Me 262 engineers over to the Me 410 but "Messerschmitt will still get some design engineers from Siebel, some of whom were loaned from Focke-Wulf. There are 34 designers. For the time being he is taking designers from the Me

262, and depending on the arrival of the newly made available designers, they will be returned to the 262. He says himself that he currently has too few with 35. He needs at least 64 designers."

## ME 262 FIGHTER-BOMBER

Voigt's project office released a new document on March 25, 1943, which gave "a brief overview of the current status of the Me 262 with special consideration of the points that have changed since the draft description P 1065 No. 3 of March 1940 and the extract from the project description of November 20, 1942".[49] It was, effectively, the third major project definition since the Me 262 project's inception back in 1938.

The opening line, under a heading 'purpose of use', said: "In contrast to the earlier specifications, in which the aircraft was only offered as a pursuit fighter, the role has been expanded to include use as a fighter-bomber. On the external structure, low-wing aircraft in all-metal construction with two engines below the wing, nothing has changed."

Detail changes, however, were: new armament, upgraded armour, increased fuel capacity, Jumo 004 B engines, the option to carry bomb loads up to 500-700kg, with "the option of bomb racks as standard", tricycle landing gear with reinforced main legs, the swept fillet between the engine and fuselage, "a thorough overhaul of the construction" to reduce weight, no pressure cabin, no ejection seat and no air brakes. The constructional redesign had also taken into account the need to transport the aircraft on a 12m railway wagon: "With the engines removed, the continuous wing with landing gear and the end of the fuselage with tail unit can be removed."

Wheel dimensions were now to be 840 x 300mm and these larger units could be accommodated by keeping the undercarriage suspension struts at an angle in their extended condition. The new backwards-retracting 660 x 160mm nosewheel would be mounted to the gun nose and would have its own brake. Full wing sweepback would be 18.32° and the engines would be Jumo 004 B-2s but with 004 Cs fitted when these became available.

The two armoured flexible bag fuel tanks, one in front of the cockpit and one behind, would now each have a capacity of 900 litres and a third unprotected tank, containing 300 litres for manoeuvring on the ground, would be added. The fuel circulation would be set up so that if one engine failed, the other could continue as though nothing had happened.

Consideration was also now being given to the use of rocket boosters for improved take-off performance. These would be Walter units and a fourth fuel tank, containing another 300 litres of rocket fuel, could be installed below the other 300 litre tank. However, solid fuel boosters were also being looked at.

Armament was now planned as four MK 108 30mm cannon in the nose, two with 75 rounds and two with 120 rounds, and "the aim is to accommodate two more MK 108 in the wing. As an alternative solution, the nose can be changed for the installation of three MG 151s or two MK 103 and one MG 151. The installation of two or four MG 131 in the wing as a replacement for the MK 108 should be possible, but has not yet been investigated in more detail. The empty ammo links and casings are collected within the aircraft. The ESK 2000 [gun camera] can be placed in the top of the gun nose". Despite not actually being included in the weapons options, graphs included with the document assumed the weight of the aircraft as fitted with six MK 108s, with a drop to four offering a performance increase.

When used as a fighter-bomber, the Me 262 was "primarily intended to take a 500kg bomb of any design with you. The bomb system can, however, be expanded by attaching a second rack for taking along 2 x 250kg bombs. Taking a BT 700 torpedo with you is possible in

terms of weight and space. For centre of gravity reasons, two weapons have to be removed from the nose. The streamlined bomb racks are suspended off-centre just below the fuselage on the section between the weapons bay and the middle part of the fuselage.

"This hanging of the bombs on 'pylons' brings a noticeable increase in speed when flying under load compared to if the bombs were hung without a gap and has the further advantage that no separate device is required for the BT 700. This gain in speed makes the Me 262 superior to enemy fighters in high-speed flight, even with a bomb, whereas the loss of speed due to a permanently attached bomb rack is hardly good for a high escape speed when the bombs have been dropped."

Within the cockpit, the usual fighter equipment was to be installed and the pilot was have a seat parachute with high-altitude breathing apparatus.

The electrical system would be powered by two 1,000W generators and the FuG 16 ZE and FuG 25 a radio equipment would be housed on a common frame behind the 300 litre fuel tank in the end of the fuselage.

The FuG 16's antenna was to stretch from the fuselage to the fin, with another antenna on the underside of the weapons bay. The antenna for the FuG 25 a would be fitted on the underside of the fuselage.

Vorwald wrote Messerschmitt a letter on March 30, ordering that the Me 410 was to be given priority over the Me 262—causing further delays which, according to the company's monthly progress overview report, meant "the plans previously submitted to the RLM will be invalid. New planning is submitted after the design engineers approved by the RLM have been assigned".[50]

The same report noted that the Me 262 V1 was now being retrofitted with Junkers 004 engines, the V2 and V3 were conducting test flights at Lechfeld, both V4 and V5 were awaiting landing gear components and V6-V10 remained works in progress.

The V2 and V3 flight tests were focused on discovering the source of the vibrations plaguing the former between 690km/h and 710km/h which did not seem to affect the latter—and the mysterious fault which caused the engines to cut out abruptly when throttled back too quickly.

## BEYOND THE ME 262

Milch and his RLM management team held a lengthy discussion about the future potential direction of jet fighter development during a meeting on March 31, 1943.[51] Milch said: "The question now arises: are the jet engines only intended for twin engine aircraft?" Pasewaldt replied: "No, not at all, but we were now investigating the question of the engine for the fighter

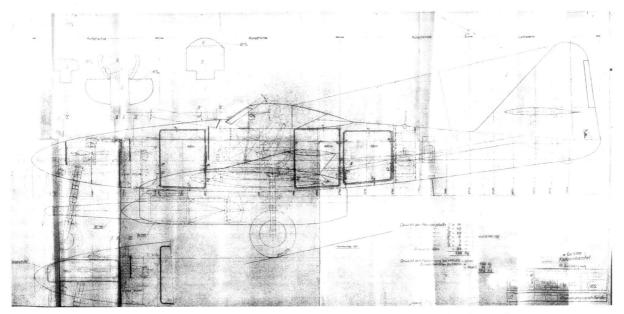

*The different features of the four Me 262 versions were presented in Projektübergabe IV. The nose could now accommodate up to six MK 108s—with two in the tip—or four MK 108s plus a 250 litre fuel tank. Fitting a new 650 litre rear fuel tank was also an option.*

directly. There are several promising approaches, especially a promising firearms arrangement."

Milch said: "In my opinion, the goal worth striving for would be for the fighter to have all its weapons positioned as centrally as possible somewhere in the middle, as the destroyer had earlier. With the single-engine design, this would allow a small aircraft size to be retained. If you couldn't do that, one day the big question would arise as to whether you don't have to basically build the fighter with two engines."

Pasewaldt: "This is, I would like to say, actually solved."

Galland, who had evidently been discussing jet fighters with Kurt Tank of Focke-Wulf, said: "I saw a design from Tank that was based on the [Fw] 190, with a jet engine."

Pasewaldt: "There are excellent opportunities to accommodate the weapons, and I believe that this will be the path that we on the fighter side should be following at the moment."

Milch: "I would very much welcome that path. It endears itself more and more to us, and we have to go with a considerable emphasis on these things. Hence my intention is to appoint a kind of Reich Commissioner or manager for the whole jet propulsion thing, as far as it lies with the companies, who can then push the uniformity of the whole thing forward and who is also a real enthusiast for it. I don't want to say yet that we'll drop the piston engine for the fighter and rely entirely on this! We are not that far along yet, but we have to consider and rethink the other thing for the future as well."

The question of the jet fighter's greater fuel consumption was then raised, and it was argued that a jet fighter flying at reduced speed—though still faster than at piston engine fighter—could achieve a reasonable endurance. Figures supplied to Schelp by Messerschmitt six months earlier pointed to an endurance of just over two hours for the Me 262 when flown economically. And these were based on the use of the Jumo 004 A which had not yet been optimised for fuel efficiency.

Milch opined: "Personally, I firmly believe that we will make significant progress in a short time ... [but] today we must tell ourselves that we have to have piston engines and jet engines next to each other until we can see very clearly; because if we were to neglect something in the piston engine area, we might end up facing a breakdown afterwards, and that must not happen under any circumstances. Hence the caution on my part—not out of pessimism, but out of sheer caution."

He then turned to the Inspector of Fighters: "Galland, what do you think of the question? What is the maximum number of horsepower you want to use for the piston engine fighter? Are your wishes covered by today's programme or do you want to continue?"

Galland: "I don't see that far yet. I believe that in the single-engine fighter the dead weight that you have to take with you [in order to accommodate an engine with greater horsepower]: propellers, engines, radiators, gasoline, which must not be forgotten, oil, coolant, etc., becomes so unfavourable that we reach a point where there is no longer much benefit. Above 2,500hp it slowly begins to become unproductive in the piston engine area."

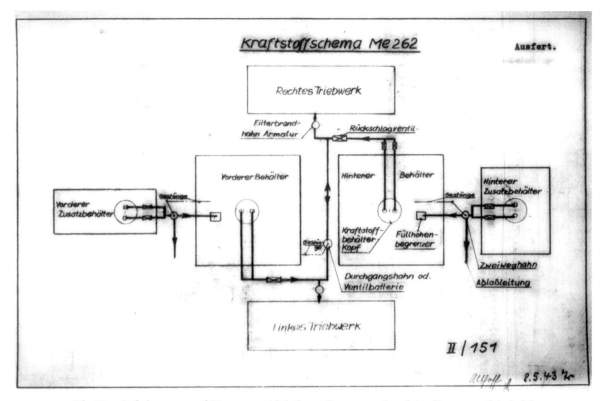

*The Me 262 fuel system as of May 1943, with both 250 litre nose tank and 650 litre rear tank included.*

Eisenlohr: "The Me 209-309 path showed that despite a considerable increase in horsepower, there are fewer and fewer advantages. Anything you put in will be eaten up again [by the extra weight]."

Later in the conversation a point raised by Milch's special advisor for tactics, Oberst Oskar Dinort, was briefly mentioned. Milch said: "Dinort suggested that you drop the Me 209 and put everything on the Me 262. We have talked about it and consider it to be premature."

Galland replied: "You can't do that."

Milch: "The run-up the 262 can be accelerated, that is possible."

Vorwald: "209 dates will be presented next Tuesday."

By April 4, the root of the vibrations and engine cut-out problems with the Me 262 prototypes had been identified and resolved. The vibrations, long suspected to have been caused by the ailerons alone, were cured by adding a fourth hinge to the ailerons and by slightly thickening the wing leading edge.[52]

The engine cut-outs were being caused by an abrupt cessation of the fuel supply. This was resolved by adding a throttle to the fuel return lines, so that when the pilot throttled back suddenly a reduced fuel supply was maintained, causing the engines to gradually drop to an idling rate of 2,800rpm.

The test report warned that while this solution prevented a complete loss of power, it would require a "new piloting technique for landing glides".

Nevertheless, the next two weeks would be spent chasing the source of yet more vibrations in the Me 262 V2 which only occurred after climbing to 8,000m, during the transition to horizontal flight, at an indicated airspeed of 450km/h. The origin of the vibrations appeared to be the ailerons again and this time the engines too but the cause could not be determined.[53]

As April went on, work on the Me 262 prototypes evidently slackened in response to Vorwald's Me 410 priority order. During a debate about Me 209 scheduling issues at the next RLM management meeting, on April 13, an exasperated Galland said: "In the case of the 262, it is also outrageous to write that it is currently running without a deadline due to the relocation of designers for the Me 410."[54]

Pasewaldt said: "We have fixed that again."

Vorwald: "That is a temporary solution until the Siebel designers are all there."

There was a further setback in the Me 262 test programme on April 18 when the V2 was destroyed in a crash, killing Messerschmitt test pilot Wilhelm Ostertag. The Me 262 V3 had meanwhile suffered a damaged undercarriage during a heavy landing and so, with no other prototypes available, flight testing came to a complete standstill again for just under a month. The V1's conversion to Jumo 004s was not expected to me completed before June, the V4 and V5 were still awaiting undercarriage components and work on the

V6-V10 had been halted by the Me 410 order.

There was a further development on April 23, 1943, when Messerschmitt presented the RLM with a new fighter design—the Me 209 H, with the 'H' standing for 'Höhenjäger' or 'high-altitude fighter'. Back in 1941, the company had worked with Daimler-Benz on a concept known as the Me 409, essentially a Bf 109 modified to accommodate a high-altitude DB 628 engine. On May 20, 1942, the RLM had ordered a new dual purpose airframe under the designation Me 155. Fitted with a DB 605 it would be a naval aircraft for use aboard an aircraft carrier and with a DB 628 it would be a high-altitude interceptor. Both low-priority projects languished in obscurity until the carrier variant was cancelled in February 1943. Now the interceptor had been repositioned as part of the Me 209 family.[55] This would become important later on.

On April 27, Messerschmitt was hit by yet more internal disruption when Alexander Lippisch's Abteilung L was dissolved—finally bringing to an end the division and antagonism that had accrued ever since the Me 163's first successful test flights. Lippisch had had 90 staff members but he took just four with him when he went, leaving the remaining 86 to be divided up across the rest of the company.[56]

## PROJEKTÜBERGABE IV

The third Me 262 project outline, Projektübergabe III, had been completed two years earlier, in April 1941, with an appendix added in April 1942. Now, in May 1943, Voigt's office produced the next update—Projektübergabe IV,[57] the end result of March 4's Protokoll Nr. 9. As with the previous three, this Projektübergabe would also be composed of pages added at various different dates.

The earliest pages were dated May 7 but most were dated May 8 and the data they contained was largely based on March 25's project description. Standard features now included either four or six MK 108 cannon armament; a reinforced undercarriage; four fuel tanks of 250 litres in the nose, 900 litres in front of the cockpit, 900 litres behind the cockpit and 650 litres in the rear fuselage; the option to carry one 500kg bomb, one BT 700 or two 250kg bombs; inner wing slats; new aileron balancing; cockpit heating; better armour and improved radio equipment.

Four different versions of the aircraft were presented as possibilities for the pre-production series. Version A would have four MK 108s, Jumo 004 B engines, just the two main 900 litre fuel tanks and 770 x 270mm mainwheels. Aircraft built to this standard would then be upgraded when the Jumo 004 C became available.

Version B would have four MK 108s, Jumo 004 C

engines, the two additional fuel tanks of 250 litres and 650 litres, the larger 840 x 300mm wheels, and fittings for the bomb racks—the racks themselves being optional. It was intended for use as a long-range fighter.

Version C would be the same as Version B but with the bomb racks fitted and was intended for use as a fighter-bomber. The last possibility, Version D, would have only one extra tank—the rear 650 litre one—but would carry two more MK 108s, for a total of six. This type would be used as a heavy fighter. All versions would be fitted with a standard Bf 109 F seat for the pilot without a pressure cabin or airbrakes.

Further details of the new undercarriage arrangement were offered, noting that with 770 x 270 wheels, the Me 262's load capacity was 2,000-2,400kg. With the 840 x 300 wheels, this rose to 2,600-3,100kg. However, the bigger wheels caused their own problems—the main landing gear legs had to be shifted outwards by 25mm and when extended the spring struts had to be inclined inwards by 10.5°. In addition, a new undercarriage locking mechanism would be needed because the inclined wheels would not be able to rest on the existing wheel well covers.

All four versions would have the tricycle undercarriage arrangement with a 660 x 160mm nosewheel, which had a load capacity of 1,560kg and a completely new strut. Owing to "the insufficient thermal capacity of the main wheels" the nose wheel was to have its own brake, but nosewheel braking would only be possible when the aircraft was rolling straight ahead. At the tail end, "frequent contact of the fuselage with the ground is to be expected; a good emergency spur must therefore be provided".

While the two main fuel tanks would be set up just as they had been on the prototypes, the two additional 300 litre tanks would each have their own header tank pumps. When starting the aircraft, all six fuel pumps would be switched on—two for each main tank and one for each additional tank. The latter would then automatically empty into the main tanks and the pilot would be able to switch off their pumps when they were empty.

A mock-up of the four MK 108 installation was needed but the basic layout was defined as four guns in the upper part of the nose, sitting on adjustable Rheinmetall-Borsig mounts. The ammo boxes would be positioned vertically under each weapon, creating a straight feed into the weapons from the inside. The uppermost pair of cannon in the centre would have 85 rounds each, while the two cannon lower down on either side would have 75 rounds each. All empty shells and belt links would be collected within the fuselage. When six MK 108s were to be installed, the additional two would fit into the extreme nose of the fuselage.

Their ammo boxes would sit side by side in the middle of the nosewheel housing, the right holding 65 rounds and the left 75 rounds.

For six cannon, five 5-litre bottles of compressed air would be required and if these could not be obtained then an alternative would be a dozen 2-litre bottles. The whole weapons bay could be accessed from above by removing the outer shell from the nose.

Possible bomb loads were one BT 700 torpedo, any 500kg bomb on one side or two 250kg bombs, one on each side. The two bomb rack attachment points would be beneath the fuselage, 400mm from the centreline on frame 2390. Each bomb rack would be shrouded with an aerodynamic cover "which should connect as neatly as possible to the fuselage and the loaded bombs. Closing the gap between the bomb and the panelling is done by sliding on a sheet metal cover with an attached rubber profile". The whole system needed to be quickly mountable and quickly removeable, and when removed "no parts should protrude from the fuselage and there shouldn't be any large holes".

Details of the aircraft's armour protection were added on May 14. All armour plates at the front would be 15mm thick, with both the cannon shells and their feeder tube protected against fire from the front. There was no side armour. The pilot was protected against fire from the front, the armour plating installed 30-40mm behind the cockpit front bulkhead. Another small armour plate was to protect against fire from above. The back armour was a flat plate with a hinged upper section and a head piece fixed to the cockpit canopy. The main tanks would have 16mm thick protection from all sides except the bottom and the lower third of their front and rear—the latter having 24mm thick protection.

Meanwhile, a Messerschmitt engineer named Träger had produced a report on May 8 concerning the detection of enemy aircraft at night using a system which picked up the sound of their engines. It was thought that since the sound frequency range of the Me 262's jet engines was higher than that of piston-engined aircraft, this acoustic system might be suitable for an Me 262 night fighter.[58]

This appears to be the earliest point at which consideration was given to such a role for the aircraft.

## GALLAND'S FLIGHT

Wendel took the repaired Me 262 V3 up for 27 minutes on May 14, recommencing the test flight programme, and the Me 262 V4 made its first flight the following day, Wendel making a 13-minute journey from Augsburg to Lechfeld. Both aircraft would soon be making multiple flights most days. Consideration was also now being given to equipping the Me 262 V5 with a fixed tricycle undercarriage for tests.

At the RLM management meeting on May 18,[59] Milch said that a situation update on the Me 262 had been handed to Göring on May 10, adding: "The question is how to give preference to the 262 programme, how to put more emphasis on it.

Friebel said that the drawings for the pre-production aircraft had been prepared and were ready to be reproduced. As soon as the first of these had been built, testing would commence and it was expected that this process would be completed by October—whereupon, all being well, approval for the start of full series production could be given.

"What is not available at the moment is the tooling for the construction and also the associated drawings," he said. "Messerschmitt still needs some help. What is also not available at the moment, but will be ready in the next few weeks, is the parts list, the equipment list for procurement, the hydraulic list and the list for the electrical system." These would be submitted by Messerschmitt within a fortnight. "This date was given yesterday by Messerschmitt," he added. "Provided that these commitments by Messerschmitt have been fulfilled, procurement [personnel] would now have to say whether the programme that is specified can then be fulfilled. This cannot be judged on the part of development [staff]."

Milch: "I have the 'non-binding' schedule here: the V3 in May and also the V4; in June V5 and V1, none in July, August and September, in October V6—for the first time with nosewheel and chassis, November ditto V7, December ditto V8, January V9 with final execution and February V10." He added: "Are these dates absolutely certain? Not according to the claims, but according to the actual status of the work?"

Pasewaldt: "I would describe it as not entirely safe, because Messerschmitt recently announced that he was a little behind again due to reallocating his resources in favour of the 410."

Vorwald: "Some designers were taken from 262 to 410 just so that we could keep even the downsized programme. In the meantime the designers from Siebel have arrived—it was 14 days ago—so that all designers are working on the 262 again as of May 10."

Pasewaldt said that even though Siebel had been told its designers were needed for a "crucial war-decisive task", the company had only handed over its "worst people", adding: "I have now instructed Messerschmitt to go there with one of my gentlemen and exchange the unfit people for suitably qualified people. That will happen in these days."

That Siebel was still trying to retain its best people, rather than handing them over to Messerschmitt, seems to have angered Milch and he threatened to "confiscate the plant and take it away from Mr Siebel" if the matter was not successfully resolved.

Alpers said that the planned construction schedule depended on the delivery date of the drawings for the tooling and the start of tool construction. He said: "The delivery schedule for the tool drawings is not yet available. If that's not there, you can't say anything about the series."

Milch: "How long does it take if he tries hard?"

Alpers: "Seiler has promised to give the schedule to me the day after tomorrow!"

Milch: "Then I would suggest that we stop here and wait for this meeting. Next Tuesday we want to talk again about how far it is. I would like to say, however, that the greatest emphasis must be placed on this. I fully agree with Vorwald, Petersen and Galland that we have to have this aircraft in a certain number. We'll need more than these few machines, if possible this year."

Alpers: "The intention was to carry out series production at the parent company in Augsburg at the expense of the 209, i.e. what is produced on 262, to do less on 209 in Augsburg. If so desired, we can still try to put the additional 209s on its licence manufacturers."

Milch: "I would definitely do that. The important thing is that we have a few of the things available besides the couple of 163s, which will also come in small series at the end of the year, but matters are still not clear about the engine."

Petersen: "Captain [Wolfgang] Späte from Erprobungskommando 16 flew the plane. He has a lot of experience on the 163 and is 300% more in favour of the 262."

Milch: "The main focus of all jet engine matters is on 262."

Four days later, on May 22, 1943, Galland travelled to Lechfeld and flew the Me 262 V4 himself. In his personal account of the war years, The First And The Last, published in 1953, he wrote: "In the early morning I met Messerschmitt on his testing airfield, Lechfeld, near the main works at Augsburg ... we drove out to the runway. There stood the two Me 262 jet fighters, the reason for our meeting and all our great hopes ... The chief pilot of the works made a trial demonstration with one of the 'birds'. After it was refuelled I climbed in. With many manipulations the mechanics started the turbines. I followed their actions with the greatest of interest. The first one started quite easily. The second caught fire. In no time the whole engine was on fire. Luckily as a fighter pilot I was used to getting quickly in and out of a cockpit. The fire was quickly put out.

"The second plane caused no trouble. I took off along a runway, which was 50 yards wide, at a steadily increasing speed but without being able to see ahead. This was on account of the conventional tail wheel with which these first planes were still fitted instead of the nosewheel of the mass-produced Me 262. Also I could not use the rudder for keeping my direction: that had to be done for the time being with the brakes.

"The runway was never long enough! I was doing 80mph. At last the tail rose. I could see. The feeling of running my head towards a wall in the dark was over. Now, with reduced air resistance, the speed increased quickly. The 120mph mark was passed. Long before reaching the end of the runway the plane rose gently off the ground.

"For the first time I was flying by jet propulsion! No engine vibrations. No torque and no lashing sound of the propeller. Accompanied by a whistling sound, my jet shot through the air. Later, when asked what it felt like, I said, 'It was as though angels were pushing'."

Despite this famously glowing review, Galland's enthusiasm for the Me 262 would quickly cool and within a short time he would make demands of the RLM that would significantly hamper the type's development.

# Messerschmitt versus the Me 262: May 1943 to August 1943

ADOLF GALLAND'S first flight in a Messerschmitt Me 262 and his subsequent report emphasising its revolutionary performance confirmed to Milch, to his managers and to Galland himself that the course they had been plotting for the aircraft was correct.

The Me 262 needed to be brought into full series production as quickly as possible and in the largest numbers possible. The question now was how to make that happen. During Milch's management meeting on May 25, 1943,[1] he said, "Galland writes to me regarding the Me 262 that the plane is a big hit," before reading out Galland's remarks. Frydag responded: "I think the decision is correct; but it is a big decision!"

Milch went on: "It's a clear path. He says the engines are completely convincing. The only thing that he himself mentions as negative is take-off and landing."

Petersen said: "We were down on Saturday. He flew the machines. It was insanely hot in Lechfeld. Lechfeld is 500m above sea level. This has an effect on jet engines, so that on that day there was a take-off [distance needed] from 1,000 to 1,100m."

Milch: "At 20m altitude or when taking off?"

Petersen: "When taking off. But the overall picture is very positive for the aircraft. People have said they have a lot less trouble with the 004 than the 605 and 109 G."

Milch: "The engine ran 100 hours at full throttle with take-off power. No engine can take that."

Petersen: "When he got out, he was excited about it. One can say that the aircraft is on average 200km/h faster than the current fighter 109 G. It is the only machine that is able to overtake the Spitfire and the high-altitude machines."

Milch: "Not only to drive away the fighters, but also to drive away the fastest Mosquitoes and the others if we had them. We have said again and again: emphasis on this machine. What personally doesn't completely convince me is the speed at Messerschmitt. That could be faster."

Pasewaldt: "He has very much leant into the matter, but only recently, when the matter was revived. I would like to support Galland's position on one point. I have the feeling that the [Fw] 190 D with 213 will come much sooner than 209 under all circumstances. For this reason, the decision should definitely be underlined. It is of course a big decision, because then we will only be standing on one leg with piston engine fighters."

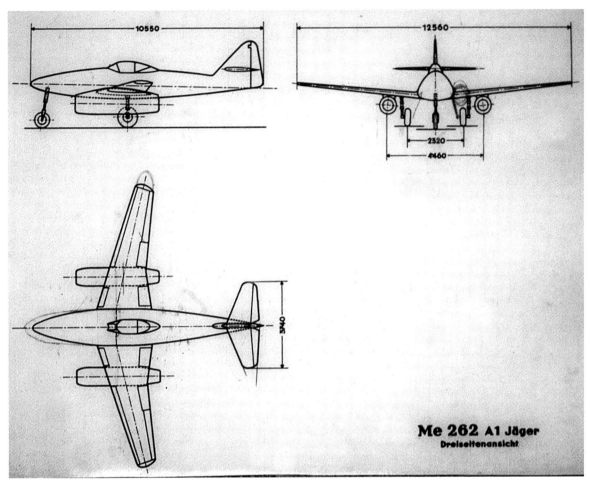

*The Messerschmitt Me 262 A-1 fighter, as it was planned during the summer of 1943.*

Milch:"We are only standing on one airframe, we are standing on several engines. I do not see the slightest hesitation in saying: under these circumstances, after the machine has blossomed: we stand on one leg with this airframe [Fw 190]. One airframe is at the end [Bf 109], the other [Fw 190] has something in it."

Vorwald:"One mustn't forget: the 109 with 605 will continue to run until 1945, even if we discontinue the 209. The 209 only comes in very small numbers in 1944. The 109 is still in mass production."

Milch:"The 109 has the highest output with 1,115 due in December 1944. Then it slowly decreases and will not have expired until autumn 1945. Then, however, the 209 should be available in large numbers."

Petersen:"The 209 already has worse climbing performance than the current 109, it takes one minute longer to climb to 9,000m than the 109. Despite the 603, the climbing performance will be a setback. It will have more armament and will be 100km/h faster."

A brief discussion about the Me 262 and Me 209 followed but Antz urged caution. No Me 262 prototype had yet been flown with the new nosewheel undercarriage and the first one to have this feature fully installed

would be the Me 262 V6, which wasn't due till October 1943. In the meantime, Antz said, "a preliminary implementation will be in the form of the V5, due this July. Of course, since the aircraft has been in development for a long time, new armament according to today's requirements must be provided. The nosewheel construction is being carried out, the new armament construction has not yet been carried out. The most important thing that is required to force the work forward is jig designers to get the jig drawings and the equipment drawings ready." He added, however: "If you stop the 209, all available jig designers etc. become free."

Milch:"Have we built jigs for the 209 yet?"
Friebel:"No!"

Schelp told Milch that no significant problems with the Jumo 004 had yet been detected and Milch asked him: "Is it ready for series production?" Schelp replied that the Jumo 004 B pre-production series was already under way.

Generalingenieur Wolfrum Eisenlohr, in overall charge of aero engine development, chipped in: "It is far more mature in series production than any engine. We have also made the preparations for production, so that we could already build a considerable number this year and in the next year."

All the stars were evidently aligned. Milch then said: "I think we are all pretty clear about it. As much as I hesitate about unimportant things, I quickly make up my mind about important ones. I am appointing Petersen as commissioner for the 262 within our framework, also with regard to industry, etc., for which only the consent of Vorwald is necessary. It is no use if we do not take a man who is interested in the matter himself, both on the engine side and on the other side. We can't do it with the companies alone."

Pasewaldt: "Wouldn't you like to take Galland?"

Milch: "No, Galland should receive every criticism, every objection, but not be responsible for the production. Then I would take from him what is most valuable to us, namely that he gives us an outside view, criticizes us sharply, tells us: 'I see it that way'. That's what I want."

Milch went on to say that "there has to be someone there who tells Messerschmitt and his men: come on, there is to be no mucking about ... I'm afraid that if we don't take a very sharp approach, it's no use. I do not accept what is said of him. The 262 must come earlier than the 109."

Pasewaldt: "I am convinced that if Messerschmitt gets room to breathe, he can definitely do it."

Milch: "The question is: is there anyone here who has any reservations about discontinuing the 209 and using the 262 instead, in accordance with Galland's request?"

He said that the fighter shortfall created by cancelling the Me 209 would have to be covered by ramping up Fw 190 production, "possibly also the 109, preferably the 190". This would buy time for the Me 262's production start-up.

RLM staff engineer Bohn urged caution: "It has to be stated that the jig construction for 209 is smaller than for 262. And the 262 has to be redesigned. Construction and design engineers; Messerschmitt must receive designers."

Frydag: "Bohn is right. But if we do the 262, then we have to make the jigs, and then I don't know where we can get the additional design capacity for the jigs. Therefore, the overall construction capacity is better utilised if we go straight to 262."

Milch: "You are for 262?"

Bohn: "Yes!"

Milch: "Then everything is fine."

But there was one person who did have very strong reservations about discontinuing the Me 209—Willy Messerschmitt. A day earlier, on May 24, the professor had written a memo headed 'Re: Me 209'.[2] He wrote: "On the occasion of General Galland's flight of the 262, the question of the accelerated start of series production

of this aircraft was also discussed. The suggestion was made to dispense with the 209 and instead let the 262 start up. General Galland now demands that the total number of piston engine fighters should not fall below the increasing [production] programme; that if the 209 is not built, the expiry of the 109 would have to be covered by the 190.

"For the standardisation of the fighters of the German air force, a transition to a single type of fighter with a piston engine is advantageous if the transition does not involve reducing the overall number of fighters and if the transition is made to the best performing aircraft. I have the following to say about this: 1) It is very questionable to me whether it will be possible to make up the shortfall of fighters in 190 factories when the 109 is discontinued. A conversion of the 109 factories to the 190 would result in a much greater break in production than a start-up of the 209, as this would lead to a complete conversion of the assembly lines. 2) Such a decision can only be made if the aircraft with the better performance has been determined by means of comparison flights. The latter is likely to drag on until the end of this year. These two questions must, however, be examined with the greatest possible care so as not to have to overturn the decision once made."

Saying nothing about the Me 262, Messerschmitt disagreed completely with the idea of cancelling the Me 209 and phasing out the Bf 109 in favour of massively increased Fw 190 production. Milch's plan was to build 190s with a variety of different engines—the Fw 190 A with BMW's 801 and the Fw 190 D with the Jumo 213, or possibly the DB 603—and convert existing Bf 109 assembly lines to the 190. Messerschmitt, while he accepted that switching the entire Luftwaffe to a single piston-engine type made good sense, thought that it should be "the best performing aircraft" that became the new standard type. And he was confident that this was the Me 209 rather than the Fw 190. At the very least, he wanted a competitive fly-off between the Me 209 and equivalent Fw 190 to decide on the winner.

## ME 262 REPLACEMENT

The Me 209 was officially cancelled on May 27, 1943.[3] Now Fw 190 production would be stepped up to compensate while the Me 262 got started. With the twin-jet Me 262 now firmly in place as the Luftwaffe's next standard fighter, the RLM development meeting of May 28 discussed plans to supplement or eventually replace it with a single-jet fighter.[4]

Focke-Wulf and Messerschmitt had each suggested fitting an existing fighter airframe, the Fw 190 and Me 163 respectively, with a turbojet to create a cheap single-jet machine. Friebel noted, however, that "working through the projects has shown that a complete redesign is inevitable and that the concept could not be carried out in its original form. This is how the new development of a single-jet fighter[5] comes about".

A specification had been issued which stipulated a climbing speed close to the horizontal speed of a piston-engine fighter, weapons installed centrally in the fuselage, one Jumo 004 engine and materials and production costs savings of 60-70% compared to existing piston-engine fighters. Projects had been received from Messerschmitt and Heinkel but Focke-Wulf's had not yet been delivered.

Milch asked how the jet-propelled Fw 190 project stood in terms of development time compared to the Me 262 and Friebel said: "It is definitely far behind." Milch replied: "The 262 is available faster?" Friebel: "Definitely!"

Pasewaldt: "Development [of the Me 262] is now completely finished, while there is nothing for the other project. The existing airframe cannot be built on. A new airframe has to be created."

Galland said that a single-jet fighter would be essential because the Me 262 lacked manoeuvrability. Friebel would go on to say that although Heinkel had offered a design, Messerschmitt seemed most suited to the task of designing and building the single-jet fighter.

Various new jet engines were discussed too—BMW's massive 3,000kg thrust 018 engine and Heinkel's HeS 011 which, it was stated, had been designed to encompass all the knowledge and experience in jet engine engineering of both Jumo and BMW as well as Heinkel itself.

Later on, Milch told his staff: "We recently talked about the introduction of the Me 262 and the elimination of the 209. The Reichsmarschall agrees with this. So everything is clear and is going as we discussed the other day."

On the same day, Messerschmitt production engineer Bley wrote a memo to Willy Messerschmitt headed "Forced approach Me 262 and its consequences".[6] It said: "Even if the further construction of the Me 209 prototypes can be restricted or temporarily stopped with the approval of the Technical Office, I would like to point out that this may not apply to any work on the standard engine.

"In the interests of the Me 210, this must be carried out at a higher speed. I would ask you, in particular, to draw the attention of the gentlemen responsible for the workshop not to give the impression that delaying the Me 209 can also delay the associated engine."

At this point the DB 603 was intended to power both the Me 209 and the Me 210—it was to be the next 'standard engine' for Messerschmitt, after the DB 605 which itself had taken over from the standard DB 601. Bley was worried that if the Me 209 got delayed, thanks to the Me 262 being pushed forward, there would be a negative effect on the DB 603's development. In other words, Messerschmitt's twin-engine Me 210 programme with all its political and financial baggage had become inextricably linked to the success of the company's next generation single-engine fighter. Messerschmitt had already had to rescue the Me 210's DB 603 once by transferring its resources from the Me 309 to the Me 209—and now that too had collapsed, though Bley did not know it at the time.

If the Me 210 alone was not sufficient to warrant the continuation of the DB 603's development, there was a very real possibility that the aircraft would be cancelled all over again. This was a scenario that Willy Messerschmitt wished to avoid at all costs, but he could not approach the RLM with Bley's concern directly since there would be many, Milch among them, who would be only too pleased to see the back of the Me 210 for a second time. He needed to find a different excuse for keeping the Me 209, and with it the Me 210, alive. And if the Me 262 had to take a hit in the process, then that was a sacrifice he was willing to make.

## JUMO'S ENGINE PROGRAMME

The RLM officially commissioned the development of Messerschmitt engineer Träger's electro-acoustic detection system for a future Me 262 night fighter on May 29, 1943.[7] Träger set about preparing a series of static experiments to determine the difference in sound frequency between jet engines and piston engines and whether that difference varied according to whereabouts the sound was recorded relative to the aircraft's position.

A meeting was held at Junkers' Motorenbau Stammwerk Dessau facility on May 31 to discuss production of engines for the Me 262.[8] Staff engineer Alexander Thoenes from the Luftwaffe's Rechlin test centre said that "the production of 100 Me 262 aircraft is ... the most important task this year". And "regarding the question of which engine types are available for the machines, Jumo reports: 004 B-1, is the emergency solution, [production] initially runs for four months (about 70 units according to the previous programme). From September 1943 B-2 starts (about 8% higher performance and the installation was unchanged). Because of the increased programme, more B-1s will probably have to be built.

"Messerschmitt explains: Dates for the prototype airframes remain unchanged. 0-series launch: November—one airframe, December—eight airframes, January—20 airframes, February—40 airframes, March—60

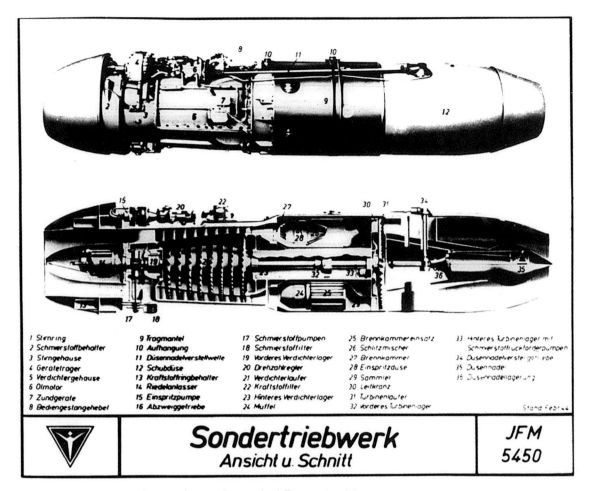

| 1 Stirnring | 9 Tragmantel | 17 Schmierstoffpumpen | 25 Brennkammereinsatz | 33 Hinteres Turbinenlager mit |
| 2 Schmierstoffbehälter | 10 Aufhangung | 18 Schmierstoffilter | 26 Schlitzmischer | Schmierstoffdruckforderpumpen |
| 3 Stirngehause | 11 Düsennadelverstellwelle | 19 Vorderes Verdichterlager | 27 Brennkammer | 34 Düsennadelverstellgetriebe |
| 4 Geratetrager | 12 Schubdüse | 20 Drehzahlregler | 28 Einspritzdüse | 35 Düsennadel |
| 5 Verdichtergehause | 13 Kraftstoffringbehalter | 21 Verdichterlaufer | 29 Sammler | 36 Düsennadellagerung |
| 6 Olmotor | 14 Riedelanlasser | 22 Kraftstoffilter | 30 Leitkranz | |
| 7 Zundgerate | 15 Einspritzpumpe | 23 Hinteres Verdichterlager | 31 Turbinenlaufer | |
| 8 Bedengestangehebel | 16 Abzweiggetriebe | 24 Muffel | 32 Vorderes Turbinenlager | |

Stand Febr. 44

### Sondertriebwerk
#### Ansicht u. Schnitt

JFM 5450

Cutaway diagram showing the different parts of the Jumo 004 jet engine.

Left side

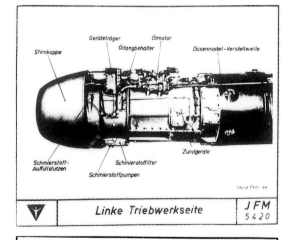

Linke Triebwerkseite — JFM 5420

Right side

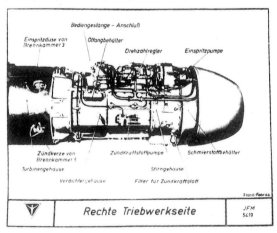

Rechte Triebwerkseite — JFM 5419

Top view

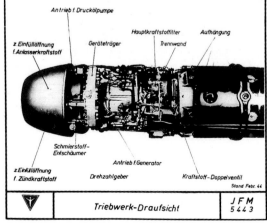

Triebwerk-Draufsicht — JFM 5443

Rear view

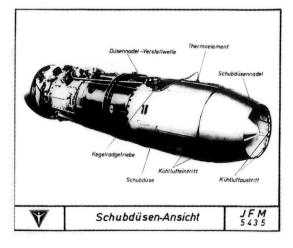

Schubdüsen-Ansicht — JFM 5435

airframes ... Required engines: double those numbers + reserve. Engine production should, if possible, have a two-month lead on the airframe programme. Jumo considers the above programme to be possible on the engine side."

The Messerschmitt delegation pointed out that using 004 B-1 engines would mean that the Me 262 could carry less armament or would need a longer runway. There was then some discussion about who would provide the engine fairings ("Decision: fairings will be supplied by Messerschmitt for [004] B engines. Junkers supplies fairings for [004] C engines") and it was stated that Junkers would supply 004 Bs with 2,000 W generators and cable support for up to 3,000 W. It was still uncertain whether 004 Cs would take 2,000 W or 3,000 W generators.

Procurement of starter motors needed to be increased and it was noted that Messerschmitt wanted to use 6-12 litre hydraulic pumps for undercarriage retraction, whereas Arado was planning to use 18-litre pumps due to the Ar 234 A's skid landing gear. For the Ar 234 B, with wheeled landing gear, Arado would "get by with 12-litre pumps".

Each Me 262 would have two constantly running fuel tank pumps. Messerschmitt and Rechlin representatives together expressed concerns that the fuel layout planned by Jumo "may cause the engine to go out in certain cases [and] contrary to the Junkers experiences, after the trial flights made by the test centres, restarting the engines at altitudes of more than 2,500m hardly seems likely to be possible. Jumo will urgently investigate the issue of restarting".

One of the 004's key technological advantages was its ability to run on low grade oil but at the meeting it was noted that capacity to produce this was "completely insufficient" and "for reasons of uniformity, the procurement office wants petrol operation for the frontline. Messerschmitt points out that running on gas oil gives a 12% increase in range. Junkers wants the first 100 airframes to run on gas oil. The adjustment of the engines to [run on] petrol is possible with the least effort (can be carried out at the front if necessary) and is planned. A decision should be made by the Technical Office shortly".

While the 004 B could run on low grade oil, there had been little requirement for the production of low grade oil in large quantities up to this point—with German production geared towards high-grade fuel for piston engines. As such, the Me 262's key fuel advantage could not be exploited without substantial changes within the already overstretched petroleum industry.

The following day, June 1, Willy Messerschmitt sent his company's Berlin office a telex asking for clarification on the Me 262's armament: "It would be a relief for us in terms of resources and construction work if we install four MK 108s instead of MG 151s from the first series 262 aircraft. I ask you to clarify in a hurry whether RLM and test centres will refrain from specifying the MG 151."

On June 2, Messerschmitt engineer Joseph Helmschrott was working on plans to make the Me 262's cabin pressure tight using a continuously emptying oxygen bottle which could be activated by the pilot, with a single pressure relief valve.[9] He wrote: "This is just to climb to altitude. The first aircraft to not receive this. The urgency for this test is great, since the behaviour of the engines at very high altitudes is decisive for later high-altitude aircraft."

## JIGS AND THE ALTITUDE QUESTION

A week later, during the RLM development meeting of June 4, 1943,[10] the Me 262/209 situation would become considerably less clear for Milch and his team. Vorwald reported that a day earlier Willy Messerschmitt had offered his thoughts on the decision to mass produce the Me 262 and drop the Me 209. These had crystalised around two points—the fact that cancelling the Me 209 would also mean cancellation of the Me 209 H variant and "the question of procurement".

Vorwald went on to point out that variants of the Fw 190 would be able to "cover against enemy bombers at altitudes of 12 to 13km until 1945" but the Me 209 H had been intended for extreme altitudes, up to 15-16km. Without it, this might become an area of vulnerability. High-altitude jet engines were being designed but it remained questionable whether they would offer the necessary performance and whether, if they did, the Me 262 would be able to accommodate them.

Petersen said: "You can only agree with the decision regarding the 262 100% and say: 100 more aircraft within a year, 1,000 and more in the next year. But I have reservations about the discontinuation of the high-altitude 209 variant. It is clear to me that it cannot be covered by the Messerschmitt group but one would have to check the matter. The 190 is 400kg heavier. We do not know whether we cover the same performance as with the 209. This has the advantage that we can introduce the modular system."

Milch said: "The 109 is replaced by the 262. The 190 can be in the intermediate stage. [Even] if I have now discontinued the high-altitude variant, the number of fighters should by no means become smaller than we have planned."

Later on, Messerschmitt chairman Friedrich Seiler,

who was present at the meeting, told Milch that in order to mass-produce the Me 262 he needed "1,000 jig and fixture designers alone, 150 for the machine tools ... given our current staffing situation, these are quite revolutionary numbers". There was also now the threat of conscription to front line units and Seiler asked that his people be given protection.

Frydag said that the urgent need for jig designers was the most pressing issue "but we have to find a way to get the right people". He went on to say: "There are a number of jig and fixture design companies; these are people who previously worked for us. They went independent and now have their own staff but they work much less productively than if we were to bring them back."

Milch: "Is it more practical to forcibly sign people up? How much work will be interrupted?"

Dr Werner, from the Speer ministry, said: "I talked to [Hauptdienstleiter Karl-Otto] Saur about it. This is difficult."

RLM staff engineer Heidtkamp: "These people also work for the army and navy, where they are deployed like shock troopers. That's why it's difficult to collect them."

Milch: "How many jig designers are missing for air force production?"

Various numbers were then shouted.

Milch went on: "Three thousand will be about right! I see a way and I want to go to it now. The Reichsmarschall has repeatedly pledged to us that he would help. I will make a practical suggestion. Maybe he'll make it happen."

Generalmajor Heinrich-Sigismund von der Heyde, chief of the Luftwaffe planning office, said: "Originally an attempt was made to bring all of the design offices over from France for aircraft development. This measure went wrong because we unilaterally terminated the Franco-German aircraft agreement. Laval[11] has taken the position that the whole aircraft deal has come to an end."

## THE ALTITUDE QUESTION PERSISTS

Milch had already dismissed the cancellation of the Me 209 H as irrelevant when Galland spoke up to say that "the question of altitude performance is one of the most acute. The performance of our fighters differs from that of our western opponents by only small values, plus or minus, at altitudes of up to 8,000m, but we are currently losing several enemy types above 9,000m.

"It is not only the question of fighting the high-altitude bomber that is acute, but also combating the fighters protecting these bombers or patrolling at these heights. The air war ... has moved out of the reach of the anti-aircraft artillery during the day. It is reaching

heights of around 9,000m and will probably go even higher. It is therefore extremely important that we get a fighter that is not designed for general performance but is a dedicated high-altitude fighter.

"It is completely irrelevant whether it is the 190 or the 209 which covers this required performance. The only thing that matters is which solution is the better up there. In my opinion, this is the only question that remains to be answered."

He said that if the solution was a high-altitude Fw 190 which came close in performance to that of the projected Me 209 H, "then I would be in favour of discussing the 209 problem no further. But this investigation must be carried out beforehand".

Milch said: "Can't Messerschmitt even comment on the questions?"

Seiler responded: "If I may first say something fundamental. We had a big debate on Monday. To my great surprise, Messerschmitt, who had been the greatest advocate of the 262 so far, was not so sure about it when he declared that, in his opinion, the dismantling of the 209 was not justifiable. We negotiated these things with the gentlemen in question[12] for nine hours in a matter-of-fact and calm manner.

"The result was such that Messerschmitt's opinion, which Lucht also strongly supported, actually coincided with the opinion that was put forward by Colonel Petersen, based on reports that we have recently received from people in the Western areas hit by bombers that we did not fight because the fighter pilots considered that there was no hope of reaching them.

"Further consideration showed that we have certain hopes of getting along a little better with the 109 [as the basis for a high-altitude type] than was originally assumed—at least on Monday. Nevertheless, it remains crucial for us that one should check the 209 question under all circumstances before dismantling this very advanced machine, which Messerschmitt gave me [details of] in writing.

"There is still 5% of the last engineering work to be done ... and the first prototype comes in mid-August. At least one has to consider whether one should cut the 209 completely, before one knows exactly whether the gap [in high-altitude capability] between 13.5 and 15km can actually be covered."

Milch attempted to get back to the question of whether the Me 209 had anything to offer as a normal fighter compared to the Me 262 and Roluf Lucht, now a Messerschmitt employee,[13] said that although the company was completely behind the Me 262, Galland had said it was a pursuit fighter, not a dogfighter. "It is essential to say," he said, "that the 262 is indispensable.

*Page from a report on stress testing the nosewheel design which appeared on the Me 262 V5.*

[But] with the 209, my opinion is that, despite these various advantages, there are scheduling risks with the 262 that can only be bridged with the 209, both in terms of time and performance."

He then tried to argue that because the Me 209 was expected to be 400kg lighter than the equivalent Fw 190, it would have a greater ceiling and rate of climb.

Milch exclaimed: "But the 209 climbs more slowly than 109!"

Lucht had a smooth answer: "Regarding the 109, it can be said that it has less armament. If you wanted to bring the same armament into the 209, you would of course not only have the same condition, but also a considerably better performance due to the DB 603's better engine power. But compared to the 190, this difference undoubtedly persists."

Lucht continued to advocate strongly in favour of the Me 209 until Milch eventually said: "We stick to our partial decision made today: the 262 with all forcefulness, the 190 high-altitude variant with all forcefulness and consideration for the 209. Comparisons between them should be presented again!"

Friebel added: "And 262 and with [high-altitude] jets."

Milch: "Of course, handle it as a question of high-altitude performance also for jets."

Galland's insistence on fighter production increasing across the board no matter what, his references to the Me 262 as an interceptor rather than a dogfighter and his demand for an extreme high-altitude fighter had kept the Me 209 alive, albeit on life support. Thanks to the Inspector of Fighters, the claimed capabilities of the Me 209 H could not be dismissed. And if the Me 209 H had to happen then it made a certain about of sense to also build the standard version of the fighter it was meant to be based on—unlocking the advantages of Willy Messerschmitt's 'modular system' of construction.

Milch remained determined to delete the Me 209 and push the Me 262 into production but Galland's politically naïve though well-intentioned pronouncements had prevented a firm cancellation.

The following day, June 5, 1943, the Me 262 V5 made its first flight with a fixed tricycle undercarriage and on June 9 Willy Messerschmitt sent an urgent telex to the company's Berlin office concerning the Me 262's fin adjustment device.[14] He wrote: "The Me 262 now has a fin adjustment device developed by the Uher company, which is not approved for series production. We need an electric fin adjustment device that has to carry a safe load of plus or minus 3,000kg at rest with a stroke of about 80mm ... the matter is extremely urgent." Bley then sent Bauer a worried memo concerning the Me 262's fuel system: "Mr Beese tells me that he can't get any further with the delivery of the linkage and fuel system for the 262, since the RLM wants to introduce new fittings, some of which are not yet available. This is of course an impossible situation and I ask you to clarify this immediately in the RLM."[15] Messerschmitt himself then sent a second telex to Berlin asking for an update on the fuel system requirements from the RLM.[16]

Two days later, on June 11, 1943, the first parts list for the Me 262 A-1 standard fighter was completed.[17] And four days after that, at the RLM development meeting on June 15,[18] Galland continued to push for a resolution on the question of his extreme high-altitude fighter: "I still have the question regarding the definition of the Höhenjäger variant 209 or 190 F."

Vorwald responded: "The question was already discussed and answered on June 4."

Milch pointed out: "We said at the time that we absolutely had to study the question. But that should by no means be at the expense of the 262 question, which should be pushed on with all our might. If the 209 were still necessary, then only as a high-altitude variant."

Vorwald: "There is still a comparison with the 190 F, which should take 14 days."

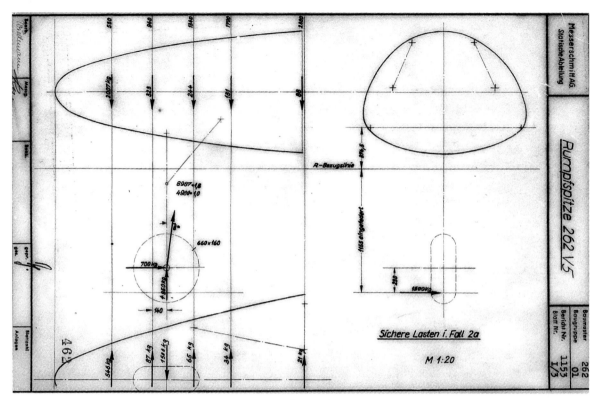

*The Me 262 V5's nosewheel position.*

## MESSERSCHMITT DRAGS ITS HEELS

On June 22, 1943, Vorwald announced to Milch's management meeting[19] that "Messerschmitt's investigations for a 100% changeover to the 262 instead of the 209 have ended. The prerequisites that are necessary for this would now have to be discussed."

Milch: "I spoke to Speer. The DE level [highest level of priority for production] has already been granted."

Alpers: "In the case of the 262, it was necessary to bring out 100 machines this year. Messerschmitt has submitted an extensive file for this programme and for the ongoing programme, which must be checked and the contents of which I want to briefly relate. Messerschmitt's investigations have shown that it was not possible to reach 100 machines this year. They could be built by May 1944 at the earliest.

"For this, Messerschmitt requires a number of conditions which are of an extraordinarily serious nature. First of all, they include the classification of the 262 beyond all programmes currently running. Then the total protection of the entire workforce, including the pilots, is required. Thirdly, the RLM should accept all the risks that lie in such a short [timescale] attempt."

Milch: "That's all nonsense. Who made the file?"

Alpers: "The file comes from Messerschmitt, it was made by Mr Bley and signed by Mr Kokothaki[20] as the manager. The individual requirements are broken down as follows..."

Milch: "We don't need that now. We just have to see what is legitimate and what we can do."

Alpers: "That has not yet been checked."

Milch: "Of course we have to do that [check it]! When we have that, we'll order them all here and Messerschmitt, Bley and Kokothaki should also come. I'll talk to you then. In no case do I agree that it should take until May."

Vorwald: "The main thing is to order materials. We have to catch up on that with a special order."

Milch: "I hope you have all ordered the items!"

Alpers: "I can't say that."

Milch: "Then call immediately afterwards and ask whether all the items that Messerschmitt needs have been placed on the order and whether something has not yet been ordered. I want a report about it. And when the gentlemen go down later, they have the shopping documents given to them. I am convinced that Messerschmitt has not yet ordered a thing, although they have known for four weeks that they should manufacture the 262. You have been wandering around for four weeks, and we are now supposed to catch up using a DE request. Are the engines coming in time?"

Generalingenieur Franz Mahnke, an engine development specialist, said: "It looks as if we won't have any difficulties with it ... It is to be expected that by the end of this year we will have a monthly capacity of 200 pieces on the Junkers side."

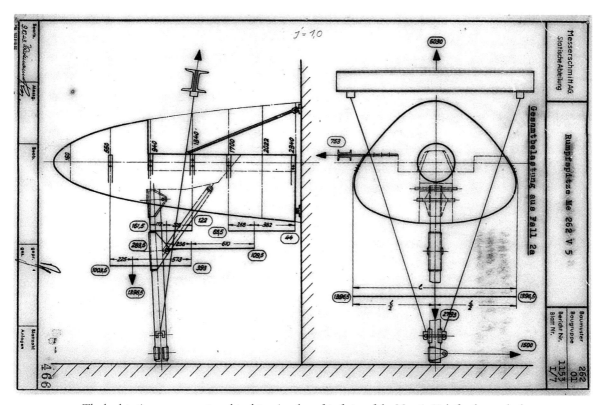

*The load-testing arrangement used to determine the safety factor of the Me 262 V5's fixed nosewheel.*

Milch: "That would be enough."

Mahnke: "The BMW series will not start until the beginning of 1945. BMW will finish development by then."

Milch: "Junkers can hold up until then. We don't need to talk about it. First of all, we have to have the Junkers engine, and that's how we get there. If the number of pieces is as you say, that's fine."

Later in the discussion, Milch made it even more plain that he felt Messerschmitt was dragging its heels on the Me 262: "What I take from their first demands is that they have not yet approached the whole thing."

Vorwald: "They have already approached it!"

Milch: "Whether all orders for 100 machines are out and also for the supply line, Vorwald, I don't trust these people!"

It seems, however, that Messerschmitt's years of neglecting the Me 262 were at the root of these delays. The aircraft may have been flying in prototype form but basic design issues remained unresolved and nothing approaching a supply chain had been established. The existing prototypes were handmade one-offs, largely composed of single-order components. The company now faced an uphill struggle to gear up for mass production, with all the tools and jigs this necessitated, while simultaneously changing and updating the design of the aircraft itself.

On the same day as the latest RLM meeting, Willy

Messerschmitt wrote to Bley concerning the acquisition of workers from an external contractor for the Me 262: "It was agreed that Rossmair would send 25 men here. Despite his written promise, he only sent 11 men here and refuses (according to Mr Beese, who was in Munich on Saturday) to send the other necessary people here.

"I draw your attention to the fact Rossmair's refusal leads to a delay in the deadline for the work on the 262."

Relocating subcontractor Rossmair's workers was only necessary, however, because Messerschmitt had changed the design of the Me 262's engine nacelles, making the drawings Rossmair had originally been sent obsolete. Messerschmitt went on: "Rossmair does all of the engine cowlings for the 262. As this is constructed of steel, close collaboration is required. All previously presented drawings had to be fundamentally changed. I request you to force the Rossmair people to come here immediately without delay. A delay is impossible because it is at the expense of the 262 dates. I personally cannot be held responsible for deadlines if I don't have the people at my disposal."

## ELECTRO-ACOUSTIC DETECTION

In a report on June 25, Träger detailed experiments carried out using microphones and measuring devices to investigate the sound spectrum produced by the Me 262's engines.[21] A measuring station had been set up using equipment from Siemens & Halske and this was

*The equipment used by Messerschmitt engineer Träger to measure the sound frequencies generated by the Me 262's engines at different positions around the aircraft.*

used to make recordings in three positions around a static Me 262—at the nose end of the fuselage, at the tail end of the fuselage and at the tip of the left wing.

It was found that "at both [engine] speeds [6,000rpm and 8,000rpm] at the nose of the fuselage, the sound pressures of the high-frequency components significantly predominate". Low-frequency sounds predominated at the tail end and the wingtip was almost exactly between the two. It was thought that the ground below the aircraft was probably absorbing the high frequency noise to the rear but further testing was required. At this stage, the best location for microphones to differentiate between high frequency jet engines and low frequency piston engines was the Me 262's nose.

## PREPARING FOR PRODUCTION

During the RLM management meeting on June 29, Milch was indeed able to question Willy Messerschmitt, Messerschmitt company engineer Bley and production director Fritz Hentzen directly about preparations for full series production of the Me 262.[22] Bley said the necessary drawings would be delivered by July 15, followed by the construction of 60 makeshift jigs for the pre-production series of 100 aircraft. The first example would be delivered in January 1944, eight more in February, 21 in March, 40 in April and then 60 in May, with the target of 100 being reached in mid-May.

Production would then continue at a rate of 60 per month until November 1944, when mass manufacturing would commence.

Production would be split between Augsburg and Regensburg, with the first full production aircraft being completed in October 1944, then five in November, 40 in December, 90 in January 1945, 140 in February 1945, 180 in March 1945—then up to 400 a month by September 1945.

When it came to licence production, Hentzen said: "We have already talked about switching on Wiener Neustadt ... We imagined that Wiener Neustadt would start the way it should have with the 209. That is now being planned. The question of whether Erla will start has not yet been decided. In Augsburg, Regensburg and with Wiener Neustadt we bring out the number of pieces that should originally have come for the 209. The question now is whether one should also switch Erla to the 262 or perhaps reserve a temporary flight for some other aircraft, perhaps a high-altitude fighter."

Vorwald: "In the first planning meeting I said that we should first plan the number of pieces as with the 209."

Milch: "It's still interesting to know what it would look like if Erla were switched on. You always have to know that we still have the high-altitude fighter question open. We do not know how far this can be covered by the 262. If this were certain, then we would go even harder on the 262. Otherwise something has to be kept in reserve. The decision to build a high-altitude variant of the Me 209 would be relatively easy if it could be done with today's 209. But I heard it can't."

Messerschmitt: "The engine should be ready, and wing inserts must be built in..."

Milch: "In German: quite a different machine! The question now is whether you can do it with the current airframe of the 190, which would be fine in and of itself to accommodate the more powerful engine and which would already have the necessary strength to be able to withstand the higher weight. It is 400kg heavier than today's 209.

"If we could manage to solve this question more easily using the 190 variant, then that would of course be an unheard of progress in terms of the application. We would get to it faster because the airframe is there—always provided that it is the airframe we already have—because it is already in production in large numbers. Then we could bridge the time until a high-altitude variant of the 262 comes up."

Messerschmitt: "That will take a long time. It looks like these engines will not be suitable for aircraft at high-altitudes in the foreseeable future."

Schelp: "That only applies to the first Jumo engine

[the 004]... and the BMW [003] engine, because these are the first performance classes. This is a question of the date of the HeS 011, when it can come. Every effort is made to get this engine ready as quickly as possible. The first one will be up and running on the test stand in the next 14 days."

Milch: "When do you think this HeS 011 is coming?"

Schelp: "We estimate that the first engines ready for installation could be there around autumn, 1944. Then a corresponding time elapses before a series can be expected."

Milch: "So another year. But that would be a reasonable future prospect. For you, Messerschmitt, it would be much happier if at any point in time you could pass over from the 109 to the 262 without any problems, first in the normal version and later in the high-altitude variant. Then you would not have to switch your whole production line over to the 209 again, purely in terms of work, construction, etc. That would also be good for us."

The discussion dragged on with Messerschmitt continually pressing the Me 209 and highlighting the Fw 190's disadvantages. Eventually, Milch asked: "How does the matter look on the [Jumo 004] engine side? Are the engines getting there in time?"

Mahnke: "After the preparations that Junkers is now making, we can expect that we are still considerably ahead of the game. This is not a bad thing with such an engine. Cambeis had the plan that by the end of the year we should get 200 pieces per month. These 200 pieces should be manufactured in such a way that each engine factory takes over several groups and that the assembly is carried out at the new location, in Neudeck."[23]

After further discussion, Petersen said: "Dr Franz from Jumo called me two or three times. Everything is going okay so far with him, but he has difficulties protecting his subcontractors [from conscription]. I referred him to the planning office."

Milch said that the RLM would take care of this problem.

## DESIGN CHANGES

Without Göring's knowledge, Adolf Hitler summoned seven key figures in the German aviation industry to attend his Berghof residence on the Obersalzburg, near Berchtesgaden, on June 27, 1943. These were Willy Messerschmitt, Ernst Heinkel, Claude Dornier, Focke-Wulf's Kurt Tank, Arado's Walter Blume, Richard Vogt from Blohm & Voss and Heinrich Hertel from Junkers.

The Führer spoke to each of them personally, behind closed doors, and offered them an opportunity to explain their work and air any grievances they might have.[24] It is unknown exactly what Messerschmitt said to Hitler

but that meeting would come to have a disastrous effect on the drive towards series production of the Me 262 before the end of July 1943.

Meanwhile, Voigt's Project Office was working on a range of new Me 262 variants. Two BMW engineers, Huber and Kappus, visited Augsburg on July 1, 1943, to discuss their company's design for a combined turbojet/rocket propulsion unit[25] which would later be designated BMW 003 R. Once they had handed over their reports, "the discussion very quickly resulted in complete agreement with regard to the extraordinary advantages of the TLR [jet/rocket] arrangement. Messerschmitt is very interested in the combined propulsion system for fighters.

"Messerschmitt has already planned a variant of the Me 262 with two Junkers jets in the wing and, in addition, a complete Walter rocket motor with 1,500kg thrust in the end of the fuselage. However, since the TLR engine combination planned by BMW offers significant advantages in terms of fuel consumption and installation compared to the above layout, Messerschmitt would prefer to use the TLR combination from BMW.

"Whether the intermediate solution of the Me 262 with TLR drive and Junkers-Walter devices is necessary or whether the combined BMW engines can be used depends on the delivery date. The prospects for a short-term development of the Me 262 with TLR drive are particularly good for the following reason: although the existing version has limited possibilities for accommodating the large amounts of fuel that are needed for the TLR-fighter, at Messerschmitt a version with a thickened fuselage, which is intended as a high-speed scout and a high-speed bomber, is already being developed.

"This variant offers the possibility of accommodating the necessary fuel quantities, so that it also represents the best airframe solution for the TLR fighter ... it was agreed that BMW would carry out the flight performance calculations for it. Messerschmitt supplies all necessary airframe-side documents. The development work for the TLR fighter is being driven forward by Messerschmitt with the greatest urgency."

Just two days later, Voigt's office produced a report comparing the performance and characteristics of several different single-jet designs with those of the Me 262.[26] It was found that although the single-jet fighters had the same range as the Me 262, the latter could carry 1,000kg of bombs whereas the former could not. And although the single-jet fighter would require a staggering 45% less material to make and could be made 10-15% quicker, its engine would be harder to access and its weapons arrangement would probably be less favourable. These single-jet fighter designs went

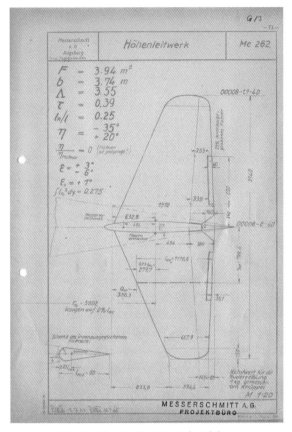

*Drawing showing the Me 262's tailplanes dated July 3, 1943. The design would change little throughout the aircraft's existence.*

no further but the potential advantages were clear and Messerschmitt would revisit the concept a year later.

On July 5, a meeting was held by Willy Messerschmitt and his engineers to discuss a variety of design changes made since the Me 262 A-1 parts list had been drawn up.[27] There were alterations to the wings, tail unit and armament.

The question of building the Me 262 as a bomber was briefly touched on during a discussion about the Arado Ar 234 jet reconnaissance aircraft at the RLM management meeting on July 9.[28] With wry sarcasm, Milch said: "Now the question of a jet bomber came up. Peltz is always humble. He has made a small demand and wants 100 of them by November at the latest."

Dietrich Peltz, Inspector of Bombers, retorted dryly: "December."

Pasewaldt said: "The Ar 234 makes a good impression in itself. We expect this machine to completely fulfil our hopes. It should be noted that the Ar 234 was developed as a scout. The variant as a bomber has recently been investigated, and the options with the Ar 234 are in any case significantly cheaper than with the Me 262, which we actually want to reserve essentially as a fighter. The current pressure on the 262 to enter service as a fighter

actually hardly justifies an intervention in the long term to create a bomber variant."

At another Messerschmitt company internal meeting with Willy Messerschmitt on July 13 it was announced that "work in the Construction Office on the preparation of the pre-production series has largely been completed" and now "various stages of further development are to be incorporated by the Construction Office immediately afterwards".[29] These jobs were: installation of fittings for solid fuel take-off aid booster rockets; two new fuel tanks—one below the cockpit and one behind the rear tank; "bomb system for Me 262 as fighter-bomber, according to the documents already delivered by the Project Office"; alternative armament of two MK 103s and one or two MG 151/15s; and finally "the first possible variant of the Me 262 is to build a prototype of the interceptor solution. Project documents will be delivered by August 15".

In fact, preliminary trials using solid booster rockets had commenced that same day with poor results. Work had begun on July 6 to fit the Me 262 V5 with a pair of Rheinmetall-Borsig 109-502 boosters. When these were tried, on July 13, it was found that the attachments were too weak and the rockets had been "lost".[30] The rebuilt Me 262 V1 made its first flight with Jumo 004 engines, and without a nose-mounted piston engine, on July 19. The only problem encountered was with the right brake, which failed to operate due to a faulty valve.[31]

Träger produced another report on preliminary testing for his electro-acoustic detection system on July 16.[32] Since the previous report on June 25, a number of flight tests had taken place using a microphone both inside and attached to the outside of Me 262 V4's nose. During the first tests the interior of the aircraft's nose was lined with 10mm thick felt "to avoid resonance phenomena" and the microphone, a type known as Nr. 21 b that had been devised by the AVA at Göttingen, was suspended within it on rubber bands. Next, a dummy microphone was attached to the nose of a Bf 110 and flown at up to 740km/h, presumably in a steep dive, to ensure that the support structure planned for the Me 262 was sturdy enough for high-speed flight.

Finally, the structure along with the real microphone was attached to the exterior of Me 262 V4. The frame, which included rubber inserts to "avoid structural noise transmission", suspended the microphone 50cm from the tip of the aircraft's nose. Further measurements of the aircraft's engine noise were then taken.

On July 20 it was decided that the Me 262's armament alternatives would be two MK 103s and two MK 108s, two MK 103s and two MG 151s or six MK 108s.[33] Messerschmitt's Project Office would now begin working out

*Dummy microphone attached to the nose of Bf 110 Werk-Nr. 4790 for flight testing as part of Messerschmitt engineer Träger's electro-acoustic detection system programme.*

*AVA Nr. 21 b microphone mounted on the nose of Me 262 V4 for flight tests.*

how best to fit these different weapons arrangements within the aircraft's nose unit.

There were four flying Me 262s at this point—V1, V3, V4 and V5—but not for long.

The V4 was demonstrated to Göring and Milch on July 24 by Messerschmitt factory test pilot Gerd Lindner at Rechlin[34] but following an interim landing at Schkeuditz on the way back to Lechfeld on July 25 the aircraft had failed to take off, overshot the end of the runway and suffered 50% damage, which was eventually deemed irreparable.[35] Whether the aircraft was still fitted with the microphone and its associated equipment at this point is unclear but there would be no further practical testing of the electro-acoustic detection system for three months after the loss of V4.

## HITLER'S FIRST INTERVENTION

Had they not been briefed in advance, Milch's staff would have been shocked, during his management meeting on July 27, 1943, to see him make an abrupt U-turn on the Me 209 and Me 262. Suddenly, the Me 209 was no longer cancelled and had taken centre stage in production planning again.[36] The Me 262 was reduced from the main focus of all production efforts to an "additional requirement".

He said: "We want to start today with the question of the [Me] 209 and [Ta] 153 fighters." He said there were three classes of fighters delineated by operating altitude—up to 8,000m was 'class 1', 8,000m to 12,000m was 'class 2' and "the third class are the actual Höhenjäger [high-altitude fighters] from 12 to about 15km."

Friebel said: "Since class 1 is relatively clear, we set up class 2 as the first task for the short-term, i.e. an aircraft armed with two MG 151/20 plus one MK 108 in a central arrangement, otherwise two 151/20s plus two 108s if a motor-cannon is not possible. A 2m per second climb rate, at least 20 minutes flight time and operational ceiling between 13 and 14km! It must be possible to derive such an aircraft from the current series with minor changes. This second class has been examined by Focke-Wulf and Messerschmitt. Both company bosses are here and can speak about it."

He was referring to Focke-Wulf's Kurt Tank and Willy Messerschmitt—who was now acknowledged once again as the leader of the Messerschmitt company, despite everything that had happened 15 months earlier.

Milch said: "You can see from the drawings that class 3, developed from class 2, brings something. But for scheduling reasons you cannot skip class 2, as it is almost a year ahead. In addition, it uses many component parts from this machine, so that this makes things easier." Addressing Messerschmitt directly, he said: "Where do you see the 209?"

Messerschmitt: "Practically every component from the 209 is in this solution."

Milch: "Then the 209, as it was planned, would no longer be necessary."

Messerschmitt: "It would cover class 1, the fighter up to 8km with DB 603 G."

In other words, the Me 209 was now back on the table as the Luftwaffe's next standard fighter. Milch said: "The difficulty of the deliberations now consists in this: we want to go through with 262 at the very least. On the other hand, with new things like the jet engine we always have to see them as something special. We cannot view them as the normal frontline fighter like the old principle aircraft is. There are so many other things in there that one should be careful in assessing."

Messerschmitt agreed: "I've always emphasized that. You can't just go straight to the jet fighter."

Milch: "We can only make it in addition to the other things."

He went on to say that the main role foreseen for the Me 262 was in combatting enemy bomber formations, while the piston-engine fighters would continue to fill the other fighter roles. He said: "I don't think we can do without the fighter with the piston engine and the

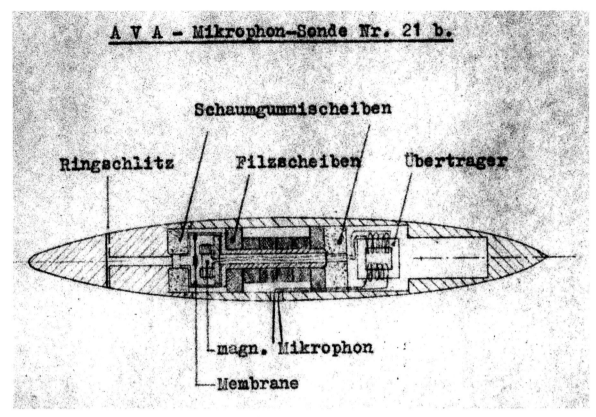

*The inner workings of the microphone used during Träger's tests.*

*The Me 262 V4's cockpit fitted with a control box for Träger's acoustic system and a Voltmeter, both in the dark area on the right. This rare view inside the cockpit of an early Me 262 prototype also shows a significantly different instrument layout compared to that of the production model.*

propeller for the moment. The answer to the question of when the jet thing will be ready is still ahead of us. I am convinced that this will be around the same time next year. Since we cannot decide today whether to rely on jet engines, we have to work on the piston-engine altitude variant. Is there anyone here who takes a different view on this matter? [Evidently no one else in the room spoke at this point] So nobody!"

Later in the meeting, Milch looked at the latest planning documents: "With the 209, by the end of 1944

there are 1,226 aircraft."

Lucht: "There should be more. A total of 3,000 are planned."

Later still, Messerschmitt said: "When it comes to jig construction, the 209 also takes over a large part of the 109, so that the licensees, Erla, Regensburg, Wiener Neustadt, of course already have a large part of the jigs required so they will not have to be manufactured."

Milch stated the obvious: "The 109 and 190 would not somehow be replaced just by the 262, but that has to be additional. So that means you have to revise the number of 262s required, doesn't it?"

Someone shouted "Yes!" in the background and he went on: "It is clear that these must of course grind against each other and that not 100% of every number, as it was in the programme, continues for each individual type."

After some further discussion, Messerschmitt said: "The main question is actually the question of the 209 in and of itself. If, as the field marshal emphasized earlier today, fighter capacity based on the piston engine should not be reduced in favour of the 262, then the capacity for the 262 would have to be reduced."

He said that the promised capacity for the Me 262 would not be kept and another Messerschmitt engineer, Mr Lead, said that plans originally laid to switch workers from the Me 410 to the Me 262 would not now proceed

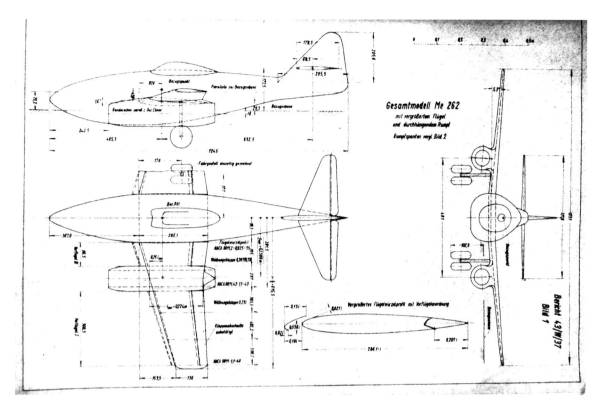

*Wind tunnel model of an Me 262 with deepened fuselage tested by the AVA. Messerschmitt's Project Office would propose the new fuselage as a means of accommodating a bomb or camera bay.*

because "the 262 is purely an additional requirement that cannot yet be covered by the current requirement 410".

Petersen, the Me 262 commissioner, could only plead: "Something has to be done for the 262."

Two and a half weeks later, during a meeting on August 17 without Willy Messerschmitt present, Milch would explain that Adolf Hitler had personally intervened in favour of the Me 209 at the expense of the Me 262.[37] He said: "At the time I accepted Galland's suggestion to discontinue the other new developments in favour of the 262 in order to tackle this matter with full force. We were so far along that we took it to the Reichsmarschall. Now afterwards, since the Führer got involved, clear instructions came to us, namely in the sense that we are not yet allowed to simply pension off the piston-engine fighter in favour of the 262. The Führer sees too great a danger in this.

"Of course he didn't say that the 262 shouldn't come. In the meeting it was also not possible to say that we can only do one thing or the other, because that is not true either. It is only if we want to produce large numbers, and very quickly, then we can only do one thing. Because we must now go along with the other two solutions [the Me 209 and Ta 153], there is definitely a handicap for the 262. This handicap must be in the number produced. That means: we have to coordinate the number of 262s we can make with the production

of the other fighters on the dates when they can come. In total we cannot go beyond 4,000 aircraft in the planning overall.

"What capacity is necessary for the construction, and so on? It is clear that Messerschmitt cannot now go 100% on the 262, as it would otherwise have been possible. A certain amount, albeit little, especially of support and development goes to the 209."

He later added, perhaps wearily: "I personally regret that I cannot build the 262 100%. Personally, I would build it and not go the way over the 209, but instead run the risk as we had decided. But I have clear orders. I am a soldier and I have to obey orders. The security that the Führer demands must be taken into account by us."

It seems likely that during his private audience with Hitler on June 27, Willy Messerschimitt stressed the importance of the Me 209 and expressed concern about Milch's ambitious plan to shift aircraft development towards jet aircraft. Hitler then met with Milch and got Messerschmitt what he wanted. But as Milch pointed out, there wasn't sufficient capacity for every fighter and the Me 262 would have to suffer if the Me 209 was to be squeezed back into the production programme.

The AVA produced a report on wind tunnel tests of an Me 262 model featuring a very deep forward fuselage on July 31, 1943.[38] The ungainly-looking design was intended to provide extra internal space which could

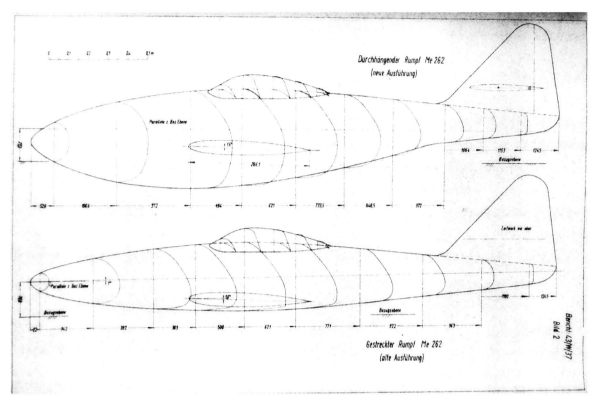

*The proposed enlarged Me 262 fuselage compared the original design.*

be used to accommodate bombs or camera equipment for reconnaissance and would appear among the wealth of new derivative designs unveiled by Voigt's team in September (see Chapter 5).

On August 2, 1943, Willy Messerschmitt was skim-reading a development history of the Me 262 and noticed two design elements which had apparently been forgotten about when the construction documents were being drawn up—heating for the weapons bay and a windscreen washer. He wrote a memo to Helmschrott, saying: "I ask for clarification and submission of the planned system so that it can be incorporated into the series documents immediately."[39]

Two days later, Messerschmitt sent out another memo, this time to Friedrich Schwarz of the Project Office concerning "special armament of our fighters and destroyers".[40] He wrote: "We are now installing the 50mm gun in the 410, which was formerly a tank gun. The same weapon is also intended for the 262 .... Since the aircraft, especially the 262, are definitely becoming more and more important for combatting the enemy tanks that might have broken through, I think it is necessary that we do not always lag behind in armament for as long as before, but that we keep in touch with the OKW directly or with the RLM, to install armour-piercing weapons in our aircraft in good time, or to investigate whether they need to be installed, or what changes will be necessary in order to be able to install them.

"You should therefore try to stay up to date so that we always have the same weapon on the plane at least at the same time as our most modern tanks. I ask for examination and an occasional presentation."

On the same day, August 4, the Me 262 V5 suffered 50% damage during a crash-landing, putting it out of action.[41]

A Messerschmitt internal report of August 7, 1943, noted that the Me 262 construction documents had been completed, as had the jig designs, but timetabling the actual production of the first 100 examples was not possible because "the requested jig builders did not arrive on schedule and most of them are still missing today".[42]

## ME 262 A-1

The Project Office produced the first full description of the Me 262 A-1 fighter on August 6, 1943, with a supplement describing the Me 262 A-2 fighter-bomber appearing two days later.[43]

The Me 262 A-1 would now be an interim design powered by Jumo 004 B-1 or B-2 engines, while the full series production model would be the Me 262 A-2 with Jumo 004 C engines. As far as Messerschmitt was concerned, "externally, the B-2 engine does not differ from the B-1 engine" except its performance was 6% higher. Each engine was attached to the wing at three points and had removeable panels for accessibility.

## Jäger A1

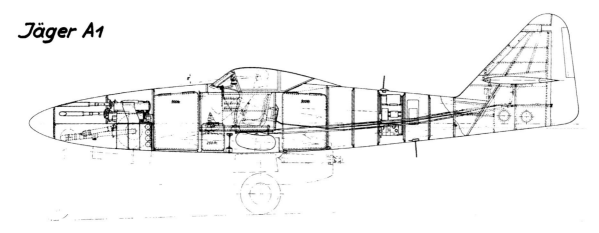

*Messerschmitt drawing number II/170, dated July 22, 1943, shows the Me 262 A-1. A month earlier the A-1 designation had applied to the standard fighter variant. Now it was applied to an interim version of the design with only two main fuel tanks, four MK 108s and Jumo 004 B-1 or B-2 engines.*

## Jäger u. Jabo

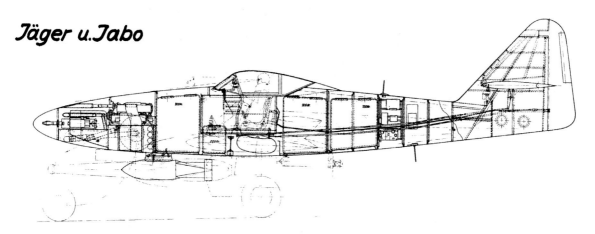

*The Me 262 Jäger und Jabo, fighter and fighter-bomber, was to receive the A-2 designation and was intended to be the main production variant. It would have three main fuel tanks, six MK 108s and Jumo 004 C engines. It appears here in Messerschmitt drawing II/173 of July 22, 1943.*

The A-1 would be limited to three fuel tanks—two of 900 litres and a third of 250 litres—and the fuel itself would be either oil or petrol, though oil was preferable. The main tanks, with two pumps each, would be accessible through covers on the underside of the fuselage and the 250 litre tank was actually mounted on a removeable hatch. The two main tanks each had a filler hatch on the top of the fuselage, one in front of and one behind the cockpit. The container for the hydraulic oil was filled through a cap on the left side of the fuselage.

Armament was planned as six MK 108s but only four could be fitted in the A-1 "due to the lower power of the B-2 engines". The rear pair would have 90 rounds each and the front pair 80 rounds each. The weapons bay was "accessible through two large flaps, similar to those found on the hood of a car". The nose itself was held on by four bolts and could be easily taken off and

swapped for another. If MK 108s were not available, a nose with three MG 151/20s could be used instead.

The cannon ammo and the pilot had 15mm of armour against fire from the front, while the latter also got a 90mm thick armoured windscreen plate set at an angle of 35°. Armour for the pilot's back was not built in but would be supplied as a kit that could be retrofitted. The cockpit, though not initially made pressure-tight, was barrel-shaped so that this feature could be added later. It was constructed as a single component and inserted into the airframe centre section.

The height adjustable pilot's seat was a standard item and the canopy centre section, unobstructed by the side frames that had featured on earlier iterations, hinged open to the right. There was a clear vision panel to the pilot's left that could be opened and in an emergency pulling a handle on the right side of the cockpit would

**Me 262** A1 Jäger
Raumaufteilung

*Shaded graphic showing the internal layout of the Me 262 A-1.*

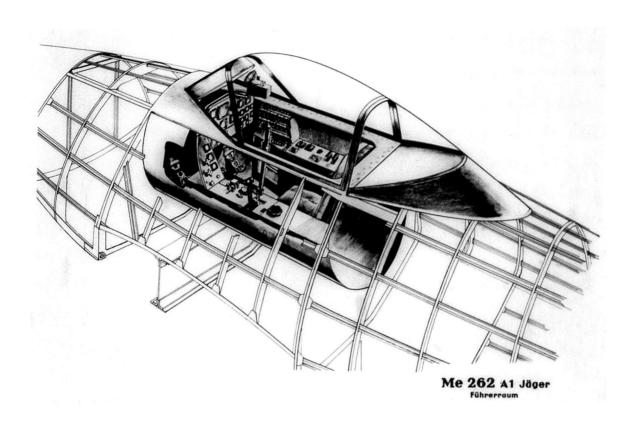

**Me 262** A1 Jäger
Führerraum

*The excellent visibility that would be afforded by the new cockpit canopy designed for the
series production model Me 262 is graphically illustrated in this image.*

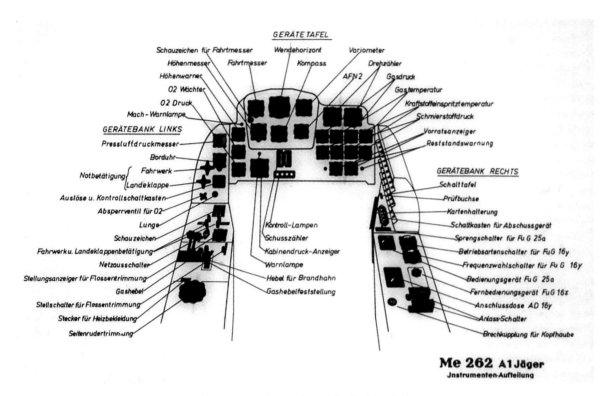

*The instrument layout planned for the Me 262 A-1.*

eject both the centre and rear sections of the canopy. The normal opening handle was on the left. The forward and downward viewing angle was 8°. Cabin and weapons bay heating was provided using hot air drawn from both engines. The unheated windscreen and right hand side window could be cleaned using a blast from the fire extinguisher or by spraying on fuel from the engine starter tank using a hand pump.

All stick controls were transmitted to the aircraft's control surfaces via push rods, with fin adjustments made using a toggle switch. A hand wheel on the left side of the cockpit was used to trim the rudder. The landing flaps were extended and retracted using two buttons, which had to be held down. When the button was released, the flap would remain in whatever position it had been adjusted to. Markings were made on the flaps themselves to indicate their position clearly to the pilot.

The buttons for the landing gear release were covered by a flap and a compressed air emergency actuation system was provided for both systems. This was powered by a single two-litre air bottle housed in the space between the left side of the fuselage and the cockpit tub.

The radio systems, FuG 16 ZY and FuG 25 a, were installed at the end of the fuselage centre section—leaving space for the additional tank behind the rear main tank—and were accessible via a hatch on the right side of the fuselage. The antenna for the FuG 16 was installed in the wooden rudder tip while the Y-antenna was in the

left wing. The antenna for the FuG 25 was on the underside of the fuselage behind the radio sets themselves. The electrics were powered by two 1,000W generators, one per engine, with a backup battery behind the pilot's seat.

The oxygen system was controlled from the left side equipment bank and the two associated two-litre oxygen bottles were on the left side of the fuselage outside the cockpit tub, refillable through an external hatch.

Five monitoring gauges per engine were provided in the cockpit along with the usual fighter performance gauges and a Mach warning indicator light to alert the pilot if the aircraft's speed rose too high. Each engine had its own a throttle lever with a start button built into the handle.

Two 500kg thrust Borsig booster rockets, actuated by a push button on the pilot's left control console, could be used for take-off with 790m of runway required. Landing speed with 4,800kg weight was 174km/h.

Top speed was 875km/h at 6km altitude. Maximum climb rate was 23.5m/s at sea level, 12.8m/s at 6km and 6.6m/s at 9km. Time to 6km was 5.8 minutes, with 9km altitude reached after 11.2 minutes. Service ceiling was 11.45km. Flight time with maximum economy was 1.46 hours at 6km altitude. With 100% thrust, flight time at 6km was 0.94 hours.

The aircraft was all-metal—mostly aluminium alloy and steel—with a take-off weight of 5,400kg when fitted with 770 x 270mm wheels. If 840 x 300 wheels could

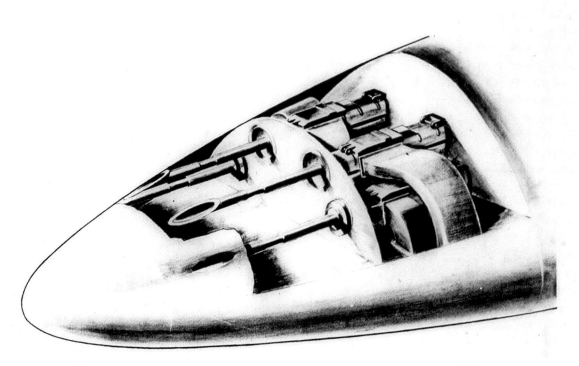

**Me 262 A1 Jäger**
Rumpfspitze 4 MK 108

*The nose of the Me 262 A-1. For the Me 262 A-2, there were to be an additional pair of MK 108s installed at the tip.*

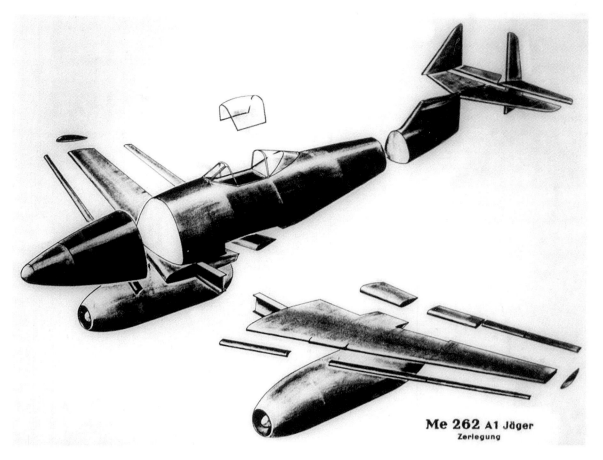

**Me 262 A1 Jäger**
Zerlegung

*Component breakdown for the Me 262 A-1, as planned in July 1943.*

be used, then take-off weight rose to 7,000kg while landing weight was 5,300kg.

The nosewheel intended was the 660 x 160 mainwheel developed for the Bf 109 but "should procurement difficulties arise, the wheel 630 x 150 can be installed without modification".

The drum brakes on the mainwheels were hydraulically actuated by the pilot using pedals but the nosewheel brake, also hydraulic, was operated using a hand lever on the left side of the instrument panel. All connections to the cockpit and the wing-fuselage junctions could be reached through the mainwheel cut-outs and the installation cover of the 250 litre fuel tank.

Jacking points were provided under the wing on the spar, to the right and left outboard of the engines and on the tail boom. And several "hand holes" were provided in the wings and tail boom allowing access to the control linkages.

The wing was a single piece that was attached at four major connection points below the fuselage and with several minor attachment points. The leading edge of the wing was swept back by 18.5°. Automatic slats were on the outer wing up to the engines and then between the engines and the fuselage. The hydraulically actuated landing flaps extended between the ailerons and the wing root, interrupted by the engines. Take-off position was 25° and landing position was 30°.

## ME 262 A-2

The Me 262 A-2 was to be a fighter-bomber with Jumo 004 C engines, these providing an 18% increase in thrust compared to the 004 B-1 and B-2. According to the report, this allowed for overthrust on take-off and "due to the greater power of the engines, the amount of fuel and thus the range can be increased, and the armament can be strengthened. There is also the possibility of using it as a fast fighter with droppable loads of up to 500kg or 700kg".

The extra fuel would be in an additional 750 litre tank behind the 900 litre main rear tank, installed through the same under-fuselage cut-out as the main tank. Armament would be six MK 108s, the two extra cannon, with 70 rounds each, being positioned in front of the other four with 15mm of armour for each new ammo box. Potential bomb loads included one BT 700 torpedo,

or one 500kg bomb on one side, or two 250kg bombs.

Plans had been drawn up to use 935 x 345mm wheels, if that was possible, or efforts would be made to develop new tyres for the 840 x 300mm wheels which could cope with a 7,000kg maximum take-off weight. The take-off itself would be made using two solid fuel booster rockets, burning for six seconds.

The cockpit would be made pressure-tight using compressed air taken from both engines behind the eighth supercharger stage and the left hand side instrument panel in the cockpit was to be kept free for the necessary monitoring instruments.

During the RLM development meeting on August 10,[44] with Willy Messerschmitt once again in attendance, Milch said: "That is one of the advantages that speaks in favour of the 209, that a considerably wider production can be achieved with operating resources. The disadvantage, however, is that we don't know where we're going to build the 262. Some other work would be necessary for that."

Messerschmitt replied: "If you want to keep the piston-engine fighter on the same level, additional capacity has to be created anyway. We gain working capacity with the 209. We save 2.5 million working hours per factory."

Alpers: "When he switches from 109 to 209."

Later on, Milch asked: "Has the 209 flown yet?" Messerschmitt replied: "No, it should fly in August. That was postponed by a month due to the 262 and the stop order."

Later still, Petersen said: "I would like to say something about [Jumo] 004 production. The engine is not okay at all."

Mahnke reported that plans to consolidate Jumo 004 production at Neudeck had failed because that facility had been reallocated to Volkswagen, Ferdinand Porsche and the production of engines for the Junkers Ju 188. No substitute facility had yet been identified.

That same day, the Me 262 V1 suffered a double engine fire which damaged both wings and its landing flaps, putting it out of action.[45] This left just the Me 262 V3 still flying and it was about to become workshop-bound during conversion work for high-speed testing.

Once again, flight testing was about to grind to a complete halt.

# 5

## Hitler and the Me 262 Fighter-Bomber: August 1943 to December 1943

THE QUESTION of how to provide Messerschmitt with more resources led the RLM to examine what capacity could be gained if types being built by other companies were cancelled. Attention had subsequently turned to seaplane builder Blohm & Voss during the RLM management meeting of August 3, 1943.[1]

The company's BV 138, BV 222 and BV 238 flying boats were cancelled the following day and during the management meeting of August 13,[2] Milch said: "What Blohm & Voss can give today in terms of designers and workers should go in favour of Messerschmitt ... Messerschmitt should not only fill his office with these people, but also get people who can approach work independently ... we have further discussed that Blohm & Voss ... is to take on a special task within the framework of Messerschmitt. We had talked about Vogt taking over all the jig construction and preparation of the Me 262.

"Then we have just talked about the question that Messerschmitt, in addition to all other tasks, gets started very quickly in a new fighter, the 209, and for this extraordinary forces are needed. We are aware that Messerschmitt also has to develop a high-altitude variant".

Milch's initial thought seemed like an elegant solution: give Blohm & Voss's capable engineers and designers, led by Richard Vogt, the sole task of creating the jigs that would otherwise be unavailable for the Me 262. At the same time Messerschmitt would be free to press ahead at full speed with the Me 209, which would in turn form the basis for Galland's indispensable high-altitude interceptor. The conversation had moved on, however.

Vogt may well have argued that his men had no experience in designing their own jigs and would be better placed to help Messerschmitt with aircraft design work instead. Milch went on: "Now it would be good if Blohm & Voss could take on a task to relieve Messerschmitt ... up to the date when the overall situation means independence for Blohm & Voss is once again made possible. Until then, the Blohm & Voss apparatus should, as far as possible, be included in the programme that is at the forefront for us: fighter and destroyer. We also said that initially all the development issues in the area of the new jet aircraft, which are highly interesting and will be discussed later, cannot be on the same level as the fighters and destroyers, but below them. As a result, first of all, all energy on the fighter-destroyer, on

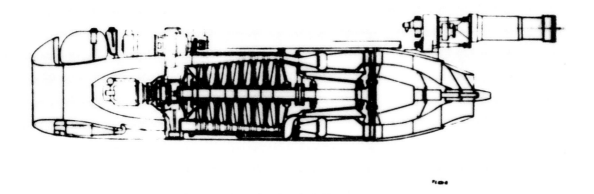

*The BMW 003 R turbojet/rocket motor combination. The practical implementation*
*of this seemingly simple concept would cause significant difficulties.*

the Reich defence programme. I suggest that we first discuss this question and that you, Vogt, say what tasks you can still take on."

Vogt: "We are completely unencumbered and are willing to take on anything that Messerschmitt considers right to hand over."

While Blohm & Voss would eventually end up receiving Me 262-related work, for now Messerschmitt had other priorities.

On August 17, a task force of USAAF B-17s dropped 82 tons of high-explosive and incendiary bombs on one of the three Messerschmitt factories at Regensburg—Prüfening—resulting in 75% damage and causing Bf 109 output to drop from 268 in July 1943 to 77 in September.[3] It was a significant blow, since Regensburg was an integral part of the plan to build both the Me 209 and Me 262, and it prompted the company to begin dispersing its assembly lines to a multitude of smaller workshops.

The office-based functions of the company, including the Project Office, would be relocated to the small town of Oberammergau in the Bavarian Alps, near Germany's southern border, and would subsequently continue operations under the codename Oberbayerische Forschungsanstalt Oberammergau.[4]

Two days after the raid, 120 Blohm & Voss designers were already working on a high-altitude piston-engine fighter "based on the Me 109/209" at Messerschmitt's Augsburg headquarters.[5]

The Me 262's lack of suitability for extreme altitudes—above 12km—was talked about during the RLM meeting of August 20.[6] Eisenlohr mentioned that BMW's TLR combination engine, the 003 R, could help.

By now it was clear that this was essentially just a BMW 003 turbojet but supplied in a nacelle that had a small rocket nozzle mounted to the upper rear, above and behind the jet outlet. He said: "If you place the rocket motor on top of the jet engine as a small rider, you can be at 12km altitude in less than two minutes with the 262 after a start with booster rockets and can then fly there for up to an hour. The rocket motor would be able to push the aircraft up to higher altitudes, but the aircraft would have to go down to 12km if the rocket fuel was all used up because that's where the jet engine can hold the aircraft in a straight line. For now, we can't go higher than 12km."

This point was expanded upon by Major Kuno Hoffmann of the Technical Office's engines section, C-E 2, during the RLM development meeting a week later.[7] He said: "The development of the jet engines, especially promoted by the Luftwaffe, led to the construction of the Messerschmitt 262 as a jet fighter, which, initially intended by the Generalfeldmarschall to replace the 109,[8] is now to come as supplemental equipment. In addition, the Me 163 B was in preparation in the other area of the rocket-engine ... The development of the jet and rocket engines took us to speeds that are astonishing and represent a very special advance compared to the speeds with piston engines."

He said that the thrust potential of jet and rocket engines was so high that "today they cannot be fully exploited with the current airframes". He went on: "I would like to refer to the combination 262 with two jet engines plus one rocket engine." This arrangement, largely a normal Me 262 but with a single Walter rocket motor in its tail, would, he said, allow the aircraft to quickly intercept enemy aircraft sighted overhead and would enable the 262 "to reach altitudes between 15 and 18km, albeit assuming that a pressure cabin is available".

He continued: "At the moment, flight over 12km seems to run into difficulties with the jet engine. The flights with the 262 had to be aborted at an altitude of 11.5 km, because irregularities in combustion have set in ... the result is a somewhat unexplored and unpredictable area: how does the jet engine behave at altitude?

"It is well known that the rocket motor gives us the corresponding thrust at altitude. It can also be used as a quick fix for our aircraft like this. The decision to be made is whether to equip the Me 262 as an experimental aircraft with a rocket motor, namely with the Hesse-Walter device, in order to carry out tests as they were carried out in the 163 B, now under further development to the 163 C."

While the Me 163 C would be much quicker and cheaper to make than the Me 262, he said, it had a flight time of only 15 minutes at altitude, whereas the Me 262 jet/rocket combination would have almost the same endurance as a piston engine fighter—43 to 45 minutes at 11-12km altitude.

## MAKING JET ENGINES

After this, Schelp gave a briefing on the difficulties being faced by the turbojet manufacturers. Chief among these was the quantity of scarce strategic materials each consumed. The Jumo 004 prototypes, he said, had each required 88kg of nickel to make—including the amounts milled off during the production process. The 004 B needed 24.4kg of nickel and the projected 004 C would need only 7kg of nickel. The savings would be made by switching from solid turbine blades to hollow blades made of sheet metal and by having less waste during production.

BMW's 003 prototypes only used 5.4kg of nickel from the outset, with 2.6kg required for the 003 A-0 series. This compared, he said, to the BMW 801 E's 4.6kg nickel requirement. There was a similar problem with chromium. The 004 still needed 10kg of it per engine and the 003 needed 19.5kg.

He said it was intended that the full series production model Me 262 would be powered by the Jumo 004 C, the Ar 234 would have four BMW 003s and the Me 262 with TLR, the interceptor, would have two BMW TLR units. However, plans were in motion to replace both the 004 and the 003 with a new engine—Heinkel's HeS 011. The 004, he explained, had already been taken as far as it could go and "we have already pumped out 16% more power than was intended". So "we tackled a successor engine in good time, which I will talk about

in more detail later. The Junkers and BMW engines will then be replaced by the Heinkel-Hirth engines, so that the future requirements with regard to the engines can also be met."

Mahnke sounded a note of caution: "We are currently still extremely poor on the production side with the jet engine. That is because we could not make any preparations for the production until a short time ago. Our inquiries that we have made so far have been answered in such a way that one does not see clearly in the whole field, so that demands for series production were not made.

"Only half a year ago it was stated that we should create two capacities of 300 engines [i.e. production of 300 jet engines by Junkers and another 300 by BMW], expandable to 500 engines per month. The systems, as they are now being built by Junkers and BMW, amount to a run of around 2,000 engines."

Milch wanted to know whether this limited supply would run out before the HeS 011 was ready: "Schelp, can you say how far along the Heinkel engines are?"

Schelp: "The first engine is running on the test bench."

Milch: "Do you have a clear picture of when the engine will be ready, at the earliest?"

Schelp: "Based on the programme for the pre-production series, I would say: at the end of 1944."

Milch: "By then we will hopefully have a larger number of Junkers 004 B engines already in operation with the 262. Then the other will first have to prove that it is so much better, so that it is worth building. Then of course Junkers can be switched [to production of the 011]."

Schelp said that the 004 B was already in series production, the 003 A-0 series was being worked on, with series production planned for February 1944, and two prototype BMW 003 R units were expected to be ready for experimental installation in an Me 262 in June 1944. Deliveries of the HeS 011 were due to begin in mid-1945. Milch said: "Couldn't this engine come earlier? It is important for our fighters. So it is still relatively far away, now two years."

## ME 262 WITH BK 5 (OR 5.5)

Following on from Messerschmitt's memo of August 4, on August 24 the Project Office was formally ordered to begin work on determining how a Rheinmetall Bordkanone (BK) 5 or BK 5.5 50mm/55mm autocannon could be installed in the Me 262's nose.[9] The test flight draught finally came to an end on September 8 when the Me 262 V3 took to the air once more. At this point it was the only airworthy example of the type.

Willy Messerschmitt had another personal audience

| Messerschmitt A.G. Augsburg | M e 2 6 2 – Jäger und Jabo / Ausführung A 2 | Blatt 38 |
|---|---|---|
| Triebwerk | 2 x Jumo 004 C | |
| Bewaffnung | 6 x MK 108 mit insgesamt 480 Schuss | |

| | | Jäger | Jabo | |
|---|---|---|---|---|
| Spannweite | | 12,65 m | | |
| Länge | | 10,6 m | | |
| Bauhöhe | | 2,8 m | | |
| Flügelfläche | | 21,7 m² | | |
| Fluggewicht $G_{max}$ | | 6891 kg | 7242 kg | |
| Landegewicht mittel / Lande | | 5196 kg | 5226 kg | |
| Landegeschwindigkeit mit G Lande | | 182 km/h | 182 km/h | |

*Data sheet showing the specifications of the Me 262 A-2—intended as the standard production model on which most of the other variants were to be based.*

with Adolf Hitler on September 9, 1943, and evidently talked the Führer through nine pre-prepared points: efforts to offset the effects of the Regensburg raid back in August; a plea to switch more resources from bomber to fighter production; a proposal to "immediately reduce the variety of aircraft types … to shorten the development and further development programmes. A merger of development companies cannot be avoided, and the aircraft will not be given a company name";[10] a proposal to have the Dornier Do 335 and Arado Ar 234 cancelled and those companies switched to Me 262 production; discussion of a recent briefing given by Oberst Dietrich Peltz at Rechlin on the use of jet bombers against England with the "fastest option based on the Me 262"; the use of the Fi 103 against England in large numbers; reorganisation of the German aviation industry into a single central group; and finally the relocation/dispersal of Messerschmitt's facilities.[11]

What Hitler made of all this is unclear—but neither the Do 335 nor the Ar 234 was cancelled and none of the German aircraft development companies were merged, though the allocation of their resources remained nominally at the discretion of the RLM. It would soon become clear, however, that Hitler had latched onto the idea of using the Me 262 as a bomber. Making the Me 262 a bomber, as far as Messerschmitt was concerned, would certainly make it less of a direct competitor for the Me 209 and Me 410.

While he was in Berlin, Messerschmitt stopped in at his company's Berlin office to send Voigt a telex.[12] His message read: "My attitude towards the single-jet fighter is still that with today's engine power it will not be sufficient to cover the constantly increasing demands for armament for fighters with reasonably satisfactory performance. I would ask you to present this position accordingly at the meeting in order to avoid further waste of German development capacity. Of course, designs and projects can still be made."

He clearly felt that the single-jet designs submitted by Focke-Wulf, Heinkel and his own company back in May ought to go no further.

## TEN VARIANTS

The Messerschmitt company regarded the Me 262 A-1 and A-2 design specification of August 10, 1943, as "decisive for the execution of the basic model" but on September 11 a new appendix was added which collated ten new variants.[13] These consisted of three potential configurations for a reconnaissance version (Aufklärer I, Ia and II), three for a bomber (Schnellbomber I, Ia and II), three for an interceptor (Interzeptor I, II and III) and one for a two-seat trainer (Schulflugzeug). Each came with its own individually dated description,[14] spanning a 52-day period from July 20 to the day before the appendix was issued—September 10.

The foreword said: "The Me 262 is the first aircraft with two jet engines to be built in series. The performance and characteristics it has shown so far give reason to investigate its possible use not only for the original purpose as a fighter and fighter-bomber, but also for use as an interceptor, high-speed bomber and reconnaissance aircraft.

"The resulting modifications of the Me 262 are intended to create a fully-fledged special aircraft for the respective application without burdening the Me 262 as a multi-purpose aircraft from the outset, with the lowest possible risk and savings in construction, testing and equipment capacity. It is therefore possible to produce special types suitable for the respective application using the greater part of the assemblies of the Me 262 with less overall effort and in a shorter time than would be possible with a completely new development … The variants below show in many cases an equivalence or superiority compared to aircraft with the

## Aufklärer I

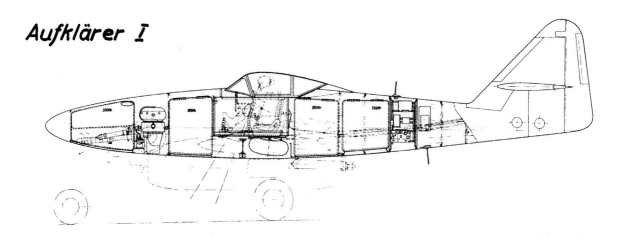

*Drawing number II/171, dated July 22, 1943, shows the Aufklärer I—a very basic conversion of the Me 262 for the reconnaissance role with two cameras in its nose and a transparent panel in the floor of the cockpit through which the pilot could identify the area to be photographed.*

## Aufklärer Ia

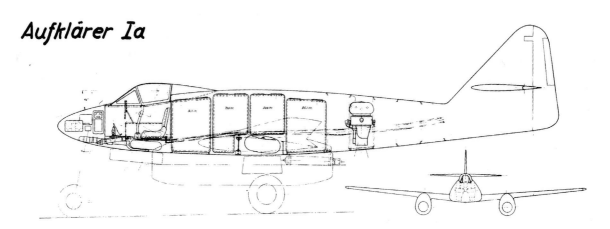

*The Aufklärer Ia design, shown in drawing II/180 of September 1, 1943, features a relocated cockpit and a camera bay for two Rb 75/30s in the rear fuselage.*

## Aufklärer II

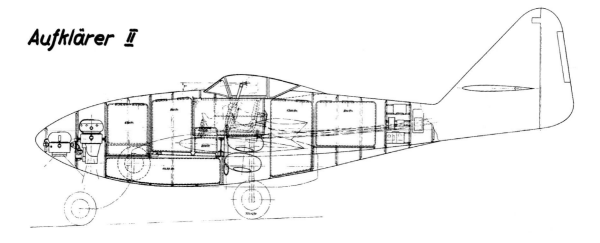

*The deepened fuselage of the Aufklärer II, appearing in drawing II/172, provided sufficient room for a huge fuel load and three nose-mounted cameras—the two Rb 75/30s being supplemented by a single Rb 20/30 in the nose tip.*

same task, e.g. Interzeptor I and II compared to Me 163 or Aufklärer I, Ia and Schnellbomber I, Ia compared to current developments.

"Since the currently running fighter series must not be disturbed, suitable capacity would have to be made available for the additional construction of the Me 262 modified model, which is still to be determined."

All versions, except for the trainer, Interzeptor II and Interzeptor III were to be powered by a pair of Jumo 004 Cs.

## RECONNAISSANCE

The Aufklärer I, dated August 2, was a relatively straight-forward conversion—the gun nose was replaced with a nose housing two Rb 75/30 cameras and a 500 litre fuel tank. The cameras would be angled outwards 11° so that the images produced overlapped from an altitude of around 1km. Alternatively, one Rb 75/30 and one Rb 20/30 could be installed. The cockpit was to have either a transparent panel in the floor, allowing the pilot direct line of sight down and forward, or a periscope. This would necessitate deletion of the 250 litre fuel tank normally fitted in this space. Frontal armour was also deleted to save weight and improve performance, though the fuel tanks were still protected and back armour could be fitted. Take-off could be assisted by four 500kg or two 1,000kg solid fuel boosters.

A top speed of 958km/h at 9km altitude was projected, with a maximum climb rate of 27.6m/s at sea level. Flight time when flown for economy was two hours 21 minutes, or one hour 44 minutes at maximum thrust.

Aufklärer Ia, dated September 9, involved a much more radical shift in configuration, with the cockpit being moved into the nose. This provided a better down-ward view and made pressurising the cabin easier. The camera setup was the same as for Aufklärer I but in the rear fuselage rather than the nose. The radio equipment was housed in the nose tip but it was possible to shift this into the tail and fit two MK 108s there instead. The space vacated by the original cockpit would be filled with two new fuel tanks of 700 and 500 litre capacities. Specific performance data was not provided.

Aufklärer II of August 2 had the deepened forward fuselage design that had been tested by the AVA earlier in the year. This allowed three cameras to be carried—the two Rb 75/30s plus an Rb 20/30. Although the accompanying drawing showed only a single seat, the description noted that "if required, accommodation of a second man behind the pilot can be arranged at the expense of range. A periscope with a downward view is installed for better orientation. In the two-seater version, a periscope is also required for the second man to see downwards". In

fact, "to improve visibility, a crew compartment located in the nose of the fuselage ... can be implemented with correspondingly greater modification effort".

Transforming a normal Me 262 into the Aufklärer II would involve some radical steps. Behind the cameras was a 650 litre tank and below that in the extended belly of the fuselage was a 1,450 litre tank. The 900 litre tank remained in front of the pilot and the 250 litre tank remained under his feet but behind him was a new 1,300 litre tank and beyond that was another 900 litre tank. The 750 litre tank in the A-2's tail was replaced with the radio equipment, which now included a FuG XVII Z transceiver.

The main landing gear struts had double 770 x 270mm wheels, the fin was enlarged and the frontal armour was omitted but again, all the tanks were protected and the pilot had rear armour thick enough to protect against 2cm projectiles.

Getting so much fuel airborne was no easy feat so it attachment points for eight 500kg or four 1,000kg rockets were planned.

## FAST BOMBERS

The Schnellbomber I design was dated July 20 and differed relatively little from the standard Me 262 A-2. The cannon were swapped for a 1,000 litre fuel tank, the rear fuselage tank was enlarged to 1,000 litres and the radio equipment was pushed further back. The main undercarriage struts would have double 770 x 270 wheels but only briefly—the extra ones would be jettisoned on take-off. The possible bomb loads were the same as those possible for the A-2 and take-off could be boosted with either eight 500kg or four 1,000kg rockets.

Schnellbomber Ia of September 10 utilised the same forward cockpit arrangement as the Aufklärer Ia but the bomb attachment arrangements were the same as those of the A-2 and the Schnellbomber I. It remained possible to fit two MK 108s in the nose, with the radio gear being rehoused in the tail.

And Schnellbomber II, from July 29, had the same deepened fuselage as the Aufklärer II—but with a 450 litre fuel tank in the nose tip instead of cameras and bombs housed internally below the nose in place of the Aufklärer II's 1,450 litre tank. And again, "to improve visibility, a crew compartment located in the nose of the fuselage ... can be implemented". The same double wheels, enlarged fin and take-off rocket arrangements of the Aufklärer II were envisioned.

The Schnellbomber II description also hinted at a variant studied at this time, and mentioned by Willy Messerschmitt in correspondence, but not offered to the RLM—an Me 262 ground-attack or 'tank-buster'

## Schnellbomber I

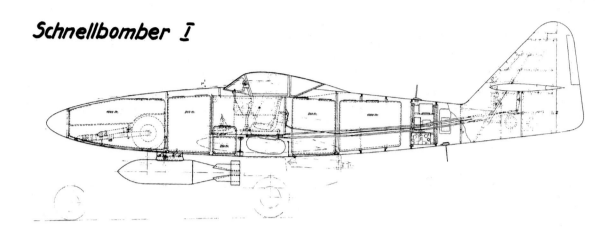

The Schnellbomber I design as it appears in drawing II/167 of July 22, 1943. The principal difference between this variant and the A-2 was the increased fuel capacity—with 1,000 litres in the nose in place of cannon and another 1,000 litres in the rear fuselage.

## Schnellbomber Ia

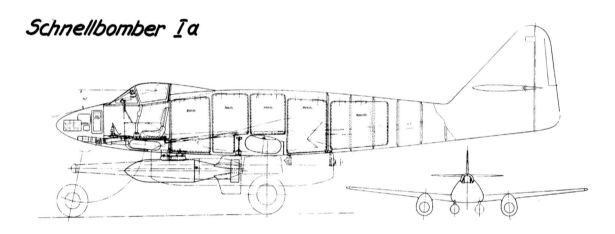

Schnellbomber Ia, like the Aufklärer Ia, had its cockpit in its nose—freeing up space in the centre of the aircraft for additional fuel tanks. The drawing, II/183 of September 10, 1943, was produced nearly three weeks after those showing the Schnellbomber I and II.

## Schnellbomber II

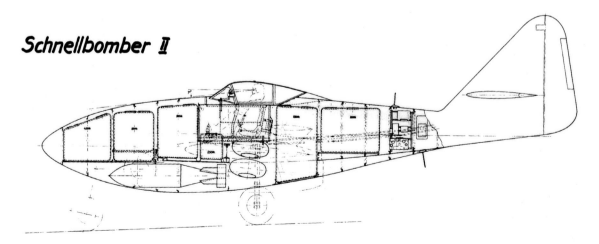

Like the Aufklärer II, Schnellbomber II had the new deepened fuselage that Messerschmitt had devised. This bulbous design offered space for an internal bomb bay plus increased fuel capacity. This is drawing II/168 of July 22.

type. It said: "The placement of imaging devices or large calibre weapons (e.g. 5cm, 7.5cm or 8.8cm) instead of bombs is being investigated and offered separately."

## INTERCEPTORS

The Interzeptor I was perhaps the oldest configuration of the ten, though the document describing it was dated July 20. The accompanying drawing depicting it was dated July 22, 1943, but the art style used was different from that of the other nine variants.[15] The Interzeptor I would be a conversion of the existing standard A-2—with an HWK RII-213/3 rocket motor installed in its rear fuselage, exhausting via a cut-out section beneath the rudder. A new forward fuel tank made of corrosion-resistant material would house 900 litres of T-Stoff for the rocket and the rearmost tank, also corrosion-resistant, would contain 625 litres of C-Stoff. A jettisonable 395 litre tank for T-Stoff could be carried suspended beneath the aircraft's nose. The 900 litre tank immediately behind the pilot and the usual 250 litre tank under his feet would hold the turbojets' fuel.

Modifications to the control lines would be needed and the pilot would get new switchgear to operate the rocket motor. Take-off would involve the same jettisonable 770 x 270mm wheels planned for the Schnellbomber I.

A fast take-off and climb could be achieved by using the rocket motor as a built-in booster. Alternatively, a normal take-off could be made on the turbojets alone and the rocket motor could be activated at an altitude of 12km to push the Me 262 above its usual ceiling. Exactly how high it could go was unclear.

The Interzeptor II of September 1 had no internal rocket motor. Instead, its Jumo 004 Cs would be swapped for BMW 003 R engines. These could simply be bolted to the same fittings as the Jumo 004s, although the wing auxiliary spar would need to be shifted slightly to accommodate the rocket nozzles. Their fuel and control lines would also need to be installed. The fuel tank arrangement was similar to that of the Interzeptor I—though the 900 litre front tank contained S-Stoff and the rear 475 litre rear tank held R-Stoff. The jettisonable tank's capacity was said to be 375 litres rather than 395, but it looked identical in the accompanying drawing. The jettisonable additional landing gear wheels were also a feature of the Interzeptor II.

The aircraft was expected to perform in much the same way as the Interzeptor I and according to the description, "Since the behaviour of the jet engines above 12km altitude is not known, at higher altitudes the jet engines were not expected to be used. According to the BMW company, however, it is likely that the performance of the jet engines will be sufficient to operate the pumps for the rocket-nozzles above an altitude of 12 km."

The third option, Interzeptor III of September 6, was a reimagining of the Me 262 without turbojets. The description stated: "The use of the Me 262 A-2 fighter with 6 x MK 108 as a pure rocket-interceptor is quite possible. The performances achieved are between those of the Me 163 B and C.

"A further improvement in flight performance can be achieved by thickening the fuselage. However, such a proposal has not been made, as the conversion effort seemed too great for this purpose and, in addition, the high fuel requirement was uneconomical. Two Walter RII-211 engines with additional nozzles for cruising were used. The attachment is in the same place as the jet engines. In order to achieve the most favourable aerodynamic form possible, the pump is housed in front of the wing and the [main] nozzle, with the cruising nozzle above it, is behind the wing in an almost centrally located nacelle."

## TRAINER

Finally, the interim Me 262 A-1, powered by Jumo 004 B-2s rather than the A-2's Jumo 004 Cs, could be converted into a two-seat jet trainer. The second seat complete with dual controls would be added directly behind the original one in the space previously occupied by the rear fuel tanks.

The student would sit up front with the instructor behind and the rear cabin's canopy section could be provided with side bulges if this was deemed necessary in order to improve the instructor's visibility. The armament in the nose would be removed and replaced with ballast—although two or four cannon could be reinstalled if the aircraft was to be used for target practice. The only radio gear fitted would be a FuG 14 and the student and instructor would be able to communicate via an intercom. This arrangement was dated August 2.

## FLIGHT TESTS

A second attempt to drop test an Me 262 fuselage from beneath the wing of an Me 323 took place in September—this time over Lake Constance. It was conducted by the other Voigt at Messerschmitt, the head of the company's theoretical and experimental flutter group Dr Herbert Voigt.

According to a postwar report,[16] "a test was performed on a fuselage and tail assembly of the Me 262 to learn of any tail flutter potentialities. The fuselage and tail weighing 2,000lb plus a ballast weight of 4,000lb were attached to the bomb shackle of an Me 323 (concrete

# *Interzeptor I*

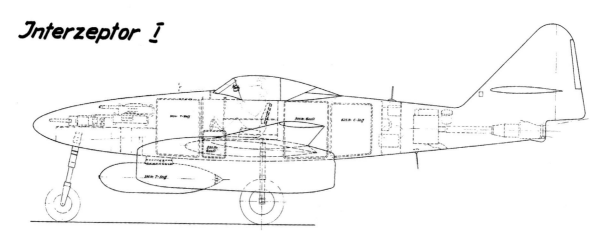

*The internal layout showcased by the Interzeptor I design could trace its lineage all the way back to the single-rocket-motor-propelled Me 262 J of November 1941. It appears here, however, in drawing II/169 of July 22, 1943.*

# *Interzeptor II*

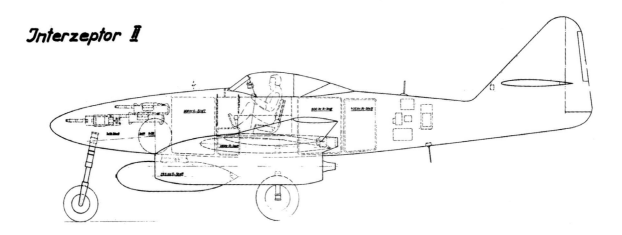

*The Me 262 Interzeptor II was chronologically the earliest of the designs shown in the Messerschmitt report on new variants—drawing II/160 being dated July 6, 1943. As such the art style used is markedly different from that of the other contemporary drawings. Like most of the others, though, it was based on the Me 262 A-2 and featured that design's six MK 108s in its nose as well as the BMW TLR engines in its wings.*

# *Interzeptor III*

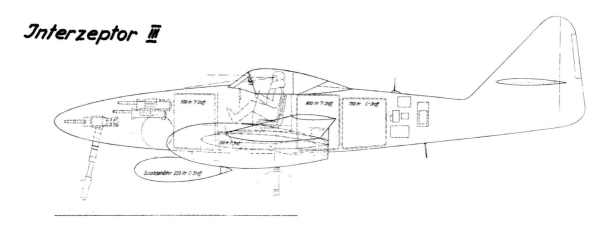

*The Interzeptor III was to be a pure rocketplane, uniquely without turbojets among its peers. Its wing-mounted nacelles each housed an HWK 509 rocket motor instead and its fuselage tanks carried rocket fuel, supplemented by another tank under its nose.*

# Schulflugzeug

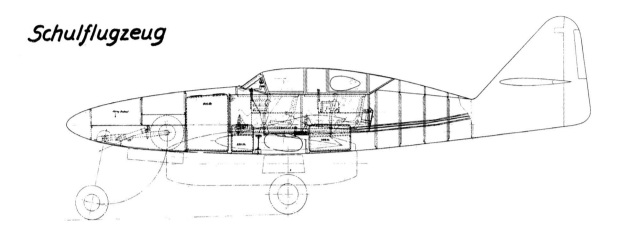

*The two-seat Me 262 trainer, the only one of the new designs based on the interim Me 262 A-1, as it appears in drawing II/175 of July 22, 1943. The nose is shown containing ballast, rather than weapons, and the instructor's cockpit to the rear includes canopy blisters for improved visibility.*

ballast was attached to the opposite wing) and flown to 23,000ft altitude assisted through towing by an He 111 Z. At that altitude the test specimen[17] was released and allowed to fall freely. A speed of 560mph or M=0.82 was attained as measured by 3 photo cameras spaced around the flight path on the ground 3 miles apart.

"At 27 or 29 seconds after start or fall an explosive bolt released the 4,000lb weight and 6 rockets with 1,100lb thrust each were fired by a clock mechanism to slow the descent (the rockets lasted for 5 seconds). Then a series of 3 parachutes were to be released to save the ship. Actually only one parachute was released so that the ship was lost in a crash in the water below.

"A compressed air hammer driven by a clock mechanism at 120cpm was installed to break down the static friction of the control system. A stylus type vibration recorder was also installed in the tail. Had this test been successful, greater velocities would have been attained through rocket assisted descent on ensuing flights.

"If these tests had been successful, they might have eliminated a 9 month period when pilots refused to fly the Me 262 at top speed. The stick was restrained loosely by rubber bands. An altimeter was installed to start deceleration at 6,500ft if the clock had not already done so."

Meanwhile, Messerschmitt's team of flight testers had been busy. During late September and into October the now repaired V1 and V3 were used to perform numerous tests and experiments, such as the use of slats to reduce both take-off distance and landing speed.[18] The V3 was involved in high-speed testing which confirmed that the vibrations plaguing earlier test flights had now disappeared.[19] In October the V3 was used to test stick forces, rolling during high speed flight[20] and pressure distribution[21] while the V1 was involved in experiments to determine the type's characteristics during a spin.[22]

The still-damaged Me 262 V5, meanwhile, was being used for static nosewheel shock tests. These showed that "excessive loads continued to cause deformation, but the safety factor was adequate for normal loads".[23]

A third aircraft, the Me 262 V6, which was the first to have a retractable tricycle undercarriage, joined the flight test programme on October 17, 1943. This was fitted with two prototype Jumo 004 B-1 engines.[24] Among its first duties were testing the effect of opening and closing the wing slats at low speed,[25] and conducting further take-off booster rocket trials. During the former it was determined that using the slats at 200km/h caused the aircraft to become unstable, while using them at 190km/h caused the aircraft to enter a dive.

During the rocket trials, "at first take-off both rockets tore from their positions. One climbed in the air while the other fell to the ground. The aircraft was not damaged and a perfect landing was made. Second flight: at a small speed in take-off the landing flaps came out but were retracted just before lifting the aircraft into the air. In flight both landing gear fairings were torn off, although the speed did not exceed 350km/h".[26] The V6 was also used for static measurements, its Jumo 004 B-1 engines assessed as delivering 1,675-1,700kg thrust—"an improvement of 60kg over earlier models of this engine". The thrust provided by the 500kg Borsig rockets was measured at 1,200kg for eight seconds.[27]

Ten days later, on October 27, the Project Office was ordered to begin working out how Heinkel HeS 011 turbojets could be accommodated within the Me 262's nacelles.[28]

## HITLER WANTS A FIGHTER-BOMBER

At a meeting with Milch on October 28,[29] Göring said: "Messerschmitt reported that if he didn't get the

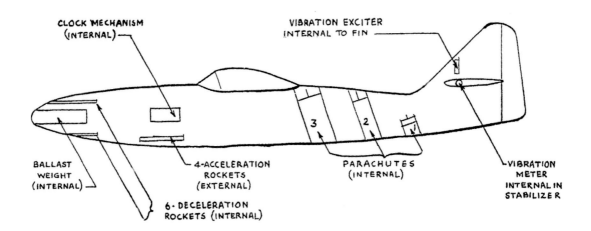

CLOCK MECHANISM (INTERNAL)

VIBRATION EXCITER INTERNAL TO FIN

BALLAST WEIGHT (INTERNAL)

4-ACCELERATION ROCKETS (EXTERNAL)

6·DECELERATION ROCKETS (INTERNAL)

PARACHUTES (INTERNAL)

VIBRATION METER INTERNAL IN STABILIZER

*Diagram showing modifications made to the wingless Me 262 V4 fuselage—including the installation of three parachutes, ten rockets and measuring devices—prior to its use in a drop test during September 1943.*

*The fuselage of Me 262 V4 suspended upside down from a bomb shackle beneath the wing of an Me 323, prior to release over Lake Constance.*

4,000 workers the 262 would come out six months later. As I said, the Führer had a shock when he heard this."

Milch: "To this day, he [Messerschmitt] has not announced a day of delay with us. He's been given absolutely top priority."

Göring: "He reported it to me. He must be interrogated immediately: why did you not pass on this report, which you made to the Reichsmarschall in Neuburg, in good time to the headquarters?"

Frydag said Messerschmitt had been assigned 7,200 workers and he had received half of them so far which "wasn't exactly as much as he asked for, but at least it was far more than anyone else got". Albert Speer, the Reich's minister for war production, said some of Messerschmitt's new workers had been acquired by shutting down other production lines, although he didn't specify which ones.

Milch: "In addition, he asked for quality workers and management staff: 120 jig makers and 260 toolmakers, everything far beyond what is possible. We shut down

other factories to give him the people ... I don't know where to get the toolmakers and the other jig makers from. He didn't even tell me or the head of the production office that he was going to be delayed. And when he is, it is because he put everything on the 209. But he doesn't tell us, but rather the Reichsmarschall and the Führer."

Later, Göring said: "Whether the Russians advance 150km further at Krivoy Rog[30] or not is not crucial, it is crucial that we start in spring at the latest with a flexibility that allows us to hold the west and not allow a second front to appear. Aviation is crucial for this. That was clearly expressed yesterday by the Führer in the presence of Dönitz. The Führer said that the decisive factor is the jet fighter with bombs, because at the given moment they can whiz along the beach and throw their bombs into the mass that has been formed there. I thought: I don't know if we'll have it by then."

This statement was, according to the stenographic report, followed by uproar. Göring then said: "Never negotiate with Messerschmitt without a stenographer, not even in private. I hereby command that. Above all, tell Knemeyer that too. Without a stenographer, Messerschmitt will not be heard, as a matter of principle."

He went on: "The Führer is a little worried and believes that the English have so many fighters that even if we build our fighters as fighter-bombers..."

Milch: "So far, they all come out like that!"

Göring: "But I don't call that a bomber."

Milch: "I don't want to decide whether to call the machine 'fighter-bomber'. It's at least a bomber like any other fighter. It's a bomb-carrying fighter-bomber!"

Göring: "A fighter-bomber is a fighter that makes a virtue out of necessity."

During the RLM development meeting the following

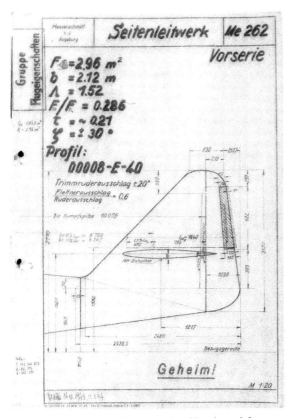

*The dimensions of the fin and rudder planned for the Me 262 pre-production series. Attention would later be focused on the size and shape of both fin and rudder when it came to correcting directional stability issues with the production model Me 262.*

day,[31] Major Siegfried Knemeyer, newly appointed head of development at the Technical Office, gave a lengthy breakdown of the situation at Messerschmitt and concluded that "you are better off with only the [Fw] 190/152 as the modern single-engine fighter, and for Messerschmitt you would say: he builds only the [Me] 262".

Milch said: "What Knemeyer says—as much as possible on the basis of the 190-Ta 152—is correct, but it also has a limit somewhere. The only difficulty I see is that we must first undertake the killing of the [Me] 209 by the highest possible path, with all the cabals that are attached to it. There will be increased partisan activity immediately."

Knemeyer: "The only one who will fight against the cancellation of the 209 would be [Willy] Messerschmitt. But all of his people are clear about the fact that they clog everything up for themselves and that they will never breathe again for sensible projects if things continue like this."

Milch: "It will not be very easy to give up after being completely wrong for selfish reasons."

A little later on, Galland queried the Me 209

production schedule: "It has been said that the 209 is way too late—it practically only just comes in [at the end of] 1944—that it should be there a year earlier."

Knemeyer: "The date of July 1 is definitely not kept for the 209 unless tremendous efforts are made ... Bringing the 209 forward becomes even more difficult if you make efforts to get more 190s and 152s out. In my opinion, Messerschmitt must put the main effort on the 262. An inquiry has now been made as to what the fighter-bomber 262 looks like."

Milch: "The Reichsmarschall said yesterday: Take a bomb on the 262!"

There was no immediate follow-up to this point as the conversation moved on to other topics but later Milch said: "I just want to clarify opinions. Galland wants the Me 209 numbers for 1945. In 1945, the Me 209 should start with 84 [in January] and be at 1,400 a month by the end of the year. Around the middle it should be between 700 and 800. Under no circumstances do you want to have more 109s delivered, but under certain circumstances Me 262 or Ta 152. If you got those, the 209 would be irrelevant to you?

Galland: "Sure."

Milch: "We have clarity now."

Meanwhile, Me 262 V1 had been fitted with a new version of Träger's electro-acoustic detection system under the codename Zwiebel or 'Onion'. This was taken up for a 24-minute test flight on November 1. While attempting to take off for further tests the following day however, the left engine suddenly suffered compressor blade failure due to foreign object ingestion after around 200m of taxiing. The aircraft turned abruptly to the left, twisting the left main landing gear leg through 90-degrees, before coming to a standstill.[32] While the airframe had suffered only minor damage, the engine needed replacing and the repairs would put the aircraft and Zwiebel out of action for more than a month.

## SUPPORT FROM GÖRING

The next meeting with Willy Messerschmitt, with a stenographer present, took place at his company's Regensburg facility on November 2.[33] Göring began proceedings in his usual style: "Gentlemen! I would like to become clear about the Me 262 today in two directions: 1. With regard to the speed at which this machine will come out, as it is currently intended, 2. What may be done, even with restrictions on other things, to bring this aircraft out even faster and therefore in larger numbers.

"The main question is then a very important technical question: how far the jet fighter is able to take one or two bombs along in order to be able to act as a surprise fighter-bomber. I would like to convey the train of thought of the Führer, who spoke to me about these things just a few days ago and who is extremely interested in completing this task.

"When the enemy tries to land in the west and on the beach when tanks, artillery and troop units are unloaded, out of the first confusion the Führer expects an extraordinarily strong fighter to emerge. These fast machines, even if there are only a few, shoot through and throw bombs into this mess. He is clear about the fact that there can be no question of precision—just that these fast machines actually appear for the first time, provided that the opponent allows us enough time before then.

"I told the Führer that I would try to solve this task with the current fighter-bombers and that it could also be solved in part despite the fighter protection, because this is only a brief targeting of the enemy. The bombs are thrown terribly quickly, and then the fighter-bomber has to sweep away immediately to fetch new ones.

"I would now like to direct the discussion the other way around. Not talk about the release mechanism etc. at first, but only discuss the technical possibility, how far the 262 can carry bombs externally—otherwise it is probably not possible—and which calibre in terms of weight and size ... The machine was designed by Professor Messerschmitt, and I would therefore like to ask you for your opinion."

Messerschmitt: "Mr Reichsmarschall! It is planned from the outset that two bomb racks will be attached to the machine so that bombs can be thrown with it, namely one of 500kg or two of 250kg each. You can also take one 1,000kg or two 500s with you. For the time being, however, because the machine should start up in series, the bomb racks and the electrical cables that are necessary for this are not installed."

Göring: "That clears the main question for the Führer. He doesn't even think about 1,000kg, but said to me again: if we could only take two 70s with us, he would be extremely grateful. Of course, he will be delighted to have two 250s with him. Now the second question: when would it be possible to retrofit the machines that are now under construction, i.e. the first examples, with these bomb racks?"

Messerschmitt: "It has not yet been designed. I would first have to design the bomb attachment and the electrical cables for it and then retrofit the first machines with it."

Göring: "You said that was already planned, so you must have thought about it."

Messerschmitt: "It is listed in the appendix to the build description. These are the different possibilities for using the bomb racks—one or two bombs, the latter on the right and left."

Göring: "Over time, more pilots have to be trained on this machine. How long do you reckon for the construction of the racks and the lines?"

Messerschmitt: "That is done relatively quickly, in 14 days. In terms of fixtures, it is not much. It is just the cladding of the bomb attachment point."

Göring: "How many machines are now ready for testing?"

Messerschmitt: "None yet in the final series form. The first machine was designed in 1938 and flown around 1941. The series production model documents were overhauled earlier this year, and some prototypes are now running. One machine totally broke and two others were badly damaged. We have the V6 here. The first machines did not have a nosewheel. One machine has now been converted to a fixed nosewheel. In terms of take-off and landing properties, however, the nosewheel is hardly better than the normal machine."

Göring asked whether construction of the first series production model aircraft had been started.

Messerschmitt: "Yes, parts of it are made in the workshop. The plan was that one machine would come in mid-January, eight in February, March 21, April 40, May 60, June 60."

Göring: "That is already above what I was hoping for."

The Reichsmarschall then pledged to give Messerschmitt as much help as possible to get the first Me 262 fighter-bombers completed. He said: "The Führer cannot, of course, do magic, neither can I, but at least the situation is very favourable because the Führer is determined, as far as he can be and I can be, to release certain people and everything that is necessary for them because of the importance of the cause."

A long discussion followed about where the Me 262's components were being made. The fuselages were to be built at Regensburg, tails at Blohm & Voss in Hamburg, wings at Augsburg and the undercarriage at Elektrometall in Stuttgart as a subcontractor for Opel. Final assembly would be at Leipheim, Gablingen and Lechfeld. Göring suggested Neuburg as another option.

Dr Franz from Jumo was also present and Göring quizzed him about the status of his engines. Franz explained the difference between the 004 A and the 004 B, then said: "About the state of development I have to say: we are relatively clear with the 004 A on the test stands. We are still in the middle of development work on the 004 B, and that is having an unpleasant effect at the moment because series production is already starting at the same time. The difficulties are: we have breaks at various points and we have certain regulatory difficulties."

Göring: "If the A-engine is okay and the B-engine is not, why can't you use the A-engine?"

Franz: "From a manufacturing point of view is it almost intolerable for large-scale production and there are also various disadvantages in terms of effectiveness and operationally, for example brazing has occurred which can be attributed to leaks, and phenomena at altitude where the performance suddenly drops off because the engine no longer works properly. All of this has been fixed in the B-engine.

"Now I have to say: in my opinion, the difficulties we have can be mastered with certainty and cleared up in a relatively short time if one can work normally in terms of development. Now the task has become more difficult for us insofar as we have to achieve a clarification of the various questions with relatively minor changes in order not to disturb the start of series production."

Göring: "Such a beautiful and comfortable development, as you imagine it to be in terms of engineering, is a wonderful thing. But I don't have the time. So get on with it!"

Franz: "That is perfectly clear to me, and that's why I also say that we have to work completely abnormally and in the middle of series production start-up we have to make certain changes which will disrupt that start-up."

After some discussion of the different engines being built, including the Jumo 004 C and HeS 011, Göring said: "So you try the B-engine and at the same time prepare to go into series production with it. Where do you build this engine now?"

Franz: "So far, 2,000 a month are planned, and up to 1,000 a month should be made in our existing factories. In order for this to be possible at all, we have distributed production to different plants. Magdeburg only builds turbines, Mino the compressor, Kassel the devices ... At the same time, the large series production plant is being built in Zittau."

The Reichsmarschall next turned to the Inspector of Fighters: "How about the pilots for the 262, Galland?"

Galland: "We'll sort out the pilots. That is by no means as bad with the training as with the 163. As soon as the test centres have enough aircraft, I'll immediately get on with the test squadron."

Milch: "The trial will take place immediately with us."

Messerschmitt interjected: "Wouldn't it be possible for General Galland to send some pilots beforehand to fly with us on the older prototypes to get a feel for them?"

Milch said: "That can happen via Galland and we are not interested in it. The machines that are to come in series have to come to us in larger numbers so that we can investigate the control problems there."

The discussion turned to exactly which aircraft types Messerschmitt should be building.

Knemeyer said: "The Generalfeldmarschall has made a new draft plan to allow the 109 to expire even further. This is the best solution if you can force it, increasing the 262 at the same time."

Milch: "There is no point in making the 209 because the company is unable to build the jigs for it in time. Second, the machine is useless."

Göring: "If the tests on the 262 work, we're not interested in the other machines."

Now that Hitler himself was personally invested in the Me 262, the tables had apparently turned. Messerschmitt asked how the gap between testing and front line service was to be bridged, presumably implying that the 209 would be the ideal stopgap machine to do it. Göring emphasised the importance of testing the Me 262 prototypes but Milch pointed out: "There is not yet a single aircraft that is very ready for series production. The current V6 is the first machine that is similar to series production."

Göring: "When can I expect machines with the same series?"

Lucht: "Around December. The V7 will arrive on November 15, and the V8 will be the first series-produced machine to be released in mid-December."

Following more discussion, Franz voiced another growing concern which went beyond technical considerations: "My development team has been rebuilt and consists almost entirely of young people. More than half of my entire team is at risk from the confiscation operation."[34]

Milch: "Last Friday I gave the express order that jet engine development didn't have to give up anybody at all. You can refuse by relying on me. The same applies to the jet fighter and jet bomber airframes. I forbade people from being taken there."

Göring: "The Führer claps his hands above his head when he hears that. If I were in his place, I would also applaud until my hands were raw. I was there when the Führer clearly emphasized what was important and what must not be withdrawn under any circumstances."

## EVERY ME 262 A FIGHTER-BOMBER

At the RLM development meeting on November 3,[35] Milch summarised Göring's orders of the day before: establish a new Me 262 commission to drive production forward, identify key requirements necessary to increase production quickly, park the precious handful of existing prototypes away from one another to prevent their wholesale destruction during bombing or as a result of sabotage, involve the Luftwaffe test centres in preliminary testing "right from the start", involve all companies concerned in the testing, and "the use of the Me 262

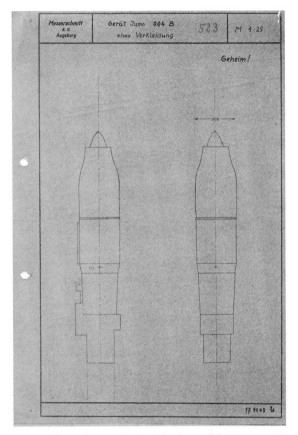

*Messerschmitt drawing showing the shape of the Jumo 004 B
engine without its nacelle, dated November 17, 1943. Outlines
such as these helped designers to ensure that the engines
shown in their aircraft drawings were dimensionally correct.*

as a Jabo [fighter-bomber] was required from the start,
as was the manufacture of two-seat training aircraft".

The order was clear—Messerschmitt was to build all
Me 262s, starting with all those already in production,
with bomb rack fittings and the associated electrical
connections. Every Me 262, early prototypes aside, was
to have the potential for fighter-bomber operations.
Willy Messerschmitt appears to have understood what
was required, though fitting bomb dropping gear to
the A-1 did go against his original plans as expressed
in the August 10 build description, which presupposed
the availability of the Jumo 004 C if the Me 262 was
to carry bombs.

However, as with every other aspect of the Me 262's
development up to this point, Messerschmitt appears
to have failed to grasp the urgency of the situation and
the potential consequences of failing to achieve this
goal set by Hitler himself. He may have thought work
on the bomb racks was largely unnecessary before the
004 C was ready, since the A-1 was not the intended
fighter-bomber model, or it may be that other work
and other priorities simply got in the way. Whatever the
case, work on the racks and fittings progressed painfully

slowly—a far cry from the 14 days he had quoted to
Göring as the preparation time required.

Later on during the meeting, Milch also pointed out
that Göring had decided to switch the main centre of
Me 262 testing from Lechfeld to Neuberg, with plans
being laid to begin Me 262 construction in the Murnau
tunnel.

During a visit to Junkers' Dessau headquarters the
following day,[36] Göring described a meeting with an
unnamed pilot flying Me 262 prototypes at Lechfeld:
"What I saw in practice in Lechfeld and heard from the
pilot was in itself quite satisfactory; the machine was
excellent ... The pilot was quite happy with the engine.
He said that there was no longer any danger when it
was throttled back. On the other hand, you have to be
careful when accelerating, especially when landing.

"If the pilot, in his excitement, pushes the throttle
in too quickly, the gearbox cuts out. In the case of the
004 B, this should be eliminated. You have to work on
it with all your energy so that the development goes
faster by eliminating the difficulties in the preliminary
tests. I have great confidence in that."

Junkers director Walter Cambeis told him: "The
relocation of the entire turbojet base from Dessau to
Zittau is currently in progress. I hope that in three weeks
we will have everything out of Dessau and safe. With
the long-term task and the urgency to accelerate the
start [of mass production], we don't want to set up new
factories with new people and equipment, but rather
switch on what is already there." He estimated that full
scale series production of the 004 B would commence
in January 1944.

The engine situation by this point was a significant
concern but not yet critical. The 40 Jumo 004 A-0
engines produced by March 1943 had been more than
sufficient to power the small fleet of Me 262 prototypes built, with some left over for development work.
However, these were steadily being used up and no more
004s were forthcoming for several months.

The first Jumo 004 B-0 prototypes had commenced
testing in February 1943 but reducing the quantity
of 'strategic' metals such as nickel within these units,
compared to the A-0, had made their turbine blades
brittle and unreliable. Only four 004 B-0s were built,
bringing the overall total of 004s to 44 by May 1943.[37]

Bench testing of prototypes for the series production
model Jumo 004 B-1 began that month—it is believed
that 15 of these were made in total[38]—and construction
of 50 pre-production 004 B-1s commenced in October.[39]

By now the first Me 209 prototype, the V5,[40] had
made its first flight—albeit with a standard Bf 109
tail because the new one wasn't ready.[41] Reviewing

a document concerning the production deadlines for the Me 262, Me 209 and Bf 109 H[42] during the RLM development meeting on November 12, 1943,[43] Milch noted: "From the text it emerges for Messerschmitt that in the area of the 262, the 209 and the 109 H the fulfilment of all deadlines is shown as being disturbed or destroyed by us. I thought of the document differently. It is awkwardly drafted and it can give the impression that GL [RLM] does not know what it wants ... In reality, of course, we know what we want. But Messerschmitt tries to play with us in this regard and puts it in such a way that everything that is good comes from him and that everything that is bad has been committed by GL.

"With that he then runs to the Reichsmarschall and the Führer and lays something right there. We have to fix this quickly and we have to realise that he has to be given the message stating that nothing will be changed in the fast work on the 262."

The Me 262 V3 was taken off the flight line on November 17 so that a camera could be fitted to its fin for a series of aerodynamic flow tests on the area between the rear cockpit canopy and the fin leading edge.[44] On the same day Messerschmitt's Project Office issued Protokoll Nr. 21, which encompassed a range of new developments for the Me 262. Among them was the ongoing development and testing of 500kg and 1,000kg thrust booster rockets for assisted take-off, and further work on firewalls between the aircraft's engines and fuselage.[45] Shortages of aluminium alloy were by now becoming all too apparent across the German aviation industry and Protokoll Nr. 21 also included details of a new wooden tail unit for the Me 262. This would be developed and prototyped by glider manufacturer Jacobs-Schweyer.

On November 23, during a meeting with Göring at his Carinhall residence,[46] Alpers was discussing the next aircraft production programme, 224, and said it "should be noted that this programme proposal, which is only a draft, does not contain the Me 209 type. We would then have to smuggle in the 209 at the expense of the other types, which should be discussed here today."

Milch said: "There is one restriction, however: the Messerschmitt company has made a significant change to the date of the 209!"

Vorwald: "There were two new models, namely the 262 and the 209, to be smuggled into Messerschmitt. Both would have to have completely new jigs. It is true that Messerschmitt and his gentlemen said half a year ago that not all of the jigs had to be rebuilt for the 209, but only 15-20%, and the rest could be taken over from the 109. But that has not been confirmed, instead 70-80% have to be built. As a result, the dates for the 209,

which were initially in mid-1944, would be postponed to late 1945 or early 1946. They would be postponed by one and a half years because the jig capacity was only sufficient to produce the 262."

Göring interjected that "you can't do both at the same time" but Vorwald said this was precisely what Messerschmitt had planned to do: "According to the old plan, in which the start-up was fixed in mid-1944, the 209 and the 262 come at about the same time, so that the jigs would have to be finished at the same time.

Frydag: "Messerschmitt wanted to bring the 209 into the business under all circumstances, made deadlines and attached conditions to them that could not be adhered to. It is the same subject that has been spoken of several times here. It was the jigs."

Milch said the earliest possible date for the Me 209 was the end of 1944 and "the bulk of the work then comes into the first half of 1945, so that he can only start building afterwards. But then the 209 is completely uninteresting."

Göring: "He sees himself making it. He also suggests doing the 262 himself?"

Vorwald: "His gentlemen, namely Hentzen, May and Seiler, with whom I spoke, suggest that."

Milch said that "Messerschmitt himself does not want to give in yet. That still has to be discussed with him". Following which, Göring grumbled: "In any case, the Führer needs the jet fighters—jet fighter-bombers, urgently."

## INSTERBURG DEMO

That same day, the Me 262 V1 and V6 plus 35 accompanying personnel arrived by train at Fliegerhorst Insterburg, East Prussia, for a VIP demonstration event arranged by the Luftwaffe test centres. Messerschmitt test pilots Gerhard Caroli, Karl Baur and Gerd Lindner, along with navigator Halenka, had arrived the night before.

Preparations for the showcase take took place throughout the 24th and 25th, with the V1 and V6 being lined up alongside a host of other aircraft in the following order: Ta 152 (actually a modified Fw 190 prototype), Me 163, Me 262 V1, Me 262 V6, Ta 154, He 219, Bf 110 with 3cm cannon, Bf 110 with 3.7cm cannon, Bf 110 with 21cm launchers, Me 410 with MK 103, Me 410 with 3.7cm Flak 43, Me 410 with 5cm KwK 39, Ju 88 with oblique firing weapons, Ju 88 with launchers, Ar 234, Ju 288, Ju 188, Ju 352, He 177, Ju 290 and Ju 390.[47] It had been planned that the Dornier Do 335 would be included, but this was cancelled.

All the central figures from the German aircraft industry had been invited: Heinrich Hertel from Junkers,

*The Me 262 V6 at the Insterburg demonstration event in November 1943.*

*Front and rear views of the Me 262 V6.*

*Close-up of the V6's nosewheel.*

Willy Messerschmitt and his production director Fritz Hentzen, Kurt Tank, Claude Dornier, Walter Blume from Arado, Carl Francke from Heinkel, Walter Cambeis and Anselm Franz from Jumo, Fritz Nallinger from Daimler-Benz, Bruno Bruckmann from BMW, Herbert Wagner and Karl Frydag from Henschel, Robert Lusser from Fieseler and Max Kramer from the DVL.

While it would appear that Messerschmitt, Hentzen, Blume, Francke, Nallinger, Bruckmann, Wagner and Frydag attended, and Dornier cancelled, whether the others turned up or not is unclear.[48]

At 11am the next day, the 12 VIP guests arrived: Hitler, Himmer, Göring, Milch, Vorwald, Petersen, Knemeyer, Generalingenieur Walter Hertel and Generalingenieur Heinrich Sellschopp plus an assistant each for Hitler and Göring. They embarked on vehicles and were taken on a five minute ride over to the aircraft line-up. The static inspection lasted 40 minutes before the party were taken back to the facility's Hall IV. Here they were able to view a Do 217 carrying a Fritz X glide bomb, an He 177 with two Hs 293 glide bombs and an FZG 76 (aka Fi 103, aka V1 flying bomb), as well as static displays of a DB 603 A, Jumo 213 E, BMW 801 E, Jumo 004 B, MG 131, MG 151/15, MG 151/20, MK 108, MK 103, Flak 43 and KwK 39.

At 12.30pm it was another ride, this time to an observation area, with a flight demonstration taking place from 12.35pm to 1pm. The Me 262 V6 was among the aircraft flown, with Lindner at the controls. The V1

*The Me 262 V6—the first prototype to have a retractable nosewheel.*

remained grounded, however, since repairs had not yet been completed. It would eventually be returned to Lechfeld by train on December 3.

Comments made by Hitler, Messerschmitt and others on this occasion would be hotly debated some six months later (see Chapter 7). Knemeyer would later claim that on this occasion it was agreed that the first Me 262s to be constructed would not need to have bomb racks—but exactly how many aircraft could be built without bomb racks appears not to have been confirmed.

## ME 209 CANCELLED AGAIN

The Me 262 V3, now with its camera installed and with thick individual tufts of wool glued to its rear fuselage to show airflow direction, made a single flight on November 29. However, it was found that a technical fault with the camera equipment meant no useful data was recorded.[49]

At the RLM management meeting of November 30,[50] Milch said that the Me 209 had been left off the production programme with Göring's blessing but that war production minister Albert Speer was being given false information about the Me 262: "Somebody had the idea that the 262 would not have been put on the programme were it not for the visit to the Reichsmarschall. At least that's how Messerschmitt reports in a letter to Minister Speer. But that is a mistake. The 262, as we have placed the greatest emphasis, has been on the programme as machine number one for about six months, since the moment you, Galland, flew it and reported about it."

Galland: "That was in May/June! That was when the 209 was killed for the first time."

Milch: "The 209 was still a question mark back then. Because you didn't know whether the 209 or the 309 would come. First came the 309, which Messerschmitt initially stated would be an excellent machine. We then found out, however, that it was not okay. Then an attempt was made to turn the 109 into a 209. In the meantime, however, the 262 had come so far that the order was given to place emphasis on it as a jet fighter. And then the 209 was killed. Now the 209 has now been offered again. When can it come into production?"

Vorwald: "Late 1945, early 1946."

Milch: "We wanted to start the 209. The Reichsmarschall has said that it has no value,[51] and he then put the machine down. That was probably also discussed with the Führer. The machine is out now."

This meeting on November 30, 1943, appears to be the point at which the Me 209 was finally removed as an obstacle to the Me 262 programme—after four months of Willy Messerschmitt's most strenuous efforts to protect it, no matter the cost.

## CONSCRIPTION

The Me 262 and Jumo 004 production programmes were further hit when the German army's conscription programme, known as 'SE 3 Action', began to bite. At the RLM management meeting on December 1,[52] with Speer in attendance, Milch heard that although a limited number of Me 262 and Jumo 004 workers were protected from conscription, there would still be disruption.

Speer's troubleshooter Dr Krome had by now been appointed to support the Me 262's development. He said: "The next point concerns total protection for the Me 262. Messerschmitt has total protection for 1,400 men, Junkers for 1,000 men. The 1,000 men have to be taken from the district. But since the district consists mainly of Junkers, Junkers has to surrender 900 men."

Speer: "In principle, total protection is such that people are drawn in and then given back. Such is the order."

Milch: "I haven't seen the order either."

Vorwald: "The first and second instalments are each 15,000 men; we have to hand them over."

Speer: "The third instalment is also 15,000!"

Vorwald: "The fourth instalment has not yet been ordered."

Krome: "That's a completely different matter. More people are being drafted by the minute; they can't do anything about it. Junkers therefore proposes to reduce the target of 3,000 men by 1,000 men. The Reichsmarschall promised Junkers that at the time. Junkers has drawn up a list of 3,000 workers. Of course, the worst were chosen. One thousand men are now protected. Nine hundred are sacrificed here. Junkers' 900 have to be handed in now."

Brückner: "That is out of the question and must be prevented."

At the RLM development meeting on December 3 fears were voiced that the British would soon put a Rolls-Royce Griffon-powered Mosquito into service.[53] Milch said: "I don't have a single aircraft that can chase the Griffon Mosquito except the [Do] 335. We would have the 262 for a short time, but with its 50-minute maximum flight time it has little chance unless the conditions are favourable, while the 335 has a long range. None of the other fighters and destroyers, including the [Ju] 388, even at its best altitude, are able to combat the Griffon Mosquito. So the opponent has practically a licence for all of Germany if he comes with it. That is why the 335 is the most important of all aircraft."

Use of the Do 335 as a night fighter was discussed and Viktor von Lossberg opined that "the 262 cannot be used at night because of the short flight time!"

Dr Krome had meanwhile been assessing the efforts of both Junkers and Messerschmitt in gearing up for series production of the Me 262. Milch said: "Krome from Speer's ministry stated quite smoothly that everything that Junkers has demanded is clear, clear and concise, so that one can only agree; everything that Messerschmitt offers is statements and assertions that are not planned through, not worked through. In a very short time, the man has 100% confirmed the impression that I have, and that the gentlemen in this meeting also probably have."

Petersen was slightly more sanguine: "It turned out that Jumo and Messerschmitt have very great difficulties and their requirements in terms of personnel and material ... These are machine tools in particular." He said that both companies were reliant on sub-contractors, who themselves worked through sub-contractors, and this complex web of interrelated companies made it very difficult to improve supply chains.

Frydag reported that he had spoken to Messerschmitt director Kokothaki: "He calls for 50 work planners and I don't know where to get them from. At Henschel I have 60, 70 men in the entire work preparation department, and now he wants to have 50 more."

Milch: "I would ask you to check these figures."

Frydag: "I wonder why he wants them now. The 209 has been deleted, the 264 does not have to be done, nothing for the 109 either. The 410 is ready. All he has to do is prepare the work for the 262, and that is a relatively small machine. I ask myself: where did he leave his work planners?"

Milch: "I would like to have that checked, but you might also involve a specialist in addition to a company. At Messerschmitt, I am of the opinion that they give him the 264 to finish when he has the 262 ready. The 264 doesn't win the war; the 262 can win it. So everything has to go to that first."

Preparations for series production of the Me 262 were well advanced by the end of 1943, despite all the problems threatening to derail it. Yet there was another dark cloud looming on the horizon. During the RLM management meeting on December 7,[54] Vorwald, who was acting chairman, asked that further consideration be given to the Me 262 as a fighter-bomber. Knemeyer replied: "The 262 can only be seen as a jet bomber."

But Petersen said: "There is still a wrinkle there, however. The fighter-bomber can only be implemented in conjunction with the 004 C."

Vorwald: "When is that coming?"

Petersen: "I do not know that. There is a chain of misunderstandings."

Nevertheless, Messerschmitt's preparations to equip the basic Me 262 A-1s already in production with the necessary wiring to accept bomb racks continued, though the design of the racks themselves remained a work in progress.

## WEAPONS INSTALLATION

Back at Lechfeld, a wide variety of minor defects with the V3 were reported including issues with the oleo undercarriage legs, the wing leading edges and the ailerons, some of these also applying to the still-static V1.[55] The V6, with its retractable nosewheel, was used for take-off and landing trials fitted with the larger 840 x 300mm main gear wheels. According to the test report: "The aircraft's take-off run to 20m altitude was measured with and without rockets. Take-off showed improvement over results obtained with V5 despite increased take-off weight. The rockets reduced take-off distance from 715m to 450m. Landing measurements were inconclusive due to faulty brakes."[56]

The near-complete Me 262 V7, fitted with four MK 108s, had been used for static firing trials towards the end of November with mixed results.[57] From November 22-23, a total of 266 rounds had been fired using one gun at a time, with 16 rounds failing to ignite and three getting stuck in the barrel. There had been two ammo feeder problems too, the cause of which could not be traced, and the issues were resolved by simply switching to a different gun. Twenty disruptions to the firing process had arisen from other causes.

December 10 saw the Messerschmitt Project Office issue Protokoll Nr. 22, which called for the construction of four new weapon noses for the Me 262 based on the work begun back in July.[58] One would trial the pair of MK 103s with a pair of MK 108s arrangement, the second would trial two MK 103s with two MG 151s and the third was to presumably be a prototype for the production version of whichever of these proved to be the most successful. The last would trial the installation of six MK 108s.

The Me 262 test squadron, Erprobungskommando 262, was established at Lechfeld on December 15, 1943, under the command of Hauptmann Werner Thierfelder,[59] with the still-under-repair Me 262 V5 being assigned for testing at the hands of Luftwaffe pilots. The following day, further firing trials took place using the Me 262 V7's nose bolted onto the incomplete Me 262 V8 airframe. For this experiment, all four cannon were fired at once ten times—with the same mixed results.[60]

## ZWIEBEL TESTS CONTINUE

The Me 262 V1 was finally declared ready to fly again on December 13 but was unable to do so due to bad weather. Eventually, after static testing on December 17,

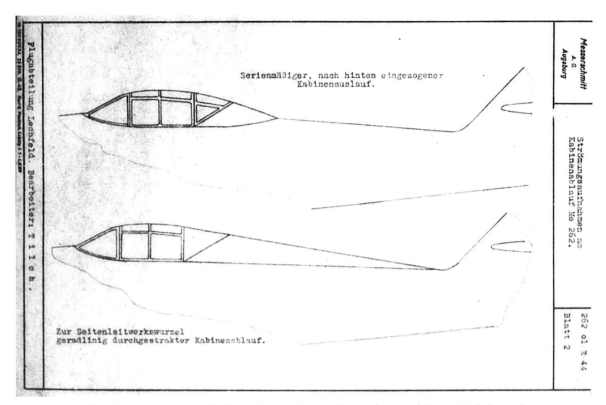

*Drawings from a report produced in early 1944 showing the rear fuselage of Me 262 V3 before and
after it was fitted with an experimental spine fairing for flight tests in December 1943.*

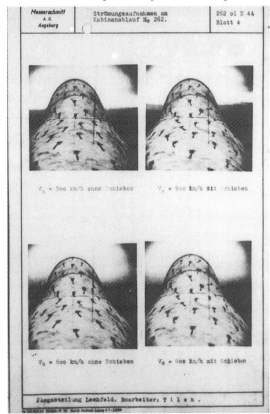

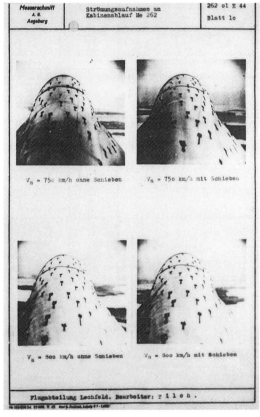

*Four views from the camera installed on Me 262 V3's
fin, looking forwards along its rear fuselage toward the
back of its cockpit canopy. Thick tufts of cotton show
the direction of airflow over its surface in flight.*

*The Me 262 V3's rear fuselage when fitted with a
fairing which gave the aircraft more of a 'razorback'
appearance, taken from a fin-mounted camera. Again,
the cotton tufts indicate the direction of airflow.*

the aircraft was able to resume testing of the Zwiebel electro-acoustic detection system on December 19. It made three test flights that day of 21 minutes, 20 minutes and six minutes, followed by three more on December 21, at 19 minutes, eight minutes and nine minutes in length.[61]

These evidently involved the Me 262 V1 tracking an Me 410 posing as an enemy aircraft and it was found that the latter could be detected from up to 750m away using the acoustic system. However, these tests were "significantly disturbed by enemy action" and "unfortunately, all documents including the evaluated measurement results were destroyed".[62]

Meanwhile, the Me 262 V7, fitted with a very basic rubber-sealed pressure cabin, had made its first flight on December 20, though whether it had its own nose on this occasion or a substitute is unclear. Its hydraulic system worked fine during the initial ferry flight from the factory at Augsburg to Lechfeld, but during a second flight at Lechfeld the landing gear failed to completely retract and when Lindner attempted to extend it again at first only the left main gear leg would lock in position. With some coaxing, however, Lindner was able to get the right leg down and locked for a safe landing. His report also complained about the engines: "The power plant is not up to standard and does not come up to the required consistency for running".[63]

In parallel to these experiments with Me 262 V1 and V7, V3 flew again with its fin camera on December 19 and 22.[64] Prior to one of these flights, a large fairing was installed over the upper rear fuselage, creating a 'razorback' slope from the upper rear of the cockpit canopy down to the leading edge of the fin. Photos were taken at speeds between 300km/h and 840km/h and later studied to see where and when the glued on threads had moved around. It was concluded that while the 'razorback' fairing improved stability, it was likely to have a negative effect on airflow to the control surfaces. The camera mount and tufts were then removed.

# 6

# Into Production:
# January 1944 to April 1944

THE RECENTLY promoted head of the Technical Office development section, Oberst-leutnant Siegfried Knemeyer, held a meeting with Willy Messerschmitt on January 4, 1944,[1] and told him that "the Messerschmitt company's most important task is to push ahead and develop the Me 262 jet fighter by all means. An attempt should be made to achieve and maintain a high technical superiority and a time advantage over the opponent under all circumstances with this type and its derivatives".

This order effectively sanctioned a continuation of Me 262 project work in three areas: upgrades for the existing aircraft, new types which used major Me 262 assemblies and plans for an eventual entirely new replacement.

The first category included work on bomb racks, cabin heating, windscreen heating, a windscreen washer, sheet metal rudders, fire prevention measures, a 6.5% inner slat extension, the Mach warning light, the air brake, new shock absorbers, the pressure cabin, installation of the BMW 003 A, installation of the HeS 011, fitment of a BK 5 or BK 5.5 autocannon in the nose and the switch to more economical wooden construction for the tail unit.[2]

It also encompassed aerodynamic improvements. Various wind tunnel tests had already hinted at the

performance gains to be had by increasing the sweep-back of the Me 262's wings but, following the meeting with Knemeyer, Willy Messerschmitt decided to take this several steps further. Throughout the course of 1944 and into 1945 the Project Office would explore ways in which the Me 262's physical form could be altered to maximise its performance potential.

The second category was a continuation of the studies that had produced the 'ten variants' report of three and a half months earlier. From this report, only the two-seat trainer, Interzeptor I and Interceptor II had progressed along the lines originally described—the latter two now being redesignated Heimatschützer ('Home Defender') I and Heimatschützer II.[3] The reconnaissance and fast bomber variants with significantly altered fuselages had not been forgotten however. Rather, it was decided that if a new fuselage was required at all it might as well be redesigned from scratch, with only the wing unit being carried over from the standard Me 262. This concept would eventually find expression in two new projects—a heavy fighter designated P 1099 and a bomber designated P 1100.

The third category, the search for an Me 262 replacement, was given the umbrella designation P 1101 and initially involved a great deal of experimenting with different wing, fuselage and engine combinations. It

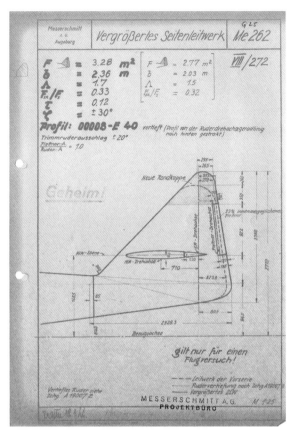

*Messerschmitt's Project Office began to consider what changes might be made to improve the Me 262's aerodynamic form during early 1944. This design for an experimentally enlarged Me 262 fin and rudder is dated January 12, 1944. The note written below the image says: "Valid for one flight attempt only!"*

would eventually result in designs for a new single-jet fighter.

During the RLM management meeting on January 5,[4] which again included members of Speer's war production ministry, Milch said that the Me 262 continued to have top priority for resources, at least as far as aircraft were concerned. The Arado Ar 234 was second and the Dornier Do 335 third.

Dr Krome was not impressed: "That may be; but I can't get the Me 262 and 004 out if I don't get the 30,000 toolmaker hours."

Werner: "We have the same problem with the engines. It bites in every nook and cranny. That is why I discussed with [director of the armament supply office in Speer's ministry Walther] Schieber yesterday evening that we would be taking stock of the situation soon so that we can find out what position we are in."

Mahnke said that production issues at Junkers were worse than anticipated: "Based on the discussion we had the day before yesterday about the jet engine at Junkers, it can be seen that the difficulties at Junkers are greater

than at Messerschmitt and will be even greater in the future. It is not to be expected with certainty that we can cover the programme for the Me 262 and 234 with Junkers. Originally it was planned to equip the Arado 234 with the BMW engine. All measures have been taken at BMW for this purpose."

He said that insurmountable problems had arisen with the Jumo 004 B-2, the model intended for mass production, and as a result "we have to get a broad flight test with the B-1 engine as soon as possible. The B-1 engine is not available because the B-2 was the engine being prepared for the series. The B-2 engine must now be changed back to B-1."

## SE 3 ACTION AND MACHINE TOOLS

RLM staff engineer Kauffmann said the conscription of engineers remained a severe problem for Junkers: "With the Me 262, we were able to quickly resolve the difficulties that arose with the airframe, as the main committee for airframes had a workforce of 550 made available until we get an exchange for the 300 soldiers who are now returning. This is much more difficult with the main engine committee. We couldn't do this in the engine sector and have to wait for the people to come back from the army."

Gunnery trials using the Me 262 V9 commenced on January 7,[5] with each of its four MK 108s being fired individually several times then all four being fired together. The Rechlin test centre weekly report for January 1 to January 7, 1944, mentions test flights with the V6 and V7 to study aileron properties and nose-wheel behaviour, noting that "V7 significantly improved. Attempts continue".[6] But this would be the first and only Rechlin report on Me 262 flight testing for more than six months.[7]

At the RLM development meeting on Friday, January 14,[8] Milch related a story about an encounter he'd had six days earlier to illustrate the ongoing problem of unilateral conscription to the army: "I went to the Führer's on Saturday and he insisted that the 262, 234 and 335 should come faster. I pointed out that it depends on the machine tools, jig makers, etc. that we want now. As I drove away from the Reichsmarschall's procession, I saw a private standing with a little suitcase in his hand. I had the impression that he wanted a ride so I let him get in. Then I asked him: 'What are you doing now?' He replied: 'I'm guarding a warehouse.' 'And what is your company doing?' 'The whole company does that!' I asked him further: 'What is your trade?' He replied: 'I am a toolmaker.' 'From which company?' 'From Henckels Solingen'.[9] 'Have you ever dealt with jig construction?' 'Yes,' he says, 'as a foreman I built these things for Junkers'.

"This was an army soldier! I also asked: 'Are there more with you?' 'In my group there is also the group leader, Sergeant Marklöhn'. 'Do you have more in the company?' 'Quite a lot!' 'Are you just keeping watch?' 'Yes indeed!' 'Wouldn't you rather build jigs?' 'With pleasure,' he replies…'Make a note of the address: Obergefreiter Heinz Klein ZGKW, Gleiskettenlager 3, Berlin N.20, Wollankstr. 54'. Sergeant Marklöhn is with the same company. We want to call on both of them and get them over as quickly as possible. Command of the Führer! We will replace them with other people."

There later followed a discussion about a demand from Göring that the Me 262 be fitted with MK 103 cannon rather than MK 108s. This caused consternation, since the MK 103 was not yet ready for service, whereas trials were already under way with the MK 108.

The same issue of conscription also came up at the RLM management meeting on January 18.[10] In spite of everything that Milch and Göring had decreed and, apparently, the wishes of Hitler himself, Frydag said, "The 262 is not fully protected from SE 3 Action."

Werner: "It is not protected. This is exactly how the jet engine is not completely protected."

Milch: "No, but it has to be completely protected, and we now have to have full protection for these works."

Frydag: "We have to make this application to Speer. So far we have taken all the people out of the air force for the 262. But we didn't get any people from the Speer Ministry, and Speer also has products that are not as urgent as the 262. I no longer know how we can still pull people out of the airframe industry."

Werner: "You have the typical example at the Gaggenau ironworks. Eighty-four people are taken away from their aviation work capacity!"

During the next management meeting, held the following day,[11] it was determined that the Me 262 would not be getting the MK 103 no matter what Göring wanted since its production was controlled by Speer's ministry. Karl-Otto Saur told Milch: "The Me 262 is not intended at all with 103, but with 108."

Milch said that there needed to be 1,500 weapons available for the Me 262 by the summer.

Saur said: "For the Me 262 there are a total of 240 MK 108 in July…"

Milch: "And how many 103?"

Saur: "None at all!"

Later on, Cambeis from Junkers reported that Jumo 004 production was being hampered by extremely attenuated supply chains. He said: "The 262 has a jet that is not built in finished factories, but rather the parts orders are distributed across several factories and countless suppliers. It is a very protracted temporary measure

because I have no replacement."

Milch: "You must have one!"[12]

Cambeis: "It's under construction. It is similar with the 262. With all these parts we live from hand to mouth and are dependent on the transport situation. The parts that are being finished are brought to where they are needed. Rail transport is neither as fast nor as reliable as the task requires. I have therefore made the suggestion that a transport organisation should be created for us with vehicles, which will be placed close to the assembly sites, preferably in the four places where our focus is: Augsburg, Dessau, Zittau and Reichenau.

"We have a similar facility on a smaller scale. However, it is no longer as effective as it used to be, because the vehicle fleet has become very strained and unusable due to relocations and aviation damage and their range is of course limited due to a lack of fuel.

"It would therefore serve us if a transport organisation were created exclusively for the purposes of the Me 262. How it should look in detail could be determined. I imagine a fleet of 30 to 40 vehicles, which would be distributed over the four main districts, whereby the individual districts should make their own agreements on transport issues."

Later still, Krome asked: "Which do we need more, A4 or Me 262?"[13]

Milch: "We need the Me 262 above all else, in front of submarines and tanks, because arms manufacturing is no longer possible without these machines. I recognise the importance as being of equal value; but you can only fix Germany with this aircraft thing. The other things can help tremendously, but do not bring us the same. Then [without the Me 262] I don't see any more tanks or submarines coming out."

Krome: "I said that four weeks ago; but the necessary conclusions have not been drawn from it."

He went on to say that 500 more machine tools were needed immediately for Me 262 production and that it might be possible to get them from Italy.

Schieber said: "The delivery of the 500 machines is completely impossible. Mr Krome knows that. Or we have to take them away from programmes where they are fixed."

Milch: "The Führer explains: I don't just want these programmes, I want more; I ask that everything be done. When we report to the Führer that we are not able to deliver the 500 machines, the Führer explains to us: I will order that they are to be returned. Then we have to call him today and inform him. The machines have to be provided, no matter where they come from."

Schieber: "Then I ask for an order. I told the minister: here are the tasks that I have; the submarine programme,

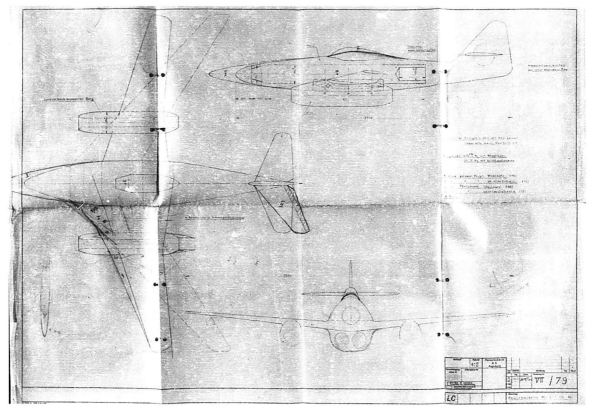

*Composite drawing showing the features of different experimental Me 262 models to be tested by the DFS in February 1944, including wings swept back at a 35° angle, swept tailplanes, a lengthened nose, a lowered cockpit canopy and both turbojets mounted in a common nacelle below the fuselage.*

the fighter programme and the Saur programme."

Milch: "Doesn't the submarine side or the tank side see that, in four or six months, one more tank and one submarine will not be able to come from a German company? Saur, don't you see that something has to be done here?"

Saur: "I can only stand up for the assault rifle programme, because the Führer has ordered that the two programmes—the Me 262 and the assault rifle programme—are the most urgent programmes for him and I told him that 60% of my capacity had been destroyed by the enemy's bombers."

## FLIGHT TESTING

The Me 262V9 made its first flight on January 19, 1944,[14] bringing the total number of flying Me 262s to six—V1, V3, V5 (now repaired), V6, V7 and V9. On take-off, the booster rockets burned the V9's FuG 25 antenna but otherwise the flight was trouble-free.

Another flight followed on January 21 and this time one of the boosters failed to ignite—a problem ascribed to the low ambient temperature. In addition, the nose-wheel required two pushes of the landing gear switch to retract and the pressure differential between the left and right engines was uneven.

A second flight on the same day was attempted but the left engine failed to run because its Riedel starter motor had failed. The pilot also noticed that air bubbles had begun to form between the windscreen's armoured glass plates, reducing visibility. The paste used to secure the glass was seen to be oozing out of the frame.

The following day, with the starter repaired, the V9 took off but now the pilot was unable to retract the nosewheel in flight. That was fixed and another flight was made on January 23. This time, the pilot noticed that the throttle levers were in different positions at full throttle. A fairing panel under the aircraft came loose and became bent and the rear fuel tank hatch was damaged because the booster rockets failed to release correctly.

While climbing aboard for a second flight on the same day, the pilot put his foot through the wing on the fuselage side of the engine because the panelling was too weak.

At around this time the Luftwaffe experimental station at Tarnewitz was informed that it would soon be involved in Me 262 weapons testing for the first time.[15]

Also on the 23rd, a report was published on the late December experiments involving the Me 262V3 fitted with a dorsal fairing. The tests had been made because

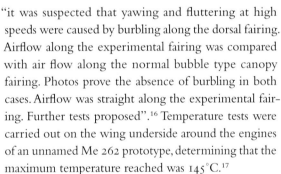

*A microphone mounted on a tripod in front of an Me 262, allowing acoustic measurements to be taken while the aircraft's cannon were fired.*

"it was suspected that yawing and fluttering at high speeds were caused by burbling along the dorsal fairing. Airflow along the experimental fairing was compared with air flow along the normal bubble type canopy fairing. Photos prove the absence of burbling in both cases. Airflow was straight along the experimental fairing. Further tests proposed".[16] Temperature tests were carried out on the wing underside around the engines of an unnamed Me 262 prototype, determining that the maximum temperature reached was 145°C.[17]

## HIGH-SPEED RESEARCH

January 26 saw the Project Office reach an agreement with the DFS to test a series of 1:5 scale models of the Me 262 in a wide variety of configurations.[18] This was the first step in Messerschmitt's new programme of aerodynamics research and five days later Rudolf Seitz was appointed to oversee it.[19]

The Me 262 V5 suffered a nosewheel failure while Thierfelder was landing it at Lechfeld on February 1, the resulting crash damaging it beyond repair.

A description of the models to be used in the DFS tests was produced two days later and in addition to a standard Me 262 form there were variants with 35° swept wings, squashed and elongated fuselages with lowered cockpit canopies and deep fuselages with both turbojets sitting side by side directly beneath the cockpit.[20] On the same day, the still incomplete Me 262 V10 was used for gunnery trials.[21]

The next phase of Zwiebel detection system experiments got underway on February 3, with ground tests to see whether firing the Me 262's guns would affect the system's sensitive microphones. The acoustic probe was mounted on a tripod in front of an unmodified Me 262, positioned at a distance from the nose tip which corresponded to what its position would be when actually installed. The aircraft's four MK 108s were then fired simultaneously several times over the course of three days. On one occasion, firing the guns resulted in a 20% error in Zwiebel's functioning but in all other instances there was no observable effect.[22]

Meanwhile, at some point between January 16 and February 6, an Me 410 had accidentally taxied into the Me 262 V1's tail, causing significant damage and putting the aircraft out of action while a new tail was fabricated and fitted.[23]

A meeting of production specialists was held on February 15 to discuss difficulties with the jigs being used to construct the first batch of pre-production series Me 262s.[24] The point where the rear fuselage and wing met was causing the most problems, with a supplemental jig having been ordered to remedy the issue. Changes to the separation point where the rear fuselage section met the tail boom had also been necessary and subcontractor Blohm & Voss, which was building the tail sections, was to be informed that the modifications had to be made from the 31st unit delivered.

Another meeting took place the following day to

discuss ongoing problems affecting the unfinished aircraft within the jigs.[25] Among the issues to be addressed were a lack of belt locks for the ammo feeder ducts; replacement of the suspension strut bushings; elevator balance weight positioning difficulties; missing covers for the hydraulic lines in the wheel wells; throttle levers supplied by Regensburg that could not be locked as intended; missing engine cowling ventilation slots; complete confusion over the radio system ("system and function is completely unclear, since nobody in the house knows about FUG 16 ZY and no documents are available. An attempt is made to clear the radio system for FUG 16, without ZY"); and cracking around the edges of the too-thin armoured windscreen plates ("the entire armoured glass installation is unacceptable in the current state for series production"). There were 47 points in all.

Schelp gave an update on the engine situation during the RLM development meeting of February 18.[26] He said that ten engines had been delivered in November, ten more in December and another ten in January. Junkers had been due to deliver 40 pre-production B-1s in February but so far only 12 of these had been completed (for an overall total of 101 Jumo 004 engines of all variants[27]).

At that time, however, only thirty-two of the 004s delivered up to the end of January remained operational. Of these, ten were at Junkers, two were at the Rechlin test centre, 16 were with Messerschmitt[28] and four were with Arado. Of the 12 engines delivered in February, three were at Dessau, four were due to be delivered to Messerschmitt and three were earmarked for Arado.

He said Junkers had been struggling to switch from the pre-production Jumo 004 B-1 to the full series production model "essentially due to the fact that the series machines of the 262 have to be equipped very largely with the development engines". At the beginning of 1943 Junkers had wanted to get more engines into the air, but now it had too few left for bench testing.

Schelp said that "it will barely be possible to prevent a gap in deliveries to Messerschmitt from occurring in the next few months…the requirement at Messerschmitt this month is 24 engines, while according to the schedule, 30 devices are to be released this month. I would ask that, in order to broaden the testing at Junkers, the remaining six engines…[40 were due for completion in February overall, but ten were automatically being kept back by Junkers] stay with Junkers, while three more engines have to be brought to Rechlin at the beginning of the next month".

Vorwald: "Messerschmitt only needs 24 engines, and there would then be six left for testing."

Petersen: "We redistribute the jet engines every 14 days. First and foremost, Franz must have some in Dessau, and he keeps back the ones he needs. Then the question is whether we will give the remainder to Rechlin or to Messerschmitt. Messerschmitt needs the engine to test its flight characteristics in order to drive the 262 further. A redistribution is valid for eight days. Then we have to make a new one. We can only decide on a case-by-case basis. Whatever happens, Cuno can distribute."

Cuno: "It's difficult to distribute because I don't know what matters to the airframes and what needs to be done. We could use the equipment better in Rechlin because there has been no flight in Lechfeld for eight days due to bad weather."

## AUGSBURG BOMBED

Feldwebel Kurt Schmidt damaged another Me 262 prototype on February 21, 1944, when he belly-landed the V7 in deep snow, reducing the test programme to three operational aircraft—V3, V6 and V9.

A review of the work carried out in readiness for the development of a high-speed research aircraft based on the Me 262 took place at Messerschmitt's Darmstadt office four days later,[29] with Seitz proposing to Willy Messerschmitt that a staged approach would be best, with the first stage being straightforward performance-enhancing modifications to an existing Me 262 airframe. Messerschmitt agreed.

That same day, during their final 'Big Week' mission, 50 bombers of the American Eighth Air Force hit Messerschmitt's Augsburg complex in two waves. The first, at 1.52pm, dropped five hundred and sixty-three 500lb high explosive bombs and the second, at 2.15pm, dropped six 1,000lb high explosive bombs plus six hundred and eight 100lb incendiaries. And that night, 600 RAF bombers hit the city of Augsburg.

According to the post-war US Strategic Bombing Survey: "The first heavy attack on the Augsburg plant in February 1944 severely damaged the storage sheds but did little damage to the machine tool shops. On the following night, a heavy RAF attack on the city of Augsburg caused great destruction to housing areas of Messerschmitt employees, and it is estimated that in the following two weeks the absentee rate rose to about 50%, during which time workers were attempting to re-establish themselves. This factor contributed to a production loss of 37% for the month of February and 15% for March, as indicated in the Messerschmitt overall report.

"The plant processes most vulnerable to attack were the machine tool shops, jig and tool manufacturing, and other machine processes. Due to the general shortage of machine equipment, and the difficulty of repairing the machines and their specialised installations, destruction of these shops would have had the most crippling effect on production."[30] A number of Me 262 airframes were damaged in the attack—reportedly including the V 10.

During the RLM management meeting on February 29,[31] Petersen explained that "Messerschmitt in Augsburg has been completely bombed" but the Me 262 airframes being manufactured there had only suffered minor damage. He said the transfer of production to Lechfeld had already been arranged but the move could not yet take place because there were still too many operational units based there.

Milch said that the RLM would assign workers to help repair the damaged airframes and it was now inevitable that prisoners of war would now have to be used for Me 262 work.

Petersen: "Then the foreign assignment with the 262! I have a letter on this."

Milch: "I've already decided that: foreigners deployed like a concentration camp, yes!"

Vorwald said: "It cannot be avoided that foreigners get an insight into jet production. Instructions are requested as to how the company should behave."

Milch: "So far the order has existed not to include foreigners in 262 production. But this order was not obeyed and they messed everything up. Now we have to make sure that this is clear. In addition, the question of the relocation of Messerschmitt must be pushed forward sharply."

Discussion then turned to what should be done with 138 draftsmen and 112 workshop personnel at Henrich Focke's Focke Achgelis company in Laupheim and Delmenhorst, who were still working on the Fa 223 helicopter. Vorwald thought they should be transferred to work on the Me 262 but Milch pointed out that Messerschmitt's existing draftsmen now had little to do: "I also ask you to make suggestions about where the draftsmen should go. I don't think the Me 262 needs draftsmen anymore; because the company recently asked for new work for 150 draftsmen."

It was asked whether Focke Achgelis should be shut down completely and Milch replied: "Temporarily shut down! You can work there again after the war. Professor Focke is supposed to work somewhere in an institute—wherever he wants. The entire staff is assigned to more important tasks."

Professor Walter Georgii, head of the DFS, said: "Focke has already touched on the question of whether he could work in an institute."

Milch: "Would you take that in hand? I am sorry for Professor Focke, but it is a war and it is necessary that every last man be made available for the new task. In the foreground is the Me 262."

Having decided to dissolve Focke Achgelis, Milch asked what other companies and programmes could be cannibalised for additional resources: "What about the other things we can sell?"

Vorwald: "The Blohm & Voss company has received its orders; the 246 is discontinued. For the 222, 238, 196 the commands are already out. Likewise for the development of the Henschel 130."

In addition to the BV 246 glide bomb, BV 222 and BV 238 flying boats, Ar 196 floatplane and Henschel Hs 130 high-altitude research aircraft, there were further proposals to expire Ju 52 production more swiftly in order to build more Ju 388s instead. Me 410 variants except for the destroyer would be dropped and the Me 323 powered cargo glider would also be cancelled.

## JÄGERSTAB

March 1 saw the launch of a new organisation within the German aviation industry—the Jägerstab or 'fighter staff', jointly headed by Milch and Karl-Otto Saur from Speer's ministry. It would be no exaggeration to say that it owed its existence to the difficulties encountered while trying to put the Me 262 into production.

As mentioned, Milch had decided to mass produce the Me 262 back in May 1943 but found that this was impossible. The first obstacle had been Willy Messerschmitt himself, using his influence at the highest level to keep the Me 209 alive and prevent the existing Bf 109 production lines from being wound down. Even with Göring on his side, Milch spent months trying and failing to overcome this unwanted interference.

That aside, the fighter production lines, with their complex networks of subcontractors and suppliers, had become so firmly entrenched by mid-1943 that attempting to make any significant change was met with strong resistance from many of those concerned with and benefitting from those production lines. And there remained many companies working on low volume non-essential aircraft types, failed projects that nobody had got around to cancelling and multiple types that were doing the same job yet shared no parts in common.

The increased frequency of Allied bombing during the summer of 1943 had necessitated dispersed production, resulting in supply chains that were more complex still. Single large factories dissolved into numerous much smaller workshops and assembly lines.

Beyond that, the RLM discovered that specialist jig builders and toolmakers had been drained away from aircraft manufacturing to work on tanks, small arms and other projects. This problem was then compounded by the German army's arbitrary conscription programme, which saw highly qualified engineers and craftsmen put into uniform and handed a rifle—even if only to guard a warehouse.

The best way to solve all these problems, it seemed to Milch, was to enlist the aid of Albert Speer's war production ministry, the RuK. At first Speer's production specialists, such as Dr Krome and Saur, had acted as external consultants but by February 1944 it was clear that this needed to go a step further.

Milch himself would later describe what happened: "Already the whole administration of armaments was in the hands of Speer's ministry. Thereby we in the Luftwaffe incurred disadvantages. The man who prejudiced us for the benefit of the army and the navy was this Mr Saur, who was department head for armament matters on the staff of Speer. For a period we engaged in weekly conferences with Speer in order to remove all these injustices. Many assurances were given, but few of them were kept.

"Speer himself had the good will but apart from him his Mr Saur made his own business flourish. And the result was that we were unable to produce sufficient fighter planes because we were not given enough assistance in all spheres. However, this support was particularly necessary for us because since July 1943 the Luftwaffe industry had been the main bombing target, especially in daytime, of the American air force and also severely at night of the English.

"As a result of this, we could only raise our plan of increasing the production of fighter planes to a certain degree and could not proceed any further. Approximately 1,000 fighter planes. However, we wanted to reach 3,000, that was my suggestion at the time, which I submitted when I took up my office. When these discussions with Speer did not show any real success—they had helped somewhat, but not decisively—Speer became severely ill at the end of 1943 and early 1944. Now Saur did not have anybody to hamper him anymore. And that was when I had the idea to establish a mutual commission between us and the Speer ministry only for the purpose of increasing the production of fighter planes. That was the only task with which the Jägerstab was charged."[32]

One of the Jägerstab's first acts, on March 1, 1944, was to appointed its own production overseer at Messerschmitt's Augsburg factory—Professor Hans Overlach, director of the Technische Hochschule Karlsruhe—much to the disgust of the company's management.

Describing what happened for the benefit of American technical intelligence officers immediately after the war, Kokothaki wrote: "In the beginning of March, the aircraft production programme was taken over by the Speer ministry. Therefore, on the 1st of March,

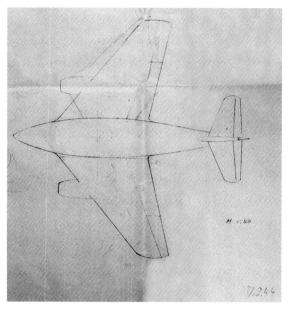

*Messerschmitt's Project Office considered a range of options for aerodynamic improvements to the Me 262 in early 1944. Among these was a delta-wing form, shown in this sketch from February 17, 1944.*

1944, a commissioner Gauamtsleiter Prof. Overlach, was attached to the Augsburg factory. From this time on, the factory's [original] management was practically put out of action because direct orders were issued by this new office."[33]

The precise accuracy of this statement—whether Messerschmitt's senior managers really were no longer able to control production at Augsburg themselves—is difficult to determine but it certainly seems clear that Overlach's appointment to this role was extremely unwelcome as far as the company was concerned.

## ONGOING DEVELOPMENTS

The Me 262 test programme suffered its second fatality on March 9, when the V6 crashed, killing pilot Feldwebel Schmidt and reducing the test programme to just two aircraft—V3 and V9. On March 11, V3 made the second of two test flights in this period to help assess the Me 262's directional stability.

The high-speed test programme was discussed again on March 14 and Seitz presented Willy Messerschmitt with his full three-stage plan.[34] The first stage involved deepening the Me 262's inner wing, installing swept tailplanes and fitting a low profile 'racing' cockpit canopy. The second stage involved leading edge root extensions, more sharply swept outer wings and improved engine nacelles. The final stage involved completely new wings with engines that were fitted 'centrally'. These three stages would soon be known as the Hochgeschwindigkeitsflugzeug ('High-speed aircraft'—usually abbreviated

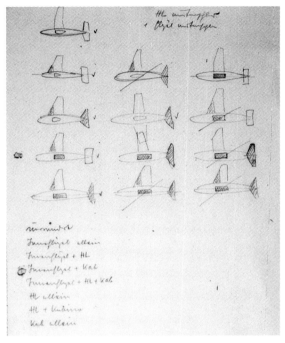

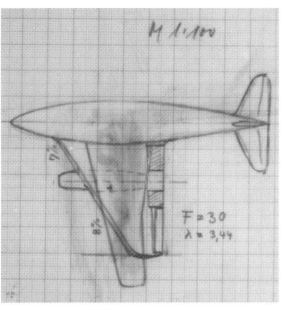

*Various different alternative forms for the Me 262's wings were considered by the Project Office.*

*Another sketch, this time undated, showing how the Me 262 might be fitted with a new delta wing.*

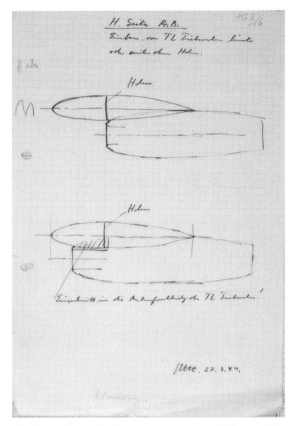

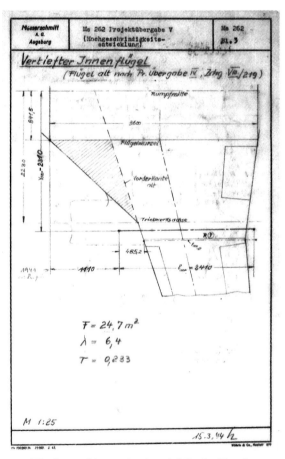

*Professor Messerschmitt was very keen to try shifting the Me 262's engines to a position where their intakes were beneath the wings, rather than protruding ahead of them, as this sketch bearing his signature and dated March 27, 1944, shows.*

*The deepened inner wing intended for the Me 262 HG I, shown in a drawing dated March 15, 1944.*

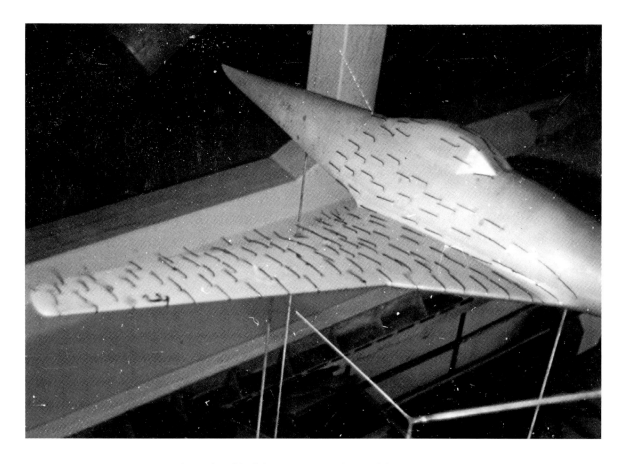

*Wind tunnel model of the Me 262 HG I's extended inner wing section.*

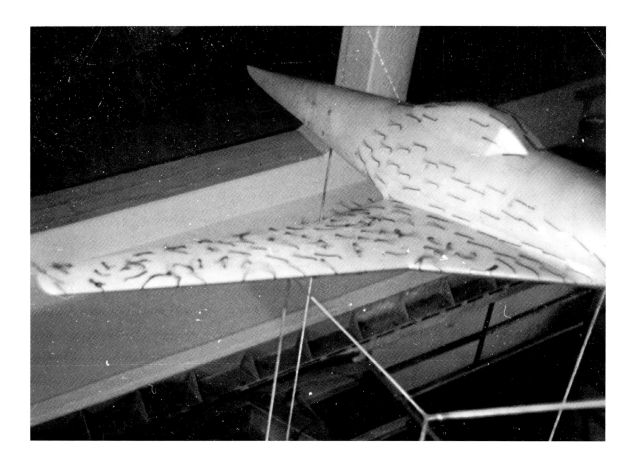

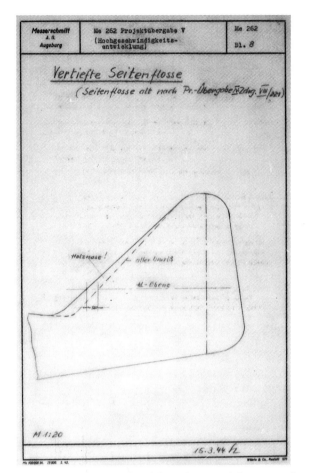 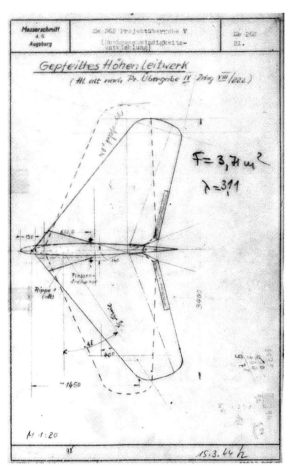

*An enlarged fin and swept tailplanes were also included in the original Me 262 HG I design.*

to 'HG') I, II and III, not to be confused with the rocket-powered Heimatschützer I, II and eventually III.

The following day another meeting was held to provide a status update on all the various ongoing projects and developments associated with the Me 262.[35] It was noted that bomb rack fittings would be installed "for the series from the sixth machine" on bulkhead 2390, with the possible option to move it to frame 1940 if the BT 700 aerial torpedo was to be used. Project work on this development was said to be complete and flight testing was to be carried out using the as yet untested Me 262 V8 with a dummy bomb.

Flight tests to determine the effectiveness of cockpit heating using hot air from the engines, previously carried out with the V7, would now be continued with the V10 and it was thought that improvements could be made by insulating the pipes used. Similar work on the weapons bay heating would also be carried out using the V10 as would work on providing an effective windscreen washer. Heating the armoured windscreen using heated fabric inserts was an aspiration that "must be tested in flight as soon as possible".

Testing to see whether a seat that could be adjusted in flight was necessary would be carried out and

Messerschmitt was working with Junkers on measures to protect against engine fires, including firewalls, a fire extinguisher based on an Arado design, and an alarm system.

There was even a project involving explosive detachment of the engines in flight as an extreme measure—as well as a project that would allow the pilot to destroy the aircraft on the ground to prevent it from falling into enemy hands.

Delivery of the Mach warning light, on order from the Fuess company, was expected in mid-April and work on the long-awaited airbrakes had been delayed indefinitely, pending service experience with the aircraft. The possibility of rockets for braking was being investigated by the Project Office.

A reliable throttle lever lock had been requested by the Luftwaffe test unit and numerous different tests were being prepared for altering the aircraft's tail surfaces to prevent oscillation around the vertical axis—including a deepened rudder, shorter fin and internally balanced elevators.

The project to introduce wooden components to the Me 262 was making good progress: "The assemblies being developed at Jacobs-Schweyer, namely fuselage

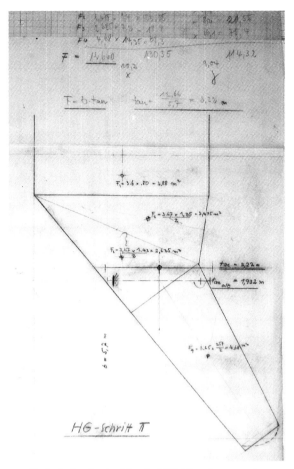

*Early design for the Me 262 HG II's 35° swept wing.*

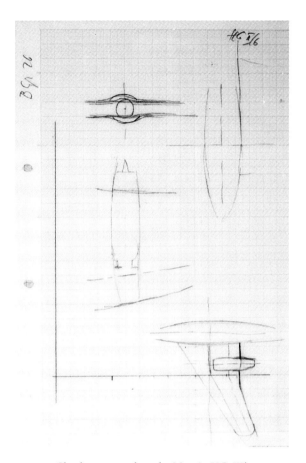

*Sketch to suggest how the Me 262 HG III's
'central' engine position might look.*

end and tail unit, are structurally 80% complete, as is the jig construction. Experimental pieces should be ready by mid-April. The wooden wing will be shelved until systematic tests with the 109 wooden wing have shown the most favourable construction method, taking into account the wheel cutouts." Plans to create longer wings for a high-altitude variant had also been shelved.

Construction documents for the two-seat trainer Me 262 were nearing completion, with a deadline of April 1, 1944, for the full set, and it had also been decided that conversion of standard aircraft to the trainer configuration would be carried out by Blohm & Voss.

Where the cockpit was concerned, the canopy glazing was to be altered and work on a pressure cabin for the series production model could only be continued after the V10's heating tests had concluded.

Installation of the ZFR 3 A telescopic gunsight was planned to commence from the 101st series production aircraft and project documents had been drawn up for the attachment of Werfer-Granate (WG) 21 aerial mortars to the Me 262 A-2's bomb racks.

The Project Office had by now completed work on arrangements for the three planned armament alternatives—two MK 103s and two MK 108s, two MK

103s and two MG 151s or six MK 108s—and mock-ups were planned. No deadline for this had yet been specified beyond the "desirable" date of no later than May 1, 1944.

Little progress had been made on the installation of the BK 5.5 cannon and only some sketchy performance data had been worked through regarding the fitment of HeS 011 turbojets.

In contrast, the first prototype Heimatschützer I—the Me 262 with a Walter rocket motor in its fuselage and a pressure cabin—was due for completion by the end of May 1944. Work on the Heimatschützer II, with two BMW 003 R engines in place of the regular Jumo 004s had yet to commence but "two TLR will be delivered at the end of April. As a preparatory work, a prototype aircraft is to be equipped with two normal BMW 003 engines in order to gain experience with BMW engines". These engines were due for delivery by the end of March.

Finally, there were plans to create a makeshift reconnaissance variant of the Me 262 with camera equipment attached to the aircraft's bomb racks in a "bomb-shaped" housing that was being "developed by the troops". The estimated delivery date for this was June 1944.

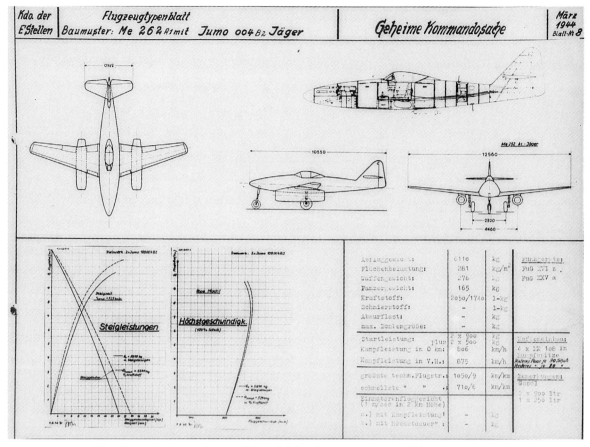

*Throughout March 1944 it was still intended that the Me 262 A-1 would be an interim type with four MK 108 cannon. This type sheet produced by the Luftwaffe test centres shows that the message had not yet filtered through about the cancellation of the Jumo 004 B-2.*

## PANZERFLUGZEUG

On March 17, the RLM development meeting heard that it was still necessary to build the extreme altitude piston engine fighter—formerly the Me 155 and now the BV 155—because the only other aircraft able to reach the same heights were the Me 163 and the rocket-propelled variant of the Me 262.[36] It was explained that the Me 262 was slightly superior because it had a flight time of eight minutes at 16km altitude and was suitable for use in bad weather, whereas the Me 163 could only manage seven minutes 30 seconds and could only be used in fair weather.

Messerschmitt's Construction Office received the project documents for the deepened inner wing and swept tailplanes of the HG I on the same day.[37] The documents for the low profile 'racing' cockpit canopy followed on the 18th,[38] with the Me 262 V8 also flying for the first time that day.[39]

Then, on March 22, no fewer than three significant Me 262 project reports were published simultaneously. One concerned a heavily armoured variant, a 'Panzerflugzeug', intended for attacking enemy bomber formations. One encapsulated all the work done up to this

point on the P 1099—essentially a new heavy fighter fuselage with Me 262 wings—and the third described the P 1100, a similarly constructed bomber.

The Panzerflugzeug proposal was made for both the Me 262 and the Me 410 at almost the same time, with separate but interrelated documents created for each.[40] According to foreword of the Me 262 Panzerflugzeug description: "Messerschmitt AG investigated to what extent it is possible to protect existing fighter aircraft types with heavily reinforced armour in such a way that a successful attack on a bomber formation from close range is possible without serious danger from the enemy defences. It turned out that the two models Me 262 and Me 410 should be suitable for this mission."

The Panzerflugzeug "can be viewed as a converted Me 262 A-1 fighter. The changes are designed to be implemented at any time on production aircraft. The armour protects the pilot against 2cm solid projectiles from the front and rear up to an all-round deviation of approximately 30°. The engines are also armoured directly from the front.

"In addition to increased protection through rubber and armour plates, the fuel tanks are fitted with a

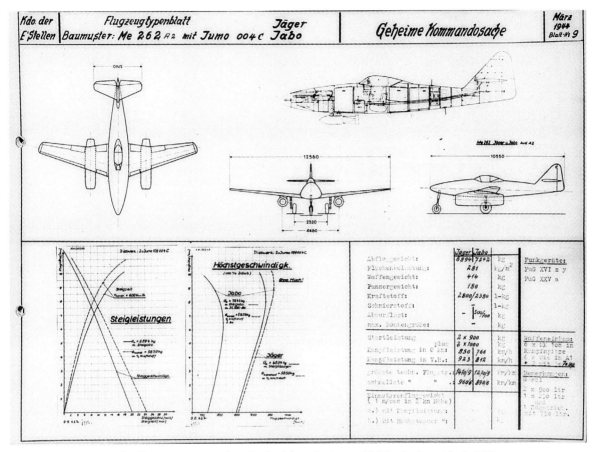

*Luftwaffe test centres type sheet for the full production model Me 262 A-2 with six MK 108s, an extra fuel tank in the rear fuselage and Jumo 004 C engines.*

carbon-acid extinguishing system. In order to save weight for the fuel protection, Messerschmitt examined a honeycomb-shaped tank, in which only the honeycombs that were shot through leaked out.

"The speeds and climb rates correspond approximately to the Me 262 A-1. In order to avoid increasing the weight too much, a reduction in flight time of 25 to 30% was accepted, but this can be changed back to the normal state of the Me 262 A-1 at the expense of other performance.

"Reinforcement of the landing gear with jettisonable double wheels...is required, however, for flight weights of more than 7.3 tons. The armament corresponds to the Me 262 A-1 with 4 x MK 108. The use of WG 21 mortars in the existing bomb rack is planned. Up to two twin tubes can be attached."

For the cockpit, 15-25mm thick reinforced steel plates would be fitted front and rear, with side plates of 12mm. The armoured tanks under the cockpit would provide protection from below. There would be a 120mm thick armoured windscreen "and at the side by foldable armour plates. In the attack position, the view to the front through the armoured pane and to the side

through the gaps that are still free must be sufficient".

Each engine intake would be extended 300mm with an armoured lip and fitted with a teardrop-shaped armoured box inside that was "dimensioned in such a way that when the first plate is penetrated the bullet is broken up before the second plate. The splinters remain in the box and cannot damage the engine". Air would flow around the box.

The ammo boxes in the aircraft's nose and their feeder tubes would get their own 25mm armour plates to protect from incoming fire from the front. In total, the aircraft would carry 465kg of armour for the cockpit, 450kg for the fuel tanks, 254kg for the engines and 75kg for the ammo. Total take-off weight with 1,400kg of fuel was 6,684kg or 7,284kg if four WG 21 mortars were also carried.

## P 1099

The P 1099 project description[41] stated that its design had arisen from two factors: the RLM's desire for a heavy fighter that could be used in bad weather or at night and the notion that jet fighters would never fly faster than Mach 0.7-0.8. If the latter were true, then a

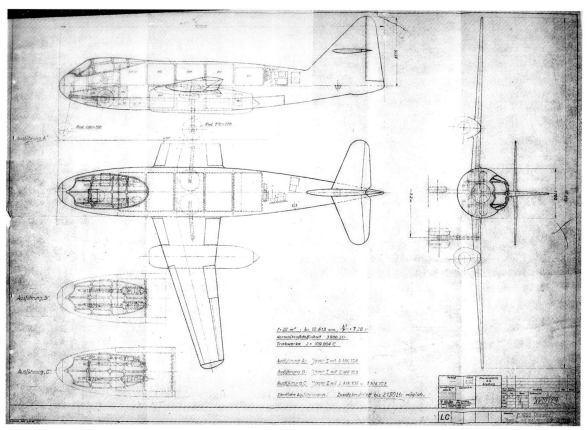

*The Messerschmitt P 1099 Jäger I of drawing number XVIII/79, dated March 22, 1944. Three different armament options are illustrated: 'A' with four MK 108s, 'B' with two MK 103s and 'C' with two MK 108s and one MK 103.*

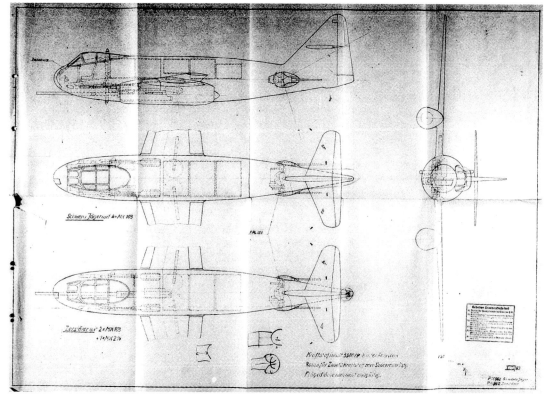

*Drawing XVIII/83 of February 22, 1944 shows heavy fighter and destroyer versions of the P 1099. The heavy fighter is armed with four MK 103 cannon while the destroyer has two MK 103s and a single long-barrelled MK 214 50mm autocannon.*

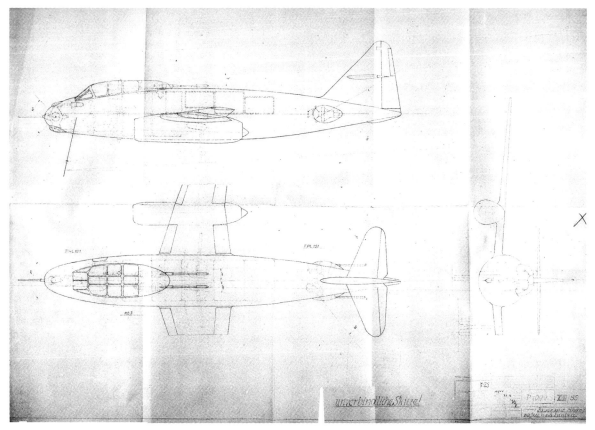

*The P 1099 variant intended for flying ahead of enemy jet bombers and shooting backwards at them is depicted in drawing number XVIII/85. It had an FHL 151 turret on its nose, FPL 151 in its tail and twin MK 103s firing over its back.*

cap was effectively set on the top speed of both German and Allied aircraft.

Messerschmitt suggested that "as a technically possible way out of this difficulty, we have the opportunity to use fighters to fight jet bombers. Flying at about the same speed they can sit in front of the bomber group and fight the enemy with a mobile weapon that fires backwards."

This idea of attacking bombers by flying along steadily in front of them was based on the difference in range and projectile travel time between the fighter's weapons firing backwards and the bombers' weapons firing forward against the flow of air. The fighters' projectiles, facing less air resistance, would have greater range and speed than those of the bombers.

Messerschmitt had worked on a variant with fixed forward-firing armament and another with turret-mounted rearward firing weapons. The report noted that "both have been designed to have essentially the same fuselage except for weaponry. It is intended to incorporate the HeS 11 engine in a later development stage with significantly strengthened armament and to adapt the wing area for heaviest armament and increased flight weights by inserting an additional section (as with the Me 109 H). The fighter or heavy fighter with defensive armament to the rear is possible for reasons of weight

only in the further development stage."

Three variants of the P 1099 fighter were detailed but at least five had been drawn up. Lösung A Jäger I ('Solution A Fighter I') was a two-seater with either two or four fixed forward-firing 3cm weapons, Lösung A Jäger II was also a two-seater but with heavier weapons, and Lösung B was a three-seater with a nose turret, dorsal turret and tail barbettes.

Lösung A Jäger I was 12m long with a wingspan of 12.613m and wing area of 22m². It had standard Me 262 wings and an Me 262 tail fin, a tricycle undercarriage with the nosewheel retracting straight back into the underside of the cockpit and the mainwheels retracting into the fuselage mid-section. It was to have two Jumo 004 Cs but "the final solution is the later HeS 11 engine" and its five fuel tanks could hold 3,900 litres. A pressure cabin would be introduced when the HeS 11 engines became available.

Armament options were four MK 108s, two MK 103s, or one MK 103 plus two MK 108s. A large empty space in the fuselage below the fuel tanks offered the option of carrying extra fuel or a bomb load. Take-off weight was 8,762-10,262kg depending on loadout.

Lösung A Jäger II had the same dimensions and engines but armament was either one MK 108 and

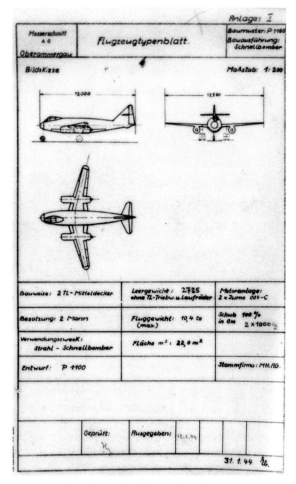

Overview of the Messerschmitt P 1100
bomber with offset canopy.

Interior detail of the P 1100 cabin mock-up, showing
the positioning of the instruments and bombsight.

one MK 112 or a single 5.5cm MK 214.

Lösung B was a sketchier design without given dimensions. According to the report: "This task is not finished yet. It is only enclosed with a general outline drawing, without any liability, showing how with this project this task could be solved."

The brief text outline of Lösung B states: "The attack armament consists of 2 x MK 103 in semi-rigid frame with limited movement (5° cone angle). The main firing direction of this aircraft is to the rear. Attempts would be made to turn the plane around 180° during the fight in order to do justice to the attacking tactics of the rear and the defence.

"In order to keep away attacking fighters and to perform the attack task undisturbed, a movable armament facing forward (FHL 151) and to the rear (FPL 151) is provided. The pilot uses a panoramic telescope to bring the aircraft into shooting range for the gunner (third man) on the semi-rigid MK 103 position. The defensive weapons are operated by the second man next to the aircraft pilot. The visor is a periscope.

"The front fuel tanks, replaced by the third man and the semi-rigid weaponry, are repositioned to the lower front fuselage. The possibility remains to use the front space as well as the entire space behind the undercarriage in the lower fuselage for the carrying of bombs."

An early draft of the report shows that Lösung A Jäger I was originally to have been a different fighter/heavy fighter while Lösung A Jäger II was a night fighter. The earlier Lösung A Jäger I would have been armed with four MK 103s or two MK 103s and an MK 214, while the Lösung A Jäger II night fighter would have had six MK 108s, with two of those firing upwards at an oblique angle. The only mention of radar was equipment of "additional devices for night fighting" and flight endurance would be increased thanks to five more fuel tanks installed in the bomb bay areas. Total fuel capacity was to be 5,500 litres.

## P 1100

The P 1100 was the successor to the Schnellbomber Me 262 projects of the year before. The foreword to its project description[42] said that the concept had arisen from four considerations: the need to "take the air war

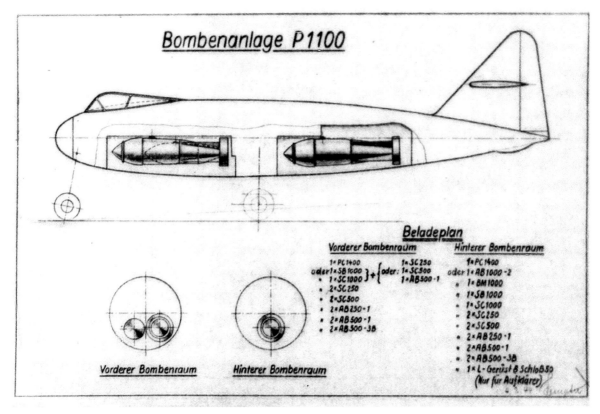

*Cutaway showcasing the proposed P 1100's substantial double bomb bay capacity.*

to the enemy", the fact that an Me 262-based bomber would be almost as fast as the fighter version, the fact that the bomber would take no more effort to build than the fighter and the fact that the enemy, while using only piston-engine fighters, would not be able to defend against a jet bomber.

As was so often the case with Messerschmitt projects, the P 1100 would be developed in stages: "This programme starts with very simple, cheap and poorly equipped designs and finally leads to a design that is as close as possible to the standards of the modern medium class bomber in terms of equipment, armament and protection."

In its earliest form, the bomber would be unarmed, mostly unarmoured and fitted with only basic equipment—focusing on performance, bomb load and ease of manufacture instead. Then, as the enemy introduced jet fighters, it could be progressively upgraded.

The P 1100's all-new monocoque fuselage had a circular cross section and consisted of four component parts—the nose containing the cockpit and nosewheel, the centre section with the fuel tanks, bomb bay and landing gear, the rear fuselage which incorporated another section of the bomb bay, and the tail end housing the radio gear.

The aircraft would have two crew in a pressure cabin—the pilot high up at the front and on the left,

and the radio operator/bomb aimer, with a Lotfe 7H sight, lower down to the rear and on the right. Their seats would be armoured against incoming fire from the rear and there were two canopy options: a narrow one offset to the left which provided visibility only to the pilot, and a wider one that stretched over both crew.

The fuselage centre and rear sections consisted of upper and lower halves. In the upper half there were five fuel tanks housing a total of 3,900 litres (3 x 900 litres, 2 x 600 litres). The lower half was divided into two separate bomb bays with a gap in the middle to house the landing gear mainwheels. Almost every standard type of bomb could be carried, up to and including 1,000kg.

At the back, before the fin, was a compartment for the radio gear consisting of FuG 16 ZY, Peil G6, FuG 101, Fu Bl 2F and FuG 25 a. Then the complete tail section of the Me 262 A-2 was stuck on the end.

The wings too were standard Me 262 A-2 units, except for the spar between them which ran through the fuselage. The P 1100's wider fuselage meant this spar would have to be lengthened by 80mm.

Controls were essentially the same as those of the standard 262, as was the hydraulic landing gear retraction system. The main gear legs each had two 770-270 wheels but the nosewheel was another standard part.

The engines were planned as Jumo 004 Cs to begin with, then HeS 011s when they were available.

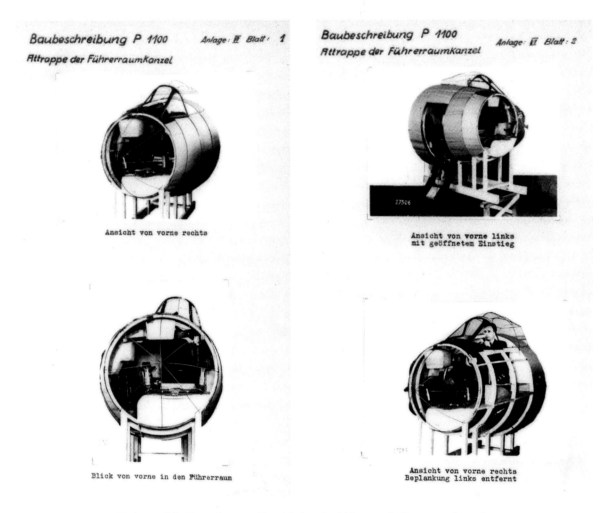

*Mock-up of the P 1100's crew cabin with the pilot high up and offset to port beneath a conventional canopy and the bomb aimer low down and to starboard.*

At take-off, four Borsig rockets with 1,000kg thrust each were proposed.

It was stated that future P 1100 developments would be fitted with FuG 120, FuG 217 and the Berlin radar system. These later versions could also be retrofitted with defensive armament, for which various options were proposed. The first was just two MK 108s—one fixed firing forwards under the pilot's seat and one fixed firing backwards in the rear bomb bay, aimed by the pilot using a periscope.

The second had an FHL 108 turret in the nose and an FPL 151 turret to the rear, now aimed by the second crewman, plus frontal armour for the crew. The third had an FHL 151 in the nose, an FDL 108 Z in the tail and one FPL 151 built into the rear of the cockpit canopy.

Voigt's office seems to have put a huge amount of work into the P 1099 and P 1100 between January and March 1944—the latter in particular reached mock-up

stage and the company seems to have had high hopes that this would become exactly what everyone seemed to want: a dedicated Me 262-based bomber. But neither went any further, particularly since their load and weight assumptions relied on the availability of more powerful turbojets. If there was to be an Me 262-based pure bomber it would need to be more closely based on the fighter—much more closely, as it transpired.

The first series production model off the Leipheim line, Me 262 S2, made its flight debut on March 28,[43] so that as March 1944 came to an end there were four flying Me 262s—S2, V3, V8 and V9—while V1, V7 and V10 were undergoing repairs. V2, V4, V5 and V6 had been destroyed but there were at least 20 more Me 262s steadily coming together in jigs at Leipheim, some having been transferred there from Augsburg, with preparations for a second production line at Schwäbisch-Hall, Hessental Waldwerk under way.

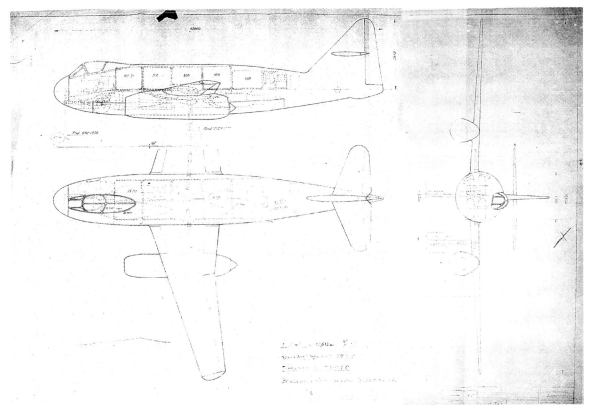

*Messerschmitt drawing XVIII/70/1 showing the P 1100 in its most basic
form—with no defensive armament and a minimum of equipment.*

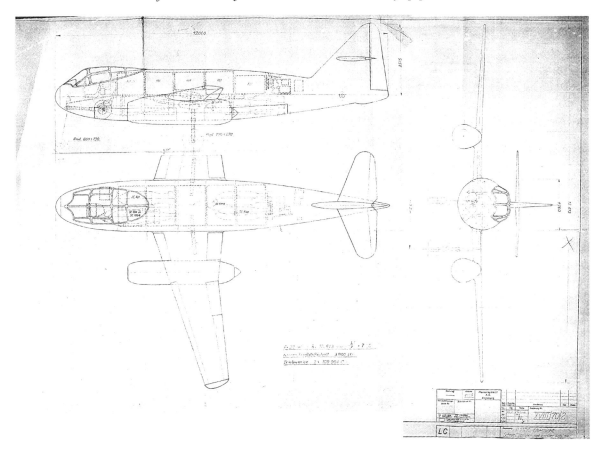

*Drawing XVIII/70/2 shows an alternative canopy arrangement for the P 1100—this time providing full visibility for both crew.*

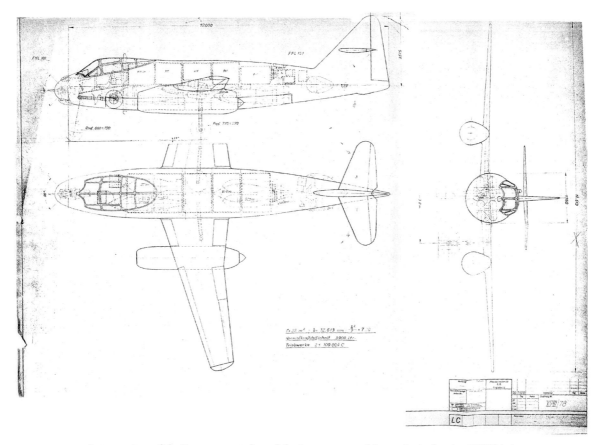

*Later versions of the P 1100 were to have defensive armament. Messerschmitt drawing XVIII/78 shows a variant with a nose-mounted FHL 108 turret and FPL 151 to the rear.*

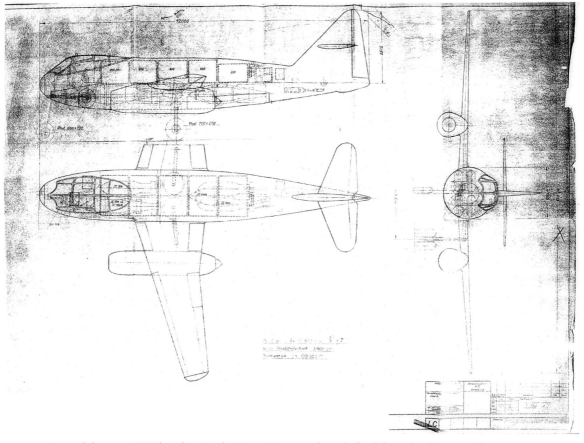

*A second drawing XVIII/79, this time depicting a P 1100 with single fixed forward and rearward firing cannon.*

# From Fighter-Bomber to Bomber:
# April 1944 to June 1944

A T THE end of March a report was compiled listing all the developmental changes being made during the construction of the first batch of production model Me 262s.

Nosewheel swivel was being reduced from 160° to just 50°, the 36-litre Barmag hydraulic pump was to be altered, the construction of the gun nose was to be "fundamentally overhauled again" to introduce rust protection for all steel components, the position of engine cowling access flaps would be altered for the series production model and gasoline had "proven its worth as a flushing liquid" for the aircraft's windscreen.

A jettisonable rear cockpit canopy section would be retrofitted to all aircraft in production, the first Mach warning light had been installed in the Me 262 S2 as a non-functional trial fixture and the pilot's control column would be reduced in length from the 22nd machine off the production line.

The installation of a signal flare launcher with eight rounds was being ground tested in Me 262 V10, which had not yet flown, and it was planned to begin adding this to the production line from the 11th aircraft. Procurement of a cover to protect the nosewheel from

the sun was "urgently required" and "a solution must be found to protect the struts and cylinders from damage caused by dirt".

The section of wing between the fuselage and the engines was still too thin and "sheet metal thickness must be increased". A ventilation flap for the cabin, a Bf 109 part, needed to be installed and "an access panel in the tail boom is required as soon as possible. The demand for retrofitting from the first machine must be expected".

A report had also been produced on the modifications necessary to transform a regular Me 262 A-1 into the Heimatschützer I, now aka Me 262 C-1, interceptor[1]—installation of the Walter rocket motor in the tail, new tanks for the C-Stoff and T-Stoff fuel, enlarged wingtips, jettisonable second wheels for the main gear, six MK 108s in the nose and a jettisonable external tank for additional fuel.

Significant progress had been made on preparing the experimental HG modifications during the last week of March 1944. Messerschmitt's Construction Office confirmed that the Project Office's proposal to lower the cockpit canopy by 150mm was feasible on March 31 but the following day Willy Messerschmitt approved a

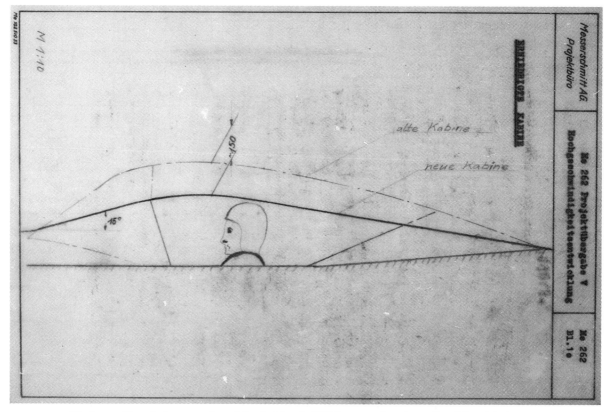

*The low profile cockpit canopy planned for the Me 262 HG I, compared to the profile of the original canopy.*

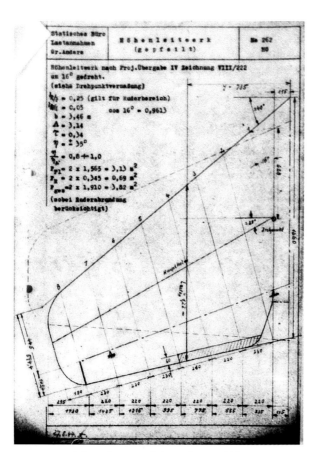

*The 40° swept tailplanes that would be
a feature of the Me 262 HG I.*

deferral of work on the deepened inner wings because all of the Construction Office's wing specialists were too busy working on the Bf 109 K.[2]

The day after that, April 2, work on the swept tailplanes was also suspended "due to other urgent work" but Professor Messerschmitt remained personally engaged with the project. He suggested that the engines should be shifted rearwards to a position still under the wings but behind the spar, previously having sketched out this arrangement towards the end of March.

Two years after the last one, April 3 saw a new project outline produced—Projektübergabe V (Hochgeschwindigkeitsentwickling).[3] This stated: "The changes mentioned [in this report] ... relate exclusively to measures that are to be carried out and tested on an Me 262 airframe to improve the performance. It is to be determined through flight tests whether and to what extent the improvement measures to be expected from the present wind tunnel measurements are influential with respect to behaviour of the airframe at high Mach numbers in order to obtain clear guidelines for the further development of the Me 262."

The changes to be made were outlined in more detail than previously: "The inner wing is deepened by attaching a new piece to the wing leading edge while retaining the wing section behind the main spar". The tailplanes were to be swept back 40° and the fin was to be deepened. Also, "in order to improve the Mach behaviour of the cockpit canopy, its structure is to be reduced to the lowest possible level". Three crucial safety features were required in this regard—the pilot had to be able to open the canopy in flight, the seat had to be height adjustable so the pilot could raise himself up to the position he would have occupied in an unmodified Me 262 and the windscreen had to be hinged so it could be adjusted.

The wing, tail and cockpit modifications would be made at the same time, then removed one by one so it would be possible to determine what worked and what didn't by the process of elimination.

By April 5, a 1:5 plasticine model of the front section and fuselage centre section had been completed but only Seitz himself and his colleague Brutscher remained working on the Me 262 HG series. Seitz complained to Messerschmitt on the 7th and the professor said that a schedule for the project needed to be established.

At the RLM management meeting held the same day,[4] it was reported that Junkers was being lined up to build 1,000 Me 262s.

Vorwald said: "This matter has to be raised again!"

Milch: "Then one more thing! I personally did not participate in the decision that Junkers should build 1,000 Me 262s. Has that also been properly planned by GL/CB?"

Vorwald: "We are only at it now!"

Milch: "I won't give my permission until that's done. We cannot yet relieve Messerschmitt of his responsibility. We also have to ask: what does Messerschmitt do with the factories then? I understand that if Junkers takes on such a thing, it will be done better, especially if it can be protected [from conscription] right away. We have had two crashes with the 262 where it has not yet been clarified what the reason could be. There are two machines that suddenly went down from a height of 1,000m. Is anything more known about it?"

Herrmann: "The investigation is in progress."

Milch: "It is entirely possible that there has been sabotage. But it is also possible that some link in the machine is too weak and breaks after a certain amount of stress. We have seen this kind of thing at the company a lot. I ask you not only to follow the matter closely, but also to examine it in detail. Why shouldn't the control pushrod break or the connecting link between the control pushrod and the tail unit or between the control pushrod and the control column? The latter is more likely to me."

Clearly the crashes that had ended the lives of Ostertag in Me 262 V2 and Schmidt in Me 262 V6 had not been forgotten, though the flight testing programme continued unabated.

During a two-day meeting from April 6-7,[5] Adolf Hitler confirmed the order that a new factory should be set up under Junkers' control, at which 1,000 Me 262s per month would be constructed. It was suggested that "due to a lack of construction workers and facilities" this should be built in France, Belgium or Holland. However, Hitler believed that it should be built "in a much safer area, namely in the protectorate" and that if there were still problems finding workers he would "personally contact the Reichsführer SS and arrange for him to raise the necessary 100,000 men from Hungary by providing appropriate contingents of Jews".

## FLIGHT TESTING CONTINUES

The first two weeks of April saw the V3 being used for ongoing directional stability tests while V8 was being used for training flights and V9 was being used for wing slot measurements.[6]

Me 262 V7, now repaired, re-joined the programme on April 7 and throughout the rest of the month was used for engine testing. V10 flew for the first time on April 15 and Me 262 S1 made its flight debut on April 19.

Meanwhile, Seitz had continued to experience problems in getting the high-speed experimental research programme going. He had arranged for work to start on a mock-up of the low-profile cockpit canopy from April 18 but the Construction Office refused to get involved. He noted in his diary on April 15: "Leinsinger refuses to schedule the construction work as there is no order for it at present (fears influence of the Jägerstabes)".

However, the following day, during an official visit to Messerschmitt's Oberammergau facility, Knemeyer provided the necessary permission and Leinsinger agreed on some dates—April 29 for the new wing leading edge pieces, May 4 for the swept tailplanes and May 30 for the lowered cockpit canopy.

## ME 262 HEIMATSCHÜTZER III

In mid-April, project work commenced on a new rocket-propelled variant of the Me 262—later to be known as the Me 262 Heimatschützer III.[7] This time the goal was to make the rocket motor and associated fuel system a bolt-on kit, rather than something that was integral to the airframe.

The single HWK 509 rocket motor would be positioned under the fuselage, behind and below the cockpit, while the volatile T-Stoff fuel would be carried in two 600-litre tanks attached to the bomb rack positioned beneath the aircraft's nose. The C-Stoff would be carried in the fuel tank behind the pilot while the petrol for the turbojets would be carried in the fuel tank in front of the pilot.

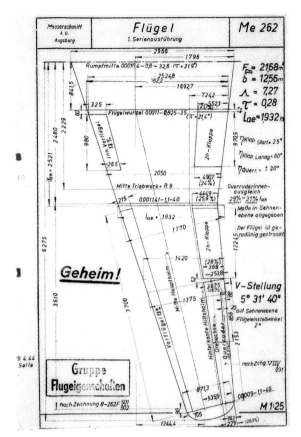

*Wing design for the full series production
model Me 262, dated April 4, 1944.*

## LETTER TO CAMBEIS

Willy Messerschmitt wrote a rather odd letter to Junkers director Cambeis on April 20 to enquire about the number of Jumo 004s likely to be available in the spring of 1945—a whole year away: "It has certainly become known to you by now that, according to intelligence reports, the British and Americans intend to equip larger units with jet aircraft in the autumn of this year. So it is a matter of life and death for all of us that we increase the number of units of the 262 with its jet engine as quickly as possible. I'll try to speed up airframe production, but I'll only be successful if I know we're getting the right number of engines.

"I would therefore be grateful if you would let me know, without obligation, of course, the probable number of engines in the programme for next spring. If you have a bottleneck that you can hope I can help with, please let me know. Your engines are currently used on our test flights. but already with a very high degree of reliability, so that from this side hardly any major setbacks can be expected."[8]

On the one hand, Messerschmitt was urging speed, but on the other he seemingly did not expect the Me 262 to hit significant production numbers for another year—despite the frantic efforts of Milch, Saur and the

Jägerstab to get it built in large quantities much sooner. Messerschmitt also skirted around the fact that his own company's management now had little control over Me 262 airframe production—it was being governed by Saur's team. And he apparently failed to understand why all concerned wanted the Me 262 so badly; at this point Hitler was still expecting it as a fighter-bomber to combat the anticipated invasion while everyone else seems to have wanted it as a bomber interceptor. No one appears to have thought that the Me 262's primary purpose would be to combat enemy jet fighters.

New drawings were made on April 20 which showed an Me 262 fitted with HeS 011 engines behind the spar on a modified wing, and the following day Voigt ordered that installation of BMW engines behind the spar should also be investigated. On April 22 it transpired that the Construction Office had mistakenly thought that the HG I was to have accommodation for a second crewmember and had been attempting to create the low profile cockpit for a two-seater. With that cleared up, work began again on a mock-up of the new canopy on April 24.

On the same day, the US 8th Air Force launched a major bombing raid aimed at three targets—airfields around Munich, airfields in the Friedrichshafen area and the Gablingen/Leipheim airfields. The latter were hit by the B-24s of the Second Bomb Division and significant, though not crippling, damage was caused to the nascent Me 262 production line.[9]

At a meeting of the Jägerstab the next day, April 25,[10] it was reported that options for the relocation of Me 262 production underground "in the case of an immediate catastrophe" would soon be outlined and Milch ordered that all film recordings of the aircraft were now banned without his personal approval.

Galland made an appearance at the next Jägerstab meeting, on the 27th,[11] to emphasise the need for an increase in production quality to go hand in hand with the planned increase in the overall quantity of fighters, stressing "the imminent introduction of the new types Me 262 (which he considers to be the same as five Bf 109s) and Me 163 … as particularly important".

Seemingly at odds with this plea for better craftsmanship, the following day Milch and Vorwald took it in turns to chair an RLM development committee meeting where the plan to build sections of the Me 262's wings as well as its entire rear fuselage and tail section out of cheap and readily available wood was discussed.[12] Schelp said there remained significant concerns about the manufacturing of hollow turbine blades for the Jumo 004 and "one should not make a change before the test with the hollow blade has been carried out on a broad basis".

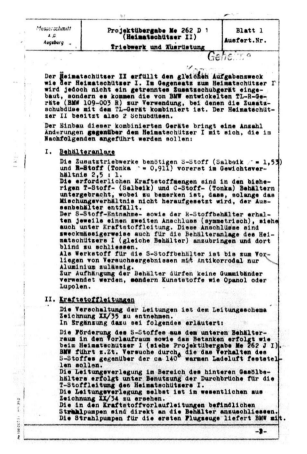

*First page from the Projektübergabe Me 262 D-1 (Heimatschützer II) document, which provides details of the type's engine and fuel tank arrangement.*

Milch said that "as long as the changeover cannot be ordered, the material for the full blade must be requested, as has already been agreed with the raw material offices".

By now, production model Me 262s had begun to roll off the Leipheim line and the number available would steadily increase throughout May. The days of struggling to keep a handful of prototypes in the air were finally drawing to an end. From the initial batch of Me 262 S1 to S22, just the S2 and S10 would be retained for development work by Messerschmitt—the rest being either involved in testing briefly before being delivered to the Luftwaffe, delivered directly to the Luftwaffe or destroyed in the bombing raid on April 24. The total number of Me 262s accepted by the Luftwaffe in April 1944 was 17.[13]

## ME 262 D-1

A new unnumbered project outline report was produced on May 1—Projektübergabe Me 262 D-1 (Heimatschützer II).[14] This began: "The Heimatschützer II fulfils the same task as the Heimatschützer I. In contrast to the Heimatschützer I, however, a separate additional rocket thruster is not installed, but the TL-R devices (BMW 109-003 R) developed by BMW are used, in which the rocket thrust nozzle is combined with the jet device. The Heimatschützer II therefore has two thrusters."

Otherwise the document gave a detailed description

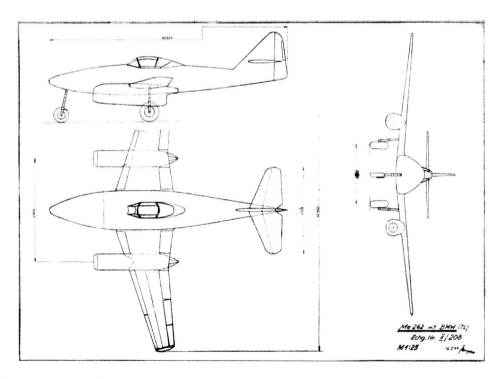

*Three-view drawing of the Me 262 D-1 (Heimatschützer II) dated May 16, 1944. The caption refers to it as simply 'Me 262 mit BMW (TL)' but the rocket motor housing can be seen protruding from the trailing edge of the wing.*

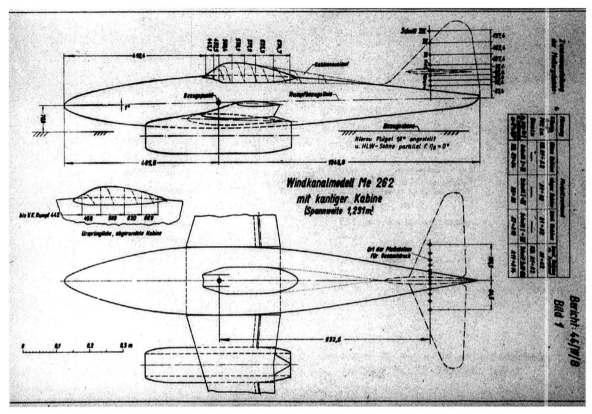

*Wind tunnel model of the Me 262 with a raised section aft of the cockpit, tested by the AVA up to May 1944.*

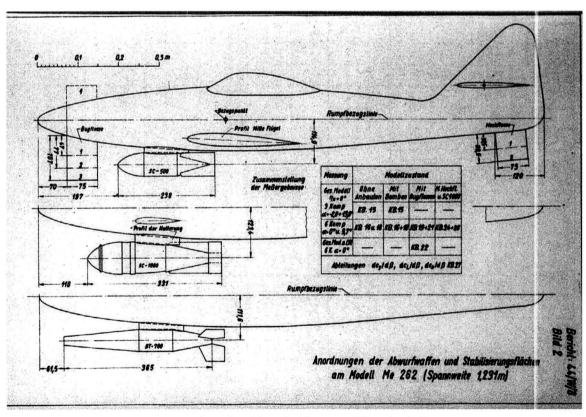

*Me 262 wind tunnel model tested with various different bomb shapes.*

of where the interceptor's fuel tanks were to be installed, what they could be made of ("until test results with anti-corrosion material are available, only aluminium is permitted as a material for the S-Stoff containers"), where the fuel pumps would go, how refuelling would be conducted, where the wiring would run and more.

The BMW 003 R engines would need to hang 50mm lower than normal 003 engines but BMW had raised the fixtures on the engine side by the required amount so no changes to the wing attachment points were needed. However, the upper section of the normal 003 engine cowling—the wing transition section—no longer fitted so a new one had needed to be designed, a mock-up being "promised for April 30, 1944".

Apart from the tanks, the wiring, new switchgear in the cockpit, fuel tubes and the wing attachment points, the Heimatschützer II was essentially a normal Me 262 A-1. It was hoped that the aircraft could be fitted with jettisonable double wheels for the main gear, specifically the same extra wheels already intended for the Heimatschützer I, but "as long as this additional undercarriage is not available, the operating weight is limited to 7,000kg".

On May 8, the AVA reported on wind tunnel tests conducted using an Me 262 model fitted with a spine extending from the upper rear end of the cockpit canopy to the base of the fin.[15] Models had also been tested with mock-ups of SC 500 and SC 1000 bombs as well as a BT-700 aerial torpedo.

That same day BMW produced a report on what effects could be expected from installing a rocket motor in the rear fuselage of an Me 262.[16] This was third party research carried out under contract in support of the Heimatschützer I programme and determined variables such as likely fuel consumption of 5.6kg/sec and a flame length of 4.5m from the nozzle.

Official variants of the Me 262 at this point were: Me 262 A-1 interim fighter, Me 262 A-2 series production fighter-bomber, Me 262 B-1 trainer, Me 262 C-1 interceptor (Heimatschützer I) and Me 262 D-1 interceptor (Heimatschützer II).

## ME 262 WITH HES 011

May 12 saw the publication of some data on how an Me 262 fitted with either Heinkel HeS 011 or Jumo 004 C engines might perform.[17] The report opened by reaffirming the Messerschmitt company's belief at this time that no aircraft would be able to fly faster than Mach 1: "Deviating from the requirement of the Technical Office to submit projected performance without considering the influence of the Mach number, the following performance figures are calculated taking into account the increase in drag resistance as a function of the Mach number.

"The engine thrusts of the Heinkel engine are too large to be able to estimate the value of the two comparison engines from flight performance data without an influence on the Mach number. The underlying increase in resistance was determined on a complete model of the Me 262 in the high-speed wind tunnel. Available but still incomplete experience from flight tests of the Me 262 confirm, up to a Mach number of 0.76 achieved in level flight, these assumptions affect the performance (loss of speed and maximum altitude)."

It was thought that increases in performance would only be possible in areas such as the aircraft's load carrying capacity, acceleration, engine weight, landing speed and fuel consumption. Speeds much above 1,000km/h were believed unattainable—imposing an absolute performance cap on all aircraft, German or Allied.

## ME 262 PANZERFLUGZEUG II

The next day, May 13, Messerschmitt issued a revised proposal for an up-armoured Me 262—the Panzerflugzeug II.[18] The foreword explained: "In contrast to the Me 262 Panzerflugzeug described on 22.3.44, the Panzerflugzeug II is more lightly armoured in order to require the least possible conversion effort as well as saving weight."

The description of the aircraft said: "The Panzerflugzeug II can be considered a converted Me 262 A-1 fighter. An attempt was made to achieve relatively good protection with the least possible means and with little conversion effort, as is the case with the Fw 190 assault aircraft converted by the troops. The additional weight of the armour is about 390kg compared to the A-1 series and is significantly higher than is the case with the Fw 190, since the current great performance superiority of the Me 262 allows this.

"It was thus possible to protect the pilot against 2cm solid projectiles from the front and rear and from an side angle of approximately 10°. In addition to the armour for the MK 108 ammunition provided for the normal aircraft, the front main fuel tank is protected by armour plates against fire from the front, 10° from the side and below, and against incendiary ammunition. The usual rubber protection was left for the other tanks.

"The speeds and climb performance correspond approximately to the Me 262 A-1. To increase the flight time, the 650 litre additional tank can be installed in the rear fuselage without the need to strengthen the landing gear."

The physical differences between the standard Me 262 A-1 and the Panzerflugzeug II involved the standard

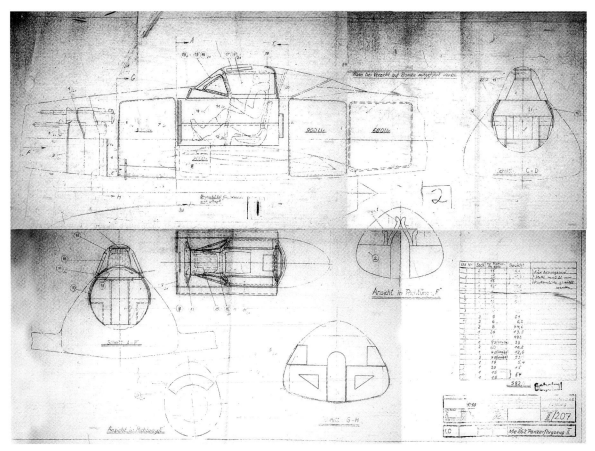

*The armour layout of Messerschmitt's Me 262 Panzerflugzeug II design, dated May 13, 1944. It was said to be more lightly protected than the original Panzerflugzeug but still carried 390kg of extra plate compared to the Me 262 A-1.*

armour plates numbered 13 (in front of the pilot's chest) and 20 (behind his upper back, neck and the lower part of his head) being thickened from 15mm to 20mm, new 6mm thick side armour plates being added, and new 40-60mm thick panes being added to the cockpit canopy. The forward fuel tank would have a 12mm thick armour plate added to its lower front section and 6mm armour on its underside and all around its base. The engines, ammunition and landing gear would receive no additional or improved armour.

The Me 262 V7 was lost on May 19 during its 31st flight. The pilot, Uffz. Kurt Flachs, was seen to jettison the cockpit canopy but did not get out. The aircraft then made a half roll to the right, which continued to steepen until it hit the ground and was completely destroyed.[19] As with the two previous fatal accidents, there was no immediately apparent cause.

May 22 saw the publication of a summary of "complaints and damage to Me 262s" for the period of May 15 to May 21.[20] Me 262 V1 remained unserviceable, V3 had made two flights for pressure distribution and speed measurements, and V7 had made one flight before Flachs' fatal crash. V9 had made four flights but there were a number of complaints about its condition—the

rudder trim tab had worked itself loose, the nosewheel was suffering severe flutter and as a result "the fuselage nose shows wrinkles and a lot of cracks". The nosewheel brake was "bad" and the deflection limiting ring "shows cracks and grooves".

There were complaints about V10 as well, which had also made four flights. The right engine, Werk-Nr. 049, had suffered burn damage; the second armoured windscreen pane, which had a heating element, had begun to crack; and when the experimental windscreen washer was activated the fluid ran between the front and mid-sections of the canopy and into the cockpit. V10, it was noted, had also been fitted with a new throttle lock, a simplified starting system and a ventilation flap.

Finally, Me 262 S2 had made two flights, during which a strong whistling sound could be heard in the cockpit—the source of which was proving elusive. The fuel tanks had also been fitted in such a way that it was difficult to remove them due to lack of space. The aircraft suffered oscillation around the vertical axis and the rudder had too much play.

Up to this point, no Me 262 had ever flown carrying a bomb. Design work on the bomb racks had been completed and there had been plans to test them on the

Me 262 V8 but this had been allocated for training flights instead. Hitler's explicit and unambiguous order that the Me 262 must be a fighter-bomber had been conveyed to Milch, by Göring, on October 28, 1943—nearly seven months earlier. The same order had been relayed clearly to Willy Messerschmitt himself on November 2 and Milch had reaffirmed the order on November 3. As far as Messerschmitt was concerned, as per the project work summary of March 15 (see Chapter 6), bomb dropping gear was being installed in every Me 262 from the sixth production example. But the RLM's senior management seem to have been unaware of this—leading to confusion at the worst possible time.

## THE PROBLEM WITH BOMBS

Göring began a three-day meeting in the Führer's dining room at the SS Barracks Obersalzberg at 11am on Tuesday, May 23, 1944,[21] by talking at length about what a disaster the Heinkel He 177 heavy bomber programme had been. The Luftwaffe could only use fighter-bombers by daylight on the western battlefields, he said ("So much for the big bomber!"), which meant that much now depended on the Ju 388 and Do 335 fighter-bombers as well as the "makeshift fighter-bomber Ar 234 and Me 262". He went on "only the new jet bomber, the [Ju] 287, will be the bomber again, a modern bomber, a type where we can carry two to three tons, with which we have a downright passable bomber again".

At some point during the day, with Hitler himself in attendance, the discussion turned to the Me 262 and Petersen, the Me 262 commissioner, evidently gave reassurances that the aircraft would indeed be available soon as a fighter-bomber.

The second day, Wednesday, May 24, also began at 11am.[22] After the usual preamble, Göring said: "We now come to our actual topic. Speer told me yesterday that he had the impression we had not told the Führer our concerns about the machine clearly enough. I think so; because the Führer said, Messerschmitt always builds too thin."

Milch: "Maybe Knemeyer can take up the discussion and then also Petersen on the worries about the strength and engine of the 262."

Knemeyer: "Regarding the use of the 262 as a fighter-bomber ... In the last few days it has been shown that the undercarriage is not quite strong enough ... If you want to use the 262 as a fighter-bomber now, you would have to lose weight. But you can't do that by taking the weapons [cannon] out from the nose.

Göring: "Why?"

Knemeyer: "The weight of weapons and tanks in the front is approximately one ton and lies in front of the centre of gravity. Then the machine cannot be flown. Even if the bomb is dropped, the centre of gravity is no longer in order. Always hang a bomb in the centre of gravity, so that no change in the centre of gravity can occur."

Göring was very quick to grasp what this meant: despite all the orders given, the Me 262 had not been developed as a fighter-bomber. His anger and disbelief at this inexplicable failure can be heard clearly through the stenographer's transcript.

He said: "The gentlemen all seem to have been deaf. I have repeatedly expressed the very clear command from the Führer that he whistles about getting the 262 as a fighter, but instead wants to take it as a fighter-bomber first."

Knemeyer: "Immediately after this order from the Führer, it was said that the machine did not have to be given a bomb rack immediately."

Göring: "That was months ago!"

Knemeyer: "It was in Insterburg at the time."

Göring: "Before that, he spoke personally in that direction. I had been to Lechfeld before, long before Insterburg, and I said that clearly and unequivocally."

Knemeyer: "That was made very clear to the company and issued as an order: the 262 will come as an A-1, as a production aircraft with the bomb rack. Only, Herr Reichsmarschall, the first samples of the pre-production series could not be changed. Frydag gives the number of 100 aircraft."

Göring: "I have to say: this is very strange considering what the Führer was told. He received an immediate reply from everyone, including Messerschmitt, that it was no problem; right from the start. Messerschmitt told the Führer that it was planned from the start that a fighter-bomber could be made out of it. Now suddenly it doesn't work!"

Knemeyer: "Messerschmitt was held to his promise and forced to have the bomb rack work flow in. Messerschmitt's remark: 'It has been provided' is wrong in that sense. He planned it as part of the project, but then had to construct the rack and calculate the force transmission of the bomb weight. We had to maintain the utmost pressure to ensure that it flowed into it at all. The statement by Messerschmitt actually only went as follows: 'The series machines that are coming out basically get the bomb rack.'"

Petersen: "I can report: Messerschmitt in Insterburg did not say that the 262 can take a 1,000kg bomb with it. A 500kg bomb was planned and entered the series. But the representation concerning the 1,000 kg bomb was not correct from the start."

Göring: "The Führer would answer: that is totally

irrelevant; 250kg is completely sufficient. The main thing at this moment is that it is suddenly declared: you cannot take a bomb in these 100 planes! Up to this very hour we were all made to believe that the machine will come out as a fighter-bomber. And now, while we are waiting for the first 20 aircraft, all of a sudden it is said: 'That doesn't work; that comes after the 100 planes.' What kind of things are these! Since when has this knowledge existed? You have to have known for a long time that the first 100 planes never get a bomb.

"The gentlemen could not have gained this knowledge just yesterday…As often as I have spoken of this machine, I have referred to the bomb, and none of the gentlemen got up and said: 'Herr Reichsmarschall, this is completely out of the question, don't make a mistake: for the first 100 there is no discussion about it at all!' If I had known that a quarter or half a year ago, I would have set a different course and everything would be okay.

"Now I can only try to put it right from this hour onwards, and this is the time you have wasted again. What are the test sites for? Each of the gentlemen knows that I want the machine as a fighter-bomber. In Lechfeld I am shown how easy it is to attach the bomb and where. Today I am told: all of this is not true for the first 100 pieces.

"It's exactly like when I need a gun that shoots 10km and that is also promised, but then it is explained: the first 100 shots do not shoot 10km, only 5km, but when that is over, you may be able to get such guns! In any case, it is absolutely apparent that the Führer was not correctly informed yesterday, but the Führer is now convinced that he will get a fighter-bomber, after what Petersen said. Yes, Petersen, you nodded as soon as the Führer said it, and said: 'It works without further ado!' You can read that in the transcript."

Petersen: "May I briefly report on the test status of the aircraft?"

Göring: "Yesterday, recorded in the transcript, you said: 'Yes, it works!' We were all excited."

Petersen: "The machine is prepared."

Göring: "When the Führer asked for the weights, you said: 'You don't need weapons in there; the machine is so fast that it does not need armour, nor does it take into account the weight that used to be 70kg.' Then the Führer said: 'I only ask for a 250kg bomb!' Then you said: 'It'll be fine!' Thereupon the Führer was reassured. Not a single note of this concern was said."

Saur chose this moment to remind everyone of the three fatal crashes suffered by the Me 262 test programme to date.

Göring: "When did the machines break?"

Saur: "The last one four days ago, on May 19."

Petersen tried to explain the difficulties that the Me 262 test programme had faced. He said that only the 10-prototype series had been constructed and "everything that had to be tested, including the weapons, was squeezed into it. What had to be flown has been flown, often with engine problems. We now have the situation that we need 3,000 flight hours to get the plane in order. We have only flown 300 of them, i.e. 10%. We couldn't fly any more than that because the planes weren't there yet. Three prototypes crashed. Three have the tailwheel, not the nosewheel. At the moment there are still V8, V9 and V10. The first four series aircraft have come off the production line but it seems that there are very great difficulties in acceptance due to construction inaccuracies.

"The horizontal stabilizer has become 8mm thicker than in the sample aircraft.[23] But that means the elevator starts flapping and also the ailerons, and it takes days and weeks to get the planes there."

Göring: "I would be grateful if you had only done 10% of your testing yesterday. That would have been very good."

Petersen: "I always reported that."

Göring: "You didn't report anything yesterday. When the Führer said: 'What is the weight?' It was said: 'So and so!' Then the Führer: 'If you take that out, you can put a 250kg bomb in?' The answer is: 'Yes!' You admitted that immediately, and for me and for the Führer the impression was that the armour and armament were simply thrown out."

Petersen: "The machine will get there, but it's still too new and I've always pointed out that we had to take the risks."

Göring: "The last report I submitted a few days ago was such that the Führer said: 'Now the thing will be done!' Unfortunately there was nothing in it about the accidents."

Petersen: "The accidents are all to be reported."

Milch interjected to say that the Me 262 would get the bomb rack already designed for the Arado Ar 234.

Göring: "Why didn't you say that immediately yesterday?"

Milch: "Maybe Petersen didn't know anything about the centre of gravity issue. It would have to be determined whether to take out or leave in the weapons and armour. I didn't know the main question yesterday either."

He said the issue of the weak undercarriage also needed to be addressed and the investigations into the three fatal accidents were still ongoing. In the case of Flachs' crash in the Me 262 V7, he said: "The pilot, who then had an accident, said beforehand: 'I don't

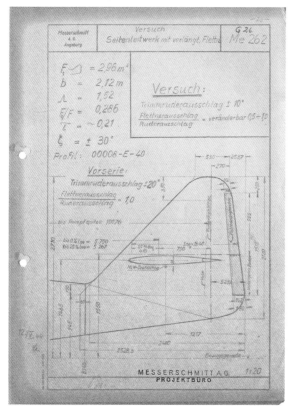

*Even as critical decisions were being made about the Me 262's role, efforts continued to refine its aerodynamic performance. This diagram dated May 12, 1944, shows a proposal for an extended trim tab.*

like the machine!' But we don't know what was going on. It was not in an extremely fast flight, so that the Mach number—the famous thing with the speed of sound—could not have been of any influence, but the machine was still in normal flight condition … flying straight ahead. Suddenly the pilot says: 'I don't like the machine!' And a few minutes later it goes upside down, makes half a roll to the side and is down. We do not know exactly what happened."

Knemeyer: "Then he threw off the canopy. The machine went into the ground with a quarter roll. It is believed that the departing canopy damaged the rudder and elevator."

Milch: "But why is he throwing the canopy off? Something must have happened beforehand so that the man wanted out. We do not know what that was. In this I personally see the main difficulty for the rapid deployment of the machine. A bomb rack can be added later, that's a small job."

Göring: "The construction for the bomb rack is finished?"

Milch: "The bomb rack is wrongly constructed. We now take the construction of Arado, of Blume."

Knemeyer: "It's mainly about the introduction of force into the fuselage, and that's done. I couldn't get the number. I was always told: the first 20 machines come without the racks, the others as A-1."

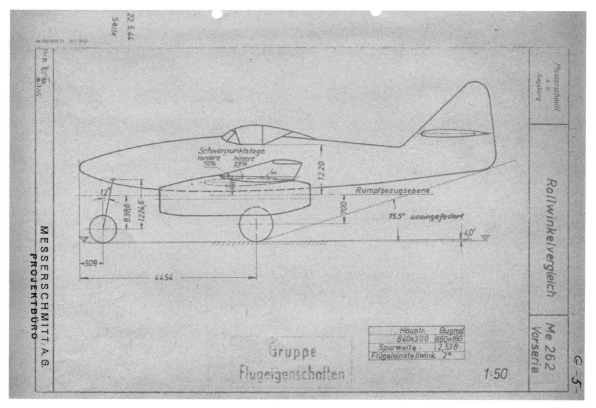

*Diagram showing the Me 262's angle of take-off.*

Göring: "May I ask: who among you knows about it at all? The head of development says 20, the other says 100 machines. If even the numbers are not subject to a certain coordination with you, I now understand why we always get such different numbers. If you get a number from any place on request, it doesn't have to be correct by any means."

Saur: "I have to say a third number. According to the previous reports, 227 machines have been verified in terms of material. If changes now result from the calculation, this material must not be used and a new one must be created. You never know what repercussions such changes have and what order of magnitude they are."

Milch, Galland, Petersen and Saur then took it in turns to explain that the shortage of prototypes from Messerschmitt had hampered the type's development but that progress was being made. Göring appears to have calmed down somewhat after his initial shock.

He said: "In any case, I would have been grateful if you had made these statements to the Führer yesterday. Read what you said yesterday in the shorthand and you will find that it is very different. What should I do there?"

Saur read out a list of production changes being made and Milch said the two "big questions" to be answered were why the three aircraft had crashed and whether it was possible to carry a 250kg bomb by removing the Me 262's armour.

Further debate followed about the armour, the weakness of the undercarriage and whether installing the long-awaited Jumo 004 C engine would improve the situation. Finally attention focused on whether removing two of the Me 262's cannon would be sufficient to free up enough weight so that bombs could be carried. Eventually, Göring said: "We want to break off the conversation. Tomorrow the designer will be here and … the question of the 262 must be clarified here with him."

## THE PROBLEM WITH BOMBS PART II

The third day of the meeting, Thursday, May 25,[24] with Willy Messerschmitt now in attendance, opened with Göring addressing the professor directly: "The 262 was originally designed and thought of as a fighter years ago, at one time, when we didn't even know the fighter-bomber concept—it hadn't been introduced to us yet. When did you start the first construction?"

Messerschmitt: "The first drafts date from 1938."

Göring: "Well before the fighter-bomber even existed! However, about a year ago the order and the wish of the Führer were made clear, both to Mr Messerschmitt and my leadership, as well as the GL, as well as me, and all of us—that the Führer does not need this type as a fighter, but as a bomb thrower, as fighter-bomber, although it

would have been enough for him if the machine could only take two 125kg bombs with it or, better yet, a 500kg bomb or a row of six or eight 50kg bombs. The order was clearly given to all bodies: the 262 is to be built as a fighter-bomber. It's a completely new aircraft. Nevertheless … very serious problems are now emerging with this aircraft that we must now talk about.

"The day before yesterday it was said that the machine could not come out as a fighter-bomber for the time being, and it was even said that the first 100 aircraft could not come out as fighter-bombers under any circumstances. The Führer then asked the question what cannon, ammunition and armour would be in the 262, had the weights determined and then pointed out that the weights [of those items together] are far higher than a bomb would make, namely over 500kg. Now he believed that by offloading his weapons and armour he would be able to carry bombs. But yesterday it was said here that this was not possible because of the centre of gravity … Various other flaws then emerged. The main flaw is in the undercarriage.

"You will not be angry with me, Prof. Messerschmitt, if I tell you that on the one hand I am very surprised and on the other hand not at all. Because when I think of the undercarriage of the 109, that was always the weakest point on the whole aircraft, and the pilots and experts attribute a lot of breakage to the weak undercarriage of the 109. But it surprises me that the knowledge and experiences from the 109 have not been used here.

"Secondly, however, it surprises me less, because the chassis, the 'legs' of the aircraft have always suffered from muscle atrophy, so that there was a certain weakness on the ground here, which, however, was against the greater force in the air. But since you first have to move away from the earth and finally have to return to the ground, the chassis also has its very decisive importance. If it is too weak, nothing is of any use, then you cannot hang on to it either. That must now be clarified and discussed. How quickly and in what way we can best bring the 262 to use as a fighter-bomber according to the wishes of the Führer.

"In addition, we have had a lot of bad luck with this machine lately; machines have crashed. You have to expect that with such new types; this is not something that would be very surprising. You always have to expect something like this to happen … But as I said, we don't have much time; because the enemy is also working on this jet engine and the decisive factor here is who comes out with it first and who has a certain advantage, even if only by half a year. So, Mr Messerschmitt, would you please generally comment on the type, and then I would ask the other gentlemen to put their questions to Mr

Messerschmitt in detail and to join the discussion."

Messerschmitt: "First of all, I can say the following about the landing gear: in two cases it happened that when a tyre burst as a result of splinters from bombs or flak on the airfield, the landing gear itself broke out of the wing above. Static tests showed that the mounting of the chassis was in order according to the applicable load assumptions. I have arranged for the point where it has broken out to be strengthened."

Göring: "Do I understand you correctly that the chassis broke as a result of a flak splinter?"

Messerschmitt: "The wheel or the tyre burst as a result of flak splinters."

Göring: "So if there hadn't been any flak fragments lying around, in your opinion, damage to the chassis would have occurred at all?"

Messerschmitt: "Probably not!"

The professor then explained the forces acting on an undercarriage strut when a tyre burst under load. Göring quizzed him on what would happen if the aircraft were stripped of armour and he replied that the centre of gravity would be unaffected. The same was true of the ammo for the cannon—the aircraft could fly fine without it.

Saur: "There are 200kg of ammunition, 276kg of weapons and 165kg of armour."

Messerschmitt: "You could take out the weapons and put ballast in the tip of the front. Then the machine would be even lighter."

Göring: "The weapons are 276kg. [But] when you take out the weapons, do you not need 276kg in the front to establish the centre of gravity?"

Messerschmitt: "No, 100kg. It could be done. But I don't think it's necessary, if you only want to use the bird for ground-attack, don't want to defend yourself, and are fast enough, you can leave out the weapons. Then the machine can of course only be used as a fighter by retrofitting the weapons."

Göring: "I have to go one step further with the testing: that the undercarriage is tested with weapons, with ammunition and with bomb weight."

Galland: "If we take out the armour and reduce the ammunition a little, we'll get there."

Messerschmitt: "I don't think that the undercarriage will cause problems in the long run. The reinforcements that are necessary are simple ones."

Göring: "Do you think that this suggestion to put 100kg in front is sufficient?"

Messerschmitt: "I think it will be enough."

Petersen: "You can't say that offhand."

Messerschmitt then made a sketch and indicated where the centre of gravity would be with 100kg ballast

in the aircraft's nose.

Göring: "What if you make a balance, if you only leave two weapons instead of four weapons and have some ammunition in the front?"

Messerschmitt: "It is clear that the machine with a 500kg bomb and full weaponry will work if the difficulties have been overcome with the sore point on the undercarriage."

Göring: "What about the 100 aircraft now?"

Messerschmitt: "It is the case that the sixth aircraft in series is fully equipped with the bomb system. It is just not attached to the external rack because it is easily removable and can even be thrown off in flight. This can be brought about quickly, but it must first start up in series production."

Göring: "But is there no longer any need to change?"

Messerschmitt: "No, not in the airframe anymore. It is only appended. From the sixth machine onwards, the machine is equipped like this: all the instrumentation, the electrical systems, the suspension points are there to hang the rack."

Göring: "That's reassuring. When does it come?"

Messerschmitt: "It's out already."

Heyne: "What's the name of the equipment?"

Messerschmitt: "It's the normal rack, [ETC] 503 or 504, with a teardrop-shaped fairing and that still needs to be built."

Heyne: "Who does the fairing?"

Messerschmitt: "Any sub-supplier. But I'm not quite in the picture. I couldn't find out if and where it started. The bomb rack is a standardized rack. But it is built into a fairing box, and I cannot say whether and where the fairing box started in series."

Göring: "Something different. So this is a bomb rack where you can hang 500 or 250?"

Messerschmitt: "Yes, or even a 1,000. But we first have to test the 1,000s to see if that works."

Göring: "We want to leave out the 1,000s entirely. Now you have a lot of space down in the fuselage. That looks very useful. One would have to think about installing a different bomb set later under certain circumstances, placing a row of 50s next to each other."

Messerschmitt: "The suspension points are designed in such a way that other sets of accessories can also be attached."

Göring: "What can we bring to the wing? Would it be worse if you still fit two 50s here, as you did with the old Jolanthe?"

Messerschmitt: "You can do it, but it slows you down. We do not yet know exactly what the bomb drag resistance is."

The professor then went on to outline the Me 262's

projected performance with and without a bomb and with different engines before going on to say: "It is the same as the Führer ordered it to be carried out, the construction drawing was made and the test installation, so that it should actually come in from the first production aircraft. It was delayed a little and it got on the sixth plane. But it could also be retrofitted from the first aircraft, if it had a purpose."

Göring: "Doing that wouldn't make any sense. This is reassuring. But is that definitive?"

Messerschmitt: "Yes. I asked the special committee by phone."

Saur: "These are machines that are coming out this week?"

Messerschmitt: "Yes, there are machines that are coming out now."

Assuming Messerschmitt was correct, the Me 262 S6 and all subsequent examples were built with the appropriate wiring and switchgear to operate with either one or two bomb racks fitted under their forward fuselage. The racks themselves, however, do not appear to have been ready to fit. And as such, no testing had been carried out. Neither does it appear that any thought had been given to bomb aiming equipment.

There followed a brief discussion about who exactly was manufacturing the fairings for the bomb racks—Messerschmitt didn't know—and the cause of Flachs' crash. Messerschmitt stated that the V7 had been fitted with a pressure-tight cabin, pressurised with air from the engines, and speculated that exhaust fumes might have leaked into the cockpit—causing Flachs to feel unwell.

Me 262 V10 made an 82-minute flight carrying a 250kg bomb on May 27, the earliest known flight of an Me 262 carrying a bomb.[25] That same day the test centre at Rechlin, presumably at Petersen's behest, put out a briefing note which stated that, "Based on a Führer order, it is planned, as already planned, to deliver the entire Me 262 series as Jabo [fighter-bomber]."[26]

## HITLER'S DECISION

It appeared as though the RLM's senior officers had been worrying about nothing. Messerschmitt had done as asked and the Me 262's future as a fighter-bomber was secured with just the first five production examples lacking bomb gear. But the round of meetings wasn't over.

Milch left Obersalzberg but the others were evidently required to remain over the weekend. On Monday morning, May 29, at 11am Göring brought his staff back together and told them Adolf Hitler had ordered that the series production model Me 262s be brought into service immediately as dedicated bombers—not

fighter-bombers.[27] He stressed that "the Führer doesn't want the aircraft to be 100% cut off from use as a fighter" but that those aircraft already in production, presumably the first 100, should be required to operate as bombers. And he then repeated Hitler's October 1943 vision, of jet bombers whizzing along invasion beaches and tossing bombs into masses of enemy troops seeking to establish an Allied foothold on the Continent.

Evidently the Führer, aware that an invasion was imminent, had got tired of waiting for his beach-skimming jet bomber.

Henceforth, the Me 262 could not be referred to as a fighter but should be called a 'super-speed bomber' instead. Further development of the type was to be overseen by General der Kampfflieger Walter Marienfeld but 10 aircraft would be set aside for continued flight testing as fighters.

There could be no ifs or buts—the Me 262 had to be a bomber first. With hindsight, the decision to use arguably most war's most powerful air-to-air combat machine exclusively for attacking ground targets seems incomprehensible. Certainly, it prevented the Me 262's use in attacking the Allied bomber formations that were remorselessly pounding Germany at this time.

In context, however, Hitler's order does not appear quite so unreasonable. Messerschmitt had discussed the aircraft's potential as a bomber with him back in September 1943 and by October the Führer had conceived of his 'bombing the beaches' concept. It appeared even then that the Me 262 was ready to put into production but as month after month passed by with barely a sign of new aircraft being built, let alone entering service, Hitler must have begun to wonder what was going on.

The genuine reasons for this delay—critical shortages of nickel, mass conscription of engineers and technicians by the army, jig-makers being requisitioned for tank production, Messerschmitt's tardiness in building prototypes and his machinations concerning the Me 209—were so numerous and complex that anyone reporting them to the Führer risked sounding as though they were reeling off a string of weak excuses.

The last straw was the mixed messages Hitler received from Göring, Knemeyer, Petersen and others regarding the Me 262 at Obersalzberg. This evident confusion presumably convinced him that the engineers and flight testers were spending overlong tweaking and fine-tuning the aircraft—oblivious to the imminent threat of invasion and all the consequences that the opening of a new front in the west would entail.

The most complete account of Hitler's justification for his decision comes from a meeting held later that month, around two weeks after the D-Day invasion. The

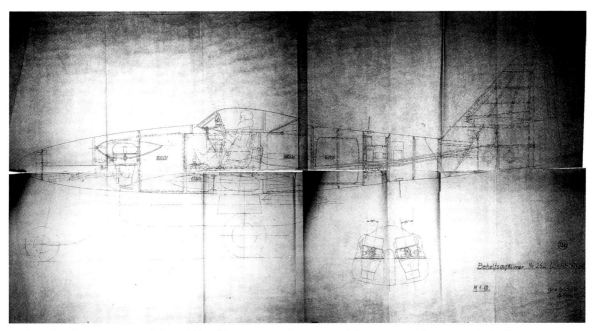

*The earliest known drawing of the Behelfsaufklärer Me 262, here composed from surviving fragments. It is dated May 30, 1944.*

minutes of that meeting state: "The Führer hopes that, in view of the considerably reduced strain on airframe and engines, owing to the initially exclusive use of the aircraft as a bomber, and by retaining steady altitude and straight line flight and, at times, reduced speed, the aircraft can immediately be made available for action.

"The aircraft is therefore to be released at once to prove its qualities in action and to go subsequently into battle, apart from being tested at home with regard to its suitability as a fighter."[28]

In other words, Hitler simply hoped that by making the Me 262's mission less demanding—no diving and no dogfighting, only level bombing—the aircraft could be brought to the front line straight away. Unfortunately, all the testing carried out up to this point had been done with the fighter role in mind. Bomb rack wiring and switches may have been installed from the Me 262 S6 onwards, but only one flight had been made with a bomb and there had been no target practice. A second bomb-carrying flight took place that same day, this time with a 500kg device.[29]

After the May 29 meeting, Willy Messerschmitt returned to Oberammergau. Me 262 V10, now scheduled for intensive bomb-carrying trials, made two flights on May 30 to assess what effect the carriage of a single 500kg bomb would have on directional stability.[30] The total number of Me 262s accepted by the Luftwaffe for May 1944 was 10—making a total of 27 accepted up to this point.[31]

A drawing was produced on May 30, presumably by Messerschmitt's Project Office, showing a "Behelf-saufklärer Me 262 (2 x Rb 50 x 30)". The 'makeshift'

reconnaissance aircraft as-shown was largely a standard Me 262 with a new this housing a pair of Rb 50/30 cameras. These would be positioned next to one another and set at an angle of 10° off centre.[32] Since the cameras did not quite fit within the existing shape of the Me 262's nose, a not-quite teardrop shaped fairing would be required on either side.

By Friday, June 2 a single Me 262 nose had been modified to house a pair of Rb 50/30 cameras, tilted outwards at an angle of 10-12°, and two further camera noses were being prepared. It was foreseen that later aircraft would have Rb 75/30 cameras installed instead and "because of the smooth running of the engines and for reasons of space, there is no spring mounting for them".[33] Heating would not be provided for the camera compartment nor would there be a viewing window in the fuselage underside so that the pilot could see what he was photographing—the nose would simply bolt onto a standard Me 262.

Evidently a tight deadline had been set for the construction of these three camera noses because "since a viewing window would require a delay in the conversion date … this is not done for the first three machines. Once the frontline experience is available, one viewing window can be installed in front of the main spar in the fuselage".

It would appear that this reconnaissance Me 262 configuration was given the designation Me 262 A-4 Aufklärer, since it appeared as such in a guide to Me 262 variants produced in November 1944. Accompanying notes state that this unarmed aircraft would have two Rb 50/30 cameras connected to an automated picture control system.[34]

# THE 14 STAGES OF ME 262 PRODUCTION SET OUT IN APRIL 1944

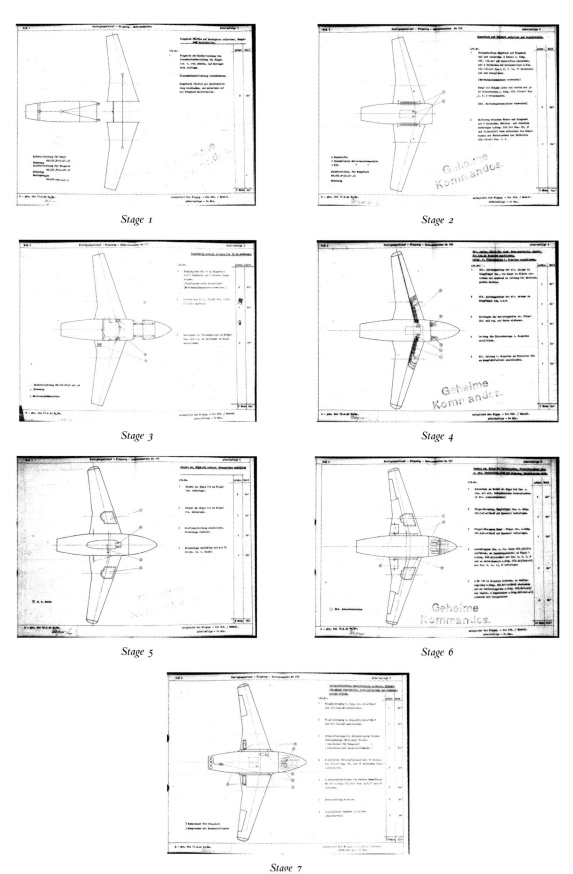

Stage 1

Stage 2

Stage 3

Stage 4

Stage 5

Stage 6

Stage 7

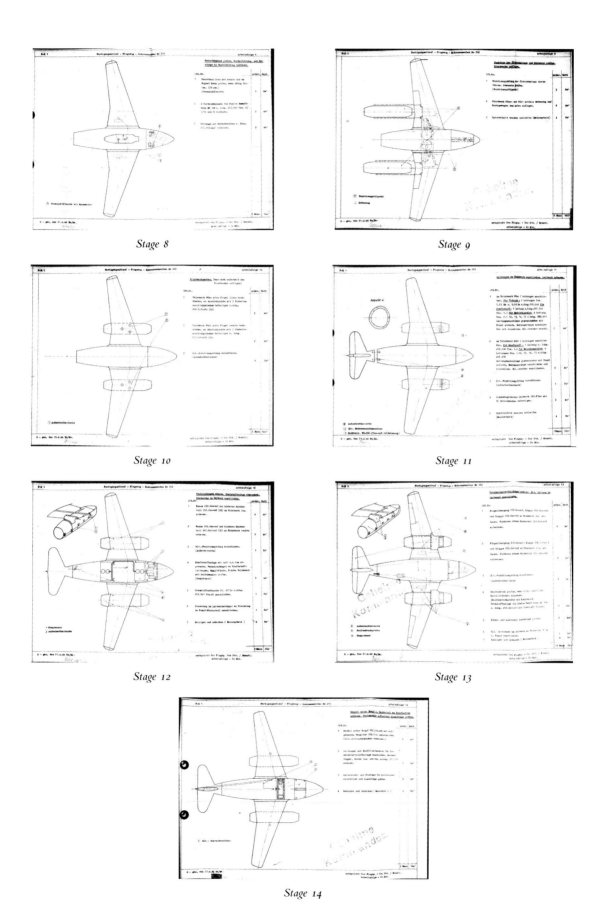

*Stage 8*

*Stage 9*

*Stage 10*

*Stage 11*

*Stage 12*

*Stage 13*

*Stage 14*

Meanwhile, at the RLM management meeting in Berlin on June 2, Günter Bock of the DVL appeared to complain about the lack of progress in making and testing wooden components for the Me 262.[35] He pointed out that no deadline had yet been given for the construction of wooden test wings for the aircraft even though "we talked repeatedly about the fact that this has to be dealt with as part of the overall planning at Messerschmitt".

Messerschmitt's representative at the meeting was Kokothaki and he pointed out that a wooden wing wouldn't work for the Me 262 because of the landing gear cut-outs. Bock retorted that the "262 has no cut-outs". The stenographer then recorded "(Contradiction)", which presumably meant Kokothaki or others had immediately shouted out: "Yes it does!"

Bock continued, unphased: "In any case, no large radiator cut-outs and for dive brakes."

Kokothaki said: "The cut-outs are big!" But Bock seemingly ignored him: "We need to get a deadline from Messerschmitt."

Vorwald, chairing the meeting, said Messerschmitt had eight days to provide a date for when wooden Me 262 wings would be ready for full series production.

Kokothaki: "The date could only be of a theoretical nature due to the unsolved problem of the wooden wing, especially the gluing!"

Vorwald: "We understand that."

Kokothaki continued to protest but was told he had until Friday, June 9, to say when the wooden wings would be ready.

The following Monday, June 5, the flight test department at Oberammergau sat down to discuss the measures necessary to get the Me 262 A-1 ready for use as a bomber.[36] These included tests to ensure that the aircraft did not top 950km/h while diving fully loaded, the expected completion date of June 12 for the Me 262's bespoke bomb rack—now known as the 'Wikingerschiff'[37]—test fitment of the new 600 litre extra fuel tank and the installation of bomb storage facilities at Lechfeld.

On June 6, 1944, as the D-Day landings were getting under way in Normandy entirely unmolested by bomb-dropping jet aircraft, the Project Office published yet another appendix to the Me 262 build description of August 10, 1943. This one was entitled 'Me 262 A1 Schnellkämpfer' or Me 262 A1 fast bomber[38]. Whether by accident or by design, almost the first word of the foreword was 'fighter': "The fighter Me 262 A-1, which is now in series production, is to be used immediately as a high-speed bomber. In the following description the performance and applications that can be achieved with the Me 262 A-1 without conversion, just by attaching the external suspension points and a simple bomb targeting system, are recorded."

Four different loadouts for the A-1 with bombs were outlined—the two with the 600 litre additional fuel tank and two without. In each case the Me 262 was assumed to have been stripped of all armour protection. 'Case I' was the standard Me 262 A-1 carrying a single 250kg bomb. 'Case II' involved the removal of two MK 108s, leaving two still in position, which freed up capacity at the nose end to carry either one 500kg bomb or two 250kg bombs. 'Case III' was the same as 'Case II' except with the 600 litre tank fitted and filled with 500 litres of fuel, and only carrying one 250kg bomb. 'Case IV' was the same as 'Case III', except the extra tank would now only be filled with 400 litres of fuel. This allowed one 500kg bomb or two 250kg bombs to be carried.

At the end of the description there was a brief mention of another configuration now being worked on by the Project Office: "For dropping bombs with the Lotfe, the possibility of accommodating a second man lying in the nose of the fuselage is being investigated. A proposal on this is made separately."

The Lotfe 7 was a bombsight developed by Carl Zeiss and commonly used on the Luftwaffe's level bombers but it required a dedicated crewman to operate. The Me 262 with 'Lotfe compartment' would be the final bomber variant of the type developed.

# 8

# Teething Pains:
# June 1944 to September 1944

HE FIRST Me 262 prototype, the V1, suffered crash damage on landing after its 95th flight on June 7, 1944. The flight test report compiled afterwards noted that "the machine (tail wheel), which was being used for Baldrian testing, broke on landing … and was partially damaged. Since the [004] A engines have been phased out, the old machine can no longer be upgraded".[1] Which is to say that it appears never to have flown again.

Baldrian appears to have been a new name for the Zwiebel electro-acoustic system—rather than being an entirely different system. Indeed, the V1's career-ending crash was by no means the end for Baldrian, with experiments continuing well into 1945 using a series of different Me 262s.

A programme was drawn up on June 8 for the airworthy test vehicles—which now included the V9, V10 and S2, plus Werk-Nr. 130015 and 130167, the latter being one of the first handful of aircraft off the new production line at Schwäbisch Hall.[2] V9 would test aileron alterations and slots; V10 would be used for directional stability testing, changes to the fin surface area, flight with bombs and hydraulics; S2 would be used to test aileron and rudder actuation, high-speed flight and fuel consumption; 130015 would test various bearings and 130167 would be used to test the seven ton take-off

weight condition as well as making flights with two 250kg bombs.

Cracking, poor adhesion and other manufacturing defects continued to be a problem in Me 262 production, with a report assessing the situation published on June 12.[3]

Between June 10 and June 16, 1944, the Luftwaffe test centre at Rechlin received its first four Me 262s, serial numbers 130018, 130163, 130168 and 130188.[4] By the end of the following week, these had been joined by a fifth machine—130172. During this time, 130163 had suffered undercarriage damage as a result of a burst tyre and both 130018 and 130168 had suffered undercarriage malfunctions.[5]

A meeting was held on June 14 at Backnang, near Daimler-Benz's Stuttgart headquarters, to discuss a new power unit known as the PTL 021 or DB 021.[6] This was effectively a Heinkel-Hirth HeS 011 turbojet used to drive a propeller as well as producing thrust via a nozzle to the rear — a turboprop. It was stated that this engine was expected to provide 1,400kg of thrust at a velocity of 720km/h and "installation is intended for the aircraft types Ju 287, Ar 234 and Me 262".

## TWO-SEAT ME 262 BOMBER
Very little effort seems to have been expended on the concept of fitting the Me 262 with Daimler-Benz 021

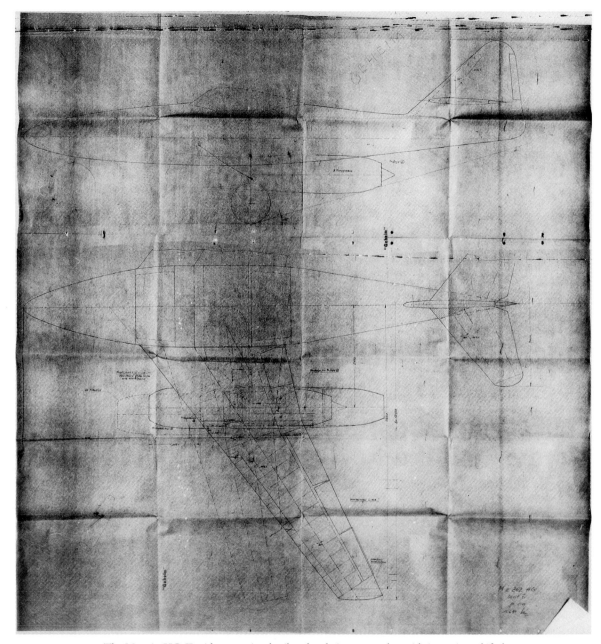

*The Me 262 HG II with conventional tail and cockpit canopy—but with its engines shifted
to the rear as per Willy Messerschmitt's instructions—dated June 15, 1944.*

turboprops. A great deal more effort, however, was spent on plans to fit the Me 262 with an effective bombsight.

Messerschmitt produced a protocol document on June 16 which called for the aircraft to be equipped with the Zeiss Ikon BZA 1 B analogue computer bombsight, modified to incorporate a telescopic vision system, and this was discussed at length during a meeting at the Rechlin test centre the following day.[7] The chief problem with the BZA was lack of capacity at the manufacturer. Zeiss was preparing to mass produce the TSA 2—another computerised bombsight designed to allow the Fw 190 to accurately launch the massive BT 1400 aerial torpedo—and it was considered that

this programme would have to be dramatically scaled back to free up capacity for the BZA. Even this would not be enough because "… if all Me 262 aircraft have to be equipped with the above-mentioned target system as standard, production capacity must be freed up elsewhere and made available for the production of BZA 1 B …"

The record of the Rechlin meeting ends with the rueful footnote: "Equipping the Me 262 with bomb sights is to be carried out within a few days according to orders. The aircraft was in the programme from the beginning as a fighter aircraft without sighting equipment."

On the same day, Messerschmitt handed over documents outlining its proposal for the Me 262 Heimatschützer III, with bolt-on rocket motor and fuel system, to the RLM's Technical Office.[8]

A two-day conference was then held at Messerschmitt's Oberammergau facility on June 19-20 to discuss the bomb sight situation.[9] According to the post-meeting report for the first day: "Efforts must be made to create a cheap periscopic sight using existing parts if possible. [Giving the pilot a] view from the underside of the fuselage initially seems appropriate for the arrangement. Oblt. Hollbeck from Rechlin reports that the Zeiss Ikon company has been commissioned to develop a design for such a periscopic sight.

"After completion of the design, the Zeiss Ikon company will immediately send its specialists to Oberammergau for installation inspection and consultation. Estimated date, June 21. On the part of Rechlin, it is pointed out that when using this simplest periscopic sight, controlled by the BZA computer, the prospects of hitting are only sufficient for the largest area targets … The uncertainty of the wind at low level also remains with this type of sighting principle … Essentially, such a device would correspond to the structure of a horizontal targeting device of the previous form. The operation of this device requires the use of both hands and thus a three-axis control for a single seat aircraft."

During the second day, "using drawings and the Me 262 mock-up, the possibilities for installing a periscope are examined again. a) Periscope with a view on the underside of the fuselage. A visual field examination by the Ob. Research Institute [Messerschmitt] shows that the field of view is unacceptably restricted by the bombs, in the event that the periscope looks out only 5cm from the underside of the fuselage.

"In view of the bombs and the visibility required, it is necessary to extend the sight about 50cm below the fuselage. In order to avoid a loss of speed, it is necessary to examine the retractability of the lower part of the scope. This increases the complexity of the structure.

"Using the mock-up and drawings, it was checked whether a simple rectilinear telescope could be placed diagonally forward through the nose of the fuselage. As a result, certain airframe changes and installation changes on the fuel tank, on the instrument panel and in other places are necessary. The total length of the telescope, according to a rough test, would be about 4m. Furthermore, the armoured discs would probably have to be omitted.

"Another possibility is giving the pilot a scope that goes straight downwards and, after deflecting twice, it is brought out on the underside of the wing. This

arrangement, however, is much more complicated than the ones mentioned above and requires an extensive optical structure.

"Drawings of the two-man cockpit with seated bomb aimer installation are shown. The mock-up should be [ready] on June 28. This version appears to bring a significant improvement compared to the arrangement where the bomb aimer lies prone."[10]

## SAUR TAKES CHARGE

Göring formalised the end of Milch's career in aviation on June 20, 1944, by ordering that Speer should take responsibility for equipping the Luftwaffe instead.[11] In practice, the formation of the Jägerstab on March 1, 1944, had seen the State Secretary rapidly lose influence on the production side but he continued to exercise full authority over development. The following day, Speer gave Milch what appears to have been an honorary position as his 'representative' and a handover period commenced which lasted until the end of July.

Since Speer himself had other concerns, Saur was now solely in charge of pushing the Me 262 forward with Knemeyer overseeing new projects and technological developments.

With this in mind, Saur chaired a meeting on June 22 where the Me 262 was the only topic up for discussion.[12] According to the non-verbatim minutes: "The Führer has ordered the Me 262 as a high-speed bomber to be brought forward and upgraded immediately and with absolute priority over all other armament projects. HDL Saur takes on this task exclusively as his personal responsibility and will ensure that now there is a change compared to the previous conditions, to achieve a real clearing up of this whole operation."

Ambitious delivery targets were set: 24 aircraft in June, 60 in July, 100 in August, 150 in September, 225 in October, 325 in November and 500 in December, with an accompanying note that Messerschmitt's own projections for what was possible "should under no circumstances be the basis for General Staff planning!"

Furthermore, "the 004 engines required for this number of units must be completed by the 15th day of the month and must have arrived at the airframe manufacturing plant during that month." On top of that a surplus of 30% in complete spare part sets and a further 30-50% in completed engines had to be delivered "for replenishment and repair".

Jumo director Walter Cambeis was appointed head of a new jet engine working committee, within the main engine production committee, to ensure that the necessary resources were focused on the 004 and also the BMW 003. His deputies would be Dr Krome for

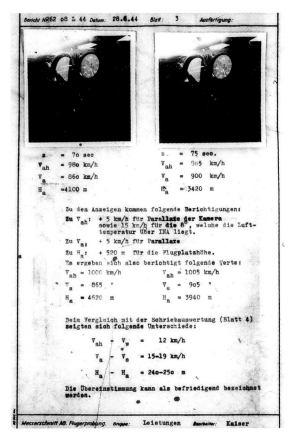

*Messerschmitt test pilot Heinz Herlitzius flew the Me 262 S2 up to 1,004km/h on June 25, 1944, setting a new unofficial world speed record. This page from the resulting report shows photographs of his instruments taken by an automatic camera in his cockpit. The dial shows 985km/h but taking various other factors into account this evidently represented a true figure of 1,004km/h.*

the Me 262 and Nauck for the Ar 234.

Extra capacity for the 004 would be achieved by transferring resources across from the Jumo 213 programme. The Ar 234 was to be the subject of a separate discussion on June 28 but Arado would get 200 Jumo 004s for testing the aircraft between September and December. From January 1945, with more Ar 234s available as bombers, more Me 262s could then be deployed as fighters because "in the end, the aim is to use the Me 262 exclusively as a fighter (see bombsight difficulties) and to cover the jet bomber sector with the Ar 234".

Any exaggeration of production numbers was "strictly forbidden! In addition to 'company information', the real values (or those estimated by the office responsible) must always be entered". Important questions for the next Me 262 meeting concerned the aircraft's tyres, brakes, fuel and the status of hollow turbine blade development for the 004.

Willy Messerschmitt, Seitz, Voigt and others sat down to discuss the experimental high-speed Me 262 HG

series on June 23.[13] Evidently it had been determined that Messerschmitt's preferred repositioning of the engines much further rearwards, with the intakes under the 35° swept back wings, was "extremely unfavourable in terms of vibration" though an intermediate solution, with the engines just moved a little further rearwards "(centre of gravity approximately on the main spar) still appears permissible in terms of vibration". Determining the best position for the engine "can only be made after the vibration calculations and static vibration tests have been completed".

During a series of dive tests to "to prove flight safety" on June 25, Messerschmitt test pilot Heinz Herlitzius managed to reach a speed of 1,004km/h in the Me 262 S2—making him the fastest man alive at that point, having fractionally topped Heini Dittmar's 1,003.67km/h record of 1941.[14] He had flown the aircraft up to 7km altitude then executed a steep dive at full throttle. An automatic camera on board had taken a photograph of his instrument panel to record his speed, confirmed by a separate DVL recording device. The report also noted that the aircraft had suffered no ill effects apart from a "slight loosening of screws".

## PROJECT STATUS

Luftwaffe test centres personnel held a meeting with Messerschmitt staff on June 28 to discuss the "open questions" concerning the Me 262.[15] The first point concerned the inclusion of bomber unit KG 51 in training at Lechfeld while the second was a list of priorities for "experimental construction". In first place, top priority, was the manufacture of 15 600-litre additional fuel tanks; second was five canopies for the pilot/seated bombardier arrangement; joint third were five Me 262 noses housing two MK 103s and two MG 151s, the installation of BMW 003 A engines and the rocket motor-in-fuselage Heimatschützer I. Languishing in fourth place, lowest priority, was Heimatschützer II with its two BMW 003 R engines.

A proposed arrangement where more ammo could be carried for the MK 108s "can be put on hold for the time being" and the Panzerflugzeug design was "currently uninteresting". The HG series and oblique firing weapons arrangements "were not discussed".

The 'development' section of the meeting was dominated by Me 262 bomber conversion work. Two ETC 504 bomb racks were ready but it was noted that "series production ETC 504 must be possible before September 1944. KdE [Luftwaffe test centres] checks the delivery situation". The next point was "bomber canopy—according to Protocol No. 34, five experimental cockpits with bombardier's seats are produced as quickly as possible". The Tarnewitz test centre, which specialised in weapons, was making a decision as to whether weapons bay heating could be omitted and "the Messerschmitt company is to conduct tests to determine how long it takes for ammunition that has cooled down to minus 30°C to warm up again". Rechlin was investigating damage caused when the aircraft touched down with its wheels stationary and was considering ways of making the wheels begin to rotate just before landing. And "a firewall between the cold and warm parts of the engine, and between the engine and the wing, is more important than a fire warning system and must be planned as a priority".

The new Mach warning system, apparently an audible alert designed and produced by Bosch "is rejected; flashing light on the instrument panel—as planned—is required". Further cockpit drop tests were to be carried out and filmed, test reports on the cabin heating system had been produced and rather ominously "in the production aircraft, the rudder proves to be insufficiently effective at low speeds, despite the high forces. Even single-engine flight is no longer possible". Quality control for the series production model aircraft would be an ongoing concern.

The ETC 504 bomb rack and two MK 103/two MG 151 gun nose reappeared in the 'manufacturing' section of the meeting and tests of the new 600-litre extra fuel tanks were required. It was stated that the Me 262's foot pedals "are to be lifted outwards so that feet do not slip off. Retrofitting [is] desired" and a self-destruct system for the engines was still wanted. The cockpit ventilation flap needed to be made "adjustable to different openings by means of a spindle (like Fw 190)".

During firing tests, some aircraft had evidently suffered wing damage from ejected empty ammo casings so "inner leading edge is tentatively reinforced with 2mm sheet metal over its entire length". There was still too much play in the aircraft's control column and the support frame for the forward fuel tank needed to be strengthened. A mudguard for the nosewheel was also a requirement "because earth is thrown into the engines" and nosewheel deflection and feedback was "finally" set at +/- 45°.

On the same day, a list was drawn up showing the planned Me 262 flight test programme. This included testing tail surfaces with internal balance compensation, different fin positions and reduced rudder deflection. Directional stability was another key area of investigation, particularly when the aircraft was carrying bombs. Measurements were to be taken with different wing slots too. High-speed flight tests would go on, as would aerobatics. Testing of the windscreen washer would also

continue—as would cabin heater, hydraulics and fuel pump tests. 'Baldrian' was on the list, as was undercarriage inspection—looking at performance when rolling over objects, deflection, forces and tyre deformation.

The Wikingerschiff bomb rack would be tried out and take-offs would be performed with an all-up weight of seven tons using booster rockets. Fuel consumption, engine settings and the extra fuel tank were also included.

The aircraft available for these tests were the 262 V9, V10, S2, S15 (presumably 130015) and S167 (which is apparently what Werk-Nr. 130167 was now being called. It would later have 'V 167' painted on it).[16] At this stage it had not yet been decided which of the five machines would be allocated for which tests.

## THE LOTFE KANZEL

The thorny question of exactly how the Me 262 could be made drop its bombs accurately onto a target was addressed at one of the last RLM management meetings chaired by Milch, on June 30.[17]

Otmar Schürfeld, an engineer from the Rechlin test centre, said: "The 262 was converted from a fighter to a bomber within a short time and was supposed to get a bombsight. Various proposals have been discussed in Rechlin and within the General Staff. The following picture emerges: assuming that the airframe is not changed, the pilot's field of vision remains eight degrees. With this, targets can be viewed from up to a maximum altitude of 3,000m.

"Mr Marienfeld [the Inspector of Bombers] requested bombing altitudes of 3,000-10,000m. In this area we can't get by with the eight degrees. The only suggestion that remains is to build a new periscope that provides a view downwards. It has been tried. It turned out that it has a length of 2.2m with a diameter of 15cm and a weight of 50kg. It would take five to six months to produce the first sample."

He said the second possibility was "the installation of a Lotfe bombsight and thus a second man in the aircraft. There were three proposals for this. The first is a horizontal arrangement, which requires relatively little effort, a slight conversion of the fuselage nose. The second is a seated arrangement, everything remains as before, only with a view downwards. The third solution, which was approved, is to move the nosewheel to the left. A mock-up will be created which will be ready to view in eight days."

To accompany this arrangement, Marienfeld had ordered the procurement of the new periscope, which was to have visibility from zero to 50-degrees at speeds of between 200km/h and 1,000km/h. Galland, meanwhile, had decided that the best interim solution was the arrangement with the second seated crewman equipped with a Lotfe bombsight previously discussed by Messerschmitt and the Luftwaffe test centres.

Petersen seemed surprised: "Did the Inspector of Fighters opt for the Lotfe? The normal fighter has the Revi [gunsight]. This cannot be a transitional solution. The Lofte requires a whole new cockpit."

Staff engineer Walter Feucht said: "I have to say that, according to Messerschmitt, the reconstruction of the cockpit would take at least six months. There is only the version with the prone observer. In relation to the seated observer arrangement, this requires a workload of 1:10. It could come in two months. But this version is rejected by Herr Marienfeld. He wants the seated observer arrangement."

Milch: "We ask for a written decision from the Inspector of Bombers."

Holbeck: "I would like to make brief comments on this question. The desire for a bombsight that is operated by the pilot alone is as old as throwing bombs in general. A satisfactory solution has not yet been found. It is not because the departments concerned or the industry are incapable, but because of the difficulty of the problem, problems of physics, throwing technology and measuring technology … It has to be considered whether the requirement to install a Lotfe really makes sense."

Von Lossberg agreed, pointing out that the chosen solution of a periscope-type bombsight was awkward and impractical: "Looking through a telescope is practically quite impossible; because that means that the pilot first has to put his machine on its side in order to see anything down below him at all, that he then has to straighten the machine again to see: how does my target appear in the periscope?"

It would be much more sensible, he thought, to "seriously consider whether you should not do the cheaper installation of the horizontal bomb aimer".

Petersen: "It's very problematic."

Von Lossberg: "My personal opinion is that the 262 is not suitable as a bomber, that the 234 is there for that and that the 262 is much more suitable as a fighter. If you want to go on the jet bomber, you have to increase the 234 accordingly."

Milch: "But the number of units is not coming as quick as for the 262, and there is the clear Führer order."

Von Lossberg: "The 262 has two options. She can do the turnip method close to the ground, especially because she arrives quietly and could make very nice surprise attacks. The depth of penetration is limited, namely the airfields must be so close to the front that in the current situation the machine is destroyed on the ground before it can be used. The second possibility, to throw from a great height, is practically only possible on very substantial surface targets.

"Any intervention in the ground combat situation from heights above 2,000m is practically impossible, especially with a machine that does not have a full vision canopy, because ground targets are hardly recognised even without today's camouflage from 2,000m. 2,000m is the limit where I can see trucks below. All that remains is to fight against area targets from great heights … which is again very problematic for this machine."

Petersen: "So the decision to march on the installation of the Lotfe is clear for the bomber."

Von Lossberg said that using the periscope meant a much longer approach run to the target.

Milch: "In addition, during that whole time he [the pilot] has no opportunity to take care of defences and such questions … [But] I would like to state once again that the Führer's demands are that the 262 initially only comes as a high-speed bomber. Any use as a fighter is initially prohibited by the Führer. He says: the tests as a fighter can continue, but the use as a high-speed bomber must not be hindered by this. The Führer has further demanded: it should be flown and dropped at 3,000m altitude outside of the light flak. The question is: what approximately can we achieve with provisional measures?"

Von Lossberg pointed out that with the standard Revi gunsight it was only possible to aim bombs up to 2,000m.

Milch: "The Führer thinks of it this way—and he was not contradicted in the discussions with the Reichsmarschall either—that the machine flies horizontally at an altitude of 3,000m and simply drops its bombs into the area below."

Von Lossberg said this meant that the pilot would have no real idea where his bombs were falling. He would simply fly to a point and let them drop.

Petersen: "There is only the possibility with Revi that he gives up some altitude and goes lower, going down below 1,500m. Then he can hit quite a bit. At the speed he can do that; the lighter flak doesn't do much there."

Von Lossberg said that using the Revi was likely to result in altitude errors and no account could be taken of wind strength or direction, stating: "This is a very crude process."

Petersen: "The Führer said: he renounces pin-point accuracy; he only values area bombing goals."

Milch: "Although he thinks that landings can be hit on the coasts."

The State Secretary then wondered: "Isn't there any way to have a section of the aircraft's underside that is glazed so that the pilot can see out of this window section, even if he is flying horizontally at an altitude of 3,000m?"

*The Luftwaffe's standard ETC 503 bomb rack with Messerschmitt adaptor fitted to an Me 262.*

*The new 'Wikingerschiff' bomb rack attached to an Me 262.*

Knemeyer: "It doesn't do him any good just to throw the bomb. A view downwards is possible; but it doesn't do anything for the bombing."

Holbeck: "These questions have been investigated in several meetings with a view to the urgency of the Führer's request and a quick solution, and it has been found that a window the size of a postcard is currently being attached to the pressure-tight tub below the rudder controls for the scouts to use. It doesn't offer any forward view because the entire space is filled up to 900 litres by the fuel tank, etc. This is more unfavourable with this machine than with any other."

Von Lossberg: "The steeply downward window is of no use to him [the Me 262 bomber's pilot]."

Milch: "What if you give him anything in the field of television equipment?"

Holbeck: "The television has been examined. A complete system was built and flown at Zeiss Ikon. You could see individual trucks and other vehicles from a height of 1,000m. It is entirely possible to install such a small-screen remote system but the effort is tremendously high ... the disadvantage is that the pilot has to constantly look at the television picture, which is not very bright."

He went on to say that the whole problem could be solved by simply putting the bomb aimer, lying prone, in the nose.

Knemeyer: "Basically! But now Rechlin is saying that the space in this machine is so tight that the man lies completely pressed."

Blecher: "I lay there in the space and noticed that you lie very tightly, that your back has 2-3cm free and that you can only turn around a little when you have pushed yourself back. If you turn your head around a little you bump it. The man no longer has freedom of movement. This is not a happy solution because it is too tight. If you build wider, you lose a lot of travel that you cannot accept."

Knemeyer said that Blecher himself was "incredibly big and broad".

After some further discussion, von Lossberg said that any form of bomb aiming device might be a waste of time since "I am of the opinion that in six months the use of the 262 as a bomber will be stopped again and the machine used as a fighter."

He went on to say: "I would suggest that this lying prone arrangement be investigated further."

Milch: "Absolutely!"

Von Lossberg: "A little bit improved and maybe limited to smaller people."

Milch: "One should do the lying thing in such a way that one loses as little aerodynamically as possible, but can still accommodate the man, taking smaller people into consideration in terms of figure."

Eick: "The advantage of the horizontal arrangement is that you can take two bombs with you."

Milch: "That seems to me to be the only possibility; the other comes too late. So we want the lying arrangement."

Galland's representative, unnamed by the stenographer, protested: "The Inspector of Fighters attaches great importance to the seated arrangement."

Milch: "He won't get that in the foreseeable future; that takes over a year before the first machine can come."

After another protest, Milch said: "It's no use. After that comes the 234 in large numbers. When she is there, the Führer agrees that the 262 will be a fighter. In a year, when it starts coming out, the 234 will be there in sufficient quantity. The seated arrangement requires the construction of a new machine. We want to be clear about that."

Galland's representative acknowledged that the prone bomb aimer arrangement was at least aerodynamically favourable.

*Wikingerschiff bomb rack as viewed from the underside.*

Milch: "I think so too. In my opinion, it is best to investigate the lying arrangement as quickly as possible and bring it into a form that is tolerable on both sides, although it must be accepted that the bomb aimer is a small, thin guy."

He asked that the decision to reject the seated bombardier design and to further develop the prone position bombardier design—which would later become known as the 'Lotfe kanzel'—be explained to Marienfeld

There was some good news on the engine front the following day, when a meeting of the Jägerstab heard that Jumo had exceeded its production target for the 004 by more than 20%—producing 121 engines against a June target of 100.[18] The total number of Me 262s accepted by the Luftwaffe in June 1944 was 33—well ahead of the target number, 24, set by Saur. This brought total airframes accepted up to 60.[19]

At Messerschmitt, on the same day, it was reported that the company's 'performance group' had produced some numbers on the Me 262 with swept back wings.[20] Their report concluded: "The current Me 262 can be made 15km/h faster by sweeping the wing and the tail unit, by improving the cabin and by retaining the current engine nacelle position.

"If relocating the nacelles eliminates the Mach influence up to Mach 0.77, a further increase in speed of 25km/h would be achieved. We draw your attention to the fact that the above-mentioned possibilities for improvement have been determined on the basis of wind tunnel measurements and must first be confirmed by flight tests."

## BOMB RACK WOES

"Important points" for Messerschmitt's flight test department were discussed on July 3, mostly echoing what had previously been said at the end of June.[21] There was to be a delay in making a reinforced suspension strut for the nosewheel because the design documents had "accidentally stayed for several weeks" before being rediscovered and sent to the manufacturers. The main gear suspension was also being strengthened and this work was progressing but had not yet been completed. A nosewheel mudguard was being worked on too.

A report on take-off distances with different bomb loads was produced on July 4—tests using Werk-Nr. 130167 showing that with a weight of 5.9 tons the aircraft needed 715m of concrete runway to take off. With booster rockets this was reduced to 460m. At seven tons, however, a 1,430m run was needed, or 900m with boosters.

During a Jägerstab meeting on July 6,[22] Saur reiterated the planned production numbers for the Me 262 but admitted that "we are considerably behind with this machine in the fourth month". On the same day Messerschmitt produced Protokoll Nr. 35, which redefined the Me 262 A-2. Formerly, this designation had been reserved for a Jumo 004 C-powered fighter-bomber. Now it would be a 'Blitzbomber' equipped with two rather than four MK 108s, a Revi 16 D gunsight and a pair of factory-fitted ETC 503 bomb racks.[23] This loosely corresponded with the 'Case II' configuration outlined in Messerschmitt's 'Me 262 A1 Schnellkämpfer' report of June 6 (see Chapter 7). The Me 262 A-3 would be the pure bomber fitted with the prone bomb aimer nose, as chosen over the two-seat bomber during the RLM meeting on June 30. It would appear that the A-4 unarmed reconnaissance variant was probably given that designation at this time too.

There were therefore now a total of seven approved Me 262 variants: A-1 Jäger, A-2 Blitzbomber, A-3 Schnellstbomber,[24] A-4 Aufklärer, B-1 Schulflugzeug, C-1 Heimatschützer I and D-1 Heimatschützer II.

By the end of the first week of July, a new specification for a single-jet fighter to replace the Me 262 had been issued by the RLM.[25] It was to be powered by either an HeS 011 or a Jumo 004 C and the first prototype had to be ready to fly by March 1, 1945. The specification was certainly sent to Focke-Wulf and may

*Top view of a Wikingerschiff bomb rack showing its attachment fittings.*

*A Wikingerschiff on the underside of an Me 262 with bomb attached.*

even have been sent to Heinkel during mid- to late-June.[26] Messerschmitt is also believed to have received it.

The relative merits of three different bomb carriage and release systems for the Me 262 were reviewed in a report published by Messerschmitt on July 9.[27] These were the 'fuselage side' release system, the Wikingerschiff and the ETC 503 with Messerschmitt adaptor.

The first of these was described as an "emergency system" that involved running a cable down the side of the aircraft from the cockpit to the bomb rack—bypassing any internal wiring or perhaps substituting for wiring that had not been installed. Either bomb rack could be fitted and actuated using this primitive method, but it suffered numerous drawbacks. Without the proper electronic connections it was impossible to tell whether the bomb racks were securely fastened to the correct fittings without "trying to remove the rack by shaking it". And if the racks were not installed in the correct order—right one first, then the left—the left one could fall out while the right one was being fitted. And when ETC 503 racks were used, if the electrical system failed to arm the bombs before they were jettisoned, the racks and the unarmed bombs would fall away together.

There were serious problems with the racks and the aircraft themselves too. According to the report: "The fuselage-side release mechanism showed difficulties in fitting the bomb racks supplied (both types) due to structural deviations of the airframe fittings and the bomb rack fittings. It is essential that gauges are provided in the individual production sites for the acceptance of the airframes and the bomb racks. Adjustment work by the troops leads to incorrect working of the latching."

Due to "manufacturing inaccuracies", it was impossible to fit standard 250kg or 500kg bombs to Messerschmitt's Wikingerschiff rack. All 18 racks delivered suffered from the same range of defects, though to varying degrees.

The situation wasn't much better with the ETC 503—a standard Luftwaffe item—because, having been designed for attachment to the underside of wings, it required an adaptor in order to fit the curve of the Me 262's fuselage. And the way in which the wooden adaptors supplied by Oberammergau had been constructed meant that they did not quite fit. Recesses had to be carved into them so that the necessary cables could be accommodated.

Meanwhile, one Me 262 had been converted to a reconnaissance configuration at Leipheim—Werk-Nr. 170006.[28] This was evidently delivered to Lechfeld for "examination of flight characteristics" on July 9 having already been rejected by the Luftwaffe BAL[29] "because the properties were not correct, especially the behaviour around the transverse axis". The aircraft was not destined to become a test mule though and had evidently been prepared outside the usual Messerschmitt/Lechfeld development process. On this occasion, Lechfeld's expert testers were being used as consultants only.

Wendel flew 170006 and discovered that "the machine in the condition in which it was delivered (two cameras, without weapons, 600 litre tank empty) was on the limit of dynamic stability". This was cured by adjusting the rudder and trim tab. There were bulged fairings over the camera positions on the nose and the Lechfeld team tested the aircraft by removing the camera nose and fitting a regular nose with ballast in its place. This made no difference in the aircraft's flight characteristics up to around 850km/h. Three test flights had been made up to July 19.[30]

The following day, Wendel produced his own flight test report on the aircraft: "Task: The aircraft was delivered here to check the flight characteristics. The main objection was that the elevator forces were too low. Condition of the aircraft: reconnaissance version with two 70x30 cameras in the fuselage nose, no weapons, no ballast, 600 litre additional fuel tank, no armour. Sheet metal elevator and rudder."

Testing did not proceed entirely smoothly, with Wendel noting: "During the first attempt to take off, the additional [fuel] tank was accidentally filled up ... The aircraft rolled backwards after 10m of taxiing. The fuselage [rear] end and the rudder were damaged. A start with [the 600 litre tank] more than 32% [full] is impossible. Then the 600 litre tank was emptied."

It was determined that filling the rear tank had changed the centre of gravity to 37%, completely over-balancing the aircraft. Wendel also complained that the aircraft appeared to have abnormal stability behaviour: "If the centre of gravity specified by Mr Keie is correct [at 26.6%] (determined by weighing), then the stability behaviour has changed significantly compared to the prototype and first series aircraft, or there are major differences in the series that are still inexplicable. Further investigations on several aircraft must be made.

"The dynamic instability around the vertical axis comes from the trim tab. Trials on other machines have shown that metal rudders are overbalanced in the tab. The tab must by no means be thicker than the rudders and the tab's axis of rotation must also be shifted to the rear by riveting on a sheet metal strip 30-40mm deep. Other complaints: 1) The fuel extraction is very uneven. It is very likely that a valve battery is leaking. 2) The trailing edge of the right middle leading edge is deformed."

Werk-Nr. 170006 would leave Lechfeld shortly thereafter, never to return, having been delivered to the Luftwaffe.

## NIGHT OPERATIONS

Preparations were made at Oberammergau on July 12 for a Messerschmitt delegation to visit the Blohm & Voss factory at Wenzendorf on July 18-19 to check on progress being made on the Me 262 B-1 trainer conversion.[31] It had been agreed beforehand that Blohm & Voss would do all the relevant testing once each aircraft was ready, based on a programme drawn up by the Rechlin test centre, but the acceptance test would be performed by a pilot from Leipheim.

Five days later, on July 17, Werk-Nr. 130015 was used in tests to assess the amount of light emitted by jet engines at various speeds at night "for eventual night operations".[32] This is the earliest known evidence that a night-fighter version of the aircraft was now seriously being considered. These experiments found that "the speed at which the strongest light is seen from behind was found to be at full throttle, 8,800rpm. At this speed, a faint glimmer can be seen from behind

from 900m. Close up you can see a roughly 2m long light. In addition, strong flying sparks can be observed. The thruster inside glows bright red. The cone dark red. When observing from a distance of 50m, the brightest fire cannot be seen directly from behind, in this case you can only see the glowing cone, but at an angle of 10-30° in the longitudinal direction you can see the bright red thruster inside. No light is visible from the front. There is no reflection on the cabin window from the glowing cone".

In other words, the Me 262 would not stick out like a sore thumb in the night sky—it would be acceptable as a night fighter. Had the engine exhausts appeared overly bright, the concept would likely have ended here.

The following day, representatives of the RLM, the Luftwaffe's Werneuchen test centre for radio and radar equipment, Telefunken and Siemens met with five Messerschmitt engineers at the company's Oberammergau facility to discuss the installation of radar systems aboard the Me 262.[33] It was stated that "the most urgent task for the installation of radio measuring devices in the Me 262 is the installation of search devices".

It was envisioned that these would be the FuG 218 G and the Lichtenstein SN 2/3 and a variety of possible antenna configurations were outlined. Early on, it was decided that while wing antennas were being looked on favourably for other aircraft, the Me 262's wing depth was probably too small for such an installation. Another possibility was the use of a 1m diameter Berlin antenna when the Me 262 was used against shipping, however "the cost in terms of weight is ... considerable, it amounts to about 250kg".

The Me 262 S2 was destroyed during a bombing raid at Lechfeld on July 19 but at least two factory-finished Me 262 A-2s, Werk-Nr. 170003 and 170004, had been completed by July 21, when they were both weighed to establish basic load data for the type.[34]

## HIGH-SPEED DEVELOPMENTS

During a meeting with Willy Messerschmitt on July 24,[35] Voigt noted that "Prof. Messerschmitt wishes for a lively exchange of experience or liaison service with the DVL and other bodies dealing with high-speed research. (The reason for this was a report that was submitted, which contained measurements from the year 1942, which have only now become known)." Voigt was to travel to Berlin and make the necessary arrangements for this 'lively exchange'.

Perhaps both Messerschmitt and Voigt had forgotten their own preoccupation with other matters during 1942—and also the fact that reports on high-speed research arriving at the Messerschmitt company during

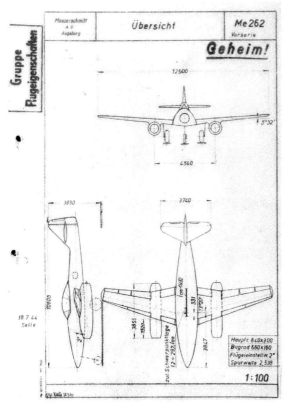

*General arrangement view of the production
model Me 262 as of July 18, 1944.*

this period from the DVL and elsewhere had largely
been funnelled into Alexander Lippisch's Abteilung L,
which Messerschmitt had then disbanded.

In addition, Voigt recorded: "Prof. Messerschmitt asks
to investigate immediately how the engine nacelles
in connection with the swept wings can be accommodated in an aerodynamically optimal manner. He
suggests arranging the engines at the root of the wing,
built into the wing." Forward swept wings for the Me
262 were also to be examined: "A rotation of the outer
wing beyond the engines to reverse the sweep is to be
investigated, but will probably not be an option for the
time being."

During a ground run on July 25, the Me 262 V3's right
engine caught fire. This was not a particularly unusual
occurrence but "incorrect operation of the stop lever
by the Jumo mechanic resulted in constant injection,
so that the fire could only be extinguished after severe
damage to the wing skin".[36] This was enough to put
the aircraft out of action while repair work took place.

A day later, on the 26th, it was confirmed in a memo
that the DVL was not in fact hiding any further useful
aerodynamics test results from Messerschmitt and the
idea of a 'lively exchange' was dropped.[37] The same
memo addressed the question of the best tail fin arrangement for the HG series aircraft: "A more favourable

arrangement of the tail unit should … be implemented
immediately, a V-tail unit appears to be the most appropriate. This should be designed immediately and go into
construction. (According to H. Prof. Messerschmitt,
construction capacity should be available for this at the
moment.)"

From the end of July onwards, there would be
no further mentions of the 004 C jet engine from
Jumo—the design having evidently been cancelled. Now
all hopes were pinned on the HeS 011 as the primary
propulsion system for the Luftwaffe's next-generation jet
fighters, with the much larger Jumo 012 being developed
for high-altitude work.

## TSA 2 COMPUTER

During early July, it was noted that the Luftwaffe test
centre at Rechlin had been testing the first pair of series
production model TSA 2 units in Fw 190 fighters and
it was further noted that 18 more TSA 2s were due
to arrive imminently.[38] The TSA 2 electronic targeting
computer incorporated both a gyroscope and an autopilot and was relatively straightforward to operate. The
pilot would identify a target using his standard Revi 16b
gunsight, set the autopilot, then fly straight towards the
target for 20 seconds. The computer would calculate
speed, altitude and flight path then sound a tone in the
pilot's earphones. The pilot would then push the bomb
release and pull up immediately. The TSA unit would
automatically release the bomb at the appropriate time
during this manoeuvre.

This new gadget had initially been rejected for the Me
262 because it was only calibrated for use up to 700km/h
and altitudes of between 0-2,000m, whereas Göring had
ordered that the Me 262 had to drop its bombs from
above 3,000m. These details appear in a telegram[39] sent
to Rechlin by the Luftwaffe high command on July 18
and in the same message it is stated that "KG 51 must
immediately stop the installation of a TSA 2 in the
Me 262, which it intends to do without permission, in
accordance with the Reichsmarschall's order of 9.7.44".
The test centre staff were, however, "asked to immediately carry out an installation study, measurement and
testing of the TSA 2 useable up to 1,000km/h in the
Me 262".

By the end of the month, one of the 18 new TSA 2s
delivered to Rechlin—presumably recalibrated for use at
speeds of up to 1,000km/h—had been fitted to Me 262
Werk-Nr. 130164, the work having been carried out at
Rechlin, based on a sketch provided by Messerschmitt,
under the supervision of Seitz[40] and monitored by a
team from Zeiss led by a Dr Schneider.

The computer itself sat in the aircraft's rear fuselage,

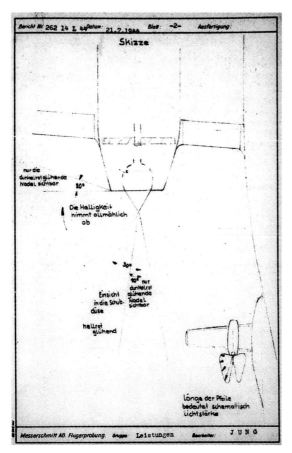

*Jet exhaust visibility in darkness was an important consideration when deciding whether the Me 262 could be used as a night fighter. This sketch was produced for a report following flight trials with Werk-Nr. 130015 on July 17, 1944.*

its presence there altering the aircraft's centre of gravity by 1.5%, linked to new control panel in the cockpit. Evidently the system was rather power-hungry since the Me 262's standard pair of 2,000W generators "are not enough … they were removed and replaced with 3,000W generators". It was fortunate that Jumo had foreseen this eventuality back in May 1943 and ensured that every Me 262 was built with a system capable of handling these higher capacity units without further modification.

Fitting TSA 2 also required the Me 262's standard pitot tube to be lengthened by 30cm "angled downwards and positioned parallel to the longitudinal axis of the fuselage". It was acknowledged that the computer would also have a detrimental effect on the aircraft's compass, being positioned in its immediate vicinity. The magnetic field generated when TSA 2 was switched on would cause the needle to move, giving a false reading.

At an RLM meeting on July 27,[41] it was confirmed that "for the two-seater version of the Me 262, an estimated 600 Lotfe 7 H will be procured. The start of the two seat production is envisaged with 10 aircraft

in November 1944". When it came to "immediate equipping of the Me 262 going to the front with TSA 2 … planning: currently a maximum of 150 units per month. If the outcome of the testing is good (decision in about 1-2 months) another decision as to whether to increase [TSA 2 installation] to two thirds of the series version Me 262 [will be made].

In addition to the 150 TSA 2s for Me 262s, a further 600 would be supplied for use with Fw 190s. But "if deployment over the next few months is not sufficient for Me 262 … [we will] cut back on deployment for Fw 190, so that the Me 262 can be equipped 100%".

## SE 4 ACTION
August 1 saw the launch of the Chef der Technischen Luftrüstung (Chef TLR for short) under Oberst Ulrich Diesing—previously Göring's adjutant. This reformed the remains of Milch's Generalluftzeugmeister organisation within the RLM and would now be responsible for aircraft design, development and testing. It would answer to the Oberkommando der Luftwaffe (OKL), the Luftwaffe high command.

Among the changes made was the appointment of former Luftwaffe chief engineer Roluf Lucht, who had caused chaos within the aviation industry with his suggestion to remove Willy Messerschmitt from his position at his own company back in April 1942, to Speer's staff with responsibility for "immediate measures".[42]

Decision-making power remained with Speer's ministry but that authority would be delegated to a new committee of technical specialists, the Entwicklungshauptkommission Flugzeuge (EHK) or Main Development Commission for Aircraft, from September 15. From November, this would be chaired by Lucht.[43]

At Saur's Rüstingsstab meeting on August 2 it was reported that there were internal disagreements between Messerschmitt's Augsburg and Regensburg plants regarding Me 262 work.[44] Saur said he had been sent letters of complaint but would be sending them all back unanswered: "I said yesterday: don't bother me with any rubbish. If Regensburg and Augsburg do not get along, then I ask you not to be involved. I have five letters in the folder … It is best to simply send it back, not to edit it at all, to put a stamp on it: only matters of importance to the war effort are dealt with."

Dr Heyne, director for aviation equipment, complained that he was struggling to maintain the Me 262 supply lines because he was being stripped of staff by the latest conscription initiative—SE 4. He said he had "suffered a not inconsiderable loss of people … but that cannot be changed; I have to get over it".

Thanks to the S2's destruction and the V3's engine

*Mock-up of the Heinkel-Hirth HeS 011 jet engine. When the Jumo 004 C fell by the wayside,
all hopes for future performance enhancements rested on this powerplant.*

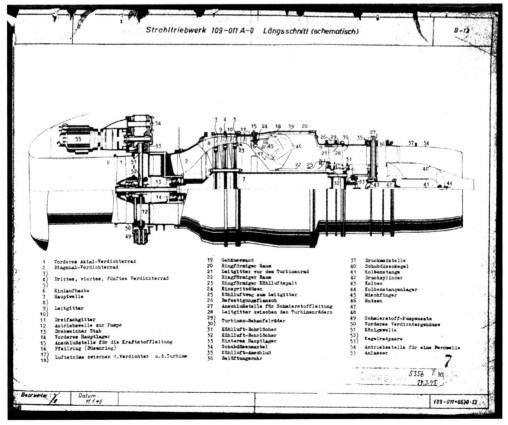

*Diagram from 1945 showing the different components of the HeS 011.*

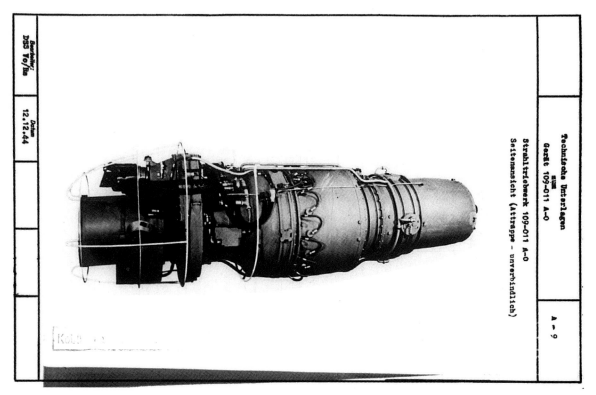

*Side view of the HeS 011 mock-up.*

fire, between July 20 and August 2 there had been just three designated Me 262 prototypes flying—V10, which had been used for bombing trials, 130015, which had been undertaking high-speed flight tests and 130167, which had been primarily used for undercarriage experiments.[45] However, the flight test department was now also able to 'borrow' aircraft assigned to Luftwaffe units for supplemental testing.

Werk-Nr. 170003, retained after being weighed, was used for directional stability investigations which focused on its sheet metal rudder and tailplanes. According to the report for this period: "The stability around the vertical axis is still not quite right on machines with sheet metal rudders."

Various trial and error methods had been used in seeking some improvement—such as reducing the amount of movement possible in the rudder and thinning its trailing edge but there had been little change. And "on a flight with W.Nr. 170003, the machine made violent vibrations around the vertical axis, so that it could not be flown over 300km/h. The cause was a missing ball bearing in the drive lever on the compensating rudder, so the trim tab had around 30mm of play."

Lateral stability—the tendency to roll—was also worse in aircraft with sheet metal covered elevators, which in "machines used as bombers ... had a very unfavourable effect". Perhaps surprisingly, "replacing a sheet metal-covered elevator with one with fabric

covering actually resulted in an improvement in the stability behaviour".

The total number of Me 262s accepted by the Luftwaffe in July 1944 was 71—11 more than Saur's target for the month—bringing the total number of airframes accepted up to 131.[46]

## LOW BUILD QUALITY

From August 3-6, V10 was used for windscreen washer tests. These showed that the aircraft's starter fuel pump was sufficient for squirting the armoured windscreen pane from take-off up to 2,000m but after that the pressure it supplied fell and a hand pump became necessary. These tests came to an abrupt end on the 6th when the aircraft suffered a mainwheel tyre blowout on landing. After 300m of taxiing, it swerved off the runway to the right and then the starboard mainwheel strut collapsed, followed by the port. It ended up with "severe deformation of the wing at the landing gear connection point" on both sides.[47] Initially, V10 appears to have been written off, but the damage would later be repaired.

Two new aircraft were now assigned to prototype work—170056 and 170079—and V9 was back in action conducting take-off and landing tests after an extended period of inactivity. While 170056 would join the programme immediately, 170079's participation was delayed by the installation of a Baldrian system.

Work on assessing the root cause of the directional

*The TSA 2 instrument panel. Two small cameras which were not part of the standard TSA setup can be seen attached to it in this photo, which comes from a Rechlin report dated October 2, 1944.*

*Lights associated with the TSA system.*

*The TSA quick activation button and main switch.*

stability issues continued, with attention focusing on the rudder, and 130015 took over from the S2 in high-speed testing up to 1,000km/h as well as trials of changes to the control column which would allow more force to be exerted by the pilot. Apparently "the 1000km/h was reached only with great difficulty because the machine could hardly be kept level at high speed".

Another aircraft, 130180, was temporarily borrowed from the Luftwaffe to test throttle setting at various altitudes after a report filed by Major Wolfgang Schenck[48] on the poor performance of his personal aircraft, Me 262 A-2 Werk-Nr. 170016. Schenck reported that its "speed is 690km/h in operational condition at 4km (the drag of a rocket that has failed to detach is taken into account, according to the estimate) [which] is very low".

It was noted that new middle and rear cockpit canopy sections installed on an aircraft being operated by the Luftwaffe's Me 262 test unit, Werk-Nr. 130017, had suddenly detached and blow away during a flight at around 780km/h. It was speculated that there was "insufficient engagement of the sprung pin connection to the upper fuselage" and that "this problem has already been found on several series production aircraft".

Furthermore, Luftwaffe test unit reports from August 10 stated that on two other aircraft—170041 and 170059—the nosewheel had got stuck part-way through retraction because the nosewheel door closed too soon. This had, naturally, also damaged the nosewheel door itself. The defect was traced to a screw being tightened too much and "since the same mistakes are being repeated on the front line, despite all the technical information, a general solution is necessary. The remedy should be the installation of a spacer tube".

Two more Luftwaffe aircraft had suffered serious problems with their booster rockets. During take-off one of 170042's rockets broke loose, entered the aircraft's left mainwheel undercarriage well, penetrated the cockpit tub and damaged the bank of controls to the pilot's left. The landing gear then retracted of its own accord and the pilot was forced to make a belly landing, tearing the right engine out of the wing. It was thought that "the cause may be traced back to the cable pull for triggering the booster rockets being too tight. It is suspected that the installation of the 600 litre additional tank caused the cable to be deflected and thus seated more tautly. Because of this, the ratchet was triggered prematurely by vibration when starting. Further investigations are being carried out".

With 170048, the right front booster rocket suspension plate had been completely torn away along with the rocket that had been attached to it. This apparently was a recurrent problem and reinforcement of the attachment point was to be carried out "as a matter of urgency".

During this same period, August 3-14, minor

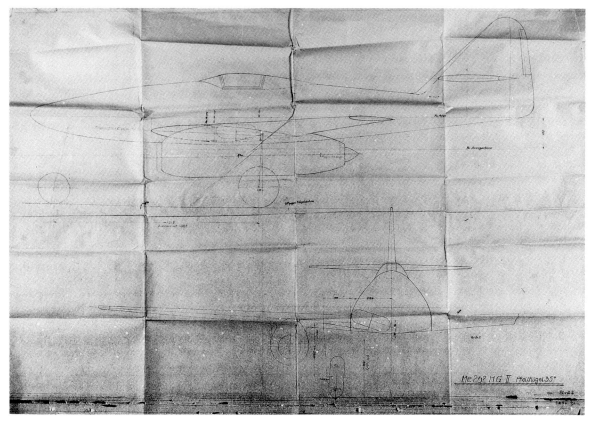

*Front and side views of the Me 262 HG II from August 1, 1944. Now the deepened fin is shown as well as the lowered cockpit canopy. The engines have been restored to a more central position.*

experiments taking place with the dedicated prototypes included the installation of a 'dirt scraper' for the nose-wheel type of 130167; new reprofiled engine nacelles, sheet metal elevators and shortened fin cap/rudder on 170056; a new adjustable control column on 130015, and an experimental firewall on the right engine of V9.

A preliminary specification for a new piston-engined bad weather day and night fighter was issued by the Chef TLR on August 4.[49] This called for a pressure cabin, wing de-icing and nosewheel undercarriage arrangement. Top speed was to be 800km/h "with additional turbojet about 60 to 80km higher speed desired". Minimum ceiling was 13km but 15km with exhaust gas turbocharger was desirable. Endurance had to be four and a half hours at full throttle. By comparison, the Focke-Wulf Ta 154's top speed was 635km/h, while the Heinkel He 219 could manage 670km/h. A crew of three was needed and armament was three MK 103s or MK 108s with Lichtenstein SN-2 target intercept radar. A further two MG 213s or two MG 151s would need to be carried in a remote-controlled turret. Carrying two 500kg bombs had to be possible too.

Clearly, meeting this specification with a piston-engined aircraft was going to be a tall order. The Me 262 could manage 800km/h and could be fitted with a pressure cabin and de-icing. It already had a nosewheel configuration and four MK 108s too—but adding a third crewman would be a challenge, as would cramming in the necessary electronics, turreted armament and sufficient fuel to get anywhere near the required endurance. Nevertheless, it is clear that the jet fighter was being seriously considered for this role.

The following day, August 5, a meeting of the Special Commission for Radio Measurement Technology, part of the Main Commission for Electric Engineering, discussed the need for low drag radar antenna on the Me 262.[50] The Messerschmitt company had proposed a series of tests with different antenna forms at the LFA's high speed wind tunnel in Braunschweig since "the circular cross-section [antenna] is unsuitable because of the great drag [it produces] both in terms of flight performance and in terms of the static strength of the rods". Evidently the best form for the antenna rods was thought to be "profile shapes with a thick, blunt trailing edge".

The company was also planning to perform "flight tests on an Me 262 with regard to the flutter behaviour of the antenna rods". Initially, individual test rods would be "attached to a harmless place on the outer wing". Tests of antenna installed within the cockpit canopy

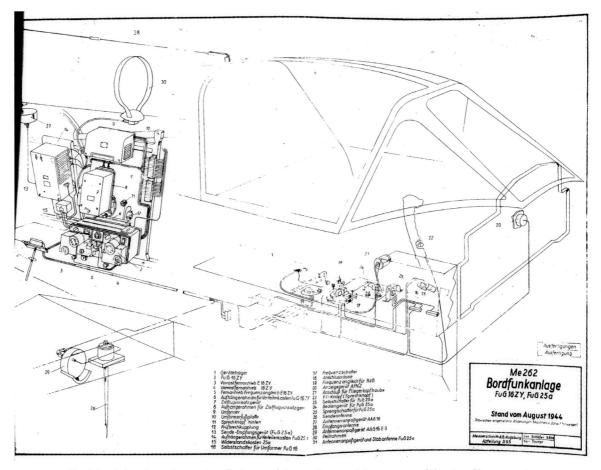

The following labels appear in the diagram legend:

| | |
|---|---|
| 1 Geräteträger | 17 Frequenzschalter |
| 2 FuG 16 ZY | 18 Anschlussdose |
| 3 Vorrastfernantrieb E 16 ZY | 19 Frequenzangleich für BzB |
| 4 Vorrastfernantrieb 16 ZY | 20 Anzeigegerät AFNZ |
| 5 Fernantrieb Frequenzangleich E 16 ZY | 21 Anschluß für Fliegerkopfhaube |
| 6 Aufhängerahmen für Verteilerkasten FuG 16 ZY | 22 FT-Knopf (Sprechknopf) |
| 7 Zielflugvorsatzgerät | 23 Selbstschalter für FuG 25a |
| 8 Aufhängerahmen für Zielflugvorsatzgerät | 24 Bediengerät für FuG 25a |
| 9 Umformer | 25 Sprengschalter für FuG 25a |
| 10 Umformerfußplatte | 26 Sendeantenne |
| 11 Sprechknopf hinten | 27 Antennenanpaßgerät AA 6 16 |
| 12 Prüfbrechkupplung | 28 Empfangsantenne |
| 13 Sende-Empfangsgerät (FuG 25a) | 29 Antennenanpaßgerät AA 6 16 E 3 |
| 14 Aufhängerahmen für Verteilerkasten FuG 25 | 30 Peilrahmen |
| 15 Widerstandskasten 25a | 31 Antennenanpaßgerät und Stabantenne FuG 25a |
| 16 Selbstschalter für Umformer FuG 16 | |

Me 262
**Bordfunkanlage**
FuG 16 ZY, FuG 25a

**Stand vom August 1944**

*The Me 262's radio equipment installation as of August 6, 1944. Many aspects of the aircraft's construction and equipment were subject to ongoing minor changes and alterations during this period.*

were also set to take place.

Test pilot Wendel reported on engine problems with two separate aircraft—Werk-Nr. 170003 and 170016—on August 7.[51] He wrote: "When flying in the above two aircraft, the right engine of the 003 and the left engine of the 016 showed malfunctions, which probably led to the previously unexplained fires in other aircraft. With extremely slow acceleration, as is only possible when the aircraft is held in place with brake pads, the engine goes to full power without any problems.

"If, on the other hand, you accelerate a little faster, but still not faster than the engines would normally tolerate, the differential pressure is only 0.5 instead of 0.62; the gas temperature goes to 700° and more. When accelerating at the start, it is almost never possible to run up the engine so slowly that this malfunction does not occur. A pilot with little experience of this type will definitely continue to take off and overheat the engine."

This problem—later identified as surging—does not appear to have been widespread, but taken together with pilots' inexperience on the new type, its variable build quality and its other weaknesses, it is not hard to see why the Me 262 appears to have had an appalling

rate of attrition through mechanical failure, in tandem with pilot error.

Messerschmitt and RLM staff met up on August 8 to discuss the installation of the new TSA 2 D computer in the Me 262, so that it could launch BT aerial torpedoes.[52] The company stated that it still had no official order for such an installation and it was agreed that an order would now be placed and that Messerschmitt would request installation documents for the TSA 2 D variant from Carl Zeiss. At the same time the RLM handed over documents detailing the BT series weapons and how they would attach to a modified ETC 504 bomb rack.

The Messerschmitt representative, Langhammer, said two main possibilities were envisioned for carrying BT weapons—either two BT 200s or a single BT 400. The latter being possible only if the aircraft's weaponry was two MK 108s, rather than four, and if the extra rear fuel tank wasn't filled up.

Carrying two BT 400s would only be possible with "further restrictons" and carrying a single BT 700 would only be possible if the bomb rack could be shifted forward by 450mm in addition to the restrictions previously mentioned.

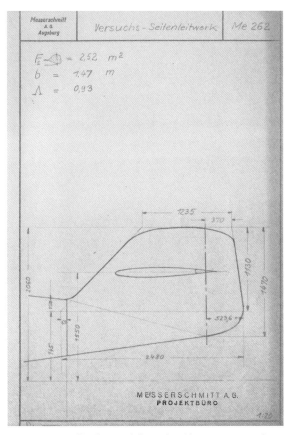

*Experimentally shortened fin and rudder arrangement for the Me 262. The aircraft allocated for flight testing changes to the vertical control surfaces was Werk-Nr. 170056.*

## ME 609 AT REGENSBURG

Up to this point, Messerschmitt's Regensburg factory had been the single largest manufacturer of Bf 109s—but on August 11 a plan was drawn up in readiness for its conversion to Me 262 production.[53] Completed aircraft built at Regensburg were to be known by the code name 'Me 609' and 14 blocks of serial numbers were allocated for them, ranging from 500001 to 502478.[54]

Meanwhile, eight new Wikingerschiff bomb racks had been delivered to Lechfeld for testing but none of them fitted properly and all had to be rebuilt. During the weekly Me 262 meeting at Messerschmitt on August 14,[55] it was noted that work on getting the ETC 504 bomb rack to fit had been completed and testing was now urgently needed. Preparations were under way to receive the first two-seater Me 262 B-1s from the Luftwaffe test centres and further testing of the windscreen washer hand pump was urgently needed.

Evidently some Me 262s had suffered rainwater ingress during bad weather because there was a new item on the agenda about "cabin seal—the separating joints are to be designed in such a way that no rainwater runs into the cockpit".

## MANUFACTURING DEFECTS

The latter half of August saw the repaired Me 262 V3 commenced high-speed flight testing on August 18, the V9 and 130167 were used for undercarriage testing—particularly concerning the nosewheel—and 170056 continued tail surface/stability testing with 130015. The new control column fitted to the latter was also assessed.[56] Speed trials were undertaken with the borrowed 130180 too.

Directional stability was now becoming a significant concern, with numerous different rudder, fin, elevator and trim tab configurations and settings tried on 170056 and 130015. According to the flight test department report: "It should be noted that each solution tried brought only a small improvement or even made things worse. The improvements were by no means even remotely satisfactory."

While these tests were ongoing, on August 18, 130015 exhibited another of the many manufacturing defects being discovered with the Me 262—a curved section of cockpit canopy glass at the upper front corner broke away. The aircraft was flying at an altitude of 7km and doing 960km/h at the time but the broken pane collapsed into the cockpit, rather than being whipped away by the slipstream.

Subsequent investigation found that the 8mm glass had broken due to a defect which caused a hollow area at the front corner where it met the canopy frame. The exact same section had previously broken away on Werk-Nr. 170116 while it was being flown at 2.5km altitude and 955km/h and comparison confirmed that the same defect was to blame. More canopies were then inspected and it transpired that all of them had the same weakness. Messerschmitt's staff office would now work out "an alternative solution for mounting the canopy glass at the front corners, with which the existing canopies can be retrofitted".

Significant progress had finally been made with the Mach warning system. It had been fitted to all five prototypes in active service and set up so that the warning light came on at Mach 0.6 (741km/h) in all cases. "With the help of tables in the aircraft, the pilots were able to check the device based on the respective speed and altitude when the light came on. The result was consistently good. Further tests will now follow at Mach 0.65; 0.7, 0.75, 0.8 and 0.85, which is probably the final setting."

The dirt scraper fitted to 130167's nosewheel had proven to be a failure since "the distance of 5mm between tyre and scraper turned out to be too small. Centrifugal force and tyre expansion caused the surface of the tyre to wear away. The distance was changed

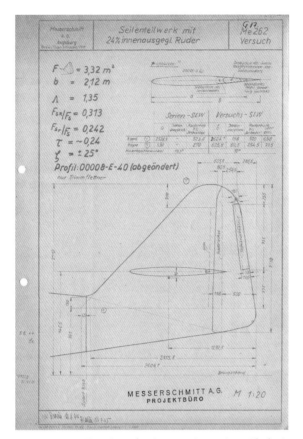

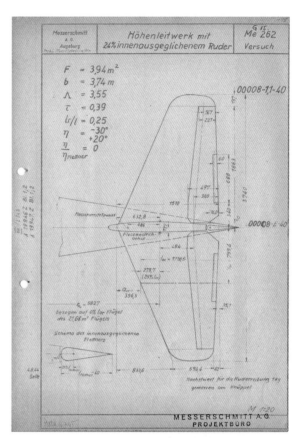

*Drawings showing experimentation with the internal balancing of the Me 262's tail control surfaces.*

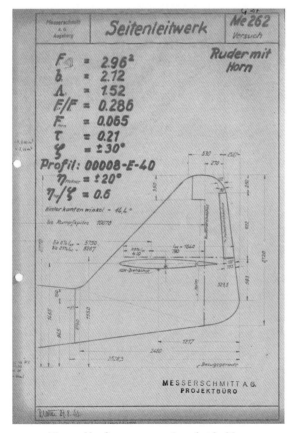

*New rudder form encompassing what had been
the top of the fin, dating from August 1944.*

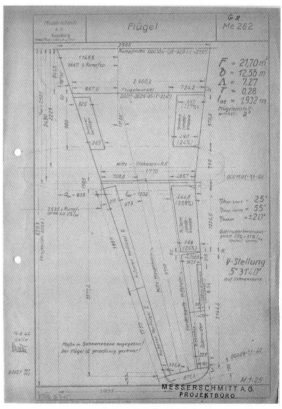

*Me 262 wing design from August 16, 1944, featuring
various detail design changes compared to that of the series
production model—including a slight increase in overall area.*

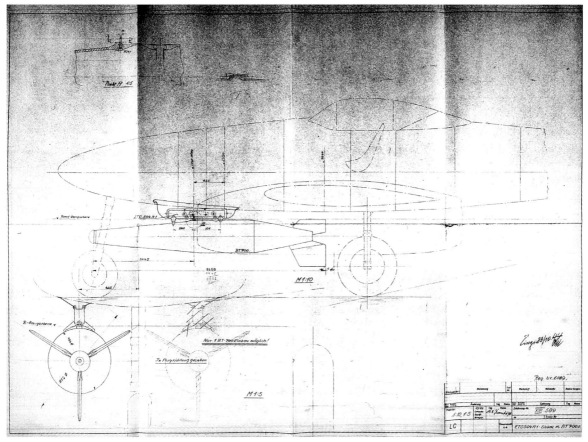

*Drawing from August 18, 1944, showing how the BT 700 C torpedo could be*
*carried by the Me 262 with an ETC 504 A-1 bomb rack.*

to 8mm and the tyre's surface was stripped off again, but to a lesser extent". It was decided that the part of the scraper plate positioned under the nosewheel fork should be left off but scraper plates on the side could be retained as "the dirt mainly sticks to the sidewalls of the tyre".

Aside from the scraper, there had been problems with 130167's nosewheel strut, which had repeatedly seized. V9's nosewheel strut had failed shortly after landing on August 23, with the aircraft tipping forward onto its nose; there was no major damage however and after a small repair to the nose tip it was able to resume flight testing. A variety of different experimental struts were subsequently tried on 130167 and V9 was fitted with a BSK 16 gun camera in its wing, but no testing took place at this time. V9 would, however, trial redesigned chutes for the spent casings from its MK 108 cannon.

Another new aircraft apparently assigned to the Messerschmitt company, 170072, suffered heavy damage before it could be involved in any testing. The accident was very similar to that of the V10: a burst tyre during a landing on August 24 caused the aircraft to swerve off the runway and onto the grass with Fritz Wendel at the controls. The left brake drum broke and the landing gear

strut was torn loose, puncturing the upper surface of the left wing. The right shock absorber was twisted through 90° and the right wing wheel well was bulged outwards.

In the meantime, further investigation of 170042's disastrous booster rocket accident had discovered that the release cable was not, in fact, being pretensioned by the addition of a 600 litre fuel tank in the rear of the fuselage. The cable was actually running too close to the pilot's seat—and when the pilot adjusted the seat upwards for comfort, it snagged the cable and activated the rockets. The simple solution was to install a tube which kept the cable away from the seat.

Yet another defect concerned interchangeability of parts: "When replacing the rudder, it was found that major structural deviations make interchangeability impossible. There are differences of up to 6mm in the bearing distances and further differences in the rudder thicknesses. So the rudder from 170079 could not be installed in 130015, since it could not be inserted into the drill hole of the fitting bolt."

## PRODUCTION SHORTFALL

Saur's Rüstungsstab meeting on August 26 noted that two days later a report was due to be received on the current state of the Me 262 "with special consideration of the question: full employment as a fighter (conversion effort)".[57] For now, Hitler's edict that the Me 262 must be used as a bomber remained in force—but serious thought was being given to what would happen should this order be rescinded.

A day later, Zeiler at Messerschmitt's central planning office wrote a memo "in order to eliminate any ambiguity" concerning the allocation of 170079 and 170072 to the test programme.[58] He said 170079 was originally to have been converted for use as the HG I, with lowered cockpit canopy and swept tailplanes, while 170072 would have been a replacement "for the destroyed V10 test vehicle".

However, "the use of the aforementioned aircraft was reversed for operational reasons". He further noted that Seitz still needed an aircraft for conversion to the HG I configuration because he "urgently needs to start the series of tests, as the necessary parts have already been completed at Oberammergau".

Presumably 170079's use as a new test vehicle for Baldrian had been deemed more important, while 170072 could no longer replace the V10 since it had itself now suffered heavy damage—though it had not been written off and would eventually be repaired.

Total Me 262 acceptances for August 1944 fell to just 37—woefully short of Saur's 100 target figure. This number likely reflects the heavy bombing of subcontractor production facilities and transport infrastructure across Germany at this time, causing 'bottlenecks' of different parts. The total number of Me 262s accepted by the Luftwaffe had now reached 168.[59]

Following on from the preliminary specification of August 4, the Chef TLR's Fl-E 2 department issued a full heavy fighter requirement to Blohm & Voss, Dornier, Focke-Wulf, Heinkel and Messerschmitt on August 28.[60] The 'Projekt neuer Zerstörer' referred to in the requirement's title was clearly intended as a replacement for the Bf 110/Ju 88 type night and all-weather fighters then being operated by the Luftwaffe. The introduction began: "The development of a new destroyer to combat enemy jet fighters in bad weather conditions during the day and at night is urgently required … Purpose: bad-weather destroyer for day and night with Lichtenstein, complete blind-flying ability including take-off and landing with the best possible flight performance including flight duration."

Again, despite the mention of enemy jet fighters, the powerplant options given were all piston engines: Jumo 222 E/F, As 413, DB 603 L or DB 613. Their "number and arrangement are not specified to ensure high flight performance. Combination piston engine/

turbojet is to be tested". And again, a crew of three was specified—pilot, radio operator and navigator/defensive gunner. Armament was four forward-firing MK 108s with 100 rounds per gun plus two MG 213s with 250 rounds each. These weapons were to be used on conjunction with the Lichtenstein system but the installation of a semi-fixed weapons system with Bremen radar had to be possible.

In addition, the aircraft was to carry a pair of MK 108s in its fuselage pointing upwards at a 70° angle plus two MG 151s with 250 rounds each in an FHL 151 turret—a total of 10 guns. It also had to be able to carry two 500kg bombs externally as an overload.

The specified electronic devices were: FuG 15, Fu Hl 3 F, Peil G 6, FuG 139, Bremen, FuG 130, FuG 226 (or 25 A to begin with) and FuG 101 A. The cockpit had to be heated, pressurised and armoured against 20mm rounds from the sides and 13mm from below, with de-icing systems for the wings and tail.

The Luftwaffe of this period seems to have had some difficulty when it came to issuing realistic specifications to industry.[61] An aircraft capable of carrying 10 guns plus their ammo, a host of hefty electronics, two 500kg bombs and enough fuel for long-range endurance was going to be enormous. And this would make the ambitious performance targets specified incredibly difficult to achieve.

## ME 262 B-2 NIGHT FIGHTER

The decision to build an interim Me 262 night fighter variant was made on September 1, 1944. This would clearly come nowhere near meeting the requirement of August 28 but was at this stage regarded as something separate.

According to Messerschmitt's Me 262 Protokoll Nr. 40, "Messerschmitt is to develop a two-seater night fighter based on the training aircraft without dual controls. The following equipment is to be considered: fuel system as with the high-speed bomber, additional external tank and consideration of drawbar tow for an additional fuel tank. Armament as for Me 262 A-1. In terms of electronic equipment, the aircraft is to be developed in two stages of development. The second stage of development should serve as the basis for the series [production model].

"First stage: electronic systems as in the high-speed bomber (FuG 25a and FuG 16 ZY, additional FuG 353 Zd Rotterdam search device). Inspection to see whether FuG 101 can be installed. Installation is only an option if there are no related difficulties.

"Second stage: equipment as listed in first stage with the following changes: instead of FuG 353, FuG 218 is installed, but only with a morning star antenna, not with SN 2. FuG 120 as a navigation device.

"Installation investigations and construction documents are to be carried out by Messerschmitt, test and sample installations created in Werneuchen[62]…The aircraft was given the series designation Me 262 B-2."[63]

The following day, September 2, Werk-Nr. 130186, aka the Me 262 Heimatschützer I rocket-propelled interceptor prototype, was delivered to Lechfeld for testing.[64] The aircraft came with its HWK rocket motor already installed in its rear fuselage but it would be some time before it actually flew using rocket propulsion.

And the mechanical issues continued to mount up with Me 262s now in service. A memo of September 6 noted that "a number of machines newly delivered to KG 51 showed the defect that when the emergency bomb drop lever was pulled to the first stop, the bomb rack was triggered and the rack carrier was unlocked at the same time. As is well known, only the rack should be released [when the lever is pulled] up to the first stop and the rack carrier only when the lever is pulled further beyond the first stop".[65]

Evidently the bomb release had previously been fine but "according to Mr Manderfeld this sequence of functions was deliberately discontinued in Leipheim at the request of control". Now it would be necessary to remove the nose of each aircraft and make adjustments to the system of cables associated with the bomb release. The release lever itself would also need to be rewelded in every case.

Saur's Rüstungsstab, having now received its Me 262 report, noted during a meeting on September 4 that "the report submitted about the Me 262 reflects the confusion that exists with this machine and the inadequate guidance. Revision of the report necessary".[66]

Meanwhile, Messerschmitt's Project Office continued to work on the high-speed Me 262 HG series, discussing an aft-rudder or 'hilfsruder' for the planned V-tail on September 7.[67] The following day it was reported that the regular swept tailplanes also planned for the HG series, when used in conjunction with 35° swept wings, would have to withstand a load 100% greater than originally forecast. The components already constructed were not strong enough for this and would need to be rebuilt.[68] Project drawings for the Me 262 HG II had been completed by September 11 but a report noted that Junkers had not been consulted about the redesigned engine intakes and that discussing them with the engine manufacturer would be necessary.[69]

That same day there was bad news for the programme from the RLM. A memo received by Messerschmitt stated that "on August 30 and September 7 you requested two Me 262 aircraft for: 1) Conversion to high speed aircraft. 2) Implementation of general test installations. After consultation with Major Behrens, it is announced that no aircraft can be made available for this for the time being.

"There are far more urgent tasks, such as night fighters, Heimatschützer etc. for which aircraft must first be made available. The order of urgency of the individual tasks is specified in the protocol dated September 1. Speed improvement work such as lowered cabin, more sharply swept wing, wing deepening, more sharply swept tailplane, etc. are clearly set behind the tasks that are important, since the excess speed is sufficient for the time being. You are asked to ensure that the processing takes place in the prescribed order."[70]

In other words, Major Otto Behrens, head of the Rechlin Luftwaffe test centre, had refused to allow the allocation of two Me 262s for Seitz's HG programme at Messerschmitt because he simply did not think the work was important enough.

## BALDRIAN FLIGHTS

The next round of Baldrian tests commenced on September 5 or September 6.[71] During the period since Baldrian's last test, installed in Me 262 V1 back in June, the system had been modified. The previously used Telefunken amplifier had been replaced with an alternative supplied by Vienna-based Radiowerk Horny, since the former was found to be extremely sensitive to moisture and proved unreliable during static tests. The Messerschmitt-devised forked nose probe had been installed on Werk-Nr. 170079, with the twin microphones at the fork tips 800mm away from one another and 1,200mm from the fuselage.

The full system complete with its 12V batteries, fitted within 170079's nose in place of its cannon, was hooked up to a Horny-developed measuring system and a cockpit display. For the first flight, the system was switched to maximum sensitivity and it was found that the direction indicator pointer remained in the zero position, with a slight oscillation of plus or minus five-degrees, with both engines running at the same revs. If one engine was slowed, "the pointer clearly deflects to the side of the faster-running engine. The pilot [Baur] states that he can use the pointer to synchronise the engines perfectly".[72]

During the second flight test, on September 7,[73] Baur repeatedly flew 170079 up behind a Bf 110 piloted by Heinz Herlitzius and the pointer on the display clearly moved in the direction of the 110, beginning at a distance of 160m, but "the difficulty for the pilot was that because of the sensitivity of the display he was not allowed to throttle the engine, so he had to fly past the

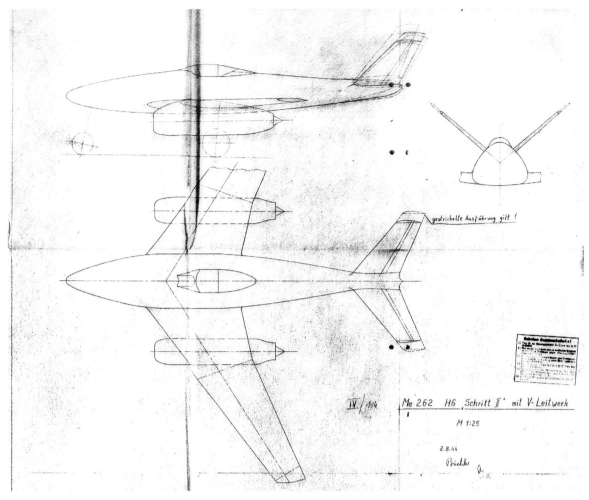

*Me 262 HG II with V-tail from drawing IV/114, dated August 2, 1944.*

Me 110 at full speed".[74]

The third test flight was on September 9, from 9.40am to 10.11am. This time the system's preamplifier was switched off and Baur again flew up behind a Bf 110. This time the engine revs had no effect on the pointer and the system picked up the Bf 110 at a distance of 350m—a big improvement over the previous test. Not only that, this time Baur was able to remain behind Herlitzius without the display being affected. The Messerschmitt summary report stated: "The pilot was able to sit at a constant distance behind the aircraft being tracked and observe the reaction of the display while turning his own machine. This experiment was carried out repeatedly. The result was always the same: at a distance of 350m, the pointer on the instrument perfectly follows the movements of your own aircraft, i.e. it always shows the position of the [other] aircraft.

"These tests have proven that direction finding based on acoustics is fundamentally possible if useful and background noise spectra differ from one another in a characteristic manner. In view of the fact that the conditions that are decisive for direction finding are only known to a limited extent, the result of a range of 350m is to be regarded as good [since it is] the first result ever in this area."[75]

Exactly why taking the preamplifier out of the equation 'fixed' the system so dramatically was "unexplained". A programme of further Baldrian work was set out in the summary report. This included tests to determine whether the probe might be better installed elsewhere on the aircraft, further test flights, modification of the system to work using the aircraft's own on-board power supply and "investigation and clarification of the phenomena that occurred during the sounding tests with regard to the use of higher degrees of amplification and the resulting engine dependency". And "after the goals set in the test have been achieved, the system should be ready for series production".

## BOMBING RAID

Having personally intervened in the Me 262's development, Adolf Hitler was now keeping a close eye on the type's entry into service. It was reported at a Rüstungsstab meeting on the same day Seitz got his bad

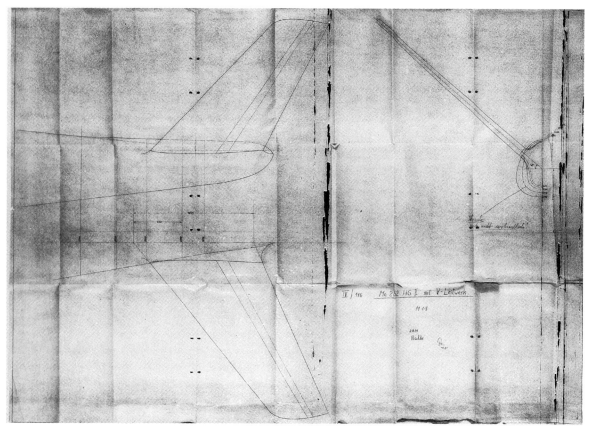

*A more detailed look at the V-tail intended for the Me 262 HG II from drawing IV/116, dated August 2.*

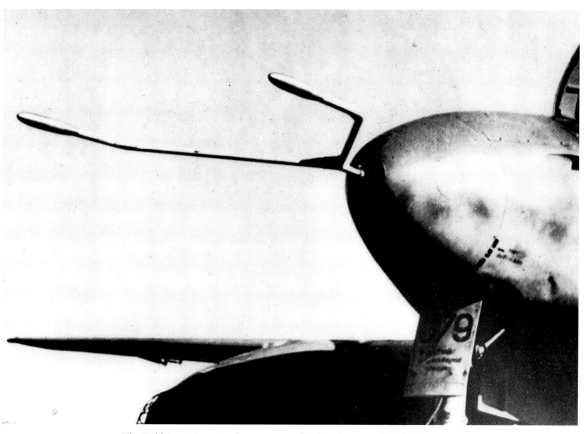

*The Baldrian twin microphone antenna fitted to the nose of Werk-Nr. 170079.*

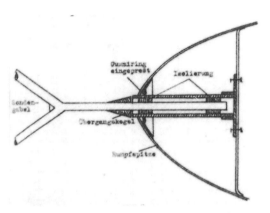

*The Baldrian system installation in the Me 262's nose.*

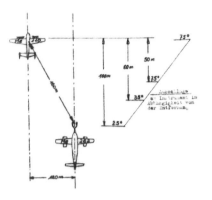

*Diagram showing the flight testing conducted using the Baldrian system in 170079 to track a Bf 110.*

news that: "The Führer has informed himself in detail about the state of the production of the Me 163 and Me 262. It was incomprehensible to him that, contrary to the first promises, these types have been produced with such meagre numbers." He was now demanding a weekly audience, every Monday, with the officer responsible for each type so that they could inform him of exactly what was causing the delays. Before that, in two days' time, the officers would be required to personally deliver a report to him on what they needed.[76]

The programme to create a single-jet successor to the Me 262, begun by early July, had been making leisurely progress up to this point and representatives of Messerschmitt, Heinkel and Focke-Wulf gathered at Oberammergau for a three-day conference to compare their respective designs on September 8.[77]

Just as this meeting was wrapping up on September 10, an identical telegram was sent to the offices of Arado, Blohm & Voss, Fieseler, Heinkel, Junkers, Messerschmitt, Siebel and Focke-Wulf, demanding designs for a new, cheap, lightweight, single-jet fighter that would be powered by a BMW 003 and armed with two MK 108s.[78]

The companies were given just three to five days to get their designs ready.

Two days later, on September 12, the Me 262 flight test programme was dealt a serious blow when the USAAF once again bombed Lechfeld. Of the eight serviceable test vehicles, the Me 262 V9 and 170056 escaped unharmed, 130015 suffered 5% damage, 130167 and 130186 (Heimatschützer I) suffered 10% damage, the Me 262 V10 took 25% damage, 170079 the Baldrian test vehicle, took 60% damage and the Me 262 V3 was basically destroyed with 75% damage.[79] The Me 262 V1, still out of commission following its crash on June 7, also took 80% damage—ending its long career permanently.[80] Yet another machine, 170110, newly assigned by the DVL, had also suffered light damage to its tail.

Had this attack occurred at the beginning of 1944 it might have spelled disaster for the Me 262 programme. Throughout the type's long years of neglect, every prototype had been a precious commodity—hand-crafted and near irreplaceable, particularly given the low priority afforded to the project by Messerschmitt. Yet now spare parts were abundant and whole wrecked assemblies could be stripped off and replaced with little difficulty. Nevertheless, it would still be three and a half days before flight testing could recommence

# Finally a Fighter: September 1944 to December 1944

ORK ON preparing for a switch from Me 262 bomber production to Me 262 fighter-bomber production was ongoing throughout the first half of September 1944. Even though Hitler's bomber-only order continued to stand, this suggests that an imminent thaw in the Führer's position may have been indicated. A weight comparison between the bomber and fighter-bomber variants, presumably the A-1 and A-2, was presented at a meeting of Saur's Rüstingsstab on September 13.[1]

At the same meeting it was noted that ministry troubleshooter Dr Krome had been transferred from the Me 262 programme to work on the Jumo 004 and BMW 003 instead. Although "September demand [for 004s and 003s] is exceeded to some extent", it appeared as though demand for those engines might, finally, be about to exceed production capacity. In other words, for the first time since the end of 1942 there was likely to be a shortage of Jumo 004s.

Another meeting was held on September 14 at Deutsche Lufthansa (DLH)'s Staaken facility to discuss construction of Me 262 night fighters using a combination of standard A-1 parts and new bespoke components.[2]

DLH would do the limited design work required itself and then produce a prototype.

It was noted that there would be two stages to the Me 262-based night fighter development—both with two seats and both with the maximum possible fuel capacity, possibly including a separate winged fuel tank towed by the aircraft. Weaponry would be the same as that of the Me 262 A-1, i.e. four MK 108s, and both would have the K 22 autopilot unit installed as well as standard Me 262 equipment. The K 22's workings had been outlined for Messerschmitt in a very scrappy description document dated September 13.[3]

On top of this, the 'Stage 1' night fighter would have the FuG 350 Zc radar plus FuG 101 radio altimeter unless the latter caused installation problems. 'Stage 2' would get FuG 218 airborne intercept radar, FuG 120 a or b radio beacon/printer, FuG 125 radio beacon signal receiver and—again—unless there were installation problems, FuG 101. Both aircraft would use the 'Morgenstern' antenna developed by E-Stelle Werneuchen and Siemens & Halske.

The first design conference for the new cheap single BMW 003-powered jet fighter, soon to be dubbed

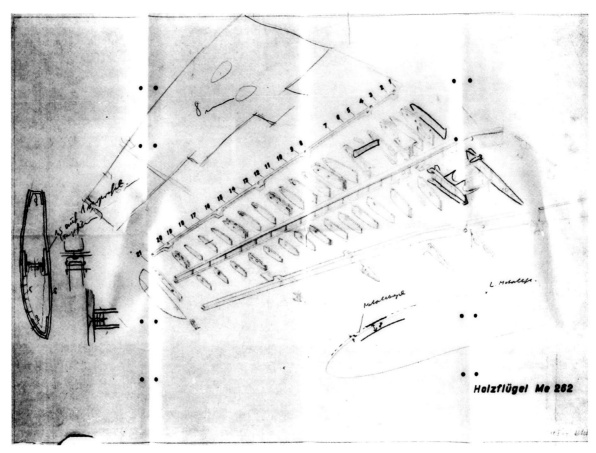

Holzflügel Me 262

*The wooden wing design intended for the Me 262.*

'Volksjäger', was held on the same day with projects tendered by Arado, Blohm & Voss and Heinkel.[4] There was no stand-out design but it was already clear that the contest was likely to be won by Heinkel's P 1073.

## WOODEN PARTS

Four days later, with repair work on the damaged Me 262 prototypes well under way at Lechfeld, a detailed memo was produced by Messerschmitt on efforts to convert some of the type's major assemblies to wooden construction.[5] It was noted that Jacobs-Schweyer at Darmstadt had now made a wooden Me 262 tail unit (see Chapter 5) and "the start of series production has already begun at the same company". The wooden fin weighed 16.2kg compared to the 15.7kg metal fin, while the all-wooden rudder was 14.5kg compared to the standard metal clad wooden rudder's 18.6kg. The trim tab was also made of wood but "for series production, a switch to plastic is desirable", though "there are still uncertainties about the delivery situation of plastic parts".

The elevators, however, could not yet be made of wood due to changing load data. While there remained an intention to make wooden wings for the Me 262, this required "the help of 10-15 experienced wooden

component designers from other companies, who have not yet arrived.

Meanwhile, as he awaited the availability of a test vehicle to upgrade with the HG components he'd had made, Seitz had calculated the likely performance enhancements they would bring.[6] With HeS 011 engines fitted, a standard Me 262's performance in a straight line at 6km altitude was expected to be 895km/h. But with 35° wing sweepback and a wing area of 25.2m², compared to the standard aircraft's 21.6m², this was expected to rise to 940km/h. And if the engine nacelles could be made to remain subcritical, a top speed of 970km/h was theoretically possible. A 45° sweepback with the same wing area was expected to yield 945km/h or 978km/h without Mach effects.

Best of all would be two HeS 011s and a 35° sweepback but with a 21.6m² wing area. In this case, top speed was calculated at 995km/h or 1,020km/h ignoring compressibility effects.

Messerschmitt's designers had come up with three different versions of the inner wing in wood and two versions of the outer wing, retaining the steel spar. A spar made of laminated wood had been examined but this "resulted in too much additional weight". Tests were now under way to determine how the plywood wings

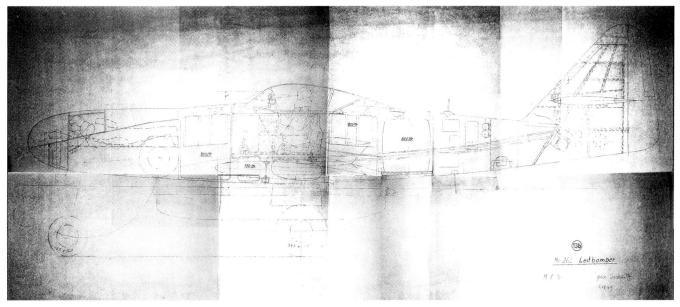

*The Me 262 A-3 with prone bombardier nose, described in the caption as a 'Leitbomber'.*
*The drawing, pieced together from surviving fragments, is dated October 5, 1944.*

could be glued to the steel spar.

Meanwhile, a meeting was held on September 21 to discuss progress on the Me 262 A-3 Schnellstbomber and its wooden bomb aimer nose.[7] It was reported that eight of these compartments were to be made in total — three for static stress testing and five for flight testing—the first of these already being fitted to 110484 with a scheduled first flight date of October 15.

## HITLER RELENTS – A LITTLE

During a series of meetings from September 21-23, Adolf Hitler ordered that "the Ar 234 is to be deployed with all speed as a bomber in the highest possible number of units" and "since it [the Ar 234] can be deployed at close range with a 500kg bomb and at long range with three 500kg bombs under much more favourable general conditions than the 262 as a bomber, the Führer confirms the promise made at the time that for every operational 234 finally approved as a bomber, an operational 262 … is made available for use as a fighter".[8]

Unfortunately, Ar 234 production—not having been subject to the same intensive effort as Me 262 production—was painfully slow at this time. The first five had been accepted by the Luftwaffe in July, followed by 10 in August.[9] Since the figure for September had not yet been determined, and since the ordered had only just come into effect, the Luftwaffe's fighter force was only allowed to now employ 10 Me 262s as fighters.

Worse still, just because the Luftwaffe was now allowed to use 10 Me 262s as fighters did not mean that 10 Me 262s were actually ready to use as fighters. According to a memo of September 29,[10] Saur had requested during

the Rüstungsstab of September 11—again, showing foreknowledge of Hitler's decision—that the 10 Me 262s built as fighters should be delivered in such a way that they were ready to fly by September 16-17. However, "the daily report from September 18 only shows the delivery of one 262 as a fighter. This example is characteristic of the manner in which individual matters are dealt with in the Rüstungsstab. As in the case mentioned above, commitments and promises are constantly being made, but these are not kept". The memo went on to point out that even this single aircraft had not actually been delivered by September 18.

Those involved in these heated discussions seem to have been unaware that it made little difference whether an Me 262 was built as a 'bomber' or a 'fighter'—the A-1 and A-2 variants being essentially the same aircraft. Plans would be laid to better adapt the A-2 for carrying bombs,[11] making it physically distinct from the A-1, but so far no changes had been made.

At the September 21-23 meetings, Hitler had also confirmed that Heinkel's P 1073 Volksjäger design, soon to receive the designation He 162, had won the competition and was "released for immediate start of series production and ordered with a provisional number of 1,000 aircraft per month".

This number appears particularly outlandish given that development of the Me 262 had begun in 1938 and six years later the total number accepted by the Luftwaffe during September 1944 was still only 111, against a target of 150. The total number of Me 262s accepted up to that point, for the six months from April to the end of September, was just 279.[12]

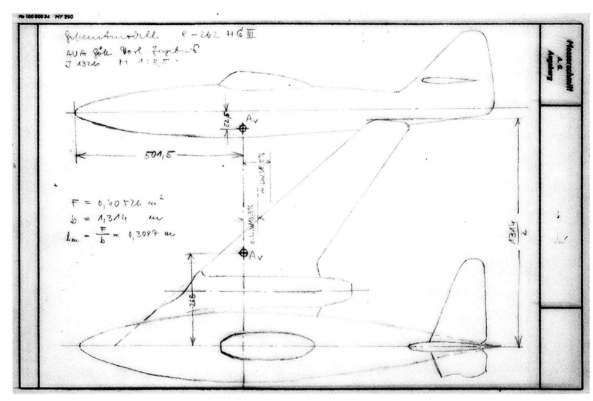

*Early drawing of an Me 262 HG III wind tunnel test model with the engines
positioned near the wingroots but not quite within them.*

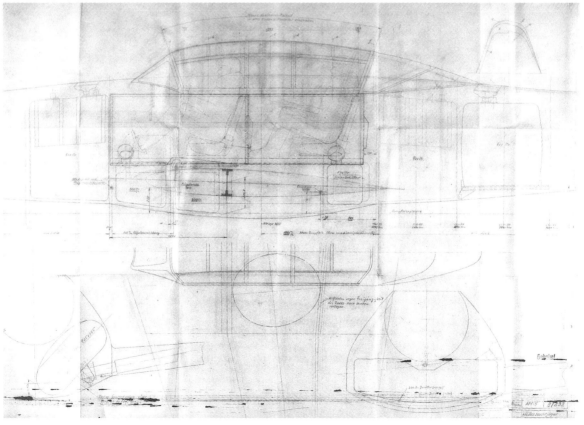

*The internal layout of what appears to be the intended production model Me 262 night fighter with extended fuselage,
drawing II/232 of October 4, 1944. It shows the awkward positioning of the aircraft's 935 x 345 mainwheels within
a pronounced under-fuselage bulge. A positive by-product of this distended belly was extra space for fuel.*

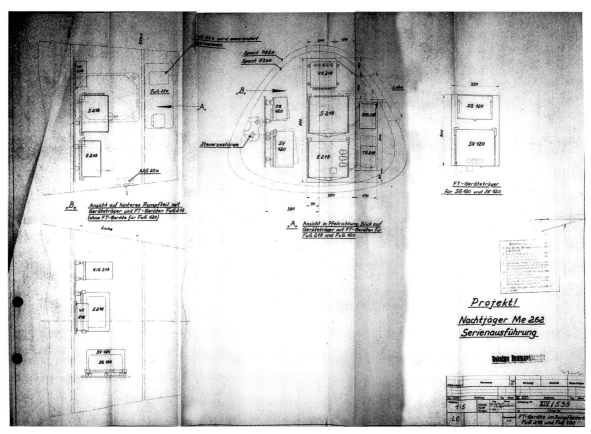

*Rear fuselage equipment installations for the night fighter shown in drawing XIV/539.*

A meeting to report on the latest Me 262 developments was held at Oberammergau on September 25.[13] The gathered company engineers heard that the ETC 504 bomb rack was still not ready to fit and that the deadline for a test installation, October 9, was rapidly approaching. It was also pointed out that adjusting the Me 262's brakes was continuing to cause problems for operational units and changes were being made to both the main landing gear suspension struts and the nose-wheel fork. Checks were to be made on whether the Mach warning device mounts made at Oberammergau had actually arrived at Lechfeld and pilots who had flown or were going to fly long range missions in the Me 262 would be asked to provide reports—presumably on the aircraft's performance.

The windscreen washer was finally about to go into series production and systems for washing the side windows of the aircraft were to be tested. There would also be further investigation on the issue of damage caused by booster rockets and the directional stability problem.

An air conditioning system for the Me 262's cabin needed to be produced "as quickly as possible" and parts made at Oberammergau for testing drawbar tow of winged fuel tanks and winged bombs would be delivered to Lechfeld on September 28.

This last project appears to have come from Professor Paul Ruden at the DFS in Ainring. Ruden and his team had been working on designs for a flying trailer that they called the 'Schleppgerät'—literally 'towing device'—since at least June 1944.[14] In its original form, this consisted of a broad rectangular wing with a pair of wheels fixed underneath. A single teardrop shaped fuel tank could be fixed above this wing and a single bomb could be fixed beneath it, slung between the wheels. The Schleppgerät was to be attached to its tug by a long rigid metal pole with a flexible joint at the aircraft end and a fixed joint at the trailer end.

Ruden had originally conceived the Schleppgerät as an add-on for either the Ju 87 or the Ar 234 but now a new version would be tried with the Me 262.

As of September 27, it was reported that three further Me 262s had suffered damage as a result of burst tyres; 170099's right tyre had burst at 180km/h, causing the landing gear leg to bend backwards and resulting in significant damage to the wing's interior. This was notable because wing reinforcement modifications intended to prevent exactly this situation from happening had already been carried out on the aircraft.[15]

Werk-Nr. 130027 had been in a similar situation, albeit with the left gear bending back, although this aircraft had not undergone the reinforcement work. 170306 had

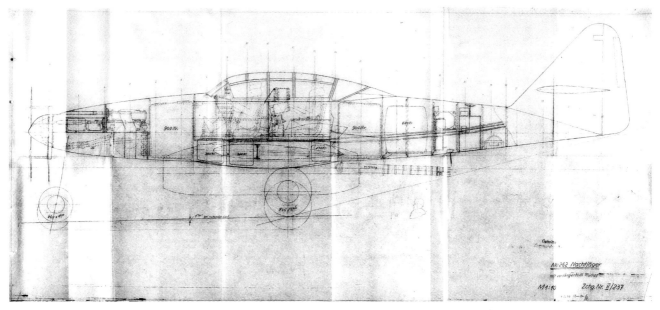

*Full side view of the production model Me 262 night fighter with extended fuselage; drawing number II/237 of October 4, 1944.*

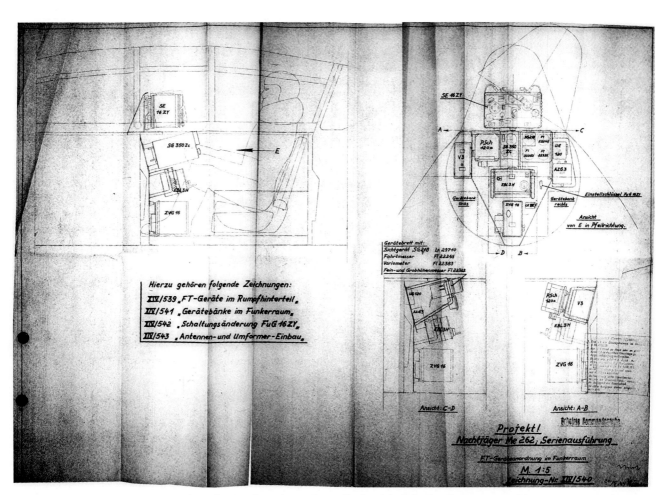

*Drawing XIV/540 showing the equipment layout for the night fighter's radar operator position.*

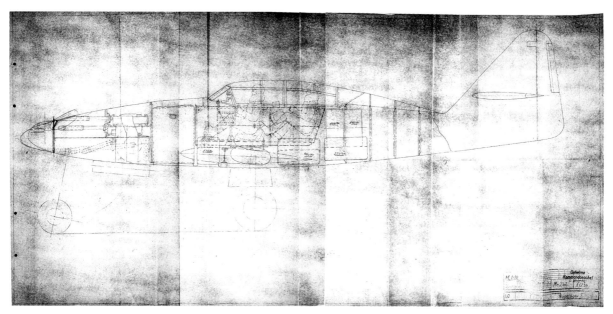

*The interim Me 262 night fighter design, based on the B-1 trainer, overdrawn to show potential changes to the nose tip. This is drawing II/236 of October 5, 1944.*

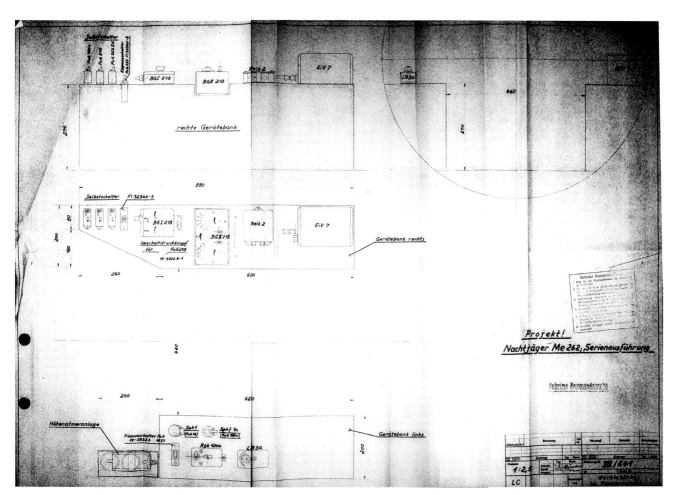

*Switchgear layout within the night fighter's cockpit, appearing in drawing XIV/541.*

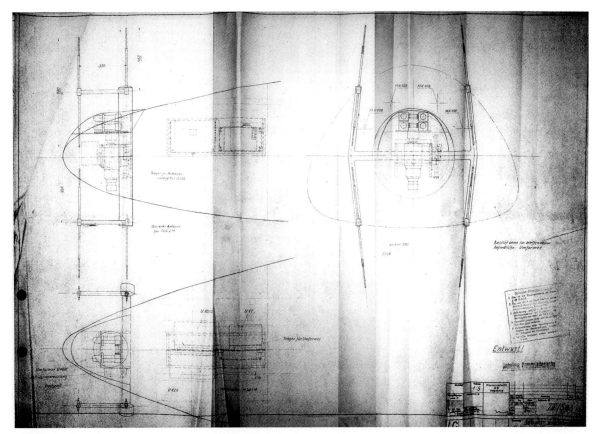

*Positioning of the night fighter's proposed antenna in relation to its four MK 108s, shown in drawing XIV/543 of October 20.*

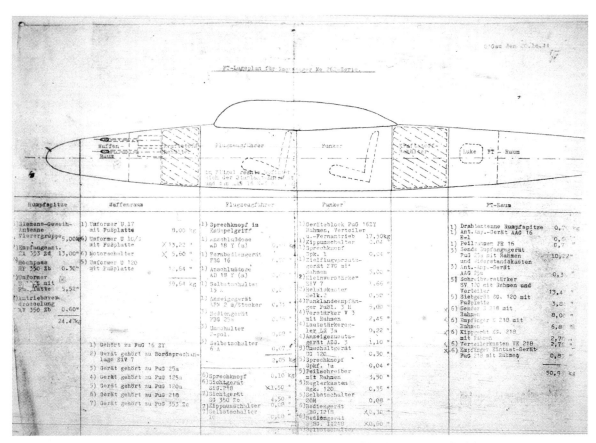

*Lists showing the large quantity of equipment to be carried by the Me 262 night fighter.*

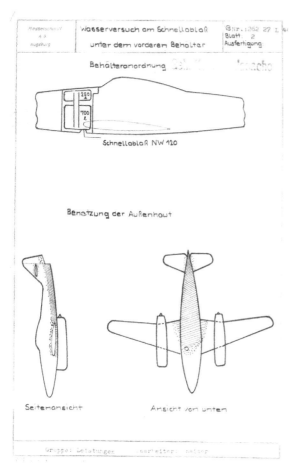

*The parts of Werk-Nr. 130186 that were coated in sticky red liquid during the emergency fuel release simulation.*

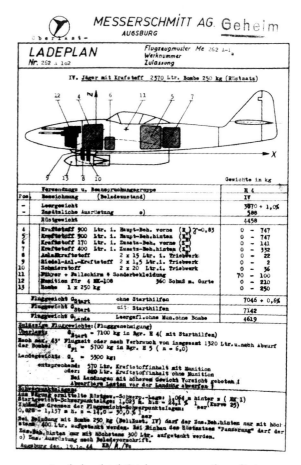

*Load plan dated October 19, 1944—the earliest known document referring to the Me 262 A-1a, with the new addition of the little 'a' denoting an Me 262 fitted with Jumo 004 engines. Machines with BMW 003s were to receive a little 'b', i.e. Me 262 A-1b.*

suffered a burst nosewheel tyre, with the nosewheel strut then being torn away from its housing. On September 29, Werk-Nr. 130167 was demonstrated for a delegation of Japanese visitors to Lechfeld.

## ANOTHER HG PLEA

Seitz's HG team presented Willy Messerschmitt with project documents describing an Me 262 with 45° swept-back wings and HeS 011 engines buried in its wing roots on October 2, 1944.[16] According to a brief account of this presentation, the radical repositioning of the engines "was justified by the fact that the advantage of the 45° swept wing only comes into effect with the best engine installation". This would become the basis for the third stage of the HG programme—the HG III.

Messerschmitt asked that a detailed investigation of the wingroot engine arrangement be carried out and until this was completed, the external engine configuration was to be retained. In the meantime, the plan to give the HG I strakes at the wingroots had been abandoned because it would have taken the Construction Office too long to produce them.[17]

The Project Office made another urgent please for an Me 262 airframe on which to test the HG components on October 5 and this time it was possible to make a more compelling argument. Even as the BMW 003-powered Volksjäger competition had been and gone, the other single-jet fighter competition—the one intended to create an HeS 011-powered replacement for the Me 262—had continued. Now the Project Office could say to the RLM: "The testing of the 35° swept wing Me 262 is of decisive importance for the further development of the Me 262 and also one of the most important prerequisites for the desired rapid/risk-free approach to the single-jet fighters. I urge you to be concerned about the procurement of a complete 262 fuselage and two engines by 25.10.44 at the latest. (Fuselage and engine are to be delivered to Oberammergau.)"[18]

## INTERIM NIGHT FIGHTER

Two new Projektübergabe documents were produced on October 5—the first[19] outlined the installation of the

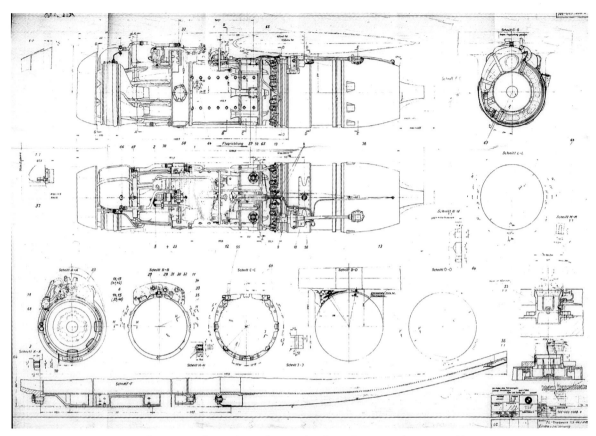

*During the autumn of 1944 it was foreseen that future Jumo 004 shortages could mean fitting large numbers of Me 262s with BMW 003 engines, as shown here.*

EZ 42 'Adler' lead calculating gunsight in the Me 262 and the second described the interim 'Stage I' model Me 262 night fighter.[20] The latter stated that "changes to the trainer aircraft should be kept to the minimum possible" though careful attention was paid to revising the fuel system. For the two-seat B-1 trainer, the second seat had been added largely at the expense of fuel capacity. Endurance was crucial for a night fighter though, so it was necessary to squeeze in as much extra fuel as possible.

In addition, the night fighter's crew compartment was to be made shorter compared to the trainer's by deleting the rear cockpit dual controls and moving the seat slightly further forwards. The partition between the two seats was to be retained but with cut-outs at the bottom for the observer's feet.

Wrapping around the underside of the rear seat would be a new 400 litre fuel tank and behind the rear seat would be two new cylindrical 140 litre tanks. Below these, the trainer's existing 250 litre tank was retained.

The trainer's wings and landing gear would be carried over unaltered but taking into account the latest design upgrades—allowing a maximum load capacity of 7,100kg with 840 x 300 wheels. The tail section would also be standard though incorporating any changes "resulting from ongoing flight tests to eliminate the vibrations around the vertical axis".

The pilot's equipment would be the same as in the Me 262 A-1 except for the right hand side panel, which would no longer contain the FuG 16 radio controls—these having been moved to the back seat control panel. In addition "UV lighting and red lighting are provided for the pilot and the observer. The normal lamps with a red cap are used as red lighting".

## COMPLAINTS

An update on the status and whereabouts of the completed but not yet installed Me 262 HG components was produced on October 5.[21] The 40° swept tailplanes needed minor modifications, the swept tail fin "has been in Lechfeld for a long time for reasons that can no longer be determined" and work was needed on the fairings that would be needed to blend it into the rest of the aircraft. The 35° swept back wings were complete and had been the subject of "little work ... in recent weeks". No fuselage had yet been secured to receive them. Similarly the low profile canopy "has been completed for a long time and is located in Lechfeld". Enquiries were being made to determine whether it could simply be attached to a standard series production

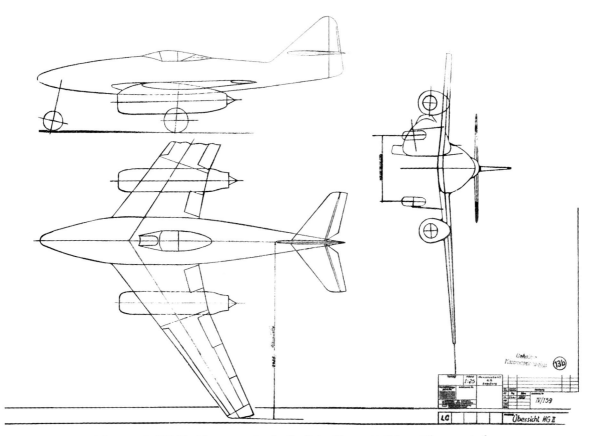

*The Me 262 HG II with a conventional tail, albeit with swept tailplanes. The concept of a V-tail appears to have been postponed indefinitely towards the end of October 1944. Oddly, this diagram has a partial second front view superimposed over the first at a 45° angle.*

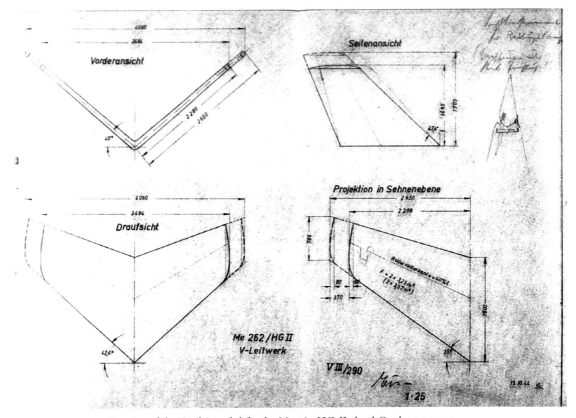

*Drawing of the V-tail intended for the Me 262 HG II, dated October 15, 1944.*

model Me 262 to get testing under way.

Lechfeld personnel visited KG 51 from October 5-7 to personally receive complaints from Major Wolfgang Schenck and his maintenance personnel about production Me 262s delivered to the unit.

According to KG 51 "a total of four brand-new aircraft from the Leipheim production facility, which were transferred at different times, had to be re-oiled immediately after their arrival. The liquid in the pressurised oil system had decomposed or formed a milky emulsion—a tacky water-clear gum". A sample had been sent to Rechlin for analysis. In addition, the oil systems of new aircraft were often found to be heavily contaminated "by mud, drilling and milling chips".

There were difficulties with the oil system on many aircraft and a certain type of hydraulic valve fitted to Me 262 A-1s but not to A-2s had a fault whereby an unexpected pressure increase could lead to "permanent, unwanted retraction of the landing gear". Another landing gear problem was the mainwheel brake hoses, which were positioned in such a way that they rubbed against the tyres and would eventually wear through.

Finally, there was a concern that new aircraft were being built with the original Siemens fuel pumps, rather than the new Barmag ones. The former were said to provide insufficient pressure and their dimensions were "unsuitable".

The Messerschmitt company wrote to the Rechlin test centre on October 6 with some circuit diagrams for connecting the TSA 2 A-1 computer to new switchgear in the Me 262. It was also noted that the new TSA 2 D-1 could be connected to the same wiring without alterations.[22]

During the period between September 28 and October 18, 35% of flights planned for the test vehicles had had to be cancelled due to bad weather.[23] When testing was possible Me 262 V10, flying again on October 1 for the first time since its landing accident on August 6, was used for brake tests and a high-altitude flight on October 7. It was then briefly taken off the flight line so it could be fitted with the Oberammergau-made parts for the DFS Schleppgerät. The first attempt to fly with this arrangement failed on October 12 when the trailer broke during a ground run.

Werk-Nr. 130015 had now been fitted with the Baldrian system, presumably having received 170079's nose while that aircraft undergoing repairs, and was used to test it on October 10-12. Four Baldrian flights were made on the 10th, another four on the 11th and two more on the 12th.[24] The same aircraft had also been experimentally fitted with the Jacobs-Schweyer wooden fin and tested with it up to 970km/h without any problems.

It would appear that after these tests the Baldrian nose was removed and 130015 got its original nose back. Certainly, the aircraft would never again be used for Baldrian testing.

Following its use as a demo machine, 130167 carried out brake tests, target approach experiments, the ever-problematic screenwash system, flight stability and diving. 170056 was also used for brake and stability testing—having its rudder forces measured.

The now repaired 170079 was used for ground tests on October 13 and 15 before taking to the air once again on the 15th for a high-altitude flight. 170303 was also on high-altitude test duties, with a revised control column arrangement in the cockpit. In fact, 170303 seems to have been the test pilots' favourite. According to the test report: "This machine was delivered with exceptionally well-tuned engines. Maximum altitude with bombs is 13.5km. Top speed without bombs at 500m is 820km/h."

The Heimatschützer I, 130186, made flights under jet power only on October 16 and 18, the latter being to test the emergency release of rocket fuel in flight—albeit using water coloured red with 0.1% methyl violet and with 0.1% sodium chloride to increase adhesion, rather than actual rocket fuel. When Baur released the liquid, those on the ground saw a "200m long red flag" extend from the aircraft. It was reported that "the outflow of the bulk of the water lasted from five to 10 minutes and this did not quite stop; there were still individual spurts during the landing".[25]

The sticky liquid completely coated the underside of the front fuel tank, the undercarriage doors and wheel well interiors, as well as the rear fuselage underside. Worse still, some of the dumped 'fuel' was sucked into the fuselage by the pressure differential and the radio equipment behind the pilot was "heavily splattered".

Unsurprisingly, the drainage system was deemed unsuitable. The experiment itself seems to have made a real mess of 130186, since "after each dump, the aircraft becomes unusable as it is impossible to clean all the wetted areas with water".

It was reported that another test vehicle—Werk-Nr. 170078—had made its first flight with BMW 003 engines on October 21, during which a piece of the engine cowling flew off. More than two and a half years after the Me 262 V1 flew with BMW P 3302 engines, a near-production model 003 had finally made its first successful flight in Messerschmitt's fighter. At this point, most BMW 003s were destined for the He 162—having originally been allocated to the Ar 234 C multirole variant. However, both the Luftwaffe high command, the OKL, and the ChefTLR seem to have been adamant that the Me 262 should be capable of accommodating two 003s.[26]

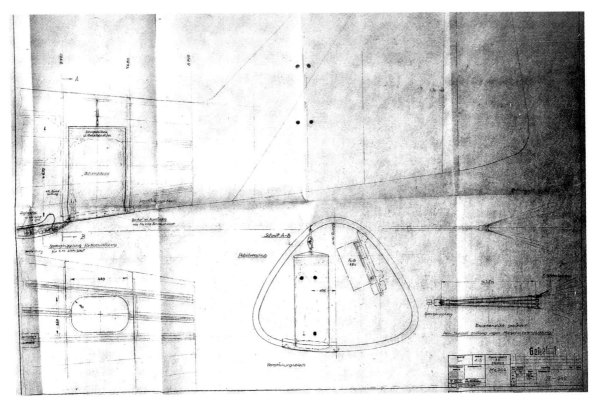

*Drawing from October 11, 1944, showing how a brake parachute could be installed within the Me 262's rear fuselage.*

*The DFS Schleppgerät (SG) 5030 attached to the tail end of Me 262 V10 via a rigid tow bar.*

*A closer look at the SG 5030. Its wing was fashioned from the wings of an Fi 103 flying bomb.*

*The Me 262-SG 5030 attachment point. The electrical connections enabled the aircraft's pilot to jettison first the trailer's wheels once airborne, then the bomb itself over the target and finally the wing and towbar.*

*The V10 taking off with Schleppgerät attached.*

*Me 262 V10 in flight with the Schleppgerät after jettisoning its wheels.*

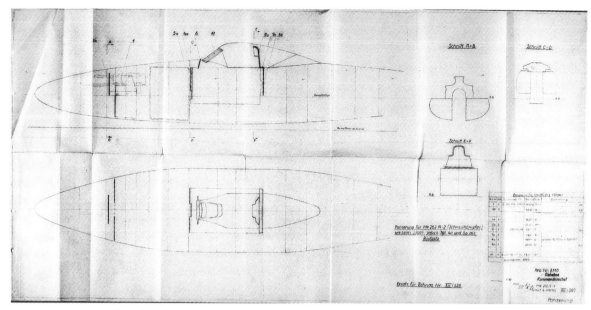

*Locations and weights of the armour plates fitted to the Me 262 A-1 from a diagram dated October 24, 1944. The A-2 was to have the same apart from the plates labelled 4a and 5a, which were optional extras.*

Directional stability remained a problem with the Me 262 and experiments with different rudder and tailplane configurations continued. Werk-Nr. 110394 had been transferred to Lechfeld but high-speed testing showed that its wings were misaligned by 3-4 degrees, making it useless for further experimentation.

A BSK 16 gun camera pod, meant to be attached to the bomb rack fittings, had been delivered to Lechfeld for testing and an investigation was ongoing to find a way of making the non-pressure cabin Me 262 canopy water-tight when it rained. Canopy construction was inconsistent and it was thought that a sealing paste might need to be applied.

## NOSEWHEEL PROBLEMS

The biggest problem now plaguing the Me 262, however, was its undercarriage—particularly the nosewheel. Me 262 V8's nosewheel had failed to extend when it was coming in to land following its 258th flight. After taxiing a short distance, the strut buckled and the aircraft slid on its nose for 150-200m before coming to a standstill. The nose itself and both engine intakes suffered heavy damage. The cause was found to be misaligned bearing journals and poorly fitted shims under the flanges of the strut bearings, resulting in seized bearings. Werk-Nr. 170052 suffered the same problem.

170306 and 130181 both suffered nose gear failure as a result of manufacturing defects related to the bearings. Each time, the breakage had been preceded by severe nosewheel 'flutter' or extreme swivelling.

Seven more aircraft—130015, 130186, 170003, 170017, 170049, 170113 and 170112—suffered a broken nosewheel

swivel stop, the part designed to prevent the nosewheel from swivelling more than 55°. 170103 and 170303 had both experienced nose deformation as a result of nose-wheel flutter and had to undergo repairs.

130027 endured a "sliding landing" as a result of a broken bearing pin on the left main gear and 170094's right main gear failed after just 35 flights. Finally, 170067 had a burst tyre on October 12, which caused a heavy landing and damage to both the right wing and engine nacelle.

## ME 262 HG I CONVERSION

Evidently there were now ongoing discussions about how to persuade Adolf Hitler that the Me 262 should finally be released for use purely as a fighter. On October 17, Albert Speer wrote to Lucht: "I have asked Mr Messerschmitt, as planned, to draw up a report on the suitability of the Me 262 as a fighter or as a bomber and to submit it to me to pass on to the Führer."

Hitler appears never to have lost faith in Willy Messerschmitt and continued to lend weight to his opinions even now. If anyone could persuade him to change course on the Me 262 it was the aircraft's nominal creator.

During the grounding of the Me 262 test fleet in early October, it appears to have been decided that V9 should be allocated to the HG programme. An update from Seitz's team on October 18 indicates that work was finally under way on assembling the first HG test vehicle—at Lechfeld rather than Oberammergau.[27] This involved fitting the low-profile 'racing' cockpit canopy and the 40° swept tailplanes.

At the same time, work was under way on a set of 35° swept back wings as well as redesigned asymmetrical engine nacelles to go with them. A drawing from the Project Office showing the V-tail had been handed over to the Construction Office that same day. Finally, the investigation required by Messerschmitt concerning the HG III's 45° swept wing arrangement, with the engines buried in the wing-roots, was reportedly near completion.

The following day it was noted that the 35° swept wing test vehicle, the Me 262 HG II, would not have a firewall installed due to time constraints,[28] and Willy Messerschmitt had been handed the results of the 45° swept wing investigation. His response was that "the arrangement of the engine can remain as it is, [and] an attempt should be made to move [it] even closer to the fuselage". It was suggested that this arrangement might suit a night fighter and that wind tunnel tests of the configuration "should be initiated immediately".[29] During the same meeting, Messerschmitt said that a standard tailplane should be used as a starting point for the HG III, with the V-tail added later.

Work was also progressing on the rocket-propelled Heimatschützer I, 130186, at Lechfeld, with ground tests of the double mainwheel arrangement taking place on October 21 and stationary tests of the rocket motor on October 25. These resulted in a demand for modifications to both the engine mounting and the fuel tank installation.[30]

## MORE COMPLAINTS

Messerschmitt personnel visited Kommando Nowotny and I./KG 51 again from October 16-20 to hear about more complaints.[31] Here they learned that Major Schenck's personal aircraft had been fitted with a replacement nose which had contained wiring that did not match up to that of the fuselage. Consequently, the unit had appointed its own weapons technician named Tigges. Tigges had apparently made an attempt "to shoot the two lower guns with the protective tubes [between the muzzle and the exterior of the aircraft] removed to determine the consequences (severe damage to the nose of the fuselage)".

The report ruefully notes that "the consequences were foreseeable given the high muzzle pressure of the MK 108. We are aware of the need for a proper protective tube holder, but unfortunately there were structural deviations during series production which made it possible to lose the protective tube. [This must be] Counteracted by retrofitting". Evidently I./KG 51 had been securing the tubes by screwing makeshift metal retainers on from the outside of the aircraft.

These situations had arisen because the Me 262 pilots had been flying bombing missions and had therefore used the cannon of their aircraft "only to a small extent, so that extensive operational experience was not yet available".

It also transpired that cannon were failing because ground crew were over-oiling them—"de-oiling to the degree of a wafer-thin lubrication supposedly brings the necessary resistance to cold" and in some cases cannon, especially those on the right, were becoming misaligned after just a few flights for reasons that were not immediately clear.

There were also complaints about ETC 503 bomb rack attachment bolts tearing at their weld seams, resulting in racks being "lost several times, with and without a bomb. According to the maintenance staff, this only happened with the ETC 503. The reason for this lies in the imprecise manufacture and fitting of these racks into the intermediate piece on the fuselage, whereby the functional reliability of the latching is not clearly guaranteed. As is well known, the ETC 503 was exclusively equipped with the intermediate carrier by the troops themselves, until this was replaced by the Wikingerschiff".

Schenck also complained that the emergency bomb release mechanism had failed to operate correctly on two occasions—"on one occasion, the emergency release lever were severely bent when it was pulled without initiating the emergency release of the rack. Another time it was only after repeated vigorous pulling to the stop that the rack was released from the aircraft".

However, consultation with the ground crew determined that these problems were caused by "improper operation by the pilot". Schenck further "urgently demands that the emergency pull handle be moved to the left side, so that the control stick hand does not change in critical moments and in the event of an emergency release".

## NEW TEST VEHICLES

A report on the BMW 003 test vehicle, 170078, was produced on October 24.[32] Within the cockpit, it was found that the switches to adjust the engine nozzle could not be reached by the pilot when his seat belt was buckled—and the handle for the nosewheel brake was in the way even when the pilot wasn't strapped in. The throttle lever was also too close to the ignition. The engine cowlings needed reinforcement and an improvised hatch had had to be added to the rear of each engine nacelle so that the engine nozzles could be adjusted. Fuel drainage holes measuring 12mm had been added to the lower cowlings and the wing-engine

# ME 262 VARIANTS AS OF NOVEMBER 1944

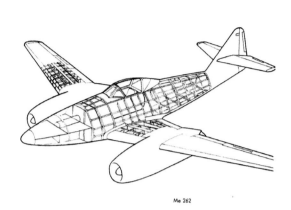

Me 262

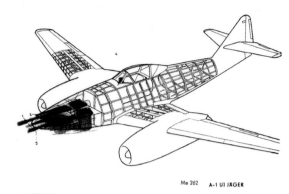

Me 262    A-1 U1 JÄGER

BEWAFFNUNG
1  2 MK 103 je 72 Schuß
2  2 MG 151 je 146 Schuß
3  bzw. 2 MK 108 je 66 Schuß
4  1 Revi 16 B bzw. 16 D

## Me 262 A-2 BLITZBOMBER (BB)

| | |
|---|---|
| BEWAFFNUNG: | 2 MK 108 je 80 Schuß |
| PANZERUNG: | 90 mm Panzerscheibe |
| | Panzerung der Waffenmunition |
| ABWURFANLAGE: | 2 × Wikingerschiff |
| | 2 × ETC 503 serienmäßig nicht vorgesehen |
| | 2 × ETC 504 |
| ABWURFBETÄTIGUNG: | TSK 244 mit ZEK später Zündumformer |

BELADEMÖGLICHKEIT:

| a) mit ETC 503: | b) mit Wikingerschiff |
|---|---|
| 2 × SC 250 | 2 × SC 250 |
| 2 × SD 250 | 2 × SD 250 |
| 2 × AB 250-2 | 2 × AB 250-2 |
| 1 × SC 500 | 1 × SC 500 |
| 1 × SD 500 | 1 × SD 500 |
| 1 × AB 500-1 | 1 × AB 500-1 |
| 1 × AB 500-3 | c) mit ETC 504 |
| 1 × BT 200 | wie ETC 503 zutalblü |
| 1 × BT 400 (bei 130 mm | 1 × BT 400 |
| vorverlegtem Schloß) | |

## Me 262 A-2/U 1 BLITZBOMBER (BB)

| | |
|---|---|
| ZIELANLAGE: | An Stelle Revi 16 D, TSA-Anlage |
| JÄGERKURSSTEUERUNG | |

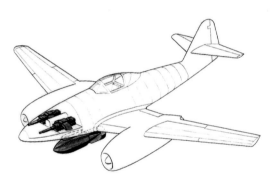

Me 262 A-2 BLITZBOMBER (BB)

## Me 262 A-3 SCHNELLSTBOMBER (SB)

Rumpfspitze in Holz mit liegendem
Bombenschützen als zweiten Mann

| | |
|---|---|
| ZIELEINRICHTUNG: | Lotfe 7 H in der Rumpfspitze |
| BEWAFFNUNG: | vorläufig keine |
| PANZERUNG: | wie Me 262 A-2 |
| BELADEMÖGLICHKEIT: | wie Me 262 A-2 Blitzbomber |
| JÄGERKURSSTEUERUNG | mit Lotfe-Aufschaltung |

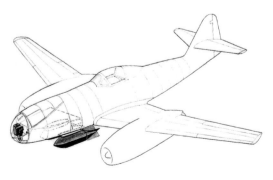

Me 262 A-3 SCHNELLSTBOMBER (SB)

## Me 262 A-4 AUFKLÄRER (A)

2 Bildgeräte RB 50/30 mit Aufsteckmotor
Bildfolgeregelung durch Intervallgeber

BEWAFFNUNG : vorläufig keine

PANZERUNG : wie bei Me 262 A-1

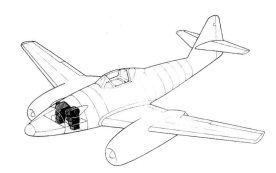

Me 262 A-4 AUFKLÄRER (A)

## Me 262 C-1 HEIMATSCHÜTZER I

Einbau Waltertriebwerk 109.509 S
Druckkabine

KRAFTSTOFFANLAGE : 1 x 900 ltr. Alu-Behälter geteilt für T-Stoff
                  1 x 900 ltr. Sg-Behälter für TL Kraftstoff
                  1 x 170 ltr. M-Behälter    „       „
                  1 x 600 ltr. Alu-Behälter für R-Stoff
                  1 x 300 ltr. Außenbehälter abwerfbar für SV-Stoff

PANZERUNG :       wie Me 262 A-1

BEWAFFNUNG :     wie Me 262 A-1

FAHRWERK        wie A 1 jedoch mit 2 abwerfbaren
                  Zusatzrädern 660 x 190

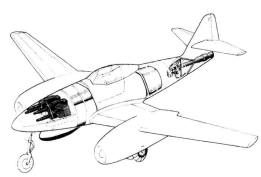

Me 262 C-1 HEIMATSCHÜTZER I

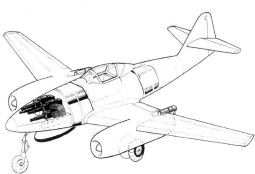

Me 262 C-2 HEIMATSCHÜTZER II

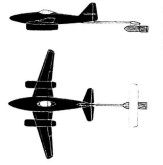

## Me 262 SCHLEPPBOMBE bzw. SCHLEPPBEHÄLTER

BELADEMÖGLICHKEIT :
Bomben bis 1000 kg (vorerst)
oder Behälter mit 900 ltr. Inhalt
Verwendbar bei Me 262 A1 - A2 - A3 - A4 - B1 - C II

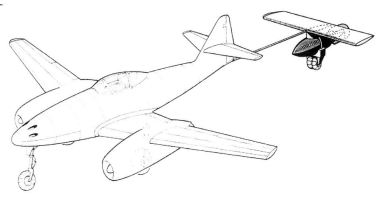

Me 262 SCHLEPPBOMBE
bzw. SCHLEPPBEHÄLTER

fillets were obstructing important maintenance panels.

On October 26, Carl Zeiss staff held a meeting to discuss the best location for the TSA 2 targeting computer within an Me 262 since it had been decided to shift it from the rear fuselage to the forward fuselage, behind the front bulkhead, where it wouldn't affect the compass.[33] Evidently "the proposed location … seems to be okay, but nevertheless this installation location is unsuitable".

This was because putting the delicate computer nearer to the nosewheel placed it under "unnecessary strain" and servicing it became "practically impossible if the cover plate has previously been screwed on (loosening 60 screws)". Retrofitting the computer was made "unnecessarily difficult because the front fuel tank has to be removed".

The best location, it was felt, remained the rear fuselage because it was then easy to fit and access via existing fuselage hatches—even though it was acknowledged that switching the device on in this position would cause the aircraft's compass to be thrown off by three degrees, or 25-degrees if the aircraft was on target approach in a shallow dive. The Zeiss team concluded that "these distractions are bearable" and suggested that as a compromise the computer could be moved even further back, resulting in the compass needle only shifting by one degree when it was switched on.

Meanwhile, E-Stelle Rechlin commander Otto Behrens, now in charge of distributing Me 262 airframes and components for testing, had agreed to a list of new allocations at a meeting with Messerschmitt company officials on October 30.[34] Junkers was to get an airframe for fuel tank fire protection testing, new noses were allocated for the repair of V9 and 170079,[35] a completed Me 262 was allocated for testing a brake parachute installation, and another would be used for testing simplified weapons control circuitry at E-Stelle Tarnewitz.

Another would be used to test carriage of the BT 700 aerial torpedo at Rechlin and two more would be used for testing the MK 103, MG 151 and MK 108 installations at Tarnewitz. One incomplete airframe was allocated to Messerschmitt for installation of parts to become the HG II test vehicle. A further three incomplete airframes would be used as the basis of the night fighter "final solution", apparently meaning the Me 262 B-2. Two of these would go to Rechlin and the last, presumably, would be sent to Messerschmitt.

Two incomplete airframes would provide the basis for Panzerflugzeug conversions, one of them at Rechlin, and two more were allocated to DLH to provide the basis for makeshift night fighters. Exactly which individual airframes would be allocated had yet to be determined.

Two other developments were discussed: Werk-Nr. 110484, fitted with the prone bombardier nose, "urgently needs to be handed over to Rechlin after the company has checked the controls and general airworthiness. Performance measurements are not of interest". And "the aircraft with BMW engines, Werk-Nr. 170078, is to be treated with priority in every respect. The following tasks are to be carried out by the company: performance measurements, tests of nacelle strength and security (cladding). It is estimated that another 1½ months will be needed to carry out these tasks, after which reports will be sent to the Rechlin test station".

Also on October 30, Gerd Lindner made the first test flight of an Me 262 (the V10 in this instance) towing a DFS Schleppgerät.[36] This took the form of an SC 1000 bomb fixed at the end of a 4m drawbar. Two wheels set 240mm apart were attached to the bomb and above it was a single-piece rectangular wing.[37]

An initial ground test, made at walking speed on grass, resulted in the wing attachment point buckling due to the trailer bumping over ruts. This was quickly repaired and a second test commenced. This time there was a break between the drawbar and the spar due to inadequate welding. This too was fixed and static testing of the explosive bolts designed to detach first the bomb's wheels, then the bomb from the wing, then finally the drawbar from the aircraft took place.

Lindner then commenced a take-off run with the trailer. Evidently it had been expected that take-off would occur at 220km/h but instead Lindner found he had to push the aircraft to 245km/h with the trailer pitching up and down on the runway. Once airborne, the trailer "hung at an angle of 10°—measured between the longitudinal axis of the fuselage and the drawbar—under the machine". Lindner reported: "My assumption that the pitching of the trailer that occurred while rolling, caused by unevenness in the ground, would subside after take-off, did not come true. The amplitude increased with increasing speed, so that the towing aircraft made unpleasant movements. Because of the low cloud base and the unpleasant behaviour of the entire tow train around the transverse axis [pitching], I blew the undercarriage off the bomb at around 420km/h."

He noticed that the pitching subsided a little with the loss of the bomb's wheels but then accidentally pressed the detonation button twice in quick succession, which detached both the bomb from the wing and the drawbar from the aircraft. The detached wing apparently then 'landed' by itself at 70km/h and was completely undamaged.

A summary of this test was published on the same day.[38] It concluded that the trailer's original wheelbase

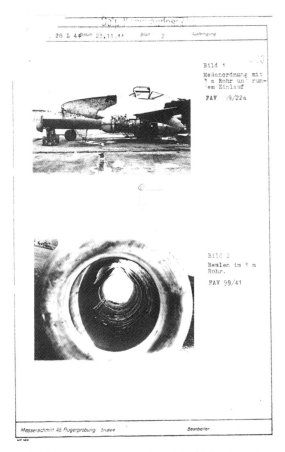

*Werk-Nr. 130015 with a 3m long tube fitted to its port engine to simulate the intake duct of Messerschmitt's P 1101 single jet aircraft. Below it is a view down the tube.*

had been far too narrow and that it should be increased to 680mm. The drawbar attachment was too weak and needed to be reinforced, while the trailer's boom, where the drawbar latched on, tended to bend during tests. The electrical system associated with the explosive bolts had also caused numerous problems.

Another aircraft test-flown during this period, on October 26, was one of the first two-seaters, 130176. Lindner took the Me 262 B-1 up to test the strength of the modified cockpit—which proved satisfactory at an altitude of 1,000m and a speed of 850km/h.[39]

## HITLER FINALLY GIVES IN

Speer had evidently allowed Willy Messerschmitt two weeks to write his report on the Me 262's suitability as a fighter or as a bomber, because he handed it over to him on October 31.[40]

Regarding the aircraft's use as a fighter, Messerschmitt wrote: "The 262 was originally designed as a fighter and is probably superior to any enemy fighter due to its flight performance (speed) ... and its modern heavy armament. This means that, if used correctly, it can destroy and drive away the escort fighters of enemy bomber squadrons and the enemy bombers themselves. Because of its high speed, it can also be used against enemy reconnaissance aircraft."

As a fighter-bomber: "Like any modern fighter aircraft, the 262 can also be used against ground targets, namely with on-board weapons and bombs (fragmentation

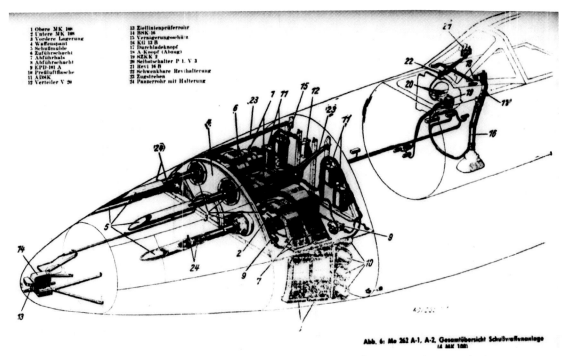

*Standard Me 262 A-1/A-2 nose with a BSK 16 gun camera installation, annotation 14, at the tip.*

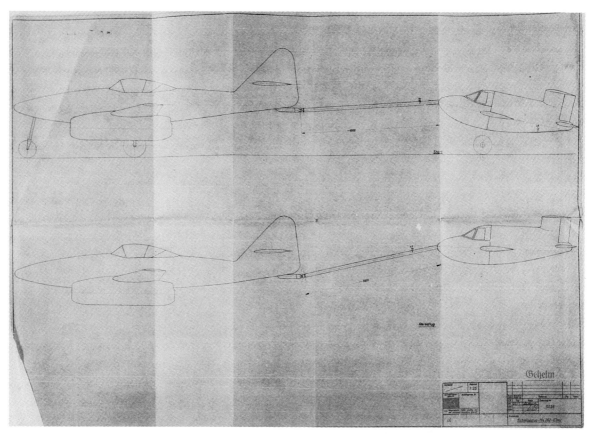

*The Me 262 as a towing vehicle for the DFS Eber, aka Schleppgerät 5026.*

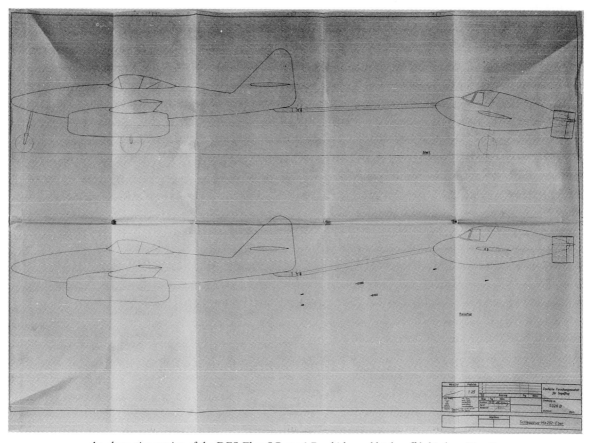

*An alternative version of the DFS Eber, SG 5026 B, which would take off behind an Me 262.*

bombs) against columns and parked aircraft in a similar way as is done today with the 109 or 190. Because of its superior speed, the 262 is unlikely to be bothered by enemy aircraft."

And as a bomber: "The 262 was not originally designed as a bomber and is currently unsuitable for high-altitude level bombing. Despite this, it is now used as a bomber. In addition, there is the order that the planes must not exceed the altitude of 4,000m, must fly no faster than 750km/h (why actually?) and may not dive. The pilot is unable to see the target hidden beneath the fuselage.

"To overcome this deficiency, a prone bombardier position was developed using the best sighting equipment available. Only this allows acceptable use of the 262 as a bomber. With this 262 used as a command aircraft for smaller or larger formations, which otherwise consist of normal 262 fighter planes with bomb racks, carpet bombing can be achieved. This bombardier position is essentially interchangeable with the fighter's gun nose.

"Conclusions: the current use of the 262 promises no success and should be discontinued. Instead, the existing aircraft should be used to ward off enemy bombers and fighters and, if necessary, as fighter-bombers similar to the 109 or 190 (attack on airfields, deployed aircraft, marching columns, etc.). After the creation of the command aircraft, which are required in relatively small numbers, it is possible to use the existing stock of fighter aircraft as a powerful offensive bomber weapon without depriving them of their use as fighters. This alternating use as a fighter or bomber is facilitated by the current conversion of bomber pilots to fighter pilots."

He went on to stress the low cost of the Me 262 and made a plea for additional resources to "ensure that through further development … our current speed advantage is maintained without interruption. I expressly emphasise this, since the deployment of the 262 is unfortunately much later than would have been possible in terms of development and because I have the feeling that the official planning at the moment does not sufficiently recognise the urgent need to further increase speed performance and maintain our lead".

This seems to have achieved the desired effect. In his summary of a series of meetings with Hitler from November 1–4, Saur noted: "The Führer agrees that the Me 262 will now be released as a fighter in all its deployments, on the express understanding that each aircraft is capable of carrying at least one 250kg bomb if necessary."

The Me 262, unquestionably Germany's most powerful fighter, had been in service for seven months by the end of October 1944. And for nearly all of that time,

despite the huge formations of Allied bombers regularly roaming across Germany to deliver one devastating raid after another, the Luftwaffe had been forced to use it as a bomber only. A record 130 Me 262s were accepted by the air force during October, bringing the total number accepted since April to 409.[41] Now the surviving examples—many had been lost in the meantime—could officially be used to take on those enemy bombers and their escorts.

## ME 262 WITH X-4 OR HS 298

A Messerschmitt memo of November 5, 1944, noted that the company had been "instructed to immediately investigate whether the devices X-4 and Hs 298 can be fitted to the Me 262".[42] Both the Ruhrstahl X-4 and the Henschel Hs 298 were rocket-propelled air-to-air missiles, the X-4 was wire guided whereas the Hs 298 used a radio guidance system.

The memo stated that "attempts should be made to accommodate 4 x X-4 or 3 x Hs 298 under the fuselage and wings. On the basis of the project documents to be created, an airworthy mock-up attachment is to be created on a test aircraft and the flight characteristics and flight performance of the type are to be checked. Following the flight test, the series documents for the airframe installations and for the attachment points are to be created and a sample installation is to be carried out".

Strict instructions had been given for the installation—the missiles had to be hung from the aircraft at an angle of between –3° and –5° from the direction of flight "so that the device can detach properly when dropped from its mount". The X-4 needed the ETC 70/C 1 bomb rack while the Hs 298 "is suspended from a launcher with slide rail developed by MWH". The latter was Metallwerke Holleischen GmbH, a company that worked largely for Messerschmitt and was associated with the Flossenbürg concentration camp located in the Fichtel mountains of Bavaria.

The Chef TLR's FL E 8/IV department was to arrange for four airworthy dummy X-4s to be delivered to Lechfeld by Ruhrstahl so that flight testing could commence as soon as possible.

## 26 OUT OF 30 AIRCRAFT LOST

Test installations during early November indicated that 1,000kg booster rockets fitted to the Me 262's usual 500kg rocket attachment points could be fired and dropped without any problems. However, a test flight on November 6 found that 2,000kg of additional thrust pushed the aircraft so hard in a straight line on take-off that the tail control surfaces became ineffective and it was actually more difficult to unstick.[43] Two

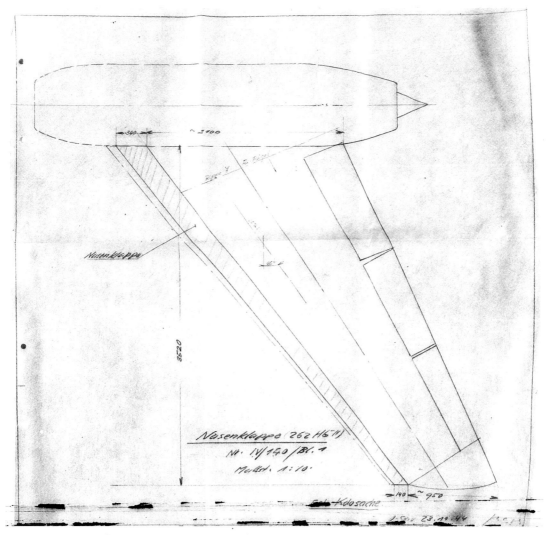

*The Me 262 HG II outer wing, shown in drawing IV/140 of November 23, 1944.*

solutions were suggested—angle the rockets so they provided a natural upwards thrust or ensure that they fired consecutively rather than concurrently, providing a steady 1,000kg of thrust for 12 seconds rather than 2,000kg for six seconds.

There was another field trip for Messerschmitt personnel from November 7-8 to observe the Me 262 being used at the front and to hear complaints.[44] This time it was noted: "In my last report, I pointed out the lack of training and leadership in this command [Kommando Nowotny]. Some of the pilots did not have any fighter training and some were deployed after just two practice flights with 8-262. Nothing has changed in this regard and after Major Nowotny also fell on November 8,[45] 1944, in a dogfight with a large number of Mustangs, probably after being shot at, General Galland was forced to take the above-mentioned order."

The unit had reportedly received 30 aircraft and had already suffered 26 losses—though one aircraft appears on the list twice, having been repaired after the first 'loss'

then 'lost' again. Technical failures were few however, and "almost all of the failures are due to operating errors. General Galland was nevertheless satisfied with the result of this mission".

It is worth briefly examining what actually happened to cause the 26 'losses'. Eight machines—110405, 110395, 170307, 110387, 110479, 110386, 110483 (presumed) and 110400 (Nowotny himself)—had been lost in combat or had crashed as a result of combat damage (110387's pilot Lt Alfred Schreiber had rammed an enemy aircraft with his Me 262 over Nordhorn, Lower Saxony, on October 29). This represents 30.8% of the total losses.

Seven (26.9%) had crashed while attempting a normal take-off or landing—110399, 110401, 170047, 110481, 170278, 170293 and 170045—and another six (23.1%) had crashed after running out of fuel—170292, 110402 (twice), 110388, 110389 and 110490. Three (11.5%)—170044, 170310 and 110403—had crashed while making a single-engine or emergency landing and one (3.8%), 110368, had crashed during a single-engine

*Front view of Werk-Nr. 110484, albeit with an engine cover borrowed from 130186. A crewman can be seen inside the glazed nose compartment posing as the prone bombardier with his eye on the Lotfe bombsight. Beneath the aircraft are two 250kg bombs on ETC 504 racks.*

*110484's bombsight aperture with its aerodynamic wooden fairing.*

*Close-up view of 110484's bombardier compartment, minus the crewman and without the wooden fairing otherwise positioned in front of the Lotfe bombsight aperture—the small set of open doors at the base of the nose. The shadowed bombsight itself is barely visible in this photo.*

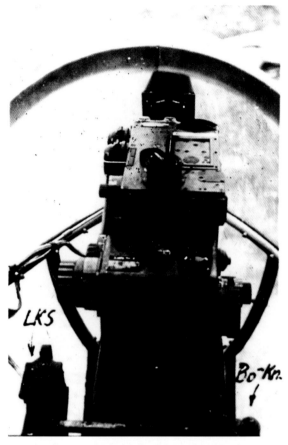

*View from inside the bombardier compartment showing the course correction switch—marked 'LKS'—and the bomb release button, marked 'Bo-Kn'.*

flight. Lastly, the pilot of 110404, Lt Franz Schall, had been forced to bail out when his "engines stopped at 9,000m without [him] changing the throttle position". Exactly what caused this is unclear and the machine was completely destroyed in the ensuing crash, so no mechanical investigation was possible.

Overall, it might be said that around 50% of the rather high operational Me 262 losses were, at this point, due to pilot error. The most significant technical complaints centred once again on nosewheel flutter but it was also the case that "the engines often stop when parts of enemy machines exploded by MK 108 cannon fire fly into one's own aircraft. After single-engine flight, the aircraft is then crashed. It must be assumed that parts flew into the engines and that the malfunction occurred as a result. The problem of protecting the engines must be examined in detail". And "even if the training of the pilots was very poor, the failures in single-engine flight give cause for concern". Lastly, it was noted that broad-shouldered pilots did not fit into the Me 262's cockpit and it was suggested that the aircraft's canopy supports could be thinned at shoulder height to make more space.

## FURTHER TESTING

Sporadic bad weather from November 9-29 resulted in 30% of planned test flights having to be cancelled during this period.[46] Both Me 262 V9 and the Heimatschützer I, 130186, were grounded for the duration—the former as its HG I refit slowly continued and the latter due to a full rocket motor replacement. A ground run of the motor on November 8 revealed a crack in the weld seam, necessitating a completely new unit. The aircraft itself suffered a deformed fuselage bulkhead and the connections where the motor joined the fuselage were bent.[47] Other changes included new fuel line valves, rearrangement of its radio systems and modifications to its pressure cabin. Ground runs with the new motor took place on November 23, revealing further problems which resulted in the replacement of a fuel pump and the T-stoff tank, which was found to be leaking.

The BMW 003 engine test vehicle 170078 managed only four flights between October 21 and November 27 and during that time had needed to have an engine removed four times—once because a Riedel starter motor was "demolished", again due to a scorched nozzle, a third time to correct leaky oil seals and finally to

*Repositioned course correction and bomb release controls within 110484's glass nose.*

repair "damage caused by foreign bodies during static running".[48] 170303 had been used for bomb dropping tests during this period and besides some loose rivets had performed flawlessly.

Werk-Nr. 130015 had developed a semi-circular crack in the front wall of the right landing gear bay, which needed urgent attention as a "repeat case", and "when the aircraft was parked on a rainy day, the rudder jammed as a result of the wooden tail unit swelling".[49] However, it remained usable as a static testbed for Messerschmitt's next generation single jet fighter programme.

There were several different configurations under consideration for this strand of development but the front runner at this time was a version of the P 1101 which had its engine housed within its rear fuselage, fed by a nose intake. This arrangement meant that air would have to travel along a 3m duct to get from the intake to the engine and there were concerns that this could lead to a loss of power. Therefore, 130015 had a 3m long tube attached to its port engine for ground testing.[50]

The engine was run up to 8,700rpm and measurements were taken with five different arrangements—the 3m tube fitted with a round inlet, the 3m tube without the round inlet, the engine without the tube, without the tube but with a protective mesh fitted and with the 3m tube plus round inlet and 'bumps' protruding into the tube. It was found that the tube, in fact, had little effect on power with a maximum loss of 3% detected.

Werk-Nr. 110499 was delivered on November 20 and work commenced on replacing its nose with a new one containing a simplified weapons installation which included the BSK 16 gun camera. And by this date a second BMW 003 test vehicle, 170272, was undergoing conversion work.[51] The test vehicle for the Me 262 A-3 bombardier compartment, 110484, made five flights from November 20-24 and was found to have greater stability than the standard Me 262 A-1s and A-2s but there were problems with the nosewheel door in the new arrangement. In addition, structural differences between the new nose and the standard one meant that normal bomb racks could not be attached, so it had proven necessary to heavily modify a pair of ETC 504s to do the job.

Me 262 V10 towed a Schleppgerät carrying a 500kg bomb without problems on November 18 but when a 1,000kg bomb was tried on November 21 there were severe vibrations and the bomb ultimately tore itself loose, causing severe deformation of the aircraft's tail unit in the process. In addition, V10 had been fitted with two big 18-litre pumps for its hydraulics—so big that the nosewheel was unable to retract in flight.[52]

The official flight test report for the period noted that the Messerschmitt "Project Office currently tries, in cooperation with Professor Ruden, DFS, to create the theoretical basis for the stability behaviour. Only on the basis of these documents can it be said in which

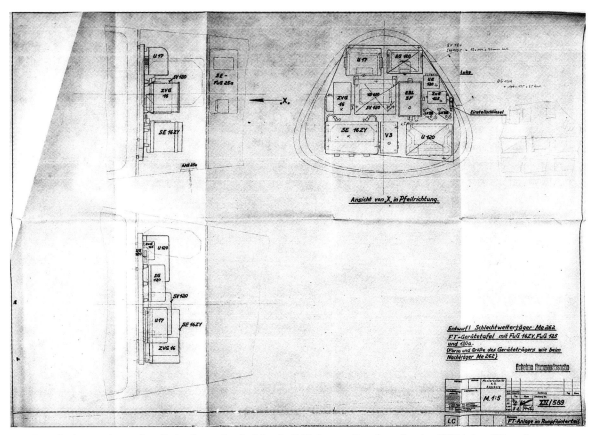

*Rear fuselage equipment installation layout for the Me 262 Schlechtwetterjäger from drawing XIV/589 of December 1944.*

direction improvements should be made". Ruden meanwhile was working to adapt the Schleppgerät principle so that the Me 262 could tow aloft a small rocket-propelled interceptor known as 'Eber'.[53]

Trial and error directional stability experiments continued throughout November, with 170056 having its internally balanced rudder reduced in depth "by cutting off the trailing edge so that a pivot position of 29% was achieved". Another configuration involved fitting a reinforced rudder of normal depth but with "a little … cut off the top", reducing the height of the fin and rudder together by a whopping 500mm.[54] The aircraft was flown by Heinrich Beauvais of the Rechlin test centre who felt it was worth pursuing this line of investigation further. 170079 had meanwhile been transferred to the Luftwaffe.

A disturbing problem had been discovered when one of 110773's bag fuel tanks had been removed. Fuel dribbling from a leaky filler cap had caused the tank's outer skin to partially decompose and detach from the inner skin. A similar issue but with even greater damage had previously been discovered during repair work on an in-service Luftwaffe machine.

Finally, it appeared as though the nosewheel shimmy problem had finally been solved—by repositioning the nosewheel fork slightly to provide an increased trail of

20mm. Three examples of this 'cranked' fork had been tested by the end of November 1944 with "very favourable results". It was found that "despite the suspension of 2 x 500kg bombs and the greatest stress while in motion (very tight turn while rolling over muddy places and uneven ground), no fluttering or tendency to flutter could be detected".

While the makeshift reconnaissance variant of the Me 262, the Behelfsaufklärer, aka A-1/U3, had been flying since mid-July and had actually been used in service from late August, Messerschmitt had only now got around to drawing up a proposal for a full series production model.[55] The design for what would become the Me 262 A-5, outlined in Projektübergabe Me 262—Aufklärer, seems to have differed little from the as-built aircraft with changes mainly focused on the fuselage cut-outs needed to accommodate the two Rb 50/30 cameras and the wiring needed to operate them.

## ME 262 WITH M-WING

The Regensburg factory was by now coming onstream with its production of the Me 262 under the 'Me 609' code name and issued a new schedule on November 24.[56] The HG group meanwhile met with Willy Messerschmitt again on November 27 and presented him with three drawings—two showing the Me 262 with

45° swept wings and HeS 011 engines built into the wingroots and one showing an Me 262 with an M-wing arrangement.[57] Presumably in the latter case the part of each wing closest to the fuselage was swept forward 45°, switching to a 45° sweepback for the outer wing section at about the halfway point.

The professor said that in terms of structure and arrangement, the 45° sweepback designs corresponded to his wishes, although "the arrangement of the engine relative to the wing is disruptive insofar as the protruding engine equipment requires a complex spar. Prof. Messerschmitt suggests pushing the engine back a little and guiding the main spar around the air intake duct on the top and bottom".

The engine manufacturer, Heinkel-Hirth, was to be contacted for details of the engine mountings necessary for this arrangement immediately and "the overall solution should be designed in such a way that it can later be used for night fighters and Panzerflugzeuge".

Messerschmitt was less impressed with the M-wing design, however: "The designs on this were discussed only briefly. Prof. Messerschmitt rejects such a solution for manufacturing reasons. However, a wind tunnel model can be created."

By the end of November another 117 new Me 262s had been accepted by the Luftwaffe, bringing the overall total accepted since April to 526.[58]

## ME 262 A-3 TESTING

December 2 saw another ground run of the Heimatschützer I's new rocket motor and the reattachment of its tail unit.[59] Two days later, a third Panzerflugzeug configuration was proposed for the Me 262—this time based on ideas originating with the Luftwaffe test centres.[60] Now the ammo in the nose would be protected by armour plates of the same size and shape as those fitted to the series production model but thickened to 22mm.

The centre fuselage assembly would be entirely made from armour, rather than armour being retrofitted to the standard airframe. The normal rubber fuel tanks would be replaced with tanks made of welded sheet steel, with the front of the forward tank and the back of the rear tank being "heavily protected". All other tank surfaces would be 2mm thick. In addition, the tanks would be larger than usual, eating up space previously allowed for routing of wiring and control lines. There would instead be metal tubes welded into the tanks through which the wires and lines could pass.

The existing main landing gear doors would be replaced with 3mm thick armour plates to protect against fire from below and the pilot would be "100%"

protected, though the precise form of this protection was to be determined using a mock-up.

The drag values of different radar antenna designs for the Me 262 night fighter had been calculated by December 3 and it had been found that the standard cylindrical antenna rods supplied by Siemens, using standard attachment brackets, would cause a monstrous flight speed reduction of 69km/h.[61] Swapping to reprofiled brackets halved this figure, however. And reprofiling the antenna rods themselves reduced the drag penalty even further, to just 8km/h. It was reported that this data had been sent to Siemens, who would now make the necessary manufacturing adjustments.

The Me 262 A-3 prototype 110484 was taken up for its first bomb release test on December 5 with Karl Baur at the controls and Bayer in the bombardier compartment.[62] According to the report summary, which also included a second test on December 10 flown by Lindner: "Following the auto-pilot control test, the Lotfe bomber nose was prepared for bomb-release tests; this entailed numerous alterations and additional fittings. The first two releases, each of one 250kg bomb on the ETC 504, gave a good result considering the bomb-aimer's inexperience. Misses were due to the influence of the side wind, the automatic correction of which assumes long-practised co-operation between bomb-aimer and pilot as well as practical experience with the auto-pilot. Visibility with the better quality Plexiglass of the test nose was said to be good."

During the second test, two bombs had been carried but one failed to release "because, owing to rattling, it was supposed that either it or the bomb rack had worked loose. After landing with the bomb, however, both parts were found to be perfectly secure".

Bayer reported that when the Lotfe bombsight was extended it was impossible to hear the voice of the pilot over the intercom above 600km/h due to the noise. The fix for this involved a wooden fairing added ahead of the extended sight, which virtually eliminated the issue. He also found the Rechlin-developed couch very uncomfortable, the report noting that "the mattress on the couch must be thicker and softer with a recess for the parachute fastening. Padded supports should be provided for the elbows in the resting position; there should be a cushion on the right hand side suitably fitted in consideration of the movements of the couch.

"The pads provided for the knees are too small. They must be large enough for bomb-aimers of different sizes and for all positions of the couch, including the working position. A head or chin support is required for the rest position and must be high enough for a comfortable view forward over the retracted Lotfe. The head support

*Werk-Nr. 170303 with extended tubes fitted to the barrels of its MK 108s. The standard Me 262
A-1 had tubes fitted which prevented overpressure from the MK 108 muzzles damaging the
interior of the nose when fired—but these only extended as far as the outer skin.*

found in the second Lotfe nose is useless. It prevents
the couch from being moved forward into the working position, is too low for the rest position and makes
it impossible to hook on the safety-belt." The second
'Lotfe nose' had evidently been completed but had not
yet been fitted to a test airframe.

The hatch on top of the bomb aimer nose was
supposed to be removable as an emergency exit but
Bayer found that when he was in the 'working position',
ready to aim, it was impossible to operate the release
lever. And it was highly likely that the bombardier would
accidentally drop the bombs prematurely—because
when he went to set the speed control his right fore-
arm would automatically come into contact with the
bomb release button. It was probable that his right elbow
would simultaneously unplug the intercom too, due to
its positioning.

The view through the Plexiglass directly in front of
the bomb aimer was poor "owing to the bad quality of
the panes" and rainwater infiltration was also a problem
because "at present the water flows directly onto the
fuse switch box".

Another variant being worked on at this time was
the Me 262 Schlechtwetterjäger or 'bad weather fighter'.
This was essentially a standard Me 262 A-1 with the
additional of a K 22 autopilot unit, the FuG 125 system

and FuG 120a. A mock-up of an Me 262 cockpit fitted
with this equipment was inspected at Oberammergau
on December 6 and some minor changes to the layout
were discussed at a meeting the following day.[63]

## NIGHT FIGHTER MOCK-UP

Another mock-up, this time of the Me 262 night fighter
configuration, was inspected on December 7.[64] It was
found that the radar operator's equipment setup was
largely fine, with only minor adjustments needed for
the sake of comfort and the omission of a variometer
as unnecessary. It was necessary, however, to find a way
of allowing the observer to switch his light on—so he
could see what he was doing—without this being visible
from outside the aircraft. The solution discussed involved
four simple black curtains, one to the front, one on
either side and one to the rear.

Another tricky aspect of the design was the one-piece
canopy which covered both crew. It had to be possible
to eject this in an emergency in such a way that it got
caught by the slipstream and whipped away from the
aircraft but without twisting sideways and hitting the
radar operator's head in the process. It was suggested that
a Junkers canopy ejection device might achieve this and
Messerschmitt's Rudolph Rentel was to investigate this.
The canopy ejection also required the cable leading from

*Another view of the extended MK 108 tubes on 170303. The longer tubes simulated the aerodynamic effect of installing longer-barrelled weapons in the Me 262's nose.*

the Naxos antenna in the aircraft's nose to be severed and experiments were to be carried out to see whether this was best achieved using a knife or blade of some sort or via a mechanism connected to the Junkers device.

No measures would be taken to ensure that the radar operator's windows didn't fog up and he would not be granted his own heating system since "a room temperature of 8° for the observer's seat is considered sufficient. It can be expected that this temperature will be reached without an additional second heating system. The rear part of the cabin is to be designed in such a way that the observer also has a good view to the rear (as with the fighter A-1)".

In the pilot's cockpit, a total of 16 signal flares were provided and a rear light could be switched on and off separately from the other lights. Beacons under the fuselage would also be provided. A single 1,000kg booster rocket would be fitted for take-off, although it would be desirable to have two which could be operated sequentially, providing 1,000kg thrust for twice as long. A K 22 autopilot unit would be fitted. Neither crewman would get back armour "for weight reasons and to maintain a clear view to the rear".

The arrangement of the electronic equipment within the fuselage was fine—with the FuG 25a IFF system as far away from the aircraft's compass as possible.

The night fighter would have two MK 108s in its nose, with more ammo than was supplied for the standard Me 262 A-1's cannon, plus two behind the cockpit pointing upwards. For the prototypes the angle would be adjustable—so that the best position could be determined—then the series production model would see them fixed in that position. However, "for the first prototype, if there is a delay, the installation of the rear weapons can be omitted. For this purpose, a normal series nose with four MK 108s is to be provided". The aircraft would also have the option to tow a Schleppgerät.

Two further mock-ups were evidently also inspected during this period up to December 8. These were an Me 262 Panzerflugzeug arrangement and a reconnaissance variant which could carry a pair of MK 108s in addition to its camera equipment.[65]

Meanwhile, the second Me 262 earmarked for A-3 bomb aimer nose conversion, 110555, arrived at Lechfeld on December 10 and two-seat trainer 170055 was borrowed from the Luftwaffe the following day as a test mule for multi-disc brake tests. During December, 37.5% of planned experimental flights from Lechfeld had to be cancelled due to bad weather but 12 Me 262 test vehicles still managed to make 159 flights, spending a total of 27 hours aloft.[66]

Unfortunately for Lindner, some of these flights

involved testing the new J2 fuel—derived from lignite, aka brown coal. He reported that the "new fuel has an offensive odour which seriously inconveniences the pilot, since gases penetrate into the cockpit. Better sealing of the cockpit against the penetration of fuel gases is considered necessary".[67]

On December 15, the Project Office issued a work order for the production of eight profiled Me 262 night fighter antennas—enough to equip two aircraft.[68]

## ME 262 HG III DESIGN

The Messerschmitt Project Office team presented Willy Messerschmitt with their latest design for the third stage Me 262 high-speed development at a meeting on December 17, 1944.[69] Burying the engines in the wing-roots had resulted in some difficulties when it came to positioning the landing gear but according to the meeting summary "Prof. Messerschmitt considers the problem to be solvable".

The engine intakes had originally been cylindrical in design for simplicity's sake but Messerschmitt "attaches particular importance to investigating a second form in which the inlet has an oval opening that is as narrow as possible". It was decided that static testing with the two proposed intake forms should take place at Lechfeld as soon as possible.

At the same meeting, Messerschmitt asked one of the Project Office team, Hans-Joachim Puffert, to contact Lippisch and the Horten brothers, Walter and Reimar, "in order to gather experience regarding the stall behaviour of swept wings". He also suggested using "spoilers" on the ailerons and rejected a suggestion to make the outer wings more slender. Boundary layer suction was to be investigated in connection with the design.

Three days later a memo was produced which summarised the HG programme's status.[70] The last component needed to complete the HG I prototype (Me 262 V9), the low profile canopy, had been modified and was awaiting despatch from Oberammergau to Lechfeld.

The 35° swept wings for the HG II were 70% complete and a target flight date of January 20, 1945, had been set although "the engines are still missing (allegedly on the way)". The special asymmetrical engine nacelles were structurally complete but their fairings were still with the Construction Office. Plans to allow for a second engine position, with the "engine moved back until the inlet is flush with the wing leading edge is not being worked on at the moment".

The Construction Office's undercarriage team were now working to "clarify wheel retraction and accommodation" in the HG III using a model and wind tunnel testing of the wingroot engine layout had begun in the low speed wind tunnel at Göttingen. Willy Messerschmitt was apparently pressing for high-speed testing to begin in order "to clarify the conditions in the engine inlet".

A programme of future work was also set out, including the creation of plasticine models and templates for the two different intake designs, preparation for performance comparisons between the HG I, HG II and HG III, the design of the proposed V-tail, the practical testing of the different intake designs, and "negotiations with the engine companies".

## ENGINE SHORTAGE

By mid-December the shortage of Jumo 004s predicted three months earlier was finally beginning to bite. When cut-down fin and rudder test vehicle 170056 crash landed on December 12, its engines were stripped out and donated to other aircraft while it underwent repairs and the reinstallation of its normal tail unit.

Similarly, the Heimatschützer I had its jet engines removed for use in other machines after its new rocket motor broke on December 18. The motor had suffered from exactly the same flaw as the previous unit—a weld seam crack. Three days earlier there had been another rocket fuel dump flight test which demonstrated that the released liquid (water for the tests) was still being sucked back into the fuselage. Now the aircraft would sit entirely engineless while it awaited its third rocket motor.

The Me 262 V9 may also have been without engines during this time, since it was parked up for the whole of December while its low profile canopy underwent revisions at Oberammergau. V10 too may have been engineless as it underwent repairs and had a reinforced Schleppgerät tow bar connection point fitted. And 170083 had its engines taken out while measuring equipment was installed to assess the performance of its undercarriage. It was noted in the December test report that the sheer number of Me 262 test vehicles sitting around without engines meant that planned undercarriage testing had had to be postponed.[71]

Werk-Nr. 170074 arrived at Lechfeld on December 20 with a pair of BMW 003 R combination engines fitted and ready to test. This was the Me 262 C-2 prototype, also referred to in contemporaneous test reports as the Heimatschützer II. Initial inspection revealed that the aircraft had been fitted with "incorrect" wiring running from the fuselage to the engines and work to correct this commenced on December 22. It was also noted that the left 003 R was to supply the cockpit with warm air while the right one powered the fuel pumps. But "since the air flow rate of the BMW engines is significantly lower than that of the Jumo engines, it still has to be clarified whether one engine is sufficient for the air and heating requirements. Discussions are being held with BMW to achieve a possible increase in air throughput".

The other test vehicle fitted with BMW engines, 170078, had made five more flights by this time and suffered two more engine failures necessitating the installation of new units—one resulting from "turbine blade fracture (perhaps due to overheating while taxiing)" and the other from "chips in the oil filter".

Also on December 22 the borrowed two-seater, 170055, was wrecked. Baur had flown it to 1,500m altitude when the left engine's rpm abruptly dropped from 6,000 down to 2,000. Adjusting the throttle made no difference so he stopped it but then couldn't get it started again. Coming in to land on one engine, the nosewheel retracted as soon as it touched the ground and both engines were torn off in the ensuing crash landing.[72] Total damage amounted to 70% of the aircraft.

It had meanwhile been noted on December 21 that work was under way on assembling the Me 262 HG II prototype,[73] based on Werk-Nr. 111538, though serious problems were being encountered because "the wing internals are poorly prepared. The engine control rods have now been fundamentally changed for the third time. The control gear and lines have to be laid for the fifth time. The fuselage is currently being built onto the wing…The promised large components, such as the nose, tail boom and engines, have not yet been received. The production date is therefore at risk".

## WINTER TESTING

Werk-Nr. 170303 was used to test the drag of "four extended MK 108 protective tubes"—presumably these extended to protrude from the aircraft's nose in the way that the barrels of an MG 151 or MK 103 might. It was found that the penalty for those longer barrels was 27km/h. Without the tubes it could manage 867km/h at 1,300m altitude; with them it could only do 840km/h.[74]

Still being possessed of "well-tuned" engines, 170303 was also used for high-speed take-offs—using a pair of 1,000kg boosters—and landings during December. Evidently angling the boosters downwards by 8° solved the earlier linear thrust problem but an additional brace against the fuselage was required to keep them in position. And 170303 had already been fitted with specially reinforced brackets for the boosters. According to the test report "the permissible tolerances are far exceeded in the series version. Remedy is urgently needed". In other words, 170303 could just about withstand 2,000kg of thrust but no unmodified production line Me 262 would be able to cope.

It also became the second Me 262 fitted with a Jacobs-Schweyer wooden fin and rudder, after 130015, but it ended up being stood in the winter rain "for a long time". The rudder consequently swelled and became stuck, requiring changes.

An inspection of the aircraft also revealed that "a large number of rivets" had come loose in the area of the rear auxiliary spar which "may be due to the high stress caused by brake testing". 130015 itself was used to measure pressure distribution on its wing leading edges and 130167 was a vehicle for disc brake tests.

As far as general testing was concerned, a "wide-ranging investigation was carried out on the ground on our own test vehicles and on Luftwaffe aircraft" to trace an issue where fuel leaked into the radio systems of some aircraft, rendering them non-functional. Further tests were carried out with sealing strips to prevent cockpit rainwater ingress and there was a common problem where "when rolling in wet snow, the same is thrown up and settles between the slide and the roller block [of the main landing gear]. When retracting the landing gear, the snow compresses and damages the leg cover and causes the clamp band to break off the roller block. Furthermore, the wheel well packs full of snow, which prevents retraction of the undercarriage".

Work on fitting a BSK 16 gun camera under the fuselage was stopped because installing it in the nose unit itself "meets the requirements".

A third attempt at bombing using the Me 262 A-3 prototype 110484 took place on December 27 with "good success". Lindner and Bayer were back as pilot and bombardier respectively and the latter noted that the Lotfe bombsight had suffered minor damage when the aircraft's nosewheel bumped over rough frozen ground. A new set of wooden wing end caps was delivered for installation and testing on December 30—another straightforward way of swapping an expensive metal Me 262 component for a cheap wooden one.

## THE FUTURE OF FIGHTERS

It had been noted on December 19 that testing of the Me 262 night fighter variant at Rechlin was not yet planned[75] but work on the Me 262 bad weather fighter was progressing, with a new document being produced on the same day which detailed exactly how and where the aircraft's electronic systems would be installed.[76]

A meeting was then held at Lechfeld the following day to discuss the current status of Me 262 development.[77] Here it was noted that the Me 262 A-3 prototype needed handing over to the Luftwaffe test stations as soon as possible and that its nose compartment needed to be updated. Three new modified nosewheel struts were ready for collection at Oberammergau to continue testing.

Despite all the difficulty involved in getting Me 262 V9 allocated as the HG I test vehicle in the first place, "since the completion takes so long, and since Stage II has now been completed, the interest is not great. For this aircraft, the swept tail must be delivered to Oberammergau again". In other words, the HG I's swept tail was now to be stripped off Me 262 V9 and sent back to Oberammergau for installation on the HG II.

But "before that... a short flight test should be carried out... the tail unit may have to be removed from the V9 and flown on another machine". Presumably this was because the V9 still languished without engines and refitting a pair would lead to even greater delays.

Multi-disc brakes were to be provided for the "15 night fighters at Offingen"[78] and the first Me 262 bad weather fighter cockpit "with a 20° window inclination" was being built at Oberammergau.

Meanwhile, the EHK had met for a two-day session on December 19 and 20.[79] The Main Development Commission was now subdivided into nine 'special commissions', each led by a high-profile figure from the German aviation industry. Willy Messerschmitt was now in charge of day fighter development, via the Sonderkommission Tagjäger, Kurt Tank of Focke-Wulf was responsible for night fighter development as leader of the Sonderkommission Nachtjäger, Heinrich Hertel of Junkers was in charge of bomber development, Robert Lusser, designer of the V1, was in charge of 'special aircraft' and so on.

In his new role, Messerschmitt gave a presentation to his fellow commission members at the beginning of the meeting on the subject of 'piston engine and jet fighter or only jet fighter?' He said, "there is a clear, uniform view that only the jet fighter can be decisive in the performance race with the foreign countries. It is known that jet fighter development abroad is roughly on the same level as in Germany. Based on this knowledge, the jet fighter with the more powerful HeS 11 engine must be developed as quickly as possible, especially since the aircraft type 162 with the 003 engine is known not to be seen as a best solution, but only as a transitional solution".

This was a significant dialling back of Messerschmitt's views on the He 162 from two months earlier when he wrote out a lengthy tirade against the Volksjäger—arguing that it should not go into production.[80] Perhaps he was being more circumspect because several of his 'colleagues' on the commission were involved with getting the He 162 into production.

It was decided that HeS 011 engine development needed to be "accelerated with very special means" and that Messerschmitt's special commission "has to make the decision about the airframe project to be carried out

at the beginning of January". Furthermore, it was still not possible to dispense with the ongoing development of piston engine fighters so the Focke-Wulf Ta 152 "must be continued on both the engine and fuselage side by all means in order to keep up with the performance of piston engine fighters abroad in the near future".

Tank then gave a speech on night fighters, stating that "the current developments of the [Ar] 234 and [Do] 335 as night fighters are makeshift solutions and are unsatisfactory for the required night use with long flight duration and sufficient navigation". He apparently failed to mention the Me 262 night fighter.

It was decided that "the development of a superior night fighter with a long flight duration (5 to 8 hours?) and sufficient navigation capability (three man crew) is particularly urgent. In January the Sonderkommission Nachtjäger (Tank) has to make clear decisions about a possible further development of the 335 using an additional jet engine as well as a fundamentally new development of the night fighter".

The development of a pulsejet-powered fighter was ruled out and attention then turned to the requirement for a point defence fighter, called 'Objektschutzjäger' in the meeting summary. It was decided that the Me 263—a rocket interceptor based on the Me 163 B but developed by Junkers—"must be accelerated by all means" and that "the finished development of the 262 with rocket propulsion should also be continued, because if the result is good, this development may make all other point defence fighters superfluous".

Rocket-propelled interceptor designs by Heinkel ('Julia') and Junkers ('Walli') were cancelled and another produced by Bachem, the Natter, could be finished in prototype form but could not enter series production. Finally, it was decided that the Jumo 222 would be cancelled since attempts to develop it further would draw much-needed resources away from Jumo 004 jet and 213 piston engine development.

A new Protokoll was issued on December 20 regarding the Me 262 A-5, requiring that the installation of an Rb 20/30 camera in the fuselage, as opposed to the nose, be investigated.[81]

## MISTEL 4

A day later, on December 21, the management report of the ChefTLR's Fl-E 2 department briefly discussed the status of the various Mistel projects being worked on by Junkers. Since mid-1943, the company had been developing and building composite aircraft for attacking large static targets on the ground—such as battleships, fortifications and bridges.

The first such combination, Mistel 1, consisted of a

worn out Junkers Ju 88 lower component, its cockpit replaced with a huge explosive charge, and a Messerschmitt Bf 109 F-4 upper component fixed to struts protruding from the Ju 88's upper surface by explosive bolts. The Bf 109's pilot would actuate the Ju 88's engines and control surfaces remotely from his 'piggyback' position above it, guiding both aircraft into the air and onward to their target. Once there, he would aim the Ju 88 flying bomb then fire the explosive bolt to detach his Bf 109 from it. Gyro-stabilisation would, in theory, ensure that the Ju 88 flew in a straight line directly into its target.

Later Mistel combinations had included the Mistel 2 Fw 190 A-8/Ju 88 G-1 and Mistel 3, a blanket designation for a variety of Fw 190/Ju 88 combinations.

Mistel 4 appears to have been an Me 262 upper component attached to a Ju 88 lower component[82] and the management report noted that an order for 25 combinations of the 88/262 was still pending as well as six lower component aircraft each for the He 162 and Ar 234.[83] These latter two were the Mistel 5 and Mistel 6 combinations respectively and each was to have the same lower component—a bespoke new twin-jet aircraft with a detachable undercarriage designed by

Junkers and known as the 8-268.[84]

The same management report noted that Knemeyer had given permission for a Japanese delegation to visit the Junkers factory, presumably Dessau, to view the following types: Ju 288, Ju 287, Ju 248 and Ju 88/Me 262.[85]

There was bad news for Messerschmitt as the year drew to a close. A company file note dated December 30, 1944, indicates that the Me 262 A-3 could not yet be cleared for series production because during static testing of a wooden bombardier compartment "the fuselage skin burst open due to poor gluing. The attempt could therefore no longer be continued. The continuation of this test is necessary for series approval".[86] In addition, it was not possible to fill up the 600 litre extra tank on the type because this would cause centre of gravity issues—negatively affecting its operational range.

As December 1944 drew to a close, the total number of Me 262s accepted for the month amounted to 144—taking the total number accepted by the Luftwaffe since April to 670 according to one source.[87] Another source gives the total produced up to the end of December 1944 as 564, with only 446 having been accepted by the Luftwaffe including 21 under repair and 17 B-1 trainers.[88]

# 10

# To the Limit:
# January to February 1945

T HE SIXTH round of army conscription from the German aircraft industry, SE 6 Action, was announced during the first week of 1945. A total of 160,000 men—half of them from armaments manufacturing and the other half from airframe construction—were to be handed over. Of these, 80,000 had to be within the age range 40-45 and the rest had to be younger. The Chef TLR noted that pleas for protection of these workers had been "rejected in principle".[1]

The Me 262 came up several times during a series of meetings with Adolf Hitler from January 3-5. On the first occasion, Saur reported that "the Führer welcomes the suggestions made by Messerschmitt [that pilots should] release the bomb rack on the Me 262, along with the two bombs, by pulling the emergency release lever twice in such a way that after the bombs have been dropped the [lower surface of the] plane is completely flat [in other words, aerodynamically clean]. It should be examined to what extent this possibility can be envisaged for other aircraft, especially with the new developments".[2]

Presumably Willy Messerschmitt, whose technical focus tended to be on performance above all other considerations, wanted to ensure that pilots were not suffering a drag penalty by leaving empty bomb racks attached to their aircraft. This meddling, encouraging Hitler to micro-manage operational considerations, is unlikely to have been welcomed either by the Luftwaffe itself or by Saur's Rüstungsstab since it failed to take account of a critical shortage of racks.[3]

Later on Saur told Hitler that, given the huge quantities of aluminium required when manufacturing bombers, "in the long run at most one American bomber can be built for every German fighter plane". So "in the future ... priority should be given to hitting the bombers, since one bomber shot down by one fighter is enough to establish parity", whereas the Americans were able to build three fighters for every German fighter. In other words, from a purely resources perspective, it made sense to focus attacks on bombers—each one shot down inflicted a greater loss of materials on the enemy.

This evidently made perfect sense to Hitler and he was again persuaded to dictate the Me 262's role. Saur wrote: "Taking this fact into account, the Führer immediately agreed to my proposal to use the Me 262 as a fighter directly against four-engined bombers."[4] This was adding insult to injury somewhat, since the Luftwaffe had wanted to use the Me 262 against four-engined bombers since May 1943—only being prevented from doing so by the production difficulties previously outlined and by the earlier decisions of Hitler himself.

*Test pilot Karl Baur takes off in Me 262 V9 to test the low-profile HG I cockpit canopy and swept tailplanes.*

## THE TEST FLEET

A combination of bad weather and a lack of engines during January 1945 grounded 63% test flights that had been planned for the Me 262 experimental aircraft at Lechfeld. Just 55 flights, amounting to a woeful 15.7 hours, were made using the 13 available test vehicles throughout the month.[5] Just one new 004 engine was delivered between January 1 and January 31.

The new J2 fuel proved to be another limiting factor since it had a tendency to freeze at extremely low temperatures. Six accidents had been caused by Me 262 fuel filters becoming clogged with ice crystals and the constituency of the fuel could not be altered without significantly degrading its performance.[6]

The test flight section was informed about the filter clogging problem by the Chef TLR and all flights ceased pending further investigation, only a handful being made with filters removed. Inspection of all filters aboard the Lechfeld aircraft showed no problems however, so flight testing resumed but only when aircraft had been kept in hangars overnight and when ground temperatures were above -15°C.[7]

The still engineless 170083 sat out the whole month and the first prone bombardier prototype, 110484, was transferred to the Luftwaffe for testing on January 7. The latter appears now to have been redesignated A-2a/U2—perhaps because the design's entry into full series production as the A-3 had now been blocked, at least for the time being.[8] 110499 was loaned to the Luftwaffe so its simplified weapons circuitry could be tested.

110555 also remained grounded. Having received the second prone bombardier nose, it was now undergoing further work to install a K 22 autopilot unit and the Baldrian system. This time, rather than having the two microphones mounted on a single forked probe, each would get its own separate probe. The aircraft's nose

compartment also received all the upgrades previously made to that of 110484—emergency ejection of the upper hatch, better seat belt adjustability, improved chin rest and better couch padding. Evidently the K 22 installation had to be abandoned at this time due to lack of parts.[9]

Exactly why an Me 262 fitted with a 'Lotfe' bombsight nose—ostensibly a bomber—would need an acoustic detection system fitted to that nose, pointing forwards, is unclear.[10]

The Heimatschützer I, 130186, didn't fly either. Installation of a new combustion chamber and quick-drain fuel system took place on January 4 but its rocket fuel lines were found to have suffered frost damage on January 12. Three days later an attempt was made to test its rocket motor but fuel leaks led to a fire and the rear fuselage had to be dismantled again. Another new combustion chamber had been fitted by January 25, and a further rocket tests took place on January 28 and 29, but then the rocket fuel tank had to be removed "in order to realign the cover that had been sucked in by the negative pressure in the tank".

All of this left eight machines that actually flew: the V9, V10, 130015, 130167, 170056, 170074, 170078 and 170303.

Baur made four brief flights to finally test the Me 262 V9's 40° swept tailplanes and lowered 'racing' canopy[11]—from 3.09pm to 3.15pm on January 17, 12.10pm to 12.17pm on January 18, 11.42am to 11.50am on January 19 and 11.30am to 11.41am on January 20.

Two days later, a Messerschmitt Project Office memo noted that the configuration had made the aircraft very tail-heavy and it was decided that the swept tail should be substituted for a standard unit so that the 'racing' canopy could be tested on its own. Similarly, the Me 262 HG II would now be tested first with a normal tail, leaving the swept tail unit unused.[12] Evidently it

*170056 pictured following its crash on December 12, 1944. Its shortened tailfin is clearly visible.*

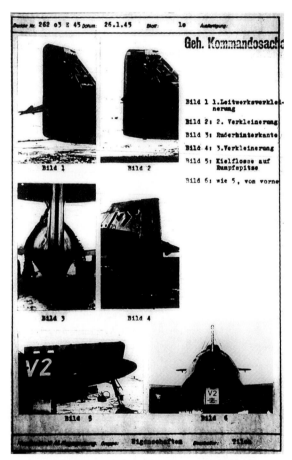

*A page of photos showing the various experiments carried out using 170056, which was briefly given the reused 'V2' designation around late December 1944.*

had not been possible to test pressure distribution over the canopy because the necessary measuring devices were in use elsewhere. In addition, Baur seems to have found the experience of flying with the lowered canopy very uncomfortable since the summary report notes: "Overall [cockpit] height is by no means suitable for the series, the test flights already have to be carried out

by the pilot in an impossible position."[13]

The Me 262 V10 had been converted to take a pair of 300-litre fuel tanks on Wikingerschiff bomb racks under its nose and these were flight-tested, commencing on January 14. As a result, "a number of fundamental deficiencies in the system were identified, and work is still in progress to rectify them."[14] There had also been further attempts to tow a 1,000kg bomb with the DFS Schleppgerät but "vibrations occurred around the lateral axis of the aircraft and trailer, which increased very sharply at a speed of approx. 650km/h. The wing of the trailer disintegrated into small scraps". The pilot had been forced to initiate an emergency release and consideration was now being given to reinforcing the wing.[15]

130015 was used to test wing slat pressure distribution as well as new 70mm wide brake pads and 130167 continued disc and shoe brake testing and testing of its internally balanced rudder. 170056 was used for lateral stability tests and then had its shortened tailfin swapped for a standard one. It was next scheduled to test a new nosewheel fork supplied by Fluggeräte Elma of Waiblingen, Stuttgart, which would enable the Me 262 to use a standard Bf 109 mainwheel, measuring 660 x 190mm, as its nosewheel.

The Heimatschützer II, 170074, only managed to get airborne once—for a fuel dump test flight using just its turbojets on January 8, the quick release outlet having now been moved to the rear of the aircraft. Afterwards it was discovered that the fuel pump for the rocket motor attached to the BMW 003 on the right was leaking and needed to be replaced. Then the ground crew encountered serious difficulty in getting either turbojet going and the Riedel starter motor on each had to be replaced twice before the problem was resolved. The 003 on the right then had to be fully replaced, on January 18, because metal chips were found in the gearbox bearing.[16]

A fuel line test using water on January 21 found that

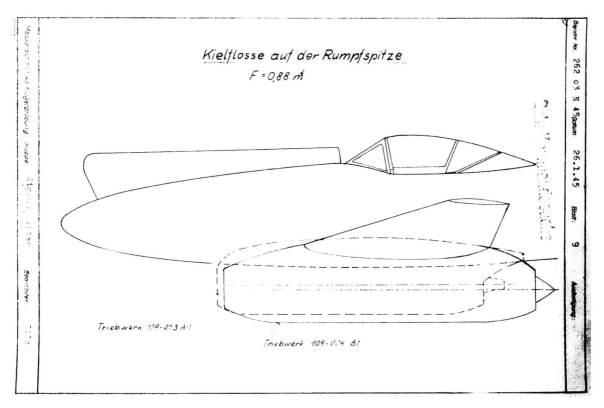

*Drawing from the January 26, 1945, report summarising the stability experiments undertaken with 170056 up to that point—including the installation of a large fin on its nose.*

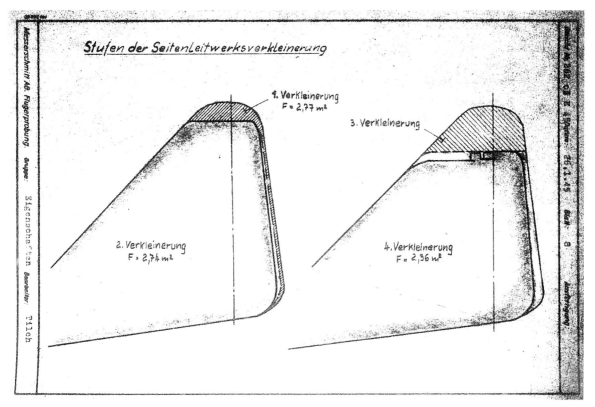

*Another drawing from the January 26 report, showing the step-by-step approach to reducing the area of 170056's fin and rudder.*

*The Me 262 C-2, aka Heimatschützer II, fires its rocket motors on January 25,*
*left, before an explosion wrecks the starboard unit, right.*

there was insufficient pressure in the system so the pressure relief valve and the fuel line itself were replaced. There was then a second water test on January 24 and it seemed as though everything was now working as required. The water was therefore replaced with actual rocket fuel and on January 25 the system was given a ground run—whereupon the rocket motor combustion chamber on the right wing exploded immediately after ignition.

The blast, which had been caused by an accumulation of too much fuel at the wrong pressure, damaged the aircraft's tail unit and right landing flap, necessitating replacements, but there were no reports of injury.

Werk-Nr. 170078 seems to have finally turned a corner with its BMW 003 engines, managing seven flights in January without any mechanical malfunctions.[17] This meant some engine performance data could be gathered and tests were conducted to assess the aircraft's lateral stability—its tendency to roll—with them installed. The results were not encouraging: "The machine's lateral stability…was judged to be particularly poor. The period of the yaw oscillation is even shorter than in the series machines." The aircraft was also fitted with the shortened fin taken from 170056 for further testing.

Lastly, 170303 was used to test take-off performance when carrying two 500kg bombs while boosted by two 500kg rockets. It had been intended that 303 would use two 1,000kg rockets installed at an angle of 8°, and 16 of these were modified in readiness, but delays resulting from bad weather meant that the 500kg boosters had to be used instead. Nine flights were made but the aircraft sustained damage, presumably on the last of these, when a booster tore itself loose. The rocket shot forwards and smashed into the rear of one of the bomb racks, detaching the bomb and leaving a hole in the underside of the fuselage.[18]

Other work carried out included testing of improved cockpit drainage strips and fitment of the Revi EZ 42

gunsight. The latter was hampered by the seemingly not uncommon problem of Me 262 components not being quite the size and shape they were supposed to be: "The installation showed difficulties due to structural deviations at the front part of the cabin, in particular the radii of the mounting brackets do not match the cabin frame profile". Four EZ 42s had been delivered and three aircraft had them fitted.

There was also some fine-tuning of the new nose-wheel fork, since it had evidently struggled with snowy conditions, and there had been complaints about the BSK 16 gun camera, where it could sometimes start up by itself if the wrong combination of cockpit controls were pressed.

## NIGHT FIGHTER COMPETITION

The OKL, the Luftwaffe high command, issued a "rough guide" to its development requirements on January 11.[19] Essentially, three new aircraft were needed—a replacement for the He 162, a replacement for the Ta 152 and a new night fighter. The latter was to be a three-seater powered by a jet engine in each wing and a single piston engine in the fuselage. Automatic blind landing was required and the aircraft had to be capable of attacking four-engined enemy bombers on piston engine power alone, the turbojets being there purely to ensure performance superiority over enemy night fighters.

Top speed needed to be 900km/h at 8-10km altitude using the turbojets or at least 550km/h between ground level and 10km altitude using only the piston engine. Endurance had to be one and a half hours using the jets or at least five hours using only the piston engine, without drop tanks.

Forward-firing armament was to be "four 3cm weapons, four MG 213/30 if possible". Oblique armament was to be two MG 213/20s. Equipment needed to include de-icing for wings, tail unit, propeller and canopy, "short and long wave on-board radio system for

*Rear view showing the damage inflicted when 170074's wing-mounted rocket motor exploded.*

touch, speech and direction finding", a navigation device, airborne intercept radar with a range of at least 10km, airborne early warning radar system, a device to track Rotterdam and Meddo (Allied airborne radar mapping systems) and a device to track enemy using jammers.

It also had to be capable of carrying the 8-344 (aka Ruhrstahl X-4 air-to-air missile), R4M rockets, Jäger-faust or "on-board rockets of larger calibre with incendiary shrapnel filling". It needed a gunsight suitable for use at night, armour protection against 20mm ammunition from the front and behind, a pressure cabin, tricycle undercarriage, ejection seat, the option to carry an overload, and rough field take-off and landing capability.

Focke-Wulf Betriebsführer Kurt Tank, in his capacity as head of the Special Commission for Night Fighters, appears to have subsequently requested descriptions of all night fighter projects then in progress and by January 19, 1945, had received them for Arado's Ar 234 C-3, N and P-1, Dornier's Do 335 A-6 and B-6, and Messerschmitt's Me 262 B-2.

The latter document, which had only been completed a day earlier,[20] stated: "The night fighter described here is a replacement for the makeshift night fighter currently under construction at Deutsche Lufthansa, which has been converted from the Me 262 training aircraft, with its short ranges and limited space.

"The night fighter Me 262, type designation B2, was

*The corrosive SV-Stoff fuel used by the BMW 003 R rocket motor stripped the paint off the side of 170074.*

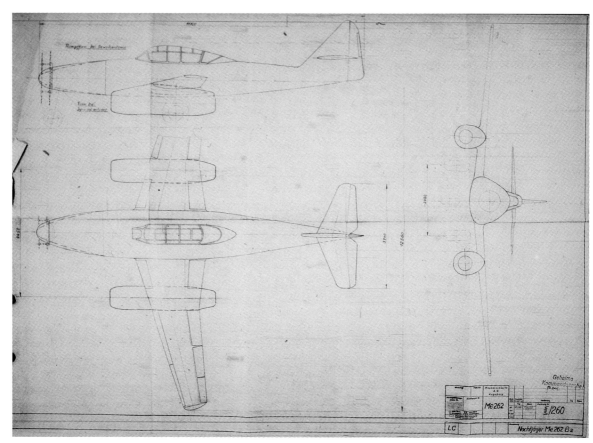

*Me 262 B-2 night fighter design from the January 18 project description. The drawing, II/260, is dated January 17, 1945.*

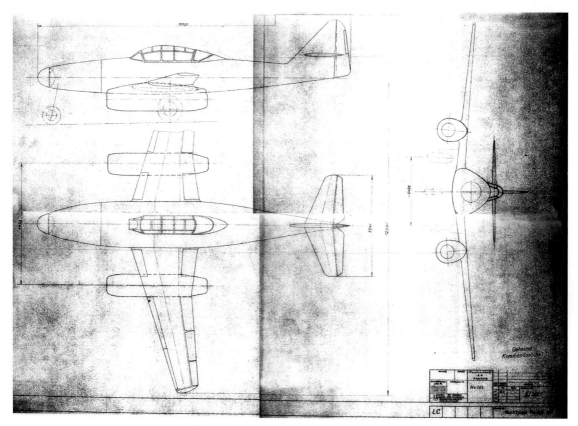

*An alternative version of drawing II/260, not included in the project description, which shows a clean nose configuration with internal dish antenna rather than the external 'antler' type.*

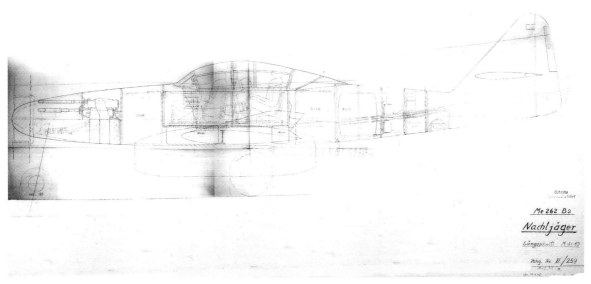

*Detailed side view of the Me 262 B-2 proposed on January 17, 1945, as seen in drawing II/259.*

developed from the basic model Me 262 fighter A1 by extending the middle part of the fuselage. In this way it was possible to accommodate the second man needed for navigation tasks and to increase the amount of fuel carried in the fuselage compared to the day fighter by about 500 litres.

"With the protected fuselage tanks the night fighter thus has a better flight time of 2¼ hours at a 6km altitude, which can be increased to approx. 2¾ hours by using 2 x 300 litre external tanks suspended beneath the fuselage and in a further development step can be increased to approx. 4 hours with larger external tanks and 'rider' tanks built onto the wing. In addition, a further increase in flight time can be achieved by using towed tanks.

"With Jumo 004 engine, the take-off run can be kept within normal limits by means of an additional thrust and, when the Heinkel HeS 109-011 engine is installed, remain in the same order of magnitude without additional thrust.

"The normal armament of 4 x MK 108 gives the night fighter considerable firepower, which can be increased by installing another two cannon or multi-barrel weapons. Since the attack by flying underneath the target is likely to be the most successful tactic, this fact is taken into account by the preparation for the installation of an angled armament in addition to a reduced horizontal armament.

"Due to the unchanged takeover of the fuselage front part of the day fighter, the night fighter also receives normal fighter armour against fire from the front, which, even if armouring should not be necessary in the near future, protects against the great disintegration effect when the enemy machines are fired on with 3cm explosive ammunition.

"The aim is to quickly install the concave dish antenna currently under development for the radar devices, which practically does not cost any speed because it can be accommodated in the fuselage. First, however, the planes will have to be equipped with the Siemens antler antenna, which in its current version entails a speed loss of approx. 70km/h. An attempt is made to reduce this speed loss to approx. 20km/h by suitable profiling of the previously round bars.

"The possibility of taking measures to increase the critical speed (high-speed development), such as swept wings with a centrally installed engine, will be taken into account later."

The fuselage extension mentioned took the aircraft's overall length from 10.6m to 11.7m and allowed an increase in internal fuel capacity from 2,570 litres to 3,100. And the two crewmen would be able to communicate with each other using the EiV 7 intercom system.

A meeting of the Main Development Commission was held on January 24 and the night fighter designs collected by Tank were discussed. The only conclusion reached was that none of them really met the Luftwaffe's requirements. Consequently, a new specification was drawn up and issued to Arado, Blohm & Voss, Dornier, Heinkel, Junkers and Messerschmitt on January 27.[21] It seems to have been a given that Focke-Wulf would also enter a design.

Once again, a crew of three was deemed essential—a pilot, navigator and radio operator who had to be "as close together as possible". The aircraft would now be purely jet propelled since "to reach the required maximum speed of 900km/h only turbojet propulsion is possible". But the number and arrangement of these engines—BMW 003s, Jumo 004s or HeS 011s—was

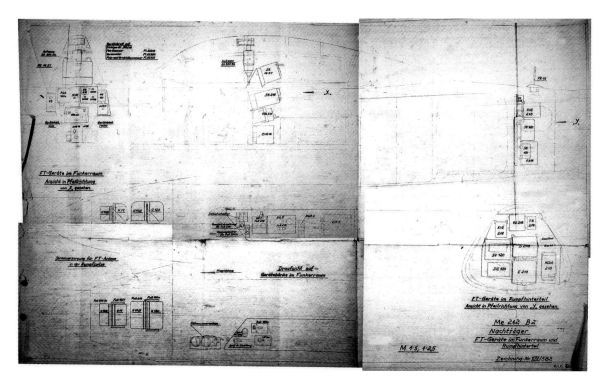

*Drawing XIV/582 of January 17, 1945, assembled from surviving fragments, shows the equipment that was to be crammed into the Me 262 B-2 both around the observer and behind the auxiliary fuel tank in the rear fuselage.*

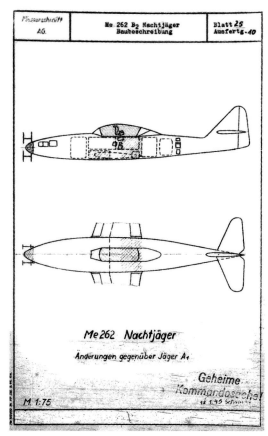

*Diagram showing how the Me 262 B-2 would utilise as much of the Me 262 A-1 in its construction as possible. Only the cross-hatched sections are entirely new.*

optional. Standard armament was four forward-firing MK 108s or MG 213/30s, each with 120 rounds. Targeting would be via EZ 42 or Bremen radar.

A further two MK 108s or MG 213/30s would need to be fitted firing upwards at an angle of 70° with 100 rounds apiece. Two remote-controlled MG 151s were to be provided for defence and it had to be possible to carry two 500kg bombs externally as an overload.

Electronic equipment that had to be carried included FuG 24 SE with ZVG 24, FuG 25 A, FuG 139, Fu Bl 3 with AWG 1, Bremen, FuG 280, FuG 218 R, FuG 101 A, Naxos and an EiV system. Armour protection from 20mm rounds to the front was required and the fuel tanks needed to be protected. Necessary safety features included a pressure cabin, ejection seats, de-icing for the wings, tail and windows, cabin heating and a fire extinguishing system.

The 900km/h top speed had to be achievable at an altitude of 8-10km and endurance needed to be four hours including climb at full throttle, without drop tanks. But "the possibility of accommodating more internal fuel for the increased performance engines must be ensured". Service ceiling needed to be at least 13km and landing speed had to be below 180km/h. Rockets could be used for take-off if necessary and when it came to building the fighter "the construction effort is to be kept as low as possible... Wood is to be used as a material to a large extent".

*Wind tunnel model of the DFS Schleppgerät designed as a towed fuel tank—an option for the Me 262 night fighter.*

While the Me 262 had no realistic chance of meeting the earlier iterations of the night fighter specification, particularly the very earliest ones dating from August 1944, the requirements seem gradually to have come closer and closer to what might be achieved through heavy modification and augmentation of the existing airframe. Deleting the piston engine stipulation was a big step in the right direction, as far as Messerschmitt was concerned, and features such as the ability to carry two 500kg bombs, a pressure cabin, ejection seats, cabin heating and a fire extinguisher system had all been at least trialled with the Me 262. There had also been a shift towards wooden construction and a top speed of 900km/h at 8-10km altitude was possible. In addition, rocket weapons such as the R4M and X-4 were no longer part of the spec.

There remained significant challenges however; a crew of three would be difficult to accommodate, oblique firing MK 108s would need to be installed somewhere and endurance was a big problem if drop tanks could not be taken into consideration. Some thought was being given to equipping the Me 262 with 'Doppelreiter' fuel tanks at this time[22]—aerodynamic containers mounted above the engine nacelles on top of the wings—but little more than basic project work had so far been carried out on this development.

Perhaps the greatest difficulty lay in reaching a service ceiling of at least 13km. Based on earlier test results, without additional rocket propulsion no fighter equipped with Jumo 004s or BMW 003s would be able to comfortably reach that altitude. It was a fundamental technological roadblock and there were no viable options for getting around it. Nevertheless, Messerschmitt's Project Office set to work.

## HITLER'S MICROMANAGEMENT

During the week of January 15-21, the Chef TLR reported that tests intended to allow "bombing against air targets with Me 262" had been successfully carried out at the Rechlin centre.[23] This involved fitting a pair of AB 500 dispensers to an unmodified Me 262's bomb racks, each filled with 24 x SD 15 Kt fragmentation bombs. The Me 262 would then be flown above an enemy bomber formation and the dispensers would be opened, allowing the bombs to fall onto the aircraft below.[24]

It was also reported that on Göring's orders test aircraft and facilities had been provided "immediately" for experiments involving the 8-344 aka X-4 missile and its new solid fuel motor—the missile originally having been developed to use a BMW 109-548 aka P 3378 liquid-fuelled rocket motor. On a less encouraging note, under the section of the report concerning aircraft repair, it was stated that "due to personnel restrictions (SE 6 Action—marching of Volkssturm units—announcement at the labour exchange on January 20 by the chief

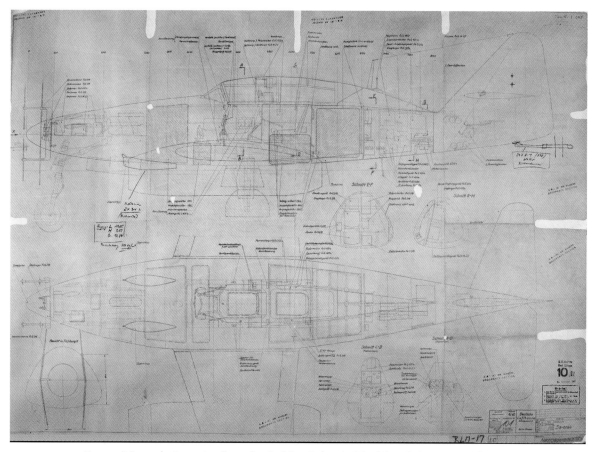

*Even as Messerschmitt continued to refine its Me 262-based night fighter designs to meet the ever-changing Luftwaffe requirement, Deutsche Lufthansa quietly got on with preparing its own designs for the Me 262 B-2. This DLH drawing is dated February 7, 1945.*

engineer of the Luftwaffe) it is no longer possible to carry out the repairs to the previous extent. Further shutdown of repair branches for less important equipment necessary".

At the end of this period, January 20, Adolf Hitler rattled off another series of edicts concerning the Me 262.[25] Saur reported that "The Führer calls for a considerable increase in the combat range of fighter planes used against bombers, in order to significantly reduce their danger. In addition to an increase in the rate of fire, which is already under way…an increase in the calibre of aircraft weapons must be carried out in an accelerated manner".

More specifically, this entailed getting the EZ 42 gunsight into mass production more quickly, "fastest completion of the development of the MK 214 A and ensuring production in the necessary quantities", introduction and accelerated start of series production of the R4M rocket with its launching devices (rail, honeycomb and automatic), increase in the firing rate of the MK 108, review of the use of the MK 112 at long range, and series production of the MG 213.

"Immediate action for the installation of the MK

214 A in the Me 262" was required, as was "immediate introduction of the series installation of six MK 108 in the Me 262". Hitler also ordered a "trial installation of the MK 112 in the Me 262" and "fastest test installation of the R4M rocket in the Fw 190, Ta 152, Me 263, Ar 234 and Do 335", the Me 262 curiously being missed off the list.

A more general order followed: "The Führer demands the fastest development and increase in performance of today's jet fighters; performance must be given priority over quantity."

Willy Messerschmitt had originally envisioned fitting a 50mm cannon to the Me 262 back in early August 1943 (see Chapter 4), and work on the project had formally commenced on August 24, 1943,[26] but the project made very slow progress and appears to have been dropped when it became clear that the aircraft would have to be operated as a bomber, rather than a fighter, circa June 1944. Now it would be a case of dusting off the documents, which had focused on the Rheinmetall BK 5 rather than the Mauser MK 214, and getting the project back on track.

The original design of the Me 262 A-1 series

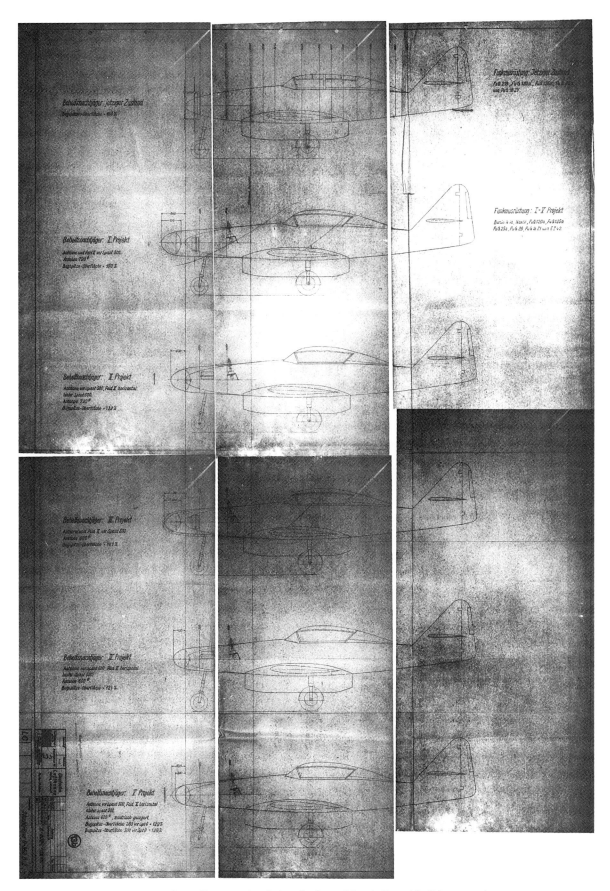

*Five Deutsche Lufthansa project designs for future Me 262 B-2 night fighter upgrades.*
*The drawing has been pieced together from surviving fragments.*

production model had called for the installation of six MK 108s once the Jumo 004 C was available and the project had commenced with Protokoll Nr. 22 of December 10, 1943.[27] However, there had been no urgent need to get the work done and the project remained incomplete more than a year later. Now this too would have to be revived immediately.

Nothing appears to have been done concerning the MK 112 so this project would have to start from scratch.

During the last full week of January—the 22nd to the 28th—the ChefTLR reported that an EHK briefing had been held to compare the interim night fighter versions of the Ar 234 and Me 262.[28] While the Ar 234 reportedly had a slight speed advantage when fitted with four BMW 003s, it also had a more vulnerable cockpit canopy and it was uncertain whether it would be worth developing an entirely new cockpit just for night fighting. The quantity of Me 262 night fighters on order remained the same, with just three due to be delivered per month.

At a meeting of the Special Commission for Night and Bad Weather Fighters on January 24, it was noted that a one-off single-seater Me 262 fitted with the FuG 218 radar system had been completed for night fighter ace Oberleutnant Kurt Welter and it was hoped that this would provide "experience for the installation of the FuG 218".[29] The first interim night fighter built by DLH at Staaken was due to be delivered at the beginning of February and the prototype for the series production model Me 262 B-2 was due from Messerschmitt in March. It was stated that "this deadline must be kept under all circumstances. A delivery programme for the other 15 aircraft ordered from Messerschmitt is not yet available. The equipment includes FuG 218 an antenna with profiled rods. The delivery of 'ring antenna'—presumably the now-familiar radar dish for internal installation—was planned. But the installation of oblique firing armament had yet to be investigated.

Meanwhile, although Hitler may have welcomed Willy Messerschmitt's suggestion that pilots should simply ditch their bomb racks along with the bombs themselves, a Rüstungsstab meeting of January 29, just over three weeks later, noted that "each drop of a Wikingerschiff [bomb rack] is too great a burden in terms of capacity; dropping is therefore only an option in an emergency".[30]

## PROJECTS IN JANUARY

None of Hitler's development orders had filtered through to Messerschmitt's Project Office by the time of its next meeting on January 22, 1945,[31] but the agenda still included a record 87 items, each one an ongoing

thread of Me 262 development. Many covered minor adjustments, such as incorrect brake hoses supplied by the Vogel company, a switch from 4mm diameter pitot tubes to 6mm, reinforced main gear suspension bearings and joints, a new standard seat, improved nosewheel shimmy brakes, adjustable aileron bearings, new rudder profiles for stability testing and whether a firewall test installation was still necessary since J2 fuel was very difficult to ignite even when it was supposed to be ignited.

The third Lotfe bomber compartment had been completed and the fourth was due for completion the following day—on January 23. Evidently the General der Aufklärungsflieger, Karl-Henning von Barsewisch, had asked "if three of these canopies are available for a special purpose. If an order is placed, the reserve canopies for bomber prototypes must be dispensed with". Exactly what purpose von Barsewisch had in mind is unknown, but it appears that the series production model of the Me 262 Lotfe bomber had by now been permanently cancelled.

Tests of a weapons nose incorporating two MK 103s, two MG 151s and two MK 108s had been interrupted because the static fuselage it was attached to at the firing range was needed elsewhere and a new airframe was having to be procured. The test nose had all six guns installed at once but it would appear that this was simply a convenient vehicle for testing the two different MK 103 installations that had been worked on since July 20, 1943. The MK 103s could be fired either together with the two MK 108s, to test that arrangement, or with the two MG 151s to test the alternative. The series production model, had it ever been made, would have had only four guns—two MK 103s plus either two MG 151s or two MK 108s.[32] In the six gun test arrangement, the two MK 103s had rather elaborate muzzle brakes and suggestions for "a more economical design" were made at the meeting with a plan being drawn up to run these through wind tunnel tests.

The other gun nose variant, with six MK 108s, had not yet been built even as a test mule and it was noted that when it was built it would be made of wood.

The unarmed makeshift reconnaissance variant, with two Rb 50/30 cameras, was to receive the designation 262 A-1a/U3 and was now scheduled for full series production at Messerschmitt's Regensburg plant, starting in May. There were also ongoing tests of wooden components—with wooden fins being trialled at both Rechlin and Lechfeld. A single wooden wing assembly was still under construction but not likely to be delivered until February while plans for a second wing assembly had been postponed pending tests of the first one.

Plans to create an experimental brake parachute

installation were still on course for March 30 but efforts were being made to expedite it by going through a different part of Messerschmitt's Construction Office.

As far as the Me 262 B-2 interim night fighter was concerned, there was "official confirmation for the construction of a further 14 aircraft promised[33]...the schedule is currently uncertain, since it is not yet clear where the night fighter will be built. Offingen will probably be cancelled".

The Luftwaffe high command, the OKL, had sent a letter to Messerschmitt on January 2 which "again demanded that [the Me 262 with BMW 003 engines] be ready for series production and found that the interchangeability with the Jumo 004 [requirement] was fully met with the exception of two points: accommodation of the starting fuel and nozzle adjustment by electrical switch".

Two other Me 262 development variants, the bad weather fighter (Schlechtwetterjäger) and the heavily armoured fighter (Panzerflugzeug), were on hold. The former was awaiting delivery of a FuG 125 unit as well as documents for the FuG 120a and FuG 101. The latter's future depended on the outcome of an imminent meeting.

## MK 108 VERSUS MK 103 + MG 151

The Luftwaffe's Tarnewitz test centre produced a report on January 30 which cast doubt on whether the twin MK 103 plus twin MG 151 nose was worthwhile for the Me 262. It posed the question: "Which armament is better for 8-262, 4 x MK 108 or 2 x MK 103 and 2 x MG 151 (15mm barrel)?"[34]

An earlier report on using the MK 108 and MK 103 in piston engine fighters and bombers, produced in 1943, had concluded that "at angles of attack of up to 15°, an MK 108 is superior to an MK 103, in particular due to the higher rate of fire, the lower weight, the smaller installation space and the shorter firing time per hit". A single MK 103 took up roughly twice as much room as an MK 108 and was roughly twice as heavy. This being the case, "instead of one MK 103, two MK 108s can be carried in a fighter. Two MK 108s are in all cases the stronger armament compared to one MK 103."

The new report set out to see whether the same findings held true for jet aircraft. It noted that "when aiming with unguided Revi [gunsight] for an angle of attack of zero degrees with four MK 108s up to 800m, about as many hits are achieved as with two MK 103s and two MG 151s. Due to the greater ammunition effect of the MK 108 compared to MG 151 the armament is more effective. At 30° flight angle and 800m combat distance, both armaments are equivalent (provided that one MK

103 hit and six MG 151 hits have the same effect as two MK 108 hits). Over 800m, combat effectiveness is out of the question because the ammunition in both cases is not sufficient to achieve enough hits".

But "when aiming with a [EZ 42] gyro sight (corresponding to the future standard equipment!), the armament with four MK 108s is superior even at large flight angles. The armament with MK 103 is therefore not suitable for conducting the fight at greater distances with better prospects. For combating air targets, four MK 108s are better than two MK 103s and two MG 151s, even when combating jet aircraft is taken into account".

Presumably this meant that the Me 262 A-1a/U1 configuration, or at least the MK 103/MG 151 version of it, was unlikely to be put into series production.

The number of Me 262s accepted by the Luftwaffe for January was around 215—a significant increase on previous monthly totals. This brought the overall total accepted since April 1944 to 885.[35] The alternative source gives 167 produced for the month, with only 116 accepted by the Luftwaffe, including nine in repair and 17 undergoing retrofit.[36] This document gives an overall total of 731 produced since April 1944, with 562 of these accepted.

## EMERGENCY PROGRAMME

Hitler sent out a notification on January 31, 1945, headed Emergency Programme of Final Armaments Production which sought to prevent any further bleeding off of manpower and resources from arms manufacturing.[37] Written in the first person, it said: "The production of those weapons that I have specified in the emergency programme is currently more important than conscripting them [the workers] into the Wehrmacht, the Volkssturm, the Volksaufgebot[38] or for other purposes.

"I therefore order that all skilled workers employed in the emergency programme, with the exception of those born in 1928 and younger, are to be released from any confiscation unless they can be fully replaced, primarily by skilled workers from closed plants. This order also applies to those productions that are necessary as basic industry and supplies for the production of the emergency programme (iron-producing industry, supply industry and for the companies that manufacture the equipment for this: optics, electrical engineering, etc.).

"The intended or planned confiscations [i.e. conscriptions] must be raised independently of this protection by the rest of the armaments industry. The transport space required for the emergency programme must be provided and may not be confiscated or withdrawn for other purposes. If possible, coal and energy are to be supplied to the emergency programme within the

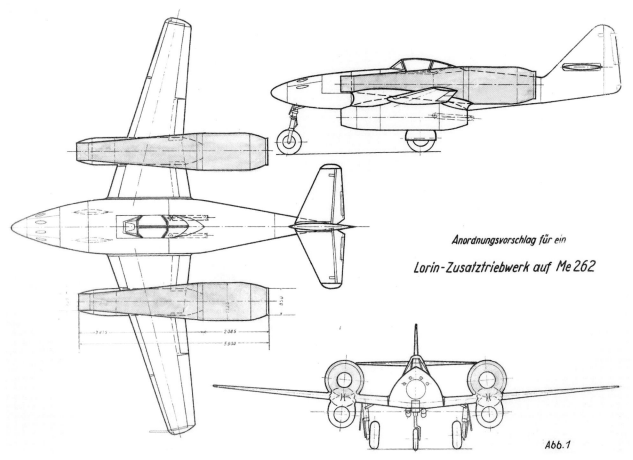

Eugen Sänger's design for an Me 262 fitted with ramjets to improve climbing performance.

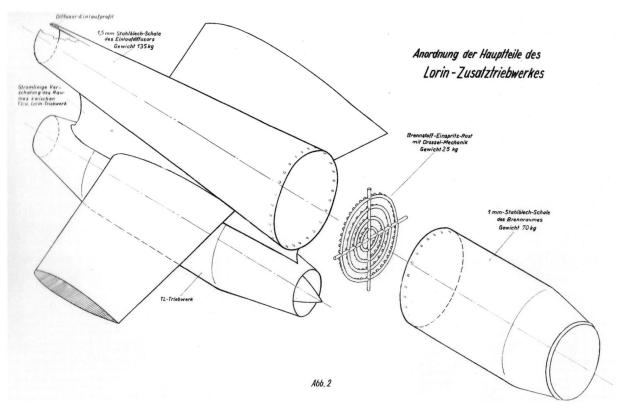

The relatively simple ramjet design, as it would attach above the Me 262's wing.

framework of the individual instructions of the Reich Minister for Armament and War Production."

Throughout the latter half of 1944, the aircraft industry had been subject to repeated attempts at streamlining, in order to free up resources for those production programmes deemed essential. Numerous aircraft types had been cancelled and now only a handful remained. Hitler's notification went on to specify those programmes which were now to be regarded as essential and of equal priority: all handguns, hand grenades and hand-held anti-tank weapons; anti-tank mines, anti-tank guns; 8cm and 12cm grenade launchers and 15cm rocket launchers; armoured cars and assault guns; trucks and tractors; generators and radio sets; submarine and ship repair, the EZ 42 gunsight and "all high-performance aircraft with a focus on 262, 152 and 190 and 109 together with [their] equipment".

Overall, just nine aircraft types were now to be spared the axe: Messerschmitt's Me 262 and Bf 109, Focke-Wulf's Fw 190 and Ta 152, Junkers' Ju 88, Heinkel's He 162, Arado's Ar 234 and Ar 396 trainer, and Dornier's Do 335.[39] Mistel combinations featuring these types would also continue to be manufactured.

Even as the Me 262 was spared, its first champion was not—Adolf Galland had by now been dismissed as General der Jagdflieger and Austrian fighter ace Gordon Gollob was appointed in his place.

## ME 262 WITH RAMJETS

At some point after April 20, 1944, Messerschmitt had received two reports from the DFS concerning the potential use of ramjets—known to the Germans as Lorin tubes after their French inventor René Lorin—as a propulsion system for fighters.[40] The company had then commissioned the DFS to "develop proposals and calculations for a possible performance increase for the Me 262 with the help of Lorin auxiliary engines" and the resulting report was produced on January 31, 1945.[41]

The DFS was working on ramjets because it had become the workplace of Austrian scientist Dr Eugen Sänger, who had been researching them since the late 1930s and had already carried out a number of practical experiments with full scale prototypes. His new report for Messerschmitt on the use of ramjets to provide a performance boost for the Me 262 noted that ramjets were poorly suited as an attachment to any existing airframe but "nevertheless, the task was tackled as a compromise solution in order to make the existing Me 262 suitable for new tactical missions by improving climb performance and ceiling with the least amount of time and effort".

It was suggested that positioning a single 1m² main frame area ramjet tube above each wing would present "the fewest difficulties of all imaginable positions" but even so "the unfavourable effects on the tailplane and on the aerodynamic wing lift are particularly noteworthy". Sänger wrote that "the tempting arrangement of the Lorin engine as a shroud centred on the turbine engine is not initially considered".

Take-off with the ramjets would involve accelerating "the aircraft to a very high horizontal speed in level flight after take-off in the immediate vicinity of the ground and only then initiating the ascent path". This would give the ramjets time to ignite and get up to speed, allowing a subsequent climb to 12,000m altitude in 7.3 minutes while burning 1,430kg of fuel.

With the ramjets active, the Me 262's maximum ceiling of 11,000m could be raised to 15,000m which "exceeds the flight altitude of [all] known combat aircraft". The Me 262's top speed, however, was limited by Mach effects. Near to the ground, top speed would be "close to 1,000km/h" but would decrease with altitude. Overall, the Me 262 with ramjets would be about 150-200km/h faster than the turbojet-only Me 262 in most scenarios.

Range, however, would suffer significantly. At an altitude of 10,000m, the normal Me 262 could be expected to achieve a range of 1,400km and a flight time of two hours 25 minutes. Using the ramjets for climbing to altitude and for a limited period of combat only, cruising on the jet engines alone at all other times, this would fall to around 470km and 50 minutes depending on usage.

Also on January 31, Messerschmitt's Project Office issued a memo concerning a miscommunication over the two complete sets of profiled Me 262 night fighter antennas—eight antennas in total—ordered more than six weeks earlier, on December 15.[42] Evidently the text of the order had been changed without the consent or knowledge of the Project Office "in such a way that it was based on the production of two complete antennas. When we pointed out that this wording could lead to misunderstandings, we were expressly informed…that a complete antenna meant the equipment for an aircraft, i.e. a total of four individual antennas.

"However, it has now turned out that the AVV only allows two individual antennas to be manufactured. Since we have to carry out flight tests with the profiled antennas very soon, it is absolutely necessary that at least two more antennas are completed in the course of this week, so that the equipment for an aircraft is complete. In addition, the production of another set of antennas (consisting of four individual antennas) is required in the near future, as we would like to make these antennas available to the companies that have taken over the manufacture of the antennas."

*Front and side views of the conical mesh shield developed to prevent ingestion of debris, as tested on 130167.*

## PRODUCTION CUTBACKS

The Chef TLR was faced with a rather bleak situation at the beginning of February 1945. It was reported that the emergency programme had been drawn up in the belief that it would receive 25,000 tons of steel for aircraft construction—but it soon became evident that only 8,500 tons would be allocated.[43] Diesing held a meeting on February 8 "to further cut the emergency programme" and it was eventually determined that 500 Me 262s and 500 He 162s would be built per month but only 370 Ta 152s and 50 Ar 234s.

There were concerns about the Me 262's compass, since the Askania laboratory where it was made was in Greifenberg, Silesia, and "no relocations from Silesia are allowed". The unwritten point being that Silesia was in the process of being overrun by Soviet forces at this time. In addition there had been a "severe slump" in EZ 42 gunsight production "due to poor planning" with only a maximum of 230 examples being made instead of the planned 1,200.

And where bullets and shells were concerned, "ammunition of all calibres is in decline due to lack of material", though production of the new R4M air-to-air rocket projectile was still proceeding.

In parallel to the Emergency Programme of Final Armaments Production, widely known as the Führernotprogramm, was a Development Emergency Programme which concerned work on the next generation of aircraft and weapons intended for the Luftwaffe.[44] In contrast to the stark production programme, this included a host of outlandish research projects which were set to continue despite the increasingly dire war situation. It did, however, see the various Mistel plans that had been on the drawing board chopped back to just one—a combination of an He 162 and a new Junkers-made twin-jet flying bomb designated 8-268 known as Mistel 5. Mistel 4, the Ju 88/Me 262 combination and Mistel 6, the 8-268/Ar 234 combination, were cancelled.[45]

## MORE BAD WEATHER

February 3 saw the publication of a rare report concerning research conducted as a direct result of combat experience with the Me 262.[46] It read: "Purpose: The troops complained that their jet engines often failed as a result of flying through the cloud of debris from a downed enemy aircraft. A protective cage is required to rectify this".

As Messerschmitt staff had discovered during their consultation with Kommando Nowotny back in November 1944 (see Chapter 9), the speed difference between the Me 262 and its targets meant pilots frequently had difficulty evading the aftermath their own attacks—resulting in engine failure due to ingestion of foreign objects. Now two conical mesh shields had been manufactured and fitted to the engine intakes of 130167, with Baur conducting comparative flight tests on February 1. These revealed that the shields knocked 5km/h off the aircraft's top speed—though it was thought that modifications to the exhaust nozzle would remedy this. The report concluded: "On the basis of this result and operational experience, the appropriate RLM departments have to decide whether the protective cage will be produced or not and whether the design and manufacture will be taken over by the engine manufacturer or by the airframe company. We consider the former to be more appropriate."

*The Heimatschützer I, 130186, finally made its first flight with both rocket motor and turbojets on February 27, 1945.*

A quarter of all test flights planned for the Lech-feld fleet during February had to be cancelled due to bad weather.[47] 170083 remained out of action, though it was finally having some engines fitted, and the Heimatschützer II, 170074, was grounded while further static testing of its BMW 003 Rs took place. 110499 never returned from its loan to the Luftwaffe—having crashed due to a reported engine fire on February 21.

The nine aircraft that did fly, V9, V10, 130015, 130167, 130186, 170056, 170078, 170303 and 110555, managed 149 flights all together, lasting for a combined total of 33.3 hours.

It proved to be a busy month for the V9. Ongoing tests seemed to indicate that the combination of a lowered cockpit canopy and swept tail resulted in extremely good yaw oscillation characteristics but the results could not be regarded as conclusive. In addition, pressure distribution tests were conducted on the V9's canopy and the aircraft was roped in for a series of bad weather visibility tests. According to the summary report, "in the case of the racing cabin, rain visibility is described as impossible. Bad at all speeds, [with the rain forming a] greasy film. Also opaque plexiglass side window panes [are] worse than normal glass. An attempt is currently being made to fit a rotating 200mm diameter disc in front of the windscreen, which hurls the rain away".

Furthermore, V9 was used to test a new component developed in the field: a series of six "ventilation gills [added] to the circumference of the front side of the engine cowling". Messerschmitt had based the installation on a sketch that had been provided, rather than the actual field-modified component.

Not everything had gone smoothly though—a ruptured pipe above the V9's main rear tank had caused a leak and the tank's rubber had been so badly eroded by

the escaping fuel that a full replacement tank was needed. And towards the end of the month, the swept tail was finally removed and replaced with a series production model unit.

V10 had been fitted with an experimental new fairing on its right engine. This was the usual shape but made of a "0.8 material 1010.2". Another modification was the installation of a new cockpit canopy front section with a 25° inclined windscreen for bad weather visibility testing—but this had not been rain tested before the month was out.

The aircraft's main task at this time, however, was to continue testing 300 litre external fuel tanks attached to its bomb racks. According to the test report summary: "As part of the external tank testing, a long-range flight was carried out by a Luftwaffe pilot. Despite not flying optimally, a flight duration of two hours was achieved, of which one hour was a loitering flight above 9km. With an optimal flight, two and a half hours seem achievable. This will be demonstrated when the opportunity arises."

During a 750km/h flight to test a new fairing for the tank attachment point, on February 25, the left tank suddenly detached itself from V10 and blew back into the left inner wing's leading edge and left engine cowling, causing minor damage. An investigation revealed that the bomb rack rear attachment point had become deformed and that the locking mechanism had subsequently torn loose.

130015 was used for engine intake cowling pressure distribution tests and was the third aircraft used for bad weather visibility trials. Whereas V9's windscreen was angled at 15° and V10's had its new 25° screen, 130015 was the 'control' with its normal 33° angle windscreen left unchanged. Test flights in rain were made and the pilot noted that visibility was bad up to 250-300km/h,

*Flight testing of 110555, fitted with the second 'Lofte' nose, commenced in February 1945.*

then slightly better from 300-500km/h, then worse again above 500km/h. The aircraft also had a wooden fin and rudder which apparently performed flawlessly over the course of flight tests totalling six hours.

Wheel brake and internally balanced rudder tests continued with 130167 and it was also fitted with an EZ 42 gunsight and BSK 16 gun camera. Five flights were made and the pilot conducted firing trials, making film recordings of the results for later analysis.

The Heimatschützer I, 130186, had its rear fuselage fully reassembled on February 2 and a static test of its tail-mounted rocket motor was made on February 3.[48] Another fuel dump test flight using just the turbojets for propulsion was conducted on February 6 but afterwards it was found that two weld seams for the T-Stoff distributor pipe had torn and the rear fuselage had to be dismantled again so that repairs could be carried out. This time a rear fuselage quick disconnection point was installed so that the fuselage end could be slipped on and off more easily. Two further rocket motor ground runs were made on February 20 with the tail off, after which it was put back on again. A turbojet ground run followed on February 22, then the turbojets and rocket motor were run together on February 23 without problems. Then the first flight using both turbojets and the rocket motor followed on February 27 and this was reported as having gone "satisfactorily".

170056 had a new windscreen washer spray nozzle—actually a borrowed Bf 109 component—installed and "the system was tested in flight and worked flawlessly". Tests with the new 660 x 190 nosewheel had gone well, showing "perfect behaviour",

though "retracting the landing gear is not possible in the current test design" and "the design of the wheel fork can be significantly improved". Evidently the two missing night fighter antennas had finally been manufactured and delivered to Lechfeld by now, since the aircraft then had a complete set fitted to its nose for aerodynamic tests.

The BMW 003-equipped test vehicle, 170078, managed four lateral stability test flights fitted with a reduced-area fin, totalling one hour and eight minutes, before being grounded due to lack of fuel on February 22. The 003 was apparently unable to run on J2 and required B4 instead, which was in short supply.[49] Even those four flights had proven valuable however. The summary report stated: "The flight characteristics of the 8-262 with BMW engines were significantly improved by fitting the smaller vertical stabiliser. The oscillation times have thus become considerably longer, while the rolling behaviour has not changed disadvantageously, unlike with the [Jumo 004-powered] series machines. The flight in gusty weather is said to be much more comfortable due to the reduction in the return moments. Unfortunately, these judgments are based on only one test vehicle."

With its unusually well-performing engines, 170303 had been used for tests to determine the optimum speed at which take-off booster rockets should be ignited. Several fully-laden take-offs were performed with the two 500kg boosters being fired at a different point during each take-off run. Once airborne, 170303 was flown up to 950km/h at an altitude of 1,500-2,000m with and without bombs so that the effects of dropping

*A closer view of 110555, in which the twin probes of the Baldrian acoustic detection system are clearly visible.*

bombs at high speed could be studied. It was found that dropping a pair of 500kg bombs at 950km/h had no ill effect—but the aircraft's landing gear covers had nevertheless broken. This was attributed to poor closing of the covers, rather than anything to do with the bombs.

This had evidently revealed another problem however. It was found that 170303's booster rocket attachment points suffered from "large structural deviations" and "we find that a large number of aircraft have these structural deviations and that the troops have not yet received any instructions for changes". The Lechfeld test station had evidently issued "special instructions" on November 12, 1944, and February 2, 1945, "which represent immediate measures to remedy the structural deviations in the launch rocket system, are also not known to the troops to this day". In other words, this was a known issue—and measures were supposed to have been put in place to offset it—but word of these measures had failed to reach the frontline units flying the Me 262.

The summary report ruefully stated: "It is necessary that the TA department, to which we have given these special instructions for the purpose of distribution to the troops, actually distributes them in order to avoid further accidents and to restore some confidence in the starting aid system."

The programme of booster rocket testing continued, but now with pairs of 1,000kg rockets angled slightly downwards. On February 28, "as a result of the front attachment point on the rocket's side tearing out, a rocket went off on its own and flew ahead of the aircraft into an open field. As a result of the booster exhaust jet, severe denting of the right inner landing flap [was caused, along with] destruction of the nose wheel shaft and simultaneous release of the right 500kg bomb…a more detailed investigation is currently being carried out".

Throughout it all, 170303 had been fitted with a wooden fin and as with 130015 this had caused no problems.

Finally, 110555 with its revised Lotfe bombardier nose and Baldrian acoustic detection system microphones had now also been fitted with a set of plywood wing end caps produced by the Behr-Wendingen company. Flight testing had commenced and the aircraft had racked up an hour and 54 minutes in the air over the course of the month.

In addition, Jacobs-Schweyer had delivered a set of wooden tailplanes for testing and these had been "mounted on a standard tail boom borrowed from the troops. This showed particularly large structural differences". In other words, the way in which the 'standard' tail boom had been manufactured differed markedly from the way Jacobs-Schweyer had made the tailplanes—even though both should have been made the same way and the parts should have fitted together seamlessly.

Testing of a new ventilation flap for Me 262 canopy's had gone well: "The improved cabin ventilation flap was rated favourably by the pilots. The flap can still be closed

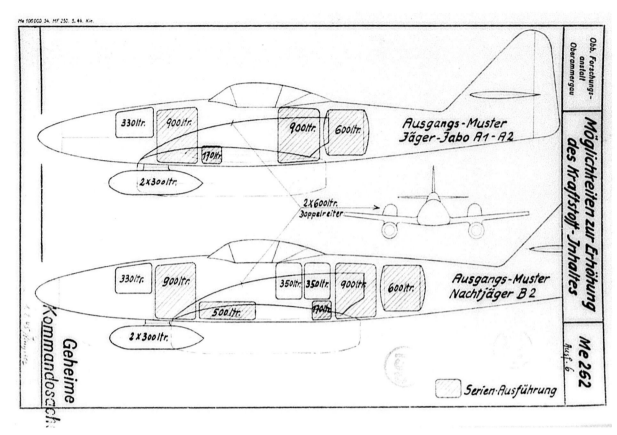

*Options for creating an extreme long-range variant of the Me 262 out of an A-1, A-2 or B-2. In the case of the latter, the rear seat would be removed to provide space for more fuel.*

**Me262 — Reichweiten- u. Lastensteigerung**
A. Möglichkeiten m. kleinen Aenderungen, kurzfristig durchführbar. **I. Jäger** *Ausf. 6*

x) Bei Fortsetzung der Belastungsversuche, evtl. noch mit den Rädern 840x300 zu decken, sonst abwerfbare Doppelräder 660x190 zusätzlich.
xx) Mit kurzen Terminen nur wenn die z. Zeit im Gang befindl. Erprobung günstig verläuft. Wie weit mit Jumo-004-Triebwerke mit Rücksicht auf Steigen kurz nach dem Abheben durchführbar, wird noch untersucht.

| | zum Vergleich: Jäger A1 | Beladezustand 1 | Beladezustand 2 | Beladezustand 3 | Beladezustand 4 |
|---|---|---|---|---|---|
| **Bewaffnung** | 4 (bezw. 6) MK 108 | 4 (bezw.6) MK108 | 4 MK 108 | 4 MK 108 | 2 MK 108 |
| Munition | 360 Schuß | 360 Schuß | 360 Schuß | 360 Schuß | 120 Schuß |
| Kraftstoff i. Rumpf | 2570 ltr. | 2570 ltr | 2570 ltr. | 2570 ltr. | 2570 ltr.+330 ltr. |
| Außenbehälter fest | – | – | 2x600 ltr. (Doppelreiter) | 2x600 ltr. (Doppelreiter) | 2x600 ltr.(Doppelreiter) |
| Außenbehälter abwerfb. | – | 2 x 300 ltr. oder 1x 600 ltr. °) | – | 1x900 ltr. (Deichselanhänger) xx) | 2 x 300 ltr. |
| **Gesamtkraftstoff** | 2570 ltr. | 3170 ltr. | 3770 ltr. | 4670 ltr. | 4700 ltr. |
| Startgewicht ausschl. Starthilfen | 7000 kg | 7550 kg | 8140 kg | 8160 kg + 1000 kg (Anhänger) | 8750 kg |
| **Größte Flugdauer** | 2,15 h | 2,55 h | 2,83 h | 3,27 h | ca 3,3 h |
| in Flughöhe | 9800 m | 8300 m | 8200 m | 7000 m | 7600 m |
| **Größte Flugstrecke** | 1200 km | 1380 km | 1500 km | 1700 km | ca 1750 km |
| Startstrecke (CINA 0m) | 1050 m (ohne Hilfen) | 1230 m (ohne Hilfen) | 1100 m (mit 1000kg) | 1350 m (mit 1000kg) | 1390 m (mit 1000kg) |
| Fahrwerk | Räder 840x300 | Räder 840x300 | 840x300 + 660x190 abwerfbar | 840x300 + 660x190 abwerfbar | 840x300 + 660x190 abwerfbar |

°) 1x600l-Behälter ist widerstandsmäßig günstiger als 2x300l-Behälter. Einbau sobald vorhanden.

Geheime Kommandosache

*Four different potential configurations for a long-range fighter based on the Me 262 A-1. The greatest endurance was achieved by limiting weaponry to just two MK 108s and carrying fuel in drop tanks as well as over-wing Doppelreiter tanks.*

| | zum Vergleich: JägerA1 | Jabo 42 Beladezustand 1 | Beladezustand 2 | Beladezustand 3 | Beladezustand 4 | Beladezustand 5 | Geheime Kommandosache! |
|---|---|---|---|---|---|---|---|
| **Bewaffnung** / Munition | 4(bezw.6) MK108 / 360 Schuß | 4 MK108 / 360 Schuß | 4 MK108 / 360 Schuß | 2 MK108 / 120 Schuß | 2 MK108 / 120 Schuß | 2 MK108 / 120 Schuß | 2 MK108 / 120 Schuß |
| **Bomben** | — | 1x 500kg od. 2x250kg | 1x 500 kg | 1x500 kg | 1x500 kg | (1x1000kg) od. 2x500kg | 1x1000kg (Schleppbombe) |
| Kraftstoff i. Rumpf | 2570 ltr. | 2570 ltr. | 2570 ltr. | 2570 ltr. + 330 ltr. | 2570 ltr. + 330 ltr. | 2570 ltr. + 330 ltr. | 2570 ltr. + 330 ltr. |
| Außenbehälter fest | — | — | — | — | 2x600ltr. (Doppelreiter) | — | 2x600ltr. (Doppelreiter) |
| Außenbehälter abwerfb. | — | — | 1x 300ltr. | 1 x 300ltr. | 1x300ltr. | — | 2x 300ltr. |
| **Gesamtkraftstoff** | 2570 ltr. | 2570 ltr. | 2870 ltr. | 3200 ltr. | 4400 ltr. | 2900 ltr. | 4700 ltr. |
| Startgewicht ausschl. Starthilfen | 7000 kg | 7550 kg | 7810 kg | 7870 kg | 9000 kg | 8145 kg *) | 8800kg + 1200kg |
| **Größte Flugdauer** in Flughöhe | 2,15 h / 9800 m | 1,90h / 8700m | 2,10 h / 8400m | 2,40h / 8300m | 3,00 h / 7000m | 1,95 h / 7300m | ca. 3,00h |
| **Größte Flugstrecke** Startstrecke | 1200 km / 1050m (ohne Hilfen) | 1000km / 1380 (ohne Hilfen) | 1130km / 1020m (mit 100kg) | 1280 km / 1050m (mit 1000kg) | 1570km / 1200m (mit 2000kg) | 1000 km / 1120m (mit 1000kg) | ca 1600 km |
| Fahrwerk | Räder 840x300 | Räder 840 x 300 | Räder 840x300 | Räder 840x300 | 840x300+660x190(abwurfbar) | Räder 840x300 *) | 840x300 + 660x190(abwurfb.) |

*Me262 — Reichweiten- u. Lastensteigerung. A. Möglichkeiten m. kleinen Aenderungen, kurzfristig durchführbar. II. Jabo*

*Six options for a long-range Me 262 fighter-bomber presented in the report of February 1, 1945.*

at speeds of up to 850km/h close to the ground, whereas this was not possible with the old version."

And the huge amount of time expended on testing of brake pads appeared to have paid off: "Up to February 15, 28 landings were made with the 70mm wide pads and 66 landings with the 85mm wide pads. With roughly the same braking effect, the service life of the wide brakes is considerably longer. According to the decision of the Rechlin test centre, the 85mm wide pads desired by Messerschmitt will be installed in series production, contrary to the earlier decision. This completes the test."

Continental had meanwhile delivered two 660 x 160 nosewheel tyres with treads, earlier nosewheels having been smooth. But "the dirt between the wheel and fork…was no greater than on the previous smooth surface. Further testing will show whether dirt is thrown up against the underside of the fuselage and into the landing gear bay".

Meanwhile, a nose unit fitted with the Mauser MK 214 V2 prototype 50mm cannon was installed on the firing range test fuselage on February 22. A total of 99 shots were fired up to March 2 with numerous instances of jamming, misfires and other problems in evidence.[50]

## ME 262 FOR EXTREME RANGE

The new fuselage required to continue testing the MK 103 and MK 108/MG 151 nose had yet to be delivered by February 1, a status update meeting that day being told that "the fuselage can be damaged, but the fuselage nose connection must be dimensionally correct".[51] Efforts were being made to begin testing an oblique-firing weapons arrangement but it was uncertain whether tests required a full fuselage installation or if the cannon

could simply be positioned at an oblique angle and test-fired. The changes made to the second Lotfe bombardier nose had yet to be carried forward to the third, fourth and fifth noses in the series and plans had been drawn up to test improved engine fittings for both the Jumo 004 and BMW 003, a mock-up now being urgently required.

The Me 262 HG II high-speed research aircraft, Werk-Nr. 111538, was still incomplete though a new tail unit transition piece was due for delivery on February 10. The aircraft's nose, wing fillets and seat were still listed as "missing". A FuG 125 unit had been installed in an unspecified airframe as a prototype for the Me 262 bad weather fighter and acceptance was "pending".

A report outlining options for increasing the Me 262's range and load carrying capacity was published on the same day.[52] This made a distinction between changes that could be made quickly and with a minimum of effort and changes that would require some development work—and between increases in fuel for the A-1 fighter variant and increases in both fuel and bomb load for the A-2 fighter-bomber. It also looked at what was possible by taking the extended fuselage of the Me 262 B-2 night fighter and turning it into a single seat long-range day fighter.

It was pointed out that when 840 x 300 mainwheels were used on the A-1, it was approved for take-off weights up to 7.85 tons—albeit only from a concrete runway. Going above eight tons was possible but only with jettisonable extra 660 x 190 support wheels or new mainwheels measuring 935 x 340. As the report pointed out though, "the use of this wheel size requires, in addition to the wheel being able to swivel relative to the strut when retracting, considerable changes to the

x) Bei Fortsetzung der Belastungsversuche evtl. noch mit den Rädern 840×300 zu decken, sonst Räder 935×340 unter Inkaufnahme von Änderungen an Rumpf u. Fläche,

**Me262**

**Reichweiten- u. Lastensteigerung**
B. Möglichkeiten deren Entwicklung in Angriff genommen ist. Jäger u. Jabo

| | zum Vergleich: 2sitz. Nachtjäger | Beladezustand 1 | Beladezustand 2 | Beladezustand 3 | Beladezustand 4 |
|---|---|---|---|---|---|
| Besatzung | 2 Mann | 1 Mann | 1 Mann | 1 Mann | 1 Mann |
| Bewaffnung | 4 MK108 | 4 MK108 | 4 MK108 | 4 MK108 | 2× MK108 |
| Munition | 360 Schuß | 360 Schuß | 360 Schuß | 360 Schuß | 120 Schuß |
| Bomben | - | - | - | - | 1× 500 kg |
| Kraftstoff i. Rumpf | 3070 ltr. | 3770 ltr. | 3770 ltr. | 3770 ltr. | 3770 + 330 ltr. |
| Außenbehälter fest | - | - | 2×600 ltr. (Doppelreiter) | 2×600 ltr. (Doppelreiter) | 2×600 ltr. (Doppelreiter) |
| Außenbehälter abwerfb. | - | - | - | 2×300 ltr. | - |
| Gesamtkraftstoff | 3070 ltr. | 3770 ltr. | 4970 ltr. | 5570 ltr. | 5300 ltr. |
| Startgewicht ausschl. Starthilfen | ~7770 kg | ~8410 kg | ~9550 kg | ~10100 kg | 10150 kg |
| Größte Flugdauer in Flughöhe | 2,3 h / 8800 m | 2,7 h / 8100 m | 3,3 h / 6400 m | ca 3,5 h / 5700 m | ca 3,3 h / 5700 m |
| Größte Flugstrecke | 1260 km | 1490 km | 1690 km | ca 1850 km | ca 1700 km |
| Startstrecke | 1300 m (ohne Hilfen) | 1250 m (mit 1000 kg) | 1450 m (mit 2000 kg) | ca 1800 m (mit 2000 kg) | ca 1800 m (mit 2000 kg) |
| Fahrwerk | Räder 840×300 | Räder 840×300 *) | Räder 935×340 | Räder 935×340 | Räder 935×340 |

Geheime Kommandosache!

*Four configurations which were to make use of the B-2 night fighter's extended fuselage for a long-range single-seater.*

wing and fuselage, with the acceptance of a flat bulge under the fuselage".

In standard configuration, the A-1 and A-2 were supposed to be able to carry 2,570 litres of fuel in four tanks—the usual 900 litres in front of the cockpit, 900 more behind, the extra 600 litre tank behind that and 170 litres in a small tank beneath the pilot's feet. The series production model two-seater Me 262 B-2 night fighter was supposed to be able to accommodate 3,070 litres, with the same three main tanks but with the 170 litre tank moved to beneath the back-seater and a new 500 litre tank added below the pilot.

In the best case scenario, cruising at 9,800m, the Me 262 A-1 could manage a two hour nine minute flight time with a range of 1,200km. But with the addition of two 300 litre external tanks on the bomb racks, this became two hours and 33 minutes/1,380km. Fitting a pair of 600 litre Doppelreiter tanks on the wings above the engine nacelles raised this still further to two hours and 50 minutes/1,500km. And adding a towed 900 litre fuel tank made it three hours and 16 minutes. The last possible step involved combining all previous steps with the removal of two MK 108s from the nose—replacing them with a fifth internal tank containing 330 litres. This gave an absolute maximum flight time of three hours 18 minutes/1,750km.

The baseline Me 262 A-2 was basically the same as the A-1, with the same tanks and the same performance. Adding a single 500kg bomb or two 250kg bombs reduced flight time to one hour 54 minutes and range to 1,000km. On the other hand, carrying one 500kg bomb but with a 300 litre external tank on the other rack evened performance out somewhat to two hours 6 minutes/1,020km. Keeping this configuration but replacing two MK 108s with the new 330kg nose tank gave two hours 24 minutes/1,280km. Adding the 600 litre Doppelreiter over-wing tanks changed this to a flat three hours/1,570km.

Dropping the Doppelreiters and swapping the 300 litre external tank for a second 500kg bomb—or even carrying just one 1,000kg bomb—knocked flight time back down to one hour 57 minutes/1,000km. The last configuration was an Me 262 A-2 with just the two MK 108s, the 330 litre internal nose tank, two 300 litre bomb rack tanks, two 600 litre Doppelreiter tanks and a 1,000kg towed bomb. This would have a flight time of three hours and a range of 1,600km.

The Me 262 B-2 in standard configuration could manage a flight time of two hours 18 minutes and a range of 1,260km. Ditching the second seat allowed the installation of two extra 350 litre fuel tanks behind the solo pilot—taking overall internal fuel capacity up to 3,770 litres. This allowed a flight time of two hours 42 minutes with a range of 1,490km. Add two Doppelreiter

*Wind tunnel model of the Me 262 HG III.*

*Partial Me 262 HG III model undergoing wind tunnel testing.*

ranks and this rose to three hours 18 minutes/1,690km. Add the two bomb rack tanks and this became three hours 30 minutes/1,850km. This appears to have been the absolute maximum range foreseen for any Me 262 variant. Finally, there was an option to swap two MK 108s for the 330 litre nose tank and swap the two bomb rack tanks for a single 500kg bomb and flight time dipped to three hours 18 minutes/1,700km.

## ME 262 HG II

The Project Office reported on February 5 that Professor Messerschmitt had personally vetoed the use of asymmetrical engine nacelles for the HG II until high-speed wind tunnel tests could be carried out.[53] And "consultation with [flight test manager Gerhard] Caroli reveals

that Prof. Messerschmitt ordered the large wheel 840 x 300 to be installed on the machine with 35° swept wing...a 40mm high bump [presumably in the underside of the fuselage] is accepted. Mr Caroli wants the larger tyres in order to be able to carry out a final test of the landing and take-off behaviour of the swept wing with operational weights". Furthermore, "Mr Caroli asks for the approval of the machine with 35° swept wing by the statics office before it is transported to Lechfeld". It was still intended that the HG II would be tested first with a normal tail unit before any thought was given to whether a swept tail should be fitted.

Three days later, a representative of the Project Office, Prager, was sent to examine 111538's undercarriage main wheel housings in person.[54] He noted that 770 x 270

*Side view of an Me 262 HG III model being tested.*

wheels had been installed with a 15mm shortened spring strut. Using his own equipment he then made some measurements by hand and found that the wheel diameter on the right hand undercarriage was 734mm, clearance against the fuselage was 42mm and clearance against the wheel well door was 62mm.

With this in mind, he noted that fitting 840 x 300 wheels would leave 4mm of clearance against the fuselage and the same against the wheel well door—an extremely tight fit.

Willy Messerschmitt wrote to his projects team on February 10 to emphasise the importance he placed on the HG II: "The work on the high-speed further development of the 262, in addition to increasing the flight performance of the 262, is extremely important in that it provides fundamental knowledge about the behaviour of strongly swept wings at low and high speeds, respectively. The partially contradictory wind tunnel results available today can be correctly assessed.

"For more than three and a half years we have been talking about swept wings. No usable test results are available today. In their urgent work on high-speed development, research and industry are, so to speak, dependent on the results of our preliminary investigations with the swept-wing 262. We must therefore do everything to ensure rapid testing of the swept wing.

"For this reason I would like to ask again for the creation of a second 35° swept wing for 262 and the design and construction of a deeper and more extended, initially fixed fore-wing (about 20% depth, extension distance up to 15%). Furthermore, the above reasons require that the intended work on 262 HG III (with 45° swept wing) is started as soon as possible. As agreed, construction work on this is to begin immediately after completion of the current Göttingen wind tunnel measurements (low speeds) if the results are satisfactory."[55]

## ME 262 NACHTJÄGER MIT HES 011

Messerschmitt offered what amounted to two new Me 262-based night fighter designs in a project description document dated February 12, 1945.[56] The first was a standard Me 262 B-2 but fitted with HeS 011 turbojets instead of Jumo 004s; the second was a standard Me 262 B-2 fuselage but with the 45° swept HG III wing and wingroot engine arrangement—the engines again being HeS 011s.

The introduction stated: "To increase combat value and performance, as a replacement for the night fighter Me 262 B2 with 2 x Jumo 004 B engines currently under construction, a night fighter has been designed with HeS 011 engines which largely meets the technical specification from January 27, 1945. The requirements in

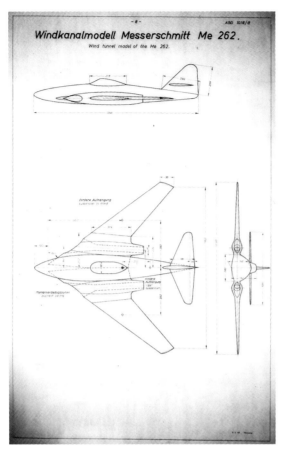

*Me 262 HG III wind tunnel model, dated January 5, 1945.*

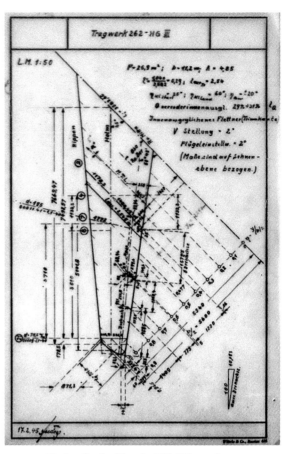

*Design for the Me 262 HG III's 45-degree
swept wing dated February 17, 1945.*

terms of speed, armament, equipment, protection and strength are already met by the B-2 night fighter after conversion to HeS 011 A engines.

"For a further increase in performance, swept wings are provided, as is also planned for the day fighter, with a simultaneous drag-reducing arrangement of the engines in the wing roots. The fuselage is that of the Me 262 B-2. The amount of fuel stored in the fuselage is also the same at around 3,100 litres. Maximum flight time when flown most economically is about two and a half hours at an altitude of 6km. The required flight duration of four hours can be achieved at an altitude of 12km with 2,600 litre external tanks.

"In both cases, i.e. the Me 262 B-2 night fighter with HeS 011 engines and the night fighter with swept wing, the requirement for the third crewman can be met by lengthening the cylindrical centre section of the fuselage without reducing the fuel content. A further increase in the amount of fuel stored in the airframe is possible at the expense of armament or the number of crew. However, it seems expedient to use this space for an extension of the FT system, the development of which is constantly in flux, and to accommodate the fuel [instead] in jettisonable external tanks or in

external tanks with as little drag as possible."

Included was an illustration showing the Me 262 night fighter with the HG III wing. This was to have four MK 108s in its nose and another two in its fuselage pointing upwards at an angle of 70°. The former would have a total of 360 rounds while the latter had 180 between them. The project description pointed out that "the use of rocket weapons...as well as the installation of other firearm calibres is possible by using a different nose". The aircraft could carry two 500kg bombs or external tanks on its bomb racks. Armour was largely the same as that of the Me 262 A-1 and the electronic equipment load was FuG 24 N with ZVG 24, FuG 25 A, FuBl 3 with AWG 1, FuG 218 R with Bremen internal dish antenna, FuG 350 Zc (Naxos), FuG 101 A, FuG 319 and FuG 280.

Other equipment included optional pressure cabin, air conditioning, heated windows, Junkers fire extinguishing system, de-icing for wings and tail, 935 x 345 mainwheels and 660 x 190 nosewheel, and attachment points for up to four 1,000kg booster rockets.

Since Kurt Tank was in charge of the Special Commission for Night and Bad Weather Fighters, his Arbeitsgruppe Flugmechanik team at Focke-Wulf

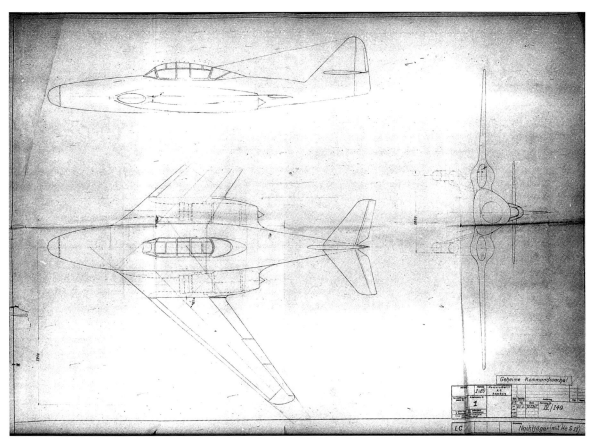

*Messerschmitt night fighter design dated February 12, drawing IV/149, with HG III wings and HeS 011 engines.*

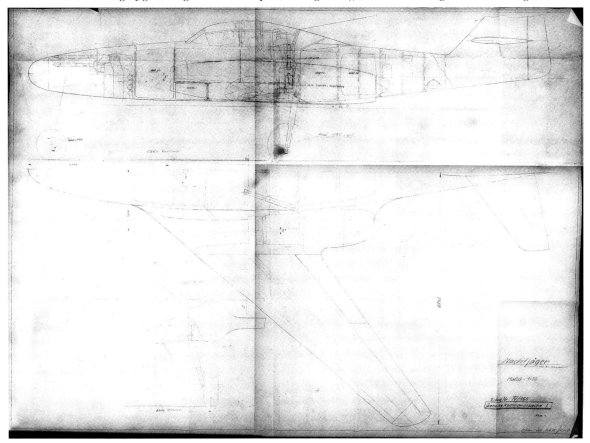

*Drawing IV/150 shows how the aircraft's enormous 935 x 340 mainwheels would fit within the fuselage.*

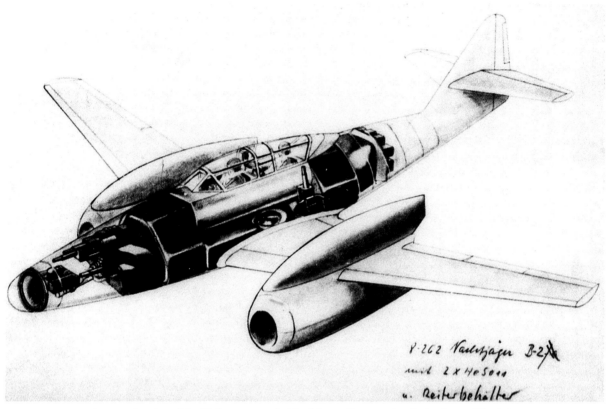

*A perspective view of the HeS 011-powered night fighter with conventional wing layout. The design also has an internal radar dish, oblique-firing MK 108s and over-wing fuel tanks.*

were given the task of comparing the projects entered as competitors for the night fighter competition.[57] Lining up against Messerschmitt's HeS-powered Me 262s were Blohm & Voss's P 215, Dornier's DoP 252/1 and DoP 254/1, and a Focke-Wulf project described as Nachtjäger mit 2 HeS 011 Entwurf II.

Unfortunately for Messerschmitt, the company's claims that a third man could be accommodated in either design were dismissed due to a lack of drawings showing the arrangement and the design as presented, with two crew, failed to meet the tender requirement. Furthermore, a detailed breakdown of weights was lacking and the Focke-Wulf men were worried that putting the aircraft's engines in its wing roots would result in a loss of rigidity in the wings and furthermore "the specified outline of the turbojet housing does not correspond to the recently enlarged dimensions of the turbojet device".

The positioning of the aircraft's oblique-firing weapons was also a major drawback: "In the Messerschmitt project, the oblique weapons are arranged on both sides of the radio operator, in such a way that the muzzle is located close to his head in the immediate vicinity of the glazing. A circumstance that will most likely lead to disturbances and complaints". And "the visor angle of 12° necessary for the full use of the EZ 42 sighting

device does not seem to have been observed".

What might have been seen as Messerschmitt's main strength—building with existing components—was also dismissed: "The present project can only fall back on existing assemblies of the previous Me 262 in very subordinate components. The overall structure of the fuselage, the new main landing gear, the strong sweepback, the novel positioning of the turbojets with the intake located in the wing leading edge, the swept tail, can be expected to give a completely different flight behaviour than the previous Me 262 version. In particular, difficulties regarding stability about the transverse axis are to be expected, caused by the arrangement of the turbojets close to the fuselage."

## ME 262 A-5A (SERIE)

Another unnumbered Projektübergabe document—perhaps the last—was published on February 21 and concerned the series production model Me 262 A-5a reconnaissance variant.[58] Fuselage installation for an Rb 20/30 camera had been rejected because it was not possible to insert and extract the camera via the existing access hatch, which left the two Rb 50/30 cameras in the aircraft's nose.

The A-5a's nosewheel installation would remain unchanged, with the cameras positioned on either side

# Endmontage 8-609

*Chart showing '8-609' assembly in nine stages at Regensburg, dated February 24, 1945.*

of it. The camera film cassettes were evidently manufactured with a 'flight direction' arrow on them so that ground crew would know which way round to install them. With the A-5's installation however, the left hand camera would have to effectively be fitted backwards, so that the flight direction arrow pointed towards the aircraft's tail rather than towards its nose tip.

Each camera inserted vertically through two hatches on the top of the nose, then toed outwards by 13° to reach their final installed position. The camera bay would be provided with electrical heating.

There would be two silicate glass panels on the underside of the nose, which would be hinged to make them easier to clean. Initially it was planned that, prior to take-off, a temporary splash guard would be fitted in front of these and automatically jettisoned when the nosewheel was retracted. However, it was considered that this might not be necessary—given that there had apparently been no complains about the windows of the makeshift reconnaissance nose being splashed while in service.

The camera access hatches would each require a teardrop-shaped protrusion since the cameras would not fit entirely within the confines of the normal Me 262 nose contours and evidently "this form was chosen because of the more pleasing appearance and a speed gain of about 2km/h".

Two MK 108s would be installed in the extreme tip of the aircraft's nose—in front of the cameras—in a position which "corresponds to the installation in the MK 103 nose". The radio system fitted would be the FuG 16 ZS rather than the standard FuG 16 ZY.

## GOLLOB'S NIGHT FIGHTER DEMANDS

The five night fighter designs assessed by Focke-Wulf were presented when the Main Development Commission for Aircraft met on February 27-28, 1945, but Gollob, representing the Luftwaffe, was apparently not satisfied by any of them and "expressed new demands".[59] Therefore it was decided that yet another new specification should be drawn up and issued to the companies, with a requirement that their revised projects should be ready by March 20 when the commission was scheduled to begin its next five-day meeting.

As it turned out Gollob's requirement, issued to Arado, Blohm & Voss, Dornier, Heinkel, Junkers, Messerschmitt and Tank's Special Commission on March 1, 1945,[60] though dated February 27, was similar in some respects to that of January 27. However, the section relating to crew had a new line added: "Arrangement: radio operator at the front, navigator at the rear. The latter must have good visibility to monitor the rear airspace".

The angle of the aircraft's oblique weaponry was changed from 70° to 80° but it was to be checked whether the defensive weaponry and the oblique weaponry could be combined—saving weight by eliminating one set of guns—and there was also a new requirement to fit R4M rockets if necessary.

Where the wording of the previous spec had simply required "ejection seat", singular, it was now spelled out that there should be an "ejection seat for each crew member, if it is possible to arrange the openings without impairing the functional safety of the pressurised cabin".

Greater endurance was also specified. It had been "four hours including climb" but now the requirement said: "Climb to 10km with full throttle, then two hours' flight at full throttle, then two hours' flight at 60% throttle".

There was more detail, too, in the construction specification: "The construction effort is to be kept as low as possible. Wood is largely used as a material. Good maintenance and repair by the troops are largely to be considered. It must be possible to park the aircraft outdoors (ground connections, etc.) The use of fuels of the poorest quality ... has to be considered constructively. (Heating devices for fuel in tanks, insulated pipes, heater, etc.)"

This new set of guidelines, along with the tight deadline, seems to have galvanised the manufacturers, including Messerschmitt, into action.

## NEW COMMISSIONER

Meanwhile, seemingly disappointed in the number of Me 262s being produced, Adolf Hitler had decided to appoint Gerhard Degenkolb as his new Me 262 commissioner on February 7,[61] though the formal announcement was not made until February 14.[62] According to Saur: "The Führer once again emphasizes the exceptional importance attached to the production of the 262 and warmly welcomes the appointment of Mr Degenkolb, who he knows to be particularly successful from locomotive production, as a special representative for the Messerschmitt circle. He expects that a combination of all measures in industry, air force and transportation will result in increased deployment of these high-performance machines under all circumstances."

The Führer was clearly also anxious to see the Me 262 fitted with high-calibre weaponry, because on February 26, Saur reported him as saying that "the output of the 5cm for the 262 and the installation work are to be pushed with all available means, emphasizing their urgency again, and increased to the greatest possible number of pieces".[63]

The Luftwaffe had accepted around 250 further Me

262s by the end of February, making a grand total of 1,135 accepted since April 1944.[64] The alternative source gives total production for February as 296 with only 187 accepted by the Luftwaffe, including 12 in repair, 47 undergoing retrofit, 13 new reconnaissance variants and three new B-1 trainers.[65] A total of 1,027 had been built, with 749 accepted.

A Chef TLR chart[66] of February 20 had noted the following Me 262 variants as either in production or intended for production: A-1a fighter, A-1a/U2 bad weather fighter, A-1a/U3 interim reconnaissance, A-5 reconnaissance, B-1a trainer, B-1a/U1 interim night fighter and B-2a night fighter. Three more types were listed as 'projects': C-1a Heimatschützer, C-2a Heimatschützer[67] and A-3a Panzerflugzeug.

Meanwhile, the Regensburg factory issued a new schedule on February 21 which listed all the 'Me 609'

variants now on its books for production—A-1 fighter, A-1/U1 fighter, A-1/U2 bad weather fighter, A-2 fighter-bomber, A-2/U1 fighter-bomber, A-3 fast bomber, B-1 trainer, B-2 night fighter, C-1 Heimatschützer I and C-2 Heimatschützer II. Evidently no one had told Regensburg that the A-3 designation had been reallocated to the Panzerflugzeug, since the fast bomber was unlikely to see production and had been given the downgraded designation A-2/U2 as a result. Similarly, the little 'a' denoting a Jumo 004, rather than BMW 003, engined variant was absent. Production codes were given for the first eight types but the columns for the latter two were left blank.[68]

In reality there would be little Degenkolb could do now other than interfere with the last few weeks of Me 262 production.

# The End:
# March to May 1945

THE WAR was rapidly drawing to a close by the beginning of March 1945. In the west, the Allies had entered Germany and were steadily pushing German forces back to the Rhine. In the east, the Soviets were driving through East Prussia en route to Berlin.

Messerschmitt's Augsburg headquarters, its base at Oberammergau and the Lechfeld airfield, all located in the south, were about as far away from either battlefront as it was possible to be in Germany. But the end was coming.

Nevertheless, the test fleet at Lechfeld continued to work through a host of developmental experiments and trials. During March it was expanded to a total of 16 aircraft — though only 10 of them flew and two of those only flew twice each.[1] The grounded machines included 170078, since there was no B4 fuel left for its BMW 003 engines, and 170083 which now had engines but was used for ground tests where it was filmed being repeatedly driven over 10cm high obstacles to measure tyre flex, shock strut movement and nose-wheel deflection. 170303 was being repaired following the torn-off booster rocket incident. 111538, the HG II with 35° swept wings, had no engines, and neither did 111857, which was described as the "improved production aircraft". A second new addition, 112355, was fitted

with a six MK 108 nose and was evidently used for static firing trials only. The nose had previously, from March 2-5, been mounted on the firing range fuselage, with a total of 618 rounds being fired before it was delivered to Lechfeld.[2]

Werk-Nr. 130186, the Heimatschützer I, flew twice using its rocket motor for a total of 22 minutes—both times on March 16—before suffering 20% damage in a low-level Allied night attack on the airfield on March 22. During the flights, "despite the rocket motor not functioning properly, it was shown that the [real life] performance corresponded approximately to performance calculations".

And 170074, the Heimatschützer II, also managed two flights totalling 12 minutes. On March 26, 1945, it made its first and only flight powered by both its turbojets and its rocket motors—the latter burning for around 40 seconds. The testers must have been thrilled because for once "ignition during take-off, take-off behaviour of the machine and combustion in flight were all correct". Things did not go quite so well during the second flight, on March 29, because neither rocket motor could be ignited. Testing came to a premature end when the very last of the B4 fuel ran out. At the end of the month the engines of both 170074 and 170078 were reported as undergoing conversion to run on J2 fuel instead.

*Werk-Nr. 170074, Heimatschützer II, pictured during ground tests. It made its first and only flight using both its turbojets and rocket motors on March 26, 1945.*

This left V9, V10, 130015, 130167, 170056, 110555 and two more new additions—111899 and 111994. Both V9 and 130015 had all been used at various points during the month to test pressure distribution on the cockpit canopy and rear fuselage. The latter had been fitted with the cut-down tail fin and rudder from 170078 in order to continue the ongoing lateral stability experiments. These confirmed that the Me 262's canopy and rear fuselage shape were having a significant negative effect on lateral stability. When an unnamed standard Me 262 was fitted with the 'racing canopy', it was found that stability noticeably improved.

130015 was also used to compare three engine nacelle intake forms—the standard 'Ruden' type already in use, a 'rounded shape' produced by Jumo and 'Type 4' produced by the AVA. Evidently the new Jumo intake had performed best and was recommended for series production. 130015 had also been fitted with the same 25° windscreen canopy previously used on V10 for a continuation of the ongoing bad weather visibility trials. It was concluded that "a direct comparison with the series version (bulletproof glass) is not quite possible, since the 25° cabin only had a plexiglass pane with a quartz glass pane in front. Nevertheless, it can be said that the forwards visibility on the 25° cabin in the rain was significantly improved by the much larger side panels, even if the windscreen itself does not bring any significant improvement. Apart from the fact that the 25° cabin is definitely better aerodynamically. It is proposed to have a number of cabins built for troop testing (bad weather fighters!)". Presumably the Me 262 A-1a/U2,

had it ever reached production, would have had a 25° sloped windscreen.

V10 itself, now with a wooden tail unit fitted, was used for testing a second set of wooden wing end caps (110555 continuing to test the first set) and took over from 170303 on the twin 1,000kg booster rocket take-off trials. It was also used for hydraulic pump investigations and a test report on these, dated March 12, indicates that it flew with weighted landing gear doors as part of the Panzerflugzeug programme, "since preparations for the flight … were very far advanced … despite the Panzerflugzeug being stopped".[3]

130167 was used for testing brakes and external fuel tanks. The EZ 42 gunsight installed in February could not be tested due to missing components and the FuG 125 system was also fitted in the meantime—as was a second engine fairing made from "0.8 material 1010.2", like the one fitted to V10 a month earlier. During one landing the aircraft's nosewheel door spring, probably weakened by months of hard use, failed to open the door correctly and the nosegear got stuck on it—preventing it from extending fully and locking into place. According to the summary report, "this resulted in landing damage. In order to avoid further accidents, a slide plate was built into the nosewheel door on all test vehicles". It is unclear exactly how badly damaged 130167 was on this occasion but it appears to have remained airworthy.

Werk-Nr. 170056 put in 23 flights during March, a total of six hours and six minutes in the air, testing various versions of the antenna intended for the FuG 218 system. These caused a reduction in flight speed of

*170056 fitted with the shaped antennas intended for the Me 262 night fighter. The aircraft retained its usual quartet of nose-mounted MK 108s during testing.*

*Test flights with 170056 found that the night fighter antennas could withstand speeds of up to 950km/h.*

*An Me 262, possibly 111899, fitted with an unpainted MK 214 cannon nose.*

around 2% and could withstand a maximum of 950km/h. This limit was discovered when, "at 957km/h, two arms of the antler antenna were suddenly bent backwards". Whether during the same flight or a different one, the entire antenna ended up snapping off—severely damaging the port side of 170056's nose in the process—possibly putting the aircraft out of action for the brief remainder of the war.

110555, with its prone bombardier nose, managed ten flights totalling one hour and 39 minutes—conducting hydraulic tests and acoustic measurements—before suffering landing gear damage. At first the landing gear got stuck and could not be retracted, then the nosewheel buckled when groundcrew attempted to tow it using the nose gear rather than the main gear. This damage was subsequently repaired and the aircraft was finally fitted with its K 22 autopilot unit.

Werk-Nr. 111899 represented the rapid fulfilment of Hitler's January 20 order to fit the Me 262 with a 5cm Mauser MK 214 cannon. With an EZ 42 gunsight and the MK 214 nose that had been tested up to the beginning of March, flight testing commenced on March 18 with Lindner at the controls.[4] Towards the end of the month the second MK 214 nose, tested on the range till March 10,[5] was installed on 170083.

With the MK 214 installed, the Me 262's nosewheel had been redesigned to turn 90 degrees while retracting

on take-off so that it lay flat beneath the cannon. This caused problems, however, with Lindner reporting that while flying at 680km/h the aircraft had become "restless"—later found to be the result of the main nosewheel door hanging loose. The restlessness vanished when the door finally tore free.

In addition, as part of the redesign a semi-circular portion of nosewheel cover had been fixed to the side of the nosewheel itself but Lindner pointed out that this "extends beyond the nosewheel radius and on uneven surfaces and when rolling over small obstacles drops cannot be avoided; this will undoubtedly happen more often". Presumably this meant that the door section fell off when the nosewheel ran over rough ground.

Lindner, together with Baur, then commenced firing trials. 111899's MK 214 was loaded with 30 rounds and the nosewheel coverings were completely removed.[6] On March 21, the pair jointly reported: "During the first flight, two single shots and three continuous shots were fired with the Revi [gunsight] switch set to 'fixed'. The flight then had to be aborted because a clasp on the weapon cover had burst open while firing.

"On the second flight, only one shot could be fired because the ignition current was interrupted by a broken spring on the retaining pin for the ignition pin. After replacing the spring, a test shot was carried out on the stand. On the third flight, the gun worked perfectly.

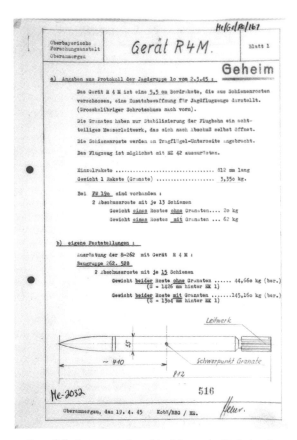

*One of the last reports issued by Messerschmitt during the war, possibly the last, concerned the R4M rocket. Dated April 19, 1945, it outlined all the drawings created to show the rockets and their launch rail fitted to the aircraft.*

The remaining 24 shots could be fired partly with single and continuous fire up to six shots without complaint.

"The Revi EZ 42 becomes unusable even when firing a single shot, because the crosshairs migrate due to the vibration. With the Revi position [set to] 'guided', the migration is more than 10° upwards and to the right. In this case you can aim more precisely [just by looking] over the muzzle brake of the barrel.

"On the next flight, the Revi EZ 42 was replaced with a normal Revi 16 B. The aiming accuracy is satisfactory after eight single shots. If you aim at the target exactly, the shots hit a little to the left of the target. It would be advisable to recalibrate this Revi on the test stand for distances greater than 150m."

Another report, this time by Baur alone, followed on March 25. He reported that the Revi 16 B had now been set up with a distance of 1,200m indicated: "Two targets were set up on the shooting range with a 30m gap (corresponding to the wingspan of a four-engine bomber). At 1,200m the two discs with the scratched marks on the Revi coincided. Shooting began at this range.

"All 30 shots hit between the targets, though as a result of inaccurate adjustment they were all slightly to the left of centre, i.e. roughly at the point where the engines would be located.

"Accurate aiming is only possible with a single shot, since the muzzle flash temporarily obscures the pilot's

*An Me 262 fitted with two underwing racks of 12 R4M rockets.*

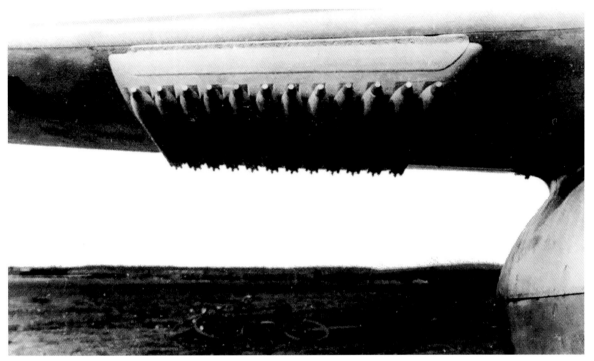

*A head-on view of the Me 262 R4M rocket rack.*

view. Nevertheless all shots hit between the targets, even with continuous fire up to five shots.

"Our fears that long-range weapons cannot be fired from the 8-262 are therefore unfounded. If you don't make the mistake of shooting at a distance of 1,500m or even 2,000m, but instead aim for around 1,200m depending on the ballistics of the weapon, then the MK 214 can easily be installed in standard airframes.

"If the operation is flown in such a way that the speed can be adapted to the bomber formation, i.e. the aircraft with the MK 214 is covered by a squadron of other machines [to defend] against enemy fighters, then several aircraft can undoubtedly be shot out of a formation one after the other."

Finally, there was 111994. This aircraft was used to test-fire Rheinmetall-Borsig R 100 BS unguided projectiles from its under-nose bomb racks. The aircraft made four flights in March totalling 50 minutes but it seems to have only fired the R 100 BSs on the ground. During one test, the exhaust from an R 100 BS evidently tore away parts of both main gear doors, necessitating replacements.

111994 was also used to test the installation of under-wing R4M rocket racks. Evidently accessibility of the electrical connections for these was "very bad" with a special tool required.[7]

One last report on this test programme was issued, by Baur, on April 3. He wrote: "During another flight, two projectiles were fired at the targets set up with a 30m gap. Both flew hard to the right of the targets. When the aircraft took off the landing gear flaps, which had

been reinforced by sheet metal that had been screwed on, were damaged again.

"The following can be said about shooting from such calibres: Aiming is like shooting 'freehand'. i.e. at the moment when the desired distance is present and the target is in the crosshairs, the shot is released. When the second shot fires automatically, with the delay of 0.4 seconds, it no longer hits the target, since the positioning is no longer correct after 0.4 seconds.

"The requirement for the R 100 BS is: each round must be fired individually. The electrical circuit is to be changed accordingly."

One more flight was made but this time an engine caught fire and had to be shut down. Baur tried to shoot his R 100 BS rounds into the ground before landing but just one ignited, forcing him to land on only one engine with the other round still sitting in its tube. He reported, evidently with some relief, that "the subsequent single-engine landing went smoothly".

## 3-SEATER NIGHT FIGHTER

Messerschmitt produced two separate night fighter descriptions on March 17, 1945—the last variants of the Me 262 to be proposed before the end of the war. The first was for a two-seater Me 262 B2 powered by HeS 011 engines similar to the design proposed on February 12[8] and the second was for an Me 262-based three-seater.[9]

The introduction to the three-seater description said: "On the basis of the technical guidelines for bad

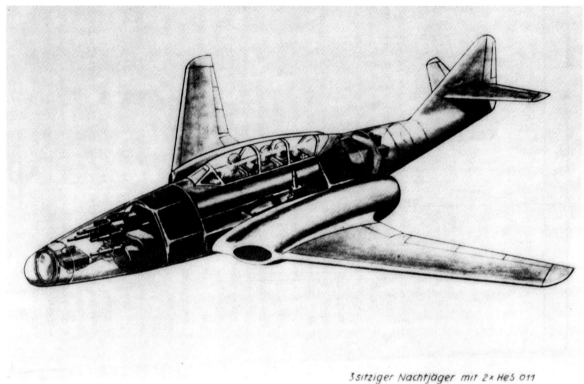

*3sitziger Nachtjäger mit 2× HeS 011*

*Perspective view of the Me 262 three-seater night fighter variant with 35-degree swept wings and engines positioned within its wingroots.*

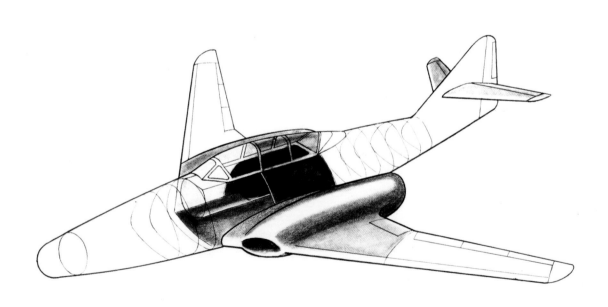

*3sitziger Nachtjäger          Änderungsumfang gegenüber 8-262 B-2*

*The shaded areas of this diagram show the new components required to upgrade the Me 262 B-2 to the new three-seater design.*

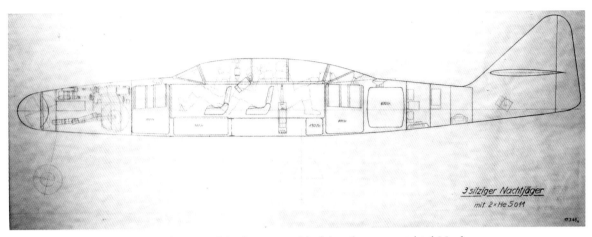

*The rather cramped interior of the three-seater night fighter, from a report dated March 17, 1945.*

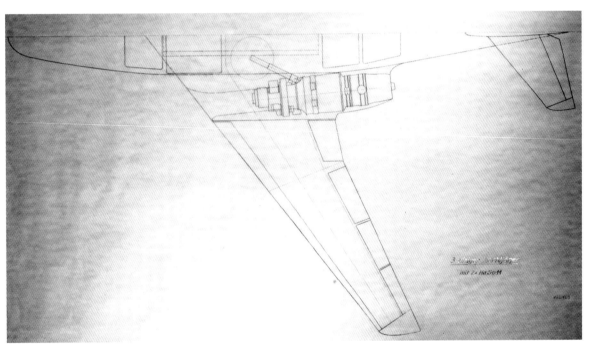

*Detail view of how the three-seater night fighter's HeS 011's engines would fit within its wingroots.*

weather and night fighters dated February 27, 1945, Messerschmitt AG proposes a further development of the previous night fighter. The advantage of this design is the use of large components from the Me 262, i.e. minimal effort in terms of testing and production capacity.

"The nose of the fuselage with nose wheel is taken from the night fighter, the tail of the fuselage, the tail boom, the outer wings, the two main tanks, [and] the 600 litre additional tank … correspond to the Me 262 A 1. In order to achieve the required maximum speed, HeS 011 engines are provided in conjunction with a swept wing, initially with a sweep angle of 35°. The area was increased to 28m² with a new centre piece using the 262 outer wings. The engines are installed centrally in the wing. Because of the simple structure and because test results with the HG II are available in a short time,

the engines can be installed under the wing first.

"The accommodation of the third man is made possible by a fuselage extension (total 2m) compared to the normal fighter. The fuel capacity of 3,200 litres in the airframe corresponds to a flight time of 2.5 hours at an altitude of 10km. With two 600 litre Doppelreiter tanks, flight duration at 10km altitude can be increased to 3.4 hours. The requirements in terms of armament can be considered to have been met by using the previously developed Me 262 nose, insofar as these can be used with the sighting device, and by using two MK 108s as inclined armament. A defensive armament to the rear was initially dispensed with. However, this can basically be installed, but at the expense of fuel.

"The electronic equipment corresponds to the specification, which coincides with the equipment previously

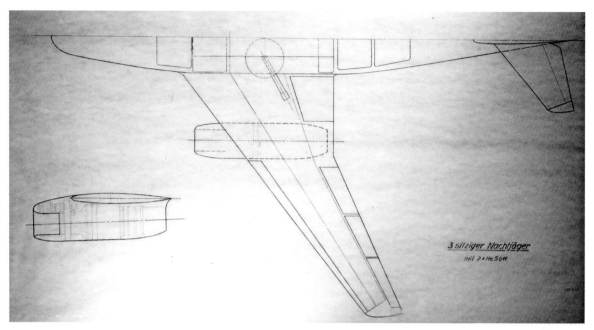

*The three-seater night fighter was also offered with engines in conventional underwing nacelles.*

planned for the two-seater Me 262 night fighter."

The four forward-firing MK 108s would have a total of 360 rounds while the two oblique-firing 108s would have 90 rounds each. In addition, "the use of missile weapons, preferably as an external equipment set, as well as the installation of other firearm calibres is possible through the use of another nose". It would be possible to carry a pair of 500kg bombs but "in this case you have to refrain from taking external fuel tanks. A defensive armament to the rear can only be realised at the expense of the fuel supply".

The electronic equipment specified was FuG 24 SE with ZVG 15 and FuG 29 for air-to-ground communication, with its antenna between the cockpit canopy and the fin tip; FuG 29 for receiving ground-to-air communications; EiV 125 intercom; FuG 25 a or c IFF with rod antenna under the rear fuselage; FuG 120k radio navigation system—using the same antenna as the FuG 29; Peil G 6 navigation system with "an iron frame under the rear of the fuselage [which] serves as the antenna"; FuG 244 radar "with concave dish antenna in fuselage nose, later Berlin system"; FuG 350 Zc (Naxos) with antenna in the cockpit canopy between the pilot and the middle crew position and "later possibly with a surface antenna on the fuselage nose"; and finally FuG 125, which also used the FuG 24's wire antenna, for bad weather landings along with FuG 101 a, which would have underwing rod antennas.

The crew compartment could be made pressure tight if required and was heated using air from the engines. The windows were heated electrically and electric de-icing would be provided. Ejection seats had been

nominally included but the designers had not accounted for the extra space these would require.

The undercarriage mainwheels would be the larger 935 x 345 size Messerschmitt had been working on for months and the nosewheel would be a 660 x 190 Bf 109 mainwheel. These sizes would allow for a take-off weight of up to 10 tons—and suspension points for four 1,000kg thrust boosters would be provided. Turbojet power would come from a pair of HeS 011 As or Bs.

Drawings included with the report partially showed two variants of the three-seater—one with the engines buried in the wingroots and the other with them in the more familiar under-wing position—but there was no full three-view nor were precise dimensions for the design included with the description. As such, it would appear to have been rejected before the final selection phase of the competition.

Unfortunately Willy Messerschmitt seems not to have been made aware of this and wrote to Lucht on March 19, apologising that he would not be present at the meeting and appointing company engineer Wolfgang Degel as his representative.[10] Degel, who had worked on the night fighter designs in his capacity as head of Me 262 development, would "present the characteristics and advantages of the night fighter to the commission. The particular advantage is that it can be introduced quickly, since the changes are not very extensive". Messerschmitt also took the liberty of ranking all the twin-jet development programme in order of priority—firstly the Me 262, then the Ar 234, then the Me 262 night fighter and its later developments and finally the "new development night fighter". It is unknown whether Degel actually

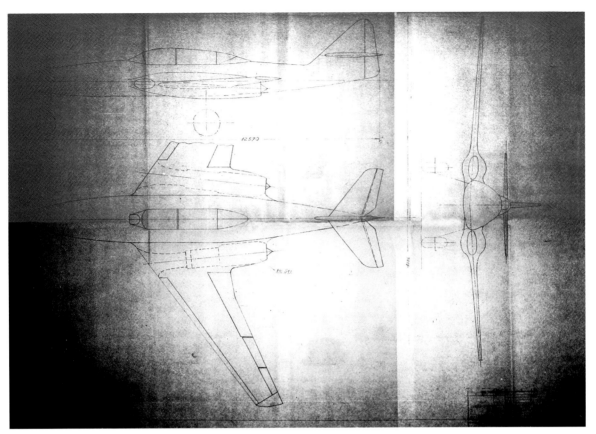

*This badly degraded image is the only known full three-view showing the three-seater night fighter. It is drawing number II/291.*

*Only seven of the 15 Me 262 B-1a/U1 makeshift night fighters ordered from Messerschmitt were actually converted to that configuration. This one is 110306, delivered to 10./NJG 11 in late March 1945. It was armed with two MK 108s. Captured by British forces, it was handed to the Americans and assigned the number FE-610. The other six B-1a/U1s were 110305, 110378, 110635, 110636, 110979 and 110980.*

attended the meeting, and if he did, whether he was asked to talk about the Me 262.

Tank convened a meeting of his Special Commission for Night Fighters to discuss the situation at Focke-Wulf's Bad Eilsen offices on March 20-21, ahead of the full EHK conference. Degel was not present. The meeting opened with the Inspector of Night Fighters, Oberstleutnant Werner Streib, outlining what he wanted and according to the post-meeting summary,[11] "the discussion led to the following statements: 1. The fight against four-engine bombers and Mosquitos cannot be carried out with one single type of aircraft. A significant increase in the cruising speed of four-engine bomber units is not to be expected in the future, so that a night fighter with piston engines is sufficient to combat them, while a jet fighter is unsuitable because of its short flight duration at low altitudes and the large difference in speed. 2. In order to combat fast aircraft such as Mosquitos and their further developments, the creation of a jet-based night fighter is required".

Under the heading of "provisional solutions" it was noted that "the piston-engined Ju 88 G-1 and G-6 are currently available. It is to be demanded that this aircraft continues in series production and its performance is to be improved as soon as possible. The suggestions made by Junkers for the G-7 series[12] can be used as a basis. In the final stage, by installing Jumo 213 J engines, such an increase in performance can be achieved that the aircraft type is still sufficient to combat four-engine bomber formations for a longer period of time.

"2. As a replacement for the Ju 88, an aircraft with piston engines must be developed that will always remain superior to the developments of the enemy on the piston engine side in the future, regardless of whether it goes to higher altitudes to avoid the jet planes, or goes to low altitudes." Dornier, it was reported, had supplied a project which met the requirement—the DoP 252, which was to have two fuselage-mounted Jumo 213 J engines driving a contra-rotating pusher prop, although there would be difficulty installing the required defensive armament in this design and further work was therefore required.

Lastly, "3. The task of combating fast enemy aircraft can be fulfilled with the Me 262 B-2 as an immediate solution for the near future with the caveat that if the enemy responds by going to greater altitudes than before, which is to be regarded as entirely possible and probable, then the altitude performance of the Me 262 B-2 with night fighter equipment is no longer sufficient. In view of the measures to be expected by the opponent, it must therefore be replaced as quickly as possible by a new development.

"Under all circumstances, it is necessary in the meantime to try to improve the altitude performance of the Me 262. This must include measures both on the engine side (increasing the full thrust of the Jumo 004) and on the airframe side (by improving the aerodynamic qualities and saving weight)."

When it came to the jet-propelled Mosquito interceptor, with the Me 262 three-seater already dismissed, the contenders were projects supplied by Arado, Blohm & Voss, Dornier, Gotha and Focke-Wulf itself. It was concluded that three designs should be given leave to reach mock-up stage: a conservative "low-risk solution" with a normal tail put forward by Arado, Blohm & Voss's tailless P 215 and "the optimal solution for the night fighter with piston engines by the Dornier company. Furthermore, the Gotha company's flying wing design should be better adapted to the tender and submitted to the ESK [the Special Commission] for processing".

But at the EHK meeting on March 22-24, it was decided that none of those designs satisfied the requirements set out on February 27[13] so yet another new specification had to be drawn up in April[14]—though whether it was ever issued is unclear. Certainly, no designs are known to have been tendered for it.

## LEADERSHIP CHANGES

While the test flight at Lechfeld continued its various trials and experiments throughout March, Hitler continued to insist that heavier armament for the Me 262 be rushed into service. On February 27, the Chef TLR's official war diary recorded: "Führer's orders: The installation of the 5cm on-board cannon for 262 is to be pushed forward and brought to the highest [production] number."[15]

Air-to-air rockets were also a top armament priority, the same report noting: "R4M airborne rocket for combating bombers (warhead with 540g explosive charge) in the first development stage without a detonator fuse. A squadron of 8-190 D 9s equipped with 24 R4M in two sets of 12 underwing rails is at test command JG 10 Parchim for operational testing."

Hitler reiterated his order on March 8, with Saur reporting: "The Führer expects to be notified of the results of the practical tests with the 5cm or the six 3cm [cannon] in 262 and submission of a start-up plan and accelerated examination of the possibility of installing at least two 3.7cm [Flak] 43 in 262."[16]

Four days later, this had filtered through to the Chef TLR, which noted: "The Führer has again ordered that particular emphasis be placed on the anti-aircraft ammunition and heavy armament of the 8-262 (5cm, 6 x 108, 2 and 4 x 3.7cm 43 respectively)."[17] While the

*A crashed Me 262 A-1a/U3 reconnaissance variant. According to a Luftwaffe quartermaster's report, a total of 25 reconnaissance Me 262s were built up to March 20.*

5cm MK 214 and six MK 108 noses were certainly built and tested, there is no evidence that Messerschmitt had ever previously been asked to trial the fully automatic 3.7cm Flak 43 for the Me 262. Indeed, it would appear that this order was never fulfilled.

The war diary for the Chef TLR stated that the emergency programme needed to be amended once again since the fuel situation was becoming increasingly dire. There were evidently plans to cease production of the Ar 234 and He 162 in order to concentrate on the Me 262, with the Chef TLR's leader Ulrich Diesing telling his subordinates that "based on the jet fuel situation, the ideal case should be built: a) If [the] 8-262 alone [is built]: about 800 per month. b) if several jet types: 8-262 550 per month, 8-234 50 per month, 8-162 200/250 per month".

In addition to this, he "emphasises the absolute priority and the war-decisive importance of the 8-262 and obliges all members of the Chief TLR to work with the utmost consistency for this sole focus".

These production numbers for the Me 262 were 'aspirational' to say the least. In reality, not only was Me 262 production way below target, it was in sharp decline. The de facto leader of the Arado company, Walter Blume, suggested scrapping his company's plans to build the Ar 234 C-3, powered by four Jumo 004s, and switching to production of the Ar 234 C-8 instead since this used only two 004s. However, the Chef TLR had countered that those C-3 "airframes can be built and Jumo engines are available due to the low 8-262 output".

Paradoxically, the low Me 262 output was ascribed to a lack of engines—not because they weren't being made in sufficient quantities but because the "procurement situation [is] bad (transport difficulties)".

Degenkolb, meanwhile, had been installed at Augsburg with his management team by March 15 and had called for an additional 100 engineers, which Diesing was supposed to supply. Degenkolb had "special executive powers for all 262 issues including engines, equipment and armament"[18] but as previously mentioned this amounted to very little in reality.

Hitler brought up the heavy weapons yet again on March 22 with more hyperbole. Saur wrote: "The Führer is extremely pleased with the success of using the 262 against bombers and sees in this machine with the reinforced armament (5cm, two 3.7cm and R4M) the decisive contribution to the entire war. He orders that a maximum output be ensured quickly and expects the new units to be fully equipped as soon as possible, particularly in the area of armament."[19]

On the same day, the Messerschmitt Bf 109, Focke-Wulf Fw 190 and Dornier Do 335 were cancelled, with "the freed capacity shifted in favour of the Me 262".[20] The only aircraft now officially approved for production in Germany were the Me 262, He 162, Ar 234, Ta 152 and, somewhat remarkably, the Ju 88.

*A closer look at the crashed Me 262 A-1a/U3, this time with an American GI sitting in the pilot's seat.*

Göring held a meeting at his Carinhall residence on March 25 to discuss the installation of heavier armament in the 262 and it was decided that "as an immediate solution" a 48-rocket R4M launcher would be developed.[21]

At around the same time, Hitler put Waffen-SS Obergruppenführer Hans Kammler in absolute control of all jet aircraft development and production for the Luftwaffe. It was an incredibly wide-ranging authority and according to the wording of the Führer's order: "Kammler reports to me personally for the execution of this order and has all the powers to do so. Here he makes use of all command posts, authorities and institutions of the Wehrmacht, the Party and the Reich, which have to obey his instructions." This completely overrode the authority of Degenkolb and on March 26 Diesing was effectively sacked from the ChefTLR, being transferred to the OKL leadership reserve. Heinrich Wittmer was identified as his temporary replacement for three days, with Generalleutnant Kurt Kleinrath being put in charge of the ChefTLR on March 29. On the same day, Kammler ordered that the Me 262s of KG 51 should be converted to carry the R4M rocket. In addition, the order cancelling the Fw 190 was rescinded. According to the ChefTLR war diary: "In a discussion with the

Rüstungsstab, it was proposed that the 8-152 model be withdrawn from the programme and that the 8-190 D model with the Jumo 213 E continue to run. Reason: Complete collapse of the start of series production 8-152 due to lost production areas. Restart would jeopardize production of the 8-262."

In a move entirely worthy of April Fool's Day, on April 1 "the reshuffle of the ChefTLR will be reversed. General Diesing resumes the leadership, while Generalleutnant Kleinrath returns to his command as the supreme commander of the parachute troops".[22]

Me 262 acceptances by the Luftwaffe fell from the all-time high of around 250 for February to about 220 for March. The total number of aircraft accepted had now reached 1,355.[23] The actual Me 262 manufacturing figure for March was 256,[24] but presumably 36 of those aircraft had not been accepted as suitable for service.

The alternative source, which only covers the period up to March 20, 1945—the date upon which the document was issued—gives a figure of 178 aircraft manufactured from March 1-20. Of these, 161 were accepted by the Luftwaffe, 10 were in repair, 43 were undergoing retrofit, 12 were new reconnaissance aircraft and three were two-seater B-1 trainers. Overall total production

*This Me 262 reconnaissance variant appears to be an Me 262 A-1a/U3 but with a single MK 108 installed in its nose tip. This does not seem to have been an official factory-approved configuration, since the A-1a/U3 was supposed to be unarmed and the series production model, apparently never built, was meant to have two MK 108s in its nose.*

up to March 20 is given as 1,205 with a total of 910 aircraft accepted—25 of them reconnaissance variants[25] and 23 being B-1s.

## ME 262 STURMVOGEL

Over the course of four days at the end of March, Messerschmitt produced no fewer than five new Protokoll documents. Nr. 63 of March 25 concerned equipment for the Me 262 night fighter,[26] Nr. 64 of March 24 was about modifying the Me 262's fuel lines to cope with lower quality fuels[27] and Nr. 65 of March 27 concerned the joint DFS and Messerschmitt towed fuel tank project.[28] Nr. 66 and 67 were both produced on March 28. The former[29] was about the material to be used for external fuel tanks attached to the aircraft's bomb racks and the latter sought to introduce a fire protection system to the Me 262.[30]

On March 26, a circular was distributed on the subject of "suggestive names for new weapons".[31] It explained that "at the command of the Führer, new, particularly high-quality weapons have been given suggestive names that particularly characterise their uniqueness. They should make these weapons known at the front and at home and increase their propaganda effect on hostile and neutral foreign countries.

"These names should primarily be used in combat descriptions and publications. In normal military correspondence, but especially in tactical and technical reports, the usual type designations are still to be used.

"In order to limit their number, only such weapons were given a suggestive name as were produced in large numbers or played a major role in combat operations due to their great effect and importance. The naming of other new weapons to be introduced is subject to the Führer's approval. All other weapons are still to be named with their usual type designation."

In other words, at this late hour, with Germany invaded and largely in ruins and with the enemy overwhelming German forces on all fronts, Hitler had decided to bestow colourful names on certain "high-quality" vehicles and weapons.

Various names for tanks and rockets were listed and the "suggestive" aircraft names were: Focke-Wulf Ta 152 Würger (Butcher Bird), Heinkel He 162 Spatz (Sparrow), Messerschmitt Me 163 Komet, Heinkel He 219 Uhu (Eagle Owl), Dornier Do 335 Pfeil (Arrow), Junkers Ju 388 Störtebecker (the surname of a famous 14th century German pirate), Messerschmitt Me 410 Hornisse (Hornet), Ar 234 Blitz (Lightning), Junkers Ju 188 Rächer (Avenger) and Messerschmitt Me 262 Sturmvogel (Petrel).

It was specified that the Sturmvogel moniker applied

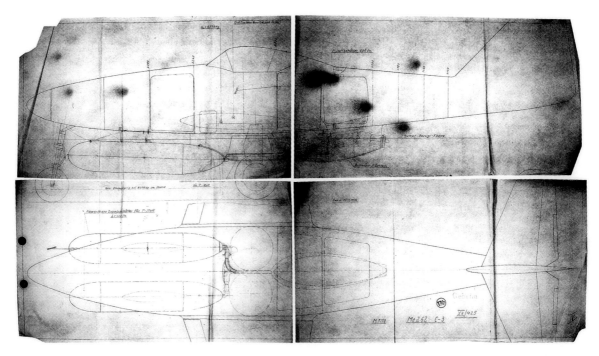

*Fragmentary drawing from February 7, 1945, showing the layout of the Me 262 C-3's bolt-on rocket propulsion gear.*

to the fighter, fighter-bomber and reconnaissance variants. It was not, however, a new name for the Me 262.
When the Luftwaffe test centres published a document
on January 15, 1945, entitled 'Testing the Me 262'—a
rather vague history of the aircraft and the test centres'
role in its development up to that point, the first of
several photos included was captioned "Picture 1: Me
262-Sturmvogel, A-2 Blitzbomber".[32] Here too, Sturmvogel seems to have applied to all Me 262s, with only
'Blitzbomber' being specific to the A-2 variant.

Going even further back, on September 25, 1944, a
supplement to the February 1944 edition of the official
German aircraft recognition chart—intended to help
flak crews and other Luftwaffe personnel recognise
friendly machines overhead—was issued. This showed
top, side, front and underside views of the Me 262 and
was captioned "Jagd-und Schnellkampfflugzeug „Sturmvogel" (Messerschmitt Me 262)".[33]

Exactly who came up with the Sturmvogel name, and
when, is unclear but it appears to be the closest thing
that the Me 262 ever had to an official name beyond
its RLM type number.[34]

## FINAL REPORTS

Werk-Nr. 170072 had been assigned to Messerschmitt
back in August 1944 but had been wrecked in an accident shortly thereafter (see Chapter 8). Ensconced at
Oberammergau, 170072 had gradually been repaired and
then, during the early part of 1945, fitted out with the
bolt-on under-fuselage rocket motor and fuel system

of the Heimatschützer III configuration first worked
on during April 1944. It now had the designation Me
262 C-3.[35]

During the test installation, the Messerschmitt team
had found that the bomb rack attachment points were
too weak to each hold a 600-litre fuel tank "and need
to be strengthened before using in flight".

In addition, the tubes connecting the tanks to the
rocket motor were too "soft" and needed support to
prevent them from moving around. And unless the nosewheel was completely straight when retracted ("during
flight operations, aircraft often take off with the nosewheel positioned sideways") it would strike one of the
fuel tanks and damage either itself or the tank or both.

The fairing covering the rocket motor needed to be
modified so that the rocket motor could "move freely"
and the lever installed in the cockpit for actuating the
rocket motor was too difficult to operate. It was stated
that the whole arrangement would be subject to another
thorough check before being used in flight operations.

A short briefing document on the Me 262 HG II
prototype, Werk-Nr. 111538, was produced on March
29.[36] This stated: "The following data will be provided
to you for the static release of the above machine: I.
State of construction. Swept wing 35° according to
drawing A 17515 S for HG II (wing weight = 1,383kg);
Engine 2 x Jumo jets with fairing according to drawing
262.610/611; 2 x 900 litre SG containers; without additional fuel tanks (170 litres, 600 litres); normal standard
fuselage nose with 4 MK 108; metal tail unit with series

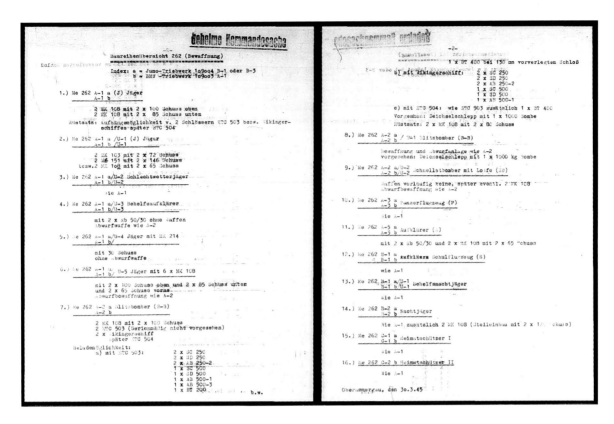

*Messerschmitt chart from March 30, 1945, showing all existing Me 262 variants and their armament.*

HVAC; complete FT system in fuselage; with armour in the nose and in the front of the fuselage; without armour behind the pilot.

"II. Weight and centre of gravity. a) Take-off weight = 6,260kg in H 4 [stress category] (without ammunition), centre of gravity = 20.5%. b) Starting weight = 6,470 in H 4 (with ammunition), centre of gravity = 17%. Since the HG II should be flown in between 20% and 25% later, loading condition a (without ammunition) is an option.

"Operating weight in H 5, weight = 5,700kg, centre of gravity = 22%. Empty weight = 4,760kg, centre of gravity = 24.5%. The starting weights include 2 x 900 litres of fuel, lubricant and starting fuel; without starting aids."

Messerschmitt's Oberammergau section issued a chart showing all 16 extant Me 262 variants and their respective armament as of March 30.[37] The key to the chart stated that, "a = Jumo-Triebwerk 109004 B-1 or B-3, b = BMW-Triebwerk 109003 A-1". Fifteen of the 16 could be fitted with either the 004 or 003—the only exception being the Me 262 C-2 Heimatschützer II, which had to be fitted 003s.

## THE END OF DEVELOPMENT

Evidently a new "Me 262 technical task force, which is used as a shock troop to increase the operational readiness of the Me 262 formations with a focus on repairing the jet engines, replenishing missing parts and for the exchange of experience between the troops" was formed on April 3, 1945.[38] In practice, this may have meant that the Lechfeld personnel, including the flight testers, were dispersed among the various operational units. In addition, anecdotal evidence suggests that Lechfeld was under "constant attack during the daytime by Mustangs and Thunderbolts. Experimental flying was thus limited to small periods near sunrise and sunset".[39]

Either way, the constant flow of flight test reports and technical documents emanating from Lechfeld appears to halt abruptly at the beginning of April 1945. The chaotic unravelling of all established organisational systems within the as-yet unoccupied portions of Germany was now in full swing.

During the first few days of April, modifications had been made to Werk-Nr. 111899, last flown on March 23. With Baur evidently no longer available, the aircraft was taken up on April 5 by Major Wilhelm Herget. He used the aircraft's MK 214 to fire six rounds at ground targets and plans were laid to use it operationally against enemy bombers. But "obtaining the live ammunition for the commanded operational testing against enemy air targets is difficult. In the entire Luftgau VII [the air district centred on Munich] there were 21 rounds available". These were picked up at Ingoldstadt and fired on April 6.[40]

## MESSERSCHMITT ME 262 DEVELOPMENT WORK IN PROGRESS

| | | Project Office | Construction Office | Testing | Series |
|---|---|---|---|---|---|
| 1 | Aluminium alloy nose with 6 x MK 108 | - | Yes | Yes | Yes |
| 2 | Steel nose with 6 x MK 108 | - | - | Yes | - |
| 3 | Nose with 1 x MK 214 | - | - | Yes | - |
| 4 | Addition R4M | Yes | Yes | Yes | - |
| 5 | Addition R 100 BS | Yes | Yes | Yes | - |
| 6 | Addition X 4 | Yes | Yes | Yes | - |
| 7 | Primitive fuel | Yes | Yes | Yes | Yes |
| 8 | K 22, closed construction | - | Yes | Yes | Yes |
| 9 | Firewall | - | Yes | Yes | Yes |
| 10 | Head armour | - | - | Yes | Yes |
| 11 | Series separation point rib 0 | - | - | Yes | Yes |
| 12 | New target frame | Yes | Yes | Yes | Yes |
| 13 | Fire suppression system | - | Yes | Yes | - |
| 14 | Messerschmitt fuel tank | Yes | - | - | - |
| 15 | BMW 003 engine | - | Yes | Yes | - |
| 16 | Hydraulic flutter brake | - | Yes | Yes | - |
| 17 | Laminated brakes | - | - | Yes | - |
| 18 | Landing wheel spinner | - | - | Yes | - |
| 19 | Brake parachute | - | - | Yes | - |
| 20 | Installation FuG 120 K | Yes | Yes | Yes | - |
| 21 | Installation FuG 29 | Yes | Yes | Yes | - |
| 22 | FuG 24 instead of FuG 16 ZY | Yes | Yes | Yes | - |
| 23 | Wooden elevators | - | - | Yes | Yes |
| 24 | Internally balanced tailplane | Yes | - | Yes | - |
| 25 | 23° windscreen slope | - | - | Yes | - |
| 26 | Improved series aircraft | - | - | Yes | Yes |
| 27 | Series reconnaissance variant | - | - | - | No |
| 28 | Series night fighter | - | - | Yes | No |
| 29 | Angled weapons for night fighter | Yes | Yes | - | - |
| 30 | Night fighter nose with Berlin antenna | Yes | - | - | - |
| 31 | Wooden wings | - | Yes | Yes | - |
| 32 | Pressure cabin | - | Yes | Yes | - |
| 33 | Climate control | Yes | Yes | Yes | - |
| 34 | 1,000kg booster rockets | - | - | Yes | - |
| 35 | Towed fuel tank/bomb | Yes | - | Yes | - |
| 36 | HG II | - | - | Yes | - |
| 37 | HG III | Yes | - | - | - |
| 38 | Jumo 004 E engine | Yes | Yes | Yes | - |
| 39 | HeS 011 engine | Yes | Yes | - | - |

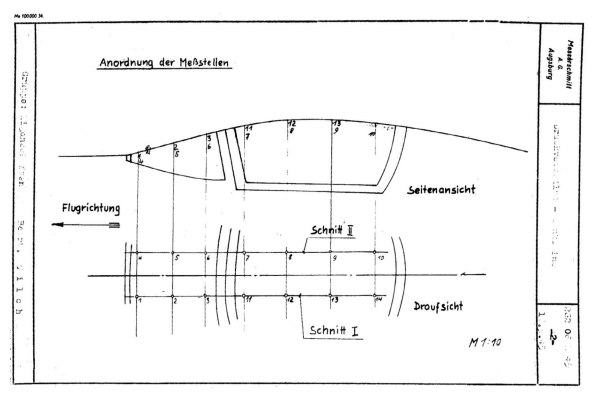

*Side view drawing of the low-profile Me 262 cockpit canopy dated March 16, 1945.
Lowering the canopy was thought to have a positive effect on stability.*

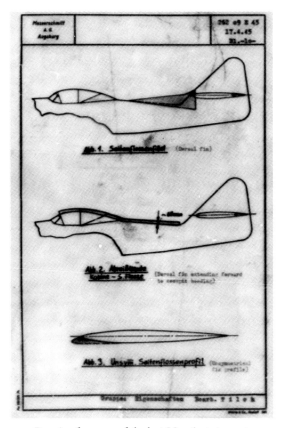

*Drawing from one of the last Me 262 test reports
issued by Messerschmitt, dated April 17, 1945, showing
dorsal fin designs intended to improve stability.*

Herget encountered some problems with the belt-fed weapon jamming up; "safety pins" supplied by Mauer had prevented the belt from falling apart and the ESK 16 gun camera "contrary to the original assumption" had worked fine in its usual nose-tip position during two test flights where rounds had been fired.

Evidently plans for further testing of the EZ 42 had been "interrupted by the deployment order" and a standard Revi 16 B gunsight "remains installed for the time being".

Oberammergau issued another chart on April 6 showing the status of all Me 262 development work in progress "according to the decision of Professor Messerschmitt".[41] Thirty-nine projects were listed and in each case it was noted whether the Project Office and/ or Construction Office had been involved, whether testing had taken place and whether the project had entered—or was intended to enter—series production.

A report was produced on April 14 outlining various problems faced in preparing a fourth MK 214 nose[42] and one of Messerschmitt's last Me 262 experimental reports was produced on April 17. This took the form of an 11-page summary compiling all the work done on lateral stability between January and March 1945.[43] The tone taken by author Tilch, Messerschmitt's senior flight test engineer for handling, was that of someone passing his research on to someone else—which indeed

*Under new ownership—the second MK 214-nosed Me 262, 170083, was given the name 'Wilma Jeanne' by the Americans.*

*The second bombardier-nose Me 262, 110555, was captured by American forces at Weimar-Nohra airfield on May 8.*

he was (see Appendix I).

According to the summary, all the "extreme" changes made to the aircraft's trim tabs, rudder and fin—shortening, reprofiling, internal balance and so on—had made relatively little difference to its turning behaviour. Thanks to the low profile 'racing' canopy, however, it had been shown that changing the form of the upper fuselage had a "decisive" effect. The work done on this so far was "not sufficient, so that the work would definitely have to be continued … measurements would be necessary to precisely determine the course of the airflow over the aircraft (possibly wind tunnel tests) in order to then change the shape of the fuselage or the course of the airflow in such a way that the turning stability is improved accordingly".

But there would be no more tests. Indeed, the most heavily modified of the test aircraft at Lechfeld and those that had been damaged appear to have remained there and would eventually be among the 80 aircraft captured by the American 92nd and 116th Cavalry Reconnaissance Squadrons when they overran the airfield on Friday, April 27.[44] These appear to have included V9, V10, 130015, 130167, 130186, 170056, 170074, 170078, 170083 and 170303.[45] All were evidently scrapped except for

130186, the rear fuselage of which was taken to Britain for study at RAE Farnborough, and 170083 which was drafted into the American 'Watson's Whizzers' unit under the name 'Wilma Jeanne' before being renamed 'Happy Hunter II' and destroyed when it crashed during a ferry flight on June 18, 1945.

110555 was captured at Weimar–Nohra airfield on May 8 after making a belly landing; 111538 was wrecked when another aircraft crashed into it;[46] 111857 was listed on the inventory of Adolf Galland's JV 44 unit on April 26; 111899 was apparently flown into combat with III./EJG 2 on April 16 but later destroyed on the ground at Salzburg on May 4; 111994 is said to have flown with JG 7 and may have been used to shoot down a B-24 Liberator and 112355 also went to JV 44 and was evidently used to shoot down three P-47s—two on April 27 and another on April 29.

Messerschmitt's Oberammergau facility was captured by the American 411th Infantry Regiment of the 103rd Infantry Division, accompanied by elements of Combat Command A of the 10th Armored Division, on April 29. They initially had no idea what they had found, with the 411th's official report for the period simply describing Oberammergau as "the home of the world famous passion play[47]—perhaps a fitting, albeit entirely accidental, allusion to the trials and tribulations of the Me 262's development.

Only around 50 new Me 262s are known to have been accepted by the Luftwaffe during April 1945, bringing the total number of series production model aircraft accepted during the full 12 month period since April 1944 to 1,405.[48] Given the contrasting figures presented in the alternative source[49] however, the accuracy of this figure must be regarded as questionable at best. The true total number of Me 262s manufactured may never be known.

# APPENDIX I

# Me 262 'Snaking'

*Most of the Me 262's technical failings had been ironed out by the time the war ended. However, there was one problem which continued to baffle the finest aeronautical minds in Germany—the aircraft's directional instability. Various theories had been proposed and tests had been ongoing but there was no agreement between the specialists.*

*This phenomenon interested British experts because the Gloster Meteor had exhibited similar traits—so thorough interviews were conducted on the topic with German technical staff by Royal Aircraft Establishment engineer Morien Morgan and J. W. J. Truran of the Aeroplane and Armament Experimental Establishment during a visit to southern Germany from July 8 to July 18, 1945.[1]*

*The following is a selection of relevant material from these interviews which also includes some interesting detail about Messerschmitt's internal workings and situation at the end of the war.*

## PERSONNEL INTERVIEWED:

- Hoffman, Lechfeld—Junior Messerschmitt test pilot
- Hoerstke, Bobingen—Junior Messerschmitt flight technician
- Baur, Augsburg—Messerschmitt chief test pilot
- Tilch, Lechfeld—Senior Messerschmitt flight technician
- Eisenmann, Oberammergau—Senior Messerschmitt theoretical man
- Doetsch, Oberammergau—Acting head of Institute of Flight Mechanics DVL Adlershof

## 3. HOFFMAN

Hoffman is a civilian test pilot, and joined the Messerschmitt group only two months before the end of the war. Previously he had extensive experience of autogyro and helicopter testing. He is essentially a tough stunt pilot, with little technical background, and speaks English reasonably well ... Owing to his limited time with Messerschmitt, Hoffman was chiefly useful to us in describing the organisation of the flight test group at Lechfeld, where all experimental work on the Me 262 was undertaken.

The technician in charge of flight testing was Kurt Zeiler. Under him were two groups dealing with performance and handling; Kaiser was in charge of the performance group, while Tilch ran the handling group. The chief test pilot was Baur, but most of the experimental flying on the 262 was done by Lindner. Hoffman was taken on as assistant to Lindner. During the few months he was at Lechfeld it was under constant attack during the daytime by Mustangs and Thunderbolts. Experimental flying was thus limited to small periods near sunrise and sunset.

## 4. HOERSTKE

Hoerstke was an assistant to Tilch on the Me 262 "snaking" tests. From all sides we learned that Hoerstke was not over bright technically, he was in fact sacked by Messerschmitts a few weeks before the end of the war. His English is sufficient for slow conversation, and during our talk with him we learned enough to confirm that he was somewhat slow on the uptake.

According to Hoerstke the firm started flight work in earnest on the Me 262 directional unsteadiness in July 1944, and he thought the work was about half done by January 1945. He had written an interim report on the work:-

Hochachsenstabilitat 8-262

Messerschmitt report number either E445 or E545

All copies of this at Lechfeld were burned. He thought a copy should be available at Oberammergau.

His interim conclusions were that the troublesome oscillation was of a period of 1.7-1.9 seconds at 700-750km/h, the main headache being the erratic nature of the damping. Improvement could be effected by taking great care that the fin and rudder profile was correct, but even when this was done some aeroplanes were still bad. He regarded it as significant that damping could be considerably improved by flying with a quite small amount of sideslip, induced by throttling back one engine slightly. They were coming round to the view that the trouble may be associated with irregular airflow round the fuselage, although flight tests with surface tufts on the rear fuselage produced negative results.

Their automatic observer recorded speed, height, rate of change of azimuth, and a pressure reading from each engine, on a time base. Cine gun records were also obtained in calm and rough air. All the original records and calculations had been burned, but most of the work had been reported on fully, and the reports may survive at Oberammergau.

Hoerstke said that his memory of detail was very vague, since he had been working as a farm labourer for weeks and was out of touch. He offered to write down all he knew at his leisure. Owing to our subsequent fairly full interviews with Tilch and Eisenmann, we did not think it worth while to take up this offer.

## 5. BAUR

### 5.1 HISTORY

Baur was chief test pilot at Messerschmitts. He speaks English fluently. He has been with the Messerschmitt firm for five years. Before that he was at the DVL (Berlin and Brunswick). In addition to being a top ranking test pilot, Baur is a fully qualified technical man. He gave us some interesting information on a scheme run by the DVL for the training of technicians as test pilots.

### 5.3 ME 262

### 5.31 SNAKING

Baur said that flight work on directional unsteadiness had been going on for about a year. They still had no conclusive answer. In his view the basic trouble lies with the shape of the fuselage, although it can be aggravated by bad manufacture of the fin and rudder. He holds to this view in spite of the fact that tufts revealed no unsteady flow round the fuselage. All the work on this problem was done on Me 262 number V9 at Lechfeld. (We saw this aeroplane, on its nose with a collapsed front leg, at the aerodrome at Lechfeld; marks where the tufts had been attached were visible, but the cameras and automatic observer had been removed).

In production the rudder trim tab often came out thicker than it should, projecting beyond the rudder profile. Bad directional unsteadiness, with perceptible rudder movement feet off, resulted from this.

Reducing the fin and rudder area by removing the top portion of fin and rudder improved matters by stretching the period. From the pilot's viewpoint this improvement in ease of sighting was far more marked when the fin area was reduced on the aeroplane with the BMW 003 engines than when the same modification was done on the variant with the Junkers 004 engines (the 003 nacelles are 85cm shorter in length than those used with the 004 units). Baur was positive that even with the reduced fin and rudder area, rudder power was adequate for flight on one engine; the rudder pedal forces were, however, too high for the engine cut case, and modifications to reduce these forces were in hand when the war ended.

Baur had satisfied himself that jet characteristics had nothing to do with the unsteadiness, by flying at greatly reduced throttle settings. He had satisfied himself that a small amount of sideslip, induced by slight differential throttle openings, improved things considerably; this was one of his reasons for thinking that unsteady flow round the fuselage was one of the root causes.

Doetsch of the DVL had been called in on the problem. He suggested that with certain heights of fuel in the tanks, the natural period of the fuel slopping from side to side coincided with the period of the yawing oscillation; the resultant resonance would produce poor damping. Baur claimed that tests at Messerschmitts with one tank completely full and the other completely empty had negatived this idea.

Baur had flown the Arado 234; he thought it better than the Me 262 from the viewpoint of directional steadiness.

The theoretical work on this problem at Messerschmitts was done by Eisenmann and Braun at Oberammergau; all flight reports should also be held at Oberammergau—those at Lechfeld were certainly destroyed.

### 5.32 LONGITUDINAL STABILITY

According to Baur this was good, even with the C.G. on the aft limit. Their main longitudinal trouble was the marked change of trim on opening or closing the throttles, arising from the low thrust line.

### 5.33 AILERONS

These gave a great deal of trouble at the beginning, when they were of the slotted variety with a fairly sharp nose which protruded for quite small upward angles; vibration and snatching resulted. This trouble largely disappeared on raising the nose of the aileron. They still had trouble with "repeatability" in production. This was met by fitting fixed metal tabs protruding beyond the trailing edge of each aileron, so arranged that on average the ailerons were too heavy. During the production flight tests progressive amounts of the tab were snipped off until an acceptable lightness was achieved; the amount to be snipped off varied of course from aileron to aileron owing to variation in manufacture.

Bad vibration was experienced on some production ailerons at 450km/h. Blunting the aileron trailing edge by inserting a channel section about ¼ inch thick was tried, but gave no useful result (the Me 262 V9 which we inspected at Lechfeld was fitted with these experimental ailerons). The trouble was eventually traced to a lifting of the rear edge of the leading edge slats, causing bad flow over the wings and resultant aileron vibration. By stiffening the slats vibration was postponed to 700km/h and above.

A "change gear" on the stick, whereby the stick gearing could be altered in flight and the pilot's mechanical advantage roughly doubled at high speeds, was tried successfully (we also inspected this at Lechfeld on Me 262 V9). According to Baur it was intended to put this into production, but the war ended before this could be done.

### 5.34 UNDERCARRIAGE

The prototype Me 262 had a conventional undercarriage. The elevator was too ineffective to lift the tail until just before take-off, resulting in an exceedingly bad view. It was decided to change to a tricycle—considered a daring innovation owing to the firm's limited experience with this type of gear; it proved a great success.

### 5.35 BEHAVIOUR AT HIGH MACH NUMBERS

Baur confirmed Lindner's story. Buffeting on the canopy starts at $M = 0.75$, the nose goes down, and by the time an M of $0.86$ is reached (the highest achieved) the buffeting on the canopy behind the pilot's head is so pronounced as to be intolerable. If the pilot could stand it, the aeroplane would probably exceed $M = 0.86$.

### 5.36 SLOTS AND STALLING

In its present form the behaviour at the stall is exceedingly mild, and no aileron snatch accompanies opening of the slots. Initially stalling behaviour was bad, and much development work was done in flight—altering the wing plan form at the root and the slot arrangements—before good results were obtained. Baur said that Eisenmann at Oberammergau had all the details.

## 6. TILCH

### 6.1 HISTORY AND ORGANISATION

Tilch has worked for the Messerschmitt concern since taking his degree in 1940. He is a pilot of light aircraft, but does no test flying. He speaks moderately good English, and struck us as being a very competent and clear headed individual. He was in charge of the 'flying qualities' test group at Lechfeld ... Tilch has been at Lechfeld for the past three years. He has been immediately responsible for all the flight tests on stability and control of the Me 262.

While the Lechfeld group had to keep up with theoretical work bearing on their flight tests, all the original theoretical analyses and detailed theoretical interpretation of the flight results were done by Eisenmann's team at Oberammergau.

### 6.2 "SNAKING" OF ME 262

We tried to obtain from Tilch a connected account of their "snaking" tests. He started off by emphasising that the war had ended before they had reached any clear cut conclusion. Many of their results were at variance with what would be expected theoretically; he amused us by saying that the mathematical "men of Oberammergau" came down regularly and pored over his results, but did not give him much help. In addition to Hoerstke's paper already mentioned in para. 4 (of which Tilch did not think very highly), Tilch himself had written a report setting out nearly all the experimental work on the job up to the end of the war: VB.262 04. E45 018 Richtungs stabilität Hochachse. A copy should be available at Oberammergau. All those at Lechfeld were destroyed.

Tilch's summary of the research was as follows:-

i.  Wendel and Baur did the early flying on the Me 262 prototype. They had no violent complaints to make about its directional steadiness.

ii.  In 1942 Beauvais of Rechlin flew the machine. After his second flight he complained that the directional steadiness at high speeds left much to be desired as compared with conventional aircraft; in particular a slight directional dither appeared to build up with feet off the rudder pedals.

iii.  For a long time Beauvais' report was disregarded, since most pilots did not complain strongly.

iv.  The first production machine snaked much worse than the prototype, feet off. This was quickly traced to bad manufacture (much unskilled foreign labour was employed), the tab being too fat.

v.  The Messerschmitt flight test team only began serious work on the problem in the spring of 1944. Strong complaints from the Luftwaffe pilots only began coming in after the Luftwaffe had heard that Messerschmitts were doing research on "snaking".

vi.  Initial tests were designed to investigate the effect of rudder and tab profile on the rudder free oscillations. It soon became obvious that behaviour was best if every effort was made to ensure a smooth profile from rudder shrouds to tab, and over the tab to the trailing edge. Various trailing edge forms were tried (U section about ¼ inch thick, split tabs 3cm chord each bent out 15 degrees in opposite direction, locking the geared tab, etc.). After each of these modifications the pilot concerned thought a big improvement had been effected, but with monotonous regularity further tests revealed that there had been no real improvement. It was found that bending both rudder shrouds made the rudder free oscillation worse; bending both out slightly made things better; bending both out more caused a deterioration.

vii.  The effect of rudder mass balance on the rudder free oscillations was examined. The standard rudder had an over mass balance equivalent to a static moment of 20kg/cm about the hinge. It was found that damping was perceptibly worse if the rudder was under mass-balanced. Putting the rudder C.G. on the hinge improved damping considerably. Over mass-balance gave little further improvement.

viii.  When the pilot held the rudder pedals fixed, and the rudder angle recorder showed no movement during the oscillations, damping was still erratic and unsatisfactory. To check that the rudder was really fixed, a positive plug and cone lock, operable in flight, was fitted between fin and rudder. The pilot could start an oscillation and then positively lock the rudder. Results showed that even with this definite rudder lock, damping was poor and erratic.

ix.  Attention was now focused on the fin, rudder movement having been ruled out. The fin had a low drag section, maximum thickness being at about 40% c. It was thought that erratic movements of the transition points on either side of the fin might give rise to trouble. Two checks were made:-

(a)  Spanwise cords were doped on both sides of the fin near the leading edge to fix transition.

(b)  A false fairing was added to the fin, altering the profile to a conventional section with maximum thickness at 28% c.

Flight tests of both these modifications gave completely negative results.

x.  Having covered the effect of fin profile, the next step was an examination of the fuselage. Damping of the oscillation was better and more consistent if the aeroplane was initially trimmed to fly with a small skid, by slightly throttling back one motor, and they thought this might result because the skid stabilised some irregular flow round the fuselage. Surface tufts round the whole rear fuselage behind the pilot were photographed in flight. No trace of irregular flow was observed during the yawing oscillations.

xi.  The firm now got down to making major modifications to the aeroplane to alter Nv, Nr, etc.

Comparative trials were run on a Me 109, Me 110 and Me 210. The Me 110 was by far the best from the viewpoint of aiming at high speeds. This was attributed to the fact that the period of the directional oscillations was greatest on this type, giving the pilot more time to correct. The reason for the lower period was quite explicable in terms of the lower speed at which the Me 110 operated.

Tilch argued that no explanation could be found for the erratic damping of the Me 262. The period however, agreed closely with what would be expected theoretically. Thus he thought the next step should be an effort to stretch the period, so that, even if the damping continued to misbehave, the pilot would have a chance of correcting the unsteadiness.

xii. First of all a vertical strake 6cm high, extending along the top of the fuselage from the front of the pilot's canopy right back to about halfway between the rear of the canopy and the front of the fin. This also did no good.

Instead of the strakes, a front fin was now added, extending on top of the fuselage from immediately ahead of the windscreen right to the nose. Ahead of the screen its height was about 1/3 the local fuselage depth, and the top edge of the fin was parallel to the fuselage centre line. This perceptibly increased the period, but not enough to improve aiming. A bigger front fin could not be tried owing to the structural strength of the front fuselage being insufficient.

xiii. Having checked that stretching the period was a good thing on the Me 262 itself, the next step was a practical modification. The top portion of the fin and rudder was removed, thereby reducing rudder fixed nv enough to increase the period at 800km/h Vi from 1.6-1.8 seconds to 2.4 seconds. This was an immense improvement. The pilot could now control the yawing oscillation. It was checked that rudder power was still adequate for the engine cut case, although the rudder was on the heavy side and more balance would be needed. It was decided to put the small fin into production, but the war ended before this decision could take effect.

Tilch dismissed Baur's story that the small fin only gave a real improvement with the BMW 003 engine, and not with the Junkers 004 units, as a red herring. He said that the fin and rudder profile was bad on the aeroplane used for the brief tests done with the 004 engines, and that that fully explained the apparently unsatisfactory behaviour.

xiv. One inexplicable feature on the standard Me 262 was a pronounced deterioration in damping as the C.G. moved aft. With C.G. at 24% c there was appreciable damping of the oscillation; at 30% c the damping was neutral, the oscillation persisting indefinitely, even with the rudder positively locked as mentioned above. Tilch mentioned that 30% c happened to be the longitudinal stability stick fixed neutral point, and thought that there may be some cross coupling between directional and longitudinal oscillations. Sideslip certainly resulted in a marked pitching moment on the Me 262.

xv. Tilch claimed to have disproved Doetsch's theory that fuel slopping was an explanation of the erratic damping, by arranging flights (a) with front tank completely full and the rear tank empty, and (b) vice versa. In neither case was any improvement obtained.

xvi. (xvi) Tilch stressed that the tests were not as systematic and thorough as he would have liked, being carried out under increasingly severe attacks on Lechfeld. He summarised his views on the work to date as follows:-

(a) Period must be greater than 2-2.5 seconds at 800km/h Vi.

(b) Periods agreed with theory. Dampings, even rudder fixed, did not. No satisfactory explanation had emerged for the erratic nature of the measured damping.

(c) Fin and rudder profile must be as smooth as possible, with well made fin, rudder and tab, and well fitting rudder and tab shrouds.

(d) The rudder must on no account be under mass balanced.

(e) No guidance had been obtained from Oberammergau on bl effects; on Messerschmitt aircraft a positive bl was a rarity.

## 6.4 DOETSCH'S "RICHTLINIEN"

Tilch had studied Doetsch's numerical handling standards very carefully. No copy was available at Lechfeld—all had been destroyed. He thought it a good effort, though possibly academic in parts—"sometimes we laughed". In his view it was very desirable for the industry to have such a document, although he felt strongly that its contents should be advisory rather than mandatory. Doetsch's paper is by no means complete; in particular Tilch thought that more attention should be paid to tests and standards at very high air-speeds—not enough was said about Mach number and aeroelastic distortion in the "Richtlinien". They did a few tests on the Me 262 on the lines of the book, but thought the aeroplane was too fast for most of the standards to apply.

# 7. EISENMANN

### 7.1 POSITION

Dr Eisenmann was the head of the Aerodynamics section of the Messerschmitt Project Office at Oberammergau. At a guess his age is about 40. His immediate superior was Voigt, who supervised the entire project department—aerodynamics, structures, etc.—and who was also being held at Oberammergau during our visit; Voigt was—we heard—probably going shortly to the United States for extended questioning.

Eisenmann only speaks English moderately well. During some of our interviews with him we had the assistance of Pickerd, a young Messerschmitt wind tunnel technician whose command of English was quite good.

### 7.2 "SNAKING" OF ME 262

Eisenmann confirmed the detailed story we obtained from Tilch. Additional information was however obtained:-

i. According to Eisenmann the basic trouble was that, even with rudder fixed, large amplitude oscillations were reasonably well damped; but instead of damping out to zero, there persisted a small residual directional oscillation of amplitude about +/- 10/2 in azimuth.

Messerschmitts were mainly concerned about this because of a project installing a very high calibre gun in the aeroplane. With such a gun, having a limited number of rounds, extreme accuracy in sighting was essential. The +/- 10/2 oscillation was quite intolerable from this viewpoint.

ii. Before the war ended the more important Messerschmitt documents were sealed up in 17 boxes and buried. After the end of the war, the American authorities succeeded in locating these boxes, which have been sent to London. All the reports we wanted on the snaking of the Me 262 would be found in boxes number 11 and 17; these boxes may also contain a copy of Doetsch's "Richtlinien".

iii. Comparative cine gun records were obtained on several aircraft during attacks on ground targets. The pilot for the sights on the target at about 1,000 metres, and held it until he had to break away at about 400 metres. On the Me 262 the speed during the attack would be about 700-800km/h.

A crude method of analysis was used consisting of drawing a mean line through the curve of directional deviation against time, and quoting the maximum deviation from the mean line during the record. Results obtained, in terms of units of maximum deviation per 1,000 units of range, were:-

- Me 109—4 units per 1,000 units of range
- Me 110—3-4 units per 1,000 units of range
- Me 410—8 units per 1,000 units of range
- Production Me 262—8 units per 1,000 units of range ("bad" aeroplane)
- Production Me 262—4 units per 1,000 units of range ("average" aeroplane)
- Production Me 262—0 units per 1,000 units of range (flown with slight skid, induced by differential throttle openings)

The yaw figure obtained with slight sideslip means that a very steady record is obtained in this case. From the viewpoint of aiming, however, this can only be utilised if the sideslip is measured by the yawmeter and fed into the sight.

iv. Eisenmann fully appreciated that the important thing is that the pilot should be able to control the heading precisely by use of the rudder. Flat spots in the rudder response curve must be avoided at all costs. When the firm laid out the Me 262 initially they decided to go for a high nv in the interests of steadiness; on the large Me 264 they put on very large fins to get a high nv, and produced a machine with excellent directional characteristics. As time went on, however, Eisenmann realised that on a small very fast machine such as the Me 262, a high nv resulted in a period of the yawing oscillation so fast that the pilot could not hope to control it. He therefore advocated a reduction of fin and rudder area on the Me

262 in order to stretch the period. As Tilch said, this proved so successful that it was going into production.

Eisenmann used a different definition of nv from that standard elsewhere, developed by himself, and based on body dimensions. In terms of this definition, he gave us the following figures from memory.

- Rudder fixed nv of standard Me 262—1.3-1.4 units (rising to 1.8 at high speeds)
- Rudder fixed nv of small fin Me 262—0.9-1.0 units
- Typical nv for small conventional fighter 0.3-0.5 units

On the Me 110, which gave fairly good results on cine gun records the period was 3 secs. at combat speed. Ideally, in Eisenmann's view, the designer should aim at a period of 4 seconds at combat speeds. On small, high speed machines this would, however, demand too small an nv from the viewpoint of structural safety at high speeds—excessive skid being introduced too easily in turns (they experienced such trouble on a later mark of the Me 109 with very large airscrew and resultant very low nv). His experience with the Me 262 had convinced him, however, that the period of directional oscillation should under no circumstances be less than 2 seconds at combat speeds.

v. The cause of the erratic damping on the Me 262 was not fully understood. Eisenmann had observed that damping was very sensitive to just what the pilot did with his ailerons during the oscillation. The marked deterioration in damping with rearward C.G. movement was also inexplicable on theoretical grounds. The small finned version also showed this effect, but to a lesser extent than the standard machine.

In his calculations on the classical basis he obtained excellent agreement with the flight results on periods, but no agreement on damping. In Eisenmann's view it may be necessary to introduce cross coupling terms, combining the directional and longitudinal motions, in order to cover the theory correctly.

His calculations of rudder free behaviour were not thorough, though more detailed work was on the programme; all the necessary equations had been established. He felt, however, that examination of the rudder free characteristics was of secondary importance to a thorough investigation of the rudder fixed case.

vi. He was convinced, from the tests made, that the snaking trouble did not arise from

(a) Mach number effects
(b) Instability of the jets or surging of the engines.

He did not agree with Doetsch that slopping of the fuel in the tanks was a major contributory cause of the erratic damping, claiming that their flight tests disproved this. They were, however, intending to try baffled tanks.

### 7.3 ME 262 AILERONS

Eisenmann was familiar with "repeatability" troubles. They attempted, after getting large variations in aileron heaviness on production aircraft, to tighten up very considerably on jigging; in particular, they laid down acceptable tolerances in aileron profile of only +/- 1mm; even so, the fixed tab snipped off progressively by trial and error had to be adopted.

Considerable trouble was also experienced on some production machines with excessive change of lateral trim with speed. Eisenmann thought this arose from wing twist in manufacture, although the tolerances were less than 25 minutes.

### 7.4 ME 262 SLOTS

When the Me 262 first flew the outer wing was swept back as at present, but the inner wing had parallel leading and trailing edges roughly at right angles to the fuselage. This gave a very bad root stall, even with slots on the inner wing, resulting in an ineffective elevator at low speeds.

The leading edge of the inner wing was then built out at the root and swept back to form a continuation of the outer wing leading edge. A great improvement in stalling behaviour resulted, and a still further improvement came with the fitting of slots to the inner wing in addition to the outboard slots.

On the Me 109 and Me 110 the slots open at a CL of about 0.8, and as they open marked aileron snatch occurs. Eisenmann claimed that the aileron snatch had been completely eliminated on the Me 262 by making the slots open much earlier at a CL of only 0.5. Choosing this low CL ensured that the slots opened much more slowly.

CLmax of the Me 262, measured in flight, is 1.35 flaps up and 1.75 flaps down.

Messerschmitts attached great importance to the stalling characteristics of fighters (we gained the impression that Eisenmann was very much a slot enthusiast). In Eisenmann's view a fighter should not drop a wing even when stalled with 10°-15° of skid—which was he contended a realistic condition. The Me 262 met this.

### 7.5 ME 262 LONGITUDINAL STABILITY — AEROELASTIC DISTORTION

At low speeds agreement between wind tunnel and flight results on the stick fixed neutral point (including effect of constant jet moments) was excellent; tunnel 0.29 c, flight 0.30 c.

If stick force at constant trim setting is plotted against q on the 262, from flight measurements, a straight line with a positive slope is obtained up to a Vi of 500km/h. The curve then kinks sharply downwards owing to aeroelastic distortion effects, and then kinks up again as Mach number effects become predominant in the region of M = 0.83.

The initial kink owing to distortion effects can be greatly modified by altering the tailplane setting.

The best man in Germany on aeroelastic distortion and its influence on flying qualities is Prof. Scheubel, who did his earlier work at Darmstadt. Fingado has worked with Scheubel for some time. Eisenmann said that the firm had not done a great deal of work on this, and no attempt had been made to correlate theory with observed flight results. In his view, once the broad effects were appreciated, detailed work was unprofitable since matters would be controlled so easily by altering tailplane setting empirically.

### 7.6 ME 262—HIGH MACH NUMBERS

Eisenmann said that the behaviour of the aeroplane at high Mach numbers tied up very well with what would be expected from the high speed tunnel results obtained at Berlin and Brunswick. In his view the aeroplane could be pushed quite a way beyond M = 0.86, were it not for considerations of structural strength. He rather poo-poohed the firm's test pilot's story that the buffeting on the canopy was so bad at M = 0.86 that they would not take it any further; if the technical staff had instructed them to go higher on the Mach number scale it would have been done (Eisenmann is not himself a pilot).

### 7.7 LARGE SWEEPBACK

He is convinced of the virtues of a large amount

of sweepback at high Mach numbers, but is very worried about the consequences of poor control and bad stalling characteristics at low air speeds. He feels that in Germany the high sweepback enthusiasts—particularly the tunnel people—have tended rather to gloss over the resultant low speed problems.

To get flight experience a wing had been designed and built for the Me 262 with 35° sweepback; the war ended before it could be flown. This was in aid of a project which was in effect a Me 262 development with more powerful units (Heinkel—1,500kg thrust), the Me 262 fuselage, and a new wing of larger span, swept back 35°.

Eisenmann feels that slots will be essential to get reasonable stalling characteristics with high sweepback. If only tip slots are used, a very high efficiency flap will be needed inboard. He was very interested in the tunnel work of Prof. Seiferth at Göttingen, who has developed a 10-20% c flap situated ahead of the aerofoil and deflected downwards through 50°-60°. In two dimensions this device gives a CL of about 0.5, large in relation to the flap area.

## 8 DOETSCH

### 8.1 HISTORY, ETC.

Dr Karl Doetsch was at the end of the war the acting head of the DVL Institute of Flight Mechanics. His age is 36. He speaks English reasonably well. He has specialised in the handling characteristics of aircraft for the past 14 years. In addition to having high technical qualifications—good degree, etc.—he is an experienced test pilot. We gathered that in Germany there is a select group of test pilots, members of which are entitled to call themselves "Flugbaumeister"—there have been 70 in all and 30 survive. Doetsch is a Flugbaumeister, and seemed very proud of it.

Towards the end of the war Doetsch's team, which had operated at the DVL Adlershof, was evacuated to Travemünde (DVL—Zweigstelle Travemünde).

After a day's interrogation we had formed a very high opinion of Doetsch's competence and knowledge.

### 8.2 "SNAKING" OF THE ME 262

Doetsch said that this had been one of his biggest headaches for the past year. The DVL had been called in early. At first he was not at all satisfied with the Messerschmitt testing procedure. He gave Lindner, the test pilot on the job, a great deal of help, and subsequently sent one of his own DVL pilots to Lechfeld to work alongside Lindner. He still felt, however, that the Lechfeld tests were not sufficiently systematic. Early this year (in February), he had a Me 262 allotted to the DVL at Travemünde for really controlled "snaking" research. The work was in full swing when the war ended. He made the following points:

i. The troublesome small amplitude oscillation on the Me 262 arises from a variety of causes. He is convinced that one trouble is the low drag section of the fin, with maximum thickness at 40% c, giving rise to erratic movements of the transition points. In his view the Messerschmitt tests with cords and a redesigned fairing over the fin to bring maximum thickness forward had been too sketchy to give any conclusive answer.

ii. He is certain that slopping of the fuel in the tanks is a partial cause of the erratic damping, and that it is owing to the alteration in the fuel distribution that the apparent deterioration in damping with rearward C.G. movement comes about. He had obtained records on the Me 262 at Travemünde which showed conclusively that the damping of the troublesome yawing oscillation depending on the height of fuel in the tanks.

He arranged to have specially baffled tank built for the DVL. This was done, but the war ended before they could be flown. The tanks should be at Rechlin.

Tests were also done at Travemünde with the C.G. at 0.25c and 0.30c, taking care that all other variables remained the same. These tests negatived the Messerschmitt findings of damping deterioration with aftwards C.G. movement.

iii. Doetsch thought another source of trouble may be interference between the jets and the tail unit. The jets were closer to the fuselage on the Me 262 than on the Arado 234.

iv. In thinking about the problem he thought that the important things were:

(a) Initial swing in azimuth on hitting a side gust.
(b) Subsequent damping.

Provided the damping was what it should be, he did not think a very fast oscillation would worry the pilot. The basic trouble on the Me 262 was that a fast period was combined with very poor damping.

He emphasised that the initial yaw on hitting a bump depended critically on just what the pilot did with his ailerons.

v. Doetsch had come to the conclusion that the quickest and most certain method of making the Me 262 an acceptable gun platform was by the brute force method of installing an automatic pilot on the rudder for use when shooting. When the war ended he was just about to start experiments on the Me 262 at Travemünde on these lines, using either one of the following two autopilots on the rudder:-

(a) Kurssteuerung (Jägersteuerung) Patin
or (b) Kurssteuerung (Jägersteuerung) LGW Hakenfelde

Both these units were in production, their purpose being to assist pilots of fighters when flying in cloud.

vi. Summing up, Doetsch's intended recommendations for the Me 262 were:-

(a) Baffle the tanks to stop fuel slopping
(b) Install an autopilot on the rudder for use when shooting.

If time had been available, Doetsch said he would have explored more fundamental cures—modifying fin profile and area, etc. The results obtained by the DVL during the flight tests from February to the end of April 1945, should be still at Travemünde.

# The Me 262 as a Combat Aircraft

*Allied intelligence gathered together numerous prisoners of war and quizzed them about all aspects of the Me 262—not just its development but also experiences of operating it as a frontline combat aircraft.*

*The result was A.D.I.(K) Report No. 323/1945 The Me 262 as a Combat Aircraft, produced on June 6, 1945.[1] It represents a collection of interesting anecdotes, recollections and nuggets of unusual information from the men who had, up until very recently, worked on and around Me 262s every day. Some of what is said rings true and some of it ought perhaps to be taken with a measure of salt.*

*The report, in common with many reports of this period, consists of sequentially numbered paragraphs—some of which are interconnected and others not. It reads as follows:*

1. The ending of the war has brought about the capture of many G.A.F. Me 262 pilots, amongst them some of the best known German fighter pilots and unit leaders, including Generalleutnant GALLAND, one of the Luftwaffe's greatest fighter aces, Inspector of the German Fighter Arm—at last in charge of J.V.44; Major BARKHORN, credited with 301 victories; Oberstleutnant BÄR, once Kommodore of J.G.3; Oberstleutnant DAHL, once in command of a famous Sturmgruppe III./J.G.3, and a host of others, including Major BRÜCKER, formerly Kommodore of S.G.4, who had flown the Me 262 as a dive-bomber and ground-attack aircraft.

2. From interrogation of these P/W it has been possible to learn much about the G.A.F's employment of its most successful jet-propelled aircraft, the Me 262. An attempt is made in this report to describe some of the features of the Me 262 as an operational aircraft with its performance, tactics, formations, and the imperfections discovered in the course of its employment. Only in the last months of the war was the Me 262 put into the hands of Germany's best pilots in J.V. (Jagd Verband) 44 and in a short time they reached definite conclusions about its usefulness.

## TECHNICAL FEATURES

3. New information of interest has been revealed by re-examination of some of the statements in A.P/W.I.U. (Ninth Air Force Advance) Report No. 49/1945 which were based solely on information suggested by a Me 262 acceptance pilot who had no battle experience in the aircraft. These present items bear partly on modifications to the Me 262 subsequently brought about by combat experience.

## TANKAGE

4. The total jet fuel tankage of the Me 262 is 2,570 to 2,600 litres, tanks being situated as follows:-

    (i) One 900 L tank ahead of the cockpit.
    (ii) One 900 L tank behind the cockpit.
    (iii) One 600 L tank behind it (ii).

(iv) One 170 to 200 L tank under the pilot's feet.

## MODIFIED CONTROL STICK

5. At speeds of about 800km/h, the ailerons and elevators of the Me 262 become very difficult to move with the ordinary control stick. A new type of control stick to give increased mechanical advantage was developed to offset this difficulty, and was installed in new models; the modification was effected by making extendable the section of the control column below the socket joint. With the section extended by moving a lever fitted to the upper part of the column, greater leverage was obtained and the control surfaces could be moved with less effort.

## GYROSCOPIC GUN SIGHT – EZ 42

6. The EZ 42 gyroscopic gun sight was fitted in many of the aircraft of J.V.44, the Me 262 unit commanded by Generalleutnant GALLAND which became operational in late March 1945, but faulty installation made the sight useless and it was locked so as to function like the old fixed reflector sight.

## AUTOMATIC THROTTLE CONTROL

7. On the Me 262s already in action the throttles had to be advanced slowly up to 6,000rpm to avoid burning out the jet units. Above 6,000rpm the throttles could be pushed all the way forward at once, because an automatic fuel flow and pressure regulator prevented a too sudden increase in the amount of fuel entering the jets and a consequent overheating. A new regulator had been developed to control the fuel flow from 0rpm to maximum, so that the throttles could be set at once at any point and the new regulator would ensure a safe and gradual acceleration to the rpm indicated by the throttle setting. The new regulator had been tested and found satisfactory.

## ROCKET ASSISTED START

8. Many experiments had been made with rocket assisted start with the Me 262; two 500kg thrust rockets shortened the distance required for start without bombs or R.P. by 250 to 300 yards. Starts with two 1,000kg thrust rockets had been effected in as little as 440 yards without bombs or R.P.

## PERFORMANCE CALCULATOR

9. The endurance and speed of the Me 262 is dependent on such variables as air temperature, barometric pressure, altitude and fuel pressure. For the purpose of calculating flying time and range a special circular slide rule was produced by Messerschmitt and issued to operational units using the Me 262.

## NEW TYPE PARACHUTES

10. The great speed of the Me 262 made it dangerous to bale out with an ordinary parachute, because the sudden deceleration might damage both parachute and pilot; so two new types of parachutes were introduced. One type, used in K.G.6, was fitted with metal rings to hold the shrouds together in pairs just below the skirt, thus reducing the circumference of the skirt and lessening the overall wind resistance. The rings were supposed to slide down gradually and allow the chute to open fully on the way down. It is not known how this arrangement worked.

11. In J.V.44 a so-called strip parachute (Bänderfallschirm) was introduced. It was constructed of spaced strips instead of one whole piece; it opened more slowly and fell more quickly than the usual parachute, and for that reason was discarded by J.V.44, whose pilots realised they were most vulnerable to attack whilst landing or taking off and therefore needed a quick opening parachute for jumping at low altitudes.

## FLYING QUALITIES

12. Because of the range of speeds at which the Me 262 can operate—250 to 950km/h—its design is a compromise, and it cannot turn as sharply as an ordinary fighter. Acceleration and deceleration in level flight are accomplished relatively more slowly with the Me 262 than with an ordinary fighter, but low wind resistance and the absence of a propeller enables the Me 262 to dive very fast.

13. At speeds of between 950 and 1,000km/h air currents around the aircraft reach the speed of sound and the control surfaces no longer influence the direction of flight; the result varies from aircraft to aircraft, and whilst some wing over and dive others dive gradually. The experiences of some pilots indicate, however, that once the speed of sound is exceeded, the phenomena disappear and ordinary control is restored. Counter measures against these tendencies have not been worked out with certainty. Vertical dives in the Me 262 are not performed because the speed of sound is reached too quickly.

14. Because of the great range of speed of the aircraft and because of the great fuel consumption, with the resultant unbalancing, constant trimming is necessary during flight as speed changes and the fuel is consumed.

15. The Me 262 flies at low altitudes with much greater speed than an ordinary fighter, speeds of 750km/h

being attainable at altitude of 100 metres. This great speed makes the 262 very sensitive to the varying currents which prevail at low altitudes, and hence flying at tree top level is dangerous.

## TAKE-OFF AND LANDING DISTANCES

16. Distances for take-off vary considerably with the factors of air temperature and pressure, but the following figures, which were considered valid for unassisted take-off by the pilots interrogated, apply to the Me 262 with full fuel load and 24 x R4M R.P.:
    Take-off: Grass field ... 1,800-2,000 yards. Concrete runway ... 1,500-1,800 yards.
17. Minimum landing distance with fuel almost expended and with no R.P. is 1,100 yards on a concrete runway or grass field.

## SERVICE CEILING

18. Altitudes as high as 38,500 feet have been reached by the Me 262 in test flights, but the operational ceiling for formations of Me 262s was set at 30,000 feet by Generalleutnant Galland, because of the difficulty of holding formation at higher altitudes and because of the possibility of the jet units cutting out at altitudes above 30,000 feet. Throttle adjustments at altitudes above 20,000 feet are likely to cause stopping of the jet unit concerned.

## SERVICING

19. The Jumo 004 jet units of the Me 262 are supposed to last from 25-35 hours, but in practice they only lasted for about ten hours' flying time. The prescribed time for changing and checking a unit was three hours, but in actual practice it took 8-9 hours because of poorly fitting parts and lack of trained staff.
20. Fuelling the aircraft could be accomplished in 8-15 minutes under operational conditions, depending on the pumping speed of the tank truck.

## OPERATION ON ONE JET UNIT

21. The Me 262 functions efficiently on one jet unit, and speeds of 450-500km/h for as long as two and a quarter hours have been attained. In attempting such flights, an altitude of about 25,000 feet should be reached before one jet is turned off, and at an altitude under 10,000 feet this unit should be restarted; landing on one unit is possible but is considered an unnecessary hazard.

## ARMAMENT

22. The standard armament of the Me 262 was four 3cm MK 108s. The close grouping of the guns in the nose was considered to be ballistically ideal, but some trouble was experienced in firing in a turn, when centrifugal force tore the ammunition belts. This was remedied by altering the feeding mechanism. Fire converged between 400 and 500 yards.
23. In combat against bombers, the Me 262s of J.V.44 carried 24 x R4M 5cm rocket projectiles, twelve under each wing. Each projectile contained 500 grams of Hexogen and had considerable blast effect. The R.P. were shot off in a space of 0.03 seconds and scatted to give a pattern covering the silhouette of as four-engined bomber at 600 yards. On several occasions victories were scored with the R4M, and it was planned to install as many as 48 under the wings of the Me 262 for greater effect. The trajectory of the R4M was almost the same as that of the MK 108; so the ordinary gun sight could be used without difficulty.

## TACTICAL EMPLOYMENT OF THE ME 262

24. The Me 262 has been employed as a fighter, fighter-bomber, shallow dive-bomber and for reconnaissance; experiments were also performed for its employment as an air-to-air bomber. Through interrogation of many experienced Me 262 pilots and unit commanders it has been possible to determine certain facts about the use of the aircraft in some of those roles.

## EMPLOYMENT OF THE ME 262 BY J.V.44 TO ATTACK U.S.A.A.F. BOMBERS

25. In January 1945, by special permission of GOERING, a new Me 262 fighter unit was formed at Brandenburg-Briest by Generalleutnant GALLAND, formerly chief of the G.A.F. Inspectorate of the Fighter Arm. This unit, known as Jagd Verband 44, or Jagd Verband GALLAND, was under training with units of J.G.7 at Briest until late March, when it moved to München/Riem and became operational. The 40-50 pilots of the unit included GALLAND himself, about ten holders of the Ritterkreuz, a dozen other highly experienced pilots and twenty-odd new pilots who showed some promise. J.V.44 was operational throughout April from Riem and moved in the last days of the war to Salzburg/Maxglan, where it was overrun by American armour on 3rd May 1945.
26. During the short time they were operational, GALLAND and his more experienced pilots developed some concept of how the Me 262 was best to be used in combat. They carried through a number of attacks on Allied bomber formations, and achieved some success, despite heavy losses inflicted

by the overpowering fighter escort that constantly harried them.

27. Rarely were more than sixteen aircraft of J.V.44 serviceable for any one mission, with the result that during any attack on U.S.A.A.F. bombers the German force was far outnumbered by the American fighter escort. The primary mission of the jet aircraft was to attack and destroy the bombers, and combat with the Allied fighters was not accepted unless unavoidable. Hence, all the tactical employment of the Me 262 in J.V.44 was hampered by numerical inferiority and strict limitation of the combat objective.

28. The large curving radius and slow acceleration of the Me 262 made the Kette element of three aircraft instead of the Schwarm (element of four aircraft the most practical basic formation; J.G.7, another unit equipped with the Me 262 did, however, fly missions in elements of four. The element of three was chosen by J.V.44 because the lack of manoeuvrability of the jet rendered it difficult for a larger element to stay together in aerial manoeuvres. When turns were made, formation had to be held by cutting inside or overshooting rather than by use of the throttles. When shifting position in a turn, the two rear aircraft of the element of three tried to pass below the lead aircraft to avoid losing sight of it, since downward visibility is poor in the Me 262.

29. The use of the element of three as the basic formation was dictated by still another consideration; as a result of the great speeds reached by the aircraft at low level and also because of its relative short endurance, assembly after take-off was more difficult to effect than with ordinary fighter aircraft. Hence it was necessary that each element should take off simultaneously, and German airfield runways were just wide enough to permit the take-off of three Me 262s side by side. In this way a scramble take-off of 24 aircraft could be completed in five minutes, after the pilots were in their seats.

30. In attacking bombers, formations of Staffel size, about nine aircraft flying in three elements of three were used. On the approach flight the formation was made up of one element leading and the other two on the flanks slightly higher and farther back. The interval between aircraft in each element was about 100 metres in climbing and 150 metres in level flight. The interval between elements was about 300 metres. If the formation was made up of more than one Staffel (9 aircraft), the other Staffeln flew on both sides to the rear and slightly higher, or were strung out in echelon on one side. Because of the great speed of the Me 262, no top cover was required as a defence

against Allied fighter attacks.

31. In the last few months of the war, Egon procedure was used to lead jet formations to Allied bomber formations. Once the bomber formation was sighted action was initiated to get behind one group to press home an attack from the rear. Getting into position was often difficult because of the great speed and large curving radius of the jet aircraft and decisions had to be made very quickly while the bomber formation was still far away. The great distances involved made it difficult to judge the altitude and course of the bombers at the same time, further complicating the problem.

32. For maximum effect it was considered advisable for one Staffel to attack each bomber group. In the case of a multi-Staffel formation, the Staffeln would separate and attack separate groups. The approach flight was best begun from a distance of 5,000 yards behind the bomber formation with an altitude advantage of about 2,000 yards, but entry into the bomber stream could be accomplished from as little as 2,000 yards behind the bombers.

33. The Me 262s formed into a column of three Ketten and dived to a position about 500 yards below and 1,500 yards behind the bombers to gain speed and then pulled up and flew straight and level for the last 1,000 yards. The purpose of the dive was to increase speed to about 850km/h, necessary on account of the Allied fighter escort, which was almost sure to be in pursuit; for best marksmanship, however, a lower speed would have been desirable. It was considered essential to hold formation and attack the whole width of the bomber group in order to split up the defensive fire of the bombers' guns.

34. Aircraft of J.V.44 used the ordinary Revi sight, but they had painted on its screen special lines so spaced as to frame the wingspan of the B-17 Fortress at 650 yards. At this point the 24 x R4M rocket projectiles under the wings were fired at the bomber chosen as a target. Fire was then opened with the four 3cm MK 108s, aim being at the general shape of the target aircraft; aiming at any particular part of the bomber was not possible because of the great range.

35. In practice it was found difficult to get directly behind the bombers and approach them from dead astern. A slight deviation to either side required a slight lead to be held in firing.

36. The three Ketten in column would attack the bomber group, closing the range to about 150 yards, at which point they began their getaway. Because of the great speed of the Me 262 they did not have to break away behind or inside of the bomber formation

but could pass through or above it, thus avoiding exposing their bellies in curving away to one side. The best getaway route was found to be a flat climb passing as close as possible above the top elements of the bomber formation so as to make it difficult for the bombers' gunners to score hits. Passing under the bombers was regarded as unwise because pieces of debris from damaged bombers may be sucked into the jet units and damage them.

37. After passing through or over the bomber formation, the Me 262s could either break off their attack and fly back to their base or repeat the attack on another formation further ahead. If they decided to depart, a shallow dive enabled them to gain enough speed to outdistance the fastest Allied fighters.

38. If the Me 262s had ammunition left they could pass on to the next bomber group ahead and attack it in a similar manner. But if too much speed had been lost in the first attack, a second was rendered perilous by the presence of the Allied fighter escort, which was usually positioned to dive from above.

39. Reassembly of the Me 262s was not usually effected after attack because the formations were too widely dispersed and fuel too low. Elements of various sizes returned home alone, depending on their speed to escape from Allied fighters.

40. Head-on attacks occurred in a few cases by accident, and it was found that the closing speed of the jet aircraft and the bombers was too great to permit of accurate sighting and firing, and there was no possibility of observing hits.

41. German pilots are of the opinion that the Me 262 would have been an effective weapon against U.S.A.A.F. daylight raids over Germany if mass employment had been possible. But numerical inferiority, fuel shortage, and lack of good pilots prevented adequate combat testing of the potentialities of the Me 262.

## USE OF THE ME 262 TO COMBAT ALLIED FIGHTERS AND FIGHTER-BOMBERS

42. The use of the Me 262 as an attack fighter against Allied bombers was dictated by the impossibility of using other German fighters for this purpose and by the necessity of doing something to stop or hinder the Allied raids, but German pilots regard the ideal role of the Me 262 to be that of a pure fighter, finding and destroying Allied fighters and fighter-bombers. They are sure that the employment of a few hundred jet aircraft against the Allied fighter escort would have forced the Allied Air Forces to use jets themselves or drastically to curtail their operations over

Germany in daylight.

43. The two principal advantages of the Me 262 as a fighter were its speed and climbing ability; it was admittedly inferior to Allied piston engined fighters in turning and close manoeuvring. These two paramount qualities of speed and climb could always be used, it is stated, to gain the two basic advantages which decide aerial combat, surprise and superior altitude. Operating at normal altitudes for fighter combat a formation of Me 262s could, upon sighting Allied fighters, accept or refuse combat as the German formation leader chose. He could climb to gain altitude and at the same time overhaul any Allied formation. When attacked from above, Allied fighters showed excellent discipline and turned into the attacking jets, but some always straggled and were shot down, and the Me 262s were usually able to pull up and repeat the attack.

44. Some Me 262s were lost when they attempted to 'dog fight' with Allied fighters, especially with P-51 Mustangs. In such cases the German pilots made the mistake of losing speed to gain manoeuvrability, and the P-51s proved still more manoeuvrable. If the Allied fighters were circling defensively, it was considered practical to dive and fire while going through a one-third or half turn with them and then to climb away. Longer turning engagements always put the Me 262 at a disadvantage.

45. When Me 262s themselves attacked from above at a range too close to permit turning into the attacking Allied fighters, the German formation had only to go into a shallow dive, put some distance between themselves and the Allied formation and then turn around and engage them. If the attack was from level rear instead of from a higher altitude, the Me 262s could easily climb away.

46. In engaging Allied fighter-bombers flying at altitudes of 15,000 feet and lower, Me 262 formations enjoyed even greater advantages than against ordinary Allied fighters. The speed advantage of the Me 262 over ordinary aircraft is most marked at low levels, and in addition the fighter-bombers were slowed down by armour and bombs. The speed of the German formation enabled it to fly low so as to sight Allied fighter-bombers silhouetted against higher clouds, and then to climb and attack from beneath, a tactic not feasible for conventional fighters.

47. Engagements with Allied fighters were undertaken by Me 262 formations only on rare occasions, when combat with bomber formations was not possible, but German unit leaders regarded the correct function of the Me 262 to be attacking the Allied fighter

escort with a view to leaving Allied bombers an easy prey for ordinary German units. But Me 262 units were only ready for combat when fuel was so short that all German fighters were ordered by the High Command to concentrate on bombers.

## USE OF THE ME 262 AS A SHALLOW DIVE-BOMBER AND GROUND STRAFING AIRCRAFT

48. One of the Me 262 pilots interrogated, Major BRÜCKER, had considerable experience as a shallow dive-bomber and ground-attack pilot. In April 1945 he was delegated by the Inspectorate of the G.A.F. Ground Attack Arm (General der Schlachtflieger) to test the potentialities of the Me 262 as a ground-attack aircraft. He was attached to K.G.51 and flew a number of missions in the closing weeks of the war.

49. The Me 262 carried a bomb load of one 500kg or two 250kg, and bombing results were as accurate as those obtained with the Fw 190. The high speed of the aircraft made it possible for it to function at low altitudes despite prevalent Allied air superiority.

50. When first operational, however, Me 262s of K.G.51 were forbidden to fly lower than 13,000 feet, to avoid their falling into enemy hands.

51. A disadvantage of the Me 262 was that the high speed made almost impossible the seeking out of very small targets like artillery positions or field headquarters.

52. Shallow dive-bombing was best performed by formations of four aircraft abreast at about 15,000 feet or lower with about 100 yards lateral interval. Targets were approached until they disappeared from sight under the right or left jet unit, and then the dive was begun. The dive was done at an angle of about 30°, using the ordinary Reflex sight for aiming. A speed of 850 to 900km/h was attained and further acceleration was prevented by pulling up the nose of the aircraft and reducing the speed of the jet units to about 6,000rpm. Bombs were released at an altitude of about 3,000 to 3,500 feet.

53. P/W [prisoner of war] noted that in all types of dive-bombing with the Me 262, it is essential to empty the rear fuel tank before pulling out of the dive, or the aircraft will be tail heavy, nose up abruptly, and the wings may break off. Several aircraft and pilots were lost in this manner in combat.

54. Several ground strafing missions against Allied troops advancing across Central Germany had been flown by one of the present P/W, who had destroyed several trucks; he does not, however, consider the Me 262 suited for this function. The MK 108 had so low a muzzle velocity that the attack had to take place at an altitude of 400 metres or less for accuracy. The total of 360 rounds of ammunition was too small for the amount of target area which could be covered by the fast Me 262. There was not enough armour to protect the pilot from A.A. fire.

## AIR-TO-AIR BOMBING WITH THE ME 262

55. Beginning in December 1944 experiments were carried on at Rechlin with the object of developing a practical air-to-air bombing technique using the Me 262. Operations were in charge of Major STAMP, now a P/W. In March 1945 the experiments were terminated because of the transfer of personnel concerned. No conclusive results had been obtained, but P/W is convinced that the methods evolved would have been successful in combat.

## BOMBS TESTED

56. Many different types of bombs were dropped over the Muritz See to establish the radius of blast, dispersal during fall, and the functioning of fuses. Little was known of the effects of blast and the velocity of bomb splinters at high altitudes, and no satisfactory experimental data was collected. Bombs tested included:

   (a) Container AB 500 filled with 370kg of Triolin.
   (b) SC 250, SC 500, SD 250 and SD 500.
   (c) AB 500 filled with 25 x SD 15 (SD 15 is 150mm gun ammunition fitted with vanes and Fuse 41).
   (d) AB 500 filled with 84 x SD 3.
   (e) AB 250 filled with SD 2.
   (f) SB 1.8 incendiary bomb filled with explosive.
   (g) AB 500 filled with 4,000 incendiary pellets (Brandtaschen) and enough explosive to throw the pellets with high enough velocity to penetrate the skin of a bomber.

57. Although experiments were inconclusive, it was decided, if the procedure was ever to be used operationally, to use the container AB 500 filled with Triolin (a).

## FUSES

58. It was finally decided to use a time delay fuse set at two seconds. The time fuse 89B with 0.6 seconds and a 3 to 10 second range was found to be the best, but other fuses experimented with included:

(a) Barometric fuse (Baro 1). This fuse was fitted with a static tube which was interfered with by the air flow around the carrying aircraft, and the idea was discarded.

(b) Acoustic fuse (Ameise). This fuse was never perfected because its too great sensitivity made it subject to damage during transport.

(c) Electric remote control fuse (Pollux). This fuse operated within the frequency range of the FuGe 16. Detonation was produced by reception of two tones on a carrier wave. Production difficulties made this device impractical.

## BOMB SIGHT

59. In the first experiments an ordinary Revi sight was used, but Dr. Kortum of Zeiss, Jena, developed in January 1945 a new sight called the Gegner Pfeil Visier (Enemy Arrow Sight GPV 1) for use with the Me 262 in air-to-air bombing; only about twenty models were produced. Values for the relative speeds of the Me 262 and the bomber formation, the relative altitude from which the bombs were to be dropped, and the necessary ballistic figures for the type of bomb being used were adjusted in the sight before start. The angle of the dive was supposed to be 20° from horizontal, but to allow last minute corrections an adjustable lever was on the left hand side of the cockpit. It was merely necessary to move the lever until its long axis was parallel to the horizontal plane in which the bomber formation was flying. The pilot sighted through a reflex sight which framed the wing tips of a B-17 Flying Fortress at 600 yards, the range at which the bombs were to be released.

## TACTICS

60. To carry out such an air-to-air bombing attack as that described above, a formation of four Me 262s was to be used. They would fly echeloned back to the right or left with 30 yards between aircraft. The bomber formation was to be approached from the front about 3,000 feet higher to avoid contact with the Allied fighter escort.

61. On the nose of each Me 262 was painted a coloured stripe slanting downward toward the front at an angle of 16° below the horizontal. When the attacking jet aircraft were at the proper distance from the bomber formation to begin their dive, the bomber formation could be lined up along the stripe. The extra 4° (20° dive – 16° stripe = 4°) was actually compensated

for by the time it took to go into the dive. The dive would begin at a distance of about 3,000 yards. Speed of the bomber formation would be set at about 350km/h and the speed of the Me 262s at about 750km/h to 800km/h. Bombs would be released with two seconds delay fuse when the bombers were 600 metres away. The Me 262s would then break away by climbing over the bomber formation and would head for home.

62. Other experienced German fighter pilots acquainted with the features of this air-to-air bombing technique regard it as highly impractical, pointing out that the Me 262 takes too long to climb to the necessary altitude with a bomb load and once at the altitude, the bomb load reduces speed so much that it could be overhauled by Allied fighters.

63. P/W believes that no Japanese agency was informed of the features of this air-to-air bombing procedure.

## FIGHTER PILOT TRAINING FOR THE ME 262

64. In November 1944, a training programme for Me 262 pilots was begun. About 50 pilots were collected from fighter and bomber units and fighter school staffs and a selection was made of promising new pilots who were about half way through their Fighter Operational Training Pool syllabus. The new pilots in the Training Pools were given a pre-jet flying course which consisted of finishing their regular 20 hours' flying time in ordinary fighter aircraft with the throttles fixed in one position, to reproduce the technical problem found in flying the Me 262, the throttles of which should not be adjusted in flight at high altitudes.

65. The training unit for actual jet training was III./Ergänzungs-Jagdgeschwader 2 [III./E.J.G.2], formed at Lechfeld from the staff of the experimental unit which had been testing the aircraft for some time.

66. Upon their arrival at Lechfeld, all pilots, both experienced and inexperienced, were given three days' theoretical instruction in the operation and functioning of jet engines, the features and flying qualities of the Me 262, as well as some practice in operating the controls in a wingless training model.

67. This introduction was followed by a course at Landsberg in the operation of conventional twin-engined a/c; pupils were given five hours' flying time in the Me 110 and Siebel 204, practising starts, landings, flights with the radio course indicator (Zielvorsatzgerät 16), instrument flying and flying on one engine. Pilots already experienced in flying twin-engined a/c did not take part in the elementary parts

of this instruction.

68. Upon the completion of the course the pilots returned to III./E.J.G.2 at Lechfeld, where they were given one more day of theoretical instruction and then began the actual experience with the Me 262. Practical instruction began with a half day's exercise in starting and stopping the jet motors and taxiing.

69. Flying instruction consisted of a total of nine take-offs as follows:

1. Half an hour of circuits with only two main fuel tanks full.

2. Same.

3. One hour aerobatics and aerial manoeuvring.

4. Same.

5. One hour high altitude flight, to 30,000 feet with full fuel tanks.

6. One hour cross-country flight at 12,000 to 15,000 feet.

7. One hour flying in element of two (Rotte), first with an instruction and then with another student.

8. Same.

9. Gunnery practice, shooting with all four MK 108 at ground targets. First approach without firing and four other approaches firing.

70. If a two-seater Me 262 was available students had the opportunity of practicing stalls with an instruction, as well as landings on only one jet and operating the landing gear with compressed air. Instrument flying in the Siebel 204 was also interspersed with the jet training.

71. Pilots who finished their course of training and were sent to J.V.44 were given further training in large formation flying, starting three abreast on a runway, scramble starts, and practice attacks on fighters and bombers, with German aircraft representing the targets. This additional training had to be encompassed in three or four starts, because of the fuel shortage.

72. The training programme outlined above was an absolute minimum one, barely adequate in enabling the pilots to fly the Me 262 without accidents and serious damage to the aircraft because of faulty operation. Oberstleutnant BÄR, who commanded III./E.J.G.2 from January to March 1945, felt that 20 starts in the training programme would have been adequate to train good pilots.

73. No great problems were experienced in the training programme. Starting and landing the Me 262 was very easy from the point of view of flying qualities but technically the aircraft was complicated and plenty of theoretical instruction and lengthy practice in starting and stopping the jet units was essential. The speed of the aircraft at low altitudes made it inadvisable to continue training when visibility at low level was bad, because pilots easily got lost on their first flights. Experienced pilots advised that new pilots afraid to land on only one jet should make a belly landing instead of attempting to come in wheels down.

APPENDIX III

# Postwar Notes on Me 262 Development

*British and American technical specialists drawn from a wide range of companies and institutions quizzing their German counterparts on their wartime work throughout the remainder of 1945. Among those subjected to in-depth questioning were the head of Messerschmitt's Project Office, Woldemar Voigt, his subordinate Rudolf Seitz and construction department manager Joseph Helmschrott.*

*One of the many fruits of this process was ADI(K) Report No. 1/1946—The Messerschmitt Organisation and Its Work During the War, a compilation of details concerning the company's technical progress, the lines of development it had been pursuing and the practical processes it used in constructing aircraft.[1] This was set out in a bullet point format with bullets grouped into loose categories. And while much of what was said concerned types other than the Me 262 or consisted of general points about Messerschmitt and its work, a number of interesting remarks were made about the twin-jet fighter.*

*What follows is a set of extracts from this report, with unrelated and irrelevant material omitted, commencing with point 105 under the heading 'fuselages'.*

## FUSELAGES

105. Wind tunnel work assessed the forces set up by suction and pressure on the fuselage, but the wind tunnel was not used to design any part of the fuselage of the Me 262 as far as normal loads on the skin were concerned. Both Seitz and Helmschrott were of the opinion that there was sufficient inherent strength in such structures to render calculations unnecessary. The frames of the rear fuselage, having fairly long flat sides, were not stressed to carry bending loads due to suction; the depth of the frames was 40mm (1.6 inches) and the depth of stringers 20mm (0.8 inches).

106. The primary reason for the triangular shape of the Me 262 fuselage was to accommodate the wheels in the retracted position. The wing-body arrangement was later found to have some merit in low interference drag between the top surface of the wing and the body.

107. The fuselage of the Me 262 is constructed in two parts and joined in the vertical longitudinal plane. One half consists of a series of segments with frames formed out of the same material as the skin at each end of the segment. These segments are joined by strips of plain skin, and so the whole series of segments is joined to make up the length of the fuselage. Holes are punched through the frames to take hat-section stringers.

109. In connection with the testing of large specimens of fuselages, informants stated that it was normally necessary to use only one specimen. This would be loaded until the deflection failed to satisfy Hooke's Law, and successive modification would be made until requirements were satisfied. The specimen

would then be loaded until it broke. Although repeated loading tests were carried out with the Me 262, this was not usually done.

## PRESSURE CABINS

110. A certain amount of work had been done in connection with pressure cabins, but they did not appear to be as far advanced as British and American manufacturers in this respect. The method of sealing around the head was to use a rubber tube constrained in place by a steel hat section running all round the joint faces of the hood. This tube was inflated by the pilot using a hand pump. Leaks in the structure of the cabin were stopped by filling them with a kind of elastic putty made by Romm and Haas of Darmstadt. Doors and other movable devices were sealed by synthetic rubber sections similar to those used in Allied aircraft.

## ENGINE NACELLES

112. In the case of the Me 262 no attempt was made to increase the torsional stiffness of the wing by using the engine nacelle, the engine was underslung and the bottom section of the wing was continuous. A steel-asbestos sheet shielded the wing structure from the engine, and a stream of cooling air between the engine and nacelle skin was employed to keep the wing cool.

113. Engines and nacelles were attached to the wing by horizontal bolts, one aft and two forward. One bolt was set at right angles to the other two, and sufficient clearance was left in the lugs to give freedom for engine expansion and flexing of the wing.

114. Hemispherical wire guards designed to protect ground personnel were usually placed over the intake ducts and removed just prior to take-off. The aircraft had occasionally been left with these guards in position without any detrimental effects to icing or any other cause.

## WINGS

115. The wings were assembled from very accurately made ribs in vertical jigs, somewhat similar in construction to those in general use in this country, each rib position being positively located in the jig. One skin was attached in the vertical jig, the other being secured subsequently in a horizontal jig. Both skins were attached by hollow rivets. It was stated that the design limits of the accuracy of the aerofoil sections was 2½mm whereas all components were actually constructed to an accuracy of less than ½mm. This high degree of accuracy was apparently obtained by special attention to detail manufacture, particularly ribs which were produced from metal dies. Compressed wood dies were used in some instances on thin material but rubber presses were not used.

116. During the initial stages of construction inspection checks were made very frequently to assure accuracy of components but as tooling progressed they became less frequent, full reliance being placed upon the jigs. Similarly, particular attention was paid to the flatness of sheets during early stages of production but as the material position became more difficult, less attention was given to defective sheets. No means of tensioning by stretching prior to riveting during the attachment to the framework was employed. Details were manufactured in the factories where components were assembled, with tools supplied from [local?] sources, and no transference of tools was permitted between assembling factories, thus avoiding damage in transit.

117. Physical interchangeability of components was made possible by referencing the construction jigs to a reference standard similar to those in this country. Accuracy of aerofoil surfaces of completed components, especially ailerons and elevators was checked in an "envelope" acceptance gauge, which provided accurate measurement at rib stations.

118. To obtain smooth surface finish normal countersunk rivets of both solid and hollow types were employed, but no undue attention was paid to special types of rivets as production was considered more important. With the Me 262 the wing skin was purposely made rather thick to ensure smoothness over and above strength requirements; it varied from .06 inches to .08 inches Dural.

119. Spanwise stiffeners (hat section) were used on top skins only, no stringers being used on bottom skins. Ribs were about 10 inches pitch. Slot skins were made up in .8mm steel outer skin with a .6mm inner skin. Slot outer skins which stretched up to 24% of wing chord were pressed up out of one sheet with no joint at the leading edge. The whole assembly was electrically spot welded.

120. On the Me 262 it was expected that the wing skin would remain smooth up to about 3.5g. When this figure was questioned, informant stated that it had been obtained with the thickness of skin and stringer arrangements quoted above.

121. Owing to the lack of Dural, steel booms were used on the Me 262 and it was found that these gave a lighter spar with the same degree of stiffness. The stress worked to in the steel was between 70 and 80

tons per square inch. Dural webs were used, as the thinness of a steel web would cause early wrinkling and the Dural could be made thick enough to be shear resistant (.064 inch+). Attempts were made to spot weld the webs to the dural angles attaching the webs to the boom, but this was later abandoned and normal riveting procedure adopted.

123. Professor Voigt was of the opinion that satisfactory jet entries could be incorporated in wing design without producing early shock-stalling, and pointed out that the internal flow would give a relaxation of conditions at low speeds. He stated that wind tunnel tests had confirmed that the flow over the wing should be satisfactory, but it was not yet certain that the flow through the entries would be sufficient.

124. He also considered that if the fairing was properly designed, the flow over the root should be no more sensitive than elsewhere along the span because of the three-dimensional flow. He did not, however, consider that Göthert's theoretical method of obtaining the fairings was correct, since it assumed an infinite body. He suggested that a practical method would be to use the water tank. The cavitation method had been used to improve the flow over the nacelles of the Me 262.

132. A set of swept-back wings was made for the Me 262, and it was found that where the sweep at 25% cord was 35° the increase in weight was about 25% (900kg as compared with 700kg), the skin thickness had to be increased due to higher torsional loads and root B.M. was higher. The large fore and aft components at the fuselage line where the spar changed direction were difficult to deal with, and the fuselage frames in the neighbourhood of the wing pick-ups had to be strengthened. Although sweep-back was convenient for cg. adjustment and aerodynamic characteristics were improved, it was felt that the large sweep-back barely justified the complexity and weight increase.

133. With the Me 262 the main spar was "floating" through the fuselage, and attachment of wing to body was by two bolts loaded at normal front and rear positions. These two fasteners dealt with vertical shears, torsion and drag loads, the spar took bending and the skin attachment angles were mainly fairing pieces, but were assumed to take about 15% of drag.

## AILERONS AND ELEVATORS

135. In the Me 262 the trailing edges of elevators and ailerons were not fitted with the usual extruded or hollow section, but were formed by riveting the ends of the two skin surfaces between flat strips, the thickness of the resulting trailing edge being 4mm. All control surface hinges were assembled after removing all components from the construction jig, but when fully tooled up, it was intended to assemble these in the jig. Pending complete tooling, hinges were fitted in an assembly jig. The design also allowed for adjustable hinges, to permit correction of flight faults arising from slight inaccuracies of manufacture. During the early stages of construction no particular attention was paid to the accuracy of shrouds to ailerons and elevators, but following trouble on flight tests, when shrouds had to be "dressed" in position, these were very closely controlled in later construction. Cord fixed to trailing edges of rudders was the only form of correction permitted. None was allowed on ailerons or elevators, flight corrections being made by adjustments to hinges and shrouds.

136. Flutter trouble was not experienced with the Me 262 controls, although servo flaps were mass-balanced. Spring tabs were not popular with the average pilot, who objected to the installation of "second pilot". Before acceptance by the Luftwaffe, aircraft were required to possess positive stability about all threes axes. The first stability tests were carried out "stick free". Pilots were said to welcome moderate tail buffeting as affording an early indication of the stall.

137. An interesting experiment was made with the Me 109 to which a "Vee" tail was fitted. The arrangement proved satisfactory but as compared with the usual horizontal and vertical surfaces, no saving in total surface was effected. With the Vee tail the elevator control was heavy, especially when used differentially. Electro-hydraulic power operation was used for the ailerons of the Me 323.

## STABILISING FINS

138. The stabilising fin of the Me 262 was made in two halves and joined in the vertical plane by means of horizontal bolts. Holes were made in the outer skin to give access to the bolts. These holes were about 1½ inches in diameter, and were covered with fabric. Trouble had been experienced through the fabric patches stripping off, and no remedy had been found for this.

139. A new type of aerial, with which satisfactory results had been obtained, had been developed and was concealed within the wooden nose fairing at the leading edge of the fin. The aerial consisted of a

small diameter rod and the maximum distance from any other metal was quoted as being 35mm.

## UNDERCARRIAGES – TRICYCLE TYPES

150. Two types of tricycle undercarriage were designed for the Me 262, one for landings with nose wheel first, and the other for landings with main wheels first and with the rear fuselage just clear of the ground (13° wing incidence).

151. The former type had been found not to be critical, as pilots always landed on the main wheels and gradually brought the nose wheel down. The aircraft was assumed to be landing with a vertical velocity of 4.2 metres/sec. and calculations were made—allowing for the spinning up of the wheels—which gave wheel loads in a direction varying from 0° to 30°.

152. The angular acceleration at the nose wheel was estimated from the moment of the main undercarriage reactions about the centre of gravity.

153. The tyre plus oleo characteristics of the whole landing gear had to be assumed. For the Me 262, at the weight of about 11,200 lbs, the maximum vertical unfactored nose-wheel load was estimated to be 11,200 lbs, and on this load factors of 1.5 and 1.8 were applied to get the ultimate design loads for the nose wheel unit and its support structure respectively. These factors were also applied to the main undercarriage and support structure.

154. On the Me 262 a failure had occurred in the main undercarriage support structure during landing, as a result of which the firm increased the 30° drag inclination during spinning up to 40° and strengthened the structure accordingly. No corresponding increase of angle was assumed for the nose wheel unit.

155. On the latter, the maximum vertical load for the second type of undercarriage was also applied at 30° backwards, together with a side load equal to 0.2 of the vertical load. Failures had occurred in the aircraft attachment points at the upper end of the nose wheel radius rod due to tension in this rod, indicating large vertical wheel loads probably combined with anti-drag loads.

157. To overcome shimmy which had occurred on snow, dampers of the friction type had been fitted. No shimmy was experienced on concrete or grass surfaces.

## RETRACTION PROBLEMS

158. Helmschrott stated that the time taken to retract the undercarriage of the Me 262 was approximately 22 sec. and a little less to lower it. In the case of the Me 410 too, the times were roughly the same. These times could have been improved by increasing the diameters of the pipe lines in the hydraulic system but they were reluctant to do this for fear of interfering with production. Even when two pumps were employed, the pipe diameters were not increased, but this was regarded as an emergency measure and they were hoping to cut down the time in due course. For emergency lowering of the undercarriage a hand pump and/or compressed air bottle were used. RLM insisted on duplicate pipes for all emergency operations.

## TYRES

166. All tyres used on Messerschmitt aircraft were supplied by Continental, of Hannover. They were made from synthetic rubber with rayon cores, the more recent having a tread design.

167. Trouble had been experienced due to cuts and bead failures caused by excessive shock absorber friction, particularly on the Me 262. This had been overcome by reducing the shock absorber pressure.

168. A tyre pressure of 4.8 atmospheres was the maximum used, but 4.0 atmospheres was more general as this gave better shock absorption. The 4.8 atmospheres limit was fixed by operation from grass surfaces. At high pressures more tyre concussion failures due to rolling over obstacles such as stones had been experienced. All tyres were made to fit a standard range of wheel sizes.

169. A certain amount of tyre trouble had been experienced due to the overheating of brakes, as a result of which disc type brakes were being developed.

## WHEELS

170. Elma of Stuttgart supplied most of the wheels used on Messerschmitt aircraft, but some of the larger wheels were supplied by VDM and by Elektron of Cannstadt.

172. The German Air Ministry required that aircraft brakes should be foot operated, and so far the two-shoe self-energising brake had been used on all German aircraft, although Messerschmitt had developed and "Elma" had manufactured a disc brake, consisting of 8 or 10 discs, the mating materials being steel on hardened steel. Very satisfactory results had been obtained, but it was generally recognised that the British and Americans were more advanced in brake design.

173. Brake operation was invariably hydraulic and only the force exerted by the pilot through the foot

pedals was employed as a rule. The Me 262 (All Up Weight 6-7 tons) was the largest size of aircraft suited to direct operation of the brakes through valves controlled by the foot pedals. These valves were in effect hydraulic variable reducing valves and were manufactured by Elma.

174. Automatic brake operation had not been tried as it was felt that any possible advantages were outweighed by the bad psychological effect on the pilot in taking away his sense of control. A hand operated emergency brake was fitted to the nose wheel of the Me 262, but braking of the nose wheel was generally considered bad practice, since it upset directional stability during landing with drift.

175. The brakes of the Me 262 were designed to withstand five consecutive landings with the shortest possible time interval with the brakes full on and the engines still producing an appreciable amount of thrust. The amount of thrust to be absorbed was not stated, but the reason appeared to be the practice of landing with the engines on. On test, the shortest landing run was about 600 metres with landing speed of about 220kph; after five consecutive landings with hard braking at short intervals the brakes were almost worn out, the greater part of the lining having been reduced to dust.

176. The first five Me 262s had tail wheels on which the brakes were assumed to have to absorb 50% of the aircraft's kinetic energy on landing. When the subsequent Me 262s had tricycle undercarriages

the corresponding figure was taken at 60%-70%.

## GUN MOUNTINGS

179. The 30mm cannon of the Me 262 were mounted on a wooden bulkhead which had very good damping properties. The wood was about 40mm (1.6 inches) thick. Recoil forces were taken into account, but it was claimed that there were no run out forces.

180. The recoil force per gun was 2,000kg. (4,400 lbs.). Loads on the gun mounting were claimed to be due to gas damping. The dissipation of this force into the fuselage was a complicated matter depending on the distribution of mass in the neighbourhood of the applied load. Messerschmitt had not gone deeply into this question, having simply accepted a design which had been tried and found workable.

181. When questioned as to the effect of more than one gun firing at one time, informants were rather uncertain as to what forces should be assumed, but suggested 4,000kg. (8,800 lbs.) at the wooden bulkhead. They were also uncertain about the dissipation of this load and suggested that a total force of 3,000kg might be considered at the bulkhead.

182. Gravity and firing loads were considered together, and informants thought that the effect of firing the guns was negligible. Partly to overcome the effects of gun blast and also to economise in Dural, most of the outside skin near the fuselage nose was made of steel.

# Cavitation research

*One of the more innovative wartime aerodynamic experiments conducted in connection with the Me 262 programme involved placing models of engine intakes and wings into the water equivalent of a wind tunnel—a channel designed for observing compressibility flow. The following is an extract from the interrogation of Woldemar Voigt.[2]*

A sharp edged ring is placed in the water stream and throws off a sharply defined compressibility bubble:-

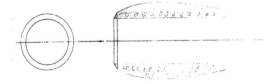

The water in the bubble, apart from being turbulent is stationary, i.e., it is not flowing with the main stream and there is no definite flow from any one part of the bubble to another; the pressures within it are therefore constant at all points; hence the pressure at all points on its outer boundary is the same. The outer boundary of the bubble therefore represents the correct shape for a constant pressure nacelle fairing. If now a wing section model is brought near to the top surface of the bubble:

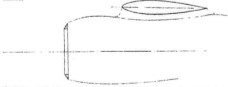

the latter will take on a new shape which will indicate the correct fairing to be used for an underslung nacelle in the presence of a wing.

A water tank test on a Me.282 revealed a bubble which could have provided additional fuel stowage space with an increase in speed

*The illustrations which accompanied the report of Voigt's interrogation concerning the use of a water channel for observing compressibility flow.*

Water channel for observing compressibility flow. This is considered to be a very useful piece of equipment, about 3.3ft x 3.3ft to take 8in to 12in models was used. Shock stalled regions can be quickly observed and modified. It can also be used as follows to find the correct shape for a nacelle in the presence of a wing at high Mach. A sharp-edged ring is placed in the water stream and throws off a sharply defined compressibility bubble.

The water in the bubble, apart from being turbulent is stationary, i.e., it is not flowing with the main stream and there is no definite flow from any one part of the bubble to another; the pressures within it are therefore constant at all points; hence the pressure at all points on its outer boundary is the same. The outer boundary of the bubble therefore represents the correct shape for a constant pressure nacelle fairing. If now a wing section model is brought near to the top surface of the bubble, the latter will take on a new shape which will indicate a bubble which could have provided additional fuel stowage space with an increase in speed.

# Me 262 Production

*Production specialist Otto Lange, an employee of Speer's armaments ministry who would also become a key figure within first the Jägerstab and later the Rüstungsstab, was asked to give an account of Me 262 production shortly after the end of the war. The result was a typed manuscript produced at Oberammergau on June 8, 1945.1 Lange identifies difficulties with jig construction and alteration as the primary reason for delays in the mass production of the aircraft, but also points to a host of other contributing factors. While his background and experience tend to lend him some credibility in this area, his views on specific technologies, such as J2 fuel and instability at high speed, ought to be treated with caution.*

If one considers that the Me 262 is a new type of jet aircraft with speeds never before mastered in technology and is also equipped with a new type of turbine engine, the output must be described as an extraordinary technical production achievement in view of the strong increase required by the programme, especially since the inhibiting influence of bombings, changes resulting from development, testing and deployment reasons cannot be neglected under any circumstances. Despite these worrying factors, the aircraft was forced into series production due to the military situation before it was ready for series production. The resulting difficulties overburdened the jig construction to such an extent that the skills of the existing specialists, especially managerial staff, were exceeded.

The capacity available in Germany in the construction of jigs, tools and gauges was extremely overstretched due to the enormous demands of the entire armaments industry. This was further increased by the requirements for aircraft construction from March 1944. The unmet need for skilled workers for this branch of industry in July 1944 was about 20,000, including about 4,000 for Messerschmitt. Despite the priority given to the Me 262, the coverage was unsatisfactory, and it was not allowed to be at the expense of the rest of the aircraft construction, because particular value was placed on the rapid increase in performance of the aircraft types already available to the troops. Nevertheless, the degree of assignment of specialists to Messerschmitt through the measures taken by the Jägerstab was considerable. Reviews of the jig construction at Messerschmitt by experts showed that the jig capacity used inside and outside the company was sufficient to implement the programme to some extent, while limiting it to the essentials and avoiding complicated or faulty designs. The curve representation of the time delay also confirms this.

Unfortunately, it was typical of the working methods at Messerschmitt that the structural side of the jig construction was in disarray and considerable rework was necessary with loss of time. In addition, there were unforeseeable instability phenomena in control of the aircraft at speeds above 800km/h. The causes were not recognised immediately and led to multiple change requirements. The jig construction was also burdened by subsequent strengthening measures required for the landing gear, wings, tail unit, nose, etc. Constant changes to the jigs and in series production were necessary. In other words, the aircraft had to be brought to technical maturity while series production was ongoing.

The bottlenecks alternated in their effect on delivery,

e.g. the output in the first and in the last three months depended on engine delivery. Around August to December 1944, on the other hand, delays arose mainly from the wings or nose units; the tail unit was also a bottleneck for a short time.

Further bottlenecks, not of manufacturing origin, appeared in the winter months from December 1944 to April 1945, which delayed deliveries to the troops. In addition, there were space difficulties due to snow, rain, destruction of the airfields by enemy action and time losses due to air raid alarms. At some airfields there were hardly more than 40 usable flight hours in the vicinity of the production sites during a winter month, and not enough airfields were available. Airfields with associated final assembly sites had to be connected to the rest of the Reich, which in turn resulted in losses of time and material due to the problems with rail transport, training of new personnel, lack of ground equipment and flight personnel, etc.

The increasing unreliability of the rail transport as a result of the bombing, which increased noticeably from month to month from December 1944, made it almost impossible, despite the preferred urgency for the handling of the transport, to still ensure the interaction of all factors necessary for on-time delivery. Loss of territory increased the difficulties, because the scheduled delivery of important individual parts from outside became disordered, although considered in themselves, impressive feats were accomplished by the companies despite the unexpected sudden forced relocation of entire factories with their skilled workers, or the involvement of other substitute factories when had to quickly start up a new production.

From January 1945, another very serious factor was added to the existing flight difficulties. The J2 fuel used

failed at low temperatures with paraffin in the fuel lines and tanks during the approach. These clogs brought about engine failure with inevitable crashes, including personnel and aircraft losses. All of these loss figures are not included in these output values shown. If this hadn't happened, I think the programme could have been fully adhered to or even exceeded.

As deliveries to the troops increased, the initial disagreements about the value of the aircraft dissipated. Only now was the special value recognised. The originally hesitant training of pilots resulted in a shortage of trained personnel. The troops therefore trained for a very long time and during this time had many aircraft losses due to take-off and landing failures.

Me 262 was developed and built as a pure fighter aircraft. After the Führer's order, it had to be converted into a bomber and delivered to the troops. The order was changed shortly thereafter to the effect that one Me 262 could be built as a fighter for every Ar 234 built, plus five trainers, every month.

Reimahg[2] joined the production programme in the third quarter of 1944 with an initially unclear programme requirement. The programme drawn up later had to be revised when Reimahg failed to keep its original promise to deliver the first 300 aircraft in December 1944 and later in January 1945. But even this greatly reduced programme was not upheld. By March 1945, Reimahg had only delivered around 15 aircraft, which were put together there from large assemblies and flown in. Messerschmitt had supplied sufficient assemblies for around 40 aircraft. This first Reimahg delivery could only be used for training purposes.

*O Lange*
*Oberammergau, June 8, 1945*

# Handling the Me 262

*Squadron Leader H. G. Morison of A.I.2.(g) produced a report on May 25, 1945, entitled Handling the Me 262 which was a set of practical pilot notes produced by Messerschmitt factory pilot Fritz Wendel.[1] Other sets of such notes exist but Wendel's are unique for the way in which he describes handling the aircraft with the delicate touch of a master.*

Several Me 262 aircraft have been captured intact and will be flown by Allied test pilots. In view of this some notes have been obtained from the offices of Messerschmitt at Augsburg, have been translated by this section and are reproduced below:

## PILOTS NOTES ON ME 262 BY FLUG KAPITÄN WENDEL

In addition to studying the condensed instruction for airframe and engines, a thorough knowledge of these notes, preferably before the first flight in a Me 262, is essential to the pilot.

### I. TAXYING

Always accelerate the engines slowly. The gas temperature must never rise above the permitted value and the engine must not "roar" (bullern). In view of this, only take corners by using the brakes, never by using the engines. Always taxi gently and never make sharp turns, otherwise control of the aircraft will be lost.

### 2. TAKE-OFF

Switch on the fuel pumps in the main tanks. Hold the aircraft stationary by applying the brakes and then slowly run up the engines, especially slowly up to 7,500rpm. The brakes must be so adjusted that they will hold the aircraft stationary up to 8,500rpm.

After releasing the brakes, push the throttle lever right forward and then check over the engines. The aircraft makes so little demand upon the pilot at the commencement of the take-off run that he is easily able to carry out this check. The check is done by eye and ear, the engines must not "roar" and the instruments must show the same values as they did during the running up or during previous take-offs. The gas pressure must be especially watched, and if it is more than 5 per cent lower than previously, do not take-off.

In such a case, it is most likely that cavitation has taken place in one of the compressor stages, that is, by running up too quickly, the compressor has been overloaded and the smooth flow breaks up, exactly as it does when a wing stalls. Cavitation takes place so easily in many compressors as a result of small constructional faults or as a result of foreign bodies that they become entirely unserviceable. If the take-off is continued when cavitation has occurred in the compressor, then the quality of air flowing through is too small, the quantity of fuel injected however is the same or sometimes even larger, as a result of which, the engine is overheated.

The directional corrections during take-off should only be made with the brakes.

The control column should remain in the neutral position.

The angle of attack of the wing, when running

on all three wheels, is smaller than the angle of attack when flying at the lowest possible speed (after becoming airborne). As a result of this, when the aircraft has reached the lowest permissible flying speed, the angle of attack must be increased, in other words the aircraft must be pulled away from the ground. If the stick is pulled back too soon, or if, at the right speed, it is pulled back too far, then there is only a rise in resistance, but no increase in lift, in fact, there may be a lessening of lift. The aircraft cannot then climb. In this case immediately reduce the angle of attack to the "running" angle, in other words, push the stick forward and then start the process again.

When will the aircraft be pulled off the ground? It is best to go by A.S.I. which should read with a fighter, fully laden i.e. 6,700kg, 190-200km/h with a bomber, fully laden i.e. 7,100kg, 200-220km/h. After becoming airborne, immediately push the stick forward slightly as the required elevator angle for pulling off the ground is greater than that for climbing at the slowest speed.

Essential for a perfect take-off is correct setting of the tailplane. The tailplane must always be trimmed nose heavy! The further back the centre of gravity moves, the more nose heavy it must be trimmed. When the 600 litre fuel tank is full, the centre of gravity is at its rearmost position. The tailplane must then be set at $+2°—+3°$ (i.e. 4-6 graduations on the indicator).

### 3. ROCKET TAKE-OFF

In order to shorten the take-off run, the rockets should be ignited 30-40km/h before the optimum take-off speed. If the take-off run need not be shorter, but there are obstacles to be negotiated after becoming airborne, then only ignite the rockets later, possibly even leaving it until the aircraft is airborne. Jettison the take-off rockets at low speeds, otherwise damage may be caused to the fuselage.

### 4. OPERATION OF UNDERCARRIAGE AND LANDING FLAPS

The undercarriage and landing flaps are hydraulically operated. The hydraulic pump has a capacity of 18 litres/min. and is attached to the port engine. Its capacity is rather too low and it is intended to fit an 18 litre per minute pump on the starboard engine. In the present state, therefore, the undercarriage operates very slowly. This is particularly noticeable when lowering. The nose wheel comes down very much later than the main undercarriage; so lower in plenty of time. The high speed of the

aircraft easily tempts one to lower the undercarriage or flaps whilst travelling too fast and this leads to damage. The permissible operating speed must be rigidly adhered to.

### 5. EMERGENCY OPERATION

Compressed air is used for emergency operation of the undercarriage and it lowers the nose wheel and the main undercarriage fairing. The undercarriage itself falls under the influence of gravity. If it does not immediately lock, then assist it by side slipping.

### 6. WARNING

The compressed air is only admitted to the undercarriage or flaps after two full turns of the operating handle have been made. With emergency operation both undercarriage and flaps lower more quickly.

### 7. FLIGHT

Always climb at the optimum climbing speed, never more slowly. The best speeds are given in the table below.

| Altitude | Speed |
|----------|--------|
| 0m | 475km/h |
| 2,000m | 500km/h |
| 4,000m | 525km/h |
| 6,000m | 550km/h |
| 8,000m | 600km/h |
| 10,000m | 650km/h |

NOTE The Me 262 has an altitude compensated A.S.I. and, therefore, the indicated speed is equivalent to the true speed above 400km/h.

The highest permissible rearward point for the centre of gravity is 30 per cent of the mean aerodynamic wing chord. If this position is exceeded, then the aircraft becomes unstable about the lateral axis, that is, it does not remain trimmed, but will automatically stall in a turn. Under normal conditions of fuel storage this position is not exceeded, but it is necessary always to watch most carefully the transfer pumping instructions. Watch particularly that the main tanks do not overflow as the J-2 fuel will run out into the fuselage and got on the wireless equipment which interferes with radio traffic.

When cruising, the tailplane must be between 0 and $+2°$.

### 8. DIRECTIONAL STABILITY

When the centre of gravity is far back and the Flettner rudder trimming tabs are not perfect, especially if the Flettner tabs are a little too thick, then the aircraft sways about the vertical axis. This movement must stop when both legs are pushed hard against the rudder pedals. If this does not stop the movement then the tabs must be altered or the trailing edge of the rudder must be bent slightly outwards. A modification is in course of preparation.

### 9. LANDING

The best approach speed is 230-250km/h. Shortly before reaching the airfield boundary, decrease the glide angle a little and reduce the speed to about 200km/h. Then flatten out and touch down normally as with an aircraft having a tail wheel. Touchdown speed is 175km/h. After touchdown, allow the aircraft to tip forward slowly. Only apply brakes when the nose wheel has touched the ground.

### 10. GOING ROUND AGAIN

It is just as easy to go round again as with other types of aircraft, but it must be remembered that by approaching slowly the engine revolutions are low and just as at take-off, the throttle lever must only be moved forward <u>slowly</u>.

### 11. SINGLE ENGINE FLIGHT

When flying on one engine only, a turning moment is developed about the vertical axis, due to the engine being offset from the longitudinal axis of the aircraft. The amount of this moment is dependent upon the power and the leverage. In this case the leverage remains constant, but the power (i.e. the effect of the running engine) changes. In order that the aircraft may remain on course, this moment must be offset, which is done by applying rudder. The amount of rudder applied must be sufficient to keep the ball of the turn and bank indicator in the centre; note this particularly in turns. Turns can be made either with or against the stationary engine.

During long single-engine flights the force on the rudder pedal may be reduced by adjusting the Flettner trimming tabs.

The turning moment imparted by the specific movement of the rudder is dependent on air-flow pressure. The smaller the pressure, the greater must be the rudder movement. In single-engine flight, with retracted undercarriage, the speed is something over 500km/h at full throttle. In this case only about 1/3 of the possible rudder movement is necessary. At 260km/h however, the full rudder movement is necessary. This low speed, however, can only occur at full throttle if one is climbing at too great an angle or if the undercarriage has been lowered.

### 12. SINGLE ENGINE LANDINGS

From what has previously been said, it will be seen that the following is necessary for a single-engine landing; minimum approach speed 260km/h, so that, if necessary, full throttle may be given. At this speed and with one engine at full throttle, the aircraft loses height with lowered undercarriage, but raised flaps at 1-2m/sec. From this, it will be seen that the undercarriage should only be lowered at such a time that it is possible to reach the airfield with little or no aid from the engine. Approach speed 260km/h. About 500m before reaching the airfield (when too high earlier, when too low later) lower the flaps and complete the landing in a normal manner. Side-slipping is possible. When landing, the Flettner trimming tabs should be set to the normal position. If it is necessary to approach under power, then the necessary force on the rudder must be exerted by the pilot. At full throttle, under all circumstances apply full rudder.

# A Note About the 'New' V-series

Most of the original prototypes—Me 262 V1 to V8—had been destroyed or retired by January 1945. V9 and V10 continued to serve but the remainder of the experimental fleet were simply airframes taken from the series production line and allocated for testing. When test reports were produced, they referred to these aircraft by their full six-digit serial numbers or the last three digits for short. V9 and V10 were still referred to as such.

The aircraft themselves typically had the last three digits of their serial number painted in large characters on the side of their fuselage, usually prefaced by a 'V', e.g. 'V186' was painted on 130186.

However, at some point between November 30, 1944, and January 2, 1945, someone appears to have decided that the new prototypes should be given the old prototype numbers. Werk-Nr. 130015 was to become the second 'V1', the now-damaged 170056 would be 'V2', 170078 was 'V4', 130167 was 'V5', the Heimatschützer I, 130186, was 'V6', 170303 was 'V7', the A-3 prototype 110484 was 'V8', V9 remained V9, V10 would still be V10, the second A-3 prototype, 110555, would become 'V11' and the new Heimatschützer II, 170074, was to be 'V12'.

The 53rd Me 262 test report summary, issued on January 2, 1945,[1] is the only document known to include these attempted redesignations and two photographs taken during this period show that 170056 had 'V2' painted on it. However, the 54th Me 262 test report summary reverts to using the earlier designations—the last three serial number digits—and photos show the prototypes, post January 1945, with those digits painted on them rather than their 'new' V-number.[2] 170056, for example, appears with 'V056' painted on it during 1945, rather than V2.

Presumably it was quickly realised that reallocating old V-numbers was a bad idea—hundreds, perhaps thousands, of reports had accumulated by now which referred to the original prototype series aircraft by their V-number. Giving that same number to an entirely different aircraft was bound to cause tremendous confusion unless every copy of every report previously issued could be amended.

As such, apart from a very brief period, it cannot really be said that there was a 'second Me 262 V1', a 'second Me 262 V2' etc. An attempt was indeed made to assert such redesignations—but it was swiftly withdrawn and the prototypes retained their own unique identities right up to the end of the war.

# Me 262 for Japan

*Japan signed an economic agreement with Germany in January 1943 and a manufacturing rights agreement in March 1944 which would lead to the Japanese acquisition of German raw materials, military equipment, manufactured goods, drawings and technical assistance. These were transferred using blockade runners—both surface vessels and submarines as well as rail communication through Siberia. The Me 262 would be included in this arrangement. The following is a excerpt from a US War Department report on technical aid to Japan which was published on August 31, 1945.*

## THE ME 262:

It was early in 1944 that Japanese representatives in Germany apparently first became aware of German development of the Me 262. While it appears that the Japanese were fully aware of the Me 262, nevertheless, their primary interest initially lay in the Me 163. This may have been a result of the features of the Me 163 which made it an aircraft particularly suitable for use in defence of Japan against air attack. Alternatively, however, it may be that Japan believed that success was imminent with its own development of turbojet units and of aircraft powered by such units.

Documentary evidence indicates that such development had been in progress in the Far East since at least 1941. The Japanese representatives in Germany, however, continued to obtain information about the Me 262, and negotiations for manufacturing rights for the Me 163 were paralleled by similar negotiations in respect to the Me 262 and German turbojet units.

The April 1, 1944, letter from Milch to Göring, referring to Hitler and Göring decisions with regard to German-Japanese collaboration, indicated close Japanese interest in the Me 262 A-1. The letter stated that, in accordance with Hitler's order, descriptions, survey sketches and illustrations of the A-1 sub-type already had been turned over to the Japanese. It is believed that those sketches and descriptive material were successfully transported to Japan, arriving there by the fall of 1944.

Japanese negotiations for manufacturing rights for the Me 262 and its power unit followed a pattern identical with those for the Me 163. In June 44, the aircraft and industrial manufacturing rights were released to Japan, the delivery, however, being subject to special orders from Göring. During that month, Japanese representatives visited Me 262 production centres, where Bringewald—in charge of Me 262 production in Germany—lectured them on the construction and special features of the aircraft. According to Bringewald, the Japanese showed particular interest in the use of wood for certain parts of the Me 262. In mid-July, Messerschmitt was ordered to prepare sets of traceable drawings and blueprints to be handed over to the Japanese for transportation to the Far East; later in the month Göring approved the handing over to Japan of a sample Me 262. In late August, however, Hitler reversed his original decision and refused the release of a sample Me 262 to Japan.

Meantime, preparation and delivery of necessary blueprints and plans proceeded, although delivery to the Japanese continued to be subject to orders from Göring. It was not until October 44 that Hitler released the Me 262. The necessary contract with Messerschmitt for sale to Japan of manufacturing rights finally was signed in December 44.

One of Messerschmitt's principal planning engineers has stated that he and four other Messerschmitt employees were the only ones who knew of a plan to transmit to Japan complete technical and production plans for the Me 262. Plans were delivered, in October 44, to Dr Thun—-head of Messerschmitt's foreign export branch—at Jettingen; a Japanese representative was present on that occasion. According to German Air Ministry records, sample parts and accessories for the Me 262 scheduled for delivery to Japan were still held by Messerschmitt in mid-September 44; their delivery to the Far East, therefore, is very unlikely. This suggests that the only drawings to reach Japan concerning the Me 262 were the preliminary survey sketches and illustrations of the A-1 sub-type which may have arrived in the fall of 1944.

There is evidence that the Japanese Army intended to go into large-scale manufacture of the Me 262. Under terms of the Army's contract with Messerschmitt, the principal work of von Chlingensperg, a Messerschmitt technician detailed for transfer to Japan, was to be that of directing the design of short-range fighters and long-range bombers at Kawasaki; as far as possible, the Army also desired to have him direct the conversion, presumably of existing aircraft factories, to the manufacture of the Me 262.

In late October the Japanese in Berlin advised the Germans that only the Army was planning production of the Me 262 and requested investigation for the Army of two production plans for the aircraft, one for 100 aircraft a month, the other for 500. Meantime, the Japanese were making arrangements for the transfer to Japan of Bringewald, a Messerschmitt technician who was to direct manufacture of the Me 262 in the Far East. At that time it appears that the Army was putting the greatest emphasis on the improvement of the Me 262 fuselage and the Jumo 004 propulsion unit. Nevertheless, first of all, attempts were being made rapidly to perfect the Me 163, principally as a means of high-altitude defence.

It is evident that Japan received little detailed information on the construction of the Me 262. However, German tactical employment and ground organisation of Me 262 fighter units were closely studied by Japanese representatives and full information on performance characteristics and tactics were obtained.

Bringewald, the Messerschmitt civilian technician, and Ruf, a Messerschmitt expert on procurement of industrial machinery, left for Japan in the U-234 and were captured when that U-boat surrender to Allied forces. They carried with them blueprints and plans

necessary for the setting up in Japan of factories adequate for the production of 500 Me 262s a month. They calculated that it would take at least 1½ years after their arrival before the first Me 262 would come off the production line and that it would require 3,000,000 man-hours to get the factory ready for production. They further stated that two Japanese engineers in Germany had given information that the Japanese were working on a turbojet unit but were meeting with continuous difficulties. It was the opinion of Bringewald and Ruf that the Japanese were not capable of building the Me 262 without receiving complete specifications and technical supervision from German specialists. They were convinced that the Japanese did not have sufficient data and information to build the Me 262, since no parts of the aircraft or its propulsion units had been sent to Japan, nor was there in Japan any German specialist who could provide the necessary assistance.

It seems possible, however, that the Japanese, if they had been able to develop a turbojet unit to the operational stage, might have built an aircraft which, although not a copy of the Me 262, was based on that aircraft. The success or otherwise of such experiments obviously depended on the successful development of a turbojet unit. That, in turn, undoubtedly was greatly influenced by the extent of the information available in Japan on the design and construction of German turbojet units, on the difficulties encountered by Germany in their development and the methods by which such difficulties were overcome. While only the Jumo 004 was used in the Me 262, the BMW 003 basically is of similar design, and information available to Japan on either of these turbojet units was a potential source of assistance to the Japanese in their own experiments.

### POSTSCRIPT

*In fact both Rolf von Chlingensperg and Riclef Schomerus, with Me 262 materials, had departed Kiel, bound for Japan, on board U-864 on December 5, 1944, arriving at Horten, Norway, four days later. After undergoing repairs for its experimental Schnorkel, U-864 eventually set off again but was attacked by British submarine HMS Venturer on February 9, 1945.*

*Hit by one of Venturer's torpedoes, U-864 broke in two and sank with the loss of all hands—including von Chlingensperg and Schomerus. It remains the only time in history that a submarine has sunk another submarine while submerged.*

*The wreck came to rest more than 150m below the surface two nautical miles west of the island of Fedje, where it remained undiscovered until March 2003. In August 2005 it was found that mercury contained in 1,857 rusting steel bottles in U-864's keel was leaking out and posed a serious environmental threat. Plans have subsequently been drawn up to either recover the vessel or entomb it and its cargo on the ocean floor.*

# Endnotes

## INTRODUCTION

1 In his 1953 book *The First and the Last*, Adolf Galland states: "…the production of the Me 262 received a further delay of six months after it had already suffered a delay of about two years, due to the previous order given in autumn, 1940, to postpone all research developments. I believe that in this way about 18 months were lost in the development of the Me 262". At a meeting on February 9, 1940 (see IWM Milch Vol. 65/7281), Göring ordered that "all raw materials and so on are to be used to the utmost in order to produce the largest possible amount of armaments as quickly as possible". And "those projects that are completed in 1940 or that promise results by 1941 at the latest are decisive". He also said that "all other long-term programmes have to be combed through again. Of particular importance is the focus within armaments… on not continuing to build individual types". Whether this had any effect on the Me 262 is unclear. The first three Me 262 prototypes were ordered a month later, in March 1940, and Messerschmitt continued to work the project up into a viable prospect for development going into June, with the prototype order being increased to 20 in July. Delays, when they eventually did occur, coincided not with Göring's order but with the pressure heaped upon the Luftwaffe by the Battle of Britain. Only then did the experimental work come to a halt—with every available resource being diverted towards improving existing types. Work on the experimental types then recommenced as the winter of 1940 approached, gaining momentum going into January 1941. On the basis of this evidence, it would appear that Galland was incorrect and Göring's 'stop' order had little or no effect on the Me 262—apart, presumably, from providing Messerschmitt with a useful excuse much later in the war to explain why progress had been so slow during the earliest stages of development.

2 The report of an interview with Messerschmitt test pilot Gerhard Lindner on May 28, 1945 (see TNA AIR 40/201 pt 2), noted: "Lindner stated that the 004 was usually run only 25 hours between overhauls, but that a considerably longer time could be reached by pilots expert in jet engine operation". See also Appendix II for some experiences of servicing the Jumo 004.

3 A Junkers chart produced in December 1944 gives the total cost of a single Me 262 jet fighter, with two engines, as RM 150,000, compared to RM 144,000 for a Focke-Wulf Ta 152 with a single piston engine. See ADRC/T-2 3429/679.

4 When interviewed by American intelligence personnel immediately after the war, Messerschmitt vice-president and finance director Rakan Kokothaki stated that: "Messerschmitt was the only airplane producer of importance not owned or controlled by the State". See ADRC/T-2 2006/2 Air Technical Intelligence USSAF Report of Technical Intelligence Survey, Messerschmitt AG, Oberammergau, Germany. 31 July, 1945

## C1. ORIGINS, 1938-JAN 1941

1 MAP/ADRC 5028/482 Junkers Schnellbericht S.103 P2625/587, Dessau, 30.7.38

2 BA-MA RL3/780 RLM LC 7/III Gegenwärtiger Stand und künftige Entwicklungsarbeit auf dem Gebiete des Schnellfluges mit Strahltriebwerk 14.10.38

3 *Air International* Vol. 10 No. 3, p135, Gestation of the Swallow by Woldemar Voigt, March 1976

4 Most surviving Messerschmitt documents from this period uniformly refer to the 'P 65', rather than 'P 1065'. However, Willy Messerschmitt himself wrote it as 'P 1065' on his earliest known drawing of the type, from October 1939, and Voigt refers to it in his later recollections as P 1065—so that designation has been used in this volume in preference to P 65 for the sake of consistency.

5 Before and during the Second World War, turbojets were such a novel innovation that no one in Germany was entirely sure what to call them. Various different terminology was used by different people and organisations at different times but eventually 'TL', standing for 'Turbinen Luftstrahl' seems to have become the most commonly used and accepted term, with 'PTL'—'Propeller Turbinen Luftstrahl'—being later used for turboprops. Pulsejets were commonly referred to as 'Strahlrohre' or 'Jet Tubes' and Messerschmitt, the principal proponent of pulsejets for manned aircraft propulsion, initially seems to have tried popularising 'SR' as the abbreviation, but this evidently failed to catch on and period German documents generally refer to a pulsejet by its official designation, i.e. As 014, or with the full word 'Strahlrohr'.

6 RLM LC 7 Nr. 461/38 (III) Technischen Richtlinien für schnelle Jagdflugzeuge mit Strahltriebwerk 3.1.39

7 Essentially the same configuration as Heinkel's experimental single-engine He 178.

8 Evidently this layout would have resulted in an aircraft similar in appearance to the Yakovlev Yak-15.

9 IWM Speer FD4933/45 I Entwicklung. 20.6.45

10 MAP/ADRC 5018/165 P 65 notes, signed by Hans Hornung 13.4.39

11 IWM Speer FD4933/45 I Entwicklung. 20.6.45

12 At least, it was the same for one of three variants being worked on at this time—these being labelled "P 65 I", "P 65 II" and "Interzeptor".

13 MAP/ADRC 5018/221 Messerschmitt Datenblatt P 65, 29.9.39

14 MAP/ADRC 5018/225 Technische Bedingungen für P 65, Entwurf Probü, Mtt A.G. 20.9.39

15 It is unclear what the P 30/7 and 30/8 actually were. Presumably, given the 'P' and the number, they were 30mm cannon projects.

16 MAP/ADRC 5018/221 Messerschmitt Datenblatt P 65, 29.9.39

17 MAP/ADRC 5018/219 Messerschmitt Datenblatt P 65, 30.9.39

18 MAP/ADRC 5018/163 Messerschmitt Reisebericht, Besprechungen im Amt; Bramo; AVA Göttingen (vom 8.10.—10.10.39), 13.10.39

19 The company's full name was Brandenburgische Motorenwerke, though everyone seems to have called it Bramo, and at this time it was in the process of being taken over by Bayerischen Motorenwerke, aka BMW.

20 The meeting summary says "reduction of the amount of

ammunition by approx. 100kg (reason: half the flight time as Bf 110)".

21 Presumably, Bramo/BMW had been intending to supply engines which could somehow 'pivot' or perhaps which allowed a measure of thrust direction control. Either way, Messerschmitt declined this 'option'.

22 MAP/ADRC 5018/209 Messerschmitt, Vorteile der ovalen Rumpfform, 27.10.39

23 MAP/ADRC 5018/210 Messerschmitt, Vorteile der dreieckigen Rumpfform, 27.10.39

24 T-2/MAP 2125/630 AVA Windkanalmessungen an Flugzeugrumpfen bei hohen Geschwindigkeiten. Auftraggerber: Messerschmitt A.G. 30.10.1939

25 MAP/ADRC 5018/208 Messerschmitt Vergleich zwischen Mittel- und Tiefdecker für die P 65 15.12.39

26 MAP/ADRC 5018/318 Messerschmitt Projektübergabe P 65, 9.11.39-15.3.40

27 A drawing number laid out in this format would appear to indicate a type intended for production —rather than a pure concept or project design—but these were not actual construction blueprints.

28 IWM Speer FD4933/45 I Entwicklung. 20.6.45

29 MAP/ADRC 5018/333 Messerschmitt Projektübergabe P 65 Schleudersitz P 65 15.1.40 / 16.1.40

30 ADRC/T-2 2221/713 Messerschmitt Flugzeugdatenblatt zur Leistungsrechnung P 70 16.1.40

31 A sketch purporting to show the P 1070 with swept wings was discovered by German writer Karl Ries during the 1960s, later being sketched by British writer Eddie Creek before the original was lost. This design was also said to have a wingspan of 8.3m—the same as the straight-winged variant for which verifiable documentary evidence exists.

32 IWM Speer FD4933/45 I Entwicklung. 20.6.45

33 MAP/ADRC 5018/340 Messerschmitt Projektübergabe P 65 Kabinenaufbau P 65 (vorläufig) 24.1.40

34 MAP/ADRC 5018/335 Messerschmitt Projektübergabe P 65 Rumpfspitze 27.1.40

35 MAP/ADRC 5018/181 Messerschmitt P 1065 stark zugespitztes Höhenleitwerk FH = $4.24m^2$ 30.1.40

36 MAP/ADRC 5018/205 Messerschmitt Festlegung des Projekts und Konstruktionszustandes P 65 8.2.40

37 *Air International* Vol. 10 No. 3, p153, Gestation of the Swallow by Woldemar Voigt, March 1976

38 MAP/ADRC 5018/337 Messerschmitt Projektübergabe P 65 Flügel (F = $18m^2$) endgültig; damit sind Blatt 4, 5 und 7 überholt. 15.2.40

39 MAP/ADRC 5018/322 Messerschmitt Projektübergabe P 65 Projekt-Richtlinien V I 17.2.40

40 MAP/ADRC 5018/330 Messerschmitt Projektübergabe P 65 Triebwerkseinbau 17.2.40

41 ADIK 129/638 BMW Arbeitsplan für die L-Entwicklung im Geschäftsjahr 1941/42 7.2.41

42 IWM FD4355/45 Vol. 5/632 LC 2 Nr. 911/40 (III) Geh. 14.2.40 TDM/Mtt/Mi. 19.2.40 P 65 Termine

43 MAP/ADRC 5018/342 Messerschmitt Projektübergabe P 65 Kabinenaufbau 24.2.40

44 IWM Speer FD4933/45 I Entwicklung. 20.6.45

45 MAP/ADRC 5018/319 Messerschmitt Projektübergabe P 65 Fahrwerkslastannahmen 6.4.40

46 MAP/ADRC 5018/324 Messerschmitt Projektübergabe P 65 Projektrichtlinien V I 6.3.40

47 MAP/ADRC 5018/336 Messerschmitt Projektübergabe P 65 Waffenkanzel 6.3.40

48 T-2/ADRC 2050/1219 Messerschmitt Projektbaubeschreibung P 1065 Nr. 3, March 1940. Note that this project build description is labelled as 'Number 3'. At the time of writing there were no known surviving copies of the first and second build descriptions.

49 MAP/ADRC 5018/294 Messerschmitt Projektübergabe II P 65 Luftbremse 29.2.40

50 MAP/ADRC 5018/271 Messerschmitt Projektübergabe II P 65 Druckkessel 5.3.40

51 MAP/ADRC 5018/299 Messerschmitt Projektübergabe II P 65 Kraftstoffanlage 5.3.40

52 MAP/ADRC 5018/308 Messerschmitt Projektübergabe II P 65 Waffenkanzel 5.3.40

53 MAP/ADRC 5018/312 Messerschmitt Projektübergabe II P 65 Projektrichtlinien V I 22.4.40

54 IWM Speer FD4933/45 I Entwicklung. 20.6.45

55 MAP/ADRC 5018/296 Messerschmitt Projektübergabe II P 65 Luftbremse 6.5.40

56 MAP/ADRC 5018/293 Messerschmitt Projektübergabe II P 65 Kraftstoffanlage 6.5.40

57 MAP/ADRC 5018/240 Messerschmitt Projektübergabe III V I mit Jumo 210 G-Einbau. It is worth noting that where the original Projektübergabe's 22 pages (29 including updates) covered a period of 127 days, from 9, 1939, to March 15, 1940 and Projektübergabe II's 76 pages spanned 72 days (of which only 54 are known to survive), from February 26 to May 8, 1940, Projektübergabe III's 21 pages (27 including page updates) cover an incredible 309 days, from May 30, 1940, to April 4, 1941. The low number of pages and the great length of time covered appear to suggest that work on the P65/Me 262 slackened off significantly during this period. In addition many of the pages in Projektübergabe III are repetitive—simply making changes to the configuration of Me 262 V I prototype or elaborating on the aircraft's design details.

58 *Air International* Vol. 10 No. 3, p136, Gestation of the Swallow by Woldemar Voigt, March 1976. In fact, Voigt states that installation details of the P 3302 and P 3303 were given. The latter seems unlikely, being a much larger engine design than the P 1065 could have easily accommodated. Perhaps he meant P 3304. After this note there is an enormous gap in Voigt's development timetable for the P 1065—from June 20, 1940, to April 8, 1941, again suggesting a period of little activity at a time when—according to the RLM's schedule—20 prototypes were supposed to be under construction.

59 MAP/ADRC 5018/242 Messerschmitt Projektübergabe III V I mit Jumo 210 G und 2 x TL 3302 21.6.40

60 IWM FD4940/45 (1) via Speer 76/746 RLM C-Amts-Programm Lieferplan Nr. 18, g. Kdos. Nr. 742/40 1.7.40

61 IWM GDC 10/9169 Tiefdecker P 65 mit Sturzflugbremsen 13.7.40

62 *Me 262 Volume 1* by J. Richard Smith and Eddie Creek, p68

63 ADIK 129/638 BMW Arbeitsplan für die L-Entwicklung im Geschäftsjahr 1941/42 7.2.41

64 Ibid.

65 IWM FD4355/45 Vol. 5/540 Messerschmitt to Reidenbach 26.9.40

66 While the Bf 209/Me 209 (the RLM tended to use the former, while Messerschmitt almost exclusively used the latter) was most famous for breaking records, it was always intended as the basis for a small lightweight fighter. See for example NARA T177-16/186 RLM LC Nr. 243/38 Betr. Flugzeugentwicklungsprogramm 3. September 1938

67 MAP/ADRC 5018/252 Messerschmitt Projektübergabe III Projektrichtlinien V I 15.10.40

68 MAP/ADRC 5018/253 Messerschmitt Projektübergabe III Projektrichtlinien V I, Forsetzung zu Blatt 9 15.10.40

69 MAP/ADRC 5018/254 Messerschmitt Projektübergabe III Projektrichtlinien V I 15.10.40

70 MAP/ADRC 5018/246 Messerschmitt Projektübergabe III V I mit Jumo 210 G und 2 x TL 3302 1.11.40

71 Involving the Messerschmitt company in the design, development and production of large long-range aircraft seems to have been a particularly ardent desire of Willy Messerschmitt. Both

Heinkel and Focke-Wulf had successfully managed to diversify this way, with the former producing numerous single-seat fighter designs as well as the He 177 bomber, and the latter similarly managing to produce the Fw 190 as well as the Fw 200 Condor. Presumably Messerschmitt wanted to join this 'club'.

72 IWM Milch Vol. 54/1591 Messerschmitt to Lucht 29.11.40

73 IWM FD4355/45 Vol. 4/267 Herrn Helmschrott—P 65 Bugrad 17.12.40

74 On page 18 of *Messerschmitt Me 262*, authors Willy Radinger and Walter Schick note that according to the report of an interrogation of Messerschmitt company chairman Friedrich Seiler dated June 17, 1945, construction of assembly jigs and individual components for the P 1065 V1 and V2 had commenced in January 1940.

75 IWM Milch Vol. 54/1587 Messerschmitt to Udet 7.1.41

76 IWM FD4355/45 Vol. 4/246 Messerschmitt—Aktennotiz! Herrn Voigt, Probü, Mitteilung Nr. 9/41 10.1.41

77 IWM FD4355/45 Vol. 4/245 Messerschmitt—Herrn Dir. Bauer. Betr.: Konstruktionsunterlagen P 65 11.1.41

78 The precise type of rocket motor to be procured by Seitz is not detailed by Willy Messerschmitt—he refers to them only as "cold". However, in his article for the March 1976 issue of *Air International*, Voigt describes "two Walter rockets of 1,653lb (750kg) thrust each". Walterwerke's RII-209, which would eventually be used to power the Me 163 A, was known to the company as 'cold' (in contrast to the 'hot' 109-509 rocket motor which would power the Me 163 B) and had a maximum thrust of 750kg.

## C2. DISTRACTIONS, JAN 1941-MAY 1942

1 ADIK 129/638 BMW Arbeitsplan für die L-Entwicklung im Geschäftsjahr 1941/42 7.2.41

2 Ibid.

3 The aircraft originally given the RLM number 8-163 or had been an unsuccessful piston-engined reconnaissance machine, of which three prototypes had been commissioned during the mid-1930s (Bf 163 V1-V3). The rocket-powered aircraft, deemed top secret, had been given the same number for to disguise its true nature and the first prototype is therefore referred to in contemporary documents not as the 'Me 163 V1' but as the 'Me 163 V4', acknowledging both the three earlier prototypes and the officially-sanctioned changeover from 'Bf' to 'Me' in the meantime.

4 *Ein Dreieck Fliegt*, Alexander Lippisch, p58

5 IWM FD4355/45 Vol. 4/236 Messerschmitt Terminverschiebungen Mitteilung Nr. 22/41 20.1.41

6 US Navy Project Squid Technical Memorandum No. Pr.-4 The Aero-Resonator Power Plant of the V-1 Flying Bomb by Ing. Günther Diedrich, translated by A. Kahane, 30 June 1948, Princeton University

7 Ibid.

8 Ibid. Diedrich would later lament that it was Schmidt's name and not his own that became attached to the invention: "The resonator engine built by the Schmidt firm after 1940 proved itself both in the Braunschweig wind tunnel and on the test stand to be neither superior nor able to compete with the Argus design. Thus it is often found in history that because of the type of competition described here, the inventor is surpassed. In the name selected by the Air Ministry, the 'Argus-Schmidt Tube', both the pioneering work of Schmidt and the forceful development of the firm Argus were duly recognised."

9 IWM FD4355/45 Vol. 5/544 Generalluftzeugmeister LC 2 Nr. 278/41(III) g.Kdos. Nachtrag zu den Richtlinien für den Entwurf eines Jagdeinsitzers. Berlin, den 16.4.41

10 While the Me 309 does appear to have been designed to meet the requirements of this specification, its early development remains something of a mystery. Most Messerschmitt designs were begun with a project number, such as P 1065 for the Me 262, but the 309's original designation is unknown. Presumably it must have fallen somewhere between P 1076 and P 1078, since the P 1075 was a heavy bomber design and work on the P 1079 had not yet commenced at this time.

11 ADIK 129/638 BMW Arbeitsplan für die L-Entwicklung im Geschäftsjahr 1941/42 7.2.41

12 IWM Speer FD4933/45 I Entwicklung. 20.6.45

13 ADRC/T-2 3754/1002 RLM LC2 Aktenvermerk zu BAL—Prüfbericht Me 262 V1 v. 17.4.1941

14 ADRC/MAP 5018/389 Me 262 mit Jumo 210 G (700 PS) + 2 x 500kg 11.5.41

15 ADRC/T-2 2217/585 Messerschmitt Flugzeuge mit Strahlrohren. Various dates 22.5.41-1.8.41

16 IWM FD4355/45 Vol. 4/197 Messerschmitt Mitteilung Nr. 88/41. Anschrift: H. Fettermann, AB. Betrifft: Me 264. 26.4.41

17 IWM GDC 10/9146 AVA Bericht 41/14/20 J 7035 Messerschmitt AG, Drei- und Sechskomponentenmessungen an einem Pfeilflügel mit Pfeilform 35° 50' (Me 262). 24.7.1941

18 USSBS Aircraft Division Air Frames Plant Report No 6 Messerschmitt AG, Augsburg, Appendix III, Report on Messerschmitt Me-262, October 24, 1945. See also IWM Speer FD4933/45 I Entwicklung. 20.6.45

19 *Me 262 Volume One* by J. Richard Smith and Eddie Creek, p83

20 ADRC/MAP 5048/29 Der Reichsminister der Luftfahrt LC 2 Festigkeitsprüfstelle Berlin-Adlershof, den 14.8.41, Auszug aus Protokoll Festigkeitsvorschriften für V-Muster Me 309

21 IWM FD4355/45 Vol. 4/99 Messerschmitt to Herr Caroli, Mitteilung Nr. 184/41 Mindestgeschwindigkeiten und Ca max Me 262 V1. 14.8.41

22 IWM FD4355/45 Vol. 5/649 Aktenvermerk Besprechung mit dem RLM. 29.8.41

23 Ibid.

24 Ibid.

25 Iowa State University Library Special Collections and University Archive MS-243 Box 17 Folder 42 Messerschmitt Projektbaubeschreibung Li P 05 27.8.41

26 IWM FD4355/45 Vol. 4/96 Messerschmitt to Voigt, Interceptor, 29.8.41

27 IWM FD4355/45 Vol. 4/91 Messerschmitt to Herr Sell, FKV. Kabine Me 262 2.9.41

28 ADRC/MAP 5018/373 262 W1 undated

29 ADRC/MAP 5018/465-477 Messerschmitt Me 262 W2 mit Walter geräten als Interceptor 2.9.41. At this stage the two most well-known Argus pulsejets, the As 014 and As 044, had yet to receive those designations. Messerschmitt reports tend to refer to all pulsejets as "Strahlrohre"—jet tubes—and abbreviate this to 'SR' in the same way that turbojets are referred to as 'TL', short for 'Turbinenluftstrahl'. The 'SR' abbreviation does not appear to have caught on, however.

30 ADRC/T-2 3358/28 Stellungnahme zum Flugbericht Rechlin E 20 by Braun September 1941

31 ADRC/MAP 5048/68 Messerschmitt Aktennotiz. Betrifft: 1. Attrappenbesichtigung Me 309. 23.9.41

32 ADRC/MAP 5048/345 Messerschmitt Besprechungsniederschrift über die Besprechung vom 22.9.1941

33 ADRC/MAP 5048/341 Messerschmitt Regensburg Besprechungsniederschrift über die Besprechung vom 29.9.41

34 *Air International* Vol. 10 No. 3, p136, Gestation of the Swallow by Woldemar Voigt, March 1976. See also IWM Speer FD4933/45 I Entwicklung. 20.6.45

35 ADRC/T-2 8089/1177 Arado Entwurfsbeschreibung E 370 18.10.41. This design would later receive the official RLM designation Ar 234.

36 ADRC/T-2 2824/536 Otter Mader Werk Sondertriebwerk T 1 Bau einer Klein-Serie by Franz 7.10.41

37 *Air International* Vol. 10 No. 3, p136, Gestation of the Swallow by Woldemar Voigt, March 1976. The October 21 date for

submission of the Me 262 reconnaissance version is also given in USSBS Aircraft Division Air Frames Plant Report No 6 Messerschmitt AG Augsburg Appendix III—Report on Messerschmitt Me 262, October 24, 1945. However, it may be that the design was actually submitted in November, see ADRC/T-2 2696/1124 Messerschmitt Vorläufiges Datenblatt Projektwerte, November 1941

38  . *Air International* Vol. 10 No. 3, p153, Gestation of the Swallow by Woldemar Voigt, March 1976

39  ADRC/MAP 5018/431-432 Me 262 J Polaren 10.11.41 and Muster: 262 J Motor: Walter Rollstrecken 11.11.41

40  IWM FD4355/45 Vol. 4/48 Messerschmitt to Voigt/Seitz, 11.12.41

41  IWM Milch 45/8188 Amtschefbesprechung bei St/GL am 12. Dez. 1941

42  The term used, verbatim, is "Tiefangriffsflugzeug".

43  Probably Luftwaffe Chief of Staff Generalleutnant Hans Jeschonnek.

44  IWM Speer 76/0756 RLM C-Amts-Programm R/TL Geräte V-Serie, December 1941

45  ADRC/T-2 8043/867 GL/C—B2 Nr 2154 gKd (I) v. 1.1.42 This comprehensive snapshot of German aircraft development as of the beginning of 1942 was unusual and nothing similar seems to have been produced before or thereafter. It is possible that it was produced for or at the behest of the new Generalluftzeugmeister Erhard Milch, in order to swiftly familiarise him with all the work set in motion by his predecessor—though there is no direct evidence to confirm this.

46  The Jumo T2 was a reworked version of the T1 which used fewer scarce 'strategic materials', particularly nickel. The T1 would later receive the designation 109-004 A (or simply Jumo 004 A), while the T2 would become the 109-004 B (or Jumo 004 B).

47  *Me 262 Volume One* by J. Richard Smith and Eddie Creek, p83

48  Known as a 'GL' or 'Generalluftzeugmeister' meeting.

49  IWM Milch 45/8163 Amtschef-Besprechung bei St/GL am 13.1.42

50  ADRC/MAP 5048/311 Mitteilung an RD—Herrn Direktor Linder. Betrifft: Me 309—Nullserie. 10. Januar 1942

51  ADRC/MAP 5048/308 Messerschmitt AG Technischer Vertrieb VT-Anweisung-Nr. 1791 Baumuster Me 309 Vorgang Nr. E/410 Betrifft: Me 309 mit Jumo 213. 14.1.42

52  Ibid.

53  ADRC/T-2 2346/898 BMW Triebwerkseinbau P 3302 V 1-10 in Versuchsträger P 1065 Geheim-Nr. 85/42 26.3.42

54  IWM Milch 45/8158 Amtschef-Besprechung bei St/GL am 20.1.42

55  IWM Milch 45/8153 Amtschefbesprechung bei St/GL am 27.1.42

56  ADRC/T-2 2768/218 Messerschmitt Funktionserprobung des Katapultsitzes in der Me 210 und Me 262. February 1942

57  *Air International* Vol. 10 No. 3, p136, Gestation of the Swallow by Woldemar Voigt, March 1976. See also USSBS Aircraft Division Air Frames Plant Report No 6 Messerschmitt AG Augsburg Appendix III—Report on Messerschmitt Me 262, 24.10.45

58  ADRC/T-2 2346/898 BMW Triebwerkseinbau P 3302 V 1-10 in Versuchsträger P 1065 Geheim-Nr. 85/42 26.3.42

59  IWM Milch 45/8143 Amtschefbesprechung bei St/GL am 10.2.42 (Nr. 11)

60  IWM Speer FD4355/45/493 GL/C-E 2 Nr. 1272/42 (I) geh. An die Firma Messerschmitt A.G. z.Hd. von Herrn Prof. Messerschmitt Betr.: P 1079 17.2.1942

61  IWM Speer FD4355/45/492 Messerschmitt An das RLM Herrn Generaling. Reidenbach P 1079 24.2.42

62  Presumably the S stood for Schlachtflugzeug or 'attack aircraft'.

63  IWM Milch 62/5167 Besprechungsnotiz Nr. 46/42 g.Kdos. 6.3.42

64  IWM Milch 45/8107 Amtschefbesprechung bei St/GL am

17.3.42 (Nr. 16)

65  ADRC/T-2 2730/1004 Me 262 V1 PC+UA Flug mit 2 mal BMW TL 3302, March 1942

66  No record of this meeting is known to survive, but March 9 was the day when Messerschmitt had been due to give his presentation on plans to cure the Me 210 by lengthening its fuselage.

67  *Air International* Vol. 10 No. 3, p136, Gestation of the Swallow by Woldemar Voigt, March 1976

68  Ibid.

69  ADRC/MAP 5012/56 Messerschmitt Flugzeug mit Strahlrohren 31.3.42

70  ADRC/MAP 5018/348 Projektübergabe III. Me 262 V2 mit Strahlrohren April 1942

71  IWM Milch 13/115 GL-Besprechung unter dem Vorsitz des Staatssekretärs Generalfeldmarschall Milch am Dienstag, dem 14 April 1942, vorm. 10 Uhr, im Reichsluftfahrtministerium

72  IWM Milch 62/5190 Besprechungsnotiz Nr. 67/42 g.Kdos. Reichsjägerhof Rominten, 19.4.42

73  ADRC/T-2 2006/2 Report of Technical Intelligence Survey Messerschmitt AG, Oberammergau, Germany 31 July 1945

74  IWM Milch 13/211 GL-Besprechung unter dem Vorsitz des Staatssekretaers Generalfeldmarschall Milch am Montag, dem 27. April 1942, Vorm. 10 Uhr

75  The 'H' designation would later be reused for the high-altitude variant of the Bf 109 and by December 1943 the Bf 109 with Jumo 213 would be redesignated Bf 109 L.

76  *Willy Messerschmitt Pioneer of Aviation Design* by Erbert, Kaiser and Peters, p178

77  Milch's strained personal relationship Messerschmitt can be traced back to a series of accidents which afflicted the Messerschmitt M 20 airliner during the late 1920s. See *Willy Messerschmitt Pioneer of Aviation Design* by Erbert, Kaiser and Peters, p65

78  An energetic, charismatic, imaginative and competent engineer, as well as being a well-regarded leader and businessman, Willy Messerschmitt made all of his company's important decisions and micro-managed much of its work. The company's management structure reflected this—with senior managers constantly looking to him for direction rather than being free to use their own initiative and judgement to work independently. Messerschmitt had met and impressed Hitler on numerous occasions during the late 1930s. On January 30, 1939, Hitler personally presented Messerschmitt with the Der Deutscher Nationalorden für Kunst und Wissenschaft—the Nazi replacement for the Nobel Prize—alongside Fritz Todt, Ferdinand Porsche and Ernst Heinkel.

79  IWM Milch 13/306 GL-Besprechung unter dem Vorsitz des Staatssekretärs Generalfeldmarschall Milch am Dienstag, dem 5. Mai 1942, vorm. 10 Uhr im Reichsluftfahrtministerium

80  IWM Milch 62/5199 Besprechungsnotiz Nr. 77/42 g.Kdos. Insterburg, den 9.5.1942, 12.35-13.30 Uhr.

## C3. TURNING POINT, MAY 1942–MAY 1943

1  IWM Milch 62/5220 Besprechungsnotiz Nr. 35/42 g.Kdos. Carinhall, 21.5.1942 von 12.40 bis 14.30 Uhr und 15.20 bis16.20 Uhr

2  GL = Generalluftzeugmeister—Milch's position but also used as a general term for the RLM's command structure.

3  ADIK 209/1006 Abdichtung der Wanne Me 262 by Geiger, May 1942

4  *Air International* Vol. 10 No. 3, p136, Gestation of the Swallow by Woldemar Voigt, March 1976

5  GL/A/C Nr. 1308/42 g.Kdos. (B-2/I) v. 19.5.42 Blatt 2 v.8—Ausfertigung 4 von 8. Via Calum Douglas collection

6  ADIK 4058/258 Besprechung bei H. Schelp RLM G1/C-E3 über TL-Sondertriebwerke für P 1065 am 9. Juni 1942. 13.6.42

7  Ibid.

8  *Me 262 Volume One* by J. Richard Smith and Eddie Creek, p88

9   *Messerschmitt Me 262* by Willy Radinger and Walter Schick, p25

10  ADRC/T-2 2439/905 Me 262 V3, PC+UC Einfliegen by Wendel, 18.7.42

11  ADRC/T-2 2824/1037 Erster Flug Me 262 by Franz, 18.7.42

12  ADRC/T-2 2006/3 Report of Technical Intelligence Survey—Messerschmitt AG, Oberammergau, Germany. Air Technical Intelligence USSAF 31 July, 1945

13  ADRC/T-2 2157/817 3 Komponenten Windkanalmessungen an gepfeilten Flügeln und an einem Pfeilflügel-Gesamtmodell. Bericht der Messerschmitt AG 20.7.42

14  ADRC/T-2 2404/914 Me 262 Untersuchung der Höhenleitwerkschwingungen; Längstabilität by Wendel, August 1942

15  ADRC/T-2 3397/272 Messerschmitt Kontrollbericht Nr. 127/42 über den Flugzeug-Bruchschaden Me 262 V3 21.8.42

16  *Air International* Vol. 10 No. 3, p136, Gestation of the Swallow by Woldemar Voigt, March 1976

17  ADRC/T-2 2159/244 DVL Hochgeschwindigkeitsmessungen am Flugzeug Me 262, 12 September 1942

18  In contrast to Beauvais' crash of August 11 (or possibly August 17), the Me 262 V2's second flight of October 1, from 10.35am to 10.51am was recorded, out of sequence, in the log books of both Beauvais and Wendel. Whether it was Beauvais or Wendel who made this second flight is unclear. However, Beauvais certainly flew the Me 262 V2 at around this time and there is no other entry in his log book for the aircraft during this period. He also gave the October 1 date in a post-war list of jet-propelled aircraft flights he compiled. If it was Beauvais who flew the Me 262 V2 at 10.35am on October 1, it is similarly unclear why Wendel would have recorded it in his own log book as though it was he and not Beauvais who made the flight. Why both of them chose to record the same flight with the same times out of sequence—when both typically noted down their flights in chronological order—is unknown.

19  *Air International* Vol. 10 No. 3, p136, Gestation of the Swallow by Woldemar Voigt, March 1976

20  ADRC/T-2 2656/724 Messerschmitt Bericht des Sonderausschusses F-2 für Monat Januar 1943

21  ADRC/T-2 2022/92 Messerschmitt Me 262 Auszug aus der Projektbaubeschreibung 20.11.1942

22  *Air International* Vol. 10 No. 3, p136, Gestation of the Swallow by Woldemar Voigt, March 1976

23  ADRC/T-2 2669/1067 Me 262 V2, PC+UB by Wendel, 9.12.42

24  NARA T321-59/0437 GL-C-Nr. 845/42 g.K. (E/J) St/GL—Befehl Nr. 480 Berlin, den 10. Dez. 1942. Betrifft: Entwicklungs- und Beschaffungsprogramm „Vulkan"

25  IWM Milch 62/5234 Besprechungsnotiz Nr. 109/42 g.Kdos. Reichsjägerhof, den 29.6.1942, 18.45–21.15 Uhr

26  IWM Milch 42/6476 St/GL/C-E 2 Nr. 5008/43 g.Kdos. Bericht Nr. 14 über die Entwicklungsbesprechung am 12.12.1942

27  IWM Milch 17/3750 GL-Besprechung unter Vorsitz von Generalfeldmarschall Milch am Dienstag, dem 22. Dezember 1942, 11 Uhr im Reichsluftfahrtministerium

28  IWM Milch 17/3830 GL-Besprechung unter dem Vorsitz des Staatssekretärs Generalfeldmarschall Milch am Dienstag, dem 29. Dezember 1942, 10.18 Uhr im Reichsluftfahrtministerium

29  IWM Milch 35/2822 E-Besprechung unter Vorsitz von Gen. d. Fl. Doerstling am Dienstag, dem 19. Januar 1943, 10 Uhr im Reichsluftfahrtministerium

30  IWM Milch 42/6450 Der Staatssekretär der Luftfahrt und Generalinspekteur der Luftwaffe St/GL/C-E 2 Nr. 5514/43 g.Kdos. Berlin, den 2.2.1943 Bericht Nr. 17 über die Entwicklungsbesprechung am 21.1.1943

31  ADRC/MAP 5039/2 Messerschmitt Aktennotiz Betr.: Me 109/DB 603 Besprechung bei Herrn Prof. Messerschmitt am 21.1.43

32  ADIK 4096/279 Messerschmitt Vergleich Me 109—309 A/IV/12/13/15/43, Augsburg, den 15.1.43

33  ADRC/T-2 2962/1019 TDM/Mtt/Mo. Vergleichsleistungen Me 109 mit DB 603 u. Me 109 mit Jumo 213. 14.11.41

34  IWM Milch 42/6450 Der Staatssekretär der Luftfahrt und Generalinspekteur der Luftwaffe St/GL/C-E 2 Nr. 5514/43 g.Kdos. Berlin, den 2.2.1943 Bericht Nr. 17 über die Entwicklungsbesprechung am 21.1.1943

35  ADIK 154/419 Bericht Nr. 64 über die Amtschefbesprechung vom 11.2.1943

36  *Air International* Vol. 10 No. 3, p136, Gestation of the Swallow by Woldemar Voigt, March 1976

37  ADIK 4062/132 Der Reichsminister der Luftfahrt und Oberbefehlshaber der Luftwaffe Protokoll Festigkeitsvorschiften Me 262 Serie 13.2.1943

38  ADIK 4059/608 Messerschmitt Me 262 Erprobungsbericht Nr. 9 by Tilch and Krauss, 12.2.43

39  ADRC/T-2 2904/1212 Messerschmitt Me 262 V2 Erprobungsbericht by Sebald, Feb 1943

40  ADIK 4059/616 Messerschmitt Me 262 Erprobungsbericht Nr. 11 by Tilch, Krauss and Jung, 22.2.43

41  ADIK 4059/636 Messerschmitt Me 262 Erprobungsbericht Nr. 12 by Tilch, Krauss and Jung, 2.3.43

42  ADRC/T-2 2008/481 Messerschmitt Me 262 Jäger und Jabo (Projektübergabe IV) May 7-8, 1943

43  ADRC/T-2 2656/705 Messerschmitt Bericht des Sonderausschusses für Monat Februar 1943

44  IWM Milch 36/3408 E-Besprechung unter Vorsitz von Generalmajor Vorwald am Freitag, dem 5. März 1943, 10 Uhr, im Reichsluftfahrtministerium

45  IWM Milch 36/3408 E-Besprechung unter dem Vorsitz des Staatssekretärs Generalfeldmarschall Milch am Freitag, dem 19. März, 10 Uhr im Reichsluftfahrtministerium

46  This conversation was recorded verbatim by an RLM stenographer but it would appear that this particular stenographer had difficulty with the numerous three-digit codes used by the RLM for engines and aircraft. The transcript of this conversation at one time calls the He 280 the '282' (the Flettner Fl 282 was a helicopter) and on another the '288' (the Ju 288 was a medium/heavy bomber designed and built by Junkers). Similarly, the Jumo T1/004 is recorded at one point as the '211'. While the 211 was used in the nose of the Me 262 prototype, it is clear that the conversation actually concerns the 004 jet engine.

47  IWM Milch 36/3686 E-Besprechung am Montag, dem 22. März 1943, 10 Uhr unter Vorsitz des Generalfeldmarschalls Milch im Reichsluftfahrtministerium

48  IWM Milch 19/4706 GL-Besprechung unter Vorsitz von Generalfeldmarschall Milch am Dienstag, dem 23. März 1943, 10 Uhr, im Reichsluftfahrtministerium

49  ADRC/T-2 2645/156 Messerschmitt Kurz-Baubeschreibung Me 262. Augsburg, den 25. März 1943

50  ADRC/T-2 2656/772 Messerschmitt Bericht des Sonderausschusses für Monat März 1943

51  IWM Milch 19/4792 GL-Besprechung unter dem Vorsitz von Generalfeldmarschall Milch am Mittwoch, dem 31. März 1943, 10 Uhr im Reichsluftfahrtministerium

52  ADRC/T-2 4035/134 Messerschmitt Me 262 Erprobungsbericht Nr. 17 v. 29.3-4.4.43

53  ADRC/T-2 2805/210 Messerschmitt Me 262 Flugbericht Nr. 913/18 by Ostertag, Apr 1943

54  IWM Milch 19/4948 GL-Besprechung unter Vorsitz von Generalmajor Vorwald am Dienstag, dem 13. April 1943, 10 Uhr, im Reichsluftfahrtministerium

55  For the full story of the Me 409 and Me 155, see *Secret Projects of the Luftwaffe: Blohm & Voss BV 155* by Dan Sharp

56  IWM Speer FD4355/45/655 Messerschmitt Mitteilung an Verteiler 27.4.43

57  ADRC/T-2 2008/481 Messerschmitt Me 262 Jäger und Jabo (Projektübergabe IV) May 7-8, 1943

58  ADIK 4079/340 Messerschmitt Elektroakustische Peilung Versuchs-Bericht Nr. 000-18-A-43 25.6.43

59  IWM Milch 20/5314 GL-Besprechung unter dem Vorsitz des

Staatsekretärs Generalfeldmarschall Milch am Dienstag, den 18. Mai 1943, 10 Uhr im Reichsluftfahrtministerium

## C4. MESSERSCHMITT VERSUS THE ME 262, MAY–AUG 1943

1 IWM Milch 20/5451 GL-Besprechung unter Vorsitz von General-feldmarschall Milch am Dienstag, dem 25. Mai 1943, 10Uhr, im Reichsluftfahrtministerium

2 IWM Speer FD4355/45 Vol.4/630 Messerschmitt Aktennotiz 24.5.43

3 Vorwald says, in the RLM development meeting of June 4, 1943, that the Me 209 was cancelled eight days earlier. The reference can be found at IWM Milch 37/3989.

4 IWM Milch 37/4053 Entwicklungs-Besprechung unter dem Vorsitz von Generalfeldmarschall Milch am Freitag, dem 28. Mai 1943, 10 Uhr im Reichsluftfahrtministerium

5 Written in the stenographic notes of the meeting as literally "Ein-TL-Jäger".

6 IWM Speer FD4355/45 Vol.4/625 Bley—Forcierter Anlauf Me 262 und seine Folgen 28.5.43

7 ADIK 4079/350 Messerschmitt Electroakustische Peilung Versuchs-Bericht Nr. 000-18-A-43 II. Teilbericht 16.7.43

8 ADIK 151/337 Junkers Niederschrift Besprechung bei Jumo am 31.5.43 über Einbau 109-004 in Me 262

9 IWM Speer FD4355/45 Vol.4/624 Helmschrott—Me 262 2.6.43

10 IWM Milch 37/3960 E-Besprechung am Freitag, dem 4. Juni 1943, 10 Uhr, unter Vorsitz des Generalfeldmarschalls Milch im Reichsluftfahrtministerium

11 Pierre Laval, former French prime minister and now head of government under the Vichy Regime.

12 Presumably this is a reference to RLM officials.

13 In a remarkable twist, the man who suggested on April 14, 1942, that Willy Messerschmitt be removed as the head of his own company—and who then went and told him the bad news in person—had himself been forced to retire on January 31, 1943. He had then been hired as factory general manager (Betriebsführer) at Regensburg by Willy Messerschmitt.

14 IWM Speer FD4355/45 Vol.4/611 Messerschmitt Fernschreiben an das Berliner Büro—z.Hd.V. Herrn Urben. Betr.: Flossenver-stellgerät Me 262 9.6.43

15 IWM Speer FD4355/45 Vol.4/613 Herrn Bley—ZA Me 262 Armaturen 9.6.43

16 IWM Speer FD4355/45 Vol.4/612 Messerschmitt Fernschreiben an das Berliner Büro z.Hd.v.Herrn Urban Betr.: Me 262 Arma-turen in der Brennstoffleitung 9.6.43

17 ADRC/T-2 2012/443 Me 262 A-1 AG-Liste 11.6.43

18 IWM Milch 37/3755 E-Besprechung am Dienstag, dem 15. Juni 1943, 10 Uhr, unter Vorsitz des Generalfeldmarschalls Milch im Reichsluftfahrtministerium

19 IWM Milch 21/5759 GL-Besprechung unter Vorsitz von Generalfeldmarschall Milch am Dienstag, dem 22. Juni 1943, 10 Uhr im Reichsluftfahrtministerium

20 Rakan Kokothaki—Messerschmitt vice-president and finance director.

21 ADIK 4079/340 Messerschmitt Elektroakustische Peilung Versuchs-Bericht Nr. 000-18-A-43 I.Teilbericht 25.6.43

22 IWM Milch 21/5673 St/GL-Besprechung am Dienstag, dem 29. Juni 1943, 10 Uhr, unter Vorsitz des Generalfeldmarschalls Milch im Reichsluftfahrtministerium

23 The former Neudecker Wollkämmerei & Kammgarnspinnerei AG works at Nejdek/Neudeck in the Czech Republic.

24 We know this because both Ernst Heinkel and Richard Vogt described the meeting in their memoirs.

25 ADIK 129/620 BMW Nr. 579 Abteilung: EZS Niederschrift der Besprechung am 1. Juli 43 bei MTT-A.G. Augsburg

26 ADRC/T-2 2009/87 Messerschmitt Technischer Bericht Nr.

90/43 Leistungsvergleich von TL-Jägern 3.7.43

27 IWM Speer FD4355/45 Vol. 4/578 Messerschmitt Anschrift: BmL 262. Betrifft: Projektübergabe; Änderungen und Ergänzun-gen 12.7.43

28 IWM Milch 22/6401 GL-Besprechung am Freitag, dem 9. Juli 1943, 10 Uhr unter Vorsitz des Generalfeldmarschalls Milch im Reichsluftfahrtministerium

29 ADRC/T-2 3754/1038 Weitere Arbeiten an der Me 262. Besprechung bei Herrn Prof Messerschmitt am 13.7.43

30 ADRC/T-2 3397/231 Messerschmitt Kontrollbericht Nr. 93/43 Betr.: Me 262 V5 Werk-Nr. 262 0005 PC+UE 4.8.43

31 ADRC/T-2 3397/229 Messerschmitt Kontrollbericht Nr. 94/43 Betr.: Me 262 V1 Werk-Nr. 262 0001 PC+UA 5.8.43

32 ADIK 4079/350 Messerschmitt Elektroakustische Peilung Versuchs-Bericht Nr. 000-18-A-43 II.Teilbericht 16.7.43

33 ADRC/T-2 3754/1041 Messerschmitt Besprechungsnieder-schrift Me 262 Nr. 26 15.3.44

34 ADRC/T-2 2656/786 Messerschmitt Monatsbericht Juli 1943 7. August 1943

35 ADRC/T-2 3397/225 Messerschmitt Kontrollbericht Nr. 98/43 Betr.: Startunfall mit Flugzeug Me 262 V4 WNr. 26200004 PC+UD mit zwei Triebwerken Jumo T1 10.8.43

36 IWM Milch 23/6831 GL-Besprechung am Dienstag, dem 27. Juli 1943, 10 Uhr, unter Vorsitz des Generalfeldmarschalls Milch im Reichsluftfahrtministerium

37 IWM Milch 24/7197 St/GL-Besprechung unter Vorsitz von Generalfeldmarschall Milch am Dienstag, dem 17. August 1943, 10 Uhr im Reichsluftfahrtministerium

38 IWM GDC 10/5370 Aerodynamische Versuchsanstalt Göttingen Gesamtmodell Me 262 mit vergrössertem Flügel und durchhän-gendem Rumpf by Scherer 31.7.1943

39 IWM Speer FD4355/45 Vol.4/525 Entwicklungsgeschichte 262 2.8.43

40 IWM Speer FD4355/45 Vol.4/524 Sonderbewaffnung unserer Jäger und Zerstörer 4.8.43

41 ADRC/T-2 2656/815 Messerschmitt Monatsbericht August 1943 8. September 1943

42 ADRC/T-2 2656/786 Messerschmitt Monatsbericht Juli 1943 7. August 1943

43 ADRC/T-2 2012/468 Messerschmitt Me 262 Ausführung A2 Jäger u. Jabo, Augsburg, den 8.8.1943

44 IWM Milch 38/4670 E-Besprechung unter Vorsitz von General-feldmarschall Milch am Dienstag, dem 10. August 1943, 10 Uhr im Reichsluftfahrtministerium

45 ADRC/T-2 2656/815 Messerschmitt Monatsbericht August 1943 8. September 1943

## C5. HITLER AND THE ME 262 FIGHTER-BOMBER, AUG–DEC 1943

1 IWM Milch 23/6488 GL-Besprechung unter Vorsitz von Generalfeldmarschall Milch am Dienstag, dem 3. August 1943, 10 Uhr im Reichsluftfahrtministerium

2 IWM Milch 24/7303 GL-Besprechung unter Vorsitz von Generalfeldmarschall Milch am Freitag, dem 13. August 1943, 10 Uhr im Reichsluftfahrtministerium

3 United States Strategic Bombing Survey Aircraft Division, Messerschmitt AG Augsburg, Germany Over-All-Report Second Edition January 1947

4 Oberbayerische Forschungsanstalt = Upper Bavarian Research Institute, a codename so bland and meaningless that even by the end of the war Allied intelligence had not guessed its true meaning. Official Messerschmitt documents from this point onwards are increasingly attributed to the Oberbayerische Forchungsanstalt Oberammergau. For the sake of clarity and consistency, the documents listed in these footnotes which bear the 'Obb Forschungsanstalt Oberammergau' mark are attributed instead simply to Messerschmitt.

5   IWM GDC 15/650 Messerschmitt Vorschlag einer Höhenjäger-
    entwicklung auf der Basis Me 109/209, July 26, 1943

6   IWM Milch 24/7066 GL-Besprechung unter Vorsitz von
    Generalfeldmarschall Milch am Freitag, dem 20. August 1943 10
    Uhr im Reichsluftfahrtministerium

7   IWM Milch 38/4610 Entwicklungs-Besprechung unter Vorsitz
    von Generalfeldmarschall Milch am Freitag, dem 27.8.1943, 10
    Uhr im Reichsluftfahrtministerium

8   This point would perhaps have particularly stuck in Hoffmann's
    mind, since he had joined C-E 2 on May 7, 1943, less than three
    week's before Milch's decision to retire the Bf 109 and replace it
    with the Me 262.

9   ADRC/T-2 3754/1041 Messerschmitt Besprechungsnieder-
    schrift Muster: Me 262. Betrifft: Stand der Arbeiten, 15.3.44

10  The issue of aircraft names seems to have been a contentious
    one, highlighted earlier by Lippisch's demand that his rocket
    aircraft's designation be given a prefix based on his own name:
    'Li 163'. Certainly, Kurt Tank of Focke-Wulf had been allowed
    to give his company's aircraft a 'Ta' prefix, i.e. Ta 152, Ta 153 and
    Ta 154. On internal Messerschmitt company documents the Bf
    109 is nearly always referred to as the Me 109, and the Bf 110
    as the Me 110. While it does not seem to have gained much
    currency initially, it would appear that at some point during
    1944 Messerschmitt's suggestion that company prefixes be
    removed was applied, albeit somewhat haphazardly. Documents
    from this period increasingly refer to aircraft types by their four
    digit RLM code, 8-XXX, i.e. 8-109, 8-190, 8-262 etc. without
    the manufacturer's prefix, i.e. Bf/Me 109, Fw 190, Me 262.
    The '8-' indicated an aircraft, whereas jet engines, for example,
    received a six digit '109-XXX' code, i.e. 109-003, 109-004 or
    109-011. Precisely what advantage or benefit was conferred by
    removing the company prefix is unclear.

11  IWM Speer FD4355/45 Vol. 1/102 Entwurf für Besprechung
    mit der Führer Hauptquartier am 7.9.43

12  IWM Speer FD4355/45 Vol. 4/441 Fernschreiben Berliner
    Büro zur sofortigen Weiterleitung an Herrn Voigt. Betr.:
    Sitzung—über Ein-TL-Jäger

13  ADRC/T-2 2012/270 Messerschmitt Me 262 Verwendung-
    smöglichkeiten Projektbaubeschreibung Anhang zur Beschrei-
    bung v. 10.8.43, 11.9.43

14  Though, as with the Projektübergabe documents, some of the
    individual pages appear to have been replaced with updated
    versions bearing a new date—making it rather difficult to defin-
    itively date any of the ten descriptions. Suffice to say that as of
    September 11, 1943, they were all regarded as 'current'.

15  The pilot, for example, is depicted with hair rather than a flying
    helmet, and the linework used to depict the aircraft itself is
    lighter and finer.

16  TNA DSIR 23/15140 Interrogation Report No. 16. Inter-
    rogation of Dr Herbert Voigt on the Flutter Organisation of
    Messerschmitt A.G., June 19, 1945.

17  Evidently the test specimen used on this occasion was the wing-
    less and heavily modified fuselage of the Me 262 V4, which had
    been wrecked three months earlier on July 25, 1943.

18  ADRC/T-2 2486/931 Messerschmitt Me 262 V1 PC+UA, Me
    262 V3 PC+UC Rollstreckenvergleich mit und ohne Innenvor-
    flügel by Lindner, September 1943

19  ADRC/T-2 2439/915 Messerschmitt Me 262 V3 PC+UC
    Hochgeschwindigkeitsflüge by Lindner, September 1943

20  ADRC/T-2 2113/111 Messerschmitt Querruderkräfte—Weich-
    heit u. Rollwendigkeit Me 262 V3, October 1943

21  ADRC/T-2 2478/525 Messerschmitt Me 262 V3 PC+UC
    Druckverteilungsmessung by Lindner, October 1943

22  ADRC/T-2 2478/492 Messerschmitt Me 262 V1 PC+UA
    Abkippuntersuchungen by Wendel, October 1943

23  ADRC/T-2 2627/811 Messerschmitt Belastung aus Bugradstoss
    an Rumpfspitze Me 262 V5, October 1943

24  ADRC/T-2 2040/503 Junkers Anhang: Motoren-Entwicklung

(Otto Maderwerk) May 14, 1945

25  ADRC/T-2 2466/150 Messerschmitt Flugbericht Nr. 986/56
    Me 262 V6 VI+AA by Baur, October 1943. See also ADRC
    2446/557 Messerschmitt Me 262 V6 VI+AA Fortsetzung der
    Vorflügelerprobung by Lindner, October 1943

26  ADRC/T-2 2478/699 Messerschmitt Me 262 V6 VI+AA by
    Lindner, October 1943

27  ADRC/T-2 2379/841 Messerschmitt Standschub Me 262
    V6 mit Ju TL 109.004 B-1 und 2 Borsig Startraketen by Jung,
    October 1943

28  ADRC/T-2 3754/1041 Messerschmitt Besprechungsnieder-
    schrift Muster: Me 262. Betrifft: Stand der Arbeiten, 15.3.44

29  IWM Milch 63/6016 Besprechung beim Reichsmarschall am
    Donnerstag, dem 28. Oktober 1943, 12 Uhr in Carinhall

30  The largest city in central Ukraine.

31  IWM Milch 39/5106 E-Besprechung am Freitag, dem 29. Okto-
    ber 1943, 10 Uhr unter Vorsitz des Generalfeldmarschalls Milch
    im Reichsluftfahrtministerium

32  ADRC/T-2 2221/749 Messerschmitt Me 262 Erprobungsberi-
    cht Nr. 35 vom 4.10.-14.11.43

33  IWM Milch 63/5961 Die Besprechung beim Reichsmarshall
    am Dienstag, dem 2. November 1943, 10.45 Uhr in den Messer-
    schmitt-Werken in Regensburg

34  A reference to the somewhat indiscriminate SE Action army
    conscription programme.

35  IWM Milch 39/5024 GL/E-Besprechung unter Vorsitz von
    Generalfeldmarschall Milch am Mittwoch, dem 3.11.1943, 10
    Uhr, im Reichsluftfahrtministerium

36  IWM Milch 63/5922 Besprechung beim Reichsmarschall am
    Donnerstag, dem 4. November 1943, 11 Uhr in den Junkers-
    Werken zu Dessau

37  ADRC/T-2 2040/503 Junkers Anhang: Motoren-Entwicklung
    (Otto Maderwerk) May 14, 1945

38  IWM Milch 41/5732 E-Besprechung am Freitag, dem 18.
    Februar 1944, 10 Uhr unter Vorsitz des Generalfeldmarschalls
    Milch im Reichsluftfahrtministerium

39  ADRC/T-2 2040/503 Junkers Anhang: Motoren-Entwicklung
    (Otto Maderwerk) May 14, 1945

40  Just as the first Me 163 rocketplane prototype was known as the
    Me 163 V4 because three prototypes of a piston-engine liaison
    aircraft designated Bf 163 had previously been planned, so the
    first Me 209 was the V5 because there had been four prototypes
    of the original Me 209 aircraft back in the late 1930s.

41  IWM Milch 26/8087 GL-Besprechung unter Vorsitz von Gener-
    alfeldmarschall Milch am Dienstag, dem 9. November 1943, 10
    Uhr im Reichsluftfahrtministerium

42  With the 'stage 3' extreme high-altitude fighter now being
    developed independently by Blohm & Voss, Messerschmitt
    had contrived to developed the 'stage 1' machine—a relatively
    straightforward conversion of the standard Bf 109 G.

43  IWM Milch 39/4922 E-Besprechung am Freitag, dem 12.
    November 1943, 10 Uhr unter Vorsitz des Generalfeldmarschalls
    Milch im Reichsluftfahrtministerium

44  ADRC/T-2 2082/201 Messerschmitt Erprobungsbericht Nr. 36
    15.11.-12.12.43

45  ADIK 153/185 Kommando der E'Stellen Entwicklungs-Auf-
    trage für Me 262 13.10.44

46  IWM Milch 64/6630 Besprechung beim Reichsmarschall am 23.
    November 1943, 12 Uhr in Carinhall

47  ADIK 157/387 Kommando der Erprobungsstelle der Luftwaffe,
    Programm für die Vorführung in Insterburg 25.11.43

48  ADIK 157/398 Kommando der Erprobungsstelle der Luftwaffe
    Rechlin, Hauptmann Blecher Fliegerhorst Interburg 22.11.43

49  ADRC/T-2 2082/201 Messerschmitt Erprobungsbericht Nr. 36
    15.11.-12.12.43

50  IWM Milch 26/7914 GL-Besprechung am Dienstag, dem 30.
    November 1943, 10 Uhr, unter Vorsitz des Generalfeldmarschalls
    Milch im Reichsluftfahrtministerium

51 It was, in fact, Milch who had said this himself—see above.

52 IWM Milch 31/514 St/GL/-Ruk-Besprechung unter dem Vorsitz des Generalfeldmarschalls Milch am Mittwoch, dem 1. Dezember 1943, 10 Uhr im Reichsluftfahrtministerium

53 IWM Milch 39/4844 E-Besprechung unter Vorsitz von Generalfeldmarschall Milch am Freitag, dem 3. Dezember 1943, 10 Uhr, im Reichsluftfahrtministerium

54 IWM Milch 27/8742 St/GL-Besprechung am Dienstag, dem 7. Dezember 1943, 10 Uhr, unter Vorsitz des Generalmajors Vorwald im Reichsluftfahrtministerium

55 ADRC/T-2 2082/201 Messerschmitt Erprobungsbericht Nr. 36 15.11.-12.12.43

56 ADRC/T-2 2402/902 Messerschmitt Start- und Landemessung Me 262 V6 by Jung, November 1943. See also ADIK 4079/147.

57 ADRC/T-2 3397/0195 Messerschmitt Kontrollbericht Nr. 181/43 November 26, 1943

58 ADIK 153/185 Kommando der E'Stellen Entwicklungs-Aufträge für Me 262 13.10.44

59 ADRC/T-2 2029/616 Kommando der Erprobungsstellen Nr.: 22150/45 g. Erprobung der Me 262, January 15, 1945

60 ADRC/T-2 3397/0183 Messerschmitt Kontrollbericht Nr. 203/43 December 21, 1943

61 ADRC/T-2 2019/941 Messerschmitt Me 262 Erprobungsbericht Nr. 37 vom 13.12.-16.1.43

62 ADRC/MAP 5003/542 Messerschmitt Elektroakustische Peilung Versuchs-Berict Nr. S 02/44 29.9.44

63 ADRC/T-2 2480/497 Messerschmitt Erprobungsbericht Me 262 V7, VI+AB by Lindner, December 1943

64 ADRC/MAP 5014/1 Messerschmitt Strömungsaufnahmen am Kabinenablauf Me 262 7.1.44

## C6. INTO PRODUCTION, JAN–APR 1944

1 ADRC/T-2 2263/872 Messerschmitt Baubeschreibungen der Weiterentwicklungen der Me 262 (mit neuern vergrössertem Rumpf) P 1099 (mehrsitzige schwere Jäger) P 1100 (mehrsitzige Bomber), 22.3.44

2 ADRC/T-2 3754/1041 Messerschmitt Besprechungsniederschrift Muster: Me 262. Betrifft: Stand der Arbeiten, 15.3.44

3 ADRC/T-2 3384/1134 Messerschmitt Heimatschützer I und II by Althoff, January 1944

4 IWM Milch 32/1166 St/GL-Ruk-Besprechung unter dem Vorsitz des Herrn Generalfeldmarschalls Milch am Mittwoch, dem 5. Januar 1944, 11½ Uhr im Reichsluftfahrtministerium

5 ADRC/T-2 3397/0170 Messerschmitt Kontrollbericht Nr. 9/44 Betr.: Beschuss der Me 262 V9 mit 4 MK 108, 10.1.44

6 ADRC/MAP 5035/301 Wochenbericht vom 1. bis 7.1.44

7 In late April 1944, the Rechlin station demanded an Me 262 test fuselage with which to resolved serious concerns about the aircraft's FuG 16 radio system. This was delivered before or during the week of May 8-13, 1944. See ADRC/MAP 5035/131 Erprobungsstelle der Luftwaffe Rechlin Abteilung E 4 Wochenbericht v. 8.-13.5.1944. The earliest Rechlin report to mention Me 262 flight testing, after the January report, is for the week of June 10-16, when an Erprobungskommandos Lärz pilot made a 13-minute flight in one. Three other examples are mentioned but were evidently not flown. See ADRC/MAP 5035/86. By the week of June 17-23, Rechlin had five Me 262s—WNr. 130018, 130163, 130168, 130172 and 130188. See ADRC/MAP 5035/75.

8 IWM Milch 40/5499 E-Besprechung unter Vorsitz von Generalfeldmarschall Milch am Freitag, dem 14. Januar 1944, 10 Uhr im Reichsluftfahrtministerium

9 At the time of writing this book, Henckels of Solingen—a company founded in 1731—was still trading.

10 IWM Milch 27/8511 St/GL-Besprechung unter Vorsitz von Generalfeldmarschall Milch am Dienstag, dem 18. Januar 1944, 10 Uhr im Reichsluftfahrtministerium

11 IWM Milch 32/1056 St/GL/-RuK-Besprechung unter dem Vorsitz des Herrn Generalfeldmarschalls Milch am Mittwoch, dem 19. Januar 1944, 10 Uhr

12 Presumably he means that Cambeis must establish a single factory for 004 assembly.

13 'A4' was the original designation of the V-2 long-range surface-to-surface missile.

14 ADRC/T-2 3397/0180 Messerschmitt Kontrollbericht Nr. 26/44 Betr.: Me 262 V9 Werk Nr. 130004 VI+AD, 26.1.44

15 ADRC/MAP 5035/360 Schwerpunkterprobungsbericht Nr. 5/44 der Erprobungsstelle Tarnewitz für die Zeit vom 30.1.-5.2.1944

16 ADRC/T-2 2749/691 Messerschmitt Strömungsaufnahmen am Kabinenablauf Me 262 by Tilch, January 1944

17 ADIK 4066/84 Messerschmitt Temperaturmessungen an der Flügelunterseite zum Triebwerksraum an Me 262 by Kraus, January 1944

18 ADRC/T-2 3604/1439 Messerschmitt Versuchsprogramm Abwurfversuche Me 262—1. Teilprogramm 14.2.44

19 ADRC/MAP 5026/121 Messerschmitt Abt.: Büro-Darmstadt Aktenvermerk Betr.: Hochgeschwindigkeitsentwicklung Me 262 Bericht für die Zeit von 10.1. bis 17.3.1944. 22.3.44

20 ADRC/T-2 3604/1439 Messerschmitt Versuchsprogramm für die Abwurfversuche mit DFS-Gleitbombenmodellen 3.2.44

21 ADRC/T-2 3397/0178 Messerschmitt Kontrollbericht Nr. 40/44 Betr.: Beschuss der Me 262 V10 mit 4 MK 108 8.2.44

22 ADRC/MAP 5003/542 Messerschmitt Elektroakustische Peilung Versuchs-Bericht Nr. S 02/44 29.9.44

23 ADRC/T-2 2019/921 Messerschmitt Me 262 Erprobungsbericht Nr. 39 vom 7.2.-12.3.1944

24 ADRC/T-2 3754/1039 Geh. Nr. 3766 Besprechungsniederschrift Betr.: Me 262—Vorrichtungsfragen 15.2.44

25 ADRC/T-2 3754/1053 Messerschmitt Besprechungsniederschrift Betr.: Änderungen an der ersten Maschine Me 262 17.2.44

26 IWM Milch 41/5732 E-Besprechung am Freitag, dem 18. Februar 1944, 10 Uhr unter Vorsitz des Generalfeldmarschalls Milch im Reichsluftfahrtministerium

27 Forty Jumo 004 A-0s, four Jumo 004 B-0s, fifteen Jumo 004 B-1 prototypes and forty-two Jumo 004 B-1 pre-production engines.

28 These were presumably fitted to the Me 262 V1, V3, V5, V6, V7, V8, V9 and V10, though the V8 and V10 had not yet flown.

29 ADRC/MAP 5026/121 Messerschmitt Aktenvermerk Betr.: Hochgeschwindigkeitsentwicklung Me 262 Bericht für die Zeit vom 10.1. bis 17.3.1944

30 United States Strategic Bombing Survey Aircraft Division, Messerschmitt AG Augsburg, Germany Over-All-Report Second Edition January 1947

31 IWM Milch 28/8918 St/GL-Besprechung unter Vorsitz von Generalfeldmarschall Milch am Dienstag, dem 29.2.1944, 10 Uhr, im Reichsluftfahrtministerium

32 Nuremberg Trials Project transcript for NMT 2: Milch Case. http://nuremberg.law.harvard.edu/transcripts/2-transcript-for-nmt-2-milch-case?seq=366

33 ADRC/T-2 2006/2 Report of Technical Intelligence Survey Messerschmitt A. G. Oberammergau, Germany 31 July 1945

34 ADRC/MAP 5026/121 Messerschmitt Aktenvermerk Betr.: Hochgeschwindigkeitsentwicklung Me 262 Bericht für die Zeit vom 10.1. bis 17.3.1944

35 ADRC/T-2 3754/1041 Messerschmitt Besprechungsniederschrift Muster: Me 262. Betr.: Stand der Arbeiten, 15.3.44

36 ADIK 42/6128 Bericht Nr. 55 über die Entwicklungsbesprechung vom 17.3.1944

37 ADRC/MAP 5026/121 Messerschmitt Aktenvermerk Betr.: Hochgeschwindigkeitsentwicklung Me 262 Bericht für die Zeit vom 10.1. bis 17.3.1944

38 ADRC/MAP 5026/122 Messerschmitt Aktenvermerk Betr.: Hochgeschwindigkeitsentwicklung Me 262 Bericht für die Zeit

vom 18.3. bis 5.4.1944

39 ADRC/MAP 2019/883 Messerschmitt Me 262 Erprobungsbericht Nr. 40 vom 13.3.-22.4.1944

40 ADRC/T-2 2028/276 Messerschmitt Me 262 Panzerflugzeug Projektbaubeschreibung 22.3.1944. See also ADRC/T-2 2277/521 Messerschmitt Me 410 Panzerflugzeug Projekt-Kurzbeschreibung 23.3.1944

41 ADRC/T-2 2251/1036 Messerschmitt P 1099 (Me 262 mit vergrössertem Rumpf) Baubeschreibung für Jäger (zweisitzig) 22.3.1944

42 ADRC/T-2 2616/508 Messerschmitt P 1100 (Me 262 mit vergrössertem Rumpf) Baubeschreibungen für Bomber 22.3.1944

43 ADRC/MAP 2019/883 Messerschmitt Me 262 Erprobungsbericht Nr. 40 vom 13.3.-22.4.1944

## C7. FROM FIGHTER-BOMBER TO BOMBER, APR-JUN 1944

1 ADRC/T-2 2666/718 Messerschmitt Rüstzustände der Me 262 C-1 Maschine, March 1944

2 ADRC/MAP 5026/122 Messerschmitt Aktenvermerk Betr.: Hochgeschwindigkeitsentwicklung Me 262 Bericht für die Zeit vom 18.3. bis 5.4.1944

3 ADRC/MAP 5026/282 Messerschmitt Me 262 Projektübergabe V (Hochgeschwindigkeitsentwickung) 3.4.44

4 IWM Milch 29/9500 St/GL-Besprechung unter Vorsitz von Generalfeldmarschall Milch am Freitag, dem 7. April 1944, 10 Uhr im Reichsluftfahrtministerium

5 IWM Speer FD.3049/49 Führerprotokolle 1942-1945 6. u. 7. April 44

6 ADRC/T-2 2019/883 Messerschmitt Me 262 Erprobungsbericht Nr. 40 13.3.-22.4.44

7 ADIK 153/185 Kommando der E'Stellen Entwicklungs-Auftrage für Me 262 13.10.44

8 IWM Speer FD 4355/45-400 Vol. 1 Messerschmitt an Cambeis, 20.4.1944

9 ADRC/T-2 2029/616 Kommando der Erprobungsstellen Nr.: 22140/45 g. Erprobung der Me 262 15.1.45

10 IWM Milch 10/5470 Reichsminister für Rüstung und Kriegsproduktion Jägerstab, Schnellbericht 25.4.44 über die Besprechung von 10-12.15 Uhr

11 IWM Milch 10/5456 Reichsminister für Rüstung und Kriegsproduktion Jägerstab, Schnellbericht 27.4.44 über die Besprechung von 10-12 Uhr

12 IWM Milch 42/6104 Entwicklungsbesprechung vom 28.4.1944 unter Vorsitz von Generalfeldmarschall Milch, zeitweise Generalmajor Vorwald

13 TNA AIR 48/2 USSBS Strategic Bombing of German Aircraft Industry November 1945

14 ADRC/T-2 2093/409 Messerschmitt Projektübergabe Me 262 D-1 (Heimatschützer II) 1.5.44

15 ADRC/T-2 2110/358 Aerodynamische Versuchsanstalt Göttingen Institut Windkanäle Gesamtmodell Me 262, Sechskomponentenmessungen mit geänderter Kabinenform, Stabilisierungsflächen und Anhängelasten 8.5.1944

16 ADRC/T-2 2053/284 BMW Messungen am Rumpfende und Leitwerk der Zelle Me 262 bei Antrieb mit R-Gerät 8.5.44

17 ADRC/T-2 2057/739 Messerschmitt Me 262 mit 2 x HeS 011-Triebwerken 12.5.44

18 ADRC/T-2 2028/293 Messerschmitt Me 262 Panzerflugzeug II 13.5.44

19 ADRC/T-2 2019/871 Messerschmitt Me 262 Erprobungsbericht Nr. 41 23.4.-20.5.44

20 ADRC/T-2 3397/168 FKV—Lechfeld Kontrollbericht "L" Nr. 20/44 22.5.44

21 IWM Milch 64/6826 Besprechung beim Reichsmarschall am 23. Mai 1944, 11 Uhr im Führerspeiseraum der SS-Kaserne Obersalzberg

22 IWM Milch 64/6901 Besprechung beim Reichsmarschall am 24. Mai, 1944, 11 Uhr

23 Presumably a reference to the V8, which was the pattern machine for the production series.

24 IWM Milch 64/6719 Göring Besprechung, 25. Mai, 1944

25 ADRC/T-2 2019/862 Messerschmitt Me 262 Erprobungsbericht Nr. 42 21.5.-7.6.44

26 NARA T321-59/0126 Kommando der Erprobungsstellen der Luftwaffe Brb. Nr. 1000/44 g.Kdos. Rechlin, den 27.5.1944

27 IWM Milch 64/6323 Göring Besprechung, 29. Mai, 1944 (a Monday). Hitler's decision appears to have been made at the end of the preceding week, since Göring sent a telegram to all those concerned at 10pm on May 27, the Saturday, giving them the gist. See AHB6-146/5664.

28 TNA FO 1078/71 FD.3353/45 Vol. 65 Discussions with the Führer between the 19th and 22nd June 1944. 23.6.1944

29 ADRC/T-2 2019/862 Messerschmitt Me 262 Erprobungsbericht Nr. 42 21.5.-7.6.44

30 Ibid.

31 TNA AIR 48/2 USSBS Strategic Bombing of German Aircraft Industry November 1945

32 ADRC/T-2 2043/687 Behelfsaufklärer Me 262 (2 x Rb 50 x 30) gez 30.5.44 Schmitt

33 ADIK 151/332 Messerschmitt Me 262 Protokoll Nr. 620/44 Betrifft: Aufklärer 2.6.44

34 ADRC/T-2 2043/682 Me 262 A-4 Aufklärer (A)

35 IWM Milch 29/9249 St/GL-Besprechung unter dem Vorsitz des Generalmajors Vorwald am Freitag, dem 2. Juni 1944, 11 Uhr, im Reichsluftfahrtministerium

36 ADRC/T-2 2012/689 Messerschmitt Besprechung am Montag 5.6.1944 über Programm Me 262 in Oberammergau

37 Period documents do regularly refer to this rack as the 'Wikingerschiff' or 'Viking ship'—undoubtedly because its aerodynamic fairing did indeed give it the appearance of a Viking longship.

38 ADRC/T-2 2045/458 Messerschmitt Me 262 A1 Schnellkämpfer Nachtrag zur Baubeschreibung vom 10.8.43, 6.6.1944

## C8. TEETHING PAINS, JUN-SEP 1944

1 ADRC/T-2 2019/862 Messerschmitt Me 262 Erprobungsbericht Nr. 42 21.5.-7.6.44

2 ADRC/T-2 2012/691 Messerschmitt Versuchsprogramm Me 262 8.6.1944

3 ADRC/T-2 3754/1088 Messerschmitt Aktenvermerk Betr.: Besichtigung gesprungener Panzerscheiben 12.6.1944

4 ADRC/MAP 5035/85 Erprobungsstelle Rechlin Betr.: Wochenbericht des Erprobungskommandos Lärz vom 10.6. bis 16.6.44

5 ADRC/MAP 5035/74 Erprobungsstelle Rechlin Betr.: Wochenbericht des Erprobungskommandos Lärz vom 17.6. bis 23.6.44

6 ADRC/T-2 2479/405 Der Reichsminister der Luftfahrt GL/C-E 2 Festigkeitsprüfstelle Az.89 / C-E 2 / FPV Nr. 38 / 44 g.Kdos. Protokoll Festigkeitsvorschriften DB-PTL 021 Besprechung am 14.6.44 in Backnang. PTL appears to have been short for Propeller-Turbinen-Luftstrahl—a turboprop engine—in the same way that TL was short for Turbinen-Luftstrahl—a turbojet engine.

7 ADIK 151/330 Erprobungsstelle Rechlin E 7 492/44 Niederschrift über die Besprechung am 17.6.44 in Rechlin

8 ADIK 153/185 Kommando der E'Stellen Entwicklungs-Auftrage für Me 262 13.10.44

9 ADRC/T-2 3754/1028 Messerschmitt Besprechungsniederschrift über Besprechung am 19./20.6.44 in Oberammergau. Betr.: Bombenzielanlage Me 262

10 Unfortunately, no drawings are known to survive showing how the seated bombardier arrangement for the Me 262 would have

worked. Presumably they would have sat behind the pilot in a similar arrangement to that of the later Me 262 night fighter.

11 IWM Milch 53/1087 Der Generalinspekteur der Luftwaffe, Berlin, den X Juli 1944

12 IWM Milch 12/6941 Bericht über die Me 262-Besprechung am 22.6.44 unter Hauptdienstleiter Saur

13 ADRC/MAP 5026/330 Messerschmitt Besprechungsniederschrift Betr.: Me 262, verstärkte Pfeilform 23.6.44

14 ADRC/T-2 2046/276 Messerschmitt Versuchs-Bericht Nr. 262 08 L 44 Nachweis der 1000km/h 28.6.44

15 ADRC/T-2 3754/1032 Messerschmitt Me 262 Besprechungsniederschrift Nr. 7 v. 28.6.44

16 ADRC/T-2 2012/668 Versuchsprogramm Me 262 28.6.44

17 IWM Milch 29/9179 GL-Besprechung unter dem Vorsitz des Generalfeldmarschalls Milch am Freitag, dem 30. Juni 1944, 11 Uhr, im Reichsluftfahrtministerium. It should be noted that several of the speakers during this meeting, such as Eick, Holbeck and Blecher and are difficult to identify. Their surnames are provided in the stenographer's transcript but not their first names, ranks or titles. Even the surname spellings are suspect, since verifiable name spelling errors are particularly common in these documents.

18 IWM Milch 9/5408 Jägerstab-Besprechung am Sonnabend, dem 1. Juli 1944, 10 Uhr unter Vorsitz von Herrn Lange

19 TNA AIR 48/2 USSBS Strategic Bombing of German Aircraft Industry November 1945

20 ADRC/MAP 5026/155 Messerschmitt Aktennotiz Betr.: Projekt Me 262 mit Pfeilflügel 30.6.44

21 ADRC/T-2 2012/663 Messerschmitt Besprechungsniederschrift 3.7.44

22 IWM Milch 9/5139 Jägerstab-Besprechung am Donnerstag, 6. Juli 1944, 10 Uhr

23 It has been suggested that the Me 262 A-2 differed from the A-1 in other ways—such as incorporating a stronger nose structure to allow heavier loads to be carried—but the Me 262 A-1 and A-2 shared a common parts list, see for example ADRC/T-2 3255/754, and a common handbook, see for example ADRC/T-2 8181/2696. Apart from leaving the factory with two MK 108 cannon instead of four and having its bomb racks pre-installed, the A-2 appears to have been physically identical to the A-1. That said, Messerschmitt certainly did have plans to adapt the A-2 more specifically for the bomber role—see ADRC/T-2 3754/1005—but these appear never to have been enacted.

24 It would appear that the Me 262 A-3 was originally known as the Me 262 A-2/U1. The basis for this hypothesis is Me 262 Protokoll Nr. 49, dated September 14, 1944, which appears on ADRC/MAP 5027/265. This document concerns armour for the Me 262 and lists three types—the "A-1 (Jäger)", the "A-2 (Schnellkämpfer)" and the "A-3 (mit Lotfe-Kanzel)", except it is clear that in the latter case someone has modified an 'A-2' to become an 'A-3' by hand and crossed out an accompanying 'U 1'.

25 ADRC/T-2 3997/583 Focke-Wulf Entwicklungsmitteilung TL-Jäger 11.7.44

26 TNA DSIR 23/14860 MAP Farren Mission to German, Appendix II He 162

27 ADRC/T-2 2101/195 Messerschmitt Abt. Flugerprobung Me 262 Abwurfwaffe 9.7.44

28 The Lechfeld test summary report appears to have been printed with a different serial number, 1X000X, with the second digit then being overwritten by hand with a '7' and the sixth digit overwritten with a '6', making 170006. Test pilot Fritz Wendel's separate flight test report on the reconnaissance prototype, dated July 20, refers to it as Werk-Nr. 130007—the Me 262 S2. The Lechfeld test summary report explicitly states that the S2 made no flights from July 6 to July 19. It seems likely, therefore, that 170006 was indeed the reconnaissance test vehicle and Wendel was simply mistaken in referring to the aircraft as 130007—the

latter never being converted for use as a reconnaissance machine.

29 BAL appears to have stood for Bauaufsichtsleitung—construction supervision—and was the short for used for the Bauaufsichten des Reichsluftfahrtministerium, the Luftwaffe's quality control and acceptance organisation.

30 ADRC/T-2 2189/1140 Messerschmitt Me 262 Erprobungsbericht Nr. 45 6.7.-19.7.44

31 ADRC/T-2 3348/591 Messerschmitt Aktenvermerk Vorbesprechung für die Musterbesichtigung Me 262 B-1 im Flughafen Wenzendorf am 18 und 19.7.44. 12.7.44

32 ADRC/T-2 Messerschmitt Beuteilung der TL-Triebwerke bei Nacht 21.7.44

33 ADRC/MAP 5041/285 Messerschmitt Protokoll Betrifft: Einbau von Funkmessgeräten in Me 262 18.7.44

34 ADRC/T-2 2346/83 Messerschmitt Deckblatt zum Ladeplan Me 262 A-1a 18.10.44

35 ADRC/MAP 5026/331 Messerschmitt Aktennotiz Betr.: Hochgeschwindigkeitsentwicklung Me 262 Besprechung bei Herrn Prof. Messerschmitt am 24.7.44

36 GDC 15/378 Messerschmitt Me 262 Erprobungsbericht Nr. 46 20.7.-2.8.44

37 ADRC/MAP 5026/333 Messerschmitt Aktenvermerk Betrifft: Hochgeschwindigkeitsentwicklung Besprechung bei Herrn Prof. Messerschmitt am 26.7.44

38 ADRC/MAP 5035/18 E-Stelle Rechlin E 7 Schwerpunktsbericht für die Zeit vom 3.-8. Jul 1944

39 ADIK 147/743 SSD LBKW 0323 18.7.44 (1630) an KDE Rechlin

40 ADRC/MAP 5027/249 Bericht über den Einbau der TSA-2—Anlage in die Me 262, Werk-Nr. 130 164, Rechlin, den 31. Juli 1944

41 147/729 GL/C-E 7 Niederschrift über die Zielgeräte-Besprechung bei GL/C-E 7 am 27.7.44

42 BA-MA R3/1749-162 Der Reichsminister für Rüstung und Kriegsproduktion, Erlass, Bildung des Rüstungsstabes 1.8.1944

43 BA-MA R3/1749-126 Entwicklungshauptkommission Flugzeuge An Chef TLR Betrifft: Organisation der EHK 22.12.1944

44 IWM Milch 9/4726 Rüstungsstab-Besprechung unter Vorsitz von Hauptdienstleiter Saur am Mittwoch, dem 2. August 1944, 10 Uhr

45 GDC 15/378 Messerschmitt Me 262 Erprobungsbericht Nr. 46 20.7.-2.8.44

46 TNA AIR 48/2 USSBS Strategic Bombing of German Aircraft Industry November 1945

47 GDC 15/382 Messerschmitt Me 262 Erprobungsbericht Nr. 47 3.8.1944-16.8.1944

48 Major Schenck was the leader of Me 262 bomber test unit Kommando Schenck.

49 ADIK 117/0731 Focke-Wulf Vorläufige techn. Bedingungen für einen Schlechtwetter- Tag- und Nachtjäger 4.8.44

50 ADRC/MAP 5041/281 der Sonderkommission für Funkmesstechnik in der Hauptkommission Elektrotechnik Aktenvermerk über die Besprechung am 5. August 1944

51 ADRC 3545/1020 Messerschmitt Me 262 Flugbericht Nr. L 83/82 7.8.44

52 ADRC/MAP 5027/251 Messerschmitt Me 262 Protokoll Nr. 39 Betrifft: Einbau TSA 2 D und BT. 11.8.44

53 ADRC/T-2 2346/456 Messerschmitt Regensburg Baulos—Aufteilung Me 609 lt. Prgr. 226 v. 15.7.44. 11.8.44

54 Quite why the Me 609 number was applied specifically to Regensburg Me 262 production is unclear. Perhaps it was intended, in order to confuse Allied intelligence, to imply that the aircraft was a Bf 109 derivative of some sort—which would make sense given the factory's reputation as a 109 producer. It is similarly unclear why there were large gaps in the allocated serial numbers. The 14 blocks of numbers are given on the August 11, 1944, document (see note 50) as follows: 500001 to 500100, 500101 to 500104, 500199 to 500280, 500422 to

500435, 500436 to 500561, 500722 to 500795, 500796 to 500889, 500908 to 501046, 501192 to 501258, 501259 to 501286, 501302 to 501444, 501492 to 501730, 501731 to 502230 and 502231 to 502478. Evidently the company only got as far as the 501192 to 501258 block by the end of the war. See *Messerschmitt Me 262 The Production Log 1941-1945* by Dan O'Connell, Classic, 2005.

55 ADRC/T-2 2012/675 Messerschmitt Me 262 12. wöchentliche Besprechung am 14. Aug. 44

56 GDC 15/524 Messerschmitt Me 262 Erprobungsbericht Nr. 48 17.8. bis 31.8.

57 IWM Milch 12/6828 Der Reichsminister für Rüstung und Kriegsproduktion Rüstungsstab Sammelbericht 26.8.44

58 ADRC/MAP 5026/346 Messerschmitt Zentralplanung Herrn Zeiler FAV-L Verwendungszweck der Flugzeuge Me 262 Werk-Nr. 170079 und 170072 27.8.44

59 TNA AIR 48/2 USSBS Strategic Bombing of German Aircraft Industry November 1945

60 ADIK 117/0909 FL E 2 Nr. 14352/44 (IIIB) geh. Berlin Betr.: Projekt neuer Zerstörer 28.8.44

61 The requirement was issued by the Chef TLR—essentially the RLM—but the underlying specification would have come from the Luftwaffe.

62 E-Stelle Werneuchen—the Luftwaffe test centre for radar equipment.

63 ADRC/T-2 2911/586 Messerschmitt Me 262 Protokoll Nr. 40 Betrifft: Me 262 als Nachtjäger 1.9.1944. See also 2090/294 and 3754/1020 for different versions of the same document.

64 GDC 15/35 Messerschmitt Aktenvermerk Betrifft: Heimatschützer I Zelle 8-262 W.Nr. 130 186 mit Junkers TL und HWK-R-Triebwerk 23.2.45

65 ADRC/T-2 2012/642 Messerschmitt Aktennotiz 49/44 geh. Falsche Einstellung der Notzugeinrichtung für Bombe und Bombenträger am Me 262

66 IWM Milch 12/6807 Der Reichsminister für Rüstung und Kriegsproduktion Rüstungsstab Sammelbericht 4.9.44

67 ADRC/MAP 5026/348 Messerschmitt Probü Aktenvermerk Betrifft: Hilfsruder für das V-Leitwerk Me 262 HG 7.9.44

68 ADRC/MAP 5026/117 Messerschmitt Probü Aktennotiz Betr.: Me 262 Hochgeschwindigkeitsflugzeug 8.9.44

69 ADRC/MAP 5026/326 Messerschmitt Abt.: KB/Scharf Aktennotiz Betrifft: Triebwerksverleidung Me 262 HG II 11.9.44

70 ADRC/MAP 5026/114 RLM Berlin an Herrn Fröhlich, Oberammergau Abschrift Betr.: Me 262 11.9.44

71 The full report on these tests states that the first test flight with the modified system was on September 5 (ADRC/ MAP 5003/542 Messerschmitt Elektroakustische Peilung Versuchs-Berict Nr. S 02/44 29.9.44) whereas the Lechfeld test flight summary for this period states that this flight was on September 6 (ADRC/T-2 2160/82 Messerschmitt Me 262 Erprobungsbericht Nr. 49 vom 1.9.44 bis 27.9.44). Test pilot Karl Baur, who flew the aircraft on this occasion, recorded the date as September 6 (a 20-minute flight lasting from 8pm to 8.20pm) in his logbook—which perhaps lends weight to the latter.

72 ADRC/MAP 5003/542 Messerschmitt Elektroakustische Peilung Versuchs-Berict Nr. S 02/44 29.9.44

73 From 6.18pm to 6.54pm according to test pilot Baur's logbook.

74 ADRC/MAP 5003/542 Messerschmitt Elektroakustische Peilung Versuchs-Berict Nr. S 02/44 29.9.44

75 The same report had also stated that during the tests at the end of December 1943, the system, as Zwiebel, had been able to detect an Me 410 from 750m. This inconsistency is somewhat inexplicable—perhaps the December 1943 tests had detected 'something' at 750m but had not been able to indicate its direction in the way that Baldrian could.

76 IWM Milch 12/6789 Der Reichsminister für Rüstung und Kriegsproduktion Rüstungsstab Sammelbericht 11.9.44

77 ADRC/T-2 2414/0527 GL/C-E Protokoll Nr. I (893/44)

10.9.44

78 ADIK 117/0886 Focke-Wulf Einstrahlige Jägerprojekte 20.9.44

79 Ibid.

80 ADRC/T-2 3397/119 Messerschmitt Kontrollbericht Nr. 2019/44 Betrifft: Schäden durch Feindeinwirkung der Flugzeuge Me 262 am 12.9.44 in Lager-Lechfeld 15.9.44

## C9. FINALLY A FIGHTER, SEP-DEC 1944

1 IWM Milch 12/6784 Der Reichsminister für Rüstung und Kriegsproduktion Rüstungsstab Sammelbericht 13.9.44

2 ADRC/T-2 3754/994 "Deutsche Lufthansa" Aktiengesellschaft, Hauptwerkstaetten Staaken, den 14.9.1944

3 ADRC/T-2 2210/973 Messerschmitt Kurzbeschreibung der LGW-Kurssteuerung K 22 13.9.44

4 ADRC/T-2 2455/0749 TLR/Fl-E 2 Nr. 9776/44 (IIIA) g.Kdos. Besprechungsniederschrift Betr.: Jagdeinsitzer 15.9.44

5 GDC 15/89 Messerschmitt Aktenvermerk Betr.: Holzumstellung Me 262 18.9.44

6 ADRC/MAP 5026/161 Messerschmitt Aktenvermerk Betr.: Me 262 / Flugleistungen mit Pfeilflügel 20. Sept. 1944

7 ADRC/T-2 3384/988 Messerschmitt Aktenvermerk Betrifft: Schnellstbomber A-3 Me 262 mit Lotfeeinb. 20.9.44

8 IWM Speer FD.3049/49 Führerprotokolle 1942-1945 21.-23. Sept.44

9 TNA AIR 48/2 USSBS Strategic Bombing of German Aircraft Industry November 1945

10 BA-MA R3/1749-165 Aktenvermerk. Berlin, den 29. September 1944

11 ADRC/T-2 3754/1005 Messerschmitt Aktenvermerk Nr. 34 Betr.: Me 262 Festigkeitsstand der verschiedenen Bauzustände 21.10.44

12 TNA AIR 48/2 USSBS Strategic Bombing of German Aircraft Industry November 1945

13 ADRC/T-2 2012/628 Messerschmitt 15. Besprechung am 25.9.44 in Oberammergau

14 ADRC/T-2 2201/128 Collection of various DFS papers on towed vehicle, dated between June and October 1944

15 ADRC/T-2 2160/82 Messerschmitt Me 262 Erprobungsbericht Nr. 49 vom 1.9.44 bis 27.9.44

16 ADRC/MAP 5026/115 Messerschmitt Aktennotiz Betr.: Hochgeschwindigkeitsentwicklung Me 262 / Besprechung bei Herrn Prof. Messerschmitt am 2.10.44

17 ADRC/MAP 5026/319 Messerschmitt Herrn Voigt, Probü Pfeilflügel Me 262 26.9.44

18 ADRC/MAP 5026/112 Messerschmitt Probü Herrn Fröhlich Me 262 / Hochgeschwindigkeitsentwicklung 5.10.44

19 ADRC/T-2 2210/925 Messerschmitt Kobü-Ausrüstung Projektübergabe EZ 42 in Me 262 3.11.44

20 ADIK 153/140 Messerschmitt Projektübergabe Me 262 Nachtjäger (Umbau Schulflugzeug Stufe I) 5.10.44

21 ADRC/MAP 5026/119 Messerschmitt Projektbüro Aktenvermerk Betr.: Me 262 / Hochgeschwindigkeitsentwicklung 5. Oktober 1944

22 ADRC/MAP 5027/261 Messerschmitt an die Erprobungsstelle der Luftwaffe E 7 Rechlin—Müritz TSA 2 A-1-Anlage in Me 262 6.10.44

23 ADRC/T-2 2611/1060 Messerschmitt Me 262 Erprobungsbericht Nr. 50 vom 28.9.-18.10.44

24 Ibid.

25 ADRC/MAP 5003/9 Messerschmitt Me 262 Wasserversuch auf Schnellablass mit dem vorderen Behälter 10.11.44. Note: This report, published more than three weeks after the experiment, states that the test was intended to help Messerschmitt's Construction Office—engine section with preparations for the Heimatschützer II. The date of the test is given as October 14 and the Werk-Nr. of the aircraft used is given as '178'. The engineer who arranged the test, Kaiser, appears to have simply got

the date and aircraft number wrong, since both the Lechfeld test summary for the period and Baur's logbook show that the flight was made on October 18 with 130186.

26 See ADRC/T-2 2688/107 Messerschmitt Baumusterbesprechung Nr. 23 8-262 22.1.45. The OKL and Chef TLR had written to Messerschmitt on several occasions, demanding that the Me 262 be made capable of accommodating BMW 003s. The earliest known example of a lower case 'a' being appended to the Me 262 A-1 designation to denote an 004-engined machine is a load plan dated October 18, 1944. See ADRC/T-2 2346/83. The Me 262 A-1 with 004 engines would become the Me 262 A-1a. With 003 engines fitted, the same aircraft would be the Me 262 A-1b. The lower case 'a' and 'b' are very seldom seen in period documents until around early January 1945, when their use becomes increasingly commonplace—the 'a' being a great deal more common than the 'b', since very few Me 262s were ever fitted with BMW 003 engines.

27 ADRC/MAP 5026/323 Messerschmitt Projektbüro Aktenvermerk Betr.: Stand der Arbeiten an Hochgeschwindigkeitsentwicklung Me 262 vom 18.10.44

28 ADRC/MAP 5026/350 Messerschmitt Probü Me 262 HG II Brandschott 19.10.44

29 ADRC/MAP 5026/322 Messerschmitt Aktenvermerk Betr.: Hochgeschwindigkeitsentwicklung Besprechung beim Herrn Prof. Messerschmitt am 19.10.44

30 GDC 15/35 Messerschmitt Aktenvermerk Betrifft: Heimatschützer I Zelle 8-262 W.Nr. 130 186 mit Junkers TL und HWK-R-Triebwerk 23.2.45. For a more detailed account, see ADRC/T-2 3397/112 Messerschmitt Kontrollbericht Nr. 2025/44

31 ADRC/T-2 2012/613 Messerschmitt Reisebericht Me 262 30.10.44

32 ADRC/T-2 3397/172 Messerschmitt Nachtrag zu Kontrollbericht Nr. 1019/44 24.10.44

33 ADRC/MAP 5027/253 Carl Zeiss Niederschrift Nr. Archiv-Nr. IV d/15 über Besprechung vom: 26.10.1944

34 ADRC/T-2 3754/1080 Messerschmitt Aktenvermerk Nr. 36 Betr.: Me 262 Flugzeugzuweisung für Entwicklung und Versuch. Besprechung am 30.10.44. 1.11.44

35 This appears to have been a retrospective allocation—170079's original nose, fitted with the Baldrian acoustic detection system, having previously been removed and fitted to 130015 while 170079's bomb-damaged airframe was being repaired.

36 ADRC/T-2 2718/215 Messerschmitt Flugbericht-Nr. L 108/110 Me 262 V10 VI+AE am 30.10.44

37 The test report describes the trailer as "SC 1000 mit V 1—Fläche". The 'V 1' in this case is a reference to the wings of the Fi 103 aka V1 flying bomb, which had been repurposed by the DFS for this variant of the Schleppgerät. While the version of the Schleppgerät tested with other aircraft types, such as the Ju 87, Ar 234 and He 177 was designated Schleppgerät or SG 5041, the simplified trailer used with the Me 262 appears to have been the SG 5030. See ADIK 4086/110, a letter from the DFS to the RLM providing details of the Me 262 trailer.

38 ADRC/T-2 3397/109 Messerschmitt Kontrollbericht Nr. 2028/44

39 ADRC/T-2 2727/830 Messerschmitt Me 262 Werk-Nr. 130 176 Doppelsitzer, October 1944

40 BA-MA R3/1749-146 Messerschmitt, Stellungnahme zu der Frage der Eignung der 262 als Jagd bezw. Kampf-Flugzeug. Oktober 31, 1944

41 TNA AIR 48/2 USSBS Strategic Bombing of German Aircraft Industry November 1945

42 ADRC/T-2 2858/699 Messerschmitt Me 262 Protokoll Nr. 53 Betrifft: Einbau der Geräte X 4 und Hs 298 5.11.44

43 ADRC/T-2 2012/587 Messerschmitt Aktennotiz 53/44. Betrifft: Starthilfen 1000kg für Me 262. 13.11.44

44 ADIK 4007/98 Messerschmitt TA-Bericht / H. Wendel Betr.: Lagebericht über den Einsatz der 8-262 in Westen 13.11.44

45 Major Walter Nowotny died on November 8, 1944, aged 23. He was credited with 258 kills.

46 GDC 15/521 Messerschmitt Me 262 Erprobungsbreicht Nr. 52 vom 9.11. bis 29.11.44

47 ADRC/T-2 3397/96 Messerschmitt Kontrollbericht Nr. 2033/44 Betrifft: Beanstandungen und Schäden an 8-262 in der Zeit vom 6.11.44 bis 25.11.44

48 Ibid. See also GDC 15/521 Messerschmitt Me 262 Erprobungsbreicht Nr. 52 vom 9.11. bis 29.11.44

49 Ibid.

50 GDC 15/265 Messerschmitt Standschub Jumo TL mit 3m Einlauf 23.11.44

51 ADRC/T-2 3397/103 Messerschmitt Kontrollbericht Nr. 1030/44 Betr.: Mustereinbau Brandschott für Jumo TL 004 nach EVA 10108 A 20.11.44

52 ADRC/T-2 3397/96 Messerschmitt Kontrollbericht Nr. 2033/44 Betrifft: Beanstandungen und Schäden an 8-262 in der Zeit vom 6.11.44 bis 25.11.44

53 ADRC/T-2 3560/197 DFS Eber assorted reports, notes and sketches, circa November 1944

54 ADRC/T-2 3397/96 Messerschmitt Kontrollbericht Nr. 2033/44 Betrifft: Beanstandungen und Schäden an 8-262 in der Zeit vom 6.11.44 bis 25.11.44

55 ADRC/T-2 2685/266 Messerschmitt Projektübergabe Me 262 Aufklärer by Althoff and Degel, Nov. 1944

56 ADRC/T-2 2346/456 Messerschmitt Regensburg Gewaltfertigung Me 609 Terminüberwachung 24. November 1944

57 ADRC/MAP 5026/329 Messerschmitt Aktenvermerk Betr.: Hochgeschwindigkeitsentwicklung 8-262 Besprechung bei Prof. Messerschmitt am 27.11.44. The drawing numbers given are IV-136, IV-137 and IV-138 but the actual drawings are not appended to the document and it must therefore be assumed that they have not survived.

58 TNA AIR 48/2 USSBS Strategic Bombing of German Aircraft Industry November 1945

59 GDC 15/35 Messerschmitt Aktenvermerk Betrifft: Heimatschützer I Zelle 8-262 W.Nr. 130 186 mit Junkers TL und HWK-R-Triebwerk 23.2.45

60 GDC 15/358 Messerschmitt Projektübergabe Me 262 Panzerflugzeug (Panzerrumpf). 4. Dezember 1944

61 ADRC/MAP 5041/270 Messerschmitt Aktenvermerk Betrifft: Widerstand von Funkmessantennen an 262 3.12.44

62 GDC 15/268 Messerschmitt Versuchs-Bericht 262-17-A-44 Bayer 10.12.44. See also ADRC/T-2 2105/707 Messerschmitt Versuchs-Bericht 262-17-A-44 Bayer 10.12.44

63 TNA AIR 40/201 Me 262 Protokoll geh. Kdos. ES/V/5506 8-262 Schlechtwetterjäger 7.12.44

64 ADRC/T-2 2858/708 Messerschmitt Protokoll Nr. 54 Attrappenbesichtigung Nachtjäger 8-262 7.12.1944

65 Chef TLR Fl-E 2 Nr. 16834/44 geh. 2. Lagebericht der Fachabteilung Fl-E 2 21.12.44

66 ADRC/MAP 4049/678 Messerschmitt Erprobungsbericht Nr. 53 vom 30.11.-31.12.1944. See also ADRC/T-2 2212/213 Messerschmitt Erprobungsbericht Nr. 53 vom 30.11.-31.12.1944

67 ADRC/T-2 2707/774 Messerschmitt Me 262 Flugbericht Nr. 133/136, Dec 1944

68 ADRC/MAP 5041/212 Messerschmitt Probü/Ausr. Arbeitsauftrag 1060, Nachtjäger 8-262 vom 15.12.44. 31.1.45

69 ADRC/T-2 2750/1051 Messerschmitt Aktenvermerk Betr.: 8-262 Hochgeschwindigkeitsentwicklung Schritt III Besprechung bei Herrn Messerschmitt am 17.12.44

70 ADRC/T-2 2750/1059 Messerschmitt Aktenvermerk Betr.: Weiterentwicklung 8-262 (Hochgeschwindigkeit) Stand vom 20.12.44

71 ADRC/MAP 4049/678 Messerschmitt Erprobungsbericht Nr. 53 vom 30.11.-31.12.1944. See also ADRC/T-2 2212/213 Messerschmitt Erprobungsbericht Nr. 53 vom 30.11.-31.12.1944

72 ADRC/T-2 2696/909 Messerschmitt Me 262 Flugbericht Nr. 135/138, Dec 44. See also ADRC/T-2 2682/233.

73 ADRC/MAP 5026/108 Messerschmitt Auszug aus "Lagebesprechung BLV-21.12.44"

74 ADRC/T-2 2114/138 Messerschmitt Widerstand von verlängerten MK 108 Schutzrohren am 8-262 22.12.44

75 BA-MA R3/1749-170 Aktenvermerk Betr.: Programm-Vorlage Nr. 17 v. 28.11.44, Berlin, den 19. Dezember 1944

76 ADIK 4007/79 Messerschmitt Projektübergabe Funkanlage 8-262 Schlechtwetterjäger 19.12.44

77 ADRC/T-2 2012/582 Messerschmitt Baumusterbesprechung Nr. 21 20.12.44

78 Presumably a reference to the Metallbau Offingen company, a subdivision of Messerschmitt, which had evidently been tasked with developing the Me 262's night fighter capability. It would appear that the company had been selected to build the first 15 examples but the precise configuration those aircraft is unclear.

79 BA-MA R3/1749-127 Entwicklungshauptkommission Flugzeuge Br. Nr. 407/44 g.Kdos. Ergebnisse der Sitzungen am 19. und 20.12.1944

80 IWM Speer FD 4355/45-10 Vol. 1 Stellungnahme zum Projekt "Volksjäger" by Willy Messerschmitt, October 1944

81 ADRC/T-2 2043/700 Messerschmitt Projektübergabe Aufklärer 8-262 A 5 a (Serie) 21.2.45

82 It is worth noting that all previously published works on the Me 262 and indeed Mistel combinations, where they mention it at all, have identified Mistel 4 as being a combination of an Me 262 two-man bomber upper component and an unpiloted explosives-laden second Me 262 airframe lower component. While primary source evidence on this design is practically non-existent, so its background and authenticity cannot be verified, it would seem that this was not Mistel 4. All known primary source material refers to Mistel 4 as a combination of a Ju 88 lower component with an Me 262 upper component. Teaming an Me 262 with another Me 262 would have made sense in terms of matching speed and fuel type but it would have involved the total loss of a brand new and sorely needed Me 262 airframe, rather than of a worn-out and otherwise obsolete Ju 88. Incidentally, there is a reference in the Chef TLR War Diary for the week of December 20-26, 1944, complaining about the installation of the 'Tonne' TV camera system in the Me 262 Mistel being delayed. Such a system would have been useful in overcoming the speed difference in an 88/262 combination—since the TV picture would enable the pilot to continue guiding the Ju 88 to its target while flying rapidly away to safety.

83 Chef TLR Fl-E 2 Nr. 16834/44 geh. 2. Lagebericht der Fachabteilung Fl-E 2 21.12.44

84 TNA AIR 40/3129 German Aircraft: New and Projected Types January 1946

85 Chef TLR Fl-E 2 Nr. 16834/44 geh. 2. Lagebericht der Fachabteilung Fl-E 2 21.12.44

86 ADRC/T-2 3384/1159 Messerschmitt Aktenvermerk Betr.: Erprobungsfluggenehmigung 8-262 A-3 (Lotfe-Bomber) W.Nr. 110484. 30.12.44

87 TNA AIR 48/2 USSBS Strategic Bombing of German Aircraft Industry November 1945

88 ADIK 156/193 Gen. Qu. (G. Abt. III) Nr. 2573/45 g. Kdos. Überblick über die Me 262 Lieferung. Stand: 20.3.45

## C10. TO THE LIMIT, JAN-FEB 1945

1 BA-MA RL3-2567 KTB der Chef TLR Berichtsraum 20.12.-26.12.1944

2 IWM Speer FD 3049/49 Führerprotokolle 1942-1945

3 BA-MA RL3-2567 KTB der Chief TLR Berichtswoche 22.1.-28.1.1945

4 IWM Speer FD 3049/49 Führerprotokolle 1942-1945

5 GDC 15/443 Messerschmitt 8-262 Erprobungsbericht Nr. 54 vom 1.1. bis 31.1.45

6 BA-MA RL3-2567 KTB der Chief TLR Berichtswoche 15.1.-21.1.1945

7 GDC 15/443 Messerschmitt 8-262 Erprobungsbericht Nr. 54 vom 1.1. bis 31.1.45

8 ADRC/T-2 2821/575 Chef TLR Erprobungsfluggenehmigung 8-262 A-2a/U2 Dec. 1944

9 See IWM GDC 15/545 Messerschmitt 8-262 Erprobungsbericht Nr. 56 1.3.-31.3.45. This shows that 110555 was not fitted with its intended K 22 till March.

10 It has been suggested that Baldrian may have been connected to the X-4 air-to-air missile in some way, since it had been planned to use an acoustic guidance system called 'Dogge' with that weapon, but no documentary evidence is known to exist which supports this notion.

11 These dates and times are recorded in Baur's logbook. By this point the Lechfeld test summaries rarely recorded individual flight dates and times.

12 ADRC/MAP 5026/369 Messerschmitt Probü Aktenvermerk Betr.: 8-262 Hochgeschwindigkeitsentwicklung 1. Erprobung Pfeilleitwerk und Rennkabine I. 22.1.45

13 GDC 15/443 Messerschmitt 8-262 Erprobungsbericht Nr. 54 vom 1.1. bis 31.1.45

14 Ibid.

15 ADRC/T-2 2688/107 Messerschmitt Baumusterbesprechung Nr. 23 8-262 22.1.45

16 GDC 15/35 Messerschmitt Aktenvermerk Betrifft: Heimatschützer II Zelle 8-262 W.Nr. 170 074 mit BMW-TL und BMW-R-Triebwerk 23.2.45

17 GDC 15/443 Messerschmitt 8-262 Erprobungsbericht Nr. 54 vom 1.1. bis 31.1.45

18 Ibid.

19 ADRC/MAP 5032/24 Oberkommando der Luftwaffe Generalquartiermeister Nr. 13215/44 g.Kdos. (6.Abt.III T) 2. Ang. Betr.: Entwicklungsforderung für Jagdflugzeug 11.1.45

20 ADRC/T-2 2009/2 Messerschmitt Me 262 B2 Nachtjäger Projektbaubeschreibung vom 18.1.1945

21 ADRC/MAP 5032/22 Fl. E F 1 Nr. 12376/45 (III E) g. Kdos. Betr.: Technische Richtlinien für einen Schlechtwatter- und Nachtjäger 27.1.45

22 ADIK 203/314 Messerschmitt Me 262 Reichweiten- und Lastensteigerung 1.2.45

23 BA-MA RL3-2567 KTB der Chief TLR Berichtswoche 15.1.-21.1.1945

24 Evidently a small unit led by Major Gerhard Stamp and known as Kommando Stamp had been established at Lärz with four Me 262s to carry out aerial bombing operations but its personnel struggled to prepare their equipment and it achieved nothing before being merged into JG 7. With JG 7, Stamp's unit would test the installation of WG 21 aerial mortar tubes on the Me 262's bomb racks—a system fully designed as part of the original Panzerflugzeug proposal back in March 1944. See Chapter 6.

25 IWM Speer FD 3049/49 Führerprotokolle 1942-1945

26 ADRC/T-2 3754/985 Messerschmitt Besprechungniederschrift Me 262 Nr. 26 v. 10.2.44

27 ADIK 153/185 Kommando der E'Stellen Entwicklungs-Auftrage für Me 262 13.10.44

28 BA-MA RL3-2567 KTB der Chef TLR Berichtswoche 22.1.-28.1.1945

29 ADRC/T-2 2911/869 Der Reichsminister für Rüstung und Kriegsproduktion Sonderkommission Schlechtwetter- u. Nachtjagd. Betr.: Besprechung über Nachtjagdausführung der Do 335, Me 262, Ar 234 am 24.1.45, 15.00 Uhr, in Berlin. The one-off single seater with FuG 218 specially made for Welter was Werk-Nr. 110304 Rote 4. He crash-landed it after take-off from Burg on the night of February 4/5, 1945.

30 Ibid.

31 ADRC/T-2 2688/107 Messerschmitt Baumusterbesprechung Nr. 23 22.1.45

32 ADRC/T-2 2060/75 Messerschmitt Baureihenübersicht 262 (Bewaffnung 30.3.45). But see also ADRC/T-2 3697/537 Baureihen-Übersicht 8-262 Stand vom 1.1.45, which appears to suggest that for a short period a production variant with all six guns fitted together was considered.

33 It appears that while a production run of 15 Me 262 B-2 night fighters had been planned, only one had actually been confirmed as ordered up to this point—the pattern aircraft, which Messerschmitt itself was supposed to supply. See Chapter 9.

34 ADRC/T-2 2101/933 E-Stelle Tarnewitz Bewaffungsvorschlag 8-262 mit 4 MK 108 oder 2 MK 103 und 2 MG 151 (15mm Lauf)—ein Vergleich 30.1.45

35 TNA AIR 48/2 USSBS Strategic Bombing of German Aircraft Industry November 1945

36 ADIK 156/193 Gen. Qu. (G.Abt. III) Nr. 2573/45 g. Kdos. Überblick über die Me 262 Lieferung. Stand: 20.3.45

37 IWM FD4355/45 Vol. 1/328 Notprogramm der Rüstungsendfertigung 31.1.45

38 Conscription to labour, such as for the construction of fortifications, rather than conscription to fight.

39 ADRC/T-2 3282/270 Sonderkommission "Zellenbau" in der Entwicklungshauptkommission "Flugzeuge" Bock an Wehrse Betr.: Fertigungsprogramm und Entwicklungsarbeiten 12.3.45

40 The two DFS reports were Über einen Lorinantrieb für Strahljäger (UM3509) by Eugen Sänger, October 1943, which can be found at ADIK 89/24, and Berechnung der Horizontalflugverhaltens eine extrem schnell steigenden Lorin-Jägers (UM3518) by W. Peterson, 20.4.44, which is available at ADRC/T-2 2042/323.

41 IWM GDC 10/5519 Deutsche Forschungsanstalt für Segelflug Leistungssteigerung der Me 262 durch Lorin-Zusatzantrieb 31.1.45

42 ADRC/MAP 5041/212 Messerschmitt Probü/Ausr. Arbeitsauftrag 1060, Nachtjäger 8-262 vom 15.12.44. 31.1.45

43 BA-MA RL3-2567 KTB der Chef TLR Berichtswoche 5.2.-11.2.1945

44 ADRC/T-2 8051/132 Entwicklungs-Notprogramm

45 BA-MA RL3-2567 KTB der Chef TLR Berichtswoche 5.2.-11.2.1945

46 GDC 15/830 Messerschmitt Schutzkörbe vor dem TL am Flug 3.2.45

47 GDC 15/655 Messerschmitt 8-262 Erprobungsbericht Nr. 55 vom 1.2. bis 28.2.45

48 GDC 15/35 Messerschmitt Aktenvermerk Betrifft: Heimatschützer I Zelle 8-262 W.Nr. 130 186 mit Junkers TL und HWK-R-Triebwerk 23.2.45

49 B4 fuel, apparently equivalent to 87 octane, was used by a wide range of Luftwaffe aircraft including the Messerschmitt Bf 109, but only the Jumo 004 was able to run on the extremely low grade J2.

50 ADRC/T-2 3397/75 Messerschmitt Kontrollbericht Nr. 1035/45 2.3.45

51 ADRC/T-2 3754/978 Messerschmitt Besprechungsniederschrift Betr.: Lagebesprechung DLV—am 1.2.45

52 US Navy 203/312 Messerschmitt Me 262 Reichweiten- und Lastensteigerung 1.2.45

53 ADRC/MAP 5026/300 Messerschmitt Projektbüro Aktenvermerk Betr.: Hochgeschwindigkeitsentwicklung—Stand 5.2.45

54 ADRC/MAP 5026/296 Messerschmitt Mitteilung an H. Prager, Probü. Betrifft: Raumuntersuchung am Pfeilflügel 35° (HG II) 8.2.45

55 ADRC/MAP 5026/295 Messerschmitt Probü Herrn Professor Messerschmitt Hochgeschwindigkeitsentwicklung. 10.2.45

56 ADIK 75/114 Messerschmitt Me 262 Nachtjäger mit HeS 011-Triebwerken Projektbeschreibung vom 12.2.1945

57 ADRC/T-2 2965/1079 Entwicklungssonderkommission „Schlechtwetter- u. Nachtjagd" Arbeitsgruppe Flugmechanik Betr.: Me 262—Nachtjäger, B u.V. P 215-01, DoP 252/1 26.2.45

58 ADRC/T-2 2043/700 Messerschmitt Projektübergabe Aufklärer 8-262 A 5 a (Serie) 21.2.45

59 BA-MA RL3-2567 KTB der Chef TLR Berichtswoche 26.2/4.3.1945

60 ADIK 117/0908 Abschrift dH/5 1.3.45 Der Chef der Techn. Luftrüstung Fl. E Nr. 12376/45 (E 2 III B) g.Kdos. 2. Angel. Betr.: Technische Richtlinien für einen Schlechtwetter- und Nachtjäger

61 BA-MA RL3-2567 KTB der Chef TLR Berichtswoche 12.2.-18.2.1945

62 IWM Speer FD3049/49 Führerprotokolle 1942-1945

63 Ibid.

64 TNA AIR 48/2 USSBS Strategic Bombing of German Aircraft Industry November 1945

65 ADIK 156/193 Gen. Qu. (G. Abt. III) Nr. 2573/45 g. Kdos. Überblick über die Me 262 Lieferung. Stand: 20.3.45

66 ADIK 120/94 OKL Chef TLR F 2 EN IV Funkausrüstung für Hochleistungsflugzeuge und Projekte 20.2.45

67 This was presumably an error, since a huge amount of additional work would have been required to create a C-2a which used a combination of Jumo 004s and rocket motors. Perhaps the chart's author simply did not know what the little 'a' stood for.

68 ADRC/T-2 2346/456 Messerschmitt Regensburg Baureihengegenüberstellung 609 21.2.45

## C11. THE END, MAR-MAY 1945

1 IWM GDC 15/545 Messerschmitt 8-262 Erprobungsbericht Nr. 56 1.3.-31.3.45

2 ADRC/T-2 3397/73 Messerschmitt Kontrollbericht Nr. 1036/45 6.3.45

3 ADRC/MAP 5004/660 Messerschmitt Me 262 Erprobung der Hydraulikanlage mit 2 Druckölpumpen 12.3.45

4 GDC 15/840 Messerschmitt Flugbericht L 160/161 18.3.1945. Lindner cites the aircraft's serial as 110499—the machine loaned to the Luftwaffe in January 1945 for testing simplified weapons circuitry—but it would appear that he was mistaken since there is no other evidence of 110499 ever being fitted with an MK 214 nose and his flight otherwise fits both the timeline for 111899 and other reports relating to that aircraft.

5 ADRC/T-2 3397/72 Messerschmitt Kontrollbericht Nr. 1039/45 13.3.45

6 GDC 15/841 Messerschmitt Flugbericht L 161/162 21.3.1945

7 ADRC/T-2 3397/5 Messerschmitt Kontrollbericht Nr. 2016/45 1.4.45

8 ADRC/T-2 2904/945 Messerschmitt Baubeschreibung Me 262 B2 Nachtjäger mit 2 x HeS 011 Triebwerken 17.3.1945

9 GDC 15/647 Messerschmitt 3-sitziger Nachtjäger mit HeS-011 A Projektbaubeschreibung v. 17.3.45

10 BA-MA R3/1749/188 Messerschmitt an Lucht, 19.3.45

11 ADIK 4085/126 Der Reichsminister für Rüstung und Kriegsproduktion Sonderkommission Schlechtwetter- u. Nachtjagd Protokoll Nr. 5 Betr.: Besprechung über Neuentwürfe für Schlechtwetter- und Nachtjagd am 20. u. 21.3.45 in Bad Eilsen. 29.3.45

12 The Ju 88 G-7 was evidently to be fitted with Jumo 213 E engines and equipped with FuG 218/220 or FuG 240 radar.

13 GDC 16/41 Focke-Wulf Entwürfe für Nacht- u. Schlechtwetterjagd 23.3.45

14 BA-MA Rl3-2568 Der Chef der Technischen Luftrüstung Fl. E Nr. 12376/45 (2/III) g. Kdos. 3. Ang. Betr.: Technische Richtlinien für einen Schlechtwetter- und Nachtjäger April 1945

15 BA-MA RL3-2567 KTB der Chef TLR Wochenbericht 26.2.-4.3.1945

16 IWM Speer FD3049/49 Führerprotokolle 1942-1945

17 BA-MA RL3-2567 KTB der Chef TLR Wochenbericht 5.3.-15.3.1945

18  BA-MA RL3-2567 KTB der Chef TLR Wochenbericht 16.3.-4.4.1945

19  IWM Speer FD3049/49 Führerprotokolle 1942-1945

20  BA-MA RL3-2567 KTB der Chef TLR Wochenbericht 16.3.-4.4.1945

21  Ibid.

22  Ibid.

23  TNA AIR 48/2 USSBS Strategic Bombing of German Aircraft Industry November 1945

24  BA-MA RL3-2567 KTB der Chef TLR Berichtsraum 16.3.-4.4.1945

25  According to A.D.I.(K) No. 313 of 18.5.45 (see TNA AIR 40/201 pt1): "Until October 1944 the well-known main factory of Flugzeugwerk Eger at Cheb was engaged on work in connection with the He 111 and the He 177, but from that time onwards it was almost exclusively occupied on the assembly and repair of Me 262s. The Me 262s assembled at Cheb were of the A-5 series designed for reconnaissance duties; the usual armament was consequently omitted and two series cameras were mounted, whilst a weight was installed in the fuselage to restore the trim of the aircraft. In order to withstand the stresses arising from the high speed at which this type of machine was to operate, the fuselage and wing tips were strengthened as compared with the normal fighter or bomber versions. A contract for 150 of these machines was placed with Flugzeugwerk Eger in the summer and autumn of 1944, but this was to be regarded as only a provisional order as the reconnaissance version had not yet been tested operationally. The first machine left the factory in December 1944 and by the end of April 1945 some aircraft had been completed. The machines were flight tested by the firm's five test pilots and were then despatched to Lechfeld airfield." Whether these were genuine A-5s or A-1/U3s is unclear, though they were most likely the latter.

26  ADRC/T-2 3397/31 Messerschmitt Protokoll Nr. 63 5./25.3.45

27  ADRC/T-2 3397/34 Messerschmitt Protokoll Nr. 64 24.3.1945

28  ADRC/T-2 3397/36 Messerschmitt Protokoll Nr. 65 27.3.1945

29  ADRC/T-2 3397/38 Messerschmitt Protokoll Nr. 66 28.3.1945

30  ADRC/T-2 3397/40 Messerschmitt Protokoll Nr. 67 28.3.45

31  NARA T321-50/4262 Luftflottenkommando 6 Führungsabteilung I Nr. 2049/45 g.Kdos. 26.3.1945

32  ADRC/T-2 2029/616 Kommando der Erprobungsstellen Nr.: 22140/45 g. Erprobung der Me 262 15.1.45

33  TNA AIR 40/201 Me 262 Part 2 Ergänzungsblatt 5 (Nachtrag 2 zur Flugzeugkenntafel Deutschland, Ausgabe Febr. 1944)

34  A somewhat less compelling case could also be constructed for the use of the codename 'Silber' or 'Silver', the Me 262 being referred to as such in a report from the Luftwaffe's Tarnewitz test centre dated December 13, 1944. See ADIK 4107/10. Another document (TNA AIR 40/201 pt 2) entitled 'Die Platzrunde auf unserem Silbervogel' refers to the Me 262 as the 'Silbervogel' or 'Silver Bird'. More curious is the name 'Schwalbe'. This is never known to have appeared on any official German wartime document relating to the Me 262. However, it does seem to have appeared in Volume 67 of British magazine *The Aeroplane* at least as early as July 1944 in reference to the Me 262. A British intelligence report, A.I. 85766 of January 5, 1945, referring to intelligence received on December 4, 1944 (see TNA AIR 40/201 pt 1), states: "There is an aircraft factory built in the KOHLBERG hill near HEITERWANG/LECH, ALGAU, which is turning out aircraft with a thermic-jet drive: Me 262 G, called "Schwalbe V". These aircraft have four small guns and two 150kg bombs, or six guns and two 50kg bombs. Their speed amounts to 800 kms per hour." The precise source of this rather inaccurate information is not given. By the end of the war, however, the press in both Britain and the US were regularly referring to the 'Me 262A-1 Schwalbe'. It may be that the nickname was applied by British journalists, rather than German service personnel, since it better suited Britain's own

system of giving aircraft colourful names.

35  ADRC/T-2 3397/64 Messerschmitt Kontrollbericht Nr. 1043/45

36  ADRC/T-2 2459/665 Messerschmitt Abschrift! 8-262 A-1a Werk-Nr. 111538 mit Pfeilflügel 35° 29.3.45

37  ADRC/T-2 2060/77 Messerschmitt Baureihenübersicht 262 (Bewaffnung) 30.3.45

38  Ibid.

39  DSIR 23/14774 RAE Farnborough Technical Note No. Aero 1673 (Flight). See notes on Hoffman interrogation.

40  ADRC/T-2 2012/577 Messerschmitt MK 214 in Me 262 6.4.45

41  ADRC/T-2 3397/11 Messerschmitt 8-262, laufende Arbeiten in der Entwicklung 6.4.45

42  ADRC/T-2 3397/16 Messerschmitt Kontrollbericht Nr. 1052/45 14.4.45

43  ADRC/T-2 3422/776 Messerschmitt Versuchs-Bericht Nr. 262 09 E 45 Seitenstabilität 8-262 (Wendedämpfung) 17.4.45

44  See *Wingfoot — Rhineland and Central Europe Campaigns — Official History 101st Cavaltry Group (Mechanized)*, Major Mercer W. Sweeney, editor. August 1945 p67

45  See *Messerschmitt Me 262 The Production Log 1941-1945* by Dan O'Connell, Classic, 2005.

46  Numerous sources report the HG II as destroyed for this reason, but no description of the precise circumstances of the accident is known to exist.

47  See Headquarters 411th Infantry Regiment Office of the Commanding Officer APO 470, US Army, 1 May 1945. Subject: Regimental History for Month of April 1945. At the time of writing this document could be viewed online at https://103divwwii.usm.edu/assets/411-narr-oprn-apr-45.pdf

48  TNA AIR 48/2 USSBS Strategic Bombing of German Aircraft Industry November 1945

49  ADIK 156/193 Gen. Qu. (G. Abt. III) Nr. 2573/45 g. Kdos. Überblick über die Me 262 Lieferung. Stand: 20.3.45

## APPENDIX I

1  TNA DSIR 23/14774 RAE Farnborough Technical Note No. Aero 1673 (Flight)

## APPENDIX II

1  TNA AIR 40/201 Me 262 Part 2 A.D.I.(K) Report No. 323/1945 The Me 262 as a Combat Aircraft June 6, 1945

## APPENDIX III

1  TNA AIR 40/2426 ADI(K) Report No. 1/1946 The Messerschmitt Organisation and Its Work During the War. January 7, 1946

2  TNA DSIR 23/15140 Interrogation No. 2. Subject: General Aeronautical Subjects—Herr W. Voigt. Tuesday, June 19, 1945

## APPENDIX IV

1  IWM Speer FD4930/45 Sup. A. Fertigung Me 262

2  REIMAHG was apparently short for Flugzeugwerke REIchsMArschall Hermann Göring—a new production site for the Me 262 established in an old sand mine under Walpersberg, near Kahla, codenamed 'Lachs' (Salmon).

## APPENDIX V

1  TNA AIR 40/2167 A.I.2.(g) reports 2284-2374 (incomplete)

## APPENDIX VI

1  ADRC/MAP 4049/678 Messerschmitt Erprobungsbericht Nr. 53 vom 30.11.-31.12.1944. See also ADRC/T-2 2212/213 Messerschmitt Erprobungsbericht Nr. 53 vom 30.11.-31.12.1944

2  GDC 15/443 Messerschmitt Erprobungsbericht Nr. 54 vom 1.1. bis 31.1.45

# Bibliography

Baker, David. *Messerschmitt Me 262*. Crowood, 1997.

Boyne, Walter J. *Messerschmitt Me 262: Arrow to the Future*. Smithsonian, 1980.

Douglas, Calum E. *The Secret Horsepower Race*, Tempest, 2020.

Ebert, Hans, Johann B. Kaiser and Klaus Peters. *Willy Messerschmitt—Pioneer of Aviation Design*. Schiffer, 1999.

Franks, Richard A. *The Messerschmitt Me 262—A Complete Guide to the Luftwaffe's First Jet Fighter*. Second Edition. Valiant Wings, 2021.

Galland, Adolf. *The First and the Last*. English translation of *Die Ersten und die Letzten* by Buccaneer Books, 1954.

Giffard, Hermione. *Making Jet Engines in World War II*, The University of Chicago Press, 2016.

Griehl, Manfred. *Jet Planes of the Third Reich, The Secret Projects Volume One*. Monogram, 1998.

Griehl, Manfred. *Jet Planes of the Third Reich, The Secret Projects Volume Two*. Monogram, 2004.

Harvey, James Neal. *Sharks of the Air*. Casemate, 2011.

Hirschel, Ernst Heinrich, Prem, Horst und Madelung, Gero. *Aeronautical Research in Germany—From Lilienthal Until Today*. Springer, 2006.

Kartschall, Alexander. *Messerschmitt Me 262 Geheime Produktionsstätten*. Motorbuch Verlag, 2020.

Kosin, Rüdiger. *Die Entwicklung der deutschen Jagdflugzeuge*. Bernard & Graefe Verlag, 1983.

Masters, David. *German Jet Genesis*. Jane's, 1982.

Mermet, Jean-Claude. *Aero Journal Hors-Serie No. 34 Messerschmitt Me 262*. Caraktère, 2019.

Nowarra, Heinz J. *Die deutsche Luftrüstung 1933-1945 Band 1-4*. Bernard & Graefe Verlag, 1984.

O'Connell, Dan. *Messerschmitt Me 262 The Production Log 1941-1945*. Classic, 2005.

Pabst, Martin. *Willy Messerschmitt Zwölf Jahre Flugzeugbau im Führerstaat*. Aviatic Verlag, 2018.

Radinger, Willy and Walter Schick. *Messerschmitt Geheimprojekte*. Aviatic Verlag, 1991.

Radinger, Willy and Walter Schick. *Messerschmitt Me 262*. Schiffer, 1993.

Sharp, Dan. *Secret Projects of the Luftwaffe Volume 1: Jet Fighters 1939-1945*. Tempest, 2020.

Smith, J. Richard and Eddie J. Creek. *Me 262 Volume One*, Classic, 1997.

Smith, J. Richard and Eddie J. Creek. *Me 262 Volume Two*, Classic, 1998.

Smith, J. Richard and Eddie J. Creek. *Me 262 Volume Three*, Classic, 2000.

Smith, J. Richard and Eddie J. Creek. *Me 262 Volume Four*, Classic, 2000.

Speer, Albert. *Inside the Third Reich*. Weidenfeld & Nicolson, 1970.

Uziel, Daniel. *Arming The Luftwaffe—The German Aviation Industry in World War II*. McFarland & Company, 2012.

Vajda, Ferenc A. and Peter Dancey. *German Aircraft Industry and Production 1933-1945*. Airlife, 1998.

Vann, Frank. *Willy Messerschmitt*. Patrick Stephens, 1993.

Zapf, Andreas. *The Jet Night Fighters—Kurt Welter & the Story of the Messerschmitt Me 262 Night Fighters*. Privately published, 2019.

Ziegler, Mano. *Hitler's Jet Plane: The Me 262 Story*. Greenhill, 2004.

# Index